T0161333

View of *Kaminoudhia* from the Neolithic site of *Teppes*, Summer 1981. The Byzantine farmstead of *Sternes* (see fig. 15.1) lies immediately to the left of the prominent "Sotira Pine," clearly visible on the horizon.

SOTIRA *KAMINOUDHIA*

AN EARLY BRONZE AGE SITE IN CYPRUS

American Schools of Oriental Research

Archaeological Reports

Gloria London, editor

Number 08
Sotira *Kaminoudhia*
An Early Bronze Age Site in Cyprus

Edited by
Stuart Swiny
George (Rip) Rapp
Ellen Herscher

SOTIRA *KAMINOUDHIA*

AN EARLY BRONZE AGE SITE IN CYPRUS

Edited by

STUART SWINY
GEORGE (RIP) RAPP
ELLEN HERSCHER

Cyprus American Archaeological Research Institute
Monograph Series, Volume 4

American Schools of Oriental Research • Boston, MA

SOTIRA *KAMINOUDHIA*: AN EARLY BRONZE AGE SITE IN CYPRUS

edited by
Stuart Swiny
George (Rip) Rapp
Ellen Herscher

Billie Jean Collins
ASOR Director of Publications

Library of Congress Cataloging-in-Publication Data

Sotira Kaminoudhia : an early Bronze Age site in Cyprus / edited
  by Stuart Swiny, George (Rip) Rapp, Ellen Herscher.
    p. cm. -- (American Schools of Oriental Research archaeo-
logical reports ; no. 08)
  Includes bibliographical references and index.
  ISBN 0-89757-064-2 (alk. paper)
  1. Sotira Kaminoudhia Site (Cyprus) 2. Excavations (Archaeology)--Cyprus--Sotira Kaminoudhia Site. 3. Bronze Age--Cyprus
--Sotira Kaminoudhia Site.   I. Swiny, Stuart. II. Rapp, George
Robert, 1930-   . III. Herscher, Ellen. IV. Series.
DS54.95.S65S68 2002
939'.37--dc21
                         2002155243

To the memory of Porphyrios Dikaios
Pioneer of the Cypriot Early Bronze Age

Porphyrios Dikaios 1904–1971

CONTENTS

LIST OF FIGURES

Chapter 1

Chapter 2

Chapter 3

Chapter 4

Chapter 6

Chapter 7

Chapter 8

Chapter 15

Chapter 16

LIST OF PLATES

Frontispiece

View of *Kaminoudhia* from the Neolithic site of *Teppes*, Summer 1981. The Byzantine farmstead of *Sternes* (see fig. 15.1) lies immediately to the left of the prominent "Sotira Pine," clearly visible on the horizon.

Chapter 1

Chapter 2

Chapter 3

LIST OF TABLES

Chapter 2

Appendix 8.1

Chapter 9

PREFACE

Even a small archaeological excavation entails awesome responsibility. In the eastern Mediterranean, monumental ancient remains as well as quantity and variety of artifacts recovered require a well-honed excavation staff, a small phalanx of specialists to study and publish the excavated materials, and the support of the antiquities service in the host country.

With the Cypriot expertise of two of the project senior staff members (Swiny and Herscher) and the well-tested interdisciplinary approach of a third (Rapp), we knew what course of action we wished to follow once our excavation permit had been secured and the money raised to mount a successful prehistoric excavation and survey in southern Cyprus. With the license to excavate and funds in hand, our attention turned to facilities, staff, and strategy, which determine the success of a project just as much as the choice of site.

The locality of *Kaminoudhia* was selected because surface finds of pottery and exploratory trenches suggested the potential for filling the then yawning gap in our knowledge of the Early Bronze Age in southern Cyprus. We understood early on that the ceramic chronology would offer us both our greatest challenge and perhaps our best opportunity for understanding the complex development of Early Cypriot culture. With our interdisciplinary and environmental approach we also hoped to shed some light on the exploitation of local resources, the nature of interregional exchange, as well as the development and status of Early Cypriot lithic, ceramic and metal technologies. The organization of this volume follows the traditional pattern of the Mediterranean region excavations with each specialist reporting on her or his studies.

ACKNOWLEDGEMENTS

We owe a major debt of gratitude to the Department of Antiquities of Cyprus and its long-time Director, Vassos Karageorghis, not only for the permission to excavate at Sotira *Kaminoudhia*, but also for his support and interest in the project. The satisfaction of undertaking archaeological fieldwork in Cyprus has much to do with the staff of the Department of Antiquities, from the Director and Archaeological Officers down to the all-important Store Keepers. This cooperation began in 1978 when Demos Christou, then an Archaeological Officer in charge of the excavations at Kourion, supported Swiny's request to the Department of Antiquities for a permit to survey the Sotira area. Once the excavations at *Kaminoudhia* were in progress it was always a pleasure to welcome V. Karageorghis either to the site or to the storerooms, for his pertinent comments would invariably contribute to our understanding of the material under study.

We also thank the Curator of the Cyprus Museum, Pavlos Flourentzos, who graciously handled our numerous requests to view objects in his custody and who visited the excavation at the close of each season for the official hand-over of finds, now housed in the Kourion Museum in Episkopi Village. Sophocles Hadjisavvas, then Curator of Ancient Monuments, saw to the preservation of the site. All researchers who have studied material in the Cyprus Museum in the past twenty five years are beholden to Gregoris Christou, the Store Keeper. Herscher and especially Swiny, who sought his assistance on many an occasion, have profited from his encyclopedic knowledge of the vast collection. His retirement left a chasm hard to fill. Without the good-natured assistance of the Custodian of the Kourion Museum, Christophis Polycarpou, the project could never have run so smoothly. His friendship with the whole Swiny family made living and working in the Episkopi area a rich intellectual and personal experience. After C. Polycarpou's retirement in 1986 Socrates Savvas assumed the position and provided the same efficient service. It was always a pleasure to reside in George McFadden's fine house in Episkopi—now part of the Kourion Museum—and to hear tales of his life and times from these persons who knew him so well. If an army marches on its stomach it is certainly true that a happy excavation requires a good cook, and nobody could better Christalla Andreou. Her earthy good humor has delighted us all. Herscher is also grateful for the hospitality of Diana Buitron-Oliver and Andrew Oliver, who offered use of their home in Episkopi during the final study of the ceramics in 1990–1992. In Nicosia, the excellent facilities of the Cyprus American Archaeological Research Institute (CAARI) and the assistance of its able Administrative Assistant, Vathoulla Moustoukki, expedited progress toward the publication in ways too numerous to mention

Living in Sotira Village in 1981 and working closely with many of its inhabitants in the years to follow was an experience none of us will ever forget. The successive village Muktars, the Agrophilakas and especially our de facto foreman Stellios Mavros, a veteran of Porphyrios Dikaios' excavations at *Teppes*, did all in their power to make us welcome. The true character of Cyprus only emerges in a village environment and we were privileged to have enjoyed the experience.

The Western Sovereign Base Area Archaeological Society assisted the project in many ways by facilitating the loan of equipment and by providing a steady flow of volunteers both in the field and in the sherd yard. Special thanks go to its indefatigable Chairman at the time of the 1986 season, Gerald Hennings, responsible for excavating most of the rather ephemeral pits in Unit 1, as well as to Don and Nancy Flint who spent many a day painstakingly restoring our badly shattered ceramics. A British Army team of surveyors graciously produced a highly accurate topographical map of the site in 1981 and later in 1983 fenced the three excavated areas thanks to the then Chairman of the Society, Major Desmond O'Connor (also a keen excavator and surveyor). The Royal Air Force was kind enough to take Douglas Kuylenstierna and Swiny on helicopter photographic runs above the site in 1983 and 1986.

In 1981 the excavation consisted of Gay Berg, Alice Greenway, Harry Heywood, Michel Khouri, Alexander Rhinelander (site photographer), Helena Swiny, Clark Walz, Deborah Whittingham (site supervisors, the latter also served as registrar), Sandy Thome (draftsperson) and John Keys (object photographer). Berg, Heywood, Walz and Thome were veterans of the Episkopi *Phaneromeni* excavations conducted between 1975 and 1978. The following persons took part in the 1983 season: Kimberle Calnan, Gregory Ewing, Alice Greenway, Harry Heywood, Ian Humphreys, Ibrahim Kouwatli, Sarah Millspaugh, Alexander Rhinelander (site photographer), Helena Swiny, Clark Walz, Antigone Zournatzi (site supervisors), Anthi Held (registrar), John Gifford (geologist) and Douglas Kuylenstierna (photographer). That summer Rip Rapp undertook a sub-surface survey of the settlement. The Brock University Archaeological Practicum led by Dianne Berrigan participated in the 1983 field season.

Credit must go to the members of the 1983 archaeological survey field crew led by Steve Held. A. Aristidou, C. Cummings, B. and I. Dispain, G. Ewing, A. Greenway, T. LaTourette, S. Millspaugh, D. O'Connor, G. Panayiotou, C. Peaple, C. Roseen, J. Thompson, and A. Zournatzi endured the rigors of funicular surveying for various lengths of time. Bill Fox assisted in part of the systematic surface collection.

We include the intensive two year and eight month environmental study by Wouter van Warmelo which had began before the excavation was planned. Upon Swiny's request he agreed to submit it as a chapter for the final excavation report since it is such a valuable addition to our knowledge of the general area.

A final, short season of excavation was organized in 1986 with Linda Hulin, Ian Humphreys, Helena Swiny in the field, Chris Hulin (artifact database), Connie Rodriguez (data input), Sylvie

Hartmann (draftsperson), Ellen Herscher (ceramics), Michael Giltenane (architect) and Douglas Kuylenstierna (photographer). Helena Swiny was the Assistant Director who always ran the excavation when Swiny made his weekly visits to CAARI. She contributed much to the overall interpretation of the site. Throughout the project logistical support in the form of transport, equipment, communication and accommodation was provided by CAARI. Needless to say that Vathoulla Moustoukki, the Institute's Administrative Assistant, was considerably involved in the excavation: she ran CAARI when the Director was in the field, she liaised, she typed the finds lists and on occasion she dug. As with most things that involve CAARI, the project as a whole and the editors in particular owe her much.

The authors wish to thank the Department of Antiquities and the Cyprus Museum for their kindness in making the metalwork from *Kaminoudhia* available and in allowing the analysis of the specimens. We are grateful to Claudio Giardino and his colleagues for their willingness to sample the metal artifacts from the site and for producing a detailed report at short notice (Appendix 8.1). Never before has the near complete metal assemblage from a Cypriot Bronze Age site been quantitatively analyzed in what is a major contribution to Cypriot archaeometallurgical studies. Thanks are due to Dr. Maria Rosaria Belgiorno who arranged for the ED-XRF instruments to come to Cyprus.

The majority of the photographs published in the volume were printed by Mark Schmidt, Editor of Photography, *University Update* (University at Albany), who obviously enjoyed the challenge of making sun-baked Mediterranean mud and deep shadow look like something! We thank him for his skill and patience.

Swiny wishes to acknowledge the private donors who supported the 1981 exploratory season. The major excavation in 1983 was funded by a matching grant from the National Endowment for the Humanities (#RO-20549-83) to the Archaeometry Laboratory at the University of Minnesota, Duluth (UMD). We are indebted to those who contributed the necessary matching dollars. The major contributors were: Charles McCrossan, Daphne Bodart, Patricia P. and John H. Wylde, George Gibson, and Mary King Ostnel. Without the support of these individuals, the excavation would not have taken place. The Chair of the University at Albany Department of Classics, Louis W. Roberts, generously provided departmental funding for the printing of the plates published in this volume. In 1990 and 1991 Ellen Herscher was awarded two Fulbright Fellowships at CAARI to prepare the *Kaminoudhia* ceramic assemblage for publication. Alice Kingsnorth received a Charles and Janet Harris Fellowship to study and publish the chipped stone from the site.

Eastern Mediterranean archaeology does not have an exemplary record when it comes to publication. Perhaps this is due in part to the difficulty in securing adequate funds for this time consuming, protracted and often-tedious sequel to field work. We have been fortunate to receive three grants to prepare this publication. Two were from the Institute for Aegean Prehistory (INSTAP), and one was from the Graduate School Research Committee of the University of Minnesota. For these grants we are particularly appreciative.

During the publication phase, we were ably assisted by Russell Rothe and the late Doris Stoessel of the Archaeometry Laboratory at the Duluth Campus, University of Minnesota. The former produced final computer-drafted figures for the pottery profiles and some of the maps, and the latter was the able editorial assistant who helped make it all come together. She also started the index that was completed by Kathy Mallak. The final version of the text was prepared by Edith Dunn at the University of Minnesota. Over the years several people have helped collate, proof and double check the data contained in the chapters written by Swiny. Marita Anderson acted as Swiny's Research Assistant in Cyprus when he was on sabbatical at the American School of Classical Studies at Athens in 1993/4 and she undertook with typical style, good humor and acuity the tedious task of entering the information contained on the hundreds of sherd count sheets. Without her dedication to the task at hand Tables 2.1a to 2.1f would not exist. The final versions of these tables were typed for publication by Teresa Quadrini. Jan Camp mounted most of the ground stone figures while Maja Zivkovich and Alessandra Swiny diligently assembled the chipped stone figures. Swiny also wishes to acknowledge Harry Heywood's pertinent comments on the areas the latter excavated in the settlement. Kathy Mallak and Jessica Fisher Neidl, a Department of Classics graduate at the University at Albany, proofread most of Swiny's contributions. Genevieve Holdridge undertook at short notice the arduous task of drawing up the chipped stone catalogue and Nicole Grandinetti verified that corrections on the last set of proofs were accurate; they too were students at the above mentioned university. The architectural plans were prepared and inked by Michael Giltanine; the sections and chipped stone were drawn and inked by Jeanette van der Post. We thank them all for contributing their time and expertise to this volume and hope they will consider that the end result was worthy of their efforts.

The photograph of P. Dikaios on page vii is from *Photomosaic. Pictures through the Years by Porphyrios Dikaios*. Cultural Services. Ministry of Education and Culture, Nicosia, 1988.

The editors thank Gloria London, Editor of the American Schools of Oriental Research's Archaeological Reports series for her support of and interest in our publication and also acknowledge the assistance of Billie Jean Collins, ASOR Director of Publications, Department of Middle Eastern Studies, Emory University. Finally, we are grateful to the anonymous readers for their constructive suggestions and corrections of typographic errors. Any errors which remain are, of course, the responsibility of the editors.

S. Swiny
G. (Rip) Rapp
E. Herscher
September, 2001

1

INTRODUCTION

by George (Rip) Rapp and Stuart Swiny

BACKGROUND

The prehistoric archaeology of Cyprus was the fortunate beneficiary of the work of the Swedish Cyprus Expedition, which began to bring order to the vast quantities of poorly-understood Cypriot antiquities that had been resting in the world's museums since the nineteenth century. Under the leadership of Einar Gjerstad, beginning in the 1920s, the Swedes' careful field methodology, prompt publication, and cautious interpretations set the standards and established the framework that continue to dominate the field. Their work also secured for Cyprus its own important identity among the earliest cultures of the eastern Mediterranean.

The contributions of the Swedish Cyprus Expedition to the Early Cypriot Bronze Age, however, were hampered by several critical limitations. They only excavated tombs of the period, thus restricting the evidence to what was present in a funerary context. Secondly, while their excavations were extensive and produced an extremely large body of material, they were for the most part geographically confined to the site of Lapithos *Vrysi tou Barba*, on the central north coast of the island. Thirdly, the absence of extended occupational stratification left the beginning of the period shrouded in mystery and its transition from the preceding Chalcolithic ill-defined. Thus, SCE's final interpretive volume on the Early Bronze Age and preceding periods, Volume IV, Part 1A (1962), included conflicting interpretations by Porphyrios Dikaios and James R. Stewart, respectively, on a distinctive early assemblage that was termed the "Philia Culture."

In the years following the publication of SCE IV:1A, these issues continued to be debated without resolution. Particularly troubling was the growing body of ceramic material available from other regions of the island (little of it scientifically excavated) that did not conform to Stewart's rigorous classification scheme. How Early Cypriot settlement assemblages might differ from those found in funerary contexts was also the subject of increasing speculation, especially as the lithic assemblages of the period remained largely ignored. These questions, and Cypriot archaeology's evolution toward a more environmental and interdisciplinary approach, set the stage for explorations at Sotira *Kaminoudhia*.

PROJECT LOCATION

The project area lies in a region about fifteen kilometers west of Limassol, five kilometers from the south coast (fig. 1.1). The village of Sotira lies six kilometers northwest of the well-known city site of Kourion (the Roman Curium), which is surrounded by a string of settlements beginning in the Early Cypriot period. The best-preserved urban remains are from the period 80 B.C.E to 330 C.E. Kourion suffered extensive destruction in the 365 C.E. earthquake.

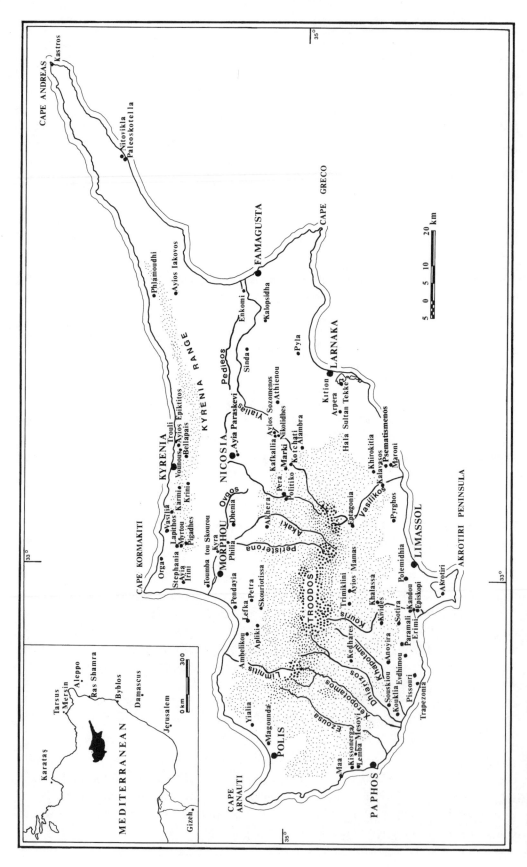

Fig. 1.1. Map of Cyprus with sites mentioned in text.

Sotira village and its predecessors were built around three perennial springs, the prime impetus for human occupation in the area. The elevation of Sotira *Teppes* is slightly greater than the surrounding territory, perhaps accounting for its choice as a habitation site (fig. 1.2). In Cyprus it is customary to name a site by appending the local toponym (in italics) to that of the village to which the land belongs. *Kaminoudhia*—meaning, "small lime kilns"—is a series of southward sloping terraces that borders the northern limits of Sotira village. The full name of the archaeological site is thus Sotira *Kaminoudhia*. More detailed descriptions of the geography, geology, climate, flora and fauna characteristic of the surrounding region may be found in Swiny 1981:51–55 and Swiny 1982:1–5.

PROJECT HISTORY

The original project was constituted to investigate the ill-defined beginnings of the Early Cypriot period, which correspond to the so-called "Philia Phase." Since the seminal publication by Gjerstad (1926) there have been major studies by H. W. Catling, K. Nicolaou, T. Watkins, N. Stanley Price, D. W. Rupp, and I. A. Todd, detailing prehistoric Cypriot settlement patterns and utilizing information from excavations and from a number of surveys. More recently, larger projects combining excavation with regional surveys have added significantly to our understanding of Bronze Age Cyprus (e.g., Todd 1982). The Sotira *Kaminoudhia* project combined excavation with a concomitant regional survey within a one-kilometer catchment area of the site to establish the relationship of the settlement to its environment. We assumed the chronology of the site to lie somewhere within the gap that separates the Chalcolithic, as defined at the nearby type site of Erimi *Pamboula*, and the Middle Bronze Age, recognized at Episkopi *Phaneromeni*, some seven and one-half kilometers southeast of *Kaminoudhia*, on the banks of the Kouris River (see fig. 1.2).

The area around the small community of Sotira was first noted as having archaeological remains in 1934, when P. Dikaios, then Curator of the Cyprus Museum, discovered a Neolithic settlement at *Teppes*, a prominent hill overlooking the modern village. He later returned to excavate the site for the University of Pennsylvania, and after its publication by the University Museum the so-called "Sotira Culture" became diagnostic of the Ceramic Neolithic in Cyprus. In the course of his 1947 investigations, Dikaios excavated a "Copper Age" tomb at *Kaminoudhia*, 400 m to the northeast of *Teppes* (see figs. 1.3, 3.1). This is briefly mentioned in the *University Museum Bulletin* for 1948 and in Dikaios' *Guide to the Cyprus Museum* (1953:12), but otherwise the finds remain unpublished.

In 1978, Swiny conducted an archaeological survey of the Episkopi region for Kent State University, Ohio (Swiny 1981). This led to the reinvestigation of the area around Sotira *Kaminoudhia* with intent to relocate the tomb dug by Dikaios and any others that might lie nearby, and to discover the settlement that likely existed in the vicinity. The general area of the "Copper Age" tomb was located and named Cemetery A (pl. 1.2). On the hillside opposite, to the east, three rock-cut looted chambers were recorded as Cemetery B.

A surface sherd scatter of Red Polished ware, many ground stone tools and some flint suggested that a settlement had once existed about 200 m to the south under a series of wide terraces on the outskirts of the modern village (pls. 1.1, 1.2, 1.3; fig. 1.3). In 1981 an excavation permit was requested from the Department of Antiquities to undertake the ASOR-sponsored Cyprus American Archaeological Research Institute (CAARI) excavations at Sotira *Kaminoudhia*. The four-week exploratory season was able to evaluate the potential of the site.

Five soundings were made in the uppermost terrace in an attempt to determine the extent and preservation of the settlement. Although the deposit only reached 0.5 m in Area A, to the north, it was here that the most comprehensive archaeological remains were recovered (pls. 1.3 and 1.4). To the west in Area B (pl. 1.3), and farther down slope in Area C (pl. 1.5), a greater depth of eroded material

4

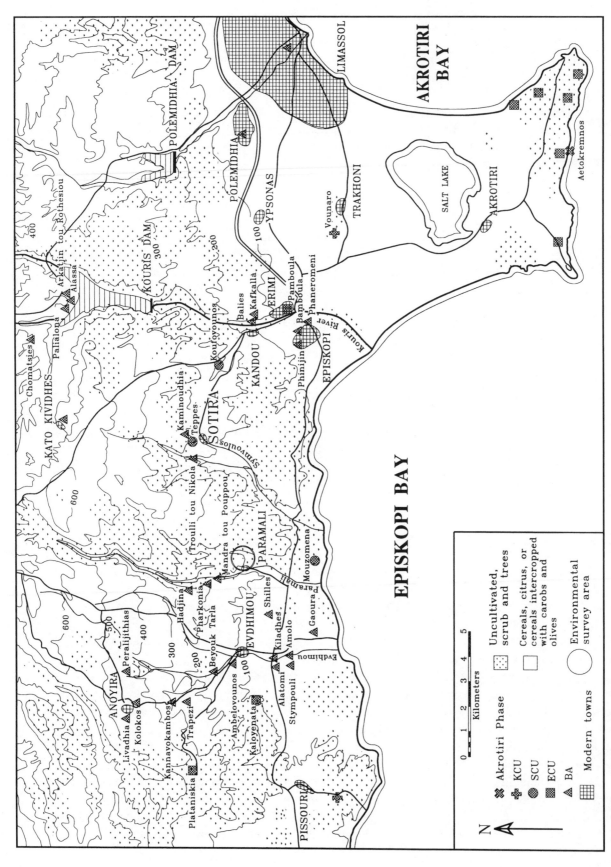

Fig. 1.2. Topographical and land use map of the Episkopi region with ancient and modern settlements and sites.

covered the archaeological strata, which as a result were better preserved. The excavations yielded a large quantity of finds, namely pottery, ground and chipped stone tools, gaming stones, terracotta spindle whorls and loom weights, the riveted butt of a copper-based dagger and other minor metal objects, picrolite personal ornaments, and a cruciform figurine of the same material. Most of the pottery belonged to the Red Polished ceramic tradition, but significant quantities of Chalcolithic sherds were also recorded.

The probes defined a settlement that covered at least a hectare. Investigations in the area around the tomb excavated by Dikaios failed to detect other burials, but a short distance farther south several eroded tomb chambers were cleared. On the flank of the hill to the east three other visible chambers were excavated. The 1981 season demonstrated that a significant portion of the settlement was preserved, and that the cemetery had the potential of yielding undisturbed tomb chambers. In order to insure that the necessary breadth of expertise was available, a joint CAARI-Archaeometry Laboratory (University of Minnesota-Duluth) team was formed to excavate the site and perform an intensive survey of the area of the site. Co-directors Swiny (archaeology) and Rapp (archaeological science) applied successfully for a Cyprus Department of Antiquities permit and for a National Endowment for Humanities matching grant.

PROJECT ORGANIZATION

The concepts of regional archaeology and an interdisciplinary approach lie at the roots of the experience of both co-directors. Swiny was the Field Director of the Kent State University excavations at Episkopi *Phaneromeni* (Swiny 1986) and its associated survey (Swiny 1978). Currently he is Director of the Institute of Cypriot Studies at the University at Albany. Rapp was Associate Director of the Minnesota Messenia Expedition (McDonald and Rapp 1972) and its excavation at Nichoria (Rapp and Aschenbrenner 1978) in Greece and later Archaeometric Director of the excavations and related survey at Tel Michal, Israel (Herzog, Rapp, and Negbi 1989). Currently he is Co-Director of a major Bronze Age interdisciplinary archaeological project at Anyang, China.

Hence, the project approach was to develop a strong interdisciplinary team of experts covering all facets of excavation methodology, survey techniques, and specialties ranging from archaeometry and geoarchaeology through paleoethnobotany and petrography to zooarchaeology. From the beginning, the co-directors firmly believed it was necessary to enlist the expertise of Herscher (1976, 1979, 1981, 1991) to anchor the ceramic studies.

THE SITE—EXCAVATION AND CHRONOLOGY

The settlement, which has two phases in Area A, consists of accretive, mostly rectilinear stone-built domestic structures, communicating with one another by means of long, narrow alleyways. Individual units consist typically of two to three intercommunicating rooms used for habitation and presumably storage. Many interior walls were abutted by rectangular hearths and low, narrow benches sometimes running their full length; the floors often had countersunk stone mortars and lime plaster bins. Several entrances were fitted with high monolithic thresholds, complete with pivot holes to support the hinged doors. It was impossible to detect specialization within units, most of which seem to have served domestic multipurpose functions, as indicated by numerous lithic, ceramic, and occasional metal finds. The bulk of these consist of querns, rubbers, pounders, etc., chert sickle blades, a broad range of Early Cypriot Red Polished bowls, jugs and amphorae supplemented by a few storage jars, terracotta spindle whorls and loom weights. Copper-based artifacts were rare, being represented by two fragmentary knives, an axe and some chisels, awls, needles, and personal ornaments. Most

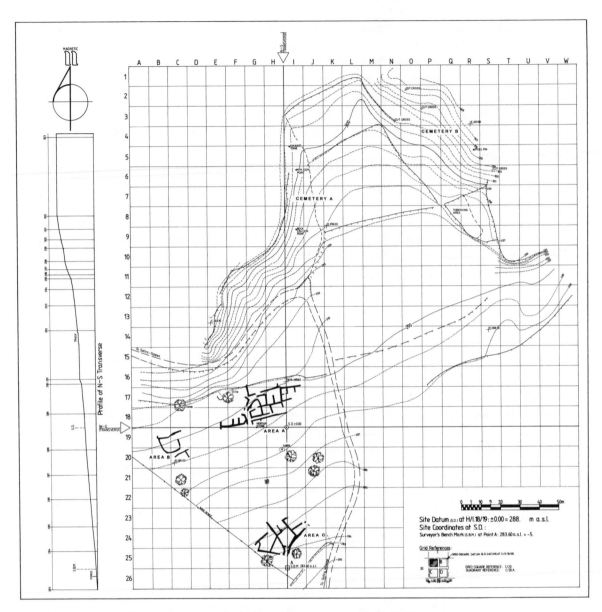

Fig. 1.3. Site plan of Sotira *Kaminoudhia*. Prepared and drawn by S. O. Held.

ornaments—pendants, beads, and enigmatic tubes—however, were made from easily carved, highly polished picrolite.

The agro-pastoral economy was based on the exploitation of cattle, reintroduced for the first time since the earliest Aceramic Neolithic phase (Guilaine et al. 1995), caprovids, pigs, and fallow deer, which provided meat and milk products, as well as the usual range of cereals and pulses, supplemented by the cultivation of the olive and perhaps the vine. *Kaminoudhia* was apparently profiting from the benefits of the secondary products revolution and many of the large spouted stone troughs may have been used for the production of olive oil.

Due to the effects of erosion and looting, only seven out of twenty-one tombs were preserved with articulated skeletal remains and grave goods: namely quantities of pottery, some terracotta spindle whorls, stone and shell personal ornaments and metal. The latter consisted of a diagnostic Philia Phase knife and an unforged billet of another knife similar in size. A series of equally characteristic spiral earrings with one flattened terminal, made from copper and tin bronze, had been worn by the deceased at the time of burial. Most unexpectedly, a pair of intertwined gold (electrum) earrings of identical type lay next to one skeleton. To date this is the earliest occurrence of gold on the island.

The ceramic assemblage at Sotira *Kaminoudhia* can be assigned generally to the Early Cypriot Red Polished tradition. The vessels from some tombs—but not the settlement—show close affinities to the Philia Phase repertory, dating to the very beginning of the Early Cypriot Bronze Age. Phase I material from Area A exhibits the earliest ceramic styles from the settlement. It is also from this level that most of the Middle and Late Chalcolithic pottery originates. The latest diagnostic object from Phase II can be assigned to Early Cypriot III.

In the course of the excavation a number of charcoal and carbonized plant samples with good stratigraphic provenience were recovered. Carbon-14 dates provide a radiometric chronology of ca. 2400–2174 B.C.E. for Phases I and II (Manning and Swiny 1994 and Chapter 17 infra), which is consistent with our archaeological observations.

Throughout this volume, the following chronological sequence has been adopted. The dates for the first three phases are based on the most recent radiocarbon determinations presented in *The Earliest Prehistory of Cyprus: From Colonization to Exploitation* (ed. S. Swiny), CAARI Monograph Series, Volume 2, American Schools of Oriental Research, Archaeological Reports, No. 5, Boston 2001.

Pre-Neolithic (Akrotiri Phase)	ca. 9825 B.C.E.
Aceramic Neolithic	ca. 8200–5800/5500 B.C.E.
Cypro-Pre-Pottery Neolithic B	ca. 8200–7000 B.C.E.
Khirokitia Culture (KCU)	ca. 7000–5800/5500 B.C.E.
Ceramic Neolithic (Sotira Culture - SCU)	ca. 4600–3900 B.C.E.
Chalcolithic (Erimi Culture - ECU)	ca. 3900–2500 B.C.E.
Early Cypriot	ca. 2500–2000 B.C.E.
(Philia Phase)	ca. 2500–2400 B.C.E.
Middle Cypriot	ca. 2000–1600 B.C.E.
Late Cypriot I	ca. 1600–1450 B.C.E.
Late Cypriot II	ca. 1450–1200 B.C.E.
Late Cypriot III	ca. 1200–1050 B.C.E.
Cypro-Geometric	ca. 1050–750 B.C.E.

STRUCTURE OF THIS VOLUME

The sixteen chapters that comprise the remainder of this volume begin with comprehensive chapters on the settlement and the cemetery. These are followed by the core ceramics chapters—typology and petrography. The ground stone and knapped stone assemblages are the next topics, followed by the metals and the terracottas. These are, in turn, succeeded by the four chapters on bioarchaeology: human skeletal remains, faunal remains, botanical remains, and the mollusks. The next three chapters cover the regional environmental aspects: the geologic and geomorphic setting, the regional survey, and the environmental survey. The volume concludes with a presentation of *Kaminoudhia's* relative and absolute chronology.

2

THE SETTLEMENT

by Stuart Swiny

INTRODUCTION

The settlement of *Kaminoudhia* covers about one hectare of the gently southward sloping terraces some 200 m north of Sotira Village (pls. 1.1, 1.2, 1.3; fig. 1.3). Architectural remains were uncovered in three areas, known as A, B, and C. The largest exposure, in Area A, corresponds to the northeastern extension of the settlement, with Area B 35 m to the west, and Area C 50 m to the south. A trial trench linking Areas A and B demonstrated that well-preserved architectural remains extend without a hiatus between the two. South of Area A the bedrock rises to the present ground level and three widely spaced trial trenches failed to detect any preserved architecture. In Operation K21D, next to the road in the east, the smooth bedrock, 1 m below the surface, had a carefully cut mortar, 20 cm in diameter and 10 cm deep, skillfully lined with a layer of lime plaster 0.3 cm thick. All the pottery recovered from this operation dated to the Bronze Age.

The architectural remains and finds were first studied by Ian Humphreys in his Master of Arts thesis submitted to Drew University in 1987 (Humphreys 1987). He undertook a detailed functional analysis of each unit in order to suggest activities that may have taken place therein and in the process prepared the plans with stratified finds, figs. 2.1 to 2.15. Humphreys concluded that most spaces had multi-functional uses. His research greatly facilitated my publication of the settlement which, with the added results provided by stratigraphic analysis and the chipped stone, ceramic and faunal studies, enabled me to advance more specific ideas—especially in connection with Area C—on the possible function of some areas.

The soil in all areas of the settlement consisted of colluvium with angular chips of bedrock. A random sample in an area 30 x 30 cm in Area C contained the following quantities: 10 pieces of 6.5 x 3 cm, three of 3.5 x 3 cm, two of 2 x 1.5 cm, in addition to a large quantity of much smaller chips. In all areas of the settlement the typical Munsell color of the topsoil is 10YR 6/2 or 7/2, described as "light brownish." Once dense wall tumble was encountered the color darkened a little to the eye, yet the Munsell reading remained similar with 10YR 6/2. Ashy occupational debris, on or directly associated with floors, was normally 7.5YR 5/2, described as "brown."

Features (Ft) consisting of hearths, lime plaster bins, rock-cut mortars etc.—but not benches—are drawn though not numbered on the site plans (figs. 2.16 [insert], 2.16a, 2.17, 2.18 [insert]), which only show spot elevations and wall identifications. They are numbered on the individual unit plans with stratified finds (figs. 2.1–2.15). Object numbers are preceded by a letter indicating their medium, e.g., B for bone, M for metal, P for pottery and TC for terracotta. When more than one item is listed the letter prefix is not repeated, e.g., S12, 6 and 27. For a variety of reasons, not all items listed under "Finds" for each unit are located on individual unit plans. In Unit 22, the sherds associated with the human skeleton have been stippled. These features and in situ (IS) items are numbered along with artifact find spots on the individual unit plans (figs. 2.1–2.15).

Note that on the section drawings figs. 2.19a to 2.21 c, the term "Room" is used instead of "Unit."

The datum for the spot elevations in Areas A, B, and C is the lowest point in each area and is not the absolute height above average sea level. Reading site plans knowing that elevations are x cm above the lowest point in this part of the site is far more meaningful. The site datum located at the intersection of H/I and 18/19, shown on fig. 1.3, is 288 m above sea level.

The excavation method used is based on the Lot system. Lots are discrete units of excavated material sequentially numbered for each Operation or Unit. Stratified finds are recorded by Unit. Unstratified finds are recorded by Operation and Lot number, the latter being underlined: e.g., H24C 6, signifies Operation H24C Lot 6.

AREA A

The northern edge of the settlement, bordered by the track leading to Sotira *Teppes* and the long, eroded east–west terrace wall, was designated Area A (pls. 1.3 and 1.4). The most extensive and complex architectural remains were discovered here, extending 40 m east–west by 20 m north–south, of which 375 m² were excavated. Unfortunately, most of the cultural deposit is shallow and bedrock is either just beneath the present ground level or at most 1 m below. The topsoil above all structures contained a few lithics and a mixture of eroded basin fragments, Red Polished, a few Drab Polished and many miscellaneous undiagnostic sherds.

Most of the pottery belonging to the Chalcolithic tradition was recovered from Area A (see Chapter 4, Appendix 4.1), and it is also here that two phases of building activity could be architecturally and stratigraphically isolated. Phase I, which furnishes the earliest evidence of Bronze Age settlement, was succeeded by Phase II, noticeable for the subdivision of large spaces and the addition of benches. Here, as elsewhere in the settlement, the clearance of a complete and fully coherent architectural plan would have required the excavation of a surface area beyond the means of the project. Area A yielded a higher percentage of caprine and pig remains in relation to those from cattle (cf. Chapter 11.3).

UNIT 1

PHASE I (figs. 2.1, 2.16 [insert]; pls. 2.1a, 2.1b, 2.1c, 2.2a)

Unit 1 occupies a central position in Area A and it was within its walls that a trial trench was sunk at *Kaminoudhia* on the first day of the 1981 season. Once interconnecting walls had been traced, it was given the designation Unit 1. As excavation progressed, it became apparent that in its original form Unit 1 covered the whole area and was subdivided by a later wall. The stratigraphy is clear in its broad lines, but is often confused in its details, due to the shallowness of the deposit coupled with extensive root action.

Unit 1 is large by *Kaminoudhia* standards, with walls oriented to the cardinal points measuring 7.2 x 6.7 m, and with a surface area in Phase I of 48.5 m². The architectural sequence in this area is complex. Unit 1 and those immediately to the east were in use for a greater period and were subject to more alterations than any others at the site.

In Phase I the unit was bounded to the north by the sturdily constructed WI, which incorporated several large, plow-scarred, boulders in its outer face (1.29 x 0.64 m). An additional alignment of fieldstones 30 cm wide flanked it to the south, preserved to a maximum height of 83 cm above Floor 2 with an average width of 60 cm, and extended almost the full length of the wall. This was perhaps a bench that could have served as a low buttress to help counter the effects of down slope soil creep that caused the wall to slip up to 27 cm south in some areas. In the northwest corner of Unit 1 two limestone slabs resting on Floor 2 were set vertically against the south face of the wall.

Up to ten courses of WI were preserved in situ, stacked like fallen dominos at 45° after having toppled downslope in a southerly direction after the structure was abandoned at the end of Phase II (see pl. 2.1a). The accumulated measurements of nine building stones (their individual widths are: 12, 12, 13, 12, 15, 13.5, 12, 12.5 and 15 cm) to which should be added at least 3.5 cm of mud mortar for bonding each course, plus the existing in situ wall stub of 45 cm, prove that WI once stood to a minimum height of 1.93 m.

In the northeast corner of Unit 1, WI appears bonded with WM that runs south, but the outer skin of the wall is now missing and the original relationship of the two walls is uncertain. WM has an average width of 60 cm, is well built of medium sized fieldstones of which a maximum of four courses survives to a height of 45 cm above Floor 2.

The meandering and poorly preserved stretch of WQ, known as WC west of WE, defines Unit 1 to the south. In the same manner as WI, it too has suffered from up slope soil pressure, with some stones of the top two courses in the WC section being displaced southwards by up to 17 cm. Even more destructive have been the effects of large carob roots snaking their way along the wall, just above bedrock. In Phase I an entrance 70 cm wide adjacent to the southern end of WB and the western extremity of WC provided the only preserved means of access to Unit 1.

The southeast corner of the room at the juncture of WQ and WM is difficult to interpret. The preserved walls are clearly not bonded, and, in the lowest corner of the unit, there is a gap of 20 cm between the two, caused either by the down slope drift of WQ or left intentionally open to serve as a drain (?). WC-WQ is preserved to a maximum of four courses and a height of 43 cm, with an average width of 60 cm.

To the west WB, on average 50 cm wide and a maximum of three courses high, is the best-preserved and constructed wall of Unit 1. The carefully aligned fieldstones in its eastern face may have been covered with a layer of mud plaster. Those in the south are larger (av. 40 x 30 cm) than the site norm (30 x 22 cm), which is found in the northern stretch of the wall. The wall is two stones wide with a small amount of rubble filling between in some places. As preserved, the northern end of WB terminates 1.24 m south of WI where it is abutted on the west by WK, the north wall of Unit 5. A single stone in the lowest course of WI, set on bedrock, protrudes from the southern face of the wall, suggesting that in Phase I the two walls (WI and WB) were connected and that the only entrance to Unit 1 was located in the southwest corner between WB and WC.

It should be noted that only one building stone with evidence for reuse was found in the Unit 1 walls (see the stone with a pecked circle in outer face of WI opposite elevation point 198, fig. 2.16 [see insert]). This is in contrast with the Phase II benches and most walls to the west of Unit 1 or in Areas B and C, which incorporate many artifacts reused as building material. This fact supports an early date for Unit 1 and suggests it was constructed before numerous stones with evidence for a prior function, such as querns and mortars, were available for building purposes.

Unit 1 walls were set directly on bedrock with no prior leveling of the uneven, southward sloping surface that served as the original Phase I floor, namely Floor 2. The only exception is a 3.5 m section of WC, between WE and WB, which is built on occupation debris up to 27 cm thick overlaying bedrock.

Phase I features in Unit 1 consist of Ft 1, a good example of a lime plaster bin, in the northeast corner and a series of cuts and holes (#1–11, see pl. 2.1b) in the homogenous white havara, all concentrated in the northeast quadrant of the room. Some, best described as "post holes," are straight-sided, circular cavities carefully cut into the bedrock. They range from 10 to 23 cm in diameter (av. 15 cm) and are up to 15 cm deep. For example #1, 16 cm in diameter, contained a few small stones lining its sides as if to serve as wedges for a wooden post. Others contained either sterile soil or a rare fragment of bone. Despite their general uniformity in size and depth, the pits failed to display a coherent pattern. Some, such as #7, were later remodeled and bisected by other cuts. More regular in shape and resembling a "flat iron" is #12 (39 x 19 cm) with its main axis running north–south. The southern end consists of a shallow step about 9 cm wide and 5 cm deep, with the remainder of the pit extending approximately 15 cm below the step. The slightly darker filling of this carefully shaped, enigmatic pit was sterile.

Roughly in the middle of Unit 1 and 1.7 m south of WI, #14 is a shallow L-shaped trench or runnel, 10 cm wide and 14 cm deep, with its main axis (one m long) oriented EW (see fig. 2.16 [insert] and pl. 2.1b on right). At its western end the runnel turns south, disappearing after a distance of 60 cm. No clues as to its function were found. This feature and all others in Unit 1 that were cut into bedrock and in use during Phase I were deliberately plastered over during the building activity of Phase II.

The lime plaster bin in the northeast corner of the unit (Ft 1) has a maximum diameter of 43 cm, an inner diameter of 30 cm, and depth of 30 cm. The base consists of a stone mortar with a deep, conical depression held in place by a collar of lime plaster 20 cm high, carefully smoothed to form a rounded rim at the level of Floor 2. It contained several pieces of animal bone. Feature 2, southwest of the center of the room, was of similar construction but slightly smaller with an internal rim diameter of 34 cm and a depth of 19 cm (pl. 2.1c). It was empty and showed evidence of several replasterings around the rim, indicating an extended period of use starting in Phase I and, unlike Ft 1, remaining in use during Phase II. In the area around Ft 2 the plaster of Floor 2 was well preserved and could be followed with ease as it ran up to and under WE. Unfortunately, in all other directions it soon disappeared as the result of root action and plowing, especially in the northwest quadrant of the room. In this corner was located Ft 3, a third plaster bin 22 cm in diameter and 15 cm deep, that contained a pounder (S668) and a small axe (S698) lying on its rim. Despite a wealth of artifacts and features, no evidence for a fireplace was recorded in this unit.

Stratigraphy

Extensive root action and the effects of plowing had seriously disturbed the stratigraphy in the western half of Unit 1 to the extent that it was impossible to separate Phases I and II, except in the areas adjacent to Ft 2 and 15 to 50 cm north of WC and WQ. The in situ Phase I deposit consisted of hard packed, fine, light brown occupation debris (7.5YR 6/3), rich in flecks of charcoal with a few sherds and some chipped and ground stone tools. In the eastern half of the room the stratigraphy was better preserved, and this deposit containing bone, chipped stone, and sherds, with a few ashy patches, was well sealed by Floor 1. Where definable, Floor 2 of Phase I consists either of the bedrock, as in the northern half of the room, or of a layer of plaster up to 2 cm thick laid on the light orange paleosol. The latter is patchy and in this part of the site never forms more than a 10 cm thick deposit above the havara. The only exception is the area close to the north face of WC, between WB and WE, where Floor 2 is laid over an accumulation of occupation debris 27cm thick. An excavated sample of this material contained chipped stone and four sherds, two of Chalcolithic types and two of Early Cypriot RP ware lying on bedrock (this area is visible on the right of pl. 2.1c).

The large size of this area, measuring 7.2 x 6.7 m, argues against it having been roofed unless posts were used to support large beams running from wall to wall. In view of the typical widths of rooms, dictated by the practical size of beams required to span them, it seems unlikely that Unit 1 was roofed in Phase I.

Finds

By comparison with the density of finds from the later Phase II, this phase was quite barren, probably because serviceable items would have been reused whenever possible. Only small areas of the undisturbed Phase I habitation surface remained intact. Pounders were the most common artifacts, numbering eight (S87, 157, 171, 201, 212, 639, 668, 686) followed by six rubber-pounders (S106, 127, 136, 164, 205, 210), two or perhaps three axes (S521, 671, 698) and three rubbers (S206, 696, 697). A cockle shell pendant (Sh2) came from the east side of the unit. The only ceramic find of note is a fragmentary RP pot stand P81, perhaps the local equivalent of the hobs so popular at Marki *Alonia* (Frankel and Webb 1996:181). The fragment of a conical spindle whorl (TC 39) came from this phase.

PHASE II (figs. 2.2 and 2.16 [insert])

The addition of narrow benches against three walls, the closure of the door in WC, and construction of WE dividing Unit 1 into two, now Units 2 (west) and 3 (east), represent building activity in Phase II. All were built on top of Phase I occupational debris (see fig. 2.19a showing the bench on the south of WI constructed over Floor 2 material), on average about 10 cm thick, but in some areas, specifically in the southwest corner of the unit where WG, the east wall of Unit 6, intersects with the south face of WQ/WC (not labeled), the accumulation above bedrock is up to 27 cm.

Compared with the construction of the perimeter walls of Unit 1, WE is of inferior manufacture. Built exactly in the middle of the room, it is preserved for a length of 4.1 m, although some coursed tumble to the north suggests it originally may have extended a little farther toward WI, though still leaving an opening for the only means of access to Unit 3. WE has a width of approximately 50 cm and a maximum preserved height of 46 cm with three courses of fieldstones. On its eastern side, 40 cm from WQ, a large tabular piece of limestone (75 x 35 x 7 cm; clearly visible in pl. 2.2a) had been carefully set on its side against the wall. WE is built on top of the well laid and preserved plaster of Floor 1 that runs up to the rim of Ft 2, the lime plaster bin. This implies that WE is slightly later than the benches resting on occupational debris sealed in places by Floor 1, which runs up against the lowest course of these benches. Unfortunately, the plaster surface of Floor 1 was only preserved in unconnected patches.

At an early stage of Phase II the doorway leading into Unit 1 from the southwest through WC was blocked and perhaps turned into a cupboard or niche. A horizontal slab of limestone, 50 cm long and level with the third course of stones in the wall, was laid upon the pisé(?) used for blocking the northern half of the door. Vertically placed stones appear to provide the sides of a niche at either end of the slab, since the space was lacking the rubble packing normally forming the core of walls. Unfortunately, the wall was not preserved to a sufficient height to confirm this interpretation.

The northern section of WB is fronted by a low bench 14 cm high with an average width of 40 cm, preserved for a length of 2.9 m. Some evidence suggests it had once extended farther south, but whether it ever reached WC is unclear. The northern section of the bench consists of three querns left in situ set into a layer of havara and occupational debris. The southernmost of these is inverted and only useful as a flat work surface. The others were right side up, but sat so close to the wall that they could not have been operational. They were perhaps seats or had been stored on the bench. Another quern also left in place in the southeast corner of Unit 3 could have served the same purpose, since it was also placed too close to the wall to be serviceable. Several artifacts lay on the bench, including two axes (S128, 132) and two pounders (S130, 139).

A bench up to 45 cm in height, made of three courses of stones with a width of around 35 cm, running along the entire southern face of WI, was constructed on top of Floor 1. Its upper surface included a flat stone with a shallow pecked depression 12 cm in diameter, and a quern rubber was built into its body. Since the tumble from the outer courses of WI completely sealed the upper surface of the bench, it was clearly not yet another reinforcing skin added to WI (see above in connection with Phase I and pl. 1.1a) and it is preserved to its original height.

There is no reason this unit should not have been roofed, since it is about 3 m wide, thus an ideal span for beams. The need for at least partial protection from the elements might be the cause for the construction of WE in Phase II, since as previously mentioned, the original unit was too large to roof with ease.

Stratigraphy

The whole unit was covered with a thin, uneven scatter of wall tumble just beneath the plow zone. Many stones were plow-scarred, and with the exception of those in situ on walls, had been disturbed at some stage. To the south of WI in the north of the room the tumble was well coursed (see description of WI above), thus sealing the debris below. This was not the case to the south, yet that is where most of the artifacts were found. Where preserved, Floor 1 consisted of packed light brown occupation debris (7.5YR 6/3), including some charcoal and a scattering of sherds and lithics.

Finds (fig. 2.2)

A glance at the plan will show the unique concentration of ground stone artifacts from the southern half of the unit. This is especially noticeable in comparison with adjoining Unit 3, with only twenty-seven stone artifacts recorded. Intact or restorable ceramic vessels, on the other hand, were rare. Atypically for *Kaminoudhia*, rubber-pounders dominate the assemblage instead of pounders (twenty-three examples: S1, 2, 3, 12, 30, 33, 34, 36, 40, 41, 42, 47, 51, 54, 56, 63, 67, 82, 83, 88, 96, 155, 164: see "Pounder" in Chapter 6). In Unit 3, pounders were the second most popular artifact type with twenty examples (S4, 11, 13, 14, 29, 43, 45, 46, 48, 49, 55, 64, 66, 70, 130, 139, 158, 170, 172, IS14) followed by six hammerstones (S58, 62, 65, 68, 92, 133), six pecking stones (S53, 84, 99, 126, 154, 169), two rubbing stones (S59, 76), two rubbers (S101, 121), five axes of various types (S9, 123, 128, 132, 159) and two artifacts suitable for use as—and with the wear marks typical of—pestles (S31, 39). The number of querns proves that grain grinding took place here. Four (S38, IS41, 42, 43) were found on the western bench, either stored there or reused as seats. The two rubbers (S5, 160) would have been used with the querns and the rubbing stone (S15). The remaining utilitarian ground stone artifacts consist of a heterogeneous assemblage of a perforated stone (S79), three palettes (S52 [very questionable], 105, 119) and a work surface (S6). Personal ornaments made from picrolite were represented by two pendants (S143, 150) and a fragmentary female cruciform figurine (S144). The figurine of typical Chalcolithic type (see Chapter 6: The Ground Stone "Cruciform figurine") is probably an heirloom. A fragment of a large (unstratified) picrolite cruciform figurine was also excavated at Marki *Alonia* (Frankel and Webb 1996b:66, fig. 4). One elongated bean pod-shaped piece of worked picrolite (S142) is of uncertain function. Of note is the presence of four spindle whorls (TC3, 6, 7, 11), an unusual concentration for *Kaminoudhia*, and two loom weights (TC1, 2). A pottery roundel, TC49, was also recorded. A spindle whorl, TC9, came from the topsoil above Unit 1.

The high number of pecking stones suggests the manufacture or shaping of stone objects, and the abundance of tools used for rubbing and pounding is perhaps indicative of other specialized activities as well. The pecking stones were also probably used for chert knapping, an activity for which strong evidence comes in the form of a fine antler hammer (B7, Appendix 11.1). Ceramic vessels were rare in this unit as diagnostic sherds from a maximum of four small RP bowls (one with a lug, P144), a RP jug and a juglet were found. Basin fragments were equally sparse and only numbered thirty-three (see Table 2.1).

UNIT 3

PHASE II (figs. 2.2, 2.16 [insert]; pls. 2.1c, 2.2a, 2.2b)

An arbitrary line between the end of WE and the northern wall WI separated the finds from Units 1 and 3. Thus on the east side of WE the area is designated as Unit 3 in Phase II where the division between the two phases is much clearer.

Floor 1 in Unit 3 is covered with a light gray (10YR 7/2) 10 to 20 cm thick accumulation of occupation debris rich in pottery, chipped stone and bone. As in Unit 1, most of the artifacts were concentrated in the southern half of the room.

A bench was constructed on Floor 1 along the entire western face of WM. It is 40 cm wide to the north where it turns west to join up with the bench along WI, but narrows to 30 cm in width in the vicinity of WQ. That any artifacts were found in situ on the bench is fortunate since its surface was just below the top of WM that in turn was very close to the plow zone.

Access to Units 1 and 3 during Phase II was via a one meter wide corridor in the northwest corner of Unit 1 (pl. 2.2b, center left). At present its northern wall, WI, does not extend more than 2.5 m west of Unit 1, this area being very close to the surface and consequently badly eroded. It probably once connected with WAL, which follows the same alignment 3 m to the west, forming a narrow passage-way 5 m long leading to Units 1 and 3.

The space between WI and WK, the north wall of Unit 5, was packed with wall tumble, but two flat rectangular stones placed horizontally on bedrock form a possible threshold extending perpendicular to WI for a distance of 75 cm toward WB. If this interpretation is correct, these stones are aligned with the east face of WB and could be part of the original wall that closed off the northwest corner of Unit 1 in Phase I.

Of note is a slab of stone 74 cm long, set against the south face of WI near the middle of the passage, clearly visible in pl. 2.2b.

Finds

As in Unit 1 Phase II, most of the finds in Unit 3 Phase II were in the southern half of the area. They consist of eight pounders (S125, 182, 189, 200, 202, 223, 645, IS15), four hammerstones (S137, 562, 647, 650), one rubbing stone (S181), three rubber-pounders (S122, 124, 187), six querns (S151, 152, IS12, 13, 46, 53) and two rubbers (S188, 696), a work surface (S196), and finally two pottery roundels (TC46 and TC50).

In the southeast corner of the unit a RP Mottled dipper (P38) and RP amphora (P24) were found in pieces amid and under the wall tumble, well above the floor level. The dipper was still sitting on the bench fronting WM and the amphora lay in the same horizontal plane, but had been displaced 20 cm to the west. The evidence suggests that its original position was on the bench. Half of two RP Mottled bowls (P113 and 125) were also recorded. Pottery seems to have been more common in Unit 3 than in Unit 1 since, in addition to the RP vessels listed, diagnostic sherds belonging to a maximum of five small and four large RP bowls, a RP jug, a cooking pot and a storage jar were recorded (Table 2.1).

U N I T 4

PHASE I (figs. 2.3, 2.16 [insert]; pl. 2.2c)

In Area A, Phase I is characterized by two large, approximately square spaces, Unit 1 already described, and Unit 4 to the east, sharing the party wall WM. This unit is bounded on the north side by an exceptionally regular and well-constructed section of WI, approximately 26 cm high with only two courses of stones. At 6.5 m from WM a cross-wall, WAV, abuts WI at right angles and with one course preserved extends south for 2.7 m, at which point it is completely eroded. All architectural remains seem to have been lost in the southeastern quarter of Area A where bedrock immediately underlies the plow zone and for this reason WAV, WD and WT all end abruptly, making it impossible fully to understand the arrangement of their associated units.

The western boundary, wall WM, already described in connection with Unit 1, is bonded at its southern end with WD, which runs east for 3.7 m before disappearing as the result of erosion. If both WAV and WD are hypothetically projected until they intersect in the southeast corner of the unit, the space enclosed would be on average 5.6 m wide by 6.5 m long with a surface area of 37 m^2, or approximately 10 m^2 smaller than Unit 1.

The rectilinear, carefully built section of WI, 60 cm wide, was laid in a foundation trench cut into the soft bedrock. It is preserved to a height of 40 cm made up of three courses, and the deliberate use of "headers and stretchers" is noted here for the only time at the settlement. WI extends to the east for 2.5 m past WAV, retaining two courses of stones, before ending in an amorphous pile of pebble-sized rubble (not drawn on fig. 2.16 [see insert]). On the south side of the wall, the foundation trench is 20 cm deep and from 15 to 18 cm wide; to the north it is on average 20 cm wide. Sherds excavated from the trench consist of Bronze Age and Chalcolithic wares. The eastern wall, WAV, 55 cm wide and preserved to a height of two courses against WI, was also set in a foundation trench cut into the soft pinkish surface layer overlaying bedrock. The 70 cm wide trench is not as deep as that for WI and the lowest course of stones abutting WI sits on the backfill of the latter. WAV was laid against the east edge of the foundation trench, presumably to provide the maximum amount of workspace for the builders.

To the south, wall WD, on average 65 cm wide with a maximum of three courses preserved to a height of 37 cm, was built on a step cut 23 cm into the bedrock on its north side. the face of the wall is between 12 to 25 cm from the edge of the cut, which has the appearance of a typical foundation trench. At its eastern end, only one course of stones is preserved.

The entrance to Unit 4 must have been through one of the now eroded walls forming the southeast corner, as none of the remaining walls have any evidence for a doorway. The only feature unequivocally attributed to Phase I is Ft 15, a lime plaster bin built around a stone mortar in the southeast quadrant of the Unit, 20 cm north of WD. Despite its poor state of preservation it contained the smashed remains of a cooking pot, P122, providing the only evidence for the function of at least some lime plaster bins (see pl. 2.3a). A plaster surface surrounding Ft 15 extends up to WD, running over its backfilled foundation trench and connecting with Floor 2, which is better preserved to the west. Patches of plaster floor were recorded throughout Unit 4—except in the eroded southeast corner—either immediately on bedrock or on sterile, pinkish white (7.5YR 8/2) sediment.

In the northeast quadrant of Unit 4, 1.3 m from WI and 70 cm from WAV, a fire-reddened circular area on bedrock, 25 cm in diameter, suggests that there had once been a fire or small hearth at this spot (Ft 32). The degree of discoloration of the bedrock indicates that considerable heat had been generated, presumably over an extended period. Had any built features existed in association with Ft 32, they were removed when the unit was remodeled in Phase II.

Stratigraphy

The whole area was covered with a thin, uneven scatter of wall tumble mixed with occupation debris just beneath the plow zone. Unlike those units to the west, where tumble was arranged in even courses, here, presumably due to the shallowness of the topsoil, no pattern could be determined. Below the tumble the soil was very compact and quite rich in sherds, chipped stone and bone. Extensive root action was noted in Unit 19 (see below) and although roots are no longer in evidence elsewhere, the whole area seems to have suffered at various stages from this form of disturbance.

Phase I is characterized by a patchy lime plaster surface, Floor 2, throughout greater Unit 4. In some places the occupation debris rests directly on the floor overlaying the bedrock, but the deposit is so shallow and disturbed that to the south of Unit 20 (see below) Floors 1 and 2 appear to merge. No well preserved sections of the Phase I Floor 2 were found immediately adjacent to WAV and it is more visible in the western half of the room, though even here bedrock sometimes serves as the original habitation surface. Few sherds were found in the hard packed brownish-gray (10YR 6/2) occupation debris with numerous ash lenses. The origin of at least some of the ash in this area is perhaps Ft 32, the hearth in the northeast quadrant. The ashy Floor 2 surface extends 4 cm under the east face of WM.

Finds

Finds were sparse, and consisted of a bone bead (B2), a pounder (S442), a biconical spindle whorl (TC18), a pottery roundel (TC 51), and a RP cooking pot (P122) smashed in the lime plaster bin Ft 15, as well as diagnostic sherds from a maximum of three small RP bowls and a RP jug (Table 2.1). The rim fragment of a coarse ware basin (P134) was also recorded.

PHASE II (figs. 2.4, 2.16 [insert]; pl. 2.2c)

Unit 4 in Phase II is the empty space south of Units 19 and 20, which were formed from the earlier Unit 4 by the construction of walls WAW, WAR, and WAO. The only addition to this area was a lime plaster bin, Ft 14. It is partially obscured by a baulk and WR, a later wall, which runs diagonally across this unit as well as Units 15 and 16. Of note from this phase is the rim fragment of a large RP bowl (P146).

UNIT 19

The building of WAO, WAR and WAW in Phase II created Unit 19 (figs. 2.4, 2.16 [insert]; pls. 2.2c. 2.3b), a small square room in the northeast corner of the earlier Unit 4, fitted with a low narrow bench against WI. Its construction thus isolated the northeast quadrant of Unit 4, which became Unit 20, arbitrarily separated from Unit 4 by a line extending south from WAR to the presumed extension of WD. Ft 16, a built hearth in Unit 20, belongs to this phase as well as a lime plaster bin, Ft 14, in Unit 4.

The eastern and southern walls of Unit 19 are, for the settlement at *Kaminoudhia*, an unusually narrow 30 cm, which emphasizes their status as partition walls. WAR, to the east, was laid on the east side of a foundation trench 11 cm wider than the wall and 10 cm deep. At its south end it turns west for 70 cm and becomes WAO, also built in a foundation trench. Following a gap 90 cm wide providing access to Unit 19, the wall, now sitting on occupation debris and labeled WAW continues up to WM. This section has no foundation trench and was built on Floor 1. As defined, Unit 19 is approximately square, measuring 2.9 m east–west and 2.7 m north–south, with a surface of 7.8 m². The entire northern wall of the room, preserved to a height of 40 cm in this area, is flanked by a low bench 20 cm wide set on the filling of the foundation trench for WI. In the southwest corner of the room an accumulation of basin fragments suggests that there may once have been a hearth here. No fire reddening was noted on the surrounding walls or floor, thus if such an installation did exist it was both insubstantial and short lived.

Approximately equidistant between the entrance to Unit 19 and WD a shallow lime plaster bin (Ft 14) incorporates a stone mortar at its base. The plaster rim, 29 cm in diameter, was carefully built up around the mortar and the combined depth of the two is 7 cm.

UNIT 20

Unit 20 (figs. 2.4, 2.16 [insert]; pls. 2.2c, 2.3c) had Ft 16, a hearth, built against the south face of its north wall on the fill of the foundation trench for WI, 95 cm east of WAR. Considering the shallowness of deposit in this area, it is well preserved and consists of two rectangular fire boxes placed side by side, fashioned from basin ware, each approximately 23 cm wide and 45 cm deep, clearly visible in the middle background of pl. 2.3c. The edges and central division are on average 4 cm thick and set in a homogenous, smooth, yellowish mud plaster that makes up the entire lower part of the feature. At 15 cm from the southeast edge, an oval depression 23 x 16 cm was cut into the bedrock. With a depth of 13 cm, it seems too shallow to have functioned as a posthole.

Stratigraphy (Units 4, 19 and 20)

Although Floor 1 of Phase II was recorded in all three units, following it in a consistent plane was impossible, especially in the southeast. It was associated with ashy lenses, sherds and chipped stone lying flat, as well as numerous small igneous pebbles, including a piece of worked picrolite (S334) and was best preserved in the western section of Unit 4. In this area it showed at least two replasterings. WAW was built on Floor 1 that runs up to the bench against WI and covers WAR's foundation trench in Unit 19. Although tracing this floor from Units 4 to 20 was impossible due to erosion and disturbance, the evidence suggests that the later floor in Unit 20, which also covers the foundation trenches for WI and WAV, is contemporary with Floor 1 in Unit 4. Feature 16 was built upon and saw use during the occupation of Floor 1, an interpretation supported by the presence of ash in this room.

The building sequence in these units is clear: WAR, WAO and the bench in Unit 19 were constructed at the beginning of Phase II. Sometime later, after occupation debris had time to accumulate on Floor 1, the wide opening into Unit 19 was constricted by the addition of WAW.

Finds (Units 4, 19 and 20)

Compared to Units 1 and 3 in Phase II, Unit 4 and its subdivisions were very poor in artifacts. This phenomenon cannot be entirely attributed to the shallowness of the deposit, since it was only a little thicker in Unit 1. Some protective tumble was recorded in Units 4, 19, and 20, enough to preserve some artifacts in place had they been present. Even in Unit 4 where the deposit was deeper, there were equally few finds.

Two pounders (S10, 586), a rubber (S581), a gaming stone (S163) from next to the plaster bin Ft 14 and a carefully shaped and vaguely phallic looking grooved stone (S531) came from Unit 4. Diagnostic sherds from one large and at most three small RP bowls were recorded along with 35 pieces of basin, perhaps eroded from Unit 20.

Unit 19 has slightly more objects surviving in situ, namely two pounders (S323, 451) a rubber-pounder (S527), a rubber (S526), a pecking stone (S528), a piece of worked picrolite (S334) and a RP bowl (P114) lying in pieces on the eastern end of the bench. It also contained diagnostic sherds from a maximum of three small RP bowls, and eighteen basin fragments.

Although Unit 20 was sparse in finds, it nevertheless yielded a pounder (S104), a spindle whorl (TC40), a pottery roundel (TC53), a RP Mottled bowl (P124), and a large bowl (P146), as well as many sherds including diagnostics belonging to a maximum of nine small RP bowls, one or two large ones, two RP jugs, a RP juglet, a RP jar/amphora, and a cooking pot. In addition, 113 basin fragments were found, a number in keeping with the presence of the hearth.

UNIT 5

Separated by wall WB from Unit 1, the irregular shape of Unit 5 (figs. 2.5, 2.16 [insert]; pls. 2.3d, 2.5a) appears to be due to the impingement caused by the construction of WO, the eastern wall of Unit 7. The room is 5 m long by a maximum of 4.3 m wide in the north, narrowing to 2.4 m in the south, with a surface area of about 16 m², excluding the threshold. To the north it is bounded by WK, from 65 to 70 cm thick and standing up to four courses high; to the south the irregular alignment of WC contains larger (e.g., 45 x 25 cm) fieldstones than in the area of Unit 1. Wall WC is 35 cm high.

The curving sweep of WO, 50 cm wide and 60 cm high, with a maximum of four courses preserved in situ, closes the room to the west. Both in terms of architecture and construction it is clear that this wall, and thus Unit 7, postdates the construction of Unit 5, which was reduced in size by 20% as a result of the construction of WO. A glance at the site plan fig. 2.16 (see insert) shows that Unit 5 was originally rectangular with a western wall continuing the alignment of the present threshold until it intersected with the now poorly preserved western end of WC. There is no visible reason for Unit 7 to have encroached upon Unit 5 in this manner. The threshold between WK and WAH is the best example of a built threshold at *Kaminoudhia* and consists of a single course of well-leveled, tabular fieldstones resting on occupational debris. It was sealed by tumble from WK and is 25 cm lower than the preserved top of the latter. Had it once stood as a wall, it should at least be preserved to the height of the surrounding structures, which is not the case. WO abuts against WC in the south, where at 0.1 m from the junction, a limestone slab (30 cm long and 4 cm thick) rested against its east face. Another slab (30 x 25 cm) lay nearby on the floor and had perhaps toppled from its position next to this slab and a third stood against the wall opposite Ft 6.

In the area where WB abuts WC there appears to have been a niche positioned 20 cm above the floor, 40 cm wide and 30 cm deep. At the back of the niche, a single fieldstone forms the east face of the wall. This niche contained a RP black-topped bottle (P74), smashed, but clearly in situ, and typologically the latest ceramic find from the settlement. All the walls in the room were set on bedrock except WO, which was built over the occupational debris filling a large shallow pit extending west into Unit 7 (see below in connection with stratigraphy).

Unit 5 contained a pair of lime plaster bins and two enigmatic features in addition to a small pit or post hole. At 80 cm from the entrance, adjacent to the south face of WK, the first bin (Ft 4), with an inner diameter of 30 cm and depth of 22 cm, was sunk into the floor. A pecking stone (S600) lay nearby, concreted to the rim.

Farther to the east a series of limestone slabs were arranged vertically against the south face of WK and the west face of WB. They were set in the floor to form a three-sided rectangular enclosure, Ft 5, measuring approximately 1.8 m on its east–west axis with a width of 60 cm (see fig. 2.5). Other slabs, bonded in straw tempered mud mortar, had been laid horizontally to form a stone-lined inner surface. Four small igneous pebbles in the northeast corner were the only finds in this enigmatic feature, built on the lime plaster floor.

A large centrally located lime plaster bin (Ft 6), with an outer diameter of 48 cm, an inner diameter of ca. 35 cm and depth of 28 cm, was lined with thin slivers of limestone. Unfortunately, root damage was evident in this area, which further complicated any attempt to interpret the surrounding plaster surface, clearly visible in pl. 2.3d. It seems to have consisted of several very shallow lime plaster troughs, possibly associated with the bin. Immediately west of the latter, the remains of what appear to be three mud bricks about 40 cm long (or wide) and 5 cm thick had once stood on edge in this spot. They were clearly discernible due to the sharp contrast between the gray matrix of the mud brick and the 2.5 m thick white lime plaster used as mortar. This feature is drawn as a series of four parallel lines, between 30 and 50 cm long, just west of Ft 6 in fig. 2.5 (see also pl. 2.4a). Also remarkable in this area was the concentration of small igneous pebbles, noted elsewhere in the Unit, especially along the west face of WB. A possible post hole (Ft 7), 16 cm in diameter, was located 1 m east of Ft 6.

Stratigraphy

The whole room was covered with an irregular scatter of wall tumble, about one stone thick corresponding to the same horizontal level as the tops of the walls. Although the occupation surface was protected by this layer, it had suffered extensively from root action.

Patches of lime plaster floor were recorded in the vicinity of Ft 5 and below Ft 6, but elsewhere it could not be consistently traced. Root disturbance was noted in the southwest corner, but nevertheless artifacts lay scattered—often lying horizontally—in a uniform, southward sloping plane throughout the room. Despite some root activity south of Ft 6, a depression with gently sloping sides was traced to the west where it ran under WO and on into Unit 7. This cavity sealed by Floor 1 could not be stratigraphically connected with Phase I in Unit 1, with which it must be at least partially contemporary.

Finds

On or above Floor 1

Unit 5 yielded an above average number of ground stone tools, namely twelve pounders (S175, 216, 217, 265, 314, 315, 317, 328, 345, 360, 374, 397), four rubber-pounders (S311, 312, 342, 678), two pecking stones (S436, 600), two hammerstones (S227, 582), a rubbing stone (S399), two axes (S272, 326), three rubbers (S509, 324, 386), twenty-six items in all. In addition were found a possible burnisher (S552), a questionable picrolite pendant (S551), and two worked pieces of the same material (S337, 339). Ceramics consist of three small RP bowls (P13, 16, 20), a RP amphora (P82), a fragmentary DPBC juglet and a RP III bottle (P74). A terracotta RP bead (TC21) and a shell pendant (Sh4) were also found. Diagnostic sherds from a maximum of one large and ten small RP bowls, a juglet and a RP jar/amphora were found. Basin ware was moderately common with forty-two fragments, demonstrating that this ware is not only restricted to units with hearths.

Below Floor 1

A single RP cooking pot (P50) was excavated below the floor in the depression that occupied the SW corner of the unit. The only distribution pattern of artifacts discernible in this room clusters along the base of walls, with two thirds of all finds recovered in such locations.

No specific function may be suggested for Unit 5, other than to note the grinding and pounding of substances. If pecking stones served as tools for shaping ground stone artifacts, then this activity may also have taken place here.

U N I T   6

The best-preserved room in Area A is Unit 6 (figs. 2.6, 2.16 [insert]; pls. 2.4b, 2.4c, 2.4d, 2.5a; sections 2.19b, 2.20b), immediately south of Units 1 and 5. Trapezoidal in shape, it measures 4.5 m on its south side along WAE, four courses high and between 40 and 50 cm wide, 3.8 m along WC to the north, 3.5 m along WW to the west and 3.2 m along WG, four courses high and 70 cm wide, to the east. The floor space thus enclosed is 14 m². Both the north and west walls are described in connection with Unit 18. The southwest corner of the room, where WAE and WW intersect, had been robbed except the lowest course of stones, when an oval pit (93 x 63 cm) was dug down from the plow zone as indicated by the lighter outline of the building stones on fig. 2.16 (see insert). The two east–west walls of the unit had tilted southwards due to slope pressure and the top course of WG had slipped 10 cm to the east of the bottom course. Neither WW nor WG are bonded into WC, which was constructed earlier. All four walls were built either immediately on bedrock or on sterile eroded material originating from the latter.

Unit 6 was approached via a long east–west corridor (Units 33 and 32) through a 1.2 m wide doorway in the southwest corner with a large stone threshold resting upon the floor. It is carefully shaped with two pecked areas, probably to accommodate the doorjambs, and has an overall length of 1.32 m, a width of 23 cm and height of 27 cm. If the depressions at both extremities were for securing the doorjambs, they would have framed an entrance 87 cm wide.

A limestone mortar, IS35, measuring 36 x 38 cm with a depth of 12 cm, sat 1 m northwest of the door and Ft 10, a large, complex but disturbed mud plaster hearth was built against the northeast stretch of WG (pl. 2.4b). Nevertheless, it was one of the better preserved hearths at *Kaminoudhia*, although the friable nature of the coarse tempered low fired "basin" material used in its construction and the substantial damage caused by wall tumble from WG—and root action—complicated and hindered its interpretation. Part of a root is visible in the upper right-hand corner of pl. 2.4b. The hearth stood on a slightly raised platform of gray occupation debris, 6 cm above bedrock, and extended 46 cm up to the top of WG. The wall face was covered with a layer 2 cm thick of reddish-yellow (7.5YR 7/8) mud plaster extending down to and covering the blackened floor of the hearth. As preserved Ft 10 consists of an L-shaped wall 14 cm high, the short arm (30 cm long; visible on the right of pl. 2.4b) joining WG at right angles and the long arm of 46 cm running off at about 100º. The inner face of the fire box is lined with a 2 cm thick skin of buff colored (10YR 8/4) basin material applied to a mud mortar support 10 cm thick. At the inner southern end, a small carefully shaped aperture between WG and the hearth wall resembles an air vent. The inner measurements of the firebox are approximately 33 x 46 cm. Although badly damaged, there appears to have been a slightly larger L-shaped feature 80 cm to the north, between Ft 10 and WC, set on the thick white lime floor plaster found in this part of the room.

Despite quantities of large basin fragments concentrated in the vicinity and scattered throughout the northern half of the room, right up to WW, no cohesive plan could be established. The sheer quantity of basin material associated with both features suggests that they were once far more substantial and complex. In the center of the northern L-shaped feature, the in situ base of a RP vessel was found.

Stratigraphy

The uneven scatter of wall tumble covering much of the room differed from that encountered elsewhere on the site. Part of WAE had tumbled northwards forming a 1.2 m line of fieldstones following a 30º angle from the top of the wall to the occupation surface (see section fig. 2.20b). Since some stones lay directly on the floor, it must have been clear of any substantial deposit of non-perishable material when the wall fell. At the intersection between the floor and the base of the WAE tumble, there is in the section a triangular accumulation of hard, compact brown soil (7.5YR 5/2). Since the falling stones did not settle first at the base of the wall and then spread outwards as is customary (see other sections from the settlement), it seems that the buff soil deposit must have been in place before the wall collapsed.

The tumble from WC, starting at the base of this wall, extends out into the room in a roughly horizontal scatter above a homogenous layer of pale brown (10YR 7/3) soil which could be roof material if WAE collapsed first, causing the roof to cave in on the habitation surface. Much the same situation may be observed in the east–west section (fig. 2.19b) where WW tumbled to the east, sealing a broad wedge-shaped deposit of homogenous gray/brown soil devoid of sherds.

A large piece of tabular limestone measuring 41 x 47 cm rested close to the east face of WW on top of the tumble in the middle of the wall, and another slab lay smashed in the southwest corner of the room. The find spots of both suggest that they had perhaps formed part of the roof edging, or lay on the roof; alternatively they could have served as shelves protruding from the upper part of the wall (see "Shelves" *infra*). Nearby, an unusually large quern (IS6), lay on its side close to an even bigger limestone slab 83 x 40 x 14 cm, also set on edge (see pl. 2.4d). Both were found on top of the tumble from WAE, but well below the plow zone. The quern may have been on the roof, but the limestone slab could equally well have served as a shelf set into the wall just below the ceiling. Unfortunately, the cultural deposit is generally shallow at *Kaminoudhia* and the variations in the taphonomy difficult to interpret; therefore, the sequence of wall collapse in Unit 6 remains ambiguous.

The habitation surfaces consisted of two floors of pale brown (10YR 7/3) compacted occupation debris. The matrix of the upper floor was rich in sherds, small pieces of chert and bone and igneous pebbles. Both easily differentiated floors were 4 cm thick; the upper corresponded to the rim of the stone mortar IS35 with its base sunk into the lower floor. The lower floor contained flecks of charcoal and other carbonized material mixed in with the otherwise sterile matrix. It seems to have been intentionally laid but was not of the usual lime plaster type encountered elsewhere at the site. Unlike Floor 1 in Units 1, 3 and 4, the upper floor in Unit 6 cannot be associated with any alterations or building activities and it simply proves two phases of occupation. The two floors could not be separated in the northern part of the room, where there was but a single occupation surface.

On this surface, at 50 cm from the middle of WC, a human femur lay next to the base of a RP vessel and from 40 cm to the east came half a human pelvis. Both bones (not studied by Schulte Campbell in Chapter 10) were almost intact, thus quite well preserved by comparison with the mass of fragmentary animal bone from all areas of the settlement. Furthermore, the reason for the discovery of these bones in a semi-articulated position is the result of a depositional history quite different from that of the animal bone found in the settlement.

Finds

The room contained a range of ground stone artifacts, consisting of eight pounders (S194, 380, 383, 410, 417, 636, 677 [an axe reused as a pounder], 681), a rubber-pounder (S377), two rubbing stones (S405, 690), three pecking stones (S198, 409, 665), a pestle (S178), three rubbers (692, 694, 695), a mortar (IS35) and an adze (S450), making a total of twenty items. There was also a necklace spacer (S473) and four intact or restorable pots, namely two DPBC vessels (P72, 109) a RP jug (P120), and an RP Mottled dipper (P62). TC 47 is a pottery roundel, which would have fitted nicely into the neck of P120. Unit 6 yielded by far the largest total of stratified sherds from Area A (1,176 including basin fragments; see Table 2.1c) as well as diagnostics from a maximum of three large and twenty-eight small RP bowls, two RP jugs, a RP juglet, a RP jar/amphora, two cooking pots and two storage jar sherds.

Metal is represented by the flat riveted butt and the pointed tip of two separate copper daggers (M27, 29) and the fragment (M28) of a copper tool-like object, either a dagger or a small flat axe. M27 was unstratified, but the shape of the butt and existence of a single rivet places it well within the EC metal repertoire. Two biconical spindle whorls (TC19, 27) were found in this room. Note the large quern (IS6) found in the tumble, perhaps originating from the roof. This assemblage, in conjunction with the existence of a large and complex hearth, as well as an above average number of basin fragments (117 pieces in addition to those directly associated with the hearth which are excluded), is primarily indicative of food preparation, from pounding and grinding to cooking and consumption if the number of bowls is significant.

UNITS 7 AND 40

These rooms are described in sequence because they form a single architectural unit (figs. 2.7, 2.16 [insert]; pls. 2.5a, 2.5b; sections figs. 2.19a and b). In plan, Unit 7 is slightly apsidal or D-shaped, with its main east–west axis consisting of WAK/WC, respectively 2.4 and 1.8 m in length. To the east, WO, already described in connection with Unit 5, curves slightly in a northwesterly direction before joining WAH which arcs sharply toward the southwest, providing this room with a maximum width of about 3.3 m. WAH, four to five courses high, with an average width of 55 cm, rests on the soft bedrock which has been cut or worn, and slopes southwards overhanging the lowest course of stones (see area of south face of WAH in section, fig. 2.19c).

To the south the room is defined by the continuation of WC, badly eroded immediately west of WO due to intensive root activity in this area. After a gap of 1.2 m, it resumes in a much better state of preservation as WAK—4 courses high and 50 cm wide—following a slightly different orientation. A low, mud plaster threshold (?) about 8 cm high spans the gap, implying that a doorway existed here to provide the only means of access to Unit 18 to the south. The overall floor surface of Unit 7 is approximately 17 m².

A double hearth (Ft 8) built against the middle of WAH was surrounded by ashy debris and a concentration of burnt clay fragments, suggesting that this feature in its original form was more substantial. As preserved it consists of a buff mud plaster packing 20 cm thick (10YR 8/4) in front of the wall face against which are backed two rectangular fire boxes, placed side by side, each measuring 18 cm wide with a maximum depth of 32 cm. The horizontal surfaces of this feature are reddish yellow (7.5YR 7/6 to 7/8) in color. The outer wall of both boxes incorporates a limestone slab (averaging 22 x 4 cm) set on edge. The hearth is visible to the left of the scale in pl. 2.5a.

In the southeast corner of Unit 7, against the north face of WC, a poorly preserved alignment of fieldstones, up to three courses high and measuring approximately 2 m long by 50 cm wide, appears to have been a badly preserved bench, work area or storage platform. On it a series of artifacts were found, including an arsenical copper needle (M30).

Two stones (IS10, 11) with flat circular depressions of 12 and 17 cm in diameter pecked into their upper surface are interpreted as post supports. IS10 was found in situ in the middle of the room 1.7 m from WO, where it would have provided a stable (and dry) base for a prop to reinforce a crossbeam spanning the gap between WAK and WC. This beam could in turn have supported a series of shorter timbers with their opposite ends resting on WO.

Stratigraphy

The entire room and the northern half in particular was sealed by a thick layer of tumble (see fig. 2.19c). The soil between and below the tumble was light brownish gray (10YR 6/2) in color, rich in occupation debris. Floor 1, consisting of compacted occupation debris, lay immediately over the southward sloping, smooth bedrock. In some areas the accumulation was 10 cm thick. No evidence for a lime plaster floor was found anywhere in Unit 7. At 40 cm from the inner northeast corner of Unit 7, a semicircular pit 20 cm deep was found beneath the floor extending south for 70 cm and west for 50 cm. It runs under WO and is part of the same pit rich in occupation debris recorded in Unit 5. Both the architectural plan and the stratigraphy suggest that Unit 7 cut into Unit 5, thus implying that the former is later than Unit 5 and that Area A seems to have developed westward from Unit 1.

Finds

There is a visible concentration of artifacts along the edges of the room, specifically in the east and south, but no specific evidence for the clustering of any type. The following ground stone tools were recorded: nineteen pounders (S211, 243, 249, 286, 296, 319, 322, 553, 655, 656, 657, 658, 659, 669, 675, 682, 685, 687, 691), a rubber-pounder (S263), a hammerstone (S366), five pecking stones (S229, 271, 303, 670, 684), a quern (S699), five rubbers (S298, 632, 702, IS9, IS17), an axe (S186), one limestone perforated disk (S667), one grinding surface (?) (S676), one mortar (S693), one unidentified grooved stone (S479), one picrolite pendant (S469) and bead (S338) and a worked piece of the same material (S458). One very small perforated bead of jasper (?) (S673) was also found in Unit 7. To these should be added three copper-based objects consisting of fragments of an axe blade (M19 and M26) and an arsenical copper needle (M30). The ceramics consisted of two small RP bowls (P15, 25), the former being very crude and small. With 750 stratified sherds recorded, Unit 7 was the third richest in Area A. The assemblage included diagnostics from a maximum of sixteen small RP bowls, one RP jug, five RP juglets, four RP jar/amphorae and two cooking pots, as well as seventy-two basin fragments. Three terracotta spindle whorls complete the list (TC16, 25, 26). All the finds combine to suggest a multi-functional purpose for Unit 7, with its wealth of pottery, hearth, grinding equipment and range of ground stone lithics, spindle whorls and a gaming stone. If our interpretation of the large flat stones with circular pecked depressions as post supports is correct, then there is evidence that at least part of this room was roofed.

UNIT 40

Unit 40 is a small trapezoidal area measuring approximately 2 m north–south and 1.6 m east–west, which functioned as a vestibule to Units 7 and 18. To the northwest it is closed by the 3 m stretch of WAQ, two courses and 38 cm high, which abuts against WAH at an acute angle where it turns sharply southward. The entrance to Unit 40 has a threshold made of two flat fieldstones laid end to end between WAQ and WAK, 29 cm below the highest preserved course of the former.

A mud plaster rectangular hearth (Ft 9) was built into the niche formed by the intersection of WAQ and WAH. The 4 cm thick walls, fired yellow (10YR 8/4) with a gray core, are preserved to a height of 18 cm. They define a smoke blackened firebox 32 cm wide and 48 cm deep, reinforced on the east side by a flat stone with a rounded, finished end. The presence of this hearth, presumably located next to the doorway to facilitate the evacuation of smoke if Unit 40 was roofed, reduced the width of the vestibule to around 1 m. If not roofed, it provided a well-defined area separate from both the communal corridor and Unit 7.

Stratigraphy

Only one period of occupation was recorded in Unit 40. The plan suggests that WAQ and the threshold were later additions, as supported by the fact that the habitation surface here is 20 cm higher than the floor in the southwest area of Unit 7. The latter would originally have been approached through the 1.1 m wide doorway between the end of WAH and north face of WAK.

Finds

In addition to a few sherds, finds consist of a possible burnisher (S470) and a perforated stone perhaps used as a weight (S489). There were also numerous basin fragments, to be expected in an area with a hearth. A pottery roundel, TC 29, came from inside the hearth, Ft 9.

U N I T 15

The area between what remains of the south wall of Unit 4 (WD) and the east wall of Unit 16, is defined as Unit 15 (figs. 2.4, 2.16 [insert]) and may have been an open space between Units 4 and 16. Figure 2.16 [insert] clearly shows that the adjacent southwest and northeast corners of these units are not structurally bonded into one another; they do not even abut and are separated by a gap of 20 cm. Part of this unit is obscured by WR, a later wall, running diagonally across the area, not indicated on the plans, but clearly visible on pl. 2.2c (see also Unit 16 below).

The whole area was covered with a thin scatter of wall tumble. Although part of the area was excavated to bedrock, on average 45 cm below the present ground surface, few artifacts were found in situ and the only feature was a cluster of three regular cavities, or mortars, cut into the bedrock by the eastern baulk of the trench, 3.7 m southeast of WD. Feature 17, the largest, still partially concealed in the east baulk, is 17 cm deep and 30 cm in diameter. Feature 18, oval in shape (30 x 24 cm), is 37 cm deep and Ft 19 is 23 cm deep and 28 cm in diameter. Features 18 and 19 are joined by a shallow runnel 6 cm wide, cut 12 cm below the bedrock surface. Such features would be well in keeping with an open courtyard area.

Stratigraphy

The habitation surface of Unit 15 was directly on the uneven bedrock, which consisted of fragmented strata approximately 9 cm thick trending gently to the southwest which had a tendency to sheer off revealing the homogenous bedrock below. No sharp soil color or density change could be recognized in the light gray (10YR 7/2) topsoil through the brown (7.5YR 5/2) to the pinkish white (7.5YR 8/2) occupation debris lying immediately on bedrock.

Finds

Two pounders (S8, 35) a rubbing stone (S7), two hammerstones (S65, 230) and a small RP bowl in many pieces (P126) were excavated from the unstratified levels above Unit 15. The bedrock habitation surface yielded three pounders (S60, 270, 395), a hammerstone (S230) and a perforated stone (S306, possibly a weight) in addition to three querns (IS37, 38, 39) and two RP bowls in a fragmentary state (P43 with a spout and P44) distributed throughout the northwest quadrant of Unit 15. In addition, diagnostic sherds provided evidence for a maximum of fourteen small RP bowls, two large RP bowls and three RP jar/amphorae.

UNIT 16

The long east–west corridor comprising Units 32 and 33 provided access through a doorway at its eastern end to Unit 16 (figs 2.8, 2.16 [insert]; pl. 1.4; section fig. 2.19b), a large square area, incompletely excavated and poorly defined. To the west and north it is bounded by WG and WQ, already described in connection with Units 1, 3 and 6. WG clearly fell to the east, as suggested by a uniform scatter of wall tumble throughout the southwest third of the room (see fig. 2.19b). Associated with this material were at least ten broken tabular pieces of limestone. Since at *Kaminoudhia* such limestone slabs never appear to have been used as building material within the body of a wall, their presence among the tumble suggests they perhaps served as long narrow shelves protruding at a certain height from the wall. In this instance, they do not seem to have been associated with the roof, as they are mingled with debris originating from mid-wall height. One slab that was reconstructed measured 70 x 40 x 5 cm and, if it were embedded in the wall to a depth of 30 cm, a sturdy, functional shelf 40 x 40 cm would thus have been created.

In the northeast of Unit 16, the tumble from WQ lay to the south of the wall, with many stones still stacked on edge, as in Unit 1. Like WG to the west, it has suffered from slope pressure and root action and now consists of a poorly preserved, meandering double line of stones on average 50 cm wide and four courses high. There is considerable evidence for root disturbance along and below the southwestern face of the wall. At its eastern extremity it is bonded with WT, which turns south and is completely robbed after a distance of 1 m, with perhaps a lone surviving stone remaining in situ a meter farther. If the line of WT is projected south toward WY, there is no evidence to indicate that they ever abutted, much less formed a bonded corner.

Although better preserved than most other walls in this unit, the fact that baulks have partially obscured it has hampered the interpretation of WY. A low bench 20 cm high and 30 cm wide runs along its north face for at least 3.8 m, its west end stopping about 1.5 m short of the door to Unit 32, the passageway. WY is approximately 70 cm wide and was constructed against a natural (?) ledge in the bedrock; its north face stands 35 cm high and that to the south, measured from the bedrock, is 70 cm. This discrepancy is due to the existence of a series of rock ledges in this area, stepping down toward the south.

If the alignment of WT is projected southwards toward WY, the enclosed area measuring 5.3 x 4.9 m is almost 27 m². Of this surface only 18 m² were excavated to the habitation surface, the remainder being taken up by baulks left in situ, or a later wall (WR) not shown on the plan. WR is visible running over Units 15 and 16 in pl. 1.4.

Unit 16 was entered from Unit 32 via a one m wide door with a monolithic threshold, 96 cm long and 16 cm wide, rising 25 cm above the floor. It is now broken and both pieces have slid apart. An oval stone 30 cm long, with a circular pecked depression 5 cm in diameter, lay next to the southern end of the threshold; both its appearance and location suggest it served as a socle or a pivot stone for a swinging door. There may have been another entrance to Unit 16 in the southeast corner, as suggested by the lack of evidence for a cross-wall protruding from WY.

In addition to the bench along WY, the only features recorded in the excavated areas of Unit 16 were two lime plaster bins, Ft 12 and Ft 13, set against WG close to the door. The thickness of their lime plaster walls varies from 1 cm near the rim to 4 cm close to the base. Feature 12, approximately 40 cm in diameter and the larger and earlier of the two, was covered by eight small pebbles with two more close by to the north. After being emptied, it was found to contain ten additional pebbles, some igneous, others of limestone. Three pounders (S358, 641, 643) lay between the bins and the wall. The south side of Ft 12 was overlain by Ft 13 of identical construction but only 31 cm in diameter. It contained three round igneous pebbles. A semicircular shelf 32 cm long protruded 16 cm from the wall about 20 cm above Ft 13, which it partially obscured. Around the rims of both features were lumps of dark brown mud, similar to that noted plastered on the wall, reaching up to the shelf.

Stratigraphy

Wall tumble was found below the plow zone in all excavated areas of the unit. Associated with this tumble and at the same level there was a later wall (WR) running diagonally across the entire area on a southwest–northeasterly bearing. It was built above WT and WD and is clearly unrelated to the Early Cypriot settlement. Unfortunately, no diagnostic pottery useful for dating purposes was associated with this structure.

In Unit 16 the southward sloping bedrock was covered with a layer of light brown (10YR 6/2) occupation debris from 5 to 10 cm thick, immediately overlain by wall tumble and sloping lenses of light chalky (10YR 7/1) and darker chalky (10YR 5/4) material. The occupation surface was covered with a scatter of small igneous pebbles, of the same shape and size as those found elsewhere on the site, but more concentrated here. An unusual assortment of finds lay on the bedrock habitation surface in the southeastern quadrant of the unit, consisting of two tubular picrolite beads/ornaments (S460, 461), an unfinished mace-head (S219), a pounder (S275) and three human long bones. No other human skeletal remains were recorded nearby, although the possibility that some may exist under the tumble of WR and/or the north baulk, both about 1 m away from the bones, cannot be excluded. As in Unit 6, the long bones were more complete than any of the faunal remains excavated in the associated occupational debris. Could these bones belong to the same skeleton recorded in Unit 6 to the west? The circumstances of discovery are very similar, namely a few well-preserved, scattered bones lying on bedrock, with no other indications that the rest of the skeleton had ever existed in the vicinity.

Finds

This unit is relatively rich in finds considering the small area excavated to bedrock. From the habitation surface came four pounders (S283, 353, 358, 421), a rubber-pounder (S455), two querns (S309, 310), a rubber (S453), a rubbing stone (S282), an unfinished mace-head (S275), a stone plaque perhaps serving as a work surface (S293), two picrolite tubular objects (S460, 461), a picrolite bead (S465) and a slightly altered picrolite pebble, perhaps intended as a blank (S209). The ceramic assemblage consisted of a RP jug (P51), and a fragmentary Brown Polished bottle, as well as evidence from diagnostic sherds for a maximum of five small RP bowls and a RP jar/amphora. A pottery roundel, TC48, came from this unit. These artifacts were scattered quite evenly throughout the room. The clustering noted along the bases of walls elsewhere in Area A is not as evident in Unit 16. Unstratified finds in and above the wall tumble consist of a pounder (S219), a quern (S495), one hammerstone (S230), one rubber-pounder (S264), a rubbing stone (S225) and a pecking stone (S279).

UNIT 18

To the south of and communicating with Unit 7 there is a large trapezoidal space designated as Unit 18 (figs. 2.7, 2.16 [insert]; pl. 2.5a, left center; sections figs. 2.19b and c). Its east–west axis is 5.5 m and the maximum width along WW, the east wall, is 3.8 m. The western boundary as defined by WAI is 2.35 m long and WAE, the southern boundary, defines an area of 17.5 m². Only the eastern third of the room, the area within G18B, has been excavated down to occupation debris; the remainder was only investigated to a depth sufficient to determine wall size and orientation.

WC and WAK on the north side of the room are party walls with Unit 7 and were described in connection with the latter. To the south, WAE is between 50 and 60 cm wide with up to five courses reaching a height of 40 cm above the occupation debris. As preserved, the top of this wall has lost many stones to the plow, and as a result it lacks the uniform shell construction of most walls at *Kaminoudhia*. WAE is bonded with WAI, which has a uniform width of 50 cm. In the northwestern corner, at the intersection of WAI and WAK, both wall faces are covered with yellowish mud plaster (10YR 8/4), which suggests the presence of a hearth on the floor beneath the tumble. To the east, the room is bounded by WW, up to six courses high and 50 cm wide. Two tabular pieces of limestone were found in the layer of wall tumble on the west side of the wall.

The southeast corner of Unit 18, at the juncture of WW and WAE, has suffered from later disturbance in the form of a pit about 1.5 m in diameter from which all building stones were removed except the lowest course (see unshaded section of wall in fig. 2.16 [see insert]). This disturbance complicated the interpretation of the only feature recorded in the room, namely an irregular construction of fieldstones, several courses high, along the north face of WAE, which may have been intended as a bench (see fig. 2.19c). The evidence is inconclusive—to the extent that the feature is not plotted on the published plan of Unit 18—and only the excavation of the western half of the room will verify the existence of this possible bench.

Stratigraphy

As in Unit 7, the disturbed light gray topsoil (10YR 7/2) was distinguishable from the darker, less disturbed soil (10 YR 6/2) associated with the even spread of wall tumble covering the entire room. The depth of topsoil was around 30 cm in the north, diminishing to 10 cm in the south where the eroded stump of WAE comes close to the ground surface. In the excavated part of the room wall tumble between 40 and 50 cm thick directly seals the occupation debris on the floor, which consists of up to 10 cm of densely packed yellowish brown material (10YR 6/4) overlying the smooth, southward sloping bedrock. All completely excavated walls rest on bedrock or on the thin chalky layer of erosional material immediately overlaying the latter.

Finds

Stratified finds from the eastern half of the unit consist of four pounders (S316, 382, 388, 411), a rubber-pounder (S376), a pestle (S392), a pecking stone (S484), an axe (S389), three rubbers (S430, 504, IS5), a jar cover? (S619), a perforated stone (weight? S491), a tethering stone or a weight (S499) and a gaming stone (S475). Two RP pots (P77 and a fragmentary jug) were found on the habitation surface close to WW in the east of the room. With 691 stratified sherds and basin fragments, Unit 18 was the third richest in Area A. This material provided evidence for the presence of a maximum of one large and thirty-one small RP bowls, a RP juglet, 4 RP jar/amphorae and eight RP cooking pots, an unusually high number. Seventy-three basin fragments were recorded and a whetstone (S466) came from the wall tumble.

UNITS 27, 28, AND 29

OPERATIONS E18C, E18D, D19A, D19B, C19B
(fig. 2.16a, sections figs. 2.20a, 2.20c)

A trial trench (25 m long and 1 m wide) was excavated between Areas A and B in order to determine whether the buildings in these discrete areas were connected. This so-called east–west trial trench (EW TT) began directly west of Unit 37, the passageway, and immediately encountered WAAC built on a north–south alignment. There followed a series of approximately 50 cm wide parallel walls, WAY, WAZ and WAAC, abutting a 13.5 m long east–west wall (WAAF) which also curves northwards to merge with WBF. The spaces so defined consist of Unit 27, apparently apsidal in shape (3.5 x 2.5 m) and bounded to the west by Unit 28, a mere 1.8 m wide and of undetermined length. The apse of Unit 27 is made up of three straight segments joined at 45°, the central one of which (WAAC) continues south in a straight line for at least 2.5 m, thus providing an architectural element for yet another construction.

The trench was widened to 1.6 m in Units 27, 28 and part of 29 to determine more accurately the width and bearings of the relevant walls. WAAF cuts diagonally across the trench delimiting the south side of Unit 29, perhaps an open space of at least 7.5 m in length, before intersecting with WBC, a cross wall bearing south. The last 2 m of WAAF are 50 cm wide and may be lined with a bench on the south face of the wall. WBC is 60 cm wide, and with eleven courses reaching 1.2 m in height, is the tallest standing wall excavated at *Kaminoudhia*.

Only the west face of WBC was excavated to floor level, and it is probable that more courses exist below the 10 cm thick occupation debris sitting on a habitation surface (see fig. 2.20a). In Operation D19B there appears to be a north–south wall protruding from a mound of tumble 5.5 m west of WBC. Three courses of this wall were excavated. In D18D 6.5 m west of WBC, another pile of tumble, starting 70 cm below ground level, signals the presence of an additional north–south wall (WBD), a little less than 50 cm wide, of which the outlines of only five stones were traced. Another 3 m west of WBD at 70 cm below topsoil and extending down to 1.5 m at the bottom of the trench, there is a concentration of tumble that might signal the presence of a wall in this area. From this point westward for another 7.5 m the whole trench was full of an uneven scatter of tumble that led up to WBE, a well preserved and unusually wide wall standing at least four courses high to within 70 cm of the present surface level. Between WBE, which follows a north–south bearing, and Unit 12 in Area B, 4 m to the west, no other architecture was recorded.

Stratigraphy

The section drawings (figs. 2.20a and c) clearly show a thick layer of random tumble covering Units 27, 28, and 29, which starts at between 20 and 30 cm below the present ground level. Unit 28 was choked with a 1.2 m thick deposit of tumble unparalleled elsewhere at the settlement. Below the tumble in this unit an accumulation of ashy occupation debris, 20 cm thick, rich in sherds, chipped stone and bone, covered a smooth, hard, whitish floor. Units 27 and 29 were not excavated down to the occupation debris. Nowhere did the trench reach the foundations of the walls or even an ashy layer of occupation debris, if such existed, to the west of Unit 29. A small probe 1.5 m west of WBC reached what appeared to be a hard packed earth habitation surface 1.5 m below the top of this wall.

Finds

The occupation debris in Unit 28 yielded the neck of a jug (P147—see discussion in Chapter 4), two pounders (S625, 626), a pecking stone (S627) and a worked piece of picrolite (S628). A pounder (S591) came from the bottom of the excavation, just above the occupation debris in Unit 29. The rest of the trial trench provided a regular scatter of lithic artifacts consisting of nine pounders (S574, 575, 576, 605, 616, 617, 622, 623, 624), three axes (S593, 615, 618), three gaming stones (S606, 608, 633), two mortars (S620, 234), a rubber (S614), a rubbing stone (S604), a picrolite pendant (S660) and a picrolite disk (S661). It also yielded a unique, carefully shaped, perfectly circular limestone disk, about 70 cm in diameter and 5 cm thick, with a pecked hole in its center.

UNITS 30, 37, AND 42

The series of alleys or passageways to the west of Units 5, 7, and 18, which connect with Unit 33, provide access to most of the structures in Area A (fig. 2.16 [see insert]; pl. 2.5b). To the north, Unit 30 connects with Unit 1 via a passage 5 m long and 1 m wide. It is closed on one side by WI, which has been completely eroded for the first 2.5 m, and on the opposite side by WK. As noted in connection with Unit 1, this passage was only in use during Phase II. To the west, Unit 30 links with the incompletely excavated Unit 38 via the narrow 1 m constriction left between the southwest corner of Unit 35 and WBA.

The area was further cluttered by the presence of a large built hearth (Ft 38) set against WAL that would have obstructed easy access to Unit 38, west of WAN. This hearth is unfortunately in a poor state of preservation with only two fire-reddened slabs of limestone remaining. The slab on the south, 70 cm long and set 74 cm out from WAL, with which it is parallel, was joined at right-angles on the west end by a single limestone slab only 24 cm long, covered on its inner face with a 2 cm thick layer of yellowish (10YR 8/4) mud plaster. The space so enclosed contained several unusually large basin fragments, suggesting that the hearth may have once supported a basin and had been used in situ for food preparation (?). The largest fragment is 20 x 9 cm, with a rim 14 cm high.

Access to Unit 5, via a built threshold, is to the southeast where the corridor narrows progressively due to the curved sweep of WAH as it merges into Unit 42. The west boundary is formed by the rectilinear 7 m stretch of WAP following a northeast–southwest bearing. East of Unit 42, WAQ is a curved later addition to WAH that reduced the corridor's width to 1 m before it bifurcated northwest toward an unexcavated area south of Unit 41 and southeast toward Unit 37. After yet another constriction opposite the built threshold to Unit 40, the vestibule for Unit 7, the passage widens to 2.8 m in Unit 37 and continues to broaden as it proceeds south into the unexcavated baulk. The western section of this stretch of the corridor, bordered by WAAC, is edged with a semi-continuous line of tabular limestone slabs. They were presumably set at the base of the wall, but since the area is not fully excavated this cannot be ascertained. In Unit 32 a similar alignment of stone slabs rested on occupation debris and not on a recognizable floor.

This series of units was only excavated to bedrock in the corridor leading from Unit 1; elsewhere the tumble-covered plow zone was cleared to a depth sufficient to determine the wall alignments. A probe 60 cm wide sunk between WAQ and WAP determined that bedrock lay 20 cm under the lowest course of the former and that the intervening fill consisted of sherds, bone and ash-filled debris, without any evidence for well-defined occupation surfaces, even at the lowest level.

Only eight registered objects were recorded from these passageways, namely two mortars (S674, 688), a gaming stone (S705), a RP juglet (P123), a tripod leg from Unit 42 (P143), two pottery roundels (TC37, 44) and a spindle whorl (TC38). To this list may be added a large quern (IS8) in Unit 30, partially blocking access to Unit 1 (see fig. 2.16 [insert] and the center of pl.2.2b).

UNIT 31

This is an area of shallow deposit, 30 cm from surface to bedrock, at the northeast corner of Area A, immediately to the east of the two course high WAV and south of WI (fig. 2.16 [see insert]). The east–west running wall WI gives way to an amorphous pile of cobbles to the east. No stratified finds were recorded.

UNIT 32/33

Units 32/33 form an east–west passageway, 11.3 m long and on average 1.2 m wide, which provides access to Units 6 and 16 (figs. 2.6, 2.7, 2.16 [insert]). For practical purposes the corridor was divided into two separate units, Unit 32 being within Operation G18C to the east and Unit 33 spanning G18B/G18D and H18A to the west. The north wall, WAE, varies in width from 60 cm in the west to 0.4 m in the east next to the stone threshold of Unit 6. At 4.4 m west of the threshold the south face of WAE was lined with a combination of six blocks and slabs of limestone resting on occupation debris 30 cm above the original floor of the passage (drawn on fig. 2.16 [see insert]). No habitation surface was detected either in section or in plan, yet their bases are all set in the same horizontal plane, which must correspond to a stage when occupation debris reached that level. At the east end of the orthostats and on the same level, a rectangular slab of limestone resembling a threshold was placed across the corridor.

WY, the south wall, was not completely excavated. It has an average thickness of 50 cm, with eight courses standing to a height of 87 m. In the middle of the passage it was also lined with two vertical orthostats set on the same surface as those opposite.

A carefully shaped, shallow rectangular depression was located 40 cm south of the threshold to Unit 6. Labeled Ft 11 and with dimensions of 50 x 64 cm and a depth of 10 cm, it would have hindered access to both Units 6 and 16 unless traffic was meant to pass over or through it. Nothing inside the trough, which was not lime plastered, gave any indication as to its function. Ft 11 is visible on both pls 2.4c and d.

Stratigraphy

Below the plow zone the passageway was packed with wall tumble originating solely from WY, because WAE fell north into Units 6 and 18. The soil associated with and immediately below the tumble is typically light gray (10YR 7/2), as in most other parts of Area A. A thick deposit of occupation debris, rich in sherds, chipped stone, bone, and flecks of charcoal, but with few artifacts, was sealed by the tumble. This accumulation of debris is particularly noticeable in the corridor where it seems to have built up rapidly in the central section, west of the doorways leading into Units 6 and 16. It seems that in this densely settled sector of Area A the corridor was one of the only spaces available for the discard of household debris. The sherds in the corridor are particularly large and the quantities of ash and bone more substantial than elsewhere (see combined totals for Units 32 and 33 in Table 2.1). A concentration of basin fragments and dark ashy soil adjacent to the easternmost vertical slab against WAE suggests the existence of a hearth in this area. Due to the presence of the slabs, the corridor is only 85 cm wide at this point, so the hearth can hardly have been very substantial. Apart from the small patch of lime plastered floor in the vicinity of Ft 11, no definable occupation surface(s) were recorded in the passage, which must have followed a measured incline because Ft 11 appears to be sunk into sterile erosional material and is 46 cm higher than the original surface of the passage 4 m west. The horizontal plane on which the row of orthostats is seated—which is later than that associated with Ft 11—fails to correspond to a recognizable surface. In the sector of Unit 32, 2.6 m west of the passageway entrance, both WAE and WY sit directly on the bedrock, whereas opposite the southwest corner of Unit 6 WAE is built on 42 cm of occupation debris, while WY remains on bedrock.

Finds

As previously noted, the passageway was rich in finds consisting of two axes (S679, 680), three pounders (S190, 363, 414), a quern (IS1), three rubbers (IS2, 3, 5), a stone with a depression

(S501) and a picrolite spacer (S662). A RP spouted bowl (P49) and a RP Mottled cooking pot (P107) were recorded on the habitation surface south of Ft 11. Stratified sherds number 1,023, which relative to the surface of Unit 32/33 and the volume of soil removed represents the greatest concentration at *Kaminoudhia*. Included in this total are diagnostic RP sherds representing a maximum of forty-three small bowls, five large bowls, one jug, seven juglets, five jar/amphorae and a cooking pot. Basin ware totals 104 pieces.

An unstratified arsenical copper chisel (M17) and a pounder (S646) were found among the wall tumble. Despite its unstratified status on the edge of a pit, the find spot of M17 is indicated on fig. 2.7 because of its rarity as an intact artifact which stylistically belongs to the Philia/EC metal repertoire.

UNIT 35

The extreme northwestern sector of Area A is occupied by Unit 35 (fig. 2.16 [see insert]) of which only three walls, WAN and WAL as well as the short and questionable stub of a wall (WBB not shown on fig. 2.16 [see insert]), have been excavated. The former, seated on bedrock and preserved for a length of 6 m with an average width of 60 cm, once continued up the bank. WAL, 40 cm wide and poorly preserved, extends westward 3.5 m in the direction of WI, with which it probably formed an integral part.

At the northern limit of the excavated area, 1.7 m north of the east end of WAL, three large stones set on bedrock appear to form the end of a wall 55 cm wide which disappears into the baulk after a distance of 70 cm. Only further excavation can determine the significance of this feature, tentatively labeled WBB. The only in situ discovery in the incompletely excavated unit was Ft 32, a fireplace made of reddish yellow (7.5YR 7/8) mud plaster. The upper part was very poorly preserved and could not be accurately reconstructed, but there is sufficient evidence to suggest that in the tradition of Fts 8 and 16 it consisted of a double hearth. The larger firebox built up against the corner of WAN and WAL was 40 cm wide with a depth of 30 cm; the second box adjoining it to the north was 22 cm wide with the same depth. The mud plaster used to make the walls dividing the fireboxes is the same material as basin fabric. A thick layer of buff colored mud plaster (10YR 8/4), discolored in places to a light red (7.5YR 7/8), had been smeared on the faces of both adjoining walls; the layered appearance of the plaster suggests the presence of multiple applications. The presence of an earlier hearth of a different plan below indicates a prolonged period of use. As preserved it consists of a mud plaster wall 18 to 20 cm high and 12 cm thick built parallel to and 43 cm out from WAN. At its southern end, there is a gap of 45 cm leading up to the north face of WAL. This gap may have been intentional or it could have been the result of disturbance in this area since the southern end of the plaster wall is unfinished, unlike the carefully rendered northern end. The space defined by this wall was packed with basin fragments, some unusually large (measuring 25 x 20 cm). The hearth was built immediately upon bedrock.

Several large pieces of shaped basin, still lying upon the upper walls of the hearths, suggest that their original height was well over the 20 cm currently preserved. Quantities of basin fragments in the general area attest to the substantial nature of the installations, as well as to the presence of basins themselves. The heat from the hearth must have been considerable, as several stones in WAL are fire-reddened despite being deeply embedded in plaster up to 20 cm thick.

The entrance to the larger firebox was partially blocked by a limestone mortar, left in situ, with a cavity measuring 19 x 19 cm and a depth of 7 cm. There has been so much disturbance in this area, particularly due to root action, that the mortar has probably been displaced and was not originally so close to the hearth opening.

Stratigraphy

Despite the shallowness of the deposit, a thin layer of wall tumble originating from WAL and WAN sealed the occupation debris which had been preserved from erosion close to the north face of WAL. Elsewhere the wall tumble lay directly on the south sloping bedrock.

Finds

No finds were recorded in situ on the habitation surface; the tumble and topsoil contained a pounder (S197), a rubbing stone (S487), an adze (S518) and a fragmentary stone dish (S446). Eighty-nine diagnostic sherds were recorded and they provided evidence for several RP small bowls, three RP jar/amphorae and a RP cooking pot. In addition to the large pieces of basin in and around the hearths, eleven other pieces were found throughout the excavated area.

UNIT 39

A small section of Unit 39 (figs. 2.8, 2.16 [insert]) was excavated between the south face of WY and the south baulk of Operation H18B, on the southeastern edge of Area A. Though restricted, the excavation was sufficient to determine that slope pressure had pushed the top of WY southwards and that it stood four courses and 46 cm high on this side. The wall had toppled in one block southwards with the stones preserved in situ on edge.

Finds

One Senet gaming stone (S330), a pounder (S248) and a rubbing stone (S378) were found below the tumble, along with 118 sherds that included a rim fragment of a small RP bowl.

UNIT 41

West of the main complex of buildings and the passageway, Unit 41 (fig. 2.16 [see insert]) appears as a large trapezoidal structure of which only the eastern portion has been excavated. In this peripheral area work was limited to wall tracing to provide a better understanding of the overall settlement plan. Unit 41 is bounded to the east by 5.5 m long WAP, on average 60 cm wide and preserved to a height of two courses. It is bonded with WBA, between 60 and 70 cm wide, which follows an east–west bearing. Probes demonstrated that both these walls were set directly on bedrock, which had been stepped to seat WBA better, excavated over a distance of 2.5 m. At the southern end of WAP a 50 cm stretch of wall runs into the western baulk, thereby further defining the size and shape of this unit.

Finds

The only artifacts recorded from below the tops of the walls inside Unit 41 were 134 sherds that included diagnostics from a maximum of eight small RP bowls and three RP jar/amphorae.

UNITS 43 AND 44

To the south Area A is bounded by the 17 m long east–west stretch of WY, unexcavated in its middle section but well preserved at both extremities (fig. 2.16 [see insert]). A cross wall (WBA) joins it 4 m before turning at right angles to the south, thereby delineating Unit 43. The area east of WBA, known as Unit 44, remains to be defined. Excavation in this area was restricted to wall tracing and no additional information exists on these two units. Just below the surface were the remains of P128, a coarse ware dipper.

UNIT 45

This unit (fig. 2.16 [see insert]) is situated to the north of the 19.5 m east–west run of WI. Most of the area consists of the steep unexcavated slope rising toward the terrace wall north of Area A. On the north side of WI a foundation trench, 10 cm wide and 20 cm deep, ran from the east of Unit 3 to the end of the wall. Occupation debris had accumulated on bare bedrock in this area that suggests that, when the site was first settled, little to no topsoil was present north of the habitations, or else it had been intentionally removed.

AREA B

On the western edge of the terraced field between Area A and the steep northeast slopes of the Sotira *Teppes* ridge, a single 1 m by 4 m trial trench was sunk in 1981 to verify whether the settlement extended this far and to determine whether any cultural remains might be preserved in situ (pls. 1.2, 1.3). The probe was successful and led to the discovery of standing architecture associated with Red Polished pottery 80 cm below the topsoil. In 1983 the excavation was expanded and Area B, located 35 m west/southwest of Area A and 50 m northwest of Area C, yielded important information on the events surrounding the abandonment of the settlement.

In this part of the site where the Bronze Age habitation surface may be 2 m below the ground surface, practical considerations made it impossible to fully excavate any of the structures south of Unit 12.

UNIT 11

A triangular section of Unit 11 (figs. 2.10, 2.17), measuring 3.5 x 2 x 4 m, was excavated through the wall tumble into the occupation debris. Unfortunately, most of the area was covered by the later wall WS (not shown on plan), only leaving a cramped space wedged between the southern extension of WAA and the east baulk available for excavation. Note that the section of WAA indicated by a dotted line is covered by the later wall WS, which followed a northeast/southwest direction (see description of WS in connection with Unit 14 below).

The occupation debris is rich in basin and RP jug fragments at approximately the same elevation as P73 from Unit 14 on the west side of WAA, which suggests that the habitation surface is not far below.

UNIT 12

The center of Area B is occupied by the large and irregularly shaped Unit 12 (figs. 2.9, 2.17; pl. 2.6a; section fig. 2.20d), which because of its size was only excavated to floor level in the southeast corner. The remaining walls were traced to provide a coherent plan of this large and unique structure.

To the north, Unit 12 is defined by the 7.5 m stretch of WAT, which meanders along a ledge in the bedrock. At its western end, where it turns north and disappears into the baulk after a distance of 1 m, WAT is 55 cm wide, but in the east of the unit it incorporates several boulders of up to 1.1 x 0.5 m in size that increase its width to more than 1 m. WAT, of which only the top two courses have been cleared, then runs into the baulk in the direction of Area A. In the west there may be an 80 cm gap, probably an entrance, between WAT and the northern end of WAM which runs southeast in a straight line for 5 m, then curves gently east for another 4 m. Unfortunately, a 1.5 m baulk separates WAM from WH, but there is no reason to suggest that the two did not connect since they are of identical (55 cm) width. Furthermore, it would be atypical for a doorway to be located at this spot, which is not near the end of a wall or a corner. WAM/WH have a maximum preserved height of 86 cm, with seven courses of fieldstones.

In the western part of C20A a section of the north face of WH, from floor level to the top of the wall, is covered with a 1.5 cm thick layer of buff mud plaster (10YR 8/4), reddened in places. For a distance of 60 cm from the west baulk the building stones are discolored by heat to within 6 cm of the outer face of the wall, which suggests that at some stage a fire had been built against the wall, presumably well before the destruction of the building, since no concentration of ash was found in this area.

At the east end of WH a quern protruded 18 cm at floor level from the north face of the wall, which, on the opposite side, is formed by two slabs of limestone and not the usual coursing of fieldstones with a rubble core in the center. In this instance, the core of the wall is composed of occupation debris and not mud mortar or perhaps pisé, which suggests that the space was either empty or full of perishable material at the time of destruction. Therefore, it may have served as a niche or cupboard since no other obvious explanation exists for this unusual form of wall construction in the settlement.

The eastern boundary of Unit 12 is formed by the 4 m stretch of WAB, one course (20 cm) high in the north but increasing in the south to a height of 59 cm, where it disappears into the baulk. It presumably intersected with WH to form a corner, but in the north its relationship with WAT is unclear and nothing suggests that it had once abutted against the latter. Perhaps another entrance existed in the northeast corner of Unit 12. It is notable that this section of WAB should be so poorly preserved by comparison with WH, since it should have been protected by both the slope and nearby mass of WAT. The coursed tumble to the west of WAB, which lay undisturbed after a section of WAT collapsed southwards, does not extend to above WAB or even visibly connect with the sparser tumble in the eastern part of the unit. The best-preserved expanse of collapse in the northwest of the operation is shown on fig. 2.17 and is visible in the right foreground of pl. 2.6a.

Thus defined, Unit 12 measures approximately 8.5 m on an east–west axis and 7.3 m from north to south which delineates an area of 62 m^2, of which 14 m^2 have been excavated to floor level.

This unit lacked features such as lime plaster bins, benches or built hearths, although a major concentration of large basin fragments, centrally located close to the large mortar S548, suggests that some structure—probably a hearth—existed here before its destruction by the collapsing wall. The above mentioned fire-reddened mud plaster applied to the southwestern face of WH also hints at the existence of a hearth or, at least, a fireplace set against the wall.

The area west of C19D was only excavated to the level of the randomly scattered tumble between 0.7 and 1.5 m below the present ground level. In this manner, it was possible to trace WAM as it runs in a northwesterly direction toward WAT. To the north of C19D the area along the southern face of WAT was excavated down to the level of the south-sloping tumble, some of which was removed with intent to discover whether WAB intersected with the former. No traces of this wall were noted and the whole area will remain difficult to interpret until baulks surrounding C19D are removed. At present the only satisfactory source for the well-coursed tumble in Unit 12, which must have fallen from a wall running east–west, is WAT, which lies diagonally and not parallel to the axis of the tumble and more than 2 m north from the first line of stones.

Stratigraphy

The most remarkable aspect of this unit is the thick, even layer of wall tumble spread over most of its surface. In places it is still arranged in neat courses clearly demonstrating how walls toppled over on their sides in large segments. Two meters south of WAT there begins a succession of seventeen courses of fieldstones, all arranged on edge with between 2 and 6 cm of mud mortar (?) between each course, representing a minimum wall height of 2.1 m. The maximum width of this coursed tumble is 1.8 m, at which point, as it approaches WAB, it degrades into the usual random scatter. When viewed in section (fig. 2.20c, pl. 2.6d), the ordered arrangement of the tumble is immediately visible. It is on average 60 cm thick and composed of three stones overlying a thin layer of white lime plaster that represents the original internal rendering of the wall. Below is rich, very pale brown (10YR 7/4) occupational debris, from 6 to 20 cm thick, overlaying the light reddish brown sterile soil (5YR 6/4). The original habitation surface on top of sterile is a mixture of hard packed limestone chips and sherds, often lying flat. Nowhere in Unit 12 was a well-defined, or well-preserved, lime plaster floor recorded. A mass of basin fragments in the south center of the unit near the mortar S548 argues for a built hearth in the vicinity, which requires further excavation to be correctly interpreted.

Finds

The stratigraphic evidence suggests that the material lying scattered on the floor of Unit 12, below the thick layer of wall tumble, is undisturbed by erosion, agricultural activity or visible root action and is therefore in situ. The patterning of some of the sixty-four artifacts recovered supports this observation. The principal feature in the southeast corner of Unit 12 is a large oval mortar (S548, pl 6.2h) 30 cm high and 50 x 44 cm in diameter, surrounded by eleven pounders (S242, 245, 247, 276, 277, 289, 295, 385, 432, 433) and a rubber-pounder (S246), one hammerstone (S437), a pecking stone (S290)—thirteen percussion tools in all—to which may be added a large axe (S238) and an arsenical copper chisel (M9). The same cluster included two rubbers (S236, 494), which may have served as small querns with the rubber-pounders—a function for which they are perfectly suited—since querns with which rubbers normally operate are lacking in this area. There was another cluster 2 m to the northwest centered on a tethering stone or a weight (S506) and two large querns (S426, 508) with a single rubber (S505) lying nearby, as well as three pounders (S343, 400, 412), a rubber-pounder (S347), a hammerstone (S401), and a weight (S456). Between these concentrations was discovered a damaged Senet gaming stone (S424), which, like the mortar, may have been intact before the destruction of the building.

In addition to these notable clusters, the habitation surface of Unit 12 was scattered with a range of objects including six more pounders (S287, 362, 368, 373, 381, 444), two rubber-pounders (S313, 355), a hammerstone (S299), a pecking stone (S407), two querns S500, 508), six rubbers (S261, 359, 361, 387, 490, 493), an adze (S418), two mortars (S239, 548), a stone weight (S456), three gaming stones (S325, 425, 467) including a rare bifacial Mehen/Senet type (S425), a picrolite pendant (S340), two pieces of worked picrolite (S462, 464), a bead (TC17), and two RP dippers (P18, P40). A badly shattered RP amphora (P83) was strewn over the southeast corner of the room. A fragmentary bone needle (B5) came from this unit. Stratified diagnostic sherds provided evidence for a maximum of twenty-six RP small and six large bowls, one RP jug, one RP juglet, one RP jar/amphora and 271 basin fragments (these figures are not entered in Table 2.1 which only lists four vessel fragments and six basin fragments). In addition to the above, thirty-one igneous pebbles, some of them perhaps intended as blanks for tools, were scattered over the habitation surface, with a concentration of ten items in the vicinity of the mortar S548. An indeterminate fragment (M15) of copper-based sheet metal 0.3 cm thick was found mixed with the tumble above the concentration of artifacts surrounding the mortar, and a pottery roundel (TC30) was found in the tumble elsewhere. From the surface above Unit 12 came another bifacial Mehen/Senet gaming stone (S530).

The size of this structure suggests that it was an open courtyard where the grinding of substances took place. The presence of so many gaming stones should indicate leisure—or even religious activities, perhaps associated with the congregation of people. More than a quarter of its surface will need to be excavated to interpret the role and function of Unit 12 fully.

UNIT 13

To the south of Unit 12 there is a long, narrow area that probably functioned as a passage or alleyway between two habitation units since it is not bisected by any walls over a distance of 11 m (figs. 2.10, 2.17; pls. 2.6a, 2.6c). Bordered to the north by WH and to the south by WN, which diverge slightly from one another, the space is about 10 m long with a width varying from a minimum of 1.7 m to a maximum of 2.5 m. WN is 7 m long and between 45 and 50 cm wide with the greatest preserved height of 76 cm. Both extremities of the wall disappear into unexcavated baulks. WH was set in a shallow, L-shaped foundation trench, only recorded along the north face of WH in the western area of Unit 12. It is not visible on the other side of the wall in Unit 13 where its south face has been excavated to foundation level.

When the western end of Unit 13 was first excavated in 1981, the well-aligned and coursed tumble with stones systematically placed on edge stretching from wall to wall, was initially interpreted as possible paving for an alleyway (compare pl. 2.6b showing street paving in Sotira Village). It was later recognized as tumble originating from WH that had fallen in a southerly direction, neatly filling the space between it and WN. In the eastern portion of Unit 13, the stones were no longer arranged in parallel orderly rows. This lack of patterning in the east of the area replicates the situation in the east of Unit 12.

Stratigraphy

Two areas of Unit 13 were excavated in depth. That to the west, a meter wide probe between WH and WN, showed that the tumble consisted of two layers of stones lying above 40 cm of pale brown occupation debris extremely rich (604 sherds in a volume of 0.92 cubic m) in sherds and bone. As in Unit 12, no well-defined compacted habitation surface was distinguishable, only slight evidence for an ephemeral surface 20 cm above the base of the wall and 20 cm below the bottom of the tumble. Sherds and a few pieces of chipped stone lay horizontally in the occupation debris. No recognizable surface was associated with the base of WH, and at 40 cm below the lowest layer of stone tumble the occupation debris grades imperceptibly into the slightly darker reddish brown (5YR 6/4) sterile soil overlaying bedrock 2 m below.

The wall tumble in the southeastern section of Unit 13, about 40 cm thick, overlay occupation debris, excavated to a depth of 20 cm below the tumble but not to sterile. It should be noted that this occupation debris was richer in bone than in the units to the south and north, suggesting that this was an open communal area such as a passageway, suitable for the dumping of refuse, a suggestion also made in connection with Units 32/33.

Finds

Four pounders (S300, 329, 367, 398), a rubbing stone (S267), a rubber-pounder (S274), two rubbers (S419, 422), an axe (S278), a gaming stone (S235) and a worked piece of picrolite (S333) were found just below the tumble in the south eastern corner of the unit. In the western probe a rubbing stone (S191), a pounder (S221) and a spindle whorl (TC24) came from below the tumble in the 40 cm accumulation of occupation debris.

UNIT 14

Unit 14 (figs. 2.10, 2.17), another large area to the south of 13, in its present state represents a triangular (5.5 x 3.3 x 6.3 m) section of a unit defined by WN and WAA, which abut each other at approximately right-angles. These walls, on average 45 cm in width, are more narrow than the norm at *Kaminoudhia*. WS is a rubble wall of late date (not shown on fig 2.17), 1.25 m wide and 80 cm high, constructed over WN and WAA. No diagnostic ceramics of any specific type and date could be associated with WS which would have to be dismantled in the hopes of obtaining material for a *terminus post quem* date. The pottery recovered from surface and plow zone levels of this trench is indistinguishable from that of other areas of the site and consists of 99% weathered Bronze Age wares with a few miscellaneous Hellenistic, Roman and undiagnostic post antique sherds. The building technique of WS—namely shell construction with small fist-sized stones between—is different from all other walls, both ancient and modern, in the Sotira area.

In the northern corner formed by WN and WAA, there was built against the latter a double hearth (Ft 34; not indicated on the plans) made of buff mud plaster (10YR 8/4) lined with slightly lighter plaster 1–1.5 cm thick. The firebox closer to WN, with which it is parallel and separated by a layer of mud plaster from 11 to 20 cm thick, was originally around 26 cm wide and perhaps 38–40 cm deep. It is separated from the next box, 23 cm wide and 22 cm deep, by a mud plaster wall 10 cm wide, now preserved for a length of 20 cm. The original depth of this box would presumably have been the same as the other. Large basin fragments filled the entire feature, the bottom of which was not reached.

Stratigraphy

A scattering of wall tumble covered the excavated area, but no well preserved coursing similar to that in Units 12 and 13 was noted and very few artifacts came from this level. Below the tumble, there were large quantities of basin fragments and several ground stone tools. The habitation surface was not reached, although the intact RP vessel (P73) associated with the hearth, Ft 34, suggests it is close to the level where excavation ceased.

Finds

From just beneath the tumble came a pestle (S199), a pounder (S218), a fragmentary quern (S307) a rubber (S318) and a rubbing stone (S233). A well-preserved RP juglet (P73) lay on its side in front of the hearth. Both the juglet and the hearth were protected by a limestone slab (65 x 45 x 10 cm) lying horizontally on occupation debris. It did not appear to be in situ and could have fallen out of an adjoining wall where it may have functioned as a shelf, perhaps even a corner shelf above the hearth. In addition to the above finds, 487 sherds were recorded from below the tumble including diagnostics from a maximum of 6 small RP bowls. The presence of the hearth would help explain the 258 basin fragments found in addition to the sherds.

AREA C

The southern border of the field in which Areas A and B are located consists of a low dry stone terrace wall running southwest–northeast which created a substantial accumulation of soil that could have afforded protection to any cultural remains set on bedrock (pls. 1.2, 1.3 and 1.5). For this reason in 1981, excavations were initiated in Area C, 50 m south of Area A and 50 m southeast of Area B. By the end of the 1983 season, 270m^2 of a well-preserved building complex had been recovered. In view of the number of units excavated down to the habitation surface, Area C was sparse in metal finds by comparison with Areas A and B. Its internal organization and range of floor plans were without parallel elsewhere in the settlement. A higher percentage of identifiable animal bone was recorded from Area C, specifically cattle (cf. Chapter 11.3), and several units present some of the most enigmatic evidence for specialized or atypical activities at the site: Unit 2, probably a courtyard, was the site of unusual activities; Unit 10, a large undefined open area, yielded a unique range of finds and Unit 21 arguably provided the best evidence for specific activities at *Kaminoudhia*.

UNITS 2 AND 25

The focal architectural feature of Area C is a large, roughly square space (Unit 2) entered from the south via a narrow vestibule, Unit 25 (figs. 2.11, 2.18 [insert], 2.21b). Although flanked on three sides by rooms, it communicates with none and as such provides yet another example of a large self-contained area approached via a narrow corridor. With its corners oriented to the cardinal points, contrary to most structures in Areas A and B, which followed a general east–west alignment, it is one of the larger units in Area C, measuring 34 m^2. WX, the 6 m long northwest wall, is irregular and poorly preserved with two to three courses attaining a height of 48 cm and an average width of 65 cm. For about 1 m WX is reduced to a single row of stones between a bench or platform in the southwest corner of Unit 22 and the outer edge of Ft 39, a hearth in the north corner of Unit 2. This does not appear to be the result of erosion, root action, nor plowing, and may be the secondary blocking of a doorway that initially connected Units 2 and 22. This interpretation is based solely on the physical appearance of the wall and not on any architectural or stratigraphic evidence.

Unit 2 is defined to the northeast by WJ, also of irregular construction, bonded with WX in the north and WA to the south. The northernmost 2 m of the wall, between Units 2 and 9, is 70 cm wide, well preserved and stands two courses and 45 cm high. The remaining section opposite Unit 17 is 20 cm narrower and of markedly different construction, as if part of a different building phase—for which there is no other evidence. In the east corner five courses are preserved, reaching a height of 68 cm. Along the entire length of its inner face, WJ is flanked by a bench between 20 and 30 cm wide and on average 20 cm high. Although such a low storage or work surface may seem of little utilitarian value and could equally well be interpreted as a purely structural feature reinforcing the base of WJ, its uniform height and level upper surface do argue in favor of its use as a bench, especially since it is bonded with a bench of equal height but greater width built along the west face of WA. Furthermore, the presence of in situ occupation debris on this surface supports the above interpretation.

The southeast side of Unit 2 is defined by WA, which in this area has a complicated construction history consisting of at least three episodes. It emerges from the southern baulk of Area C and only its west face was articulated during the excavation of Unit 25. It is poorly preserved and increases in width to 1 m opposite the wide door between Units 2 and 25. Two meters further northeast the wall is flanked by a low bench on the west and a 2 m long step or buttress on the other side, to be described later in connection with Unit 10. At 1.30 m from the east corner of Unit 2 by a later pit, 80 cm in diameter has destroyed the inner face of WA, along with the bench.

To the southwest, Unit 2 is bounded by WL, a well-built and well-preserved wall 5.2 m long, 50 cm wide on average with a maximum of four courses of large stones rising to a height of 63 cm. The common size of the fieldstones used for this wall is 44 x 29 cm, whereas the site average is 30 x 22 cm. Unlike other walls of the unit, which are shell built, WL, in the manner of WI in Area A, is of crude header and stretcher construction. At its southeastern extremity before curving south, it is abutted by the 1 m long WAC, a cross wall which defines Unit 25, a vestibule 3.3 m long by 1.3 m wide. WAC is 50 cm wide, four courses and 55 cm high, and it creates a doorway 1 m in width between the two units. The entrance to Unit 25—and by extension Unit 2—is fitted with a large stone threshold, 1.17 m long and 17 cm wide, rising 27 cm above the bedrock. On the left side, when facing the entrance, the threshold has two circular pecked depressions, one of which, 6 cm in diameter and 4 cm deep, is very smooth and obviously supported the door pivot. If the width of a wooden doorjamb is taken into account, then the door opening may have been about 80 cm, but if it closed directly against the west face of WA, which is quite feasible, the width increases nearly 10 cm. All walls were set directly on the smooth hard bedrock, which was not leveled to provide a better footing for the foundations. A single lime plaster bin, Ft 20, 22 cm in diameter and 15 cm deep, incorporating a stone mortar at its base, was located in the southeast corner of Unit 2, 90 cm north of the door.

In the northern corner of the unit at 1 m from WJ, a 40 cm long slab of limestone was set vertically in mud mortar at right angles against WX. The west face of the stone, the adjacent area of WX as well as a patch of mud plaster 50 cm in diameter, are all fire-reddened, indicating the presence of a poorly preserved hearth (Ft 39). Quantities of gray ash mixed with numerous basin fragments provide further evidence for a fireplace, the only one recognized in Area C.

Stratigraphy

The southeastern sector of the northwestern quadrant of Unit 2 was not excavated to bedrock and a 4.5 m^2 up to 25 cm thick sample of the occupation debris was left in situ.

Both Units 2 and 25 were sealed by an irregular scatter of tumble, located 40 cm on average below the present ground level. Since the upper surface of some stones had been scarred by the iron socle of traditional plowshares, which cannot penetrate to a depth of 40 cm below the surface, the level of the field must have risen either through terracing or as the result of some other agency, such as erosion. No coursed tumble was recorded in this area and it would appear that WJ at least, disintegrated gradually in situ, with its stones tumbling in an uneven scatter to either side of the original wall alignment. In the central, eastern sector of Unit 2, a thin white layer of lime just below the stone tumble may have been the remains of wall plaster. Similar plaster was noted below the sections of walls that had collapsed in one piece, specifically in Unit 12.

Throughout both units the wall tumble was spread on top of a thick deposit of ash-rich occupation debris, which had accumulated on the original lime plaster, terra rossa (7.5YR 3/2) and bedrock habitation surface. The thickness of this deposit, which contained many sherds, much bone and chipped stone, varied from 25 cm to 55 cm, and the density of ash ranged from pockets of dark gray carbonized material (5Y 4/1) to a mixture of brown ashy soil (2.5Y 7/1). There are at most two identifiable strata in the occupation debris (see fig. 2.21b), which do not appear to correspond to separate phases of habitation but simply to a greater admixture of ash and soil in the upper level by comparison with more concentrated, darker ashy material below. Unit 25 had a similar thick deposit of ash overlaying bedrock.

In Unit 2 the irregular scatter of ceramic, lithic, metal, and terracotta artifacts fails to suggest any depositional pattern or associations. In addition to a few objects just below the tumble, the majority of finds were on or just above the habitation surface, the most notable exception being P86, a large spouted bowl sitting on 30 cm of ashy deposit in the eastern half of the unit (pl. 2.7a).

When did this ashy deposit accumulate? Was it during the life of the settlement, in which case it would presumably have built up gradually with abandoned or lost artifacts incorporated in the matrix, or did it build up rapidly—as in Unit 8—surrounding the vessels sitting on floors? Unless the bowl was abandoned by a person who visited the site after a conflagration which resulted in the departure of the inhabitants, it is difficult to explain how it got placed on ashy debris 30 cm *above* the habitation surface, yet below the wall tumble in an open courtyard.

Finds

The relative paucity of lithic artifacts in Unit 2 by comparison with Unit 12, the other large open space, in Area B, is noteworthy. On the other hand, sherd material is the densest of any unit at *Kaminoudhia*, especially with reference to small bowls as discussed below. The 14 m² of habitation surface excavated in Unit 12 yielded sixty-four artifacts, whereas only thirty-three were recovered for the 29.5 m² excavated in Unit 2.

Stratified finds consist of one bone needle with an eye (B1, see Appendix 11.1), three pounders (S129, 131, 375), a rubber-pounder (S94), two rubbing stones (S93, 588), a quern (S428) and three rubbers (S32, 61, 384), an axe (S416), two possible stone weights (S497, 502), a mortar (S280), a possible jar cover (S110), a perforated disk (S474), a stone with a depression (S111), a Senet gaming stone (S71), a rare bifacial Mehen/Senet gaming stone (S72) and two pieces of worked picrolite (S146, 463). The unusually large number of seven intact or restorable vessels came from this unit. They consist of a RP spouted amphora (P127), a RP miniature bowl (P39), a RP juglet with relief decoration (P55), a RP Mottled cooking pot (P116), two RP Mottled bowls (P131, 145), a large RP spouted bowl (P86), a DPBC tankard (P85) and a DPBC juglet (P88).

In addition to the above, 2,123 stratified sherds were recorded, including rim sherds from a maximum of 92 RP small bowls as well as one large bowl, one RP jar/amphora, and a cooking pot. Fragments of at most forty vertical handles and six trough spouts were also noted. These figures represent approximately one-fifth of all the small bowls and vertical handles included among the ca. 17,000 stratified sherds from the entire settlement.

Four terracotta spindle whorls (TC14, 15, 20, 28), two sherd roundels (TC52, 54), a copper-based awl (M4) and an awl-like copper tool (M8) complete the list. An almost intact Mesopotamian fallow deer antler lay on the floor parallel to the bench along the west face of WJ, 30 cm southwest of S502. The antler, which only lacked its burr, was 49 cm long and displayed four tines.

The above objects do not suggest any specific function for Unit 2, but they do imply that whatever activities took place therein, many small bowls were required along with other receptacles for containing and/or pouring liquid (hence the six trough spouts, probably from jugs or juglets). The deep spouted bowl (P86) is the largest of its kind from the site.

When viewed as a group the vessels from Unit 2 stand out due to their atypical characteristics. There was little grain grinding activity since only one quern and very few of the associated handstones were discovered. Of note is a slight emphasis on spinning and perhaps even weaving, if the stone weights are correctly interpreted. The size of the area suggests it was unroofed and is thus an open courtyard similar to Unit 12. Also of note is evidence to suggest that the walls of this courtyard were rendered with lime plaster (see "Lime plaster" *infra*). This was a costly material to produce, which with one other exception was not found on interior or exterior walls at *Kaminoudhia*, so its use here may attribute a particular status to this courtyard. Dazzling white walls framing an enclosed space open to the sky would contrast sharply with the usual drab mud colored surfaces of other structures. Could it be a coincidence that the only additional record of lime plaster was in Unit 12, also a large courtyard, in Area B?

From above the wall tumble in the east corner of the unit came an adze (S177). The only stratified finds from Unit 25 were fragments of two small limestone mortars (S308, 554) and a pecking stone (S555).

UNIT 8

Both in terms of shape and taphonomy Unit 8 (figs. 2.12, 2.18 [insert], 2.21a, 2.21b) is unique. No other triangular room with a curvilinear element was excavated at the settlement, and no other had such a thick ashy deposit with so many in situ ceramic vessels.

Its main north–south axis measures 6.8 m as defined by WAR and WL, which converge at a 35° angle. The former, 6.2 m long, on average 50 cm wide with three courses standing to a height of 63 cm above bedrock, is the most regular and best-preserved wall in Unit 8. It abuts against the 4.1 m long and 55 cm wide section of WAJ, which follows a general east–west bearing. In places this three-course, 55 to 70 cm high, wall has suffered from erosion, with many stones slightly displaced. At the eastern end of WAJ, there is a 1.2 m wide opening with a low rock-cut threshold that provides the only means of access to the room. To the east it is bounded by the 7.8 m long WL, which curves to the south for the last 2 m and ends with a short 30 cm return protruding from its west face and acting as a door jamb for the entrance. (This feature was already described in connection with Unit 2.) All walls are built directly on bedrock, or in the intervening areas, on terra rossa. Because of the hardness of the limestone in this area and the gentle, regular southward slope, no preparation for seating the foundations was necessary. Unit 8 has a floor space of 19 m².

Most of the habitation surface consisted of hard, karstic limestone with a smooth weathered surface and pockets of terra rossa. The southern half of the unit where the bedrock becomes uneven is covered with a well-preserved, thick lime plaster floor running up to the base of WAJ.

At approximately 2 m from the north corner of the room, a complex and unique series of features (Ft 23a and b) was set against WL. The northern end (Ft 23a) consisted of a stone and rubble platform protruding 70 cm from the wall, 30 cm high and 60 cm wide. Adjoining it to the south was a rectangular space 33 cm wide and 60 cm long, defined on the outside by two stones set on edge. This three-sided trough was full of occupation debris, therefore empty at the time of abandonment. A mud pisé platform of the same height as Ft 23a, also lined on its outer face with field stones set on edge, provides a second rectangular platform to the south (Ft 23b). The interface between this pisé platform and WL corresponds to a gap in the wall stones, which as the only such gap in the entire length of the wall cannot be viewed as a coincidence. That the void was filled with mud mortar or pisé, identical to the material used for the platform, suggests this could be the plastered base of a blind niche, similar to that described in the southeast corner of Unit 5. The original height of Ft 23b at the time of abandonment was around 30 cm.

Although no objects were found in immediate association with these features to provide clues as to their function, three rubbers (IS31–33) and a rectangular slab of limestone (IS34 measuring 48 x 20 x 5 cm) surrounding the southern end of Ft 23b had perhaps been displaced from its surface. There is also a rock-cut mortar (Ft 22), 28 cm in diameter and 19 cm deep, situated 48 cm south of Ft 23b. It is the type usually connected with pounding, although no handstones—pounders or rubber-pounders— were recorded nearby. Since its dimensions are similar to those of post supports, it perhaps served this function and not that of a mortar. Perhaps there is a connection between Ft 23 and Ft 21, a large pedestal basin or mortar 48 cm high with a central cavity 24 cm in diameter and 21 cm deep. It sat on the bedrock 1 m to the west. No other mortar of this type was found in the settlement and although its basic function is obvious, the same activities could probably have been performed in any one of the rock-cut or lime plaster mortars found in many units.

In the middle of WAJ the lime plaster floor gives way to a carefully shaped, shallow rectangular trough (50 x 46 x 8 cm), Ft 40, also fashioned out of lime plaster (see figs. 2.12 and 2.21a). Its smooth inner surface sloped down toward the wall face.

For a large room containing such varied features the absence of a hearth is unexpected at *Kaminoudhia*. Not even a fire-reddened patch of floor on bedrock was recorded—as in Unit 20 for example—either during excavation or in the following years after winter rains had scoured the plaster and bedrock.

Stratigraphy

Much of the unit is covered with an uneven scatter of wall tumble, clearly visible in fig. 2.21a. As in Unit 2 none of the tumble was coursed and its absence in the vicinity of WAJ in the lower part of the room would suggest that this wall toppled in a southern direction. Figure 2.21a, the north–south section running through the center of Unit 8, unambiguously demonstrates that no clear succession of levels is distinguishable, merely the disturbed plow zone above the tumble, on average 40 cm below the surface, followed by ash, sherd, bone and chipped stone rich occupation debris extending down to the floor and without any internal sub-stratification. Pockets of purer, darker, ash are common (10YR 6/2:dry; 10YR 5/1:damp), but only very small, scattered lumps of charcoal were noted. If this occupation debris had accumulated gradually as the result of regular discard patterns, at least some secondary lenses corresponding to floor areas, which became more compacted (as in Units 1 and 5 for example), should be recognizable. None were detected in Unit 8.

The wall tumble directly overlay the ash-rich material in places from 30 to 50 cm thick. Few artifacts, except a copper awl, came from on top of the debris; the remainder, apparently in situ, were concentrated in the eastern half of the room and lay on the habitation surface. The stratigraphic evidence suggests that the ash built up around the vessels and the few other objects sitting on the floor. Since none of the vessels are thick-walled, sturdy storage jars, and since the ashy material shows no signs of internal stratification, it appears to have built up rapidly as the result of a single event.

If the ash originated in this manner, and not through the gradual accumulation of occupation debris as recognized in most units at the settlement, then the most likely source for the ash is the accidental burning of the roof or of combustible material stored within the unit. Since no evidence for the latter exists, or is likely to exist, the roof destruction scenario seems the most plausible. Unfortunately, there is no unequivocal evidence for a roof other than the presence of ash in the occupation debris, which provides a circular argument. No carbonized bits of in situ beams and no impressions of sticks or reeds in fire-hardened mud were recorded here or elsewhere at the site (see Le Brun 1987:292, fig. 9, for an example from Khirokitia *Vouni*). The lack of such impressions is not surprising, since wet mud applied to a wooden or reed support is not the procedure used for large covered spaces.

If the structures at *Kaminoudhia* were covered in a manner similar to traditional Cypriot flat mud-roofed buildings, then a thick layer of dry soil would have been packed on top of reeds, brush or seaweed, supported by more substantial branches or slats laid across the roof beams. Such an arrangement is unlikely to leave telltale soil impressions, even in the presence of a conflagration, unless the soil was very wet at the time (see "Roofs" *infra*).

In conclusion, explaining satisfactorily how such a quantity of ash accumulated in Unit 8 is impossible. It seems most likely to have been the result of a conflagration that buried everything left in the room when the roof caved in. It is ironical that the unit with the best evidence for a burnt roof appears to have been lacking a fireplace.

Finds

The discard pattern of artifacts in Unit 8 is unusual. For its size, very few stratified lithic finds were recorded—nine in all—whereas it exhibited the settlement's largest concentration of in situ intact or largely restorable vessels in addition to sherds and basin fragments.

The only lithics consist of two pounders (S602, 603), five rubbers (IS31-3, S266, 704), a mortar (S556) and a piece of worked picrolite (S335). In addition to the above-mentioned cluster of querns south of Ft 23, there was another concentration of two pounders and a mortar in the extreme northern corner, an area so constricted that it can hardly have served any function other than for storage. In the southeast corner of the room were arranged close to or against the east face of WL, five RP jugs of varying size and shape. Two (P33 and 60) were intact while the others (P69, 70, 106) were smashed in situ. A RP bowl restored from many pieces (P129) came from the same area. The pattern noted in Unit 2 is repeated somewhat in Unit 8 where the 972 stratified sherds provide evidence for a maximum of thirty-eight small RP bowls, eight large RP bowls as well as nineteen RP closed vessels of different types (including a fragment of a RP juglet, P138) and twenty-one vertical handles. An important find was the rim of a large, and rare, RP storage vessel (P140). The same unit yielded a pithos handle, probably from another storage vessel since the handle of P140 *may* have been horizontal (see discussion of this piece in Chapter 4). In addition to the above listed material, a copper awl (M5) was recovered from just below the tumble, and therefore well above the floor, a RP bead (TC13) and an incised spindle whorl (TC36) were also recorded. Basins are more common in units with fireplaces, but Unit 8 is an exception to the rule with 253 pieces of this ware.

From a study of the artifacts and features recorded in Unit 8 one may suggest that grinding and pounding took place here in addition to the storage of a substance(s), requiring the use of at least one pithos, of which a few sherds were noted in the northern corner of the room (P140). By comparison with Units 2 and 10 (see below), the number of small bowls is unremarkable but, in relation to the typical numbers recorded in Areas A and B, it is high. We can only surmise that these bowls were used for the consumption of food and drink, in which case a greater amount of eating and drinking seems to have taken place in the abovementioned Area C units.

UNIT 9

Only the southwestern section of Unit 9 (figs. 2.14, 2.18 [insert]) has been excavated, thus its original size and shape are unknown. On the present evidence, it is a long rectangular room with at least two low benches, but, in view of the uneven shapes of many units at *Kaminoudhia,* this is mere speculation. A 1 m wide probe in the southeast determined that WAD extends for at least 6.5 m more to the northeast. To the southwest the unit is defined by a length of WJ, which was described in connection with Unit 22. Only a 3 m section of WV, the northwest wall, on average 65 cm wide and two courses high, could be investigated before it entered the north baulk. The total excavated surface of Unit 9 is 22.5 m².

An irregular stretch of masonry, approximately 2.5 x 1 m with the main axis running northeast-southwest, occupied the center of the room, consisting of a post Bronze Age wall only one course high. It was built 35 cm above the floor and no specific pottery type could be associated with it. The building technique employed in its construction is that of the Bronze Age walls at *Kaminoudhia,* thus quite different from WS, the later wall cutting across Units 11 and 13. Further excavation to the northeast may explain its presence.

All the other walls of Unit 9 were built directly on the gently south-sloping bedrock without any prior preparation of the smooth surface that also served as the floor for most of the room. Where the limestone is eroded or replaced by deep pockets of terra rossa, it is covered by a 2 to 3 cm thick layer of crumbly lime plaster.

The southeast section of WJ is fronted by a 2.2 m long bench, narrowing from a maximum width of 40 cm against WAD to 30 cm at the opposite end. It stands 27 cm above the floor. On the other side of the unit another bench 30 cm high and 30 cm wide was built against the south face of WV. Close to the bench and 50 cm from WJ, Ft 27, a natural solution hole in the bedrock, had been reworked to form an oval mortar (30 x 38 cm), the base of which, 22 cm deep, was packed with limestone chips.

Stratigraphy

The entire unit was covered with an irregular layer of tumble approximately 50 cm below the present ground surface. Patches of ash-rich debris were found throughout, starting just below the tumble. Only the northwest corner of the room seems to have been free of ash. The occupation debris covering bedrock was the usual mixture of sherds and chipped stone with a higher than usual amount of bone.

Finds

Few artifacts were recorded in situ on or just above the habitation surface. The most important is a restored RP jug (P117), lying close to WAD with a small fragmentary mortar (S503) nearby. From the northeast of IS54, a shallow mortar (50 x 40 x 6 cm) half way between WAD and WV, came a stone with a depression (S492) and a mortar (S513). The remaining objects, a bone point (B9), a pecking stone (S403), a rubber-pounder (S448) and a picrolite pendant (S468), came from the occupation debris below the tumble but were well above the floor. They may have originated on the roof. There were 499 stratified sherds, including a maximum of thirteen small RP bowls and forty-four basin fragments.

UNIT 10

Unit 10 (figs. 2.11, 2.14, 2.18 [insert], 2.21a, 2.21b; pl. 2.7b) is located east of the 16 m stretch of WA and consists of two triangular areas, I24B and I24C, each measuring approximately 5 m on the diagonal by 4 x 4 m on the other sides, respectively adjoining Units 17 and 2. WA is not of uniform construction and varies in width from 1.1 m in the southeast corner of Unit 2 to under 50 cm in the northeast corner of Unit 17. Between, it incorporates Ft 30, a 2.2 m long and 50 cm wide buttress or shelf reinforcing the wall opposite Unit 2, which in turn is flanked by Ft 31, a bench 40 cm wide and 40 cm high. The upper surface of the feature is eroded to the same height as the top of WA (see section) so it is impossible to determine whether it was originally built to the same height as WA or served as a shelf at least 80 cm above the habitation surface. To the north of Ft 30, WA narrows to 50 cm in width up to WJ and after that for a distance of 2.5 m it appears to have slumped and spread to a width of 80 cm, perhaps due to slope pressure. The last 2 m of WA, standing up to 77 cm and five courses above bedrock, are slightly less than 50 cm wide.

No cross-walls abutting WA were encountered, suggesting that Unit 10 was a large open space adjoining the southeast side of the Area C building complex and as such it extends at least 3.5 m away from WA (i.e., a right-angle measurement from WA to the southeast corner of I24B). The area was lacking features except Ft 30 and Ft 31, which form an integral part of WA. The hard karstic limestone consists of smooth ridges and gullies mostly in the same horizontal plane with terra rossa between. Sometimes small areas of the bedrock and the terra rossa are covered with a 2 cm thick layer of poorly preserved crumbly white lime plaster (5YR 8/1) which does not appear to have ever extended over large areas.

Stratigraphy

Little wall tumble was recorded in the south of I24C, but to the north in I24B it was heavy, especially in the northeast corner where the upper surface of the tumble is on average 60 to 70 cm below the present ground surface. Underneath, the soil remained ash free and pale brown (10YR 6/3) down to the habitation surface. A few objects were recorded in and among the tumble, specifically P67, a worked sherd, possibly a pot support or mold, and S259, a work surface or perhaps the cover for a storage jar. Everything else came from on or just above the habitation surface.

Finds

The habitation surface of Unit 10 yielded an even scatter of artifacts, mostly small ground stone pounders, associated with occupation debris rich in pottery, chipped stone, bone (including the remains of a kestrel *Falco tinnunculus*: see Chapter 11), and an abundance of small, igneous water-smoothed, ovoid pebbles, averaging 5 x 4 x 2 cm. In I24B alone 29 pebbles were distributed among three clusters and many more littered the area.

The abundance of pounders is noteworthy and indicative of some specific activity (or activities) requiring the pulverizing and pounding of substances, perhaps as well as knapping. Twenty-one were recorded (S25, 50, 57, 69, 100, 113, 116, 135, 244, 251, 252, 253, 284, 292, 294, 321, 346, 364, 413, 415, 420), followed by three rubber-pounders (S54, 80, 344), a pecking stone (S44), a whetstone (S117), and two axes (S254, Type 3, 327, Type 1). One quern (IS26) and three rubbers (S107, 112, 118) were recovered along with four rubbing stones (S97, 138, 228, 292), a work surface (S259), a possible burnisher (S148), and three pebbles (S90, 103, 147) of uncertain usage though here interpreted as possible blanks, one of which (S90) displays an area of high polish. Three clusters of pebbles near S292 (n=16), S364 (n=7) and S232 (n=5) were recovered from the area. Were they also blanks, or had they some other function, possibly ritualistic (see below)? A remarkable, in fact unique, concentration of seven gaming stones of Senet type (S77, 78, 80, 102, 109, 114, 234) was noted in the area. One picrolite bottle-shaped (S140) and one oval (S542) pendant along with a spacer (S663) of the same material conclude the list of stone finds, to which must be added a poorly preserved RP juglet (P30) and a large and unique flat bottomed basin (P121, pl. 2.7b) with extensive signs of wear on its inner surface. It was sitting on bedrock, apparently in situ, 2 m to the east of WA with the handle and body fragments of a large storage jar—also unique—lying nearby (P141). Two terracotta objects, a "tripod foot (?)," TC8, and a roundel, TC43, were also recorded.

The occupation debris in Unit 10 yielded the fragments of four large RP bowls, one of them spouted (P135), and 1,250 stratified sherds which suggest the presence of a maximum of ninety-three small bowls (including P132), two juglets and five jar/amphorae, all of RP ware. There were also twenty-four vertical handles belonging to closed vessels and 182 basin fragments (not included with the sherd total).

The most unusual and significant discovery from the area was the moderately well preserved upper cranium and horn cores of a cattle skull, 1.2 m east of WA, opposite the southeast corner of Unit 17 (pl. 6.4d). The facial bones had been cut away so that the horns could have easily been attached to the top of a person's head. In this respect the cranium is quite different from those excavated at many Bronze Age Cypriot sites and interpreted as masks or wall fixtures (Karageorghis 1982:101).

The wealth, density, and diversity of finds in Unit 10 equal, and in most instances surpass, those recorded in rooms and courtyards elsewhere in the settlement, thereby identifying this as an area with a high level of activity. Further excavation should be able to determine whether it was indeed an open space at the edge of the structures in Area C, or whether it was circumscribed by more buildings to the east. Note, however, that when the cart track 20 m east of WA was asphalted in 1993, its eastern scarp was re-cut and shaved smooth from ground level to bedrock, and no evidence of buildings was visible. This suggests, along with the 1 x 4 m trial trench sunk in K21 which was without architecture, that the settlement never extended further east, at least south of Area A.

The presence of abnormally high numbers of small bowls, coupled with containers for liquids, the seven gaming stones and especially the mask/cattle skull invites speculation about the activities which could have taken place here as well as in adjoining Unit 2. It seems likely that not all were concerned with food processing and production, and that some were probably of a non-domestic nature. The numerous drinking vessels, along with the unusual concentration of games, which could have had a religious connection (Swiny 1986:50), suggests that feasting—perhaps ritualistic—may have taken place here. Also significant is the curious 2.2 m long bench, Ft 31, flanking another unusually high bench, or more plausibly a shelf, Ft 30. Features such as these could have served a range of non-domestic functions and it should be remembered that only 3 m away was found the cattle skull/mask, and that three gaming boards (S77, 80 and 117) surrounded by small bowl fragments, lay on the habitation surface less than 1 m from the lower bench. The link between large bowls especially, and wine drinking in EC and MC Cyprus has recently been discussed in some detail by Herscher (1997). However, Herscher has also suggested that pottery making may have occurred in this area (see Chapter 4 "Miscellaneous Shapes: Pot support/Mold [?]").

Despite the 1.3 m of deposit above bedrock in Unit 10, further excavation is necessary to understand the reasons for this unusual and intriguing assemblage of finds.

UNIT 17

Located to the east of Unit 2 and south of Unit 9, Unit 17 (figs. 2.14, 2.18 [insert]) has been only partially excavated to floor level. Trial trenching, however, determined with a reasonable degree of confidence that it consisted of a rectangular room with its long axis running northwest–southeast. To the north Unit 17 was bounded by WAD, preserved to a height of 62 cm and four courses on its south side, already referred to in connection with Unit 9, and to the south by the northernmost extension of WA, from 50 to 80 cm wide, discussed in connection with Unit 10, and WJ, the southwest wall, described in connection with Unit 2. On its north face, however, WJ was on average four courses and 63 cm high. Probes in the eastern part of the unit located three wall segments determining the exact alignment of WAD, which ends with a short 40 cm right-angle turn to the south, thus providing the doorjamb for the 1.4 m wide entrance. All the above-described walls were built directly on bedrock. The overall internal dimensions of Unit 17 are 6.5 m in length with a width varying from 3.3 m in the west to 2 m in the east, enclosing an area of approximately 17 m², just over half of which, or 9 m², has been excavated to floor level.

A single feature was recorded in the Unit, namely Ft 29, a shallow mortar with a diameter of 18 cm, cut into an irregular protuberance of the bedrock and rising 28 cm above the floor in the center of the room, 1.8 m from WJ.

Stratigraphy

The entire excavated area of Unit 17 was covered with a thick accumulation of random wall-tumble starting on average 40 cm below the ground surface. The tumble overlay an intricately mixed deposit of gray dark ashy soil (5Y 4/1) with patches of lighter material (2.5Y 7/2) and whitish soil and havara (5YR 8/1). The darkest (ashiest) deposit was concentrated just above the bedrock, terra rossa and lime plaster floor, and was up to 0.3 m thick in places with lighter colored ashy soil above or intermixed with it. The maximum depth of ash recorded was 54 cm.

Percentages of artifacts recovered from the different strata are significant in that the mixture of light colored ashy and pale brown soil (10YR 7/3) immediately under the tumble contained proportionately more sherds than the underlying stratum of dark ash. The lowest stratum on and just above the floor contained the same proportion of sherds as the material under the tumble, with, in addition, most of the non-ceramic artifacts.

There are important differences between the taphonomy of Unit 17 and Units 2 and 8, which have equal amounts of wall tumble and ash. In these latter units, the ashy debris forms quite a homogenous stratum below the tumble, with the lighter ash separated by a gently undulating, roughly horizontal interface from the darker material below. In Unit 17 the interface between dark ash, light ash and white material is, in contrast, confused, clearly as the result of a different depositional history. The lack of any horizontal layering within the ash would suggest that its genesis was the result of a single event such as the combustion of beams and brush supporting a flat mud roof, which collapsed, thus causing the intermingling of ash and soil.

Finds

An average number of finds was recorded on the habitation surface. The point of significance is that, except for a mortar (S331) from within the tumble, thus perhaps reused as building material, and a picrolite pendant (S165) found in the sieve, all artifacts lay on the floor. These consist of three pounders (S173, 222, 402), a rubber-pounder (S95), a worked plaque (S354) and two picrolite artifacts, one a pendant (S165) and the other simply showing signs of shaping (S457). To the above may be added TC10, a Red Polished spindle whorl. No intact or restorable ceramics were excavated although the density of stratified sherds numbering 413, including a maximum of five small and two large RP bowls and eighty-seven basin fragments, are typical for *Kaminoudhia*. It is rare to find a room without querns, but since only half of the floor surface was excavated, they may have been located in the remaining unexplored area. On the floor in the southwest section of the unit, twelve small igneous pebbles were found in association with the other artifacts.

UNIT 21

The westernmost extension of Area C consists of the large, trapezoidal, incompletely excavated, Unit 21 (figs. 2.13, 2.18 [insert], 2.21b). To the east it shares a party wall (WAR) with Unit 8 and to the south it is bounded by the 5 m continuation of WAJ, still up to three courses high, despite its generally poor state of preservation. The unexcavated southwest corner was defined by the intersection of WAF and WAJ which created a triangular space that became a separate entity—Unit 26—with the addition of WAS, a curvilinear partition wall 40 cm wide. In this part of the unit, only the upper courses of the walls were traced; thus no stratigraphic information is available, and it is not known from which side Unit 26 was approached. The overall extrapolated lengths of WAJ and WAF would have been 8.3 m and 10 m. At its northeastern end the 60 cm wide and one course high WAF abuts against the 3.9 m stretch of WAG, of later construction, built on a 5 to 10 cm thick deposit of occupation debris. WAG is not aligned with any other structure, yet in conjunction with wall WL, it provides a functional, though architecturally ungainly, access corridor to Unit 21. Its north face is lined with three slabs of limestone, an arrangement also noted on the opposite face of WL. The western ends of both WAG and WL are unexcavated. Unit 21 has a maximum surface area of 47 m^2, reduced to 42 m^2 if Unit 26 is subtracted. No built features or lime plaster bins were recorded in the eastern excavated half of the Unit, but approximately in its center a very shallow mortar (?), Ft 35 (diameter 10 cm, depth 1.5 cm), was hollowed out of the bedrock.

Variations in wall thickness in relation to function are notable. WAR, a party wall with Unit 8, is 50 cm wide; the two outer walls, WAF and WAJ, are on average 60 cm wide and the partition wall delimiting Unit 26 is a diminutive 40 cm in width. The difficulty of roofing a space from 4 to 6 m wide would argue in favor of Unit 21 being open. The smaller dimensions of Unit 26, on the other hand, suggest that it could easily have been covered.

Stratigraphy

A thin, irregular scatter of wall tumble covered the southern portion of the unit at 50 cm below the present ground surface. The northern sector, between WAG and WL, was lacking tumble, perhaps because of the more shallow deposit in this area and the possible removal of fieldstones for agricultural purposes. Below the tumble and plow zone the soil turned more ashy with some darker pockets, but never so dense as in Unit 8. The ash was mixed with occupation debris directly overlaying the smooth, southward sloping bedrock that served as the floor in the excavated area. No well-defined habitation surface could be linked with the later construction of the short section of WAG, which represents a specific architectural event that was not stratigraphically isolated in the excavated area.

Finds

Only the northeastern sector of Unit 21 was excavated to the habitation surface, and this is where most of the finds were concentrated. The excavation of the remainder of the unit is a high priority for future seasons because of the unusual concentrations of animal bone (see Chapter 11.3) consisting of 135 identifiable pieces—whereas most units did not exceed 26—and the evidence for chert knapping (see below).

Ground stone is well represented with six pounders (S557, 559, 560, 561, 564, 570), a rubber-pounder (S569), one rubbing stone (S572), two rubbers (S701, 703), two hammerstones (S558, 571), two querns (S700, IS19) in addition to three rubbers and two other querns left in situ, three mortars (S565, 567, 568), and two work surfaces (S510, 664). A terracotta figurine fragment or part of an unusual tab handle (TC22—it was associated with the upper wall tumble of Unit 21), a pounder (S408), and a worked piece of picrolite (S459) were found associated with wall tumble, from below which came two RP bowls (P36 and P87, the latter possibly part of a composite vessel), the neck of a DPBC juglet (P137), a fragment of a stone bowl, a gaming stone, a pecking stone, and a hammerstone (S393, 546, 390, 571). P87 was level with the top of WL, well above the habitation surface. It may have been on the roof or on a shelf protruding from the west face of this wall. A single spindle whorl, TC35, was recorded.

Of note was a large sherd with the inner surface very worn, so that the coarse pebble tempering stood proud of the surface, in the manner of P121 from Unit 10. Unit 21 had 996 stratified sherds—but only one piece of basin—which included a maximum of four small RP bowls and eight jar/amphorae, the latter number in accordance with the twenty-five pieces of vertical handle recorded. The presence of several large RP bowls was also noted.

The study of the knapped stone (Chapter 7 *infra*) isolated what may be a knapping station in this area, which contained both the raw materials and the tools required for such an operation. It provides the strongest evidence for this specific activity so far recognized in the settlement; evidence that is reinforced by the presence of four artifacts made from bone (see Chapter 11, Appendix 11.1), three points (B3, B6 and B8) and above all a much used and broken antler hammer (B4). The unusually high percentage of animal bone also hints at specialization within the walls of this large and probably unroofed area.

UNIT 22

The northwest wall of Unit 2 (WX) is shared by Units 22 (figs. 2.15, 2.18 [insert], 2.21c) and 23 and, although separated by WZ, may prove to be part of the same structure. Unit 22 was only defined on three sides: therefore, its original plan and dimensions are not yet determined. To the northeast it is bordered by the 3.5 m stretch of WU, which to the south merges with WJ described in connection with Unit 2. WU, between 60 and 70 cm wide and faced with several tabular pieces of limestone, has a maximum of two courses of fieldstones preserved to a height of 30 cm. It turns at right angles to the northeast where it becomes WV and forms the northwest wall of Unit 9. Determining whether WU extended farther northwest was not possible, since bedrock is only 56 cm below the ground surface and the remaining wall could have been robbed without leaving a trace. The problems associated with the poorly preserved stretch of WX have already been discussed (see Unit 2). WZ is a wall 35 cm wide that runs parallel to WU, 3.1 m to the west. At 3.5 m from WX, it abuts against Ft 25, a protuberance of the bedrock containing a mortar and a gaming board. It would not appear that WZ extends farther north than Ft 25, in which case it should be seen as a partition wall—an interpretation suggested by its narrowness—separating a larger space into Units 22 and 23. The northern limits of Unit 22 remain unexcavated and undetermined, but it is at least 6 m long, as demonstrated by the lack of any cross wall within the area dug to bedrock. The corner formed by WU and WV suggests that the space was L-shaped. As currently defined, about 14 m^2 of Unit 22 has been excavated, only 10 m^2 of which are, strictly speaking, intra mural.

The most prominent feature in Unit 22, located at the northern end of WZ, is the limestone outcrop Ft 25. It measures about 100 x 55 cm and there is a circular cavity—22 cm deep and 31cm in diameter with the sides slightly undercut below the rim—cut into the smooth upper surface, 22 cm above the floor. Next to the mortar the bedrock has been pecked away, seemingly to direct liquids toward the cavity. This reworking slightly damaged a perfunctory, yet clearly visible, Senet gaming board pecked into the upper surface of the outcrop. It is the only rock-cut version of this game at *Kaminoudhia*. On the east side of Ft 25 another small shallow mortar, 16 cm in diameter, was cut into the rock. A third example, Ft 26, 20 cm in diameter and 10 cm deep, was located 70 cm to the east in the middle of the room.

In the southwest corner of the unit a platform or bench, or perhaps even a buttress, approximately 60 cm square and 20 cm high, was faced to the north with tabular pieces of limestone. Since the feature is eroded to the same level as the surrounding walls its original height and function remain undetermined.

Stratigraphy

Little wall tumble was recognized in this unit, which consisted of light brown topsoil (10YR 7/3) extending down to and merging imperceptibly with the more ashy (2.5Y 7/1) occupation debris on bedrock. In the northwest sector a few fieldstones lay immediately on bedrock, 60 cm below the present ground surface. In this part of the settlement the bedrock is mostly very smooth, but where it is uneven because of deep solution holes filled with terra rossa it was covered with a lime plaster floor from 1 to 10 cm thick. The edges of these patches of floor are always worn and uneven, so much so that on occasion it was difficult to determine whether the surface was cultural or natural.

An extensive layer of ashy soil, up to 18 cm thick, stretched across the center of the room, then phases out before picking up again just north of WX, where a well-preserved human skeleton was found. This deposit was generally poor in pottery, bone and chipped stone. In the center of the unit, a large stone mortar (S427) lay upside down on the floor. Its base, 52 cm below the present ground surface, was scarred by iron plowshares. This damage can only have occurred when the ground surface was at least 25 cm lower than at present, because under normal circumstances a traditional ard will not penetrate more than 20 to 30 cm into the plow zone.

In the southern corner of the room, next to the platform, the skeleton of a young woman lay in a contracted position on her right side facing the southern wall (see Chapter 10 "Skeletal Remains from the Settlement: Unit 22"). Her skull was wedged up against the platform, both hands were raised to her face and the left leg partially covered a large, smashed shallow bowl (see fig. 2.15, pl. 10.5b). This RP bowl (P110), of unusual dimensions for the settlement had been mended in antiquity prior to the event, which resulted in its breakage and dispersal over an area of about half a square meter. Both skeleton and bowl were surrounded by the light gray, ashy debris (2.5Y 7/1) covering the floor, but the sequence of events leading to the positions in which they were found is unclear. Some of the bowl sherds rested upon the floor, as did the woman's skull, but other pieces and most of the skeleton were incorporated in the ashy matrix *above* the habitation surface (fig. 2.21c).

This does not appear to be a burial. The skeleton faces south and not the usual east, grave goods do not accompany it and, uniquely, it lies partially *on top* of a large bowl, which was apparently smashed before hand. Finally, the corpse was covered with the ashy occupation debris common to the rest of Unit 22.

It is pertinent to determine whether the ash predates the breakage of the bowl. It does appear to have been smashed and scattered first, before the arrival of the body, but it remains unclear whether the ash accumulation precedes one or both events. Parts of the bowl do sit on ash, but the ash could have filled the empty spaces around the sherds in the same manner as it replaced the flesh as the corpse decayed. Unfortunately the skeleton is not covered with well-coursed tumble, similar to that recorded in Units 1 and 12 for example; therefore seismic activity is not an obvious cause for its presence in Unit 22.

A unique assemblage of seven knapped stone objects was found scattered along the north face of the platform, immediately to the west of the skull. They are of excellent quality raw material, different from all the other knapped stone from the site (see Chapter 7, "Human skeleton" *infra*). The most intriguing aspect of the group is that Kingsnorth describes three specimens (f26, 87 and 89) as possible projectile points.

The thick ash deposit in this unit is no easier to explain here than elsewhere in Area C, except that the space defined by WU, WX and WZ is 3 m wide, therefore easily covered with a roof that could have produced the ash if it had been burned. Perhaps the roof with its heavy capping of soil collapsed in flames trapping the woman below, an unconvincing scenario since traditional buildings with stone walls do not "explode" into flame, and ample warning should have been provided for her to leave the room, unless the conflagration occurred as the result of an earthquake, or for some reason she was forced to remain inside a burning building. The presence of three possible arrow heads, unique to *Kaminoudhia*, found in close proximity to the cranium, is a remarkable coincidence if there was no connection between them, the ash, the shattered bowl, and the demise—but not burial—of a young woman in the deepest recess of a long narrow room.

Finds

The rest of the assemblage of artifacts from Unit 22 is varied but unremarkable. More unusual, however, is the unprecedented concentration of egg-sized igneous pebbles, which are not artifacts, but were intentionally imported to the site for a purpose. Several dozen such pebbles recorded in the southern end of the room represent the largest single concentration from the site. In the southwest corner of the unit, just north of the skeleton, a concentration of ten pebbles was found on the lime plaster floor and in the other corner a second group of fourteen was excavated.

The lithic finds from Unit 22 consist of eleven pounders (S237, 273, 348, 349, 350, 439, 441, 443, 478, 481, 534), a rubber-pounder (S260), a hammerstone (S438), a pecking stone (S536), three axes (S369, 524, 549), and two mortars (S427, 550). One large quern (IS25) sat approximately in the middle of the room and two diagnostic quern rubbers (IS24, 30) were left in situ. From the topsoil above Unit 22 came a Senet gaming stone (S281).

A single terracotta spindle whorl (TC33) also lay among the ashy debris on the floor. Unit 22 had more in situ complete or almost complete RP bowls than most (P71, 108, 110) in addition to a RP jug (P136). Of the 547 stratified sherds recorded, only one RP small fragment of a bowl rim was noted; this dearth of small bowls is atypical and may have something to do with a lack of post abandonment disturbance in Unit 22 which meant that the sherds from vessels in the room at the time of abandonment remained within the unit. Only three basin fragments were recorded (included in the above sherd total).

UNIT 23

Only the southern section of Unit 23 (figs. 2.15, 2.18 [insert]) has been excavated to the bedrock habitation surface (figs. 2.15, 2.18 [insert]). As preserved, it consists of a long narrow space defined to the east by the partition wall WZ—described in connection with Unit 22—to the south by the western, 2 m extension of WX and to the west by WL. The latter, preserved for a distance of 6.2 m runs into the northern baulk, so that the room remains undefined at this end, in the manner of Unit 22.

Thus defined, Unit 23 measures at least 6 m long by 2 m wide. The only feature in the excavated area is a low bench 35 cm wide abutting against the southernmost 3 m of WL.

Stratigraphy

No tumble was found sealing the thin ashy deposit immediately overlaying the patchwork of smooth bedrock and terra rossa. So little of this unit has been excavated that no further comments can be made.

Finds

The stratified artifacts consist of a pecking stone (S391), a pounder (S352), a picrolite pendant (S542), a rubber (S507) and two RP bowls (P115 and 130). P115 was found next to the bench. The unit yielded 372 stratified sherds, including a maximum of five small and three large RP bowls, one RP juglet and one RP cooking pot. Twenty-two basin fragments were recorded (included in the above sherd total).

CONCLUSIONS

When Chalcolithic pottery was recorded from stratified levels in some quantity (cf. Table 2.1a) during the first season of excavation in 1981, it was, logically enough, thought to belong to the Chalcolithic period, thus providing evidence for an early phase of the settlement. Later, with the final and detailed publication of the Chalcolithic sequence from Lemba *Lakkous* (Peltenburg 1985), it became clear that the diagnostic Chalcolithic pottery from *Kaminoudhia* was predominantly attributable to the Middle Chalcolithic, which discounted the possibility of unbroken occupation from the Chalcolithic to the Bronze Age at the site.

How then is the presence of Chalcolithic pottery at the *Kaminoudhia* settlement explained, when it is absent from all funerary deposits excavated to date (see Chapter 3) or from elsewhere in the vicinity of the site? Indeed, intensive survey (see Chapter 15) and twenty-five years of field walking by the present writer in the neighborhood of the settlement and cemeteries have failed to detect additional Chalcolithic cultural material.

A study of the frequency with which Chalcolithic pottery occurred in the different units of the settlement demonstrated that it was far more common in Area A, where 883 of the 952 stratified sherds were recovered. But no diagnostic circular architecture or purely Chalcolithic levels were recorded.

Although all units rich in pottery yielded some Chalcolithic sherds (Table 2.1c), the main concentration was centered around Units 1, 3, 6 and 16, with the numbers dropping as the distance from this focal point increased. Only 24 stratified Chalcolithic sherds were recorded to the west from Area B, with a similar density from Area C to the south, where a larger area excavation was undertaken. This distribution pattern suggests a focus of Chalcolithic activity in the center of Area A, but since no associated cultural remains in the form of architecture, burials or diagnostic lithics—with the exception of a single cruciform figurine (S144)—have been recorded, it is impossible to determine the exact nature of the Chalcolithic presence. The size of the densest Chalcolithic sherd scatter would indicate a small area of occupation, perhaps represented by a single habitation unit at most, if the material, although mixed with Bronze Age deposits, remains close to its place of origin. On the other hand, the lack of Chalcolithic architecture or pure deposits suggests that all the cultural material could have eroded down slope, and is not in situ. If the sherds did erode into their present position in the northeastern sector of the later EC settlement, their only logical source of origin is the small triangular area—now a field—measuring 35 m north–south and a maximum of 40 m east–west, immediately above and to the north of Area A. This area of shallow deposit is now bounded on both sides by a 3 m wide dirt road set on bedrock (which was asphalted after completion of the excavation). Since no Chalcolithic sherds were recovered on the barren hillside above the road or in the fields to the east of it, the extent of the original Chalcolithic presence appears to have been extremely limited.

Evidence from all three excavated areas suggests that the settlement suffered from earthquake damage, a conclusion that was independently reached by Rapp (Chapter 14). The walls with well-coursed tumble (Units 1, 6, 12) fell to the south, suggesting that the shock waves were traveling in this direction, in other words along a north–south bearing. Most earthquakes affecting southern Cyprus have their epicenters south of the island, well out to sea (Soren and Lane 1981).

It is difficult to determine the magnitude of this destruction since only some walls provided coursed tumble. Others may have remained standing, especially if they followed a general north–south direction and were thus at right angles to the shock waves. It is also interesting to note that those walls evidencing coursed tumble are always long ones. Shorter stretches braced by numerous cross-walls are without coursed tumble, and may not have collapsed at that time.

The factors favoring a catastrophic end to the settlement are as follows:

1. The settlement was abandoned, never to be reoccupied by squatters or others.
2. The presence of human skeletal remains in three rooms (Units 6, 16 and 22).
3. The evidence suggests that the roof of at least one structure (Unit 17) collapsed as the result of fire, and others (Unit 6) collapsed with artifacts still in place.[1]
4. Quantities of ash covered the floors of many structures. Although ash is a byproduct of normal domestic and/or many manufacturing activities, it could also have resulted from a conflagration

---

[1] When structures are simply abandoned, serviceable beams are normally retrieved after removal of the soil covering. The author was able to witness this pattern of beam retrieval and salvage in numerous traditional houses abandoned in the Kyrenia district in 1974.

associated with an earthquake. When earthquakes occur in the winter, at a time when fires are lit indoors, the chances of a conflagration are far greater.[2]

5. In her exhaustive study of the chipped stone, Kingsnorth noted that three quarters of the chipped stone from some deposits was burnt (Chapter 7, *"Heating")*, which suggests that it was exposed to a fire. The sheer quantity of burnt material argues for much of the settlement having gone up in flames. Since burning occurs in all three areas, well separated from one another, it can hardly have been accidental and was probably caused by an event that affected all parts of the settlement, contiguous or not.

Finally, there is some evidence to suggest a special status for Units 2 and 12: both were open courtyards which appear to have had lime-plastered or whitewashed walls. Elsewhere in the settlement neither interior nor exterior walls were treated in this fashion.

Unit 2 was entered via an antechamber, contained much ash (not from a burnt roof since it was most likely too large to have been covered), numerous small (drinking?) bowls, a large spouted bowl, and other vessels often of uncommon types. If a special status is to be associated with cult, then this area on the edge of the settlement (and perhaps courtyard Unit 12 as well) is a good candidate for such an activity.

BUILDING PRACTICES

FLOORS

No large expanses of well-preserved, intentionally laid floors were excavated at Sotira *Kaminoudhia*. Commonly the bedrock served as the original habitation surface for all buildings, and occupation debris immediately overlay bedrock, or, as in Areas A and B, it sat on sterile eroded material. In some sectors of Area C patches of terra rossa separated bedrock from the habitation surface. Small patches of a lime plaster surface were recorded in Units 4, 5, 6, 8, 17 and 22. In Unit 17 it was between 1 and 3 cm thick and in Unit 22 it varied from 1 cm to an unusual 10 cm.

Most walls are founded directly on bedrock, which resulted in the accumulation of occupation debris starting at the same level as the masonry, except in Unit 7 where the bedrock slopes up to the south face of WAH. In this instance, it seems that the soft chalk was intentionally cut down at the foot of the wall to provide a more horizontal habitation surface in an area where the bedrock originally sloped south. This leveling of the room's floor must have corresponded with the original phase of construction because the hearth, (Ft 8), in use throughout the period of occupation, was also built below the level of the base of the wall. Where foundation trenches have been dug, the occupation debris runs up over the backfilled trench (e.g., in Unit 20).

The range of features associated with floors, namely pits (some perhaps used as post holes?) and bins cut down into the bedrock, as well as hearths, benches, clay and lime plaster troughs, will be described at the end of this section.

WALLS

Following the classificatory system adopted at Alambra *Mouttes* (Coleman et al. 1996), the settlement walls at *Kaminoudhia* may be separated into three categories: namely exterior walls, party walls, and partitions.

---

[2] This fact was often discussed in earthquake-prone Iran and Afghanistan (personal observation).

Exterior walls are not always easy to isolate because the excavations did not extend far beyond the structures making up most architectural units. Some walls categorized as "exterior" may be the party wall of an alley, passage, or large space such as a courtyard, the other side of which has not been excavated. Following these criteria, there are a) walls which define the perimeter of a cluster of structures, and b) those which constitute the outer wall of a building fronting on a passageway.

a) In Area A sections of WI and WY, 60 and 70 cm wide, in Area B WAT and perhaps WAM, 55–100 cm and 50 cm wide respectively, and in Area C WA and WAJ, 70–100 cm and 55 cm wide, are the sturdiest walls recorded at *Kaminoudhia*. It is significant that the most obvious exterior walls, WA, WY and WAT, are also those with the greatest thickness. WAM is narrow for an outer wall, and it is quite possible that to the west it abuts an alleyway similar to the one leading into Unit 13.

· b) In Area A the exterior walls *within* a building complex are WK (Unit 5), WAH (Unit 7), WAI and WAE (Unit 18), and WAP (Unit 41), from 50 to 70 cm in width; in Area B, WH (Unit 12) and WN (Units 11 and 14) are respectively 50 and 55 cm wide, and in Area C, WAF (Unit 2) and WV (Unit 9) are from 60 to 65 cm in width.

Party walls shared by two contiguous units are by far the most common type in the settlement. Of the eighteen examples recorded, eight are 50 cm wide, five are 55 cm wide, four are 60 cm wide and one is 65 cm in width. Sections of two walls increase to 70 cm from their average respective widths of 50 and 60 cm. The preferred width for such walls is around 50 cm with few examples much exceeding this dimension. The party walls in Area C, except the slightly later WAG, are generally more regular both in construction and width, a fact that is probably due to the single phase of occupation in this part of the site.

Partition walls are uncommon and noticeably more narrow. Unit 4 in Area A was subdivided by the creation of Unit 19, a small space initially defined by the construction of WAR and WAO, which was further closed off by the later addition of WAW. All these walls are 30 cm wide, or approximately half the usual width of many party walls. In Area C the southwest corner of Unit 21 was partitioned off by WAS, a curvilinear wall 40 cm wide. Units 22 and 23 may constitute a large space subdivided by WZ, only 35 cm wide. Partitions always abut against and are never bonded with the walls of the units they subdivide. Occasionally, such as in Unit 19, they are stratigraphically later additions, a point that cannot be demonstrated in Area C.

Orthostats. Large tabular slabs of limestone, or orthostats, either singly or in alignment, stood against the base of many walls onto which they had presumably been affixed with mud plaster. In Area A two were noted in the northwest corner of Unit 1 against WI, with a third much larger orthostat 2.5 m west in the corridor. In Unit 3, a single orthostat stood against the east face of WE, not far from WQ. A series of slabs was associated with the east face of WO in Unit 5, others lined stretches of both sides of Unit 33, the passageway, and more were set against WBF in the corridor west of Unit 33.

No orthostats were recorded in Area B, but in Area C they were common. The east face of WU, above the bench in Unit 9, had an alignment of tabular slabs and a single example was recorded on the west face of the wall in Unit 22. Several smaller slabs were set against the north face of the square platform or buttress in the southwest corner of this unit. Another cluster was noted in Unit 38a, lining sections of both sides of this corridor leading into Unit 21.

The use of orthostats does not appear to follow any obvious pattern, except that they are usually found in the narrow passages and not in the wide alley in Area B. Because they were recorded facing both internal and external walls, it cannot be argued that their function was specifically to protect walls against rain splatter. When used in roofed areas they may have served as a remedy against peeling mud plaster caused by rising damp. It is also possible that some slabs were not bonded into walls and were simply leaning against them, as in storage, awaiting another use.

Height of wall preservation. Well-preserved wall collapse from sections of WI in Unit 1, WAJ in Unit 12, and WH in Unit 13 provided minimum heights for the *Kaminoudhia* domestic structures and supplementary information on construction methods. In all three instances, a section of wall had toppled southwards as a unit where it lay undisturbed, with each course of stones remaining in situ. WH, with ten courses preserved, must have stood at least 1.93 m high. In Area B, where a greater deposit of topsoil has resulted in less weathering and agricultural disturbance, a section of wall at least 2.1 m high and 1.8 m wide lay on the floor of the courtyard. Since the fieldstones are all arranged on edge, roughly parallel to WAJ, this tumble should be part of WAJ. There is, however, a 2 m wide gap without tumble, either random or coursed, between the wall and the unit of coursed masonry. A standing baulk has complicated the interpretation. If it is argued that the wall collapse is in situ, and that more tumble would have originally extended to near the base of WAJ, then this courtyard wall once stood an unlikely 4 m high. Further excavation in the area might provide a clearer picture of the original wall height.

Equally well-coursed tumble originating from WH filled Unit 13, the space between the latter and WN. The west section of Unit 13, where the tumble is still arranged in vertical courses, was 2.5 m wide to which must be added the present standing height of WH, providing a minimum total height of 3.04 m for this wall.

Traditional rubble masonry, single story buildings, throughout Cyprus in general and Sotira Village in particular, are around 3 m high. The evidence from the *Kaminoudhia* settlement suggests that some of its stone walls stood to at least 2 m and probably closer to 3 m in height, without any use of mudbrick or pisé.

FOUNDATIONS

Most walls at *Kaminoudhia* were founded directly on bedrock or on the sterile eroded material overlaying the latter. In Area B the deposit was up to 2 m thick below WH and WN, but nowhere else in the settlement was such an accumulation of colluvium noted.

Short stretches of some walls (such as WAW, WC/WQ and WAE as well as all of WE) were built on occupation debris. The excavated length of WAG was also on occupation debris that varied from a few centimeters to 27 cm in depth.

Foundation trenches were cut out of the soft bedrock to better seat the eastern section of WI, all of what remains of WAV, and all of WAR/WAO (see Netzer 1992:17 for a general discussion on foundations). These trenches were 15 to 20 cm wider than the wall, which was either built in the center of the cut, such as WI, or up against one face, as with WAV. Elsewhere, especially in Area C, the bedrock was far too hard to cut without considerable effort, and with such solid ground, foundation trenches were judged superfluous. In two instances where the bedrock slopes and laminates along the strata, walls have been set in L-shaped trenches, presumably to provide a horizontal footing for the first course of masonry. This is the case for the short preserved section of WD and perhaps also for the easternmost stretch of WY, north of Unit 39. Another L-shaped cut, this time in the hard-packed colluvium, seated the southwest section of WH.

ROOFS

No direct evidence for the manner in which buildings were roofed was discovered at *Kaminoudhia*. Although several units appear to have been destroyed by fire (especially Unit 17), no partially charred beams nor the telltale impressions of reeds or brushwood on fire-hardened clay were found. One reason for the lack of molded impressions is that the main material used for roofing was most probably not mud plaster, but dry soil. This presumes building activity was carried out between spring and autumn. If the roofs constructed by the inhabitants of *Kaminoudhia* resembled those used in traditional vernacular domestic architecture of coastal areas in Cyprus and the eastern Mediterranean up to the 1950s, the methods and materials described below would have been employed.

The area to be roofed was first spanned by wooden beams spaced from 16 to 30 cm apart—the norm being around 20 cm—covered by densely packed reeds or branches laid at right-angles and covered in turn with a layer of vegetable matter (brush, or for buildings close to the sea, seaweed). On this well trampled bed is applied a 10–13 cm thick layer of *dry* earth sealed by a 5–7 cm layer of chaff-tempered mud plaster protected by a thin rendering of well-tamped clay renewed every year. Depending on the materials used, the total thickness of a flat roof of this type varies from 20 to 40 cm (see especially Ionas 1988:156, fig. p. 160; Ragette 1974; Aurenche 1981, fig. 125). The floor and roofing materials of the type described here can be seen in pls 2.7c and 2.8b showing traditional village houses 6 km west of Sotira.

Although the term "flat" is used for roofs of this type, they are actually pitched toward one of the long walls to ensure the proper drainage of rainwater. Since the dry earth was only applied to brushwood, usually fine-branched shrubs such as thyme or spiny burnet, it would not be expected to leave impressions, even under ideal firing conditions.[3] On rare occasions reed impressions from roofing materials have been recorded in Cyprus, from the Neolithic at Khirokitia (Le Brun 1995:19) to the late Bronze Age at Maa *Palaeokastro* (Karageorghis and Demas 1988:53, pl. LXX). The weight of such a roofing system is approximately 500 kg m^2, a serious consideration when determining the width of a room and the size and availability of beams.

On several occasions between 1969 and 1995, I have been able to study traditional Cypriot houses that had recently burnt. In 1985, a single-roomed house in the abandoned village of Old Paramali caught fire during a military exercise (pl. 2.8a). The interior measurements of the structure were 3.20 x 9.50 m, with an interior height of 2.5 m. It had been built early in the twentieth century using the traditional materials of the region: stone bonded in mud mortar for the walls, Phoenician juniper or olive for the lintels, and cypress beams for supporting the earth roof. The dry beams and brush had burnt fiercely until the weight of the earth roof, some thirteen tons (see above) caused it, in this instance, to fall as a whole. Careful investigation of the interface between the charred beams and myrtle branches and the roughly 20 cm thick layer of earth failed to reveal any fire-hardened impressions of vegetable material. If this structure were to be excavated in the distant future, it would fail to provide any evidence of the type we sought at *Kaminoudhia*. Over a period of time the carbonized beams would be broken up by root action, only leaving specks of charcoal similar to those commonly found on shallow Cypriot archaeological sites.

All the houses in Old Paramali Village seem to have used myrtle branches between the beams and the earth. Traditional houses closer to the coast had brush or reeds beneath a compacted 2 cm thick layer of seaweed (Neptune Grass, *Posidonia oceanica L.*). More substantial (grander) houses built by

[3] Personal observation in Old Paramali Village. See also Wright 1992: 494 and especially Netzer 1992:24 ff. for problems of flat mud roofs supported by pole rafters.

wealthier individuals would have about 4 cm of seaweed and ca. 40 cm of earth providing a better-insulated, more waterproof roof.

ROOM SIZES

Excepting Units 2, 12, 21 and possibly 16, which would have been difficult to roof without the assistance of post supports like those found in Unit 7, there is no reason that most units should not have been roofed. The taphonomy within several units—specifically Unit 17—suggests that roof debris filled the interior space. Because of the accretive architectural tradition at *Kaminoudhia,* few units were entirely excavated and many of those which were had irregular shapes. The average width of a room, based on the measurements of those which are sub-rectangular in shape, is 3.5 m. For example, Unit 17 measured 6.5 x 3.4 m, proportions very similar to many traditional one-roomed dwellings in the region.

If a space is intended to be covered to protect it from rain and sun, the availability and physical characteristics of suitable materials for supporting the roof, in this case wooden beams, will influence its size. Not only is it necessary to take into consideration the load bearing properties of individual woods (for example, cypress is superior to poplar), but issues concerning procurement, transportation and installation are also important. A seasoned cypress beam weighs about 8 kg per m. Allowing for average room widths of 3.5 m with the beams embedded in each wall for about 40 cm, most roof beams would typically measure around 4.5 m and weigh between 36 and 40 kg. A tree of this size and weight is easy to fell and to transport (two per donkey); a maximum of two people can also maneuver it into place.[4]

For comparative purposes the traditional houses at the abandoned village of Old Paramali were studied (see Appendix 2.1). A random sampling of five houses provided room widths of 3.25 m, 3.37 m, 3.37 m, 3.05 m and 3.2 m, the average being 3.34 m, which is slightly narrower than at *Kaminoudhia*. All rooms at Paramali had a roof supported by roughly adzed cypress beams which spanned its width (pls. 2.7c, 2.8b). The room 3.05 m wide was 7.68 m in length, with twenty-six beams separated by an average distance of 30 cm (from center to center); that with a width of 3.2 m was 11.05 m long, with forty-two beams separated by an average distance of 26 cm (from edge to edge). The average diameter of fourteen beams used in the roof of this last room was 12.2 cm, their diameters ranging from 10.5 to 13.5 cm.

In the Episkopi region, cypress trees were traditionally planted along the edges of irrigation ditches, both to serve as windbreaks for crops and to provide valuable and quick growing, straight timber. The beams used in Paramali houses built about a century ago appear to have come from a similar source, since most belong to young, fast growing trees. Note in Appendix 2.1 that the samples collected in Nicosia and presumably from that district had grown more slowly, probably due to the general scarcity of water in the Mesaorea (ca. 30 cm a year). Information on the dimensions and ages of roof beams has not previously been recorded. The number of houses with traditional beams available for study is ever decreasing as the old earth roofs are replaced with tiles or cement slabs. New sawn beams, rectangular in section, are normally used instead of cypress or pine poles. Commonly the traditional houses are abandoned or pulled down to make space for modern buildings. For more information see Appendix 2.1.

---

[4] Donkeys carrying a pair of long poplar beams tied together in front and splaying out behind the animal were a common sight in the mountainous rural areas of Turkey, Iran and Afghanistan. I have also been informed by builders in these countries and Cyprus that it is much easier to utilize beams which can be moved with ease by two people.

DOORWAYS

Nine well-preserved doorways, recorded in Areas A and C, range from 80–90 cm to 1.2 m in width, with a preference for the larger opening (three examples). They are usually placed at the corner of rooms but two entrances (leading into Units 18 and 19) were in the middle of walls. The most notable feature of doorways at *Kaminoudhia* was the three monolithic thresholds, two of which (leading into Units 6 and 25) were complete with well-used pivot holes. The largest, in Unit 6, was 1.32 m long, 23 cm wide and rose 27 cm above the floor. Similar thresholds have not been recorded at Marki *Alonia* (Frankel and Webb 1996b:58 with comparanda) or Alambra *Mouttes* (Coleman et al. 1996:27).

CONSTRUCTION MATERIALS

Stone

All the walls at *Kaminoudhia* were built of angular fragments of the locally abundant tabular limestone, generally described as "fieldstones." The limestone strata in the *Kaminoudhia* area are often 10 to 15 cm thick which, when eroded out of position and shattered, provide ideal building material. The plans show that the preferred size was a typically quadrangular block of around 30 x 22 x 10 cm, followed by a larger and less common module of 55 x 30 x 15 cm. These averages are based on a total count of building stones on the top of randomly chosen walls in Area C. The total number of stones counted was eighty-four, of which seventy-two (86%) belonged to the smaller and twelve (14%) belonged to the larger category. Igneous cobbles, which had to be imported to the site, were only rarely used for building purposes. A few artifacts, such as querns and the larger types of handstones, were occasionally found built into walls, a practice not encountered in the earliest structures of Area A.

The walls are of "shell" built, random rubble type, using untrimmed fieldstones. For a good example of this technique which remained in use on the island until the 1950s, see pl. 2.8b. Here chinking has also been used and is clearly visible in the wall to the right. According to this building tradition the space between the carefully constructed faces was packed with rubble (see wall on left in pl. 2.8b) bonded in the same manner as the roughly coursed fieldstones with a liberal application of mud mortar (for the method see Wright 1992:500 ff.). Wider, heavier walls generally had a more substantial rubble core, whereas partitions were reduced to a double line of facing stones.

Stones often protrude beyond the median line of the wall and interlock to form a crude system of headers and stretchers (for example WI, WM, WAP, WH, WL and WAR), a technique which would have greatly increased the structural rigidity of the whole. On rare occasions, a stone spans the entire width of the wall, thus serving as a binder or parpen. In other instances, the walls were constructed of smaller fieldstones with a greater admixture of mud mortar, for example, WC, WY, WD, WJ and WA.

This building tradition which does not use chinking to secure the individual blocks is only efficient if plentiful mud mortar—normally between 3 and 4 cm thick at *Kaminoudhia*—is applied to both bed and rising joints.

Mudbrick

No sun-dried mudbrick was used in wall construction. Such a building material was known, however, as demonstrated by the discovery of what appear to be chaff tempered mud bricks near Ft 6 in Unit 5 (pl. 2.4a). The bricks, 5 cm thick and either 40 cm long or wide (no entire bricks were excavated) were set on edge as part of some enigmatic feature. It was not determined whether they were form-made or handmade.

Mud Mortar

Although it proved impossible in terms of color or consistency to distinguish between mud mortar and the surrounding soil when the latter was not ash-rich occupation debris, the rubble walls had, by definition, to be bonded with this material: "Such masonry is dependent for its strength on the mortar retaining its cementitious properties" (Wright 1992:409). It could not be determined whether the mortar had initially been tempered with chaff, or a mixture of gravel and chaff (which is more likely), because no telltale straw impressions were noted in the wall mortar, which was always thoroughly permeated with small roots because of its proximity to the surface. If chips or gravel had been used for tempering, they were equally difficult to diagnose since the surrounding soil is full of similar sized stones. However, straw tempered mud was used for building purposes as proved by the presence of chaff impressions in the mortar bonding the tabular blocks of Ft 5 in Unit 5.

Paddled mud, also known more commonly—and incorrectly—as pisée or pisé (Wright 1992:377), was only tentatively identified in three instances at the settlement. The first was the threshold between Units 7 and 18, built of a homogenous mass of mud, without occupational debris, which is most likely to have been pisé. The final diagnosis of this feature will await full excavation of Unit 18. The second occurrence was in connection with Ft 23 in Unit 8, where mud packing seems to have been used to build part of the feature and again served to fill a void in WL, the wall behind. Pisé was used in the third instance in Unit 1 to fill a similar void that appears to have been a blocked Phase I doorway in WC.

Hearths were not built out of mud mortar, as might be expected, but made from the same material as basins and then coated with mud plaster (see below). Buff colored (Munsell 10YR8/4 "yellow") soft, poorly levigated clay with heavy inorganic tempering is the typical basin fabric at *Kaminoudhia*.

Mud Plaster

Mud plaster, made of clay or marl, is the same material as mud mortar, but used differently and to serve another function. Instead of bonding materials together, when used as a plaster it is applied to a surface as a rendering or protective layer. No evidence for the consistent rendering of either interior or exterior walls with mud plaster was recorded at *Kaminoudhia*.

Except for a small area of plastered wall above the lime plaster bins, Fts 12 and 13 in Unit 16, and Ft 15, the enigmatic rectangular construction in Unit 5, mud plaster seems to have been reserved for the manufacture of hearths. In Ft 15, the plaster consisted of brown, chaff-tempered mud, presumably identical to that used as mortar for the walls.

The mud plaster employed in the manufacture of hearths is of a very pale brown color (10YR 8/4)—different from that described above—without noticeable chaff tempering. It is, in fact, the same material used for the manufacture of coarse ware basins (see *infra* in connection with "Hearths").

Mud plaster was thus used to fix in place the sides of hearths and to cover the bottom of the fire boxes in Unit 7 Ft 8, Unit 40 Ft 9, Unit 6 Ft 10, Unit 20 Ft 16, Unit 35 Ft 32, Unit 14 Ft 34, Unit 30 Ft 36, and the poorly preserved hearth in Unit 2. The same pale brown material was used to plaster the wall faces around and above hearths in Units 12 and 35, and probably indicates the presence of a similar hearth below the tumble in Unit 18.

Lime Plaster

There are serious problems with the identification of lime plaster versus gypsum plaster—also commonly known as "Plaster of Paris"—in Cyprus and elsewhere in the Near East (see Wright 1992:386 ff. for a useful and lucid synopsis; Kingery et al. 1988). Lime plaster is made by mixing some form of tempering such as sand, ground limestone, or other materials, with water and quicklime. The latter is produced by calcining limestone to 800-900° C. Gypsum plaster is made by heating alabaster or gypsum rock at a temperature of 150–400° C.

The two can be easily differentiated, both from the parent rocks and from each other, by optical study of their microstructure using a scanning electron microscope (Kingery et al. 1988:222). The lack of gypsum deposits in the Episkopi area (Bear 1963b:146 ff., fig. 7) strongly supports the interpretation of our "white" lime plasters as lime based. Local availability of raw materials, such as limestone or gypsum, affected their use both on the island and the mainland (Kingery et al. 1988:236).

At *Kaminoudhia*, slaked lime was used for the manufacture of circular and sub-rectangular bins, as a flooring material, and probably also as a wall rendering. All ten lime plaster bins were, by definition, made from this material. In addition to this category, a shallow sub-rectangular trough, Ft 38 in Unit 8, was the only other feature made from lime.

There is no evidence to suggest that any units were entirely floored with lime plaster. Patches of carefully laid and smoothed plaster were recorded in Units 1, 2, 4, 5, 6, 8, 20 and 22, the largest expanse being in the southern half of Unit 8.

In two instances (Units 2 and 12), a line of whitish material associated with wall tumble was interpreted as slaked lime wall plaster. To be certain of this identification optical analyses are necessary. It should be noted that both occurrences were associated with the inner walls of structures interpreted as courtyards.

ARCHITECTURAL FEATURES

Benches

The inhabitants at *Kaminoudhia* appear to have considered that long, narrow benches were important domestic features. Out of the nineteen units either completely excavated or sufficiently cleared to provide an accurate picture of the architecture, ten, or more than 50%, were fitted with benches of some sort, which in four instances fronted more than one wall.

Two types of structures described as benches or platforms were recognized at *Kaminoudhia*. The first, and most common, was low, long and narrow, varying in width from 20 to 40 cm and in height from 20 to 50 cm (ten examples recorded). The average width of benches was around 30 cm, with several examples varying from 40 to 30 cm over their length. Heights cannot be grouped in any preferred category, the average being 31.5 cm. One bench was 50 and another 45 cm high; the remainder were considerably lower. Such benches usually ran along the entire wall span (e.g., WJ in Unit 2, WM in Unit 3, WY in Unit 16, WI in Unit 19), but were sometimes only built along part of it (e.g., WB in Unit 1, WA in Unit 2, WU in Unit 9 and perhaps WA in Unit 10). An insufficient amount of Unit 9 has been excavated to determine whether the bench along the east face of WU continued for the full run of the wall.

The second type of bench, short and broad as in Units 7, 8, 22 and perhaps also Unit 10, is problematic for several reasons. That built against the entire length of WC in Unit 7, 42 cm high and 50 cm wide, was poorly preserved, although it did seem to have served as a storage space because several objects were discovered on its upper surface. Feature 23 in Unit 8 is difficult to interpret and may be a platform, 30 cm high, 60 cm long and 70 cm wide, separated by a 33 cm wide gap from another pisé platform of similar dimensions, both of which were built against the west face of WL. In Unit 22 a squarish corner buttress or platform, 60 cm to a side, was built in the angle formed by WX and WZ.

Although faced on one side with limestone orthostats, it was eroded to the same 20 cm level above bedrock as the surrounding walls, which prevented its interpretation as either a bench or a buttress standing to the full height of the wall. No finds lay on its upper surface, further complicating its interpretation. Both as a buttress and as a square corner platform this feature is unique at *Kaminoudhia*. The whole arrangement of the buttress and bench, Fts 30 and 31 in Unit 10, is unusual, therefore open to differing interpretations. Being absolutely certain that Ft 30 is a buttress is not possible since the wall was only preserved to around 50 cm in this area, which makes the explanation of Ft 31 equally problematic. As preserved it consists of a bench 40 cm high and wide extending the full 2.2 m length of the buttress. With the density of artifacts recovered from this obviously much utilized area, a bench does seem a likely and useful feature.

Hearths

The distribution of hearths at *Kaminoudhia* does not appear to follow any specific pattern, as noted, for example, in Anatolian megaroid structures or EB II Tarsus domestic units. Except for Ft 32, the circular patch of burning on the bedrock of Unit 20, all of the nine hearths excavated belong to Phase II. They consist of coarse buff, grit-tempered clay, identical to that used for basins (see above in connection with "Mud Mortar").

Coincidentally, Ft 32 provided the most basic evidence from the settlement for intentional fire-making in one spot. It consisted of a patch of fire-reddened bedrock, 25 cm in diameter, which was not associated with any built features and could have predated the earliest phase of the settlement. Alternatively, if it had been a circular built hearth, all structural remains would have been removed when Floor 2 was laid.

Rectangular double hearths made of mud mortar seem to have been the most popular, with four examples (Fts 8, 16, 32, 34). The inner dimensions of the individual fireboxes ranged from 18-40 cm wide and 22–45 cm deep, with a preferred width of around 23 cm and depth (length) of 22, 32 or 40 cm. The variations in depth emphasize the lack in consistency, presumably based on personal choice or function.

Three hearths (Fts 9, 10, 38) consisted of rectangular boxes with the long side built against a wall and an opening at one end. The best-preserved example is Ft 9 in Unit 40, 32 cm wide, 48 cm deep with walls 18 cm high. Ft 10 in Unit 6 was badly damaged and difficult to interpret. The firebox, 46 cm wide and a minimum of 30 cm in length, was preserved to a height of 14 cm. That the mud plaster extended up the wall for 46 cm, would suggest a larger—and more complex—installation in its original form. The large rectangular hearth in Unit 30, the passageway, suffers from the same problems of interpretation as Ft 10. As preserved it is 74 cm wide by 70 cm in length and mostly built of fire-reddened slabs of limestone, the clay mortar having been disturbed.

The patch of discolored bedrock, 50 cm in diameter, next to a limestone slab set at right angles to the wall (Ft 21) on the north side of Unit 2, is all that remains of a built hearth. This area has suffered from severe disturbance that could have destroyed a hearth built of basin fabric.

Evidence for localized and protracted burning, consistent with hearths, or a concentration of basin fragments hints at the presence of several other fireplaces in the settlement. Fire discolored wall plaster was noted in the northwest corner of Unit 18 and on WH, the south wall of Unit 12. Substantial accumulations of basin fragments associated with dark ashy soil were recorded in the southwest corner of Unit 4, in a central position in Unit 12, and against WAE in the passageway, Unit 32.

The association of basins with hearths, already noted at Episkopi *Phaneromeni* (Swiny 1979:49), was reinforced by the excavations at *Kaminoudhia* where every hearth was filled and often surrounded to a greater or lesser degree with basin fragments of varying sizes. Since the hearths are manufactured from the same material as basins, it was sometimes impossible to determine whether the fragments belonged to one or the other. Most hearths incorporated slabs of limestone in their side walls, held in place by basin material. The whole was covered with a layer of mud plaster.

In contrast to Marki *Alonia* (Frankel and Webb 1996b:181), no clay hobs, whether associated with hearths or not, were excavated at *Kaminoudhia*. A single fragment of a circular flat bottomed pot stand (P81), which is 7 cm high and 19 cm in diameter, came, perhaps significantly, from Unit 1 Phase I, the earliest material from the settlement which would put it closer in time to the introduction of foreign elements (see Herscher, Chapter 4). Nothing as elaborate as the Marki hobs was recorded (Frankel and Webb 1996b:figs. 8.1, 8.2; pl. 32). Another dissimilarity between Marki *Alonia* and *Kaminoudhia* is in the form of the hearths. At Marki most of the cooking seems to have been done on hobs used in conjunction with plaster hearths (Frankel and Webb 1996b:59). The hearths themselves are circular or oval plaster features, or are areas discolored by burning without associated structures. It is noteworthy that no rectilinear hearths were recorded at Marki whereas they are common at *Kaminoudhia*.

No hobs came from Alambra *Mouttes* either, which also appears to lack the carefully plastered multiple hearths of *Kaminoudhia*. Coleman et al. (1996:28) report three built hearths and six other places where burning was recorded. The most elaborate example is a square stone feature, 40 cm across, set against the wall of a room believed to have been used for "food storage, preparation and perhaps cooking" (Coleman et al. 1996:71, fig. 21). Another hearth built of stone is L-shaped and seems incomplete since it lacks sides to form a rectilinear firebox (Coleman et al. 1996: pl. 6.d, fig. 20). A connection between trays (called basins at *Kaminoudhia)* and hearths is seen at *Mouttes* (Coleman et al. 1996:259), but not specifically at Marki *Alonia* (Frankel and Webb 1996b:173).

Circular Lime Plaster Bins

Carefully shaped circular depressions made from slaked lime, similar to shallow mortars were sunk into the floor of four units. The role of these so-called "lime plaster bins" remains to be satisfactorily determined, but there is circumstantial evidence to suggest that they served various functions.

Nine out of the ten examples were concentrated in Area A, where they are generally grouped in pairs. Phase I in Unit 1 had been outfitted with two (Fts 1, 2) and perhaps even three bins (Ft 3, in use in Phase II, may have been built in the preceding period). Unit 5 had a pair of large bins (Fts 4, 6) and Unit 4 had a bin (Ft 15) in Phase I, which continued in use in Phase II along with a second bin, Ft 14. Unit 16 had two bins (Fts 12, 13) constructed against its west wall. Although Ft 12 is the earlier of the two, in that Ft 13 cuts into its wall, both appear to have been simultaneously in use. The sole lime plaster bin from Area C came from Unit 2.

The inner diameter of the cavities varies from 22 to 37 cm, the average being 29 cm. Depths vary from 15 to 30 cm, with an average of 21 cm. Four bins (Ft 1, Unit 1; Ft 20, Unit 2; Ft 14 and Ft 15 Unit 4) incorporated a stone mortar at their base, which suggests that they were intended for some form of grinding or pounding. Feature 6 in Unit 5 was lined with limestone chips, much like the pot supports at Marki *Alonia*, and probably served this function. The shape and size of the bins, especially those which do not incorporate mortars, suggest that they may have served as pot supports, an interpretation supported by the discovery in Unit 4 of a cooking pot, P122, smashed inside Ft 15 (pl. 2.3a). It should be noted that Ft 15 also incorporated a stone mortar, which hardly seemed ideal for supporting the base of a clay pot. Perhaps manufacturing the bins with a stone at their base was easier, or else they were considered as multipurpose features depending on the need.

Several bins were associated with ground stone tools, pounders especially, or concentrations of water smoothed igneous pebbles (Fts 3, 4, 12, 13). The presence of the pounders suggests some form of pounding or grinding activity either in or around the plaster bins. Note however that the bins most closely associated with stone percussion tools were not those reinforced by a stone mortar at their base!

Shelves?

Several large slabs of tabular limestone were discovered among the tumble, sometimes associated with artifacts. Both their size and shape suggest they could have served as wall shelves.

Slabs of this type were excavated in Units 6, 14 and 16. Although most preserved wall stumps are too low for shelves to be found in situ, they could, however, have existed at a higher level, as suggested by even a cursory survey of preserved vernacular architecture in Cyprus and the Aegean. Where large tabular slabs of stone are readily available as a building material, as in the Sotira region, horizontal stone shelves protruding from mid- to upper-wall height are common features. They are usually embedded from 20 to 40 cm into the body of the wall and may protrude up to 60 cm from its face (Kloutsinakis and Faraclas 1984: pls. 27, 30; Ionas 1988:94; and 1996:11:115, left). There is no reason why such a practice could not have been in use at *Kaminoudhia*.

Utilization of the Bedrock

A series of unique cavities, grooves and runnels were cut into the soft bedrock during Phase I in the northeast corner of Unit 1, Area A. Some deeper cavities may have served as postholes, but the majority provides no clue as to their purpose.

The bedrock in Area C, far harder than elsewhere, contained a series of circular mortars supplementing the common movable type discussed in connection with the ground stone industry. Features 22, 25, 26, 27, 29 and 35 varied in diameter from 16 to 31 cm and in depth from 12 to 22 cm. Feature 27, oval in shape (30 x 38 cm) was unusually large, and Ft 35 was merely a smooth circular shallow depression 1.5 cm deep in the bedrock. It was perhaps not a mortar at all.

Up against the east baulk of Unit 15 three mortar-like depressions (Fts 17–19), with diameters of approximately 30 cm and depths of less than 20 cm, were cut into the soft bedrock, the only such features in Area A.

SOTIRA *KAMINOUDHIA* AND THE CYPRIOT BUILDING TRADITION

At the time of the transition from round house building (later third millennium) it seems that sub-rectangular housing was organized in the agglutinative manner—i.e., rooms being added in any and every manner—without any regard for part or whole. (G. R. H. Wright, *Ancient Building in Cyprus*, 1992:305)

This statement, which specifically refers to Sotira *Kaminoudhia*, is correct as it describes a building tradition that would survive in southern Cyprus for six centuries, as so clearly demonstrated by the LC I settlement at Episkopi *Phaneromeni* (Carpenter 1981:73; Swiny 1986: fig. 3). The architecture at *Kaminoudhia* bears little resemblance to the preceding Chalcolithic tradition with its consistent use of a circular model (Peltenburg et al. 1985, 1991), despite rare occurrences of rectilinear walls.

The earliest known Bronze Age settlement is probably at Vasilia *Alonia* on the north coast, where a diagnostic Philia Phase flat axe and dagger were excavated along with quantities of Chalcolithic and some EC pottery (Karageorghis 1966:326, figs. 70–72; Swiny 1997:180; see also Chapter 8 "Dagger," n. 6). Unfortunately, the rescue excavation did not note the existence of any architecture. Despite plentiful evidence of a Philia Phase presence as demonstrated by several burials at Kissonerga *Mosphilia*, no settlement remains have yet been excavated, thus nothing is known of the contemporary building plans.

According to the stratigraphic evidence and the ceramic assemblage recovered from the trial excavations at Kyra *Alonia* in the western Mesaorea, a Philia Phase settlement had once existed at this spot. Although no buildings were recorded in the four trenches of 4 m² each, "floors and intermediary layers which included ashes have been observed" (Dikaios 1962:152).

The excavations at Marki *Alonia*, south of Nicosia, have yielded well-preserved architecture belonging to the end of the EC or beginning of the MC period (Frankel and Webb 1996b),[5] therefore later than the settlement at *Kaminoudhia*. The excavated structures that concern us here cover a plateau, specifically its eastern edge which overlooks the Alykos River (Frankel and Webb 1996b:figs. 4.1, 4.40). They consist of rectangular units with party walls built of mudbrick set on stone footings. The plan of the latest phase is a stratigraphically complex amalgam of walls built at different intervals and ultimately all in use together. Clearly, the overall architectural tradition consists of rectangular units, from 5 to 6 m long and 2.4 to 3.4 m wide, with connecting doorways. One squarish room (XXVIII) measured approximately 2.3 x 2.5 m and another (XV), with an entrance corridor in one corner, closely resembled Unit 5 at *Kaminoudhia* in size, shape, and the manner in which it was formed by subdividing a larger unit.

Features common at *Kaminoudhia*, such as low benches, monolithic thresholds, lime plaster bins and double hearths are rare or unknown at Marki *Alonia*, which in turn used clay hobs and elaborate clay hearths unknown in the south. Both sites share many common traits in terms of ground stone (specifically both types of gaming stones), ceramics, terracottas, modified sherds and coarse ware trays, just to name a few. When the architecture at Marki *Alonia* and Sotira *Kaminoudhia* is compared, despite repeated rebuilding and additions, the former gives the impression of a more formalized tradition using a smaller range of room shapes and sizes.

The excavations at Alambra *Mouttes*, 8 km southeast of Marki *Alonia*, yielded extensive remains of an early MC settlement (Coleman et al. 1996). A comparison of the architecture from both sites will help to determine whether the development noted between *Kaminoudhia* and *Alonia* continues at the later settlement of *Mouttes*.

A study published before the excavations at Marki *Alonia*, that emphasized the similarities between the bipartite row houses at *Mouttes* and EB II Tarsus (Schaar 1985), would no doubt have found it difficult to accommodate the architectural evidence from *Alonia* that does not follow this model, yet precedes the *Mouttes* settlement. If it is argued that there exists anything more than a mere similarity in the general arrangement between *Mouttes* and EB II Tarsus—separated as they are by more than half a millennium—then the nearby *Alonia* settlement theoretically should fit into the sequence, and this is not the case.

In essence the early MC house form at *Mouttes* consists of a rectangular portico with walls perhaps in antae, providing access to an inner area of similar proportions reserved for domestic activities. This last may be subdivided into one or more smaller rooms, possibly used for storage and utility purposes (Coleman et al. 1996:33–107), whose layout differs in each case. Most units are interpreted as serving a domestic function, but manufacturing activities, perhaps connected with metallurgy, were thought to be concentrated in the large Building III, of a different plan.

Despite the lack of connections between the house forms at *Kaminoudhia* and Area A at Alambra, both sites share other architectural features, such as stone thresholds, lime plaster bins and long, low, narrow benches. Benches of greater width and a "slaked lime hearth" (more plausibly a shallow lime plaster bin) were recorded in the apparently contemporary single structure excavated 500 m southwest of Area A by E. Gjerstad (Gjerstad 1926:20 ff.; Coleman et al. 1996:7).

Although excellent building stone was available on site, the inhabitants of *Mouttes* used mud brick, which could be interpreted as another progressive development. However, Alambra *Mouttes*, like Marki *Alonia*, shares many aspects of the material culture—such as ground stone (including games), terracottas, and pottery—with *Kaminoudhia*.

Much closer to the architectural plan of *Kaminoudhia* is the early MC site of Ambelikou *Aletri*, with its complex of at least two courtyards (#I and II as determined by their size) surrounded by rooms (Dikaios 1960: pl. 29c), most of which are incompletely excavated. Several pits and benches were recorded along with numerous ground stone tools and restorable ceramic vessels lying on the floors. The site was interpreted as an industrial smelting complex rather than a settlement in view of the finds and perhaps because of the large (#I measures 12 x 6 m) adjacent courtyards (Dikaios 1960).

The large apparently free standing MC III domestic structure at Kalopsidha in the southeast Mesaorea consists of a central court surrounded by domestic quarters and workrooms (Gjerstad 1926:29ff., fig. 3; Åström 1969:75). As interpreted by the excavator, it stands apart from the architectural tradition currently known to exist in pre-Late Bronze Age Cyprus.

More typical of the Cypriot architectural tradition are the plans of the late MC settlement at Dhali *Kafkallia* southeast of Nicosia (Swiny 1972), with its random scatter of different sized domestic (?) units, and especially LC IA Episkopi *Phaneromeni* (Carpenter 1981; Swiny 1986). The house form visible at *Phaneromeni*, 7 km from but 600 years later than *Kaminoudhia*, suggests that in southern Cyprus little development had taken place. The accretive plan of *Phaneromeni* Settlement A, with meandering walls forming a range of different shaped rooms of varying size, only lacks the curvilinear features noted at *Kaminoudhia*. The antecedents of the low narrow benches, lime plaster bins, clay hearths, gaming stones, as well as some of the ground stone, terracottas and ceramic types (Swiny 1979) can all be traced back to *Kaminoudhia*.

FOREIGN RELATIONS

In order to draw parallels between Sotira *Kaminoudhia* and contemporary sites in surrounding countries, chronological synchronisms must first be established. The absolute date for the latest occupation of the settlement at *Kaminoudhia* is ca. 2200 B.C.E. (Manning and Swiny 1994), which falls within the Early Bronze IV in Palestine and the late Early Bronze IIIA in southern Anatolia, Cilicia in particular.

A study of the exhaustive synopses of Anatolian, southern Syrian and Palestinian architecture undertaken by Naumann (1971:336–88), Bonn (1977), Harif (1974), Ben Tor (1992), and especially Wright (1985), with one exception fail to reveal any close parallels between EC Cyprus and the mainland, either to the north or to the east. The agglutinative, or accretive, style of planning so characteristic of *Kaminoudhia* is without obvious antecedent in the surrounding countries, but in EB II and Intermediate Early/Middle Bronze Age Palestine a similar architectural layout does appear occasionally. One problem, however, with the search for comparanda is the need for substantial area excavation of accretive architectural complexes to discover what pattern, if any, governed their development. Domestic architecture in the Levant traditionally has not attracted the attention of excavators and, as a result, few sites can boast an extensive exposure of the often deeply buried EB structures. The sites of Arad, Byblos, Megiddo and Tell el-Far'ah are notable exceptions to the rule and, if relevant, will be discussed in the present study.

Ras Shamra is the closest major Levantine site to Cyprus with evidence for EB occupation, but the third millennium levels have only been the focus of limited excavations. Level III A3, dated to ca.

2250–2000 B.C.E. (Schwartz and Weiss in Ehrich 1992:240), was reached in a deep sounding which measured approximately 27 x 25 m, excavated by de Contenson (1969:45–89). He concluded that the architecture from this period had suffered much from erosion and suggested that the site may have been abandoned before the MB period. The preceding Level III A2 was also sparse in architectural remains, with nothing more than a few long, disjointed wall sections uncovered (de Contenson 1969:58, fig. 8).

The only other information from Ras Shamra of relevance to the present inquiry comes from Courtois' EB sounding in a small trench measuring 3.2 x 1.4 m (Courtois 1962:415–75). This excavation fortuitously came upon an EB olive oil press but contained no information on domestic architecture. Even if structures of a domestic nature had been discovered, the area was far too small to reveal anything of the overall plan (for a review of the Early Bronze Age Level IIIA, see Schaeffer 1962:225).

The other prominent coastal settlement with contemporary levels is Byblos, 150 km to the south, which has yielded a wealth of EB domestic architecture, apparently covering much of the site (Dunand 1952:82–90). Unfortunately the remains of this period suffer from the same problems of interpretation as do those from other levels, and few conclusions may be drawn from the published material, including—and especially—the plans (Saghieh 1983:X, XI; Wright 1985:287). Dunand (1952:84, 86, pl. II upper right hand corner) describes individual structures with a central hall flanked by rooms on both sides as belonging to the late phase of the EB, but not the very end which was characterized by single room structures (Dunand 1952:86, pl. I, pl. II: A, B, C; Wright 1985: fig. 216 for both types). Neither of these self-contained house units with their carefully planned and typically jogged rectilinear walls (Wright 1985:287, fig. 261) are remotely similar to those at *Kaminoudhia*.

The selective review of Levantine domestic architecture in the EB period will be completed with a study of the contemporary inland sites of Alalakh, Hama and Tell el-Far'ah, the material from Arad being considered too distant from Cyprus to be relevant to the present inquiry.

Only a small expanse of domestic architecture was excavated at Alalakh, Level XIII of EBA date (Woolley 1955:15, fig. 5). Although the scale and accretive arrangement of the structures are similar to those at *Kaminoudhia*, the plans of the sub-rectangular rooms are far more regular, resembling Alambra *Mouttes* more than *Kaminoudhia*. Of interest is the common tradition of long, low narrow benches (40 cm wide and 20 cm high), and simple hearths resembling Ft 9 in Unit 40.

Period 3 at Tell el-Far'ah of EB II date (ca. 2700 B.C.E., see Ehrich 1992: fig. 16) has an accretive style of domestic architecture reminiscent of that at *Kaminoudhia*, but it consists of a series of two interconnected units arranged in an L shape fronting onto narrow alleyways (de Vaux 1961:584, pl. XXXIV; Wright 1985: fig. 213: 6, 7, 8). The basic architectural unit is therefore a single rectangular room, quite different in concept from the norm at *Kaminoudhia*. The settlement was not occupied in the succeeding EB III.

A study of the architecture from Hama, Level K1, dated to around 2400 B.C.E. (Ehrich 1992:187, fig. 3) reveals a series of poorly preserved, mostly disjointed walls. When they can be connected to form coherent structures, the resulting plan exhibits clusters of sub-rectangular rooms without an overall pattern (Thuesen 1988: fig. 34). An insufficient number of doorways are preserved (or indicated on the plan) to enable any comments on the manner in which these units were approached and subdivided. The architecture of Level J at Hama, dated from ca. 2400 B.C.E. to 2000 B.C.E. (Ehrich 1992:187, fig. 3), has a more intelligible sequence of domestic architectural remains, following the same alignment and general layout of the earlier Level K1. The houses consist of large units of up to 12 x 8 m (Fugmann 1958: fig. 63, R2, 5 and 7) approached via narrow streets. The description of the architecture is cursory (Fugmann 1958:59ff.) and few doorways were defined or represented on the plan; therefore, it is difficult, even after careful scrutiny, to isolate individual habitation units. The multi-roomed complexes, however, are analogous, though more formalized versions of those at *Kaminoudhia*.

Wright (1985:288) sees the possibility of a dual tradition in EB Palestine and southern Syria with the pre-urban *Breitraum* detached house existing side by side with the multi-roomed town house marked by squarish rooms, neither of which have any parallels with EC Cyprus. Ben-Tor's chapter on EB dwellings in the latest comprehensive study of architecture in the eastern Mediterranean supports this conclusion in Palestine (1992). However, it appears that the EC agglutinative tradition does have echoes on the mainland, probably due to social and economic factors. A multi-roomed accretive tradition was widespread throughout the EB II period in Palestine, especially in the Negev. Two or three mostly quadrangular rooms, more or less arranged in a row, characterize the so-called "Frontal-space House" built to the same scale as the units at *Kaminoudhia*. It is unnecessary to postulate any direct connections between these two traditions. Their appearance is probably a reaction to similar environmental and social conditions, a situation that some contemporary Aegean settlements suggest (see *infra*).

In western Anatolia and the islands of the east Aegean the "megaroid" style of domestic architecture predominated, as demonstrated at EB III Karataş (Mellink 1968, 1973) and all contemporary sites in this area (Warner 1979). The characteristic features of a megaron are two long freestanding walls with cross walls inserted to form one or two rooms, always entered axially on the short side. The front walls—and sometimes the rear ones as well—end in antae, forming a porch of varying depth. A central and sometimes elaborate circular hearth in the front room is a regular fixture (Warner 1979:135).

In central Anatolia, however, a less rigid building tradition is noted, as exemplified by the EB domestic structures at Alaca Hüyük, where two four-roomed houses were excavated (Koşay 1966: pl. 137). Although not adjoining each other, their irregular sub-rectangular plans are reminiscent of a more ordered version of the settlement at *Kaminoudhia*.

No architecture earlier or contemporary with the Philia Phase or the EC period was excavated at the Cilician site of Mersin in the latter phases of Level XIIa (2600–1900 B.C.E.) "except for scanty traces on the outskirts of the Tepe" (Garstang 1953:192). Because of Mersin's proximity to Cyprus—and to Tarsus—and the potential for connections between both areas, the lacuna is unfortunate.

In view of the irrefutable contacts that existed between Cyprus and EB II Tarsus (Swiny 1985 for bibliography; Mellink 1989:323–24; 1991), the domestic buildings from the later EB II levels of this site are the most likely to have served as models for the new architectural canon introduced to the island at the beginning of the Cypriot Bronze Age. If the amount of Cypriot pottery found in some of the nine EB II phases can be taken as an indicator of links between Tarsus and the island, then Phases 5–6 provide the most substantial evidence. From a mere three small rooms (Goldman 1956: pl. 6, nos. 103, 105, 107), only one of which was fully excavated, came five Red and Black Stroke Burnished sherds. The total surface of these rooms represents less than one quarter of the excavated area of domestic structures, a fact which underlines the frequent occurrence of Cypriot imports in these two phases. The earlier Phase 3 yielded a RP bottle and jug, generally considered of Cypriot origin (not mentioned in Mellink 1991, however, but they appear more Cypriot than Anatolian, cf. Swiny 1986a:35). No stratified Cypriot sherds were recovered from the later EB II phases, although absolute levels of the find spots attributed to two Red and Black Stroke Burnished pieces without provenance (Goldman 1956:130, nos. 372, 373) would suggest that they came from Phase 8 (Goldman 1956: Plan 8).

In conclusion, it would appear that the domestic architecture of Anatolia that could have influenced Cypriot building traditions in the mid-third millennium BC is more formalized, consisting of either freestanding megaroid structures or row houses with party walls.

Despite the modular tradition of Tarsian EB II two room houses fronting on streets, quite unlike the random settlement plans at *Kaminoudhia,* a number of common features may be cited. Whenever possible, comparisons will be drawn with the Tarsus EB II Phase 5–6 settlement (Goldman 1956: Plan 6) of a mid-third millennium date (Mellink 1991: fig. 1), thus predating Phase II at *Kaminoudhia* by at least two centuries. Since the EB II building sequence shows strong continuity

(Goldman 1956:346) throughout the period—Phases 5–6 adhere closely to a building tradition already apparent in Phase 1 around 2700 B.C.E.—some parallels will be noted with earlier and later EB II phases. To avoid confusion between Tarsus and *Kaminoudhia* in the following discussion, without the constant referencing to one or other site, it should be noted that all mentions of Rooms 98, 112 etc., allude to Tarsus and of Units 2, 16 etc., to *Kaminoudhia*.

The most striking common trait between both traditions is the rejection of freestanding, self-contained megaroid units. In this respect the buildings at Tarsus EB II, 5–6, with their party walls and irregularly arranged rooms of varying size (e.g., Rooms 98, 100, 103 and 105) are echoed by the layout at *Kaminoudhia* Area A of Units 1, 3, 7 and 18 in particular.

Although the Tarsian row houses generally have two-room units with the larger front room entered directly from the street, of the eighteen well-preserved houses from different EB II Phases published on Plans 4–8 (Goldman 1956), only eight were approached in this manner. The more common layout of entranceways consisted of front porches, corridors or antechambers, the latter being arranged similarly to those at *Kaminoudhia*. Room 103 at Tarsus (only 2 m wide) as shown on Plans 6 and 7, serves as an antechamber to Room 107, and therefore serves the same function as Units 25 and 40 at *Kaminoudhia*. The short 1–1.5 m wide corridors leading into Rooms 98 and 95 at Tarsus (Plans 6 and 8) embody the same concept as the much longer but equally narrow corridors, which provide access to multiple units, e.g., Units 1/3 or 6/16 at *Kaminoudhia*.

The positioning of doorways within a structure is never a random decision by the builders, since it significantly affects the use of and circulation within spaces. Doorways may be placed in the run of the wall, as between Units 7 and 18 or 4 and 19 at *Kaminoudhia* and in megaroid structures, for example, or they may be located in a corner. At both EB II Tarsus and *Kaminoudhia*, doorways are usually placed in the angle of a building, sometimes adjacent to a short spur wall or return (compare the doorways to Rooms 98, 103 at Tarsus with those to Units 8 and 17 at *Kaminoudhia*). Of the twelve unequivocal door openings at *Kaminoudhia*, eleven are adjacent to a wall. The width of EB II doorways at Tarsus tended towards a standard 70 cm. At *Kaminoudhia* their dimensions were far less standardized and varied from 87 cm to 1.30 m, the average for the nine best-preserved doors was 1.01 m.

Over half the nineteen fully excavated units at *Kaminoudhia* had low benches, either long and narrow (seven units) or broad and square to rectangular (three units). Identical features were recorded at EB II Tarsus—coincidentally few in Phases 5–6, which lack houses south of the street—but otherwise common in both earlier and later phases. A few parallels will suffice to illustrate the point: Rooms 112 and the room east of the forecourt leading into Room 115 (Plan 5) had narrow benches along two adjacent walls identical to those in Unit 2 and Unit 1/3 at *Kaminoudhia*. Broader benches fronting a single wall were noted in Rooms 99, 100 and 105 in the manner of those in Units 2, 7 and 23. At Tarsus short, broad benches were often associated with hearths, a fine example coming from Room 99 (Goldman 1956:26, figs. 84-5, Plan 6), which is reminiscent of Ft 23 in Unit 8 and the structure in the southwest corner of Unit 22, if this is a bench or platform.

The significance of these simple utilitarian features at both sites should not be overemphasized, especially since the Tarsus benches were broader and generally of more elaborate construction. Although not diagnostic, they were nonetheless common at both sites and, unless it is argued that the buildings were provided with furniture made from perishable materials, the benches would have played an important role as one of the most practical means of elevating and storing objects above the floor. It is interesting that benches were not usual features at other contemporary or earlier sites in the region. Of the large number of domestic structures excavated in level J6 at Hama (Fugmann 1958: fig. 63), only one room (R.2) may be equipped with a bench. None are visible on the plan of the EB houses at Byblos (Dunand 1952: pl. II) and at Tell el-Far'Ah de Vaux only notes a single occurrence of a ca. 40 cm wide bench (preserved to a height of 7 cm?) surrounding three sides of a room (de Vaux 1961:584, pl. XXXIV, #609).

Another little noticed feature perhaps shared by *Kaminoudhia* and EB II Tarsus is the "pot support." The lime plaster bin is quite a common feature at *Kaminoudhia,* where it may have served a variety of functions. In at least one instance, Ft 15 of Unit 4, a bin contained the remains of a pot, which was presumably abandoned in its place of use. A single occurrence of "A large and beautifully worked limestone pot support was set into the floor" in Room 98 is singled out but Goldman suggests elsewhere that they were quite common (1956:346 and 16, fig. 68). In both its size (D ca. 35 cm) and appearance it closely resembles the *Kaminoudhia* examples made of lime plaster, sometimes reinforced with a mortar at their base, in which case they may also have served as mortars. A depression described as a "jar rest" with an inner diameter of ca. 25 cm and packed with gravel and limestone chips was noted by Goldman (1956:17, Plan 4) in Room 115. This description is reminiscent of Ft 6 from Unit 5, a large lime plaster bin lined with slivers of limestone.

In light of the above, the common occurrence of benches as well as the postulated existence of pot supports at EB II Tarsus and *Kaminoudhia* further emphasize the similarities between the sites.

Evidence for connections between the Aegean and Cyprus in the Early Bronze Age, as demonstrated by a few western imports in Cyprus (Grace 1940, Dikaios 1940), has been the subject of many studies that in the past fifty-five years have merely cited or reevaluated the same minuscule body of material repeatedly. The presence of a MM I bridge-spouted jar from an EC IIIB burial and two EC IIIB daggers of Aegean origin are the earliest imports (Stewart 1962:277, 280; Karageorghis 1982:46). None of these items need have reached Cyprus directly and the paucity of Cypriot EC/MC I objects in the Aegean, more than 500 km to the west, argues against protracted contacts. There is no evidence for links contemporary with or earlier than the *Kaminoudhia* settlement; therefore any connection between the architectural traditions of the two areas is highly unlikely (Åström 1979; Herscher 1979:7; Merrillees 1979:25; Swiny 1979:29; Swiny 1997).

Nevertheless, a generic connection is evident between the layout of the Cretan EM II hilltop settlement at Myrtos-Phournou Khoryphi (Warren 1972:1992) and *Kaminoudhia.* Although Phournou Khoryphi is large by comparison, consisting of more than ninety units divided into six individual family clusters, the "houses [are] joined to each other in a cellular structure" (Warren 1992:198). The clusters which could be isolated include a work room (sometimes used for spinning or weaving), kitchen and storeroom. The site's lack of planning and clusters of irregular units of widely varying sizes with meandering walls, does bear comparison with Areas A and C at *Kaminoudhia.* The presence of long, narrow, low benches (30 cm wide, 28 cm high) is another feature shared by both sites (Warren 1972, Schematic plan opp. p. 11). Nevertheless, here the comparison must end because despite its lack of individual structures, Phournou Khoryphi was organized into specific function areas, something undiagnosed at *Kaminoudhia.* The similarities exhibited by Phournou Khoryphi are probably due to factors such as the uneven terrain, space constraints and above all to the lack of a strict building tradition at this small hilltop settlement, far from the major centers of power and wealth. When the domestic architecture of Phournou Khoryphi is compared with contemporary EM II Vasiliki, with its large, carefully planned and built rectangular, multi-roomed structures (Zois 1992:276, fig. 41.1, 2), its rural character is emphasized. It is this last point and the fact that Myrtos-Phournou Khoryphi lies at the beginning of an architectural tradition—outside Knossos no EM I domestic architecture has been preserved—that connect Phournou Khoryphi and *Kaminoudhia.*

 Even farther afield, on the eastern Aegean islands of Lemnos and Lesbos, large areas of EB II domestic architecture have been uncovered. The Verde level at Poliochni on Lemnos displays architecture of a domestic nature similar to the Cretan accretive tradition (Bernabò-Brea 1964: Tav. 23, Plans 10, 11, 12). The large irregularly shaped stone built structures comprising two to seven rooms (Isled XVII, XXIV, XXV and Edificio XXIII) were separated by winding narrow streets or alley ways from 1.10 to 2 m wide. Rooms were mostly 3–4 m long, with exceptional occurrences of 7 m and from 1.5 m to an average 2.8 m wide. They are usually quadrangular in shape, but irregular triangles and pentagons also occur. The doorways were generally located in corners, but almost half were positioned in the run of a wall. Built-in features such as benches or hearths, common at most EB settlements, are not represented on the plans.

No such parallels may be noted with the contemporary EB II architecture in levels I–III at Thermi on Lesbos (Lamb 1936: Plans 1–4), which from the beginning (Plan 1) is reminiscent of the western Anatolian tradition, with long regular single room structures sharing party walls. The early EB III buildings of Thermi IV continue the same tradition, despite major changes at the site (Lamb 1936: figs. 15–16).

If more extensive area excavation had been undertaken at Sotira *Kaminoudhia* it is probable that large clusters of units separated by alleys or passageways would have been clearly defined. For example, Units 1, 3, 4, 5, 6, 7, 18, 19, 20, 31 and 40 could be seen as one cluster separate from Units 27–29 and perhaps Units 35–41. All of Area C, defined as it is on two sides by WA and WAJ, could be seen as belonging to a single, perhaps even self-contained cluster.

Although it is not suggested that any connection existed between EB Lemnos and Cyprus, some 850 km apart, the contemporary domestic architecture on these two islands and on Crete at Myrtos-Phournou Khoryphi displays the same general characteristics in terms of scale and settlement layout.

In the following tables, 2.1a–2.1f, BTB (i.e. "Black Topped Bowl") sherds should, by definition, belong to bowls. In these tables, however, the BTB definition has been broadened to include all sherds from Black Polished vessels, closed or open.

Table 2.1a. Stratified sherd totals from Sotira *Kaminoudhia* by ware and shape.

WARE	RP	DPBC	BTB	COARSE	BASIN	RW	R&B/B	CHALCO	TOTAL
Body Open	5359	38	291	184		282	69	203	**6426**
Body Closed	6714	82	43	163		304	60	18	**7384**
Small Bowl	496	4	21	3		2	5	2	**533**
Large Bowl	76		3	5					**84**
Jug	9								**9**
Juglet	18	1	2						**21**
Jar/Amph	54	1	2	15		1		1	**74**
Cook Pot	23	1		6					**30**
Store Jar	8	1		29					**38**
Basin	44				1819				**1863**
Round Base	10	1							**11**
Flat Base	159	4	2	18		3	1		**187**
Pointed Base	7								**7**
Vert Handle	222		2	7					**232**
Lug	34			2					**36**
Trough Spout	26	1	1			134	367	432	**28**
TOTAL	**13259**	**134**	**367**	**432**	**1819**	**592**	**135**	**225**	**16963**
Percentage	**78.2**	**0.8**	**2.2**	**2.5**	**10.7**	**3.5**	**0.8**	**1.3**	**100**

Table 2.1b. Stratified sherd totals from Area A by ware and shape.

WARE	RP	DPBC	BTB	COARSE	BASIN	RW	R&B/B	CHALCO	TOTAL
Body Open	2251	37	86	144		271	45	190	**3024**
Body Closed	2667	72	4	71		290	40	31	**3175**
Small Bowl	229	4	10	1		2	3	4	**253**
Large Bowl	27	1	2	3					**33**
Jug	9								**9**
Juglet	17	1							**18**
Jar/Amph	31			10		1		1	**43**
Cook Pot	15								**15**
Store Jar	4	11		27					**32**
Basin	28				698				**726**
Round Base	8	1							**9**
Flat Base	70	2		8		3	1		**85**
Pointed Base	5								**5**
Vert Handle	84			4				1	**89**
Lug	17			2					**18**
Trough Spout	9	1							**10**
TOTAL	**5471**	**120**	**103**	**270**	**698**	**567**	**89**	**227**	**7545**
Percentage	**72.5**	**1.6**	**1.4**	**3.6**	**9.3**	**7.5**	**1.2**	**3**	**99.8**

Table 2.1c. Stratified sherd totals from individual units in Area A.

WARE	RP	DPBC	BTB	COARSE	BASIN	RW	R&B/B	CHALCO	TOTAL
Unit 1	272	14	7	2	33	60	5	1	394
Unit 3	286	5	10	13	18	133	5	27	497
Unit 4	190	5	7	3	28	15	8	0	256
Unit 5	395	9	8	4	42	33	6	0	497
Unit 6	809	14	23	72	117	65	16	60	1176
Unit 7	598	2	2	17	72	59	0	0	750
Unit 15	126	6	1	4	9	44	2	0	192
Unit 16	428	20	3	25	6	83	12	71	648
Unit 18	534	4	1	28	73	25	2	24	691
Unit 19	59	0	1	1	18	1	0	0	80
Unit 20	444	4	6	8	113	20	3	8	606
Unit 31	211	1	0	33	33	4	4	0	286
Unit 32	258	0	6	10	25	5	5	0	309
Unit 33	492	12	18	43	79	13	21	36	714
Unit 35	44	21	10	2	11	1	0	0	89
Unit 39	104	2	0	2	4	6	0	0	118
Unit 41	113	1	0	3	17	0	0	0	134
Unit 46	18	0	0	0	0	0	0	0	18
TOTAL	5381	120	103	270	698	567	89	227	7455
Percentage	72.2	1.6	1.4	3.6	9.4	7.6	1.2	3	100

Table 2.1d. Stratified sherd totals from Area B by ware and shape.

WARE	RP	DPBC	BTB	COARSE	BASIN	RW	R&B/B	CHALCO	TOTAL
Body Open	592		11			6	5		66514
Body Closed	725					7	6		738
Small Bowl	17		4						21
Large Bowl	4								4
Jug									0
Juglet									0
Jar/Amph	2			1					2
Cook Pot									1
Store Jar									0
Basin					444				444
Round Base	1								1
Flat Base	7		1						8
Pointed Base									0
Vert Handle	23								23
Lug									0
Trough Spout	6								6
TOTAL	1377	0	16	1	444	13	11	0	1862
Percentage	74		0.8		238	07	06		100

Table 2.1e. Stratified sherd totals from Area C by ware and shape.

WARE	RP	DPBC	BTB	COARSE	BASIN	RW	R&B/B	CHALCO	TOTAL
Body Open	2594	1	205	43		6	21		2870
Body Closed	3368	10	35	92		7	13	3	3528
Small Bowl	251		6	2			2		261
Large Bowl	45		1	2					48
Jug									0
Juglet	3								3
Jar/Amph	23	1		5					29
Cook Pot	8	1		5					14
Store Jar	4			2					6
Basin	22				699				721
Round Base	1								1
Flat Base	82	2		10					94
Pointed Base	2								2
Vert Handle	127		1	3					131
Lug	17								17
Trough Spout	12								12
TOTAL	6559	15	248	164	699	13	36	3	7737
Percentage	84.8	00.2	3.2	2.1	9	0.2	0.5	0.04	99.9

Table 2.1f. Stratified sherd totals from individual units in Area C.

WARE	RP	DPBC	BTB	COARSE	BASIN	RW	R&B/B	CHALCO	TOTAL
Unit 2	1972	9	48	81	174	4	6	3	2297
Unit 8	904	0	51	13	205	0	4	0	1177
Unit 9	419	1	8	24	44	3	4	0	503
Unit 10	1178	2	18	38	182	4	10	0	1432
Unit 17	319	1	2	3	87	1	0	0	413
Unit 21	909	0	83	1	1	1	1	0	996
Unit 22	525	1	16	0	3	0	2	0	547
Unit 23	333	1	22	4	3	0	9	0	372
TOTAL	6559	15	248	164	699	13	36	3	7737
Percentage	84.8	0.2	3.2	2.1	9	0.2	0.5	0.04	100

APPENDIX 2.1

ROOF BEAMS IN CYPRIOT VERNACULAR ARCHITECTURE

I wish to thank Ian Humphreys and Helena, Philip and Alessandra Swiny for their interest and help in gathering the data on house beams. All the beams discussed here retain their basic tree trunk shape and are thus more or less circular in section. Those from Paramali were recorded in 1987, the rest in the following years up to 1990.

The measurements of beams from houses in Paramali, Episkopi, and Nicosia provided thirty-seven minimum age and maximum diameter determinations. Counting the visible tree rings determined the ages. Thus, a minimum age was obtained since trees might lose a few outer rings along with the bark through adzing, or in the case of the Nicosia beams, through planing. In the interest of economy a minimum amount of wood would have been removed, thus the beams are not uniform in diameter.

The data collection in Paramali Village was sadly facilitated by the fact that the beams in many of the houses were being cut at either end by chain saw to be used as fence posts. In this manner, one beam in two had been removed, leaving enough in place to prevent the roof from collapsing immediately, on top of the chain saw operator! We visited the village shortly after this operation had taken place, and the cuts were still fresh and the rings easy to count. The information from Nicosia was obtained from beams removed from the Cyprus American Archaeological Research Institute when it was being renovated in 1989/1990, and from a building yard specializing in reused materials. Smoke-blackened adzed beams, slightly pointed at both ends, which also tend to be worm eaten, are characteristic of traditional Cypriot roofing materials and therefore easy to identity. The planed beams used for part of the McFadden house, Episkopi Village, built in the 1930s (now the Kourion Museum), have an average diameter of 12.7 cm and are placed between 16 and 18 cm apart.

	PROVENANCE	MATERIAL	FUNCTION	DIAMETER (CM)	AGE (YEARS)
1	Old Paramali Village	Phoenician juniper	door lintel	15	87
2.		id		15.5	108
3.		id		14.5	60
4.		id		14	147
5.	Old Paramali Village	cypress	roof beam supporting 1st floor	13	17
6.	Same house			13	14
7.	Same house			12	22
8.	Same house			14	20
9.	Same house			13.6	32
10.	Same house		heavily adzed beam	14	61
11.	Same house			10.5	23
12.	Same house			10.8	20
13.	Same house			10.7	20
14.	Same house			10.5	20

15. Same house			10.8	14
16. Same house			12.6	14
17. Same house			14.2	24
18. Same house			14	45
19. Same house			10.2	23
20. Same house			11	15
21. Same house			12.6	14
22. Same house			13.2	21
23. Old Paramali Village	cypress	roof beam	11	42
24. Episkopi Village	cypress (adzed)	roof beam	13.4	27
25. Nicosia, CAARI;	cypress (planed)		10.5	26
26. id.			9.8	40
27. id.			10	19
28. id.			11	37
29. id.			11	28
30. Nicosia	cypress (adzed) original provenance unknown*		15.8	32
31. id.			17.5	31
32. id.			16.2	43
33. id.			16.5	27
34. id.			16.4	30
35. id.			17.5	30
36. id.			14.2	31
37. id.			15	32

* The structures from which these beams were removed were located within the town of Nicosia. They were found in 1990 stockpiled in the courtyard (near the Old Airport Roundabout, south of Navarino Street) of Mr. Kotchas, a merchant of second-hand building materials, who specialized in sandstone blocks, traditional floor and roof tiles, wooden doors, etc.

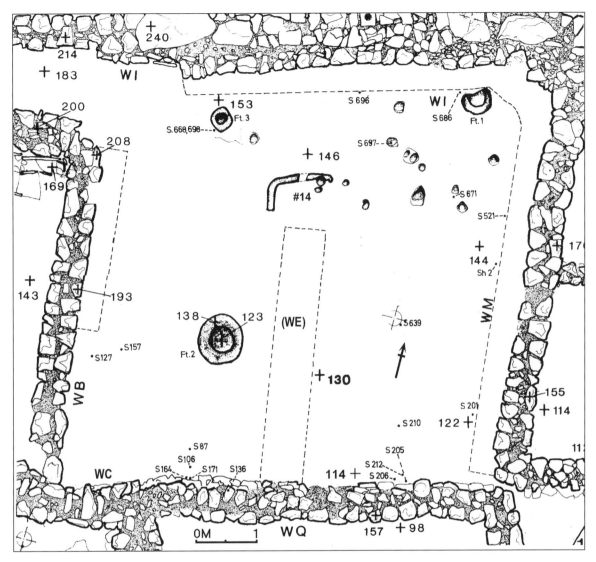

Fig. 2.1. Area A. Unit 1, Phase I. Stratified finds in situ.

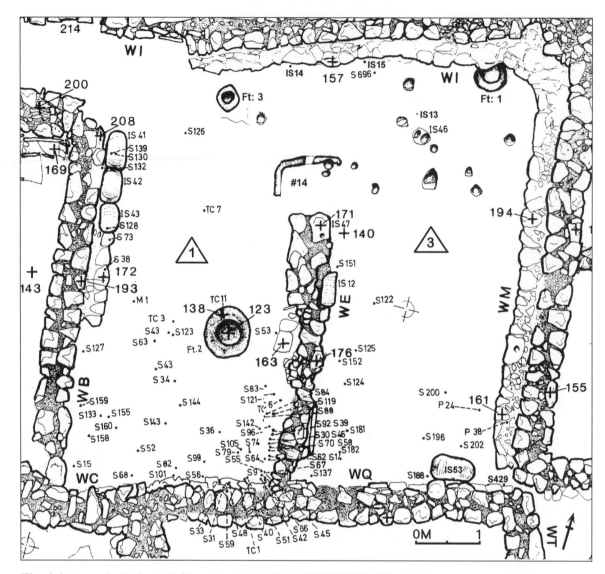

Fig. 2.2. Area A. Units 1 (left) and 3 (right), Phase II. Stratified finds in situ.

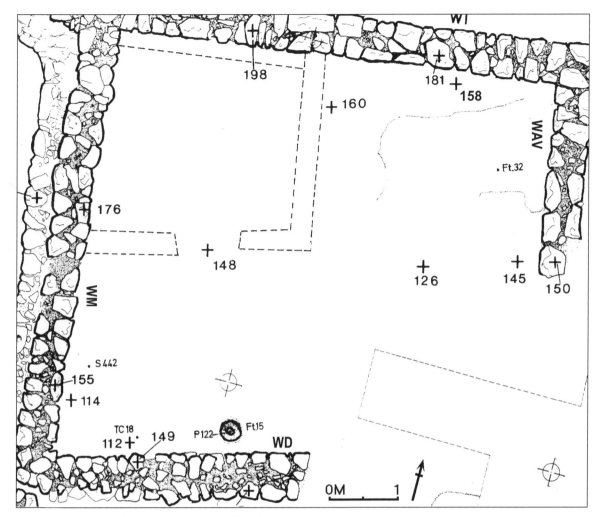

Fig. 2.3. Area A. Unit 4, Phase I. Stratified finds in situ.

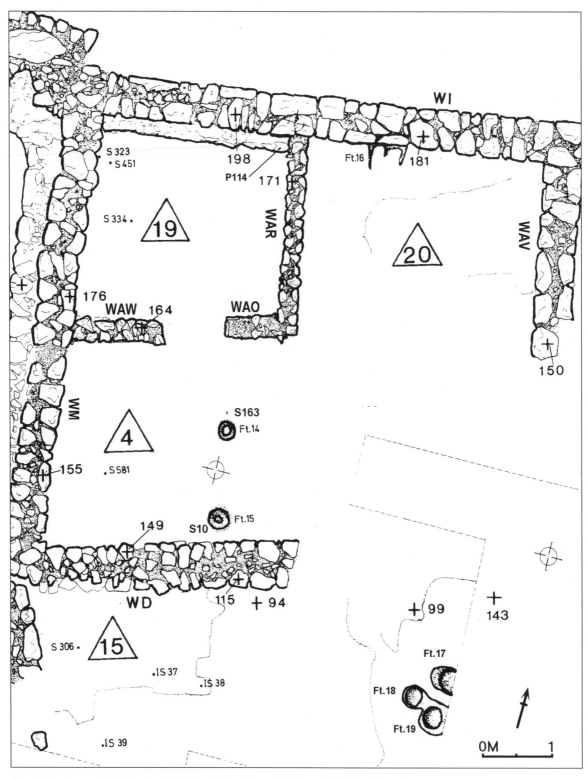

Fig. 2.4. Area A. Units 4, 15, 19 and 20, Phase II. Stratified finds in situ.

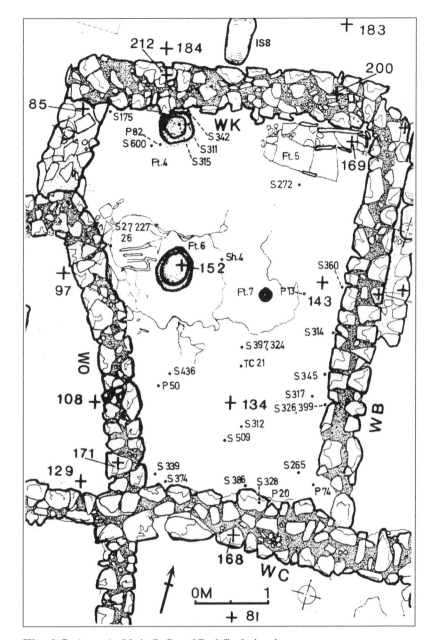

Fig. 2.5. Area A. Unit 5. Stratified finds in situ.

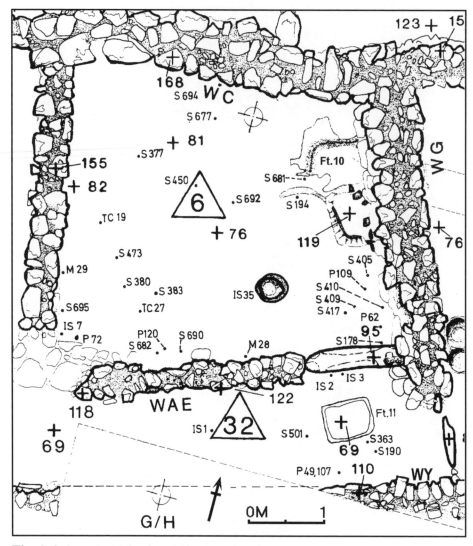

Fig. 2.6. Area A. Units 6 and 32. Stratified finds in situ.

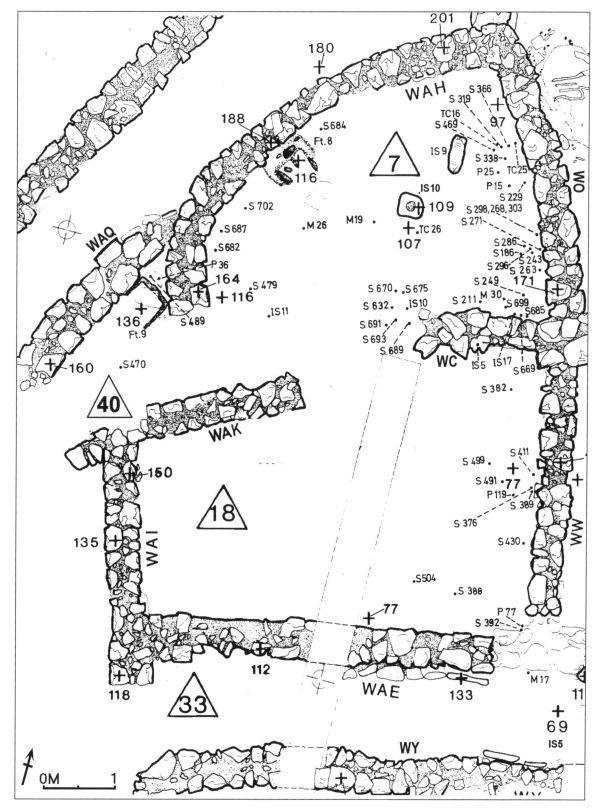

Fig. 2.7. Area A. Units, 7, 18, 33 and 40. Stratified finds in situ.

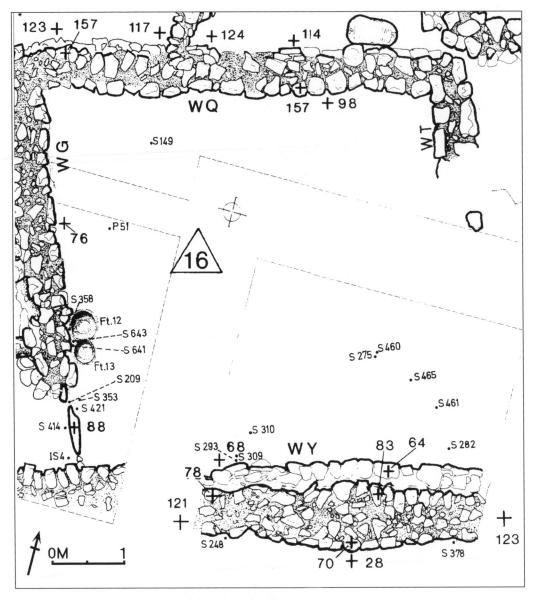

Fig. 2.8. Area A. Unit 16. Stratified finds in situ.

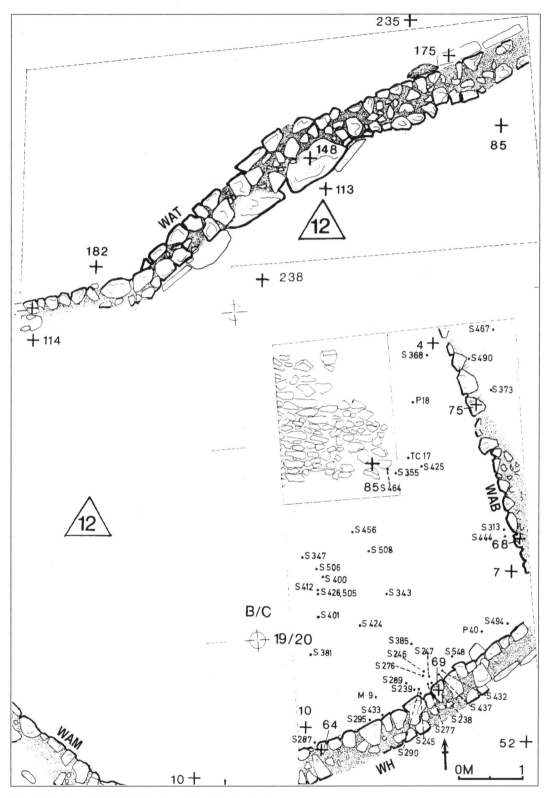

Fig. 2.9. Area B. Unit 12. Stratified finds in situ.

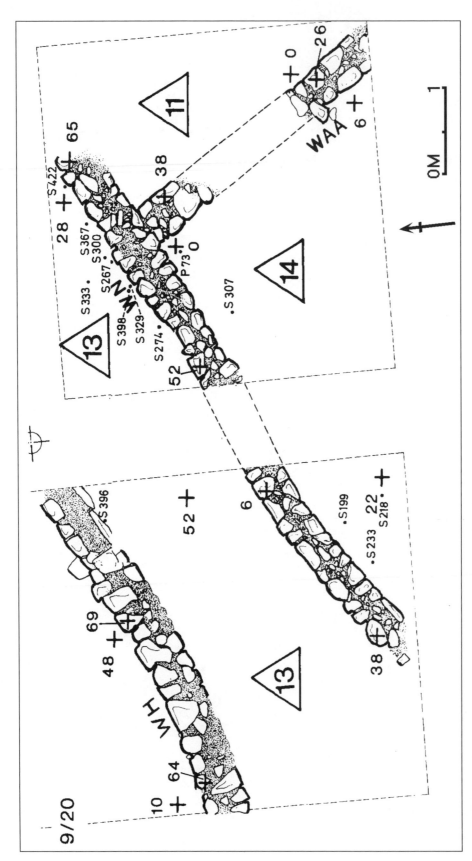

Fig. 2.10. Area B. Units 11, 13 and 14. Stratified finds in situ.

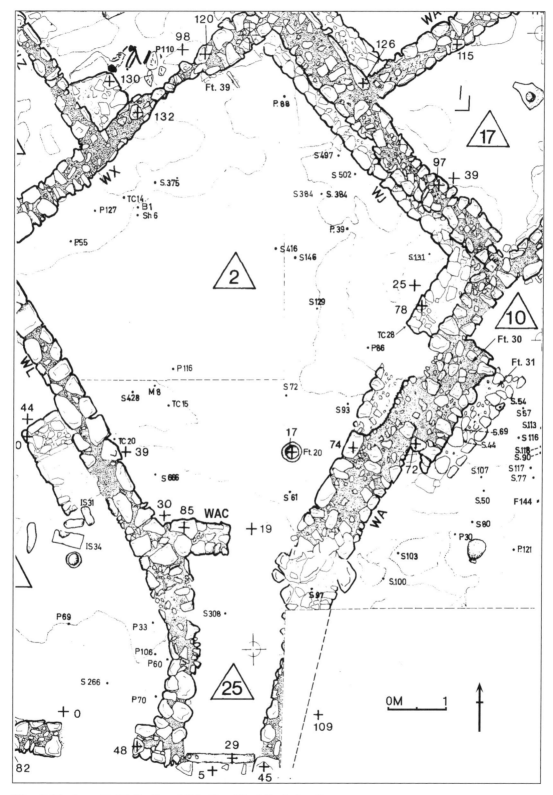

Fig. 2.11. Area C. Units 2 and 25. Stratified finds in situ.

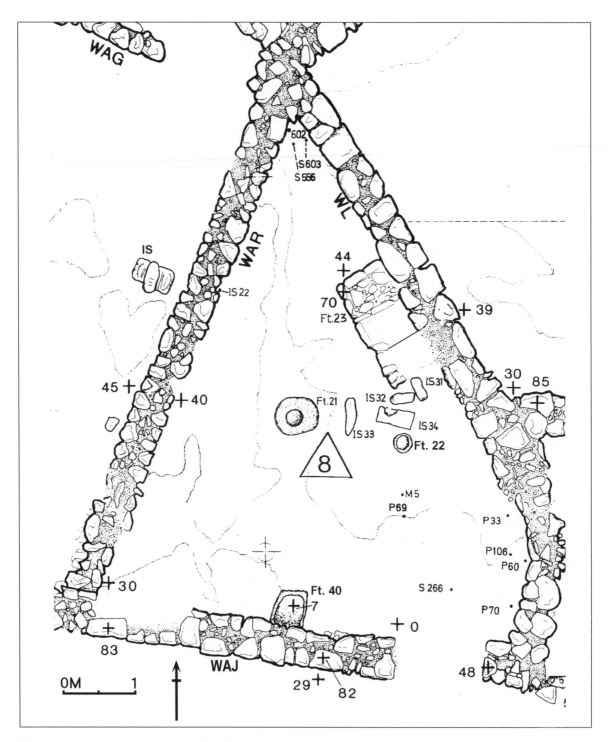

Fig. 2.12. Area C. Unit 8. Stratified finds in situ.

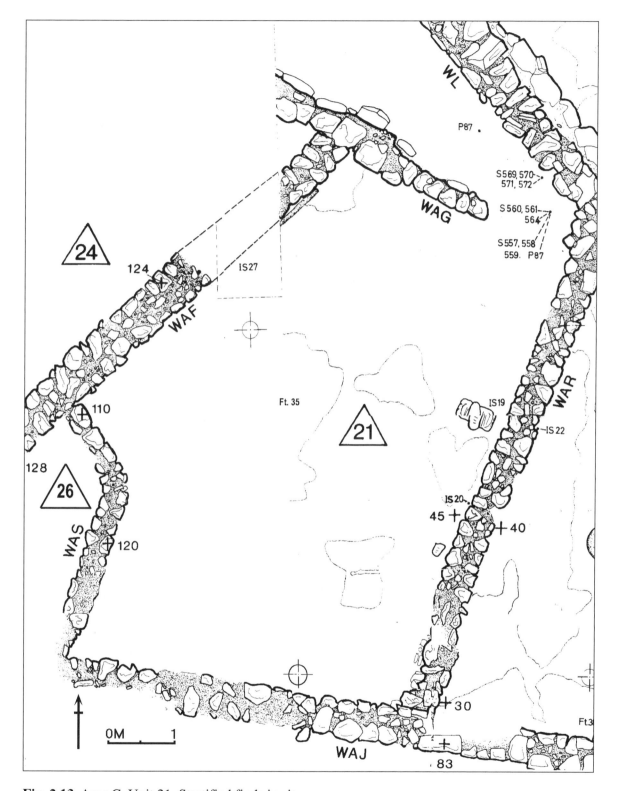

Fig. 2.13. Area C. Unit 21. Stratified finds in situ.

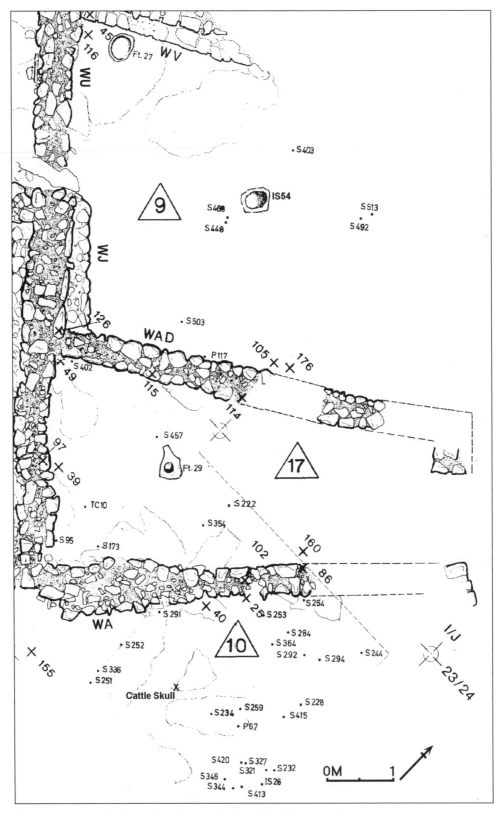

Fig. 2.14. Area C. Units 9, 10 and 17. Stratified finds in situ.

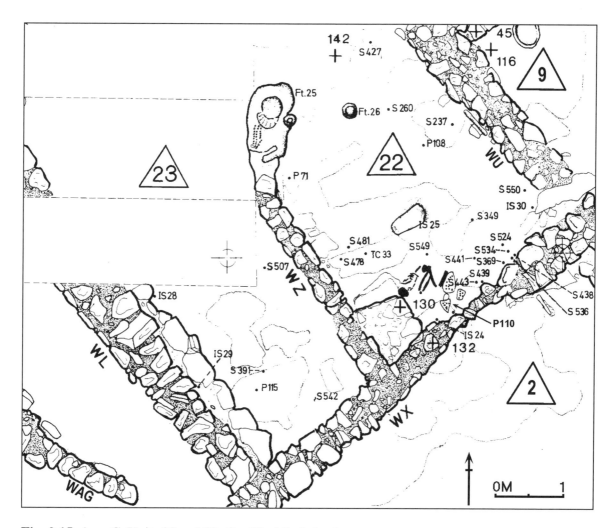

Fig. 2.15. Area C. Units 22 and 23. Stratified finds in situ.

Fig. 2.16. [See insert.]

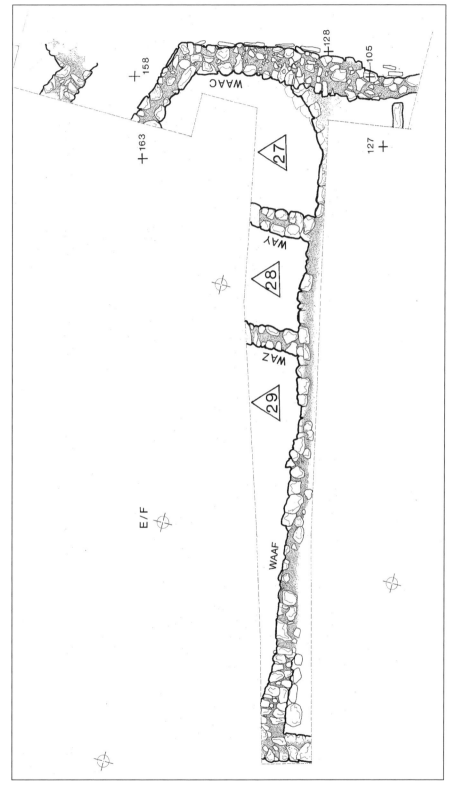

Fig. 2.16a. Western Extension of Area A (East–West Trial Trench). Section DD' runs through Units 27–29.

Fig. 2.17. Plan of Area B.

Fig. 2.18. [See insert.]

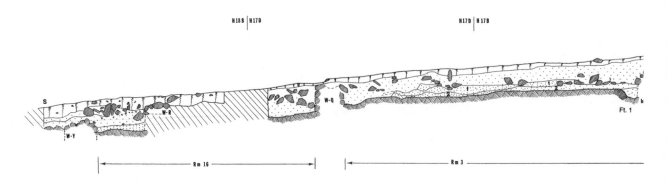

Fig. 2.19a. Area A. Section AA' looking west, from bank above Area A to WY in south. WR is later.

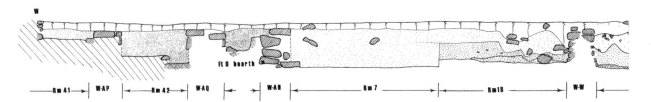

Fig. 2.19b. Area A. Section BB' looking north across entire area.

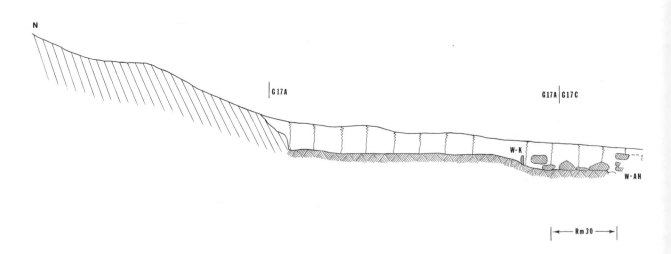

Fig. 2.19c. Area A. Section CC' looking east.

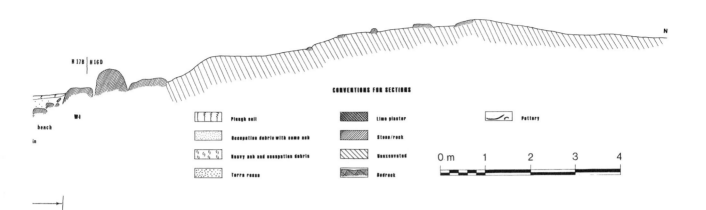

CONVENTIONS FOR SECTIONS

Plough soil	Lime plaster	Pottery
Occupation debris with some ash	Stone/rock	
Heavy ash and occupation debris	Unexcavated	
Terra rossa	Bedrock	

0 m   1   2   3   4

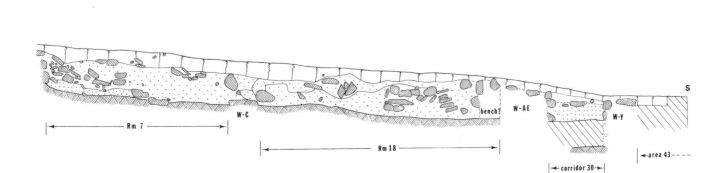

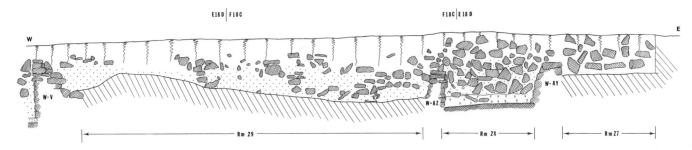

Fig. 2.20a. Area A. Section DD' looking north.

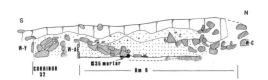

Fig. 2.20b. Area A. Unit 6 looking west.

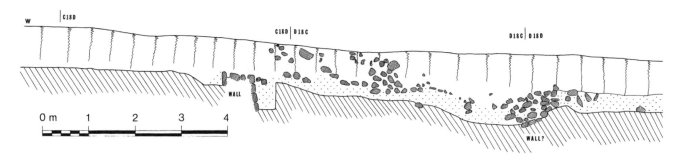

Fig. 2.20c. Western extension of fig. 2.20a. North baulk of East–West Trial Trench.

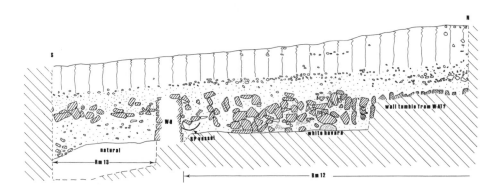

Fig. 2.20d. Area B. Section AA' looking west.

D18D | E18 G | E18 D

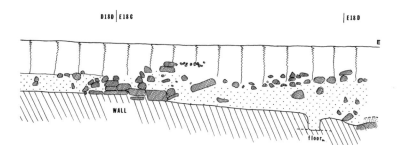

WALL

floor

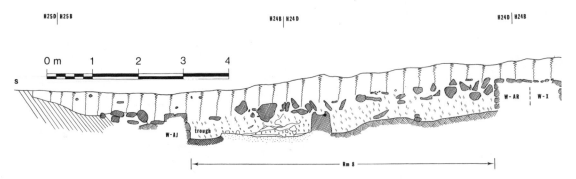

Fig. 2.21a. Area C. Section AA' looking west.

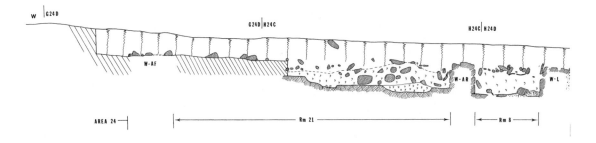

Fig. 2.21b. Area C. Section BB' looking north.

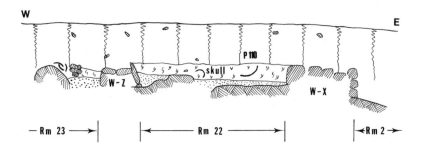

Fig. 2.21c. Area C. Section CC' looking north across Unit 22.

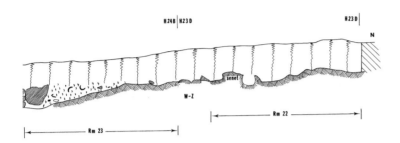

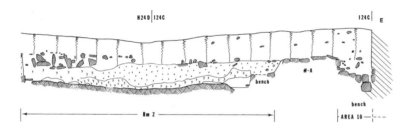

3

THE CEMETERY

by Stuart Swiny and Ellen Herscher

INTRODUCTION

The excavations of the burial ground at Sotira *Kaminoudhia* were first described by Kimberle Calnan in a Master of Arts thesis submitted to Drew University in 1984.[1] The section of her study dealing with the tombs and their contents was then reworked and reinterpreted by Swiny. Each tomb description is followed by a list of finds in which the entries for the ceramics and the discussions of the relative date of the burials have been prepared by Herscher. Ceramic and lithic finds from Cemeteries A and B which were found outside tomb chambers are listed at the end of the chapter. Carola Schulte Campbell presents the detailed discussion of human skeletal remains in Chapter 10, and Paul Croft deals with the faunal remains from funerary contexts in Chapter 11. Although the ceramic, lithic, metal, and terracotta finds from the cemeteries are listed and described tomb by tomb, they are also discussed in greater detail in the respective chapters focusing on these materials.

The burials stretch across a narrow valley approximately one hundred meters north-northeast of the settlement (fig. 1.3, pl. 3.1), in an area which has been recognized as a Bronze Age cemetery ever since Porphyrios Dikaios uncovered a tomb here in 1947 while directing the excavations at Sotira *Teppes* (Dikaios 1948: 23, pl. VIb). At that time the three empty chambers of Cemetery B must have attracted his attention and the surface pottery in the vicinity would have provided an approximate Early Bronze Age date for the interments. How the burial in Cemetery A came to be excavated by Dikaios is not recorded, but the local villagers already knew that burials with pottery existed in the immediate area. Over 60 years ago the grandfather of one villager recovered from this spot a black colored pot with incised decoration, which appealed to him so much that he used it thereafter to keep honey for the table.[2]

Most of the funerary chambers and cist graves appear to have been excavated out of the east or west sloping hillsides, although others, now covered by the intervening terraces, are known to exist in the valley floor. Indeed, the sinking of a probe in the middle of one such terrace led to the discovery of a dromos and two chambers (T11 and T20) cut into the valley floor, and in 1985 after heavy winter rains, a hole suddenly appeared on the western edge of a terrace due east of the burial excavated by Dikaios. This anomaly was presumably the result of the collapsed roof of a tomb chamber dug at least

---

[1] Calnan 1984. The thesis was based directly on her meticulous and exhaustive study of the excavation note-books, which saved Swiny many hours of tedious work with field notes written by different people over the course of two field seasons.

[2] Information supplied by Stellios Mavros in 1981, whose grandfather found the pot. The same year his wife Eleni showed me a RP bowl that she had "found in the vicinity" of Cemetery A at the base of a carob tree.

one meter below the present surface.[3] As a result of these discoveries there is good reason to believe that the cemetery originally consisted of an unbroken scatter of tombs stretching from Cemetery A in the west across the valley floor up to Cemetery B in the east (in pl. 3.1 Cemetery A is the white area in the center and Cemetery B is slightly to the south in the right of the picture).

Despite an intensive, systematic survey of the area around the settlement (see Chapter 16), no other cemeteries or evidence for individual graves have been recorded in the vicinity: thus it appears that the inhabitants of *Kaminoudhia* only buried their dead in this particular sector of the valley, a short distance north of the settlement.

The present vegetation consists of Cyprus pine and carob with a thick ground cover of cistus, thyme and spiny burnet; above the cemetery on both hills clumps of lentisc are common.

In Cemetery A the topsoil is typically light brownish yellow (10YR 6/6) with many limestone pebbles and cobbles. This material is a mixture of terra rossa originating from the hillside above and eroded limestone debris. Below the topsoil, lenses of almost pure eroded limestone, yellowy white (2.5Y 8/2) to light gray (10YR 7/3) in color, are common. Cemetery B being closer to the crest of a hill had little terra rossa and all loose material consisted of more or less concreted secondary limestone. The intervening terraces were composed of light brown sediment, which is a mixture of imported terra rossa and secondary limestone. Inside tomb chambers the matrix may vary from dark brown (10YR 4/3) to light brownish gray (10 YR 6/2) depending on the admixture of terra rossa and eroded, thus secondary, limestone. No particular significance could be attributed to these color variations, which changed from tomb to tomb and appeared to be determined by the local topography rather than human agency. The color and lensing is thus a factor of the percentages of terra rossa and secondary limestone, which became mixed in the processes of moving down slope. In this report Munsell color descriptions will be used to designate different soil colors—e.g., "light gray" (i.e., 10YR 7/3)—but in most instances will not be followed by the alpha Munsell numeric reference code.

Finds drawn on plans and sections are referred to as follows: #6-P94, which indicates that #6 on the plan or section is item P94 listed in the object catalogue. The caption for each figure includes a concordance for the finds listed thereon.

The funerary architecture at Sotira *Kaminoudhia* belongs to a generic tradition common to Cyprus from the Bronze Age to the Christian era. Tombs were always hewn out of the bedrock and they usually consisted of a dromos (a bathtub-like depression of varying depth) with a roughly circular opening in one side, known as the stomion, which provided access to the domed, roughly circular burial chamber. There was always a step down from the bottom of the dromos to the horizontal floor of the chamber. The stomion was normally blocked by a large stone slab, or plaka, or more rarely, a rough wall of fieldstones.[4] In Cemetery A several less elaborate alternatives, in the form of cist graves, were also noted, and indeed many of the burial chambers did not seem to have been approached via a dromos.

---

[3] The hole could be seen to penetrate about 80 cm into the soil forming the terrace.
[4] The words *dromos, stomion* and *plaka* are such commonly used Greek words that they have not been italicized in the present publication.

CEMETERY A

DIKAIOS TOMB 1

The results of excavations in Cemetery A (pls. 3.1, 3.2a) begin with a description of the work undertaken by Dikaios in 1947, which was only published in a cursory manner. His report is worth quoting in full:

> During the same campaign a cemetery of the Copper Age was discovered on the slopes adjoining the Sotira hill on the east. Owing to lack of time, only one tomb was cleared (pl. VI, b). It contained Red Polished pottery of early types and dated approximately to the middle of the third millennium B.C. This discovery shows that Sotira continued to be inhabited in the third millennium B.C. and gives hopes that settlements of the Erimi period may also be brought to light in the same neighborhood.[5]

A site plan[6] published with this description places the tomb, labeled as T.1, approximately 2.5 m north of the dromos of T14 in I5A (figs. 1.3, 3.1). Because a dry stone wall has been built in this area since 1947 and evidence of Dikaios' excavation is no longer discernible, it was impossible to locate the position of the tomb with greater accuracy. Although plate VIb, showing "The dromos of the Copper Age Tomb" is clear and sharp, none of the salient features represented thereon could be recognized in 1981. Since this photograph is the only visual record of the excavation known to the writer, it is necessary to describe it in some detail.

The site plan published by Dikaios shows the position of the tomb on the west flank of the valley. From the lay of the land visible in the photograph and the position of the shadows, the camera must be pointing west, as the ground rises in that direction. The foreground is dominated by a large slab of stone standing on edge, aligned north–south, which in both shape and size is consistent with the plakas used to seal burial chambers at *Kaminoudhia*. Since the ground climbs behind the slab a normal arrangement would be for the dromos to lie in front of it with the chamber behind, and indeed the caption of the plate is "Dromos of Copper Age tomb." A cut in the bedrock marked by shadow, perhaps 1 to 1.5 m behind and to the left of the plaka, probably represents the actual chamber, the roof of which is now missing. Unfortunately, no grave goods are visible on the floor of the tomb, which is entirely obscured by the plaka. Indeed, the only ceramic item visible in the photograph is the neck of a jug with a cutaway spout and broken vertical handle, which was not included with the other items stored in the Cyprus Museum (see below). Behind the chamber there appears a makeshift stone wall, about 40 cm high, aligned north–south with another large slab standing up against its west face. This arrangement of slab, or plaka, with a rough wall in front is commonly found as a means of securing the entrance to tomb chambers, so it is possible that another chamber had once existed in this spot. No other features of significance are visible within the excavated area, which is surrounded to the south and west by small boulders, loose stones, and low bushes that climb up the slope. Scale is provided by a small pick standing up against the baulk, to the left of the wall; the handles of such picks may vary in length from 40 to 50 cm, but are very rarely any longer.

---

[5] Dikaios 1948:23, pl. VI, b. No plan of the tomb or notes could be located in the Cyprus Museum Archives when a search was undertaken by the author in 1977. The Director of the Department of Antiquities graciously made the finds from the excavation kept in the Cyprus Museum storerooms available for study and publication.

[6] Dikaios 1948:17, see the upper right-hand corner of the plan for the location of the trench that contained T.1.

The finds from the tomb are described below in order to provide a complete picture of all the material recovered from the cemeteries at *Kaminoudhia*.[7]

1. RP cooking pot. Pl. 4.6a; Swiny 1979: fig. 68:1. H: 26.4; D: 27.0. Flat base (D: 12), globular body, short wide cylindrical neck, plain vertical rim; two opposed vertical handles, round in section, from rim to upper body. Undecorated. Clay not very hard, dark brown to dark gray, with many inclusions, some of them large, and organic temper; fairly thick smeared slip, with some luster preserved, worn, varying in color from black to dark brown to dark red-brown; interior also slipped, a more uniform dark red-brown. Cooking Pot Type B.

2. Red Polished jug (?). H (est.): ca. 25. Fragmentary, incomplete; flat base (D: 9.0), inverted piriform body (approx. one-third preserved); additional preserved sherds of handle, neck and probable cutaway spout (cf. Dikaios 1948: pl. VIb), but not restorable. No decoration preserved. Soft clay, mostly gray with light yellow-brown surface, with much fine organic temper and some large gray inclusions; trace of lustrous dark red-brown slip.

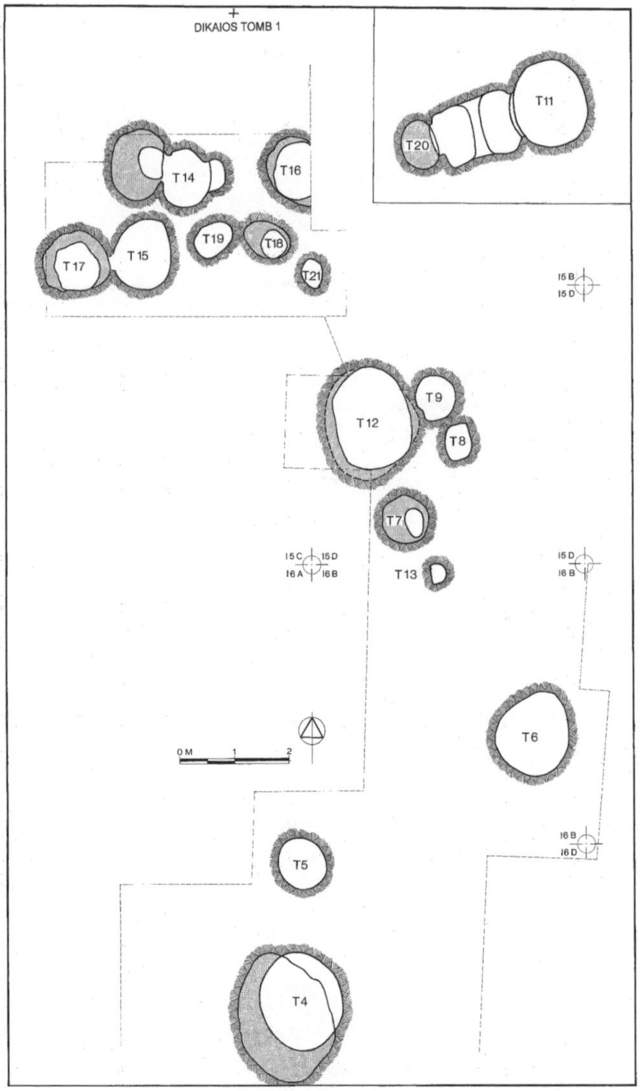

Fig. 3.1. Plan of Cemetery A with inset of Tombs 11 and 20.

3. Red Polished Philia spouted bowl. Fig. 4.3; Swiny 1979: fig. 68:3; H.W. Swiny 1982: fig. 11 (left). H: 17.0; D: 19.5. Flat base (D: 8.4), deep ovoid body, plain rim (chipped); tubular spout with straight end rising diagonally from mid-body; horizontal handle, round in section, at mid-body opposite handle. Undecorated. Hard dark red-brown clay with many black and white inclusions, some quite large; dark red-brown slip with very irregular burnishing strokes clearly visible on interior and exterior, large black area on one side; much worn. Spouted Bowl Type A.

4. Red-and-Black Polished (?) bowl. D (rim): ca. 12. Fragmentary, incomplete; deep straight-sided bowl with plain rim, preserved to a height of about 6 cm. Soft heavily straw-tempered clay, mostly

[7] The finds from the tomb were first described in Swiny 1979:264 ff.; fig. 68:1, 3, 5; fig. 69:1, 2. Herscher subsequently studied them in preparation for their publication here in Chapter 3. For discussion of the ceramic types, see Chapter 4.

very dark gray with light brown surface in places; oxidized band (max. width ca. 4 cm) around rim (interior and exterior), with black lower body; no traces of slip preserved.

5. Red Polished Philia bottle. Swiny 1979: fig. 69:1–2. Fragmentary, small sherds only preserved, not restorable. Rim (D: ca. 2.2) appears straight, no indication of base. Incised decoration of parallel lines and herringbones on body. Fine soft gray clay with organic temper, surface mostly gray-brown with black areas (lower body may have been black, upper body, neck and rim brown or red-brown); little surface preserved, traces of lustrous dark brown slip. Bottle Type D.

6. Red Polished bowl. Fig. 4.1; Swiny 1979: fig. 68:5. H: 8.0; D: 16.5. Broken, repaired, incomplete. Somewhat irregular shape; flat base (D: 8–9, not precisely circular), wide conical body with straight sides, plain rim; no lug or handle preserved. Undecorated. Soft brown to red-orange clay with one large dark gray area, thick light gray-brown core, many fine and some large inclusions and fine organic temper; traces of red-brown slip. See Chapter 4, "Unclassified Small Bowls."

Chronology

This Philia Phase tomb displays clear connections to the Chalcolithic period in the shape of bowl no. 6 and the fabric of cooking pot no. 1. The shape of the cooking pot is new in the Philia Phase, as is the horizontal handle added to spouted bowl no. 3. The fragmentary bottle no. 5 seems to be the distinctive Philia type. More elusive is the identification of no. 2, which may be a jug with cutaway spout: the preserved sherds are inconclusive, but such a jug was illustrated in Dikaios' report of his excavation.

EXCAVATIONS OF 1981 AND 1983 (fig. 3.1)

Excavations in Cemetery A undertaken in 1981 and 1983 yielded substantial amounts of artifactual, architectural and skeletal material. In 1981 a series of trial probes was opened in I4, I5, I6, I7 and I8, with only I4C and I6D yielding evidence of Bronze Age cultural activity, the most significant discovery being that of T4 in Operation I6. In 1983, the balance of tombs to be excavated was located in I4, I5, and I6.

The tomb chambers and their contents were generally quite well preserved, although all had suffered from varying degrees of roof collapse. Only one well-defined dromos was found; in some instances surface erosion may have destroyed the evidence but in other instances this feature appears to have been lacking. Most of the larger chambers contained skeletal remains and, with the exception of T20, which was sealed, but completely empty, all yielded artifacts which have been drawn on the published plans.

OPERATION I 7 (fig. 1.3)

The two probes in I 7 failed to produce evidence for funerary activities, either artifactual or architectural. The first was a narrow east–west trench, 0.5 m wide and 8.2 m long, placed along the edge of I8, near some fairly recent pits presumably dug by tomb prospectors. Hard bedrock sloping east was encountered between 20 and 50 cm below the surface. The only finds consisted of six RP Mottled sherds, and the absence of any funerary architecture demonstrated that the recent attempts to locate tombs in this area had been unsuccessful. A similar probe 5 m further north in I 7 hit bedrock just below the surface and was devoid of any finds at all.

TOMB 4 (Plan and section: fig. 3.2)

Operation I6D began as a 5 x 5 m trench 15 m south of Dikaios' Tomb 1 (fig. 3.1, top) in Cemetery A. The inhabitants of Sotira village mentioned that attempts to locate tombs had been made in the general area within the past thirty years, particularly in and around I7.

As the topsoil was removed, unusually high concentrations of large RP, RP Mottled, and DPBC sherds (n = 405) appeared throughout the operation, followed by a scatter of bone. The first of these concentrations occurred 55 cm below the surface, near a series of cuts in the bedrock associated with fragments of large tabular slabs of limestone, which could have been the remains of plakas. At a depth of 50 cm below the surface the soil became softer and sherds less common (n = 51). A more substantial cut in the bedrock, later labeled as T4, was noted close to two stones and the neck of an incised vessel.

Location and Dimensions

T4 is located approximately 17 m due south of Dikaios' T.1, just west of where the terraces reach the western slope of the valley.

The tomb chamber consists of an irregular oval, 1.84 x 0.70 m in size, aligned north–south. The maximum preserved height is 1.08 m. Although no dromos was preserved, by analogy with T1, T11, T14, and T20, the shape of the chamber suggests that one probably existed on the eastern down-slope side, which is now severely eroded.

Stratigraphy and Finds

The upper fill of T4 contained 54 sherds and a pounder (S85), found 26 cm below the conjectured roof of the chamber. Below was found a quantity of RP, RPSC and RP Mottled ware sherds (n =140) and a griddle fragment. A few pieces of human bone were mixed in the fill, with a concentration of skull fragments noted 50 cm below the preserved roof, 73 cm from the north wall. The fill to the south and southeast yielded 17 sherds, mostly RP ware, and four very fragmentary and intermixed Brown Polished bottles and RPSC flasks (#2-P26, P27, P28 and P29) as well as the remains of a RP jug (#1-P8) associated with more bone fragments and teeth. The floor of the chamber lay approximately 87 cm below roof level. Several fieldstones mixed with the tomb fill may have formed part of a wall blocking the dromos, should one have existed, but they could also have been thrown into the tomb at a later date. The upper fill of T4 was looser and sandier than that below, which was composed of compacted roof debris. The lack of in situ finds suggests that the chamber had been disturbed prior to the collapse of the roof. The chronological range of the bottles and flasks further suggests that the material was mixed since there is only evidence for one burial, albeit in a very fragmentary condition (see Chapter 10, Tomb 4).

The RPSC incised flask, P28, was partially reconstructed from sherds scattered throughout the area, above, inside, and surrounding T4. It is most likely to have come from T4, but could have originated from T5 or some other unrecorded—i.e., eroded—chamber nearby.

Catalogue

P8. Red Polished jug. Fig. 4.4; Swiny 1985a: fig. 7:1; Karageorghis 1982b: fig. 83: no. 7 from left. H:39.0; D: 24.0. Flat base, ovoid body, concave neck, flaring rim; vertical handle, oval in section, from mid-neck to upper body. Incised decoration: on handle, three transverse lines at top, "X" at mid-point. Fairly soft thick light brown clay with a small amount of black inclusions; some organic temper that

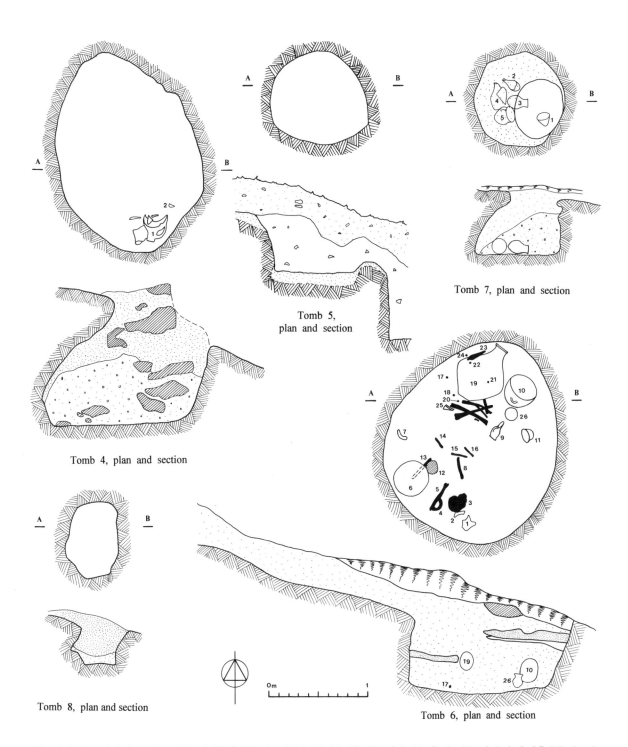

Tomb 5,
plan and section

Tomb 7, plan and section

Tomb 4, plan and section

Tomb 8, plan and section

Tomb 6, plan and section

Fig. 3.2. *Tomb 4:* **1.** RP jug, P8; *2.* RPSC flasks, P26, 27, 28, 29; *Tomb 5:* No finds. *Tomb 6:* **1–2, 25.** RP sherds; **3.** Skull; **4.** Mandible; **5.** Humerus; **6.** RP Philia ear-lug pot, P94; **7.** RP handle; **8.** Radius or ulna; **9.** RP beak-spouted juglet, P14; **10.** RP Philia spouted bowl, P52; **11.** RP bowl, P22; **12.** Rubber-pounder, S231; **13–15.** Long bones; **16.** Copper-based awl, M10; **17.** Gold hair rings, M6, M7; **18, 21.** Bronze earrings, M21, M13; **20, 22, 24.** Copper-based earrings, M23, M14, M22; **19.** RP Philia storage vessel, P53; **23.** Copper-based knife billet, M12; **26.** RP Philia ear-lug pot, P11. *Tomb 7:* **1.** RP bowl, P21; **2.** RPSC flask, P80; **3.** RPSC flask, P76; **4.** RP Mottled juglet, P12; **5.** RP cooking pot, P23; *Tomb 8.* No finds.

has burned out in firing; core not visible; rather thin somewhat lustrous slip, red-brown with brown areas; very worn, none preserved on large portion of body. Jug Type B.

P26. Red Polished South Coast flask. Fig. 4.9. H (pres.): 6.4; D: 8.0. Round, slightly flattened base, squat piriform body; neck and rim not preserved. Decoration: deep wide incision filled with white; group of four horizontal lines on upper body, groups of short oblique lines around mid-body (five preserved) and lower neck, interrupted by opposed double vertical lines. Thick soft gray clay with many small white and some black inclusions, fine organic temper, some areas of surface slightly browner; thin lustrous slip, dark gray to dark brown, worn and poorly preserved.

P27. Brown Polished bottle. Fig. 4.10. H (pres.): 6.0; D (est.): ca. 9.0. Base, neck, and rim not preserved; piriform body; no indication of handle preserved. Incised decoration with a few traces of white filling: on body, horizontal multiple (4) zigzags, groups of short parallel and dotted lines filling the spaces; multiple horizontal lines (at least 3) below neckline. Fairly soft brown clay with gray exterior surface, a few small white inclusions and some fine organic temper; thin lustrous dark brown slip with some lighter brown areas. Bottle Type A. Cf. P29.

P28. Red Polished South Coast flask. Fig. 4.9. H (pres.): 14.0; D (est.): ca.10.6. Base not preserved, body shape uncertain (probably globular), short slightly concave neck, flaring rim. Decoration (pres.): wide deep incision filled with white; lower body not preserved, double horizontal line at mid-body; on upper body, two opposed multiple (4) horizontal zigzags with opposed groups of short parallel lines between; on neck, zigzag formed by parallel lines. Soft brown clay with dark gray interior, small black and white inclusions and much fine organic temper; thin lustrous brown slip with some black areas, worn.

P29. Brown Polished bottle. Fig. 4.10. H (pres.): 13.3; D: 7.6. Round base, piriform body, slightly conical neck, flaring rim. Fine incised decoration with traces of white filling: body as P27, but with puncture-filled lozenges filling the spaces; on neck (pres.), vertical puncture-filled band, vertical double row of punctures; group of four horizontal lines below rim. Fabric as P27. Bottle Type A. Cf. P27.

Chronology

The finds associated with Tomb 4 represent a broad chronological range, in keeping with its disturbed condition. Of the five ceramic vessels sufficiently preserved to be catalogued, four are flasks or bottles, an unusual distribution that may have significance regarding the original purpose of this deposit. The two Brown Polished bottles (P27, P29) closely resemble those found in the settlement and date to early in EC III. The other three pots, including two RPSC flasks (P26, P28), should date to the previous phase of the *Kaminoudhia* cemetery, EC I/II. The jug from the tomb (P8), with a potmarked handle, has general similarities to RP I and II jugs from *Vounous*; the potmark itself has an exact parallel (reversed) at Psematismenos *Trelloukkas*. Among the sherds from Tomb 4 was the ear-lug from a RPSC ear-lug pot (cf. Stewart 1962: fig. CII:5) and other RPSC (flask?) sherds, which also probably belong to this EC I/II group. A few sherds of incised RP Philia ware were also found in this tomb.

TOMB 5 (Plan and section: fig. 3.2)

Location, dimensions, and stratigraphy

Immediately north of T4, a semi-circular cut in the bedrock yielded five RP sherds, but nothing else. Still further north, at 1 m from the mouth of T4, was found a shallow depression 90 cm in diameter and 5-10 cm in depth, which was probably the eroded floor of a small chamber, labeled T5. The gray-brown fill of the depression and that in its immediate vicinity contained a few sherds belonging to P26, most of which had been recovered from T4. Since T4 and T5 are barely one meter apart it is possible that either the tombs were looted at approximately the same time and their contents scattered in the vicinity, or that through erosion some of the ceramics from T5 were washed down-slope into the open chamber of T4.

TOMB 6 (Plan and section: fig. 3.2; pl. 3.2b)

Operation I6B was opened in 1983 in order to follow a cut in the bedrock east of T5. The topsoil consisted of backfill from the previous season's excavation, overlying the original undisturbed mixture of terra rossa and limestone containing fragments of two vessels and a number of sherds. On the east side of I6B two cuts in the bedrock suggested the possibility of a pair of chambers. In between lay an expanse of compacted chunks of limestone interpreted as the remains of a collapsed chamber roof, which after excavation proved to be that of Tomb 6.

Location and dimensions

T6 is 5 m northeast of T4 and 2.5 m southeast of the T7-T13 cluster. At floor level the chamber consisted of an irregular oval measuring 1.55 x 1.37 m, with its long axis oriented north–south. The maximum preserved height on the east side of the chamber was 80 cm. Excavation undertaken to the east of the chamber in an attempt to locate any evidence for a dromos yielded 151 sherds of different wares but no remains of a dromos, perhaps due to erosion of the bedrock. Half of the chamber lay immediately below a much-used footpath leading north from the village.

Stratigraphy and finds

Beneath the layer interpreted as collapsed roof was found a horizontal expanse of large RP body sherds (n = 137) as well as the flat bases of two vessels. Below there was a thin layer of whitish, homogenous secondary limestone containing 98 sherds. A RP bowl (# 11-P22) and a RP beak spouted jug (#9-P14) were found 80 cm below the present ground surface at the eastern limit of the excavation. At the same level, but 70 cm to the southwest, a large fragmentary RP ear-lug pot (#6-P94) was surrounded by a poorly preserved skull and long bones (#3, 4, 5, 8, 13). The skull (#3) lay on its right side, facing south and one long bone lay partially inside P94, suggesting some degree of disturbance, but not sufficient to totally disassociate the bones from their original anatomical positions. The long bones closest to the skull were humeri, with radii and ulnas (#8, 14, 15) closer to the concentration of leg bones to the north. Next to P94 lay a discoidal rubber-pounder (#12-S231). Articulation of the skull and mandible produced several miniature red and white beads, approximately 3 mm in diameter, augmented by numerous other (n = 646) beads and three spacers (of a total of six) recovered from water sieving of the surrounding fill, all of which were catalogued as S208, a bead necklace with spacers. Several human teeth were found, and since they are not associated with either the skull cavity or the mandible, they provide further evidence for some form of disturbance.

A concentration of hard white limestone similar to the bedrock walls was noted in the approximate center of the cavity and interpreted as the remains of the collapsed chamber roof. North and northwest of this deposit were found an ear-lug pot (#26-P11) and a RP spouted bowl (#10-P52), lying next to a large half preserved RP storage vessel (#19-P53). P53 lay slightly above a concentration of human long bones roughly arranged in anatomical order (pl. 3.2c), surrounded by a scatter of metal artifacts consisting of an awl (#16-M10) found near where the pelvis should have been, the billet of a dagger (#23-M12) from the northern edge of the chamber, and a scatter of bronze and copper-based spiral earrings (#18, #20, #21, #22, #24 = M21, M23, M13, M14, M22) extending over an area of about 45 cm in diameter. On the west side of this scatter was found a pair of interlocked gold earrings (#17-M6 and M7: pl.3.3a), identical in shape, and a scatter of miniature beads, probably part of S208, the same necklace mentioned in connection with the skull #3. Two spacers were associated with the beads in this area.

The floor in the southern half of the tomb consisted of bedrock gently sloping southward. Chunks of limestone, perhaps part of the roof, were intermingled with the fill in the north side of the chamber. Despite the effects of erosion, most of the artifacts were in good condition. Erosion, not systematic looting, seemed to have been the primary agent of disturbance here since a number of intrinsically valuable items were recovered and the bones remained in roughly anatomically correct positions. It was clear that the single skeleton had been laid out on its right side in a flexed position facing east. Why the hair ornaments and a substantial number of beads were found in the vicinity of the feet remains unexplained. It should be noted that some beads were found in the vicinity of the skull where their presence could be explained as that of a necklace. The beads near the feet could plausibly have been part of anklets, but this does not provide a satisfactory explanation for the earrings so frequently found in association with skulls. Since there is no evidence for a second burial with its skull placed in this part of the chamber, it can only be suggested that these intrinsically valuable offerings/ornaments, along with the dagger billet, were carefully placed at the feet of the deceased.

Catalogue (pl. 3.6a)

P11. Red Polished Philia ear-lug pot. Fig. 4.12; Karageorghis 1984: fig. 133:3; Swiny 1986a: fig. 1:31. H: 10.5; D: 9.0. Crudely shaped with irregular surface, stands off-axis; small flat base, squat inverted piriform body, wide concave neck, slightly flaring rim; two opposed horizontal lug handles (?), not preserved, on upper body; two opposed holes (D: ca. 0.5) below rim. Crude incised decoration, filling uncertain: horizontal herringbone band at mid-body and neck, double broken vertical zigzags on upper body and lower neck. Thick hard red-brown clay with thick dark gray core, some gray, black, or brown areas, fairly large black, gray, and white inclusions; fairly thick dark red-brown slip, now matt and poorly preserved. See Chapter 4, "Unclassified Ear-lug pot."

P14. Red Polished juglet. Fig. 4.7; Karageorghis 1984: fig. 133:1. H: 18.1; D: 10.0. Wide flat base, slightly articulated by pinching; globular body, conical neck, beak spout (rim chipped); vertical handle, round in section, from rim to upper body. Undecorated. Fabric as P11 but slightly softer, more brown areas; core not visible; slip as P11, with black and brown areas, worn and poorly preserved, especially on body. Juglet Type D.

P22. Red Polished bowl. Fig. 4.1; Karageorghis 1984: fig. 133:2. H: 8.4; D: 11.7. Crudely formed, irregular shape; flat base, deep globular body, slightly flaring rim (chipped). Undecorated. Soft brown clay, core not visible, with small amount of black and white inclusions, impressions of organic material (straw and seeds?) in surface; thin red-brown slip, now matt, worn and poorly preserved. Bowl Type H.

P52. Red Polished Philia spouted bowl. Fig. 4.3; Karageorghis 1984: fig. 133:5; Swiny 1986a: fig. 1:21. H: 23.0; D: 27.7. Flat base, inverted piriform body, plain incurving rim; tubular spout with plain end rising diagonally from below rim; horizontal handle below rim at point of greatest diameter, round in section, with wide groove on outside. Undecorated. Hard well-fired light gray-brown clay, slightly grayer in thick areas, with a small amount of small black and white inclusions; fairly thick dark red-brown slip, worn and surface damaged, burnished irregularly ("stroke-burnished") on interior and exterior. Spouted Bowl Type A.

P53. Red Polished Philia storage vessel. Fig. 4.14. Karageorghis 1984: fig. 133:4. H: 48.5; D: ca. 43.5. About half preserved; flat base, rather squat ovoid body, wide conical neck, slightly flaring rim; one (preserved) horizontal handle, round in section, on upper body. Undecorated. Medium hard brown clay with gray core, moderate amount of small black and white inclusions; fairly thick dark red-brown slip, now matt and worn. Storage vessel Type A.

P94. Red Polished Philia ear-lug pot ("mosque lamp"). Fig. 4.12. H (est.): ca. 40; D (est.): ca. 25. Extremely fragmentary, incomplete; flat (?) base, inverted piriform body, short conical neck, plain rim; handle(s?) not preserved, from mid-neck to upper body. Incised decoration (pres.): appears to be on upper body and neck only; multiple parallel lines, some with "feather" borders and herringbones. Very soft light red-brown clay with thick dark gray interior, many white and gray inclusions; traces of thick lustrous dark red slip; surface extremely worn and damaged. Ear-lug pot Type C.

M6. Earring. Fig. 8.3; pls. 8.d, 8.e; Karageorghis 1984:938, fig. 134; Swiny 1986a:38, fig. 3:18; Swiny 1995:33; Swiny 1997:191, fig. II: 9. D. (of spiral): ca. 1.3, W: 1.1, Th.: 0.03. Electrum. One of an identical pair. One end pointed, the other flattened.

M7. Earring. (Same references as above). D: (of spiral) ca. 1.3, W: 0.9, Th.: 0.3. Electrum. Identical in shape to M6 above, except that the spiral turns in the opposite direction to form an antithetical pair.

M10. Awl. Fig. 8.1. L: 8.5, W: 0.5, Th.: 0.4. Intact. Copper-based. Rectangular in section, the tang is thicker and less tapering than the other extremity.

M12. Dagger billet. Fig. 8.2; pls. 8.1b, 8.1c; Swiny 1989:189 (3rd from right); Swiny 1995:32 (3rd from right). L: 6.2, W: 2, Th.: 1. Intact. Copper-based. See detailed description and references in Chapter 8.

M13. Earring. Fragmentary. D: .4, Th.: 0.2. Copper-based. One end pointed, the other flattened.

M14. Earring. Fragmentary. D: 1.2, Th.: 0.2. Copper-based. See M13 above.

M21. Earring. Fragmentary. L: 1, W: 6.5, Th.: 1.3. Tin bronze. Identical in shape to M6 and M7.

M22. Earring. Eight fragments from 0.7 long to 0.6 wide; Th.: 0.1. Copper-based. See M6 above for shape.

M23. Earring. Seven fragments from 0.6 long to 0.2 wide; Th.: 0.1. Copper-based. See M6 above for shape.

S208. Beads and spacers. Fig. 6.16, S208: 1-5l; Swiny 1995:35. Jasper, white limestone, siltstone, and picrolite. Six hundred forty-six with single perforations and six spacers with three perforations each. See more detailed description in lithic catalogue and discussion in Chapter 6, "Necklace."

S231. Rubber-pounder, Type 2. Igneous. Intact. L: 11.3, W: 9.0, Th: 4.2. Discoidal. Fine-grained, dark gray. Both faces smooth from rubbing. Both ends and circumference pitted and slightly faceted from pounding. This object has a very regular shape.

Chronology

Tomb 6, with its distinctive features of the typical "mosque lamp" (P94), the crude truncated juglet (P14), beak spout fragments (Jug F) and multiple spiral earrings, is probably the best example of a Philia Phase tomb found by the CAARI excavations. Similar small beads are well attested in the Philia Phase, although they also have a long subsequent history (cf. Tomb 18 below; Swiny 1986:30; Stewart 1962:260, fig. 105:1–4).

TOMB 7 (Plan and section: fig. 3.2; pl. 3.3c)

Location and dimensions

Tomb 7 is upslope, 3.6 m northwest of T6, in a cluster formed with Tombs 8, 9, 12, and 13. The average diameter of the tomb chamber at floor level was approximately 80 cm. The maximum preserved height from the floor to the overhang above was 50 cm. Access to the chamber was via an oval aperture of 54 x 46 cm with its long axis aligned north–south. No evidence for a dromos was recorded and in view of the curvature of the roof, it is very unlikely that one ever existed.

Stratigraphy

Removal of the topsoil in the area north of T6 revealed two cuts in the bedrock 5 cm below the present surface. Beneath an initial layer of loose, reddish topsoil, a much harder layer of buff/white secondary limestone sloped westwards, down from a lip in the bedrock towards the opposite side of the oval aperture which provided access to the chamber.

Finds

The chamber contained six RP vessels of varying size and shape: a bowl (#1-P21) lay immediately beneath the mouth of the chamber, with the rest—two incised flasks (#2-P80 and #3-P76), a cutaway spouted juglet (#4-P12) and a cooking pot (#5-P23)—clustered beneath the overhang, but without apparent order. Inside the cooking pot was found P31, a finely incised deep conical bowl.

Water sieving of the contents of the chamber failed to produce a single bead or so much as a sliver of bone, which suggests two ways of interpreting the deposit. The first is that no interment had taken place here despite the presence of six vessels of types frequently deposited in graves. The second, more likely interpretation is that the small chamber belonged to an infant or neo-natal whose soft bones and teeth have completely decayed. This interpretation is slightly weakened by the absence of the cusps, some of which normally survive decomposition even when they belong to neo-natals. No concrete evidence favors one or the other interpretation. If the chamber had been approached via a dromos, it has now been fully eroded; alternatively, it is quite possible that dromoi were judged unnecessary for small pits of this nature, which could still have been sealed by a plaka.

Catalogue (pl. 3.6b)

P12. Red Polished Mottled juglet. Fig. 4.7. H: 23; D: 12. Flat base, ovoid body, conical neck, short cutaway spout; vertical handle, round in section, from rim to upper body. Conical knob to right of lower handle attachment, otherwise undecorated. Fairly hard brown clay with many black, gray and white inclusions; fairly thick dark red-brown slip, traces of luster, much worn, small dark gray areas. Juglet Type C.

P21. Red Polished bowl. Fig. 4.1. H: 9.9; D: 12.9. Small flat base, deep inverted conical body, plain rim; pointed pierced vertical lug at rim. Undecorated. Hard brown clay (interior not visible), straw impression on exterior; fairly thick matt slip, mottled red-brown, brown, dark gray and black; worn on base; smear marks on interior and exterior. Bowl Type A.

P23. Red Polished cooking pot. Fig. 4.15. H: 16.3; D: 13.5. Flat base, ovoid body, short wide slightly concave neck with slightly flaring rim; two opposed vertical handles, oval in section, from rim to upper body. Undecorated. Thick rather soft red-brown clay with many black, gray and white inclusions; core not visible; may have been cracked in firing; fairly thick red-brown slip, with a little luster, many black areas; straw and seed (?) impressions in surface, fingerprint in slip near base; surface worn and damaged. Cooking Pot Type A.

P31. Red Polished South Coast conical bowl. Fig. 4.8; Swiny 1995:31 (lower left). H: 8.3; D: 7.1. Round-pointed base, deep inverted conical body, plain rim; two opposed hooked lugs on rim. Decoration: wide deep white-filled incision; group of horizontal lines at mid-body and below rim either side, groups of parallel oblique lines on lower body, rows of punctures on either side of upper body; below lugs, groups of punctures. Fairly soft clay with small black and white inclusions, mostly gray, brown at top; thin lustrous slip, mostly black, red-brown at top; worn.

P76. Red Polished South Coast flask. Fig. 4.8; Swiny 1995:31 (lower right). H: 20.0; D: 13.1. Flat base, inverted piriform body, slightly conical neck, flaring rim; two holes (preserved) side-by-side below rim; only half preserved. Decoration (preserved): same style as P31, above, probably by same hand; wide deep incision with traces of white filling; on body, group of five vertical lines below holes, two large groups of parallel oblique lines either side; on neck, two groups of semicircular punctures below holes, multiple horizontal lines either side; groups of vertical lines below rim either side of holes. Fairly soft dark gray clay with brown exterior surface, small black and white inclusions; thin lustrous brown slip with some dark gray areas, slightly worn, possibly some organic impressions.

P80. Red Polished South Coast flask. Fig. 4.8. H: 16.8; D: 9.8. Small flat base, inverted piriform body, conical neck, slightly flaring rim; most of rim and part of body not preserved. Decoration (preserved): wide deep incision with traces of white filling; groups of horizontal lines at lower body (3), point of greatest diameter (4) and neckline (4); middle group has row of short vertical lines below; on neck, only a group of oblique parallel lines preserved. Quite soft dark gray clay with some light brown areas, a few small black and white inclusions; small amount of thin lustrous brown slip preserved; probably most slip was black, but none preserved; surface very worn and damaged.

Chronology

Tomb 7, dating to EC I/II, contained the only conical bowl (P31) found by the CAARI excavations. This shape can be compared to "tulip bowls" of EC I and II at *Vounous* and other sites, although P31 is smaller than most of them and bears the regional RPSC style of decoration. The cooking pot (P23) is an early type, but clearly shows its derivation from the Philia cooking pot (Type B, e.g., P91) and is different from early cooking pots from *Vounous*.[8] Small bowl P21 resembles RP I bowls from *Vounous*, while retaining a flat base. Of the two RPSC flasks (P76, P80), P80 particularly shows descent from Philia Phase flask shapes and style of decoration.

TOMB 8 (Plan and section: fig. 3.2)

Location and dimensions

T8 belongs to the same cluster as T7 and is 1 m to the northeast of the latter and 0.6 m east of T12. It consisted of a roughly circular, straight-sided depression approximately 50 cm in diameter and 30 cm deep. There was no evidence for an associated dromos.

Stratigraphy and finds

The cist was about 5 cm below the surface of the footpath leading north from Sotira Village. Buff colored, undifferentiated secondary limestone filled the entire depression.

The only finds consisted of two pieces of dentalium shell, a fragmentary Brown Polished bottle (P79) and four RP sherds from a larger vessel which were perhaps intrusive. No skeletal remains, including teeth, were recovered despite water sieving all the material within the cist.

T8 was the smallest and most eroded cist grave to contain putative funerary offerings. The problems associated with the interpretation of these small chambers are discussed at the end of the chapter, under "Conclusions."

Catalogue

P79. Brown Polished bottle or juglet. Extremely fragmentary and poorly preserved. Probably Bottle Type B; very similar to P98 (Tomb 12).

Chronology

The only pot found in this tomb, the Brown Polished bottle, dates the deposit to the EC III period, approximately contemporary with the date of the settlement.

TOMB 9 (Plan and section: fig. 3.4)

Location and Dimensions

Tomb 9 is located immediately north of T8 and east of T12. It consisted of an irregular oval depression measuring 80 x 95 cm, with its long axis aligned north–south. The floor of the cist slopes sharply from the east down to its maximum depth of 45 cm in the west. Since erosion had destroyed the

---

[8] Which have a small articulated base: cf. Stewart 1962: figs. CXX:12–14, CXXI:1–9.

upper part of the chamber, the original shape remains undetermined, as well as any evidence for a dromos.

Stratigraphy and Finds

The fill of the chamber consisted of a mixture of soft eroded limestone and terra rossa. The finds lay on bedrock, between 40 and 50 cm below the present ground surface.

Two fragmentary vessels, a RPSC flask (#1-P32) and a RP bowl (#2-P17), were recovered from the cist. Water sieving failed to yield any skeletal remains and in this respect T9 is closely comparable to T7 and T8.

Catalogue

P17. Red Polished bowl. Fig. 4.1. H: 13.5; H (rim): 11.4; D: 16.0. Approximately half preserved; flat base, deep ovoid body, plain rim; small horizontal handle, round in section, rising vertically from rim. No decoration preserved. Soft red-brown clay with gray core in thickest place (base); medium amount of large black, white and gray inclusions; straw impression; traces of quite thick lustrous red-brown slip, surface very worn and damaged. Bowl Type A.

P32. Red Polished South Coast flask. Fig. 4.8; Swiny 1995:31 (bottom, second from right). H (pres.): ca. 19; D: 11.5. Flat base, globular body, conical neck, rim not preserved. Decoration: deep wide white-filled incision; on body, two opposed groups of vertical lines with a horizontal zigzag of parallel lines between, group of horizontal lines above zigzag, double vertical row of punctures on one side, zigzag repeated on neck. Soft thick red-brown clay with gray exterior surface, dark gray core, many large white and gray inclusions; small amount of thin dark brown slip preserved, with some traces of luster preserved; surface very worn and damaged.

Chronology

A probable date for this deposit is provided by the RPSC flask (P32), placing it in EC I/II. The bowl (P17) still has a flat base, but the appearance of a (somewhat rudimentary) horizontal handle at the rim may preview the later common type of small bowl (cf. e.g., Todd 1986: fig. 26: 2–10).

TOMB 10 (Plan and section: fig. 3.3; pl. 3.3b)

Investigations in the northern part of Operation I4C produced many RP Mottled sherds, probably washed down from disturbed tombs on the western slopes above. In the center of the operation, a large tabular slab of limestone resembling a plaka in shape and size was propped up at a 45° angle, suggesting the presence of a tomb chamber in this area. South of the plaka a circular area of softer material contained a few sherds and small patch of ash which extended down to bedrock, but was probably secondary and the result of an open pit at some stage in the past.

Location and Dimensions

T10 is located 6 m northwest of T14 and the main cluster of tombs in Cemetery A. The exact size and shape of T10 remain to be determined since the hardness of the deposit combined with the sparseness and fragmentary state of the finds caused the operation to be halted before excavation of the entire area which might have encompassed a chamber. The identification of the large limestone slab set at a 45° angle as a plaka is convincing; the accumulation of the surrounding hard-packed deposit had prevented it from falling to a horizontal position. The southern edge of the tomb was clearly defined in bedrock and the postulated western edge rises to a height considerably above the present level of the plaka. Any further funerary remains should be sought in this area. The northern edge of the chamber was not determined; although the northeastern quadrant did curve down to intersect with the plaka. Excavations to the east of the latter revealed only bedrock, indicating that the dromos had long since been eroded. No evidence for the tomb roof, even in the form of an incipient inward curvature of the walls, was recorded.

Stratigraphy and finds

It is likely that there was a burial chamber west of the plaka because a depression appeared immediately after removal of the topsoil. The first object encountered within the depression was a RP spouted bowl (#1-P64) standing upright in a limestone matrix identical to that of the surrounding bedrock in terms of both density and color. This visual similarity of secondary fill and bedrock complicated the excavation of the tomb in general and the defining of its walls in particular. The next object to be discovered, immediately north of P64, was a badly crushed ear-lug pot (#2-P65) with incised decoration. To the north of P65, a RP cooking pot (#3-P66) lay on its side next to a rubbing stone (#4-S288). If in situ, the latter offers a rare occurrence of a stone tool in a funerary context, but the chamber is so eroded that it may not belong to the original deposit. Poorly preserved human long bones and rib fragments were found just below P64 and P65, further strengthening the funerary nature of the ceramics found within the depression.

To all appearances this chamber had suffered roof collapse resulting in its contents being exposed to the elements and probable disturbance by human agency, followed by the gradual infilling of the cavity with compacted secondary limestone interspersed with lenses of terra rossa. The compacted nature of the fill suggests that the process had occurred in the distant past.

Catalogue

P64. Red Polished Philia spouted bowl. Fig. 4.3. H: 21.5; D: 22.0. Flat base, deep ovoid body, plain rim; tubular spout with plain end rising diagonally from below rim; horizontal handle, round in section, at mid-body opposite spout. Undecorated. Thick soft brown clay with many black and white inclusions, core not visible; fairly thick lustrous red-brown slip with some brown and black areas. Spouted Bowl Type A.

P65. Red Polished Philia ear-lug pot (?). H (pres.): 31.5; D (base): 9.4. Crushed and fragmentary, incomplete, not restored; flat base, body and neck shape indeterminate, flaring rim; handle not preserved. Incised decoration (preserved): multiple herringbone pattern and zigzags on upper body. Probably Ear-lug pot Type C.

P66. Red Polished cooking pot. D (rim): ca. 18.0. Broken, incomplete, not restored; base not preserved, body not restored, short wide concave neck, slightly flaring rim; two opposed vertical handles, approximately round in section, from rim to upper body. No decoration preserved. Hard red-brown clay with dark gray core, many small black, white and gray inclusions; fairly thick dark red-brown mottled slip, now matt and poorly preserved, surface damaged. Cooking Pot Type B. Cf. P91 (Tomb 15).

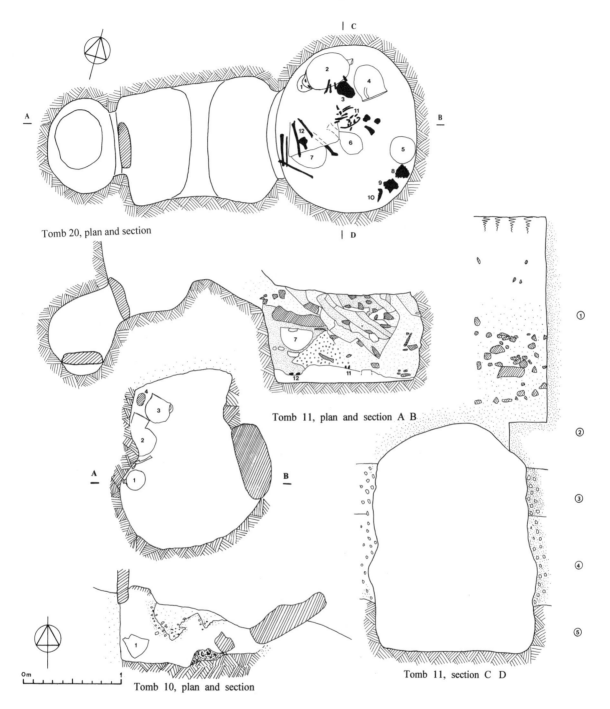

Tomb 20, plan and section

Tomb 11, plan and section A B

Tomb 11, section C D

Tomb 10, plan and section

Fig. 3.3. *Tomb 10:* **1.** RP Philia spouted bowl, P64; **2.** RP Philia ear-lug pot, P65; **3.** RP cooking pot, P66; **4.** Rubbing stone, S288. *Tomb 11:* Section C-D from topsoil to bottom of chamber, (1) Terrace fill, (2) Brown sediment, (3) Dark brown sediment with many small stones, (4) Yellow lime-rich sediment with many stones, (5) Secondary limestone. *Tomb 11:* 1. RP bowl, P47; **2.** RP spouted bowl, P63; **3.** Skull; **4.** RP cooking pot, P92; **5.** RP bowl, P56; **6.** RP jug, P57; **7.** RP jug, P58; **8–10.** Faunal remains (Fragments of skull, 8, 9; Mandible, 10); **11.** Rib and pelvis fragments; **12.** Long bones. *Tomb 20:* No finds other than a single fieldstone.

S288. Rubbing stone. Igneous. Fragmentary. L: 10.0, W: 8.0, Th.: 5.5. Ovoid in shape and sections. Fine-grained, light gray/brown.

Chronology

The sparse remains recovered from Tomb 10 included three vessels of Philia types: the spouted bowl (P64), a probable ear-lug pot of "mosque lamp" type (P65), and a cooking pot (P66). The tomb appears to be roughly contemporary with Tombs 6 and 15.

TOMB 11 (Plan and sections: fig. 3.3; pls. 3.4a, 3.4c)

Location and Dimensions

Tomb 11 is located immediately east of T20 with which it shares the same dromos. It lies 25 m northeast of T6 in the middle of the artificial terrace spanning the narrow valley between Cemeteries A and B. The floor of the chamber lay 4 m below the present surface of the terrace.

The overall dimensions of the oval chamber at floor level were 1.54 m on the long north–south axis with a width of 1.26 m. The original maximum height of the chamber remained undetermined, but by analogy with T20, it must have been at least 1.5 m. The dromos was 1 m wide and measured 56 cm from the step leading down into the dromos to the stomion, which was 70 cm above the floor of the chamber.

Stratigraphy

The circumstances of discovery of T11 were unusual in that it was found as the result of a probe sunk by one of the expedition's geologists, J. Gifford, to define the stratigraphic sequence of soil deposition in the terrace separating the two cemeteries. The trench opened for this purpose measured 1.5 x 1 m and was intended to be excavated down to bedrock. At a depth of 1.86 m in the northeast corner of the probe, an underground cavity was discovered when the floor caved in to reveal a 20 cm void between hard-packed sediment and a cone of loose fill and fieldstones. On the west side of the cavity a dromos cut was just discernible. The ensuing excavation determined that the loose sterile mix of fieldstones and fill (probably a mixture of terrace soil and natural sediment) was 1.1 m thick and overlay 0.8 m of material that had been washed or eroded into the chamber. All artifacts were recovered from the lower layers of fill (see fig. 3.3, T11, section) which consist of five or six lenses of brown, pale brown, pale yellow, and light gray soil that had eroded into the chamber via the stomion after a considerable amount of silt had already been washed in, presumably around the edges of the ill-fitting plaka. A tabular, irregularly shaped slab of limestone with a maximum length of 52 cm and average thickness of 12 cm lay with other limestone cobbles below and between the lenses and the stomion. The relative positions of the slab and the lenses suggest that the former was the plaka which broke and then fell inwards, thus allowing material to erode into the chamber. Below the slab lay a RP jug (#7-P58), 30 cm above the chamber floor, human bone fragments, and a RP jug (#6-P57, not in the section). It is obvious that considerable silting had already occurred before the plaka fell—or was pushed—into the chamber. The skeletal remains and all the vessels, with the exception of P92, lay on a layer of silt up to 20 cm thick covering the chamber floor.

The dromos had probably been cut into the havara lying under the surface formed by the hard, dark brown sediment with many small stones—level (3) in the section on fig. 3.3—which was probably a paleosol. The layer of havara in formation (4) made up about half of the chamber. The artificial terrace above (1) merged imperceptibly with the fine light brown sediment (2) covering the floor of the valley, in this area at least, at the time of the terrace building, empirically determined as Roman or Byzantine. The fine sediment of which (2) is composed may be the result of soil erosion caused by agricultural activity prior to the placement of the terrace.

It would appear that despite considerable silting, a substantial air cavity remained within the upper part of the chamber of T11, the entrance to which was somehow blocked prior to the transport and deposition of soil for the terrace. At some stage the roof collapsed, and the cavity moved upwards like an air bubble in water. This process, in the writer's opinion, best explains the existence of a cavity well *above* the original roof of the chamber, some 2.1 m from the floor. No EC or MC tomb chamber anywhere on the island has been recorded as having an interior height of over 2 m, therefore it is extremely unlikely that T11 would be an exception by such a large margin.

After the single burial had been deposited, the chamber seems to have remained undisturbed while silt gradually filtered in via the stomion, perhaps adding to material eroding from the soft, yellow, lime-rich walls above the limestone bedrock. Some pots, such as the large jug #7-P58, seem to have remained on top of the silt layer (see section fig. 3.3), while others retained their floor level positions. At this stage of the tomb's existence the plaka fell in or was pushed in immediately on top of P58, which allowed for the presumably rapid, and certainly well differentiated, layers of silt to accumulate at an angle sloping down from the stomion. This process, which must have occurred either before or (more plausibly) during the building of the terraces, would also have involved the filling of the dromos. If the plaka was moved in the course of building the overlaying terrace, then the fill consists of intentionally dumped terrace building material filling a tomb that was not considered worth emptying of its contents,[9] since the burial and grave goods were not visibly disturbed, either by erosion or human agency.

The dromos on the western side of the chamber was full of light yellowish brown (2.5Y 6/4) sterile soil without visible internal stratification. The difference between the fill of the dromos and chamber argues against them being of the same origin.

Finds

Although the skeletal remains were poorly preserved, they were nevertheless sufficient to determine that a single burial had been laid out in a flexed position on its right side with the skull (#3) to the left of the entrance. A RP bowl (#1-P47) lay opposite the rib cage in front of the skeleton next to a large spouted bowl (#2-P63) that once had been propped up against the side of the chamber, immediately behind the skull. Under P63 lay P45, a bowl similar in size and shape to P47. In the area of the feet, but above them, was found a large RP jug (#7-P58) and another RP jug (#6-P57) had been placed at the back of the skeleton along with a RP cooking pot (#4-P92) behind the skull. A RP bowl (#5-P56) was found next to the wall in the southeast quadrant of the chamber along with a concentration of faunal remains (#8-10) consisting of skull and mandible fragments. These last were probably food offerings for the deceased (see Chapter 11).

Despite the depth of deposit covering the burial and attendant grave goods, the bones and the pottery in particular, with the exception of P63, were extremely poorly preserved even for *Kaminoudhia*. Was this caused by above average quantities of lime-rich ground water seeping into the chamber that

---

[9] Had some of the tombs been investigated or destroyed in the course of terrace building, which seems inevitable, their contents at that time would surely have been considered of little intrinsic value by comparison with the far more lucrative rewards of rifling metal-rich Iron Age cemeteries. For this reason the builders of the terrace may not have bothered to investigate the chamber.

lay in the bottom of the valley in the path of seasonal runoff, or were the ceramics deposited in the chamber unusually poorly fired? The former explanation seems the most plausible.

Catalogue

P45. Red Polished bowl. Fig. 4.1; Barlow and Vaughan 1999: pl. IVf. H: 7.4; D: 12.6. Small flat base, hemispherical body, plain rim; pointed vertical lug at rim, pierced from either side with a very small hole (does not appear to go all the way through). Undecorated. Fairly soft red-brown (?) clay with many small black, white and gray inclusions (interior fabric not visible); fairly thick dark red-brown slip with some luster preserved, a few small brown and black areas; surface worn. Bowl Type B.

P47. Red Polished bowl. H: 10.3; D: 13.8. Small flat base, ovoid body, plain rim; vertical slightly pointed lug at rim, unpierced. Undecorated. Soft fine brown clay with dark gray core in some places, a few very small black and white inclusions, fine organic temper; thin lustrous dark red-brown slip with a few small black and brown areas. Bowl Type A.

P56. Red Polished bowl. Fig. 4.1. H: 7.8; D: 22.2. Cracked and very fragile; flat base, shallow conical body, plain rim; narrow horizontal ledge lug preserved at rim, other lugs possible but rim inadequately preserved. Undecorated. Very soft fine light brown clay with light gray core, many white and some gray and black inclusions; thick lustrous dark red-brown slip, little preserved, surface worn and damaged. Bowl Type C.

P57. Red Polished jug. Fig. 4.6. H: 38.0; D: 28.0. Flat base, ovoid body, conical neck, flaring rim; vertical handle, oval in section, from mid-neck to upper body. Undecorated. Very soft fine light brown clay with thick gray interior, many white and some black and gray inclusions; rather uneven lustrous dark red-brown slip with some brown and black areas, worn. Jug Type D.

P58. Red Polished jug. Fig. 4.4. H (pres.): ca. 45; D: ca. 30. Wide flat base, body incomplete, inverted conical neck, flaring (? not preserved) rim; vertical handle, oval in section, from mid-neck to upper body. Decoration: neat, smooth and deep incision on handle, opposed interlocking vertical zigzags (3 X's in a vertical row). Very soft light brown clay with light gray interior, small amount of large black, white and gray inclusions; rather thin, uneven slip, red-brown with some brown areas, some luster. Jug Type A. Cf. P3 (Cemetery B).

P63. Red Polished large spouted bowl. Fig. 4.3. H: 16.5; D: 41.0. Flat base, wide conical body, plain rim; short tubular spout with flaring end, rising diagonally from below rim; semicircular horizontal ledge lug rising diagonally from rim opposite spout, pierced with two holes. Undecorated. Hard dark red-brown clay with many small black and white inclusions, interior fabric not visible; thick lustrous dark red-brown slip with small black areas; worn in places, especially on base, as though used. Spouted Bowl Type C.

P92. Red Polished cooking pot. D (base): ca. 7.3; D (rim): ca. 24. Fragmentary, not restored; very thick-walled vessel; flat base, apparently globular body, wide plain flaring rim with rounded edge; two opposed (?) vertical handles, thick oval in section, from rim to upper body. Decoration: finger impression at lower handle attachment (only one preserved). Very soft red-orange clay with many large white and gray inclusions; thick dark red-brown slip with dark gray areas on interior and exterior, some luster; worn especially on interior. Unclassified Cooking Pot.

Chronology

Tomb 11 has been dated EC III, although none of the certain diagnostic features of this phase at *Kaminoudhia* is present. The jug P58 has been classified as Type A, although its decoration is careless and less developed than that customary for Type A jugs. Narrow necked jugs (cf. P57) become common on the north coast in EC III, although the closest parallels to P57 are without secure provenience. The presence of P57 and P58 in the same tomb deposit demonstrates the variety of jugs in contemporaneous use. The small bowl P56 and the spouted bowl P63 display the shallower shape and ledge lugs that become common in EC III, while still retaining flat bases. Parallels to P56 occur in Kalavasos Tomb 46 and in the EC III levels at Marki; parallels to P63 are found in Alambra Tomb 102 and Lapithos Tomb 302B, both dated EC III. Cooking pot P92 was not restored, but there was no indication that one handle was larger than the other: if so, this vessel may represent the earlier Type A.

TOMB 12 (Plan and section: fig. 3.4)

Location

This is the largest and most important chamber of the cluster, of which it occupies the northwest corner, 6 m to the northwest of T6. In this area, the bedrock slopes up more steeply to the west. T9 was separated by 10–15 cm from the east edge of T12, which provides an idea of the clustering in this area.

Dimensions

The decanter-shaped, oval chamber with its longest axis pointing north–south measured 2 m x 1.6 m, with a maximum depth from the mouth to the south sloping floor of approximately 1.4 m. The mouth of the chamber, as preserved, was circular with a diameter of about 90 cm, roughly 20 cm below the ground level at the time of excavation, but erosion has certainly increased its dimensions due to the softness of the bedrock in this area.

No evidence for a dromos was found around the mouth of the chamber and it would seem that the large plaka lying close by to the west had once sealed its opening. The deep accumulation of soil around the plaka suggests that it had not been removed from its original position in the recent past.

Stratigraphy

The chamber contained fine eroded limestone with light brown lumps of havara and some larger fieldstones. A greater concentration of fieldstones was found in the upper layer (see section fig. 3.4), which probably represents a separate episode of erosion beginning after the removal of the plaka or some other more recent disturbance. At 30 cm below the chamber's mouth a Roman sherd indicated that the upper level had certainly been contaminated. The rest of this level and that below, extending down to the scatter of fieldstones, contained few sherds (n= 4).

Beneath this southward trending layer, there was a lime-rich, fine-grained deposit, which extended down to the stratum of fieldstones and pebbles covering the funerary deposit. Whether this material was intentionally thrown into the chamber after burial as backfill or whether it represents gradual silting of the unsealed chamber is impossible to say, but it is denser and finer than the upper layer which it obviously predates.

Finds

Below the compact layer of rock fragments there was a mixture of limestone chunks of different hardness in a matrix darker than that above the rock lens, sealing a scatter of sherds from a single large RP jug (#8-P99), crushed in situ on the floor almost in the center of the chamber and associated with a small quantity of human bone. Also scattered around the floor were the better preserved remains of six vessels: two RP bowls (#1-P84 and #6-P97), a RP amphora (#2-P100), a DPBC tankard (#3-P95), a RP spouted bowl (#4-P96), and a Brown Polished bottle (#5-P98). A rubber-pounder (#7-S635) was found in the northern part of the chamber, as well as a terracotta spindle whorl (#9) nearer the center. Insufficient human bone was preserved to determine the original orientation of the burial.

Catalogue (pl. 3.6c)

P84. Red Polished Mottled bowl. Fig. 4.1. H: 12.1; H (rim): 10.9; D: 17.1. Small flat base, ovoid body, plain slightly incurving rim; small horizontal handle, oval in section, rising diagonally from rim; slightly horned horizontal ledge lug on rim opposite handle, pierced twice; when resting on base, bowl is considerably off-axis. Undecorated. Hard brown clay with small black and white inclusions, straw impression; thick mostly lustrous slip, red-brown mottled with black, brown and dark pink, well preserved with signs of wear around base and handle. Bowl Type B.

P95. Drab Polished Blue Core tankard. Fig. 4.7. H: 21.0; D: 15.2. Round base, globular body, wide cylindrical neck, flaring rim; vertical handle, thick oval in section, from rim to upper body. Undecorated. Very hard fine blue gray clay with light orange surface, quite a few small straw impressions; thin matt light orange slip with a pinkish-gray area on side of body. Tankard Type A.

P96. Red Polished Mottled spouted bowl. Fig. 4.3; Swiny 1986a: fig. 1:32. H: 17.4; D: 24.2. Flat base, deep ovoid body, plain rim; small vertical handle, oval in section, from rim to upper body; short tubular spout with flaring end rising diagonally from below rim. Undecorated. Fairly hard brown clay with many small black and white inclusions; thick dark red-brown slip with large dark gray area on either side; base worn. Spouted Bowl Type B.

P97. Red Polished Mottled bowl. Fig. 4.1. H: 9.1; D: 13.5. Small flat base, ovoid body, plain rim. Undecorated. Hard brown clay with many small black and white inclusions; thick somewhat lustrous slip, dark red-brown mottled with dark gray, light gray, light brown and dark pink; rim and base worn. Bowl Type A.

P98. Brown Polished bottle. Fig. 4.10. H (pres.): 14.5; D: 8.9. Round base, globular body, inverted conical neck, flaring rim; two opposed holes below rim. Fine incised decoration: on body, a horizontal panel framed by groups of three horizontal lines, containing a horizontal double zigzag filled with groups of transverse lines (almost a checkered effect); on neck, three groups of three horizontal lines, one at neck bottom, two on upper half, and on lower neck a multiple herringbone motif alternating with a checker-filled lozenge (two each); groups of short oblique lines below rim. Fine soft light gray to light brown clay with a small amount of small white and a few dark red inclusions; traces of thin lustrous black to dark brown slip; surface worn. Bottle Type B. Cf. P79 (Tomb 8).

P99. Red Polished large jug. Fig. 4.4. H: 43.5; D: 31.6. Broken, repaired; flat base, ovoid body, conical neck, flaring rim with flattened edge; vertical handle, rectangular in section, from mid-neck to upper

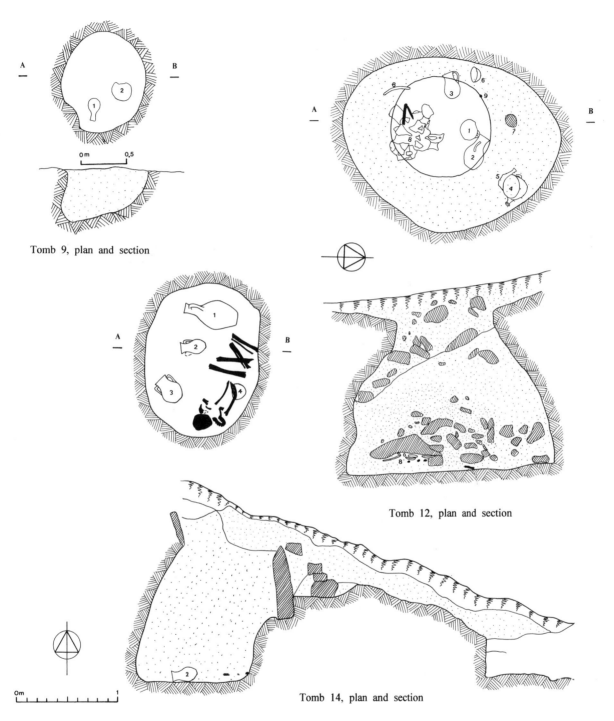

Tomb 9, plan and section

Tomb 12, plan and section

Tomb 14, plan and section

Fig. 3.4. *Tomb 9:* **1.** RPSC flask, P32; **2.** RP bowl, P17. *Tomb 12:* **1.** RP Mottled bowl, P84; **2.** RP amphora, P100; **3.** DPBC tankard, P95; **4.** RP Mottled spouted bowl, P96; **5.** Brown Polished bottle, P98; **6.** RP Mottled bowl, P97; **7.** Rubber-pounder, S635; **8.** RP large jug, P99; **9.** Conical terracotta spindle whorl (no terracotta catalogue number). *Tomb 14:* **1.** RP jug, P118; **2.** RP amphora, P68; **3.** RP amphora, P90; **4.** RP bowl, P93.

body. Decoration: relief band at neckline; deep wide smooth incised decoration on handle: patterns of joined lozenges, five at upper handle and eight at lower, two oblique hatched bands between. Soft light brown clay with light gray interior, many quite large black, white, and gray inclusions; thick lustrous dark red-brown slip, poorly preserved. Jug Type A.

P100. Red Polished amphora. Fig. 4.14. H: 26.5; D: 19.3. Flat base, ovoid body, slightly conical neck, flaring rim; two opposed vertical handles, rounded square in section, from mid-neck to upper body. Undecorated. Quite soft thick light pinkish brown clay with many quite large gray and some white and black inclusions, straw impressions; thick lustrous dark red-brown slip with some brown to gray areas, stroke burnished; little slip preserved, surface worn. Amphora Type A.

S635. Rubber-pounder, Type 2. Igneous. Intact. L: 11.2, W: 9.5, Th: 4.2. Discoidal. Tertiary use as a hammerstone.

TC. A fragmentary spindle whorl, #9, was found on the floor of the chamber but fell apart and disintegrated in the process of drying out and was not recorded in the Terracotta Catalogue.

Chronology

This deposit from a single burial provides the paradigm for an assemblage of the latest material found at *Kaminoudhia*, dating to early in the EC III period according to the standard terminology. The most diagnostic features include an undecorated DPBC tankard (P95, the only DPBC vessel found in the cemetery), a Brown Polished bottle, and a fine example (P99) of the distinctively decorated Type A jugs. The bottle and the tankard mark the appearance of round bases. The bowl (P84) displays two new features that become popular in EC III: a horizontal ledge lug and a horizontal handle rising from below the rim. The Type B spouted bowl (P96), clearly evolved from Type A, has other south coast parallels, and can be compared to similar EC III bowls from *Vounous* (where, however, they have the standard north coast round-pointed base). Of all the finds, the amphora (P100) exhibits the earliest features, with parallels as early as EC I and a stroke-burnished surface.

TOMB 13 (fig. 3.1)

Location

A shallow depression 50 cm southeast of T7 may be the remains of a small, eroded cist grave, which was designated Tomb 13.

Dimensions and stratigraphy

The depression measured 35 x 28 cm with a depth of 20 cm and in this respect, it closely resembled T8. Two boulders roughly measuring 50 x 50 x 20 cm covered the depression, which was devoid of ceramic or osteological remains. Nearby was found a RP bowl (P19) which may have been an offering associated with the putative T13 or with T7, or alternatively could be a find abandoned by a pre-modern looter. The soil matrix surrounding P19 appeared to have accumulated over an extended period. In view of the small, irregular size of the depression and the complete lack of any cultural material, the identity of T13 as a grave, even an unused one, must remain open to question.

Catalogue

P19. Red Polished Mottled bowl. H: 10.1; D: 14.0. Round base (very slight flattening), ovoid body, plain rim; pointed vertical lug at rim, unpierced. Undecorated. Fairly hard light red-brown clay with small amount of small black inclusions; thick slip with traces of luster in some areas, mottled dark red-brown, dark gray, dark pink and brown. Bowl Type A.

Chronology

The single find from this "tomb," a Type A bowl, does not provide evidence adequate for firm dating. The fact that the base of the bowl is only slightly flattened, i.e., nearly round, may indicate a date in EC III.

TOMB 14 (Plan and section: fig. 3.4; pl. 3.4b)

Location

T14 belonged to a cluster of six and possibly seven (if T21 is considered a grave) tombs, the center of which was located 4 m northwest of T12. It defined the northwest limit of this cluster and is the only tomb in Cemetery A to include a well-preserved dromos. To the east lay T16 and to the south T15 and T19.

Dimensions

At floor level the overall dimensions of the roughly oval chamber were 1.28 m north–south by 94 cm east–west, with a maximum preserved height of 1.2 m. A hemispherical dromos, 90 cm long, 1 m wide and 20 cm deep, provided access to the stomion of T14. The dromos was preceded by a shallow step 25 cm deep and 55 cm wide.

Stratigraphy

The dromos was packed with slabs of limestone which on the south side abutted against the in situ plaka (pl. 3.4b). The exact definition of the dromos was complicated by the nature of the matrix surrounding the limestone slabs that consisted of eroded bedrock in the process of recalcification. Although the plaka remained in place, the top of the chamber had collapsed allowing the accumulation of a hard-packed deposit of almost sterile eroded bedrock.

On the floor of the chamber, 1.35 m below the top of the plaka, lay a single undisturbed burial surrounded by four funerary offerings. The contents of this chamber did not seem to have been disturbed by human agency.

Finds

The relatively well-preserved skeleton had been placed in a flexed position on its right side with the skull to the south, thus facing east. In front of the lower torso was found a RP bowl (#4-P93), and a RP jug (#1-P118) had once stood by the feet. Behind the skeleton had been placed two RP amphorae (#2-P68 and #3-P90). The jug and the amphorae all faced west, either because they had been deposited in that manner or, which seems more likely, they had fallen over in this direction from an original standing position. No metal, beads or pendants accompanied the ceramic grave goods, although a chert flake, perhaps part of a sickle, was associated with the burial.

Catalogue (pl. 3.7a)

P68. Red Polished small amphora. Fig. 4.14. H: 20.7; D: 12.4. Broken, incomplete; flat base, ovoid body, inverted slightly conical neck, flaring rim; two opposed pointed vertical handles, approximately triangular in section, from mid-neck to upper body. Undecorated. Fairly soft thick light red-brown clay with gray interior, small amount of small black inclusions; thick lustrous dark red-brown slip, poorly preserved; surface worn and damaged. Amphora Type B.

P90. Red Polished amphora. Fig. 4.14. H: 22.2; D: 17.1. Broken, repaired; flat base, globular body, inverted conical neck, flaring rim; two opposed angular vertical handles, one round and the other rounded rectangular in section, from mid-neck to upper body. Undecorated. Thick soft red-orange clay with many black, white and gray inclusions, some very large; interior fabric not visible; thick lustrous dark red-brown slip, poorly preserved; surface worn and damaged. Amphora Type A.

P93. Red Polished bowl. Fig. 4.1. H: 10.0; D: ca. 15. Broken, repaired, incomplete; flat base, irregular ovoid body, plain rim; small conical knob at rim (rim incomplete so uncertain whether there were lugs or handle). No decoration preserved. Very soft brown clay with thick dark gray core, a few small white and dark red inclusions, fine organic temper; thick lustrous dark red-brown slip, very worn and flaking. Bowl Type A.

P118. Red Polished jug. Fig. 4.6. H: 41.2; D: 24.4. Broken, repaired, partly restored; flat base, ovoid body, slightly concave neck, slightly flaring rim; vertical handle, oval in section, from mid-neck to upper body (attached crookedly, with lower end to right of top). Shallow hemispherical knob on upper body to right of lower handle attachment, otherwise undecorated. Thick soft light pinkish-brown clay with many black, white and gray inclusions; thick lustrous dark red-brown slip with a few small black and brown areas; poorly preserved, worn and damaged. Jug Type C.

A chert flake was also found associated with the burial.

Chronology

Tomb 14 appears to be EC I/II in date, although it lacked the RPSC ware typical of this phase.[10] It contained two amphorae (P68, P90), comparable to EC I examples from *Vounous*[11] and an amphora from Psematismenos *Trelloukkas*. The jug P118 has general similarities to Philia Phase jugs from Philia *Vasiliko* and RP I jugs from *Vounous*, but is best paralleled at *Trelloukkas*. The fourth object from the tomb is a Type A bowl (P93) of RP I type.

---

[10] Perhaps this absence is simply accidental, although it is possible that it is an indication of a date early in the EC I/II phase. The visible burnishing marks on amphora P100 may also signify an early date.

[11] EC IB or C, according to Stewart 1992:100, 114.

TOMB 15 (Plan and section: fig. 3.5; pl. 3.5a)

Location and Dimensions

The tomb lay in the T14-T21 cluster between T17 to the west and T19 to the east, immediately south of T14. The overall measurements of the oval chamber at floor level were 1.24 m north–south by 1.06 m east–west. The depth from the highest preserved point of the roof to the floor was 0.68 m, which is 0.9 m below the present ground level.

Stratigraphy

The first suggestion of a burial chamber in this area was in the form of a concentration of cobbles associated with a vaguely circular depression below the pale brown topsoil (0). Beneath were found a layer (1) of light reddish soil with limestone inclusions and a large cobble. This in turn gave way to an extremely hard, slightly laminated limestone deposit (2), which, in its upper layers, appeared to be the remains of the chamber's collapsed roof. This material was so homogenous that it proved impossible, as was often the case at *Kaminoudhia*, to differentiate between it and the eroded limestone surrounding the skeletal remains and funerary offerings.

The contents of T15 had obviously been disturbed since the burials took place. It would appear that skull no. 3 (#8 on plan) and the accompanying long bones had been pushed aside to make room for the later burial(s) of skulls nos.1 and 2 (#12 and #14 on plan). This scenario is supported by the fact that a fine dagger (#7- M18), an intrinsically valuable object, was left next to skull no. 3 (pl. 3.5a) and not removed as would probably have been the case if the disorderly arrangement of the skeleton was due to looters' activities. It is impossible to determine whether the absence of finds in the northeastern quadrant of the chamber is due to looting or natural agencies, or whether it is a simple coincidence since few grave goods were deposited in T15.

The fact that T17 abutted T15 to the west and that T14 and T19 were each about 40 cm to the north and east meant that the only place for a dromos providing access to T15 would have been to the south. Since erosion had removed at least a third of the chamber, it could also have obliterated any evidence for a dromos in this area, because none existed at the time of excavation. As T14 was provided with a dromos on the usual down-slope side of the chamber, T15 could be expected to have been approached in the same manner had it been preceded by a dromos. Thus, it would seem that T15 was most likely to have been entered via the roof in the manner of T12 and probably T17.

Finds

The remains of three disarticulated skeletons lay on bedrock, surrounded by grave goods mostly located in the southern half of the chamber. Skull #8 (no. 3) lay amid the main concentration of long bones at the western edge of the chamber, where a 25 cm wide aperture communicated with T17. There is no evidence to suggest, however, that both chambers were originally connected, and the narrow aperture could have been caused by erosion or weathering. Next to this skull lay a copper-based dagger with a flat tang (#7-M18), the fragment of a saddle quern (#6-S297), a large RP jug (#1-P103), and a RP cooking pot (#2-P91). Skulls #12 and #14 were found with a few long bones in the southeastern quadrant of the chamber. If the burials in T15 had adhered to the local custom of placing the corpse on the right side facing east, then this is approximately where the skulls should be located. One shell and seven picrolite anthropomorphic figurines (#16-#18-S471; not all the find spots are indicated on the plan), apparently belonging to the same necklace, were close to skull #14 and mandible #15, next to

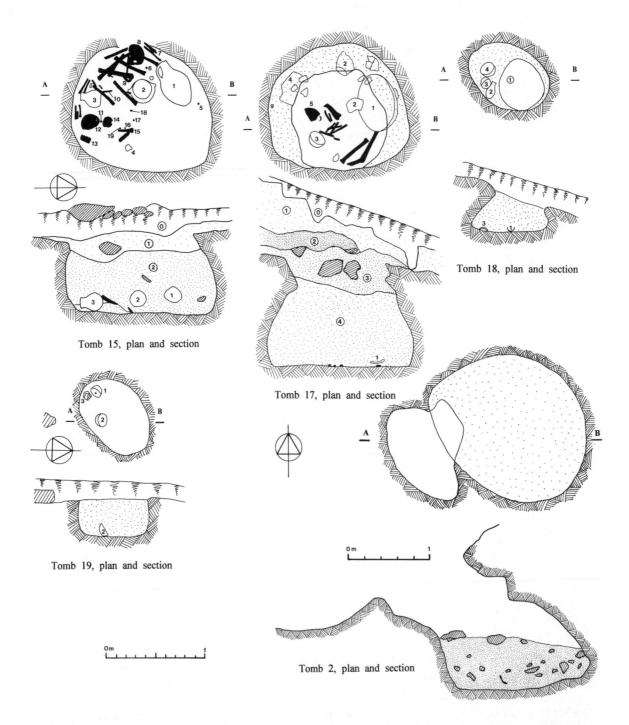

Tomb 15, plan and section

Tomb 17, plan and section

Tomb 18, plan and section

Tomb 19, plan and section

Tomb 2, plan and section

Fig. 3.5. *Tomb 2:* No finds preserved in situ. *Tomb 15:* **1:** RP jug, P103; **2.** RP cooking pot, P91; **3.** RP Philia ear-lug pot, P102; **4.** RP Philia bottle, P75; **5.** Biconical bead, TC 23; **6.** Fragment of a saddle quern, S297; **7.** Copper-based dagger, M18; **8.** Skull #3; **9.** Mandible #3; **10.** Copper-based awl, M11; **11.** Copper-based earring, M20; **12.** Skull #1; **13.** Mandible #1; **14.** Skull #2; **15.** Mandible #2; **16–18.** Picrolite anthropomorphic pendants, S471; **19.** Copper-based earring, M16. *Tomb 17:* **1.** RP Mottled large bowl, P104; **2.** RP sherds; **3.** RP bowl, P89; **4.** Limestone slab; **5.** Skull fragment. *Tomb 18:* **1.** RP bowl, P59; **2.** RPSC flask, P61; **3.** RP Mottled bowl, P48; **4.** RP bowl, P78. *Tomb 19:* **1.** RP Mottled bowl, P46; **2.** RP bowl (uncatalogued); **3.** Brown Polished bottle, P105.

which was found a spiral copper-based earring (#19-M16). Between pendants #16 and #17, 7.5 cm apart, a distinct line of black, white, and brown miniature beads was recorded in situ (S543). These beads, 132 in number, obviously formed part of a necklace with the anthropomorphic figurines. The find spots of these small objects, some obviously undisturbed since burial, and M16 the earring, which would easily have become embedded in the chamber floor, lend support to the argument that the deceased were originally placed with their necks, and thus heads, in this area. Nearby lay a RP ear-lug pot (#3-P102), a copper-based awl (#10-M11), an earring (#11-M20) between skulls #12 and #14, and the poorly preserved remains of a RP Philia bottle (#4-P75). A single biconical bead or a small spindle whorl (#5-TC23) was found at the northern edge of the chamber near the base of P103. The northeast quadrant of the tomb was devoid of finds, a fact that cannot be attributed to erosion since it was no closer to the surface than the remaining quadrants.

Catalogue

P75. Red Polished Philia small bottle. Fig. 4.10. H (pres.): 4.8; D: 5.1. Incomplete; round base, squat ovoid body (tapering to inverted conical neck?); neck and rim not preserved. Traces of incised linear decoration: short parallel oblique lines? Fine quite soft thick light gray-brown clay, light brown at base, a few small white inclusions; no slip preserved, surface extremely damaged. Bottle Type D.

P91. Red Polished cooking pot. Fig. 4.15; Swiny 1986a: fig. 2:10. H: 23.7; D: 22.8. Flat base, globular body, short wide slightly concave neck, plain rim; two opposed vertical handles, oval in section, rising slightly from rim to upper body; stands considerably off axis. Undecorated. Moderately hard brown clay with many black, white and gray inclusions, some large; traces of fairly thick dark brown to red-brown slip with some luster, worn and poorly preserved. Cooking Pot Type B.

P102. Red Polished Philia ear-lug pot. Fig. 4.10, pl. 4.5a. H: 19.9; D: 16.8. Broken, repaired, incomplete; flat base, ovoid body, short wide inverted conical neck, flattened rim; two opposed large horizontal semicircular lugs, pierced, on upper body. Incised decoration: on upper body, horizontal panel, framed by herringbone bands, containing a band of joined hatched lozenges; on neck (nearly indistinguishable) groups of short oblique lines (?). Soft brown clay with thick dark gray interior (completely gray at neck and upper body), moderate amount of small black and white inclusions; thin lustrous slip, dark red-brown with brown areas on body, black on neck and upper body; worn and poorly preserved, surface damaged. Ear-lug pot Type B.

P103. Red Polished large jug. Fig. 4.6. D (rim): ca. 11; D (base): ca. 12. Fragmentary, incomplete; flat base, body not restored, short wide slightly tapering neck with straight vertical rounded rim; vertical handle, thick oval in section, from rim to upper body. Undecorated. Medium soft fabric with dark gray interior, light brown exterior, large gray and white inclusions; some fairly lustrous dark red-brown slip preserved, very worn. Jug Type E.

M11. Awl. Fig. 8.1. L: 9.5, W: 0.5, Th.: 0.4. Copper-based. Pointed end slightly damaged. Rectangular in section. The tang is thicker and less tapering that the other extremity.

M16. Spiral earring. Ten fragments of a spiral earring. Largest piece 0.7 x 0.7 x 0.1.

M18. Dagger. Fig. 8.2; pls. 8.1a, 8.1c; Swiny 1989:189 (4th from right), 1995:32 (4th from right). L: 16.2, W: 3, Th.: 0.4. Copper-based. Intact. Flat straight tang, straight shoulders, and slightly concave blade. Flat mid-rib running full length of blade. See Chapter 8, "Dagger" for a full description.

M20. Spiral earring. Fragmentary. L: 1.1, W: 0.75, Th.: 0.1. Narrow at one end, broadening to a spatula like extremity.

S297. Saddle quern. Fragmentary.

S471. Anthropomorphic figurines. Fig. 6.16, pl. 6.4a. Six made of picrolite, one of shell. Mostly intact. Length ranges from 1.8 to 2.8 cm. Drilled perforations. Hourglass in section with horizontal striations. (For individual dimensions see the Ground Stone Catalogue in Chapter 6.) **#1.** Surface gray and polished. Both faces show diagonal scratch marks from original manufacturing process. **#2.** Same surface treatment as #1 only slightly broader head. **#3.** Same surface treatment and color as #1. Where the foot has been broken off the light green picrolite is visible. **#4.** Light green. Same surface treatment. Without a shaped head. If there had once been a head, which broke off during manufacture, the "broken" edge was left in a well-rounded and symmetrical state. **#5.** Light gray and smaller, otherwise identical to the others. **#6.** Same color as #5. Foot is slightly rounder, instead of flat like others and the "head" is slightly damaged. **#7.** White shell, matt on one face, lustrous on the other. Slightly convex on the matt (outer) surface. The shape is different with the addition of the "arm stubs." The horizontal striations of the drill holes are very visible on this piece.

S543. Beads. Jasper, white limestone, and siltstone. One hundred thirty-two beads with single perforations. See more detailed description in the Ground Stone Catalogue and discussion in Chapter 6, "Bead (minature)."

TC23. RP bead, biconical, undecorated. Fig. 9.1. Three-fourths preserved. H: 1.8, max. D: 2.7, hole D: 0.4–0.5, pres. wt: 8.1 gr. est. wt: 11 gr. Pink (5YR 7/4) fabric with fine grit temper. Pinkish gray (5YR 6/2) core. Light red (10R 6/8) slip (see Chapter 9 for full discussion of terracotta beads).

Chronology

Tomb 15 is closely similar to T6 and belongs to the Philia Phase. It contained a distinctive Philia type bottle (P75), cooking pot (P91), an ear-lug pot with characteristic herringbone decoration (P102), and a necklace (S471) of distinctive Philia type pendants (see Chapter 6, "Anthropomorphic Figurine"). The copper-based dagger (M15) with its flat mid-rib is of a type to date only found in Philia Phase burials (cf. Chapter 8, "Dagger").

TOMB 16 (fig. 3.1)

Location and Dimensions

The tomb chamber lay 90 cm east of T14 and 50 cm northeast of T18. The dimensions of the roughly circular, poorly defined chamber were approximately 1 m north–south and 0.9 m east–west, with a maximum depth of 0.6 m.

Stratigraphy

Below the topsoil the ephemeral outline of a depression filled with dark brown soil (10YR 4/3) containing 26 sherds suggested the possibility of either a dromos or a tomb chamber in this area. Beneath was found a compact mass of limestone which probably represented the collapsed roof of a tomb chamber. The presence of a large stone slab at the eastern edge of the depression along with 19 RP and 4 RP black-topped bowl sherds strengthens the possibility that this depression once served as a grave.

Beneath the postulated roof collapse the fill consisted of undifferentiated eroded limestone with a few bone fragments and human teeth, but no pottery. The eastern half of the chamber had been destroyed by a footpath and could not be planned. No finds were reported from this area.

TOMB 17 (Plan and section: fig. 3.5)

Location and Dimensions

Tomb 17 is adjacent to the west side of T15. At floor level the overall measurements of the approximately circular chamber were 1.08 m north–south by 1.20 m east–west. The highest preserved point of the domed roof was 74 cm above the floor and 74 cm below the present ground level.

Stratigraphy

Although T17 must have remained open for a time in order for the skeleton to be disturbed and the vessels to be shattered and scattered around the chamber, there is no evidence that it had suffered from any recent intrusion as noted in the description of the material overlaying the chamber mouth (see below, "Finds From Outside Tombs In Cemetery A").

Despite the lack of evidence for a dromos providing access to T17, one could have existed to the north, west, or south, but has now been completely destroyed by erosion. The chamber walls that curve inwards on all sides and are well enough preserved to exhibit the original tool marks of an adze-like instrument—the only such occurrence at *Kaminoudhia*—argue against the existence of a dromos. When chambers are entered from a dromos via a stomion, as in T11 and T14 for example, the wall face below the stomion always curves *outward* towards the ledge on which the plaka was set (see the section of T14, fig. 3.4, in this connection). Based on these observations it seems most likely that T17 was entered via the roof in the same manner as T12.

Finds

Immediately to the south of the chamber mouth there was an accumulation of cobbles and a single limestone slab which may once have been used to seal the chamber, had the initial aperture been smaller. The upper fill (4) to within 50 cm of the floor contained 43 RP sherds that must have eroded into the chamber after displacement of the plaka and initial exposure of the grave goods and skeleton. Alternatively, it could be argued that the chamber was back-filled after the interment with soil that already contained RP sherds from earlier cultural activities in the vicinity. The first object to be located in the chamber was a large RP bowl (#1-P104) with its rim resting on the floor and base propped up against the northern wall of the chamber. On or just above the floor were the semi-articulated skeletal remains with a RP bowl (#3-P89) placed in front of them and a fragmentary RP jug (#2) lying in pieces behind. On the south side of the chamber, 12 cm from the skull, was found a thin sub-rectangular slab of limestone (#4) measuring 28 x 17 cm that may have originally been placed under the head. Although the skeleton was incomplete and relatively poorly preserved, it had obviously been laid out in a flexed position on its right side, head to the south, looking east. Also associated with the fill at floor level were two chert blades displaying silica gloss. These objects may have been hafted in a sickle deposited with the burial.

Catalogue (pl. 3.7b)

P89. Red Polished bowl. Fig. 4.1. H: 10.6; D: 14.7. Broken, repaired, small part of rim not preserved; slightly flattened base, ovoid body, plain rim; pointed vertical lug at rim, unpierced. Undecorated. Fine quite soft light brown clay with small amount of small black and white inclusions; thin lustrous slip, mostly brown with dark red-brown areas; worn and surface damaged. Bowl Type A.

P104. Red Polished Mottled large bowl. Fig. 4.2. H: 21:7; D: ca. 45. Broken, repaired; very irregular in diameter; flat base, wide ovoid body, plain rim; two opposed semicircular ledge lugs at mid-body, one pierced vertically. Undecorated. Moderately hard red-brown clay with small amount of black and white inclusions; thick lustrous dark red-brown slip with a few small black areas; worn, surface damaged, poorly preserved. Large Bowl Type A.

Two chert blades with silica gloss.

Chronology

Tomb 17 dates to EC I/II. The small bowl with pointed lug (P89) and the large bowl (P104) resemble EC I types from *Vounous*, and have parallels at Psematismenos *Trelloukkas* and in EC I/II deposits at Marki *Alonia*.

TOMB 18 (Plan and section: fig. 3.5; pl. 3.5b)

Location and Dimensions

The tomb lies 45 cm. southwest of T16 and east of T19. The overall measurements of the oval chamber at floor level were 74 cm along a northwest–southeast axis by 52 cm in width. The maximum depth was approximately 30 cm, which resulted in an overall depth below the sloping ground surface of 50 cm.

Stratigraphy and Finds

Below the topsoil, a small oval depression in the bedrock was found full of light gray sterile soil, which at a depth of 25 cm yielded a series of ceramic vessels and numerous stone beads. All the finds were on the floor of the depression (pl. 3.5b). They consisted of a small RP bowl (#1-P59), a RPSC flask (#2-P61), and to the west, two more RP bowls (#3-P48 and #4-78). Water sieving of the fill produced 80 miniature black and white limestone and brown jasper beads (S710), but no bone fragments or teeth. Despite the lack of any skeletal remains, including teeth, the presence of a necklace and four clay vessels in a depression with incurving walls, which were very unlikely to be the result of natural erosion, suggests that T18 served a funerary role. Of note is the fact that the four vessels were small and crudely made which would make them more appropriate as offerings for a child. The depression resembles a miniature tomb chamber with access through the roof and may either have contained an infant or child burial or was used solely as a repository for funerary offerings. Unless it is argued that a neo-natal or an infant was interred therein, water sieving should have recovered at least a few teeth.

Catalogue (pl. 3.7c)

P48. Red Polished Mottled bowl. Fig. 4.1. H: 6.9; D: 10.5. Small flat base, ovoid body, plain rim; two opposed small semicircular ledge lugs on rim, one pierced twice vertically. Undecorated. Hard brown clay with many small black and white inclusions, interior not visible; thin red-brown slip, now matt, mottled with dark gray, worn and surface somewhat damaged. Two leaf impressions (olive?) in surface, one to left of pierced lug, other below and to right of it (pl. 4.6b). Bowl Type A.

P59. Red Polished bowl. Fig. 4.1. H: 7.4; D: ca. 8 (irregular). Very crudely formed; flat base, deep ovoid body, plain rim; semicircular lug rising diagonally from rim (chipped), with six irregular punctures in top (not pierced through); rim opposite lug slightly thickened; otherwise undecorated. Thick soft yellow-brown clay with one small dark gray area, many black, white and gray inclusions, many holes from burned out organic temper; thick dark red-brown slip, probably originally with some luster, worn and poorly preserved. Bowl Type H.

P61. Red Polished South Coast flask. Fig. 4.8; Swiny 1995:31 (bottom, second from left). H: 15.0; D: 8.0. Flat base, ovoid body, inverted conical neck, slightly flaring rim; two pairs of holes opposed below rim. Deep wide incised decoration: on upper body and neck, groups of short parallel lines, some horizontal and some oblique. Fine soft light brown clay, perhaps a small amount of small black and white inclusions, interior not visible; thick dark red-brown slip, slight luster preserved; surface worn and damaged.

P78. Red Polished bowl. Fig. 4.1. H: 10.1; D: 14.5. Small slightly flattened base, globular body, plain rim, pointed vertical S-shaped lug at rim, unpierced. Undecorated. Fairly hard red-brown clay with many black, white and gray inclusions; thick lustrous red-brown slip with two small dark gray areas, impressions of straw and grass on surface, considerably worn in places. Bowl Type A.

S710. Eighty miniature black and white limestone and brown jasper beads. See Chapter 6, "Beads (miniature)."

Chronology

The four small ceramic finds suggest a probable EC I/II date for this tomb, although none of them is precisely diagnostic. Two of the bowls (P48, P59) are of unusual types, and the third falls within the broad range of Type A bowls. The flask (P61) has been classified as RPSC, but it is somewhat smaller than the other examples and the decoration is not as formalized. The small beads (S710) are identical to those from Tomb 6, a type which is known to have a wide chronological range, from the Philia Phase through Middle Cypriot; another EC I occurrence is from Arpera (cf. Swiny 1986:30; Stewart 1962:260–61, fig. 105:5).

TOMB 19 (Plan and section: fig. 3.5)

Location and Dimensions

The tomb lies between T15 and T18, due south of T14. At floor level, the overall dimensions of the oval chamber were 72 cm along a northeast–southwest axis with a width of 50 cm and a maximum depth of 50 cm. The deposit of topsoil above the chamber was on average 20 cm thick.

Stratigraphy and Finds

Below the topsoil a small oval depression in the bedrock was filled with light gray sterile soil, which at a depth of 20 cm yielded three ceramic vessels sitting on the horizontal floor of the cut. RP bowls (#1-P46 and #2, which disintegrated after removal from the tomb) were accompanied by a Brown Polished bottle (#3-P105). Water sieving yielded a tooth belonging to a juvenile. This single tooth may be viewed as intrusive, but could equally be all that remains of a sub-adult burial. Its presence in a chamber of similar dimensions to T18 supports the suggestion that both were graves for juveniles, in which the skeletal remains, not as robust as those of adults, had almost completely decayed.

Catalogue

P46. Red Polished Mottled bowl. H: 9.5; D: 12.7. Flat base, globular body, plain slightly incurving rim; pointed vertical slightly S-shaped lug at rim, unpierced. Undecorated. Hard red-brown clay with many (?) small black, white and gray inclusions (interior not visible); thick lustrous dark red-brown slip with a few small dark gray areas; well preserved with some worn areas. Bowl Type A.

P105. Brown Polished (?) bottle. Fig. 4.10. H (neck): 4.5; D (rim): 3.1. Very fragmentary; round base, body not restored, inverted conical neck, flaring rim; two opposed holes below rim. Incised decoration (preserved): broken horizontal multiple zigzag on body and neck; group of four horizontal lines on body below neckline, group of three on neck below rim. Somewhat soft light gray clay with a very small light brown area, small black inclusions and very fine organic temper; traces of dark brown and dark gray lustrous slip. Bottle Type C.

Chronology

The Brown Polished bottle (P105) was too poorly preserved to permit definite conclusions about its type, but it may be somewhat later than the other Brown Polished bottles from the cemetery (see Chapter 4, Bottle Type C, below). The only other vessel in the deposit was a Type A bowl of good RP Mottled fabric. Both the finds suggest a date well into EC III.

TOMB 20 (Plan and section: fig. 3.3; pl. 3.5c)

Location

In the course of excavating the dromos of T11, a second tomb chamber with its plaka still in place was discovered immediately west of T11. It was designated T20.

Dimensions

The small oval chamber measured 86 cm at the level of the stomion along its north–south axis and 63 cm east–west. The maximum height from the top of the stomion to the bottom of the chamber was 86 cm. As can be seen in the section, the floor of the chamber was concave either by intention or because the tomb was unfinished. All other chambers at *Kaminoudhia* had flat floors. The small size of the chamber would have precluded the burial of an adult in the normal flexed position favored in Cemetery A.

It was impossible for an average sized adult to work in the chamber with comfort, and there was certainly insufficient room to swing an adze or pick, though a hammer and cold chisel would have been manageable. Due to these size constraints it is most likely that a child or small adult had been responsible for its excavation.

The sub-rectangular dromos, 1 m wide and measuring on average 7 cm from the step leading into the dromos to the stomion, had been carefully shaped and was larger than the actual burial chamber.

Stratigraphy and Finds

Removal of the plaka revealed an intact chamber empty of silt or other objects with the exception of a fieldstone carefully placed in the middle of the floor.

It would seem that this miniature chamber had been excavated in anticipation of a child burial. All debris had been carefully removed and the fieldstone placed horizontally on the bottom of the chamber, which was then sealed with a plaka. It is impossible to determine whether a ritualistic significance should be attached to this unique discovery.

TOMB 21 (fig. 3.1)

Location and Dimensions

The tomb is located between T12 and T16, 50 cm southeast of T18. It consists of a small oval depression measuring 50 cm north–south and 38 cm east–west with a depth of 25 cm.

Stratigraphy and finds

The depression was filled with light gray soil, which yielded two cobbles and six RP sherds from a closed vessel. No human skeletal remains were recovered, so the exact function of this depression remains questionable. The presence of six sherds from the same vessel does not specifically demonstrate that an infant burial had been deposited here, as the sherds could have washed in accidentally or the vessel could have been intentionally placed in the shallow depression excavated in the bedrock.

FINDS FROM OUTSIDE TOMBS IN CEMETERY A

The following section describes the location and associated stratigraphy of material from Cemetery A which was not associated with any of the funerary chambers or cists.

In Operation I6D (fig. 3.1) the topsoil interspersed with limestone lenses to the west of T4 was rich in sherds (n = 171). Here a thick deposit of secondary limestone seems to have accumulated after disturbance of T4 or other, unlocated tombs in the vicinity, as indicated by numbers (n=545) of RP sherds. Two meters west of T4 were found a pounder (S91), a RP Philia ear-lug pot (P7), a RP flask (P101) and a very fragmentary RP Philia flask (P9), and nearby a copper-based spiral earring (M2) well embedded in the secondary limestone. From the general area came another pounder, S85. A piece of bone, presumably human, was found immediately beneath P7. All lay directly on or just above bedrock 80 cm below the present surface in an area of boulders and fieldstones which do not form a recent accumulation, thereby indicating that these objects are not the result of recent tomb looting. Note that all the accurately datable finds belong to the Philia Phase. Fifty-two sherds were also recovered from this deposit. Since these finds, and Tomb 4, are at the base of a slope it is most probable that the material originated in a long since eroded or looted tomb containing diagnostic Philia Phase ceramics and metal located higher up the hillside.

From the undisturbed terra rossa mixed with limestone pebble topsoil in Operation I6B, north of T4, were found the fragments of a RPSC flask (P34) intermingled with a RP Philia flask (P35) along with 242 sherds, mostly of RP ware. It is quite possible that some of this material, especially P35, came from the eroded upper portion of T6.

A probe in Operation I4C was opened next to a cut in the bedrock which appeared to be part of a tomb chamber. The dark brown loose topsoil yielded a few RP sherds concentrated in the middle of the operation, which belonged to a smashed spouted bowl (P42) lying below. Excavation around this bowl revealed a small RP bowl (P10) immediately to the east. Both were embedded in compacted topsoil and fine secondary limestone, 40 cm below the surface. Removal of P42 uncovered a few poorly preserved RPSC sherds within the bowl, suggesting it had once contained a smaller vessel. The pattern of placing one vessel inside another was noted at both *Kaminoudhia* cemeteries. The area around the vessels, which consisted of compacted layers of terra rossa rich soil and eroded limestone, was excavated down to bedrock, demonstrating that these vessels did not belong to a funerary deposit. Their placement in this location was not recent and, in view of the compacted nature of the surrounding matrix, it could well have occurred during the life of the cemetery

In the area of Operations I5A and I5C, about 11 m northwest of T4 and immediately above T17 (see fig. 3.5, Tomb 17), the pale brown topsoil (0) containing 7 sherds mostly of RP ware was followed by (1) a layer of calcium carbonate-rich soil mixed with limestone pebbles with a darker lens (2) of light reddish soil rich in limestone pebbles. The area around the chamber mouth of T17 had a deposit (3) of loose reddish sandy soil containing a fragmentary RP Philia ear-lug pot (P41), a few large sherds, a biconical spindle whorl (TC12) perhaps of Philia Phase type,[12] and several cobbles followed by brownish gray fill (4) that became increasingly calcified and hard towards the chamber floor.

The artifacts from stratum 3, which ends about 60 cm above the T17 funerary deposit, are not associated in any way with the underlying burial. They somehow came to rest in the depression partially articulated by the mouth of T17, either by human agency or by eroding down the slope. P41 would initially have been deposited with a Philia Phase burial, or left on the surface at that time, and thus predates the in situ material in T17. From the topsoil in I5B came a Philia Phase bowl, P54, which could well have come from an eroded tomb chamber—such as T15—in the vicinity.

Excavation of the topsoil in I5D around the chamber of T12 produced yat may have been a jar stopper, S320, just below the surface to the west of the chamber mouth. A concentration of 125 sherds, mostly RP ware, was noted to the northeast of the mouth.

Catalogue

P4. Red Polished Mottled bowl. Swiny 1985a: fig. 4:1. Fragmentary, incomplete; flat base, ovoid body, plain incurving rim; no lug preserved. Undecorated. Found on the surface within the confines of Cemetery A.

P7. Red Polished Philia ear-lug pot. I6D <u>10</u>. (Found with P9 and P101 west of Tomb 4.) Fig. 4.12; Karageorghis 1982b: fig. 83 (second from right); Swiny 1985a: fig. 7:2. H: 33.4; D: 24.2. Flat base, ovoid body, conical neck, slightly flaring rim; two opposed large vertical rectangular lugs, pierced, on upper body (one not preserved). Incised decoration: two pairs of short vertical lines on lug. Thick soft light brown clay with many black, white and gray inclusions, some of them large, interior not visible;

---

[12] No exact parallels are known from Philia Phase tombs and the decorative motif could indicate a later type, although it is not recorded at Episkopi *Phaneromeni* (Swiny 1986).

thick dark red-brown slip, stroke burnished, poorly preserved; surface worn and damaged. Ear-lug pot Type A.

P9. Red Polished Philia flask (?) body and neck fragments. (Found with P7 and P101.) Fig. 4.9. Incised decoration.

P10. Red Polished Mottled bowl. I4C 2. (Found above Tomb 10 with P42.) H: 10.2; D: 14.3. Flat base, ovoid body, plain rim; no lug preserved. Undecorated. Quite hard orange-brown clay with many small black and white inclusions, interior not visible; thick lustrous dark red-brown slip with some dark gray areas; surface of one side and some other areas much worn and damaged. Bowl Type A.

P34. Red Polished South Coast flask (?) body fragment. I6B-D 2. (Found in topsoil immediately west of Tomb 6.) Fig. 4.9. Incised and punctured decoration.

P35. Red Polished Philia flask (?) body sherd. (Found in topsoil immediately west of Tomb 6, not same vessel as P34.) Fig. 4.9. Incised decoration.

P41. Red Polished Philia ear-lug pot. I5B 11. (Found in deposit above Tomb 17.) Fig. 4.12. H: ca.15; D: 11.1. Flat base, ovoid body, wide inverted conical neck, flattened rim edge; two opposed large vertical lugs, one semicircular and the other squarish, pierced, on upper body. Incised decoration: five horizontal lines between lugs on either side, row of "feathers" below lines on one side, above and below lines on other side; on neck, groups of parallel oblique lines, at least one of them with a "feathered" edge. Soft gray to gray-brown clay with many small black and white inclusions; thin lustrous dark brown to black slip, worn and poorly preserved, surface damaged. Ear-lug pot Type A.

P42. Red Polished spouted bowl. I4C 2. (Found above Tomb 10 with P10.) H: 15.1; D: 23.5. Flat base, deep hemispherical body, slightly incurving rim; tubular spout with flaring end rising diagonally from below rim; handle not preserved. Undecorated. Fabric and slip as P64 below. Spouted Bowl Type B.

P54. Red Polished Philia bowl. I5B 4. (Found near surface.) Fig. 4.1. H: 11.7; D (rim): ca. 14. Fragmentary, about half preserved; flat base, deep ovoid body, plain rim; no lug or decoration preserved. Thick soft brown clay with thick gray core, many black, white and gray inclusions, some of them large; thick dark-brown to dark red-brown slip, stroke burnished, worn and poorly preserved. See Chapter 4, "Unclassified Small Bowls."

P101. Red Polished Philia (?) flask. (Found with P7 and P9 above Tomb 4.) Fig. 4.8. H: 14.6; D: 9.7. Flat base, globular body, wide cylindrical neck, slightly flaring rim; two opposed pairs of holes below rim. Deep wide incised decoration: groups of horizontal, vertical and short oblique parallel lines. Thick soft dark gray-brown clay with small amount of small white inc usions; thin lustrous black slip, poorly preserved; surface worn and damaged.

M2. Earring. I6D 6. Fig. 8.1. D: 1.2, Th: 0.2. (Found with P7, P9, P101 and S91.) Copper-based. Fragmentary. Flattened strip of metal narrow at one end and broadening towards the other.

S85. Pounder. Type 1. I6D 3. Igneous. Fragmentary. L: 11.9, W: 6.1, Th: 4.4. Fragment of a rubber. Fine-grained, gray/green. One end rounded, the other missing. One face concave, the other flat. At the extremity of both faces, there are traces of pitting from use as a pounder.

S91. Pounder. Type 1. I6D <u>8</u>. (Found with P7, P9, P101 and M2.) Igneous. Intact. L: 12.7, W: 6.1, Th: 5.0. Elongated: triangular in transverse section. Fine-grained, gray/green. Pitting on both extremities from use as a pounder. Marks of pitting on one face from secondary use as a hammerstone.

S320. Jar stopper? 15D, unstratified topsoil, to west of T12. Limestone. Intact. L: 3.4, W: 3.5, Th: 2.2. Cylindrical. Cream-colored limestone. Thick disc with reasonably carefully worked circumference. function unknown. Could have served as jar stopper?

TC 5. RP decorated conical spindle whorl. 14C <u>3</u>. (See Chapter 9, Terracotta Catalogue, for full description).

TC12. RP decorated biconical spindle whorl. 15B<u>6</u>. (See Chapter 9, Terracotta Catalogue, for full description).

CEMETERY B

The hill overlooking Cemetery A to the east displays a horizontal row of three wind-worn cavities, the remains of long-since opened tomb chambers which were numbered T1, T2 and T3 (fig. 3.6). In pl. 3.1 the open chambers are clearly visible as a row of three black dots near the middle right edge of the aerial view. As noted in the Introduction, according to local tradition they had last been investigated some 60 years ago, and there is no reason to believe that tombs located in such an exposed position would not have been open for centuries. Since these were the only visible remains of funerary architecture at *Kaminoudhia*, and because the area had a fair deposit of topsoil which might hide other chambers, it was in Cemetery B that the search for undisturbed chambers began in 1981.

Choosing the row of chambers as the point of departure, five trenches (fig. 3.6) were sunk in their vicinity wherever bedrock did not reach the surface, namely to the north, southeast and west. The stratigraphy in all the operations was similar and consisted of a thin layer of eroded limestone mixed with varying degrees of terra rossa, overlying pure deposits of more or less compacted and dense secondary limestone. The similarity of this material to primary limestone has already been commented on in connection with tombs in Cemetery A, and were it not for the presence of pottery therein it would often have been difficult, if not impossible, to determine whether it was primary or secondary. Operation R4C, southeast of the chambers, yielded a scatter of RP sherds (n=13) and a single RP bowl (P1) 29 cm below the interface between the topsoil and secondary limestone. Immediately north of this find Operation R4A contained two RP juglets (P2 and P3) and two RP bowls (P5 and P6), one placed within the other (pl. 4.3b), buried in the same deposit. Six RP sherds, perhaps from the same vessel, were the only other artifacts from R4A. The trenches to the north and west of the chambers were excavated down to hard secondary or even primary limestone, but they failed to yield any remains of funerary architecture and the only artifacts consisted of scattered potsherds. These investigations demonstrated that there was no evidence for any funerary architecture within a 20 m radius of the existing chambers.

The six vessels excavated in Operations R4A and R4C were all embedded in a compacted secondary limestone matrix which was not of recent date. The same is true of the finds from Cemetery A east of Tomb 4 (see above). Although it was impossible to determine when the pots were last handled, it was certainly not when the neighboring tombs were disturbed, if this event occurred within the past century. No stratigraphic or other evidence argues against the deposition of these vessels on the surface in the vicinity of burial chambers when the cemetery was still in use. If this were the case, and in the absence of other chambers nearby, these vessels were then left on the exposed hillside between five and ten meters below the nearest chamber, namely T3.

Catalogue of Cemetery B Pottery from Outside Tombs

P1. Red Polished Mottled bowl. Swiny 1985a: fig. 4:2. H: 9.1; D: 14.7. Flat base, ovoid body, plain slightly incurving rim; no lug preserved (rim chipped). Undecorated. Hard brown clay with many small black and white inclusions; thick lustrous dark red-brown slip with some gray areas; worn in places, surface somewhat damaged. Bowl Type A.

P2. Red Polished juglet. Fig. 4.10; Karageorghis 1982b: fig. 83 (fourth from left); H.W. Swiny 1982: fig. 11 (right); Swiny 1985a: fig.4:3; Swiny 1986a: fig. 1:34. H: 16.0; D: 10.0. Flat base, globular body, inverted conical neck, flaring rim; vertical handle, rectangular in section, rising slightly from rim to upper body. Incised decoration: on upper body, horizontal double line, broken opposite handle, with opposed multiple triangles above and below it; below this band, on mid-body, multiple short oblique lines alternating with groups of small squares; on body and neck opposite handle, vertical row of short zigzags alternating with double small squares; on body under handle, two herringbone groups; double horizontal line at neckline with row of punctured triangles pendent below it; on neck, groups of short oblique lines, group of five horizontal lines below rim; on handle, motif of four transverse lines alternating with groups of five small squares. Thick soft light gray to light gray-brown clay with many small black and white inclusions; fairly thick lustrous slip, one side apparently black, the other dark brown, poorly preserved; base worn, surface worn and damaged. Juglet Type B.

P3. Red Polished juglet. Fig. 4.7; Swiny 1985a: fig.7:3. H: 21.7; D: 13.0. Flat base, ovoid body, cylindrical neck, slightly flaring rim; vertical handle, oval in section, from mid-neck to upper body. Incised decoration: on handle, two antithetical intersecting vertical wavy lines. Thick soft light orange-brown clay with many black, white, and gray inclusions, some straw impressions; thick lustrous red-brown slip, very worn. Juglet Type A.

P5. Red Polished Mottled bowl. Fig. 4:1; pl. 4.3b; Swiny 1985a: fig.7:5. H: 6.2; D: 11.3. Slightly flattened base, hemispherical body, plain rim; vertical semicircular lug, pierced, below rim. Undecorated. Fairly hard bright orange clay with many small black and white inclusions; thin slip, now matt, light red-orange with dark gray band and dark red top; slip worn and damaged. Bowl Type B.

P6. Red Polished Mottled bowl. Swiny 1985a: fig.7:4. (Fused inside P5: pl. 4.3b.) H (est.): 6; D: 10.2. Base not visible, hemispherical body, plain rim; semicircular vertical lug at rim (or below, rim chipped), pierced. Undecorated. Soft bright pinkish-orange clay with a few small black and white inclusions; thin dark pinkish red slip with gray areas; worn, interior surface damaged. Bowl Type B.

TOMB 1 (fig. 3.6)

Dimensions

Tomb 1, which was found empty of debris, had suffered considerably from eolian erosion and for that reason was only plotted on the Cemetery B plan, fig. 3.6. Its dimensions at floor level were 1.77 x 1.5 m with a maximum height of 1.1 m.

THE CEMETERY

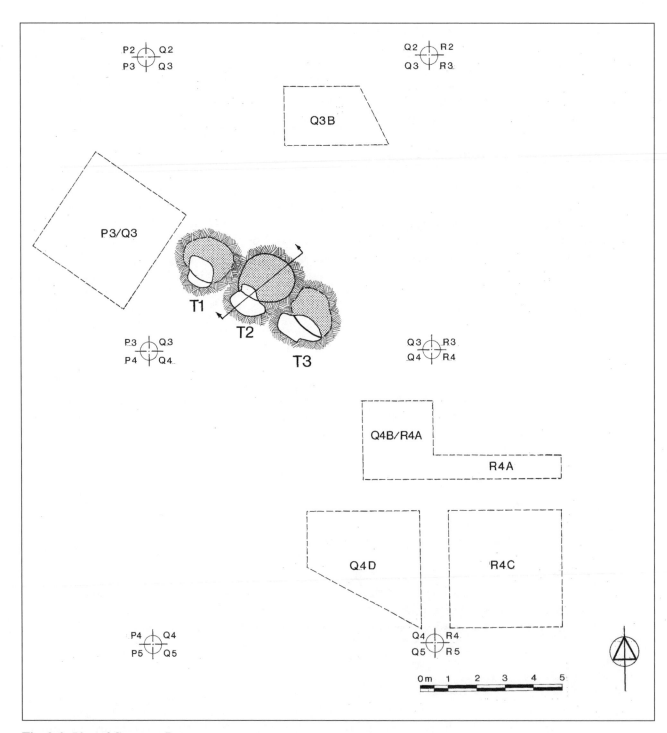

Fig. 3.6. Plan of Cemetery B.

TOMB 2 (figs. 3.5, 3.6)

Dimensions

As excavated, T2 was an irregular oval depression measuring 1.9 x 1.75 m with its main axis oriented northwest–southeast. The maximum preserved height of the chamber was 1.1 m. The D-shaped dromos, 60 cm wide and 20 cm deep, was ill-defined lengthwise and could have been up to 1.25 m long.

Stratigraphy and finds

Prior to excavation the chamber was noted to be half full of eroded debris and a shallow dromos appeared to precede the much-weathered stomion. Clearance of the dromos yielded nine large RP sherds. The chamber contained a 60 cm deposit of well-differentiated, loosely packed, eroded limestone, a few fieldstones, pebbles, 21 sherds and some human bone, including three teeth.

The presence of sherds—some of them quite large—and bone in T2 argues against the chamber having lain open for centuries perhaps like those of T1 and T3. Since this chamber lies between the two sterile chambers, it is difficult to see why it should differ from them so markedly. The tombs were in an exposed, thus vulnerable, position and would have been prime candidates for rifling, if not for gain, at least out of curiosity. It seems likely that the sherds and fragments of human bone contained within the relatively soft matrix of T2 had been deposited there in the recent past as the result of unrecorded looted chambers presumably located up-slope.

TOMB 3

The eroded dromos and chamber of T3 contained a shallow deposit of compacted totally sterile secondary limestone. The tomb was only plotted on the Cemetery B plan (fig. 3.6).

CONCLUSIONS

When skeletons were well enough preserved to yield information on the original disposition of the bodies, they appear to have been arranged in a flexed position on their right side. In the chambers of Cemetery A they are placed with their heads to the south, thus facing east (T6, T14, T15, T17). In T11, at the bottom of the valley, the body had been placed in the same position with the head to the left of the entrance, but because of the orientation of the chamber and dromos this meant that the skeleton faced northwest. It is interesting to note that in the three instances where the skeletons were well to relatively well-preserved in situ (T14, T17 and T11) a small bowl was found in front of the body with the remaining vessels placed behind. In T14 and T11 large jugs were found in the area of the feet, and in T11 a large bowl was placed by the skull, whereas in T17 a large bowl was placed near the feet. The number of well-preserved excavated burials is insufficient to determine whether these apparent trends are real or coincidental.

The interpretation of the small chambers and cist graves such as T7, T8, T9, T13, T18 and T19 as features intended for a funerary purpose is problematic. The complete absence of any skeletal remains, including slivers of bone or the cusps of infants' teeth, raises questions about the identity and function of the cavities. The presence of ceramics, typical of those normally deposited in tomb chambers, and specifically of dentalium shells, as in the case of T8, strongly suggests burials, presumably infant burials in view of the size of most chambers. This suggestion is supported by the small size (and perhaps the poor quality as well) of the vessels in T18. Were grave goods deposited in these chambers *without* a corpse, or is the chemical composition of the soil such that it destroyed the bones of an infant or neonatal over a 4,000 year period?

The presence of sometimes well-preserved ceramic vessels and other artifacts embedded in compacted secondary limestone, often at some distance from tomb chambers, may be interpreted in several ways. That they were surrounded by secondary limestone sealed by topsoil would suggest their presence predated the formation/deposition of the limestone and was not the result of recent tomb disturbances, as the formation of such material is a process that requires many centuries. It is possible that the artifacts were dispersed from their original locations within tomb chambers as the result of erosion occurring relatively soon after the cemetery went out of use. Some pieces, however, were well-preserved, and two bowls (P5 and P6) still sat one inside the other, which would argue against their findspots being the result of natural agencies. As already noted prior to the detailed study of the cemetery (Swiny 1985a:14), the explanation that best fits the evidence at hand argues in favor of many, if not all, of these objects being intentionally placed on the ground within the confines of the cemetery, perhaps as part of Early Cypriot funerary rites.

4

THE CERAMICS*

by Ellen Herscher

INTRODUCTION

Excavations at Episkopi *Phaneromeni* beginning in 1975 were the first systematic investigations to reveal the high degree of regionalism that existed in Cyprus during the earlier part of the Bronze Age (Herscher 1976, 1981). The ceramics recovered there during four seasons of work immediately demonstrated that the long-accepted standard classification system for Early and Middle Cypriot ceramics, as elaborated by J. R. Stewart (1962) and based mainly on material from the north coast cemeteries of Bellapais *Vounous* and Lapithos *Vrysi tou Barba*, was not applicable to southern sites. Furthermore, understanding of this period continued to be hampered by the overwhelming preponderance of funerary evidence and almost total lack of excavated settlements. Earlier brief trials in the *Phaneromeni* settlement had led to the conclusion that pottery made for deposit in tombs was totally different from that in domestic use, a view that gained wide acceptance (Weinberg 1956:121; Merrillees 1974:45).

Intensified research in the south and other parts of Cyprus in the past 27 years has begun to provide a fuller, more detailed picture of the complexities of Cyprus in the Early and Middle Bronze Age. Tombs continue to come to light, but some in previously poorly known regions have been subjected to systematic examination (e.g., Todd 1986; Karageorghis 1974). More important, two centrally located settlements have been explored and comprehensively published (Coleman 1996; Frankel and Webb 1996b). With the publication of Sotira *Kaminoudhia*, one more piece is put in place that will help provide the outlines of a restructured view of pre-Late Bronze Age Cypriot society.

Several significant features characterize EC south coast ceramics, especially as represented at Sotira *Kaminoudhia*. Strong continuity from the Philia Phase assemblage is apparent in the wide flat unarticulated bases (at *Vounous*, bases become small and articulated, then round-pointed), deep bowls with rising tubular spout, and ear-lug pots. Incised decoration is uncommon, with the notable exceptions of Red Polished South Coast ware—which continues the parallel lines and herringbone motifs of the Philia style—and Brown Polished ware. At *Kaminoudhia*, at least, both of these wares seem to be for special purposes, and may possibly be imports from other southern sites. The region appears not to have developed the techniques for locally producing real Black Polished ware or the controlled black-topped version of Red Polished ware.

FABRICS

The Bronze Age pottery excavated at Sotira *Kaminoudhia* mainly consists of varieties of Red Polished ware, with a small amount of Drab Polished Blue Core ware. It was possible to isolate three

---

*A complete list of catalogued pottery from *Kaminoudhia* appears in Table 4.1. The catalogue of pottery from the settlement appears at the end of this chapter. Cemetery pottery is catalogued in Chapter 3.

distinct varieties of Red Polished ware: RP Philia, RP South Coast and RP Mottled, but further divisions within the heterogeneous corpus of Red Polished ware did not prove to be workable.[1] In addition, a number of pieces seemed to fall between the established categories. Brown Polished ware could also be considered a variant of RP, although its distinctive features of fabric technology (seen especially in the consistent brown firing of its slip), shape, and decoration are here considered to warrant separate terminology.

RED POLISHED WARE (RP)

The pottery classified simply as RP ware at *Kaminoudhia* represents a continuum of fabrics.[2] It varies from quite soft to moderately hard clay; light orange to dark red-orange (5YR 5/6, 6/6, 6/4) in color,[3] generally not fully oxidized (the core is usually gray). Inclusions consist of black, white and gray particles of various sizes, sometimes with added organic temper. The slip is usually quite thick, dark red-orange to dark red-brown (5YR 5/4, 10R 4/6, 2.5YR 5/8), with some luster although not highly lustrous; normally the surface has some dark gray and/or brown areas, evidence for irregular firing conditions. Bowl P16, from the settlement, has a fairly uniform dark gray interior, perhaps evidence for stacking during firing; bowl P15, also from the settlement, appears to have been misfired or burned while in use.

A wide variety of common shapes occur in RP ware: small, large and spouted bowls, jugs, juglets, amphorae, and the unique hob (P81). Versions of this fabric were in use at all periods of settlement and cemetery use at *Kaminoudhia*. Examples from both cemetery and settlement showed signs of wear, usually on the base;[4] the interior of cooking pot P92 appeared to be worn from use.

Decoration on RP ware from the cemetery is scanty. The most is found on juglet P2 (fig. 4.10), from Cemetery B but unfortunately without context. The only other significant decoration is on jug P99 (fig. 4.4), with the standard scheme for Type A jugs on the handle and a relief band at the neckline. The simple incision on the handle of jug P8 (fig. 4.4) is most probably a potmark; the decoration on the handles of jug P58 (fig. 4.4) and juglet P3 (fig. 4.7), similar motifs of interlocking lozenges, may be related to the Type A jug scheme, or could be potmarks as well. The only other relief decoration recorded from the cemetery was a single knob near the handle of jug P118 (fig. 4.6), again possibly a potter's sign.

Decoration on RP ware from the settlement was somewhat more plentiful, but still consisted mainly of simple forms. Again there is one elaborately incised pot (the fragmentary amphora P82, fig. 4.13), and several examples of Type A jugs with incised necks and handles and relief bands at the neckline (P120, P136, P70: figs. 4.4, 4.5). These jugs display various degrees of care in the execution of the decorative scheme. Relief decoration is also combined with incised handles on amphora P83 (fig. 4.14), which has a crescent on the shoulder. Two fragmentary unclassified juglets also combined relief and incision: one with groups of lines on the neck (as on jug Type G) and at the neckline a relief band incised with a zigzag, and the other with a punctured relief band at the neckline and upper handle.

---

[1] Red monochrome sherds without features distinctive of the specialized varieties were classified simply as RP: cf. Webb and Frankel 1999:14–15. For nomenclature of sub-groups, cf. Merrillees 1991.

[2] As also observed at Marki: cf. Frankel and Webb 1996b:113–15.

[3] Color designations according to Munsell 1975, determined in natural light, open shade. The numbers used in these descriptions are the most frequent readings obtained, but all the Sotira *Kaminoudhia* fabrics had considerable variation in color (often even within a single vessel), as is normal for primitive ceramic technology.

[4] Wear was noted on the bases of bowl P21, large spouted bowl P63, and juglet P2, from the cemetery, and jug P69 (pl. 4.1a) and large bowl P110 from the settlement.

Groups of short incised lines are found on the lugs or handles of large (P110, P133: fig. 4.2) and small bowls (P129 and P132: fig. 4.1, P144), and spouted bowls (P43, fig. 4.3). Groups of short parallel lines appear on the body, neck and handle of jug P33 (fig. 4.6) and on other fragments of Type G jugs (the motif also occurs in RP Mottled fabric). The "X" on the handle of juglet P30 (fig. 4.7) is probably a potmark.

A few other examples of relief decoration—these not accompanied by incision—were found on RP ware from the settlement. They include a pair of conical knobs at the base of the handle on juglet P73 (fig. 4.7), a plain relief band at the neckline and on the neck over the upper handle attachment on juglet P138 (fig. 4.7), a small crescent on the shoulder and a short vertical line on the handle of juglet P55 (fig. 4.7), and conical knobs with punctured centers and a vertical wavy band on the shoulder of jug P106 (fig. 4.6).

Some RP vessels provided evidence for methods used in their manufacture. From the cemetery, the slip on bowl P21 was smeared as though applied with a cloth and burnishing marks were clearly visible on amphora P100. Cooking pot P23 preserved a fingerprint in its slip, while the surface of several vessels[5] retained impressions of various organic materials, such as straw, grass and seeds.

Settlement vessels also showed evidence for burnishing (bowls P132 and P144) and straw impressions (spouted amphora P127). The *interior* of two vessels (amphora P83, pl. 4.1b; spouted amphora P127) was slipped and smoothed as well as the exterior, although in a somewhat thin and smeared manner; amphora P83 also had a groove around the rim interior (pl. 4.2a). While most vertical handles—where the method could be ascertained—were attached in the typical Cypriot Bronze Age manner, with the lower end inserted through the pot wall (e.g., P8, fig. 4.4; P30, fig. 4.7; cf. Webb and Frankel 1999:18), the handles of several vessels were inserted at *both* ends, sometimes smoothed on the interior and other times left protruding.[6] The alternative method of handle attachment—affixing the handle ends to the exterior of the pot body—is perhaps reinforced by finger impressions at one or both handle attachments, e.g., on cooking pot P92, jug P33, and a fragmentary amphora. The large bowl P110 provided evidence for ancient repairs (pl. 4.3a).

The section of the base of jug P120 (fig. 4.4) indicates an unusual method of manufacture. While flat on the exterior, it is totally round on the interior, thus becoming very thin in the center and very thick toward the outside edge of the base. It appears that the base was originally made round and then scraped off to become flat. A second fragmentary Type A jug from the same unit (Unit 6) had a similar base, although it was not quite so thin in the middle. The base of bowl P125 appeared to have been made in the same manner.

When the lugs on bowls were pierced, it was usually done horizontally with a round instrument, although one unstratified bowl lug from Cemetery A was pierced at a considerable slant. Another lug from Area B Unit 12 was not pierced all the way through. Evidence for different kinds of piercing tools includes a tapering pointed tool (seen on a fragmentary lug from Unit 1 Phase II whose hole has a tapering triangular section), and a thin wide tool (seen on a fragmentary lug from Unit 3 Phase II).

RED POLISHED MOTTLED WARE

Red Polished Mottled ware is one of the most common fabrics of the Early and Middle Cypriot periods, having been identified at sites throughout the island.[7] It occurs in both the settlement and

---

[5] Bowls P17, P22 and P78; amphora P100, and cooking pot P23.
[6] Smoothed: amphora P83 (pl. 4.2b) and jug P70 (fig. 4.5); protruding: jug P136 (fig. 4.5).
[7] E.g., Herscher 1981:80–81; Swiny 1981:58-59; Todd 1985:60–71; Todd 1986:131; Herscher 1988:142; Herscher and Swiny 1992:73–82; cf. Merrillees 1978:26.

cemetery at Sotira *Kaminoudhia*, where it is a hard to moderately hard fabric, usually containing many small black and white inclusions. The fired clay is generally red-brown or dark red-brown in color (2.5-5 YR 5/4-6), sometimes varying to brown or orange; frequently there is a thick dark gray unoxidized interior or core. The slip is normally moderately thick and quite lustrous, dark red-brown or sometimes brown (2.5YR-10R 4-5/6), relatively sparsely mottled with dark gray or brown areas.[8] A coarser, less well-finished version is sometimes used for storage vessels.

In comparison to the Red Polished Mottled ware from the nearby site of Episkopi *Phaneromeni* (Herscher 1981:80–81), that from *Kaminoudhia* normally has a thicker and more lustrous slip, is frequently somewhat less hard, and shows less color variation in the surface mottling. Such differences may only indicate localized varieties of the fabric or could represent chronological distinctions related to the evolution of firing technology, as higher temperatures may have been attained at the later site of *Phaneromeni* (Shepard 1965:124).

Most RP Mottled ware occurs in open shapes, such as bowls of various sizes, spouted bowls, and dippers. In both the settlement and the cemetery, small bowls were the most common type, a few of them spouted. A wider variety of shapes came from the settlement, including several dippers, a few cooking pots, a large coarse basin (P121), a sherd from a large closed vessel reworked into a pot support or mold (P67) and one catalogued example each of a jug and juglet (P51, P60). Most vessels display the irregularity to be expected from handmade ceramics, although a few pieces are particularly misshapen, such as large bowl P104, and the small bowl P84 which stands considerably off-axis.

Most RP Mottled ware from Sotira *Kaminoudhia* is undecorated. However, a few pieces from the settlement displayed a minimal amount of incised or relief decoration, usually on handles or similar attachments. These include a tankard (P40, fig. 4.7) and spouted bowls (P43, fig. 4.3; P49, fig. 4.4) with a single vertical line incised on the handle, a similar incised line on the lugs of small bowls (e.g., P25, fig. 4.1), and on cooking pot handles (cooking pot P116, fig. 4.15, also bore a group of punctures on its handle top). Double lines were incised on the handle of a storage vessel (P141, fig. 4.16). Groups of three incised lines appear on the ledge lug of a small bowl (P13, fig. 4.1), on the handle, neck or upper body of Type G jugs (e.g., fig. 4.6: P33, P51), and on the upper body to the right of a handle attachment on a fragmentary coarse RP Mottled storage jar. An incised rectilinear motif appears below the handle on another storage vessel (P140, fig. 4.16). A small tripod leg fragment (P143, fig. 4.15) had a scheme with multiple lines. The few examples of relief decoration recovered include a horizontal band below the rim of a deep spouted bowl (P135, fig. 4.3), and impressed relief bands on two rim sherds from large bowls.

From the cemetery, the only RP Mottled vessel that might be considered decorated is the juglet P12 (fig. 4.7), which has a single conical knob on the body near the handle (or this might be considered a potmark). Accidental traces left from the manufacturing process include a straw impression on bowl P84, and two olive leaf impressions on bowl P48 (pl. 4.6b). Most probably the small bowls were stacked inside one another when fired, although it cannot be assumed that the fusion of the two bowls actually found attached (P5, P6: pl. 4.3b) occurred during the firing process or through some later activity. Bowl P84 shows signs of wear on its base and handle, spouted bowl P96 shows wear on its base, and bowl P97 on both rim and base.

Several vessels from the settlement provide evidence for the manufacturing process. At least some storage vessels (e.g., P142, fig. 4.16, and another similar fragment from Area C Unit 2) were built on mats, the impression of which is preserved on the base, but a similar but unimpressed fragmentary base from Area A shows that this method was not universal. A similar mat impression appears on the exterior sides of a fragmentary unstratified griddle (pl. 4.5b). Variations on the usual method of handle attachment were observed on storage vessel P141 (pl. 4.4c), for which the lower handle end

---

[8] For a color illustration of ware, see Morris 1985: pl. 12.

was pushed through the pot wall, but then was smoothed on the interior. For jug P147, the upper handle end was inserted through the neck and smoothed (pl. 4.4b), and the neck was inserted into the body then secured by adding clay on the exterior of the join (pl. 4.4a). Griddle P139 showed clear marks of burnishing. Wear observed on RP Mottled vessels from the settlement included the base of bowl P114 and the handle of storage vessel P141.

RED POLISHED PHILIA WARE (RP/P)

All the Red Polished Philia ware identified at *Kaminoudhia* came from the cemetery, with the exception of one sherd identified from Area A of the settlement.[9] It generally conforms to the fine, well-levigated, fairly soft-fired fabric known at other Philia sites.[10] The clay is light-colored brown or red-brown with a gray core and a small amount of small black and white inclusions. The unclassified ear-lug pot P11 has a notably harder and darker fabric than normal. Slip is a lustrous dark red to dark red-brown, usually fairly thick, with an alternative version of thin matt slip.[11] Both standard and pattern burnished varieties occur at *Kaminoudhia*; when the burnishing strokes are visible, they were applied either in even bands or in an irregular pattern in all directions. Pattern burnishing is attested on ear-lug pots, small bowls, spouted bowls, and jugs.

A coarser version of the RP/P fabric was used for cooking pots (Dikaios 1/1, P66, P91), but it is still relatively soft in comparison to that used for later cooking pots. The large quantity of inclusions suggests intentional modifications to meet the thermal requirements.[12]

A wide repertoire of Philia shapes is attested at *Kaminoudhia*.[13] These include the small bowl, spouted bowl, jug, large jug with round spout (P103, fig. 4.6), neck juglet, bottles, ear-lug pots, cooking pots, and a storage vessel (P53, fig. 4.14). Notably absent, however, is the jug with long beak spout, so characteristic of Philia Phase sites elsewhere, especially the type site of Philia *Vasiliko*. All have flat bases except for the small bottles (Dikaios 1/5 and P75 from Tomb 15).

The flat base of juglet P14 (fig. 4.7) is unusual, with its slightly flaring articulated appearance. Since the vessel was intact, it was not possible to examine the interior in order to determine the method of manufacture: the base may have been flattened by pressing down on a hard surface, or it may have been made separately and then applied to the pot bottom (cf. Webb and Frankel 1999:18). Evidence for the method of base construction can be seen on the interior of the ear-lug pot P102 (Type B, pl. 4.5a), which has ten or more shallow linear depressions on the inside of its flat base. These depressions (0.7 cm maximum diameter and 0.35 cm deep) appear to have been made with a stick, not the potter's fingers.

---

[9] Also from Area A came a worked sherd roundel that may be of RP Philia fabric (TC51, see Chapter 9), as may be some of the pottery from the settlement identified as "RP Pattern Burnished" (see Appendix to this chapter). The difficulty of identifying RP Philia ceramics in sherd form should also be kept in mind: cf. Frankel and Webb 1999:95.

[10] Frankel and Webb 1996b:149–53; Bolger 1991:33–34; Peltenberg et al 1986:37. For a full discussion of RP/P ware see Webb and Frankel 1999:14–23, 39 and Table 2. For a quite accurate color illustration see Morris 1985: pl. 8.

[11] Webb and Frankel (1999:18) have noted the bimodal distribution of the finish on RP/P—either very lustrous or matt—whereas the luster of regular RP falls into a continuum on a unimodal curve, with most classified in the middle (i.e., slightly lustrous).

[12] Cf. Webb and Frankel 1999:28–29 ("RP Coarse Philia"); for thermal properties of cooking pots, see Frankel and Webb 1996b:167–69; cf. Taramides 1999:47–97.

[13] For a synthesis of the standard Philia repertoire, see Webb and Frankel 1999: figs. 3, 5. They suggest (p. 39) that the new pottery types introduced with the Philia Phase may be related to new eating/drinking rituals.

While the lower end of most jug and juglet handles was attached by the typical Philia (and later RP) method of insertion through the pot wall, there is at least one exception (P103), perhaps an indication that some degree of experimentation was still taking place. Further evidence for manufacturing techniques comes from the ear-lug pot P94, which has a small air pocket inside the rim, parallel to the lip, indicating how the rim was formed by folding over toward the exterior.

Several vessels display the distinctive complex Philia style incised decoration composed of parallel lines, multiple zigzags and herringbones (cf. Webb and Frankel 1999:23). It seems that the use of decoration is closely tied to the type of vessel: all Philia ear-lug pots,[14] flasks (P101, fig. 4.8; P9, P35: fig. 4.9) and bottles are decorated, but not jugs or bowls. Of particular interest is the ear-lug pot P41 (fig. 4.12), found above Tomb 17, which retains some traditional Philia design elements (parallel lines, herringbone), but is also beginning to evolve into the more structured style of RPSC (cf., e.g., flask P80 from Tomb 7; fig. 4.8).[15]

RED POLISHED SOUTH COAST WARE (RPSC)

Red Polished South Coast ware was first (and presciently) defined by Stewart, although few examples were known at the time.[16] Later excavations at *Phaneromeni* confirmed the south coast origin of this ware and provided further evidence for its characteristics (Herscher 1981:80). Lubsen-Admiraal (1999) has now undertaken a study of the ware, in which she provides many additional examples although they are unfortunately of unknown provenience. All the RPSC found at *Kaminoudhia* came from the cemetery, with the exception of three possible sherds from Area A of the settlement.

The fabric of RPSC at *Kaminoudhia* is generally quite soft and poorly oxidized, displaying a mostly gray core, with a small amount of fine inclusions and sometimes fine organic tempering. The slip is thin, most commonly red-brown to dull red, usually with a low degree of luster (cf. Stewart 1988:60). Impressions of organic materials were observed on the surface of at least one vessel (P76).

Red Polished South Coast ware sometimes occurs in a variation that is virtually all black in surface color. But this is not a highly lustrous true black like Black Polished ware, as defined by Gjerstad and Stewart,[17] and which is particularly common at Dhenia, but rather a very dark gray or very dark brown. RPSC, even in its "red" version, always has at least some irregular black areas of various sizes, and many of the mostly "black" examples have at least a small red area. So there has been no attempt to divide the classification of the *Kaminoudhia* South Coast ware into Red Polished and Black Polished versions, by virtue of the assumption that the differences in appearance are not due to an intentional effort to produce a "Black Polished" ware, but rather are due to the nature of the firing conditions and lack of control thereof. Indeed, black or dark brown is the most common surface color among the *Kaminoudhia* RPSC pots. The one example that does appear to display a controlled firing technique is the conical bowl P31, on which a black-bottomed effect was produced.

---

[14] Although the ear-lug pot P7 has only simple incision on the lug.

[15] Evolution in the Philia style of decoration may also be suggested by a jar from Kissonerga *Mosphilia* (Peltenberg 1983: fig. 2b), on which the decoration seems less developed than the standard scheme: does this indicate an early stage of development?

[16] Stewart 1962:270, 359; for the nomenclature, cf. Merrillees 1991:238. As further evidence for the ware's chronology has become known, it has seemed advisable to drop Stewart's use of "I" in the name, since it does not really seem to be a regional variant equivalent to the standard (north coast) RP I. (Stewart [1988:60] was also aware of its possible EC II date.)

[17] Gjerstad 1926:131; Stewart 1962:227, figs. CLII–CLIV; for a good rendition of the color of Black polished ware, see Morris 1985: pl. 19.

While a wide variety of shapes has been attested in RPSC (cf. Lubsen-Admiraal 1999), at *Kaminoudhia* a single shape—the flask—dominates. The only other types identified were a conical bowl (P31) from Tomb 7, and an ear-lug sherd from Tomb 4 (cf. Stewart 1962: fig. CII:5 [provenance unknown]). Most significantly, there is no evidence at *Kaminoudhia* for the elaborate, often multi-necked vessels and rhytons so characteristic of previously known RPSC (with the possible exception of what may be a bracket fragment: see below).

Most RPSC ware is highly decorated, although a few undecorated examples have been identified (Lubsen-Admiraal 1999: figs. 7, 31). The usual decoration consists of linear and punctured patterns, executed with a broad, round flat-ended tool, arranged in groups of parallel lines, bands or individual motifs of zigzags and chevrons, and rows of punctures (cf. fig. 4.9). The decoration appears to have connections to the Philia style, for example in its use of the herringbone pattern and groups of diagonal parallel lines, but the overall effect is more structured.[18] RPSC decoration also is characterized by more elaboration than that of Philia vessels, with the addition of punctures and circles, although this tendency is not as pronounced on the *Kaminoudhia* examples as on those known from elsewhere. The shape repertoire also differs from that of the Philia Phase. RPSC decoration, especially as it appears in the simpler versions (as is typical of *Kaminoudhia*), also has similarities to some RP I vessels from *Vounous*, particularly a number of flasks and bottles with linear and punctured decoration.[19]

Despite the additional evidence provided by *Kaminoudhia*, the majority of known RPSC is still without scientific context;[20] nevertheless, there are strong grounds for concluding that it was widespread in southern and western Cyprus. It is well attested at Episkopi *Phaneromeni*[21] Paramali,[22] and Anoyira (Stewart 1962: fig. LXXIII.1,2), and has now been found within the city of Limassol (*Katholiki* quarter).[23] Other examples apparently also come from somewhere in the Limassol area.[24] The easternmost example is that said to be found "near Amathus" (Stewart 1962: fig. CVII.4). To the west, a number of RPSC vessels have been reported to come from Yialia or elsewhere in the Paphos District.[25] An example said to be from Dhenia appears to be the most northerly occurrence, if this attribution is correct (des Gagniers and Karageorghis 1976: pl. V:2). In central Cyprus, a fragmentary example has now been excavated at Marki *Alonia* (Frankel and Webb 2000: fig. 4 [P13740]).

---

[18] Stewart originally observed this style's links to Philia pottery: 1992:84–85; 1962:270.

[19] Cf., e.g., Stewart 1962: figs XCIX.6, C.11, CII.2, CIII.4, CV.5, CVI.7, CVII.3; Stewart and Stewart 1950: pl. LXVI.b. Hennessy (1973:14, fig. 5.3–5) singled out this group and noted its connections to both RPSC and Philia pottery.

[20] E.g., des Gagniers and Karageorghis 1976: pls. V:1, VI.2; Karageorghis 1991: pl. CXIX.3; Karageorghis 1985a: Nos. 23, 26, 27, 30; Taramides 1999: pls. 13, 15–16, 18–19, 22.

[21] Herscher 1981: fig. 4.1; Weinberg 1956: fig. 11; Swiny 1995:31 (top row). Probably removed from *Phaneromeni* in ancient times is the piece found in the Archaic altar at the Kourion Sanctuary of Apollo Hylates (Buitron-Oliver 1996: fig. 45.A1). Other finds are likely to have come from the *Phaneromeni* area: e.g., Dikaios 1940: pl. LIV.7,8; Stewart 1962: figs. LXXIII.3; CVII.1, 2; CXLII.19; Karageorghis 1985a: No. 22; Lubsen-Admiraal 1988:127–28, pl. XXVIII.1–3, figs. 1–2.

[22] Herscher and Swiny 1992:74–75, n. 22 (with references); pls. XII.2, XIII:1. The ware is also said to come from the nearby site of Evdhimou *Kiladhes* (Karageorghis 1976:851, fig. 20).

[23] Christou 1993:725, figs. 26 and 27; Christou 1998a:74, figs. 30 and 31 (incorrectly labeled as figs. "26" and "27").

[24] E.g., Papageorghiou 1991:794, fig. 24; Lubsen-Admiraal 1999:35; Christou 1998b:80, fig. 39.

[25] Karageorghis 1968:286–287, fig 56; des Gagniers and Karageorghis 1976: pl. VI.1; Karageorghis 1975:817–18, fig. 31; Karageorghis 1988:804, fig. 29; Stewart 1992: fig. 10.7.

A much wider variety of shapes is attested in the coastal regions of the south than were found at the more inland site of *Kaminoudhia*, further evidence to support Stewart's belief that RPSC originated there. He also remarked upon the rather soft fabric of these vessels and the impractical, nonfunctional shapes of many of them, thus concluding that they were for purely ceremonial or funerary use (Stewart 1988:60; cf. Weinberg 1956:121). However, the examples of RPSC found at *Kaminoudhia* were almost entirely simple flasks and made in a harder version of the fabric that is clearly functional. Furthermore, they were equipped with holes at the rim, presumably to facilitate some method of closing the pot's opening and protecting its contents. Because of these factors, it may be suggested that these flasks represent the EC I/II predecessors of the Brown Polished and north coast black-topped bottles which appear to have been containers for some widely traded substance in the EC III period (cf. Herscher 1991).

BROWN POLISHED WARE

A highly standardized type of small bottle found in both cemetery and settlement at *Kaminoudhia* was made of a distinctive fabric that has been called "Brown Polished ware" in this study. While such vessels have previously been termed "Black Polished" ware (e.g., Karageorghis 1940–1948:130–32, figs. 14.11, 15, 17, 18, 19)—and they may in fact represent the south coast's regional attempt to produce Black Polished ware—they are distinctly different from the standard Black Polished as well known on the north coast and at Dhenia.

Brown Polished ware is made of fine soft light gray-brown (7.5YR 6/4, 10YR 7/4) clay with a small amount of fine black, white and organic temper (and sometimes a few small dark red inclusions); frequently a distinction between the browner core and a gray exterior surface can be seen. The surface is covered with a thin lustrous dark brown to grayish-brown (7.5YR 3/2, 10YR 3/2) slip, sometimes with a few small lighter areas (cf. Herscher 1991:47).

All Brown Polished vessels found at *Kaminoudhia* are small bottles with round bases (one of the few round-based types found at the site), globular or piriform bodies, narrow neck with flaring rim which is pierced by two opposed holes (Bottles Types A and B, fig. 4.10 [P27, P29, P98]). At other sites (most notably Kalavasos) a few other shapes are attested, but the bottle remains overwhelmingly the most common. Additional shapes found at Kalavasos include an ear-lug pot, small bowls, a juglet, and spindle whorls.[26] The only other shape known is an amphoriskos, said to be from Arpera (MacLaurin 1980: fig. 82.9). All are decorated with fine incision in a limited and standardized repertoire of multiple zigzags, rows of dots, and chevrons filled with dots or parallel lines.[27] It is likely that the Brown Polished bottles from *Kaminoudhia* were imported for their contents from elsewhere in southern Cyprus (perhaps the Kalavasos area: cf. Herscher 1991).

DRAB POLISHED BLUE CORE WARE (DPBC)

Drab Polished Blue Core ware occurs rarely at *Kaminoudhia*, represented by only one vessel (tankard P95) in the cemetery and a few incomplete vessels from the settlement. All of the examples display the distinctive thick gray or bluish-gray core produced by the reduction technique by which it

---

[26] Karageorghis 1940–1948: figs. 14.19, 18:GI, 5.6; Todd 1986: fig. 36.5–7. In Tombs 9 and 10 a total of 20 bottles were found along with a bowl and amphora (Karageorghis 1940–1948:130–32, figs. 14.11, 15, 17, 18, 19).

[27] A few juglets from other sites (Alambra, Larnaca, *Phaneromeni*) of typical fine RP fabric are decorated in a similar style: cf. Coleman 1996: fig. 72.F631; Herscher 1988: fig. 3.8; Herscher 1991:46.

was fired (generally only the surface itself has been oxidized). The pyrotechnology used to produce DPBC ware appears more advanced than that of the usual varieties of RP ware found at *Kaminoudhia*, and it is assumed to be imported from elsewhere on the island (most likely from somewhere in the general southwestern region).[28]

The fabric of the DPBC ware at *Kaminoudhia* is hard to very hard, pinkish-orange (2.5YR 6/4, 5YR 6/6) when oxidized, with many white and some dark red inclusions. Most vessels retain traces of a thin lustrous light orange to pinkish-brown (2.5YR 6/6) slip, sometimes with visible burnishing marks (e.g., tankard P72, jug P109). The slip often has an irregular, smeared appearance, suggesting that it was applied by wiping. Straw impressions are visible in the surface of P95. Often the surface is poorly preserved and flaking off (cf. Rye 1981:114).

The DPBC shapes from *Kaminoudhia* also appear to be more advanced than the local RP ones. Its bases are either round, pointed, or occasionally "dimple," "nipple," or small flat and articulated,[29] but never the plain, flat unarticulated bases that are otherwise the norm (see especially Unclassified Jugs and Unclassified Juglets, below). Tankard P95 (fig. 4.7) is one of very few round-based vessels from the cemetery: the others are the highly specialized brown or black-topped bottles (otherwise only the round-pointed base of RPSC conical bowl P31 is not flat).

The only DPBC shapes attested at the site are large jugs (P109), juglets (P137, P88), and tankards (P85, P95, P72)—six nearly complete vessels and several additional fragments. The presence of three examples of the unusual tankard (Types A and B), the forerunner of an advanced shape with a long continuation into later periods, is further indication of the precocious nature of DP ware. The only indication of an open DPBC shape at *Kaminoudhia* was an unstratified lug from a small bowl found in the area of Cemetery A.

Frankel and Webb have noted the unusual method of attaching the neck of DP vessels, by placing the neck cylinder *outside* the body (1996b:156–57). This probably accounts for the fact that DPBC necks generally appear less articulated than those of RP vessels. The bands and punctures that frequently occur as decoration at the neckline would also serve to help seal the pieces together. The usual practice of attaching the lower handle end by insertion through the body can be seen on juglet P137.

Decoration appears to be more common on DPBC ware than on the RP ware from *Kaminoudhia*. This includes plain and impressed relief bands (P137, fig. 4.7; P109, fig. 4.6) and rows of punctures (P72, fig. 4.7). The lug of the unstratified small bowl from Cemetery A has three short lines incised on top.

Drab Polished Blue Core ware is still mainly known from chance finds and rescue excavations, so its internal chronology remains poorly understood. But the examples from *Kaminoudhia* demonstrate that the type with simple crude punctured decoration, or entirely plain, can be dated to Early Cypriot III (for full discussion of chronology, see Chapter 17).

COARSE WARE

While many vessels are made of a coarser fabric, they have been classified as Red Polished because of the presence of a burnished slip. Only one coarse vessel, the dipper (?) P128 (see Unclassi-

---

[28] For discussion of DP ware, with references, see Herscher and Fox 1993; Frankel and Webb 1996b:155–60, 179. For other contemporary south coast examples, found even further to the east (at Kalavasos), see Karageorghis 1940–1948: figs. 21.CI; 23.CVII; 24.8.

[29] E.g., large unclassified jug P109 and a similar fragmentary base, slightly larger in diameter, from Area C, Unit 9.

fied Cooking Pots) appeared to be without any slip whatsoever: rather the surface appears to have been simply smoothed, mottled black to dark red-brown from firing. The large amount of sand inclusions present in the clay suggests that it was intended to withstand heat. The single handle preserved was incised, and the flat base showed signs of wear.

SHAPES

The ceramic types found at *Kaminoudhia* represent a limited range of simple shapes, most of them well suited to the everyday utilitarian tasks of eating, drinking, food preparation, transport and storage.[30] Only a few types might be seen to serve some more specialized function—for example, the highly decorated flasks, bottles, and conical bowl—but such an interpretation is by no means necessary. All the shapes display some irregularity and the lack of standardization that is normal for hand-made pottery: occasionally a vessel is extremely misshapen (e.g., large bowl P104). The vast majority of the ceramic repertoire has flat bases, with the exception of the bottles, the DPBC vessels, and the RPSC conical bowl.

SMALL BOWLS

Small bowls (fig. 4.1) are the most common pottery type at *Kaminoudhia*, found in all three areas of the settlement[31] as well as in the cemetery. They were particularly prevalent in Units 2, 8 and 10 in Area C, where they far outnumbered all other types of vessels (see Chapter 2, above). The normal diameter for "small" bowls is estimated to be 10–15 cm, in contrast to "large" bowls with an estimated diameter of approximately 35–40 cm.[32] Small bowls vary widely in shape, fabric and added details (usually lugs). All are undecorated except for occasional small incisions, which should probably be considered as potmarks rather than decoration.

All small bowls from the cemetery have small flat bases (although the bases of P5 and P19 are only slightly flattened). Bases from the settlement are either flat, round or impressed "dimple" bases. No bowl from the settlement is definitely without an added lug, but the lugless shape is clearly attested in the cemetery (P97). Only on bowls from the settlement are the lugs occasionally incised, impressed or punctured (e.g., P132, P25, P13, P129, P59). Only Types A and C are attested in both cemetery and settlement, but it should be noted that Bowl Type A is an extremely heterogeneous and inclusive class, while the two examples of Bowl Type C are not very close parallels.

Bowl Type A. The most common small bowl type, but not highly standardized, is found in both the cemetery and the settlement (only in Area A, where it is still less common than in the tombs), in RP and RP Mottled fabrics. All have deep ovoid bodies, plain rims and small flat bases (although occasionally, for example P19, there is only a very slight flattening of the bottom). Height: ca. 9–11 cm; diameter: ca. 13–15 cm. In at least one case, P97, the bowl has no added lug; several other examples have no lugs preserved (P1, P10, P54, P114, P125), but since their rims are not complete, one may originally have

---

[30] The distribution of the various shapes within the settlement is discussed in Chapter 2 and shown on Table 2.1a–f.

[31] However, they were poorly represented in Area B, with only a few sherds and no identifiable types recovered from the excavated area.

[32] In sherd form, the fragments are usually too small to permit an accurate reconstruction of the original diameter. In these cases, bowl sherds were classified as "small" or "large" on the basis of rim thickness: small bowls always have a distinctly thinner rim.

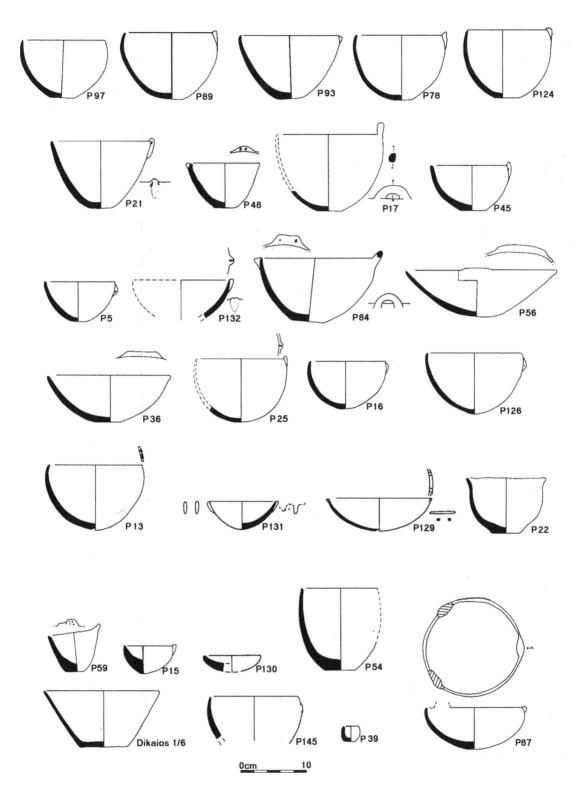

Fig. 4.1. Bowls Type A (P97, P89, P93, P78, P124, P21, P48, P17); **Bowls Type B** (P45, P5, P132, P84); **Bowls Type C** (P56, P36); **Bowl Type D** (P25); **Bowls Type E** (P16, P126); **Bowl Type F** (P13); **Bowls Type G** (P131, P129); **Bowls Type H** (P22, P59, P15, P130); **Unclassified Philia Phase Bowls** (P54, Dikaios 1/6); **Bowl with unusual lug** (P145); **Composite Vessels** (P39, P87).

been present. Lug forms include unpierced pointed vertical lugs at the rim (P89, P19, P47) and a plain, conical knob at the rim (P93). Three examples (P78, P124, P46) have more globular bodies, with S-shaped or pointed lugs at the rim. The type also includes a more conical variation (P21, P125), sometimes with a pierced pointed lug. Another more conical example, P48, is smaller than most of the bowls in this class, and has two semicircular ledge lugs at the rim, one of them pierced twice. These bowls, especially those from the cemetery, are generally comparable to RP I bowls from *Vounous* and occur frequently at other south coast sites.[33] The body of P17 is deeper and more ovoid than usual, and has a horizontal handle rising from the rim.

> Illustrated examples (fig. 4.1): P97 (and pl. 3.6c), P89 (and pl. 3.7b), P93 (and pl. 3.7a), P78 (and pl.3.7c), P124, P21 (and pl. 3.6b), P48 (and pl. 3.7c), P17.
> Additional catalogued examples: P1, P4, P10, P19, P46, P47, P113, P114, P125.

Bowl Type B. Hemispherical bowl with flattened base, smaller and shallower than Bowl Type A, in both RP and RP Mottled fabrics. Height: 6–7.5 cm; diameter: 10–13 cm. The sufficiently preserved examples all have lugs, sometimes pierced and one (P132) incised on the top. None of the few examples comes from a good context, but it may occur in Area C of the settlement as well as in the cemetery area. A similar bowl but somewhat larger than is usual for the type (P84) has a pierced horned horizontal lug and a horizontal handle opposed at the rim.[34]

> Illustrated examples (fig. 4.1): P45, P5, P132, P84 (and pl. 3.6c); pl. 4.3b: P6.

Bowl Type C. A shallow bowl with flat base and at least one narrow horizontal ledge lug at the rim. Height: 7–8 cm; diameter: ca. 19–23 cm. Examples are known from both the cemetery and the settlement (Area C), in RP and RP Mottled fabrics. A similar ledge lug incised with three alternating pairs of parallel lines (cf. P133, Large bowl Type B) was found unstratified in a trial trench east of Tomb 10. A few similar bowls have been recognized at other sites.[35]

> Illustrated examples (fig. 4.1): P36, P56.

Bowl Type D. Similar to Type A in all respects, except that the base is round. All sufficiently preserved examples have a pointed lug at the rim, sometimes pierced or with an incised line on the top of the lug (P25, P144). Found only in the settlement, Areas A and C, in RP Mottled fabric. This shape is deeper than the usual EC III–MC I knob lug bowl (cf. Type E) and probably represents a somewhat earlier version (cf. Frankel and Webb 1996b: fig. 7.3 [P5613]; Karageorghis 1940–1948: fig. 18:AIII).

> Illustrated example (fig. 4.1): P25.
> Additional catalogued examples: P108, P115, P144.

---

[33] E.g., Stewart 1962: fig CXXXVIII:25–28; for comparable examples from other sites, see, e.g., Todd 1985: fig. 6:38, 51, 52; pl. IX:6; Todd 1986: fig. 35.2; Frankel and Webb 1996b:117, fig 7:3 (P3602, P3167, P3687, P6352, P7086); Frankel and Webb 1999: fig. 6: P11665, P11945; Karageorghis 1940–1948: fig. 18:AII; Herscher and Swiny 1992: pls. IX:4; XI:3; Vavouranakis and Manginis 1995: fig. 4:3; for P48, cf. Georghiou 2000: fig. 3:16.
[34] Somewhat similar bowls from *Vounous* have two lugs and no handle: Stewart 1962: fig. CXLII: 15, 17.
[35] Cf. Frankel and Webb 1996b: fig. 7:3 (P3798); Todd 1986: fig. 24:8; somewhat similar, but with pierced lug, Stewart 1962: fig. CXLII:17.

Bowl Type E. Similar to Type B, except that the base is round and most examples are slightly larger (height: ca. 7.5–9 cm; diameter ca. 12–15 cm). Lugs are a plain convex shape and placed below the rim, sometimes pierced (P126). All examples came from Area A of the settlement, in Red Polished fabric. These appear to be the local version of the knob-lug hemispherical bowls with round bases that are ubiquitous throughout Cyprus beginning in EC II and continuing into MC.[36] Cf. Dipper Type A (below).

Illustrated examples (fig. 4.1): P16, P126.
Additional catalogued example: P44.

Bowl Type F. A deep ovoid body similar in size and shape to Type D, in RP Mottled fabric, but the round base has an impression ("dimple") in the center. Both examples have a slight thickening on the rim impressed with three transverse lines. The two examples of this distinctive type are both from the settlement, Area A Unit 5, perhaps suggesting that they are made by the same hand. A fragmentary somewhat smaller bowl with a similar impressed base was found in Area C Unit 2. This base type seems to occur occasionally throughout the island beginning in EC III, and appears on a variety of small vessel shapes.[37]

Illustrated example (fig. 4.1): P13.
Additional catalogued example: P20.

Bowl Type G. Two examples with a shallow hemispherical body and holes below the rim, perhaps for hanging the vessel.[38] Each has opposed lugs at the rim, pairs of vertical ones on P131 and incised horizontal ledge lugs on P129. Bases are round, or impressed as Type F. Both are of RP fabric, from Area C.

Illustrated examples (fig. 4.1): P129, P131.

Bowl Type H. Grouped together in this type are four crudely shaped, irregular small bowls, from both cemetery and settlement, the fabrics of which can generally be classified as RP. The horizontal lug at the rim of P59 is decorated with rough punctures. The two bowls from the settlement, especially P15 from Area A, show signs of misfiring, or perhaps later burning. Along with juglet P14 (from Tomb 6, like P22), these vessels suggest experimentation or children's efforts (Frankel and Webb 1996b:125). However, the similarity of P130 (from Area C) to Philia Phase "dishes" should also be noted.[39]

Illustrated examples (fig. 4.1): P15, P22 (and pl. 3.6a), P59 (and pl. 3.7c), P130.

---

[36] E.g., Stewart 1962: fig CXXXIX:2–42; Coleman et al 1996: fig. 72:F638, F640; Frankel and Webb 1996b:117, 121, fig. 7:4; Karageorghis 1940–1948: fig. 18:AIV.
[37] Cf. Coleman et al. 1996: fig. 72:F639, from Tomb 105: a juglet with the same base type comes from the same tomb; Frankel and Webb 1996b:117; Vavouranakis and Manginis 1995: fig. 6:2; Herscher 1988: pl. XXX:9 (a jug base); possibly Hennessy et al. 1988: figs. 19:1, 21:12; Karageorghis 1940–1948: fig. 18:BV (with horizontal handle).
[38] For similar holes below the rim, see Stewart 1962: fig. CXLII:18.
[39] Cf. Dikaios 1962: fig. 82:14; Stewart 1962: fig. CXLVIII:4; Bolger 1983: fig. 2:12; Hennessy et al. 1988: figs. 9:20, 15:6, 41:2; Peltenburg 1998: fig. 76:7.

Unclassified Philia Phase Bowls. The incomplete and unstratified bowl P54 (fig. 4.1), to which Dikaios Tomb 1/4 is somewhat similar, has a general resemblance to Type A bowls, but its fabric and deep shape are distinct from the vast majority of these. The closest parallels are to Philia Phase bowls in RP and Red-and-Black Polished fabrics.[40] However, because P54 is not intact, it is quite possible that it originally had a lug or even a spout.[41]

Another unclassified vessel, Dikaios Tomb 1/6 (fig. 4.1), also assigned to the Philia Phase, is a low conical RP bowl with flat base, straight flaring sides and plain rim. No lug is preserved, but the rim is not complete.[42] This shape has its origins in the Chalcolithic and disappears early in the EC period. A similar bowl from Nicosia *Ayia Paraskevi* has a small horizontal lug (Bolger 1983: fig. 2:10).

Lugs. A number of lugs that originally belonged to small RP and RP Mottled bowls were found among the stratified sherds from the settlement. These were most common in Area A, in a wide variety of shapes, but generally in the form of a vertical lug, flattened at the top and pierced, attached to the bowl at the rim.[43] Sometimes the top of the lug rises slightly above the rim in a point and is then flattened on the interior side. One example from Area C had a deep vertical incision along its entire length. While most of the pierced holes are circular, two examples indicate that a tapering pointed object and a thin wide object were used as tools in those cases. A deep crude puncture was added to the flat top of one lug. One RP lug from Unit 4 Phase I, with a well-made hole and visible burnishing strokes, seems to have been attached below the rim of the bowl, but the amount preserved is insufficient for determining whether it comes from a Stroke-Burnished bowl.[44]

From Area B came a RP pointed vertical lug, similar to a horned lug, attached below the bowl rim and flattened against the side of the vessel, only partially pierced (cf. Stewart 1962: fig. CXXXVII:22). Area C produced two RP flat-topped vertical lugs, rising slightly above the rim and pierced, like those from Area A. In addition there was a pierced pointed lug, attached at the rim, with a deep vertical incision running the full length of the lug. Of particular interest, from Unit 2 of Area C, is a fragmentary bowl, P145 (fig. 4.1), with a small unpierced lug below the rim, in an unusual RP Mottled fabric that has several characteristics of DPBC ware.

COMPOSITE VESSELS

Two bowls were found in Area C that may have originally comprised parts of composite vessels (fig. 4.1). The RP Mottled bowl P87 has broken areas at the rim suggesting attachments for an unusual handle arrangement that may have connected this bowl to one or more similar vessels.[45]

The tiny bowl P39 was found in an extremely damaged state, and may simply be another crude vessel like those grouped as Bowl Type H above. However, it is worth noting that in shape, size and fabric P39 is very closely similar to an attachment on a White Painted IA (Philia) "cult vessel" from

---

[40] Stewart 1962: fig CXXXI:16; Dikaios 1962: figs. 80:5, 83:12; for Dikaios 1/4, see Dikaios 1962: fig. 83:10.

[41] As, for example, Dikaios 1962: figs. 80:1, 83:3; Hennessy et al. 1988: fig. 17:9; Webb and Frankel 1999: fig. 6:10-11.

[42] Cf. Dikaios 1962: figs. 64:62, 72:5; Hennessy et al. 1988: fig. 11:10; Peltenburg 1986: fig. 2.5; Webb and Frankel 1999: fig. 6:9.

[43] For chronology and distribution, cf. Frankel and Webb 1996b:120.

[44] Cf. Stewart 1962:224, fig. CLI:1–3; Dikaios 1962: fig. 83:3–4; Hennessy et al. 1988: figs. 11:21, 17.5, 9, 19:10.

[45] E.g., Dikaios 1940: pls. XXVI, XLI:b; for similar profile and lug, see Frankel and Webb 1996b: fig. 7:3 (P2909).

Ayia Paraskevi (Stewart 1962: fig. CLV:9; Hennessy et al. 1988: fig. 16:3). While this piece is cata-logued here as RP ware, the fugitive condition of the slip does not preclude the possibility that it may also be WP ware (although otherwise no WP ware was found at *Kaminoudhia*).

LARGE BOWLS

Few large bowls without spouts were found in the *Kaminoudhia* cemetery, a striking contrast to the well-known EC tombs at *Vounous* where large bowls were extremely common.[46] They were much more common in the *Kaminoudhia* settlement, especially Area C where they were most plentiful and diverse, an indication that their function here was probably domestic (although some ritualistic use should not be excluded). Only Type A is attested from both the cemetery and the settlement (Area A only). One example of Type C also came from Area A. Types B and C as well as some unclassified examples came from Area C. Area B produced no identifiable examples.

Large Bowl Type A. Type A is the only large bowl type (without spout) attested from the *Kaminoudhia* cemetery, with one classifiable example, P104. It is very irregularly formed, with a flat base, hemi-spherical body and two opposed semicircular ledge lugs at mid-body, one of them pierced vertically (D: ca. 45 cm; H: ca. 22 cm). The bowl is undecorated, and made of a fabric that suggests a cross between RP and RP Mottled, perhaps a transitional technique. This seems to be an early—and prob-ably local south coast—form of the large bowl type, which by EC III usually is equipped with ledge lugs at the rim.[47]

A possible example of the same type from the settlement is P146, from the upper level in Area A, although its poor state of preservation does not permit a secure comparison. P146 is made of a good early RP Mottled fabric, is slightly larger in diameter than P104, and its lug is thinner and more sharply curved. The preserved lug was not pierced.

Illustrated examples (fig. 4.2): P104 (and pl. 3.7b), P146.

Large Bowl Type B. This type, in RP fabric from Area C, is shallower, with a more conical body than Type A (D: est. 40–50 cm). It has horizontal handles above the midpoint of the body, instead of the ledge lugs of Type A, and has additional ledge lugs with incised decoration at the rim. The only com-pletely preserved example, P110, was associated with the skeleton of a young woman in Unit 22 (see Chapter 2) and its importance is further suggested by the presence of several ancient mending holes (pl. 4.3a). Large bowls with flat bases and horizontal handles are known from *Vounous* in EC I (e.g., Stewart 1962: fig. CXXIX:3), but these have plain rims: the incised ledge lug at the rim of these Type B bowls is more typical of later (RP III) bowls. A fragment of a similar bowl, with incised lug at the rim and horizontal handle below, was found at Evdhimou *Beyouk Tarla* by the Kent State University sur-vey.[48]

---

[46] The shape is called "basin" by Stewart: cf., e.g., 1962: figs. CXXIX, CXXXX. For a recent discussion of their possible funerary function, see Herscher 1997:28–35.

[47] The best parallels come from Psematismenos *Trelloukkas*: Todd 1985: fig. 8:11, 13, 23; Georghiou 2000: fig. 5:14; a bowl with one similar lug handle from Dhenia: Nicolaou and Nicolaou 1988: fig. 18:1; at *Vounous* a similar handle occurs on a deep spouted bowl: Dikaios 1940: pl. XLIV:1, while a bowl almost identical in shape and size has horizontal handles rather than lugs: Stewart 1962: fig. CXXIX:2. Perhaps also of comparable shape are fragmentary large bowls from Marki *Alonia* (Frankel and Webb 1999: fig.6:P12095, P12096, P12282).

[48] Unpublished; for survey, see Swiny 1981:73–74.

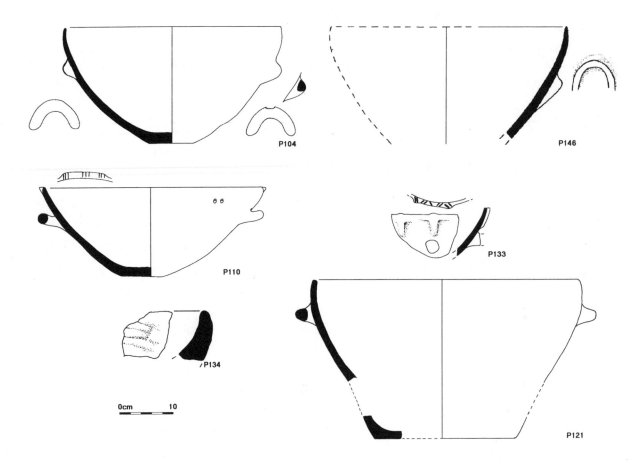

Fig. 4.2. Large Bowl Type A (P104, P146); **Large Bowl Type B** (P110, P133); **Large Bowl Type C** (P134, P121).

Other possible examples of this type are extremely fragmentary, so that it is not certain that they did not originally have spouts. Nevertheless, included here are several fragments that differ from P110 in having flat rim edges. Bowl P133, an unstratified fragment from Area C, had a horizontal handle set well below the rim with an incised horned ledge lug at the rim above it; short relief bands descend from the ledge lug.[49] Two other sherds of large bowls with flat-edged rims came from Unit 10. Another, from Unit 21, had a horizontal impressed relief band below the rim, as did another from a trial trench west of the main settlement in Area A.

Illustrated examples (fig. 4.2): P110, P133.

Large Bowl Type C. A coarse heavy "basin-like" vessel with a flat base and two opposed horizontal handles on the upper body, a diameter of approximately 50 cm and height of about 30 cm or greater. The lower interior of the only well-preserved example, P121, from Area C, is heavily eroded to expose

---

[49] This relief decoration may be related to what Dikaios has called "inverted horns of consecration" that appears on many large bowls from *Vounous*: Dikaios 1940:104–5, pls. XI:c, f, XLV:3; cf. Stewart 1962: fig. CXXX:7–13.

the large pebble inclusions, suggesting that this part of the vessel was either subject to severe abrasion or perhaps contained a corrosive substance that destroyed the fabric. The type appears to be rare, but that may be due to its probable domestic (rather than funerary) function (cf. Dikaios 1940:160-161, pl. LV:2, from Arpera). The only other example of this type, the fragment P134, comes from the earlier phase in Area A. It has a more rounded rim than P121 and is insufficiently preserved to show that it conforms to all aspects of the type, but has been included because it is a large coarse bowl.[50]

Illustrated examples (fig. 4.2): P121, P134.

Unclassified Large Bowls. Two additional stratified large bowl rim sherds from Area C, Units 10 and 17, are of interest although too small to be classified. Both are of unusual fabric, with characteristics of DPBC ware and Red-and-Black Stroke Burnished ware. The rims are plain and rounded; the profiles of the bowls seem to have been fairly shallow. Estimated diameters range between 34 and 45 centimeters. On the sherd from the larger bowl the end of a vertical relief band is preserved, perhaps one of a pair descending from a ledge lug such as on P133 (cf. fig. 4.2).

SPOUTED BOWLS

Spouted bowls from the cemetery all have flat bases and are undecorated. Examples from the settlement frequently have a small amount of decoration, such as simple incision on the handle. Some settlement examples may have round bases, although the state of preservation does not make this completely certain.

Spouted Bowl Type A. Securely attested only from the cemetery, Type A consists of a broad flat base, deep ovoid body, tubular spout with straight end, and horizontal handle opposite the spout. Both spout and handle are set low on the body. The size varies quite widely, with heights ranging from approximately 17 to 23 centimeters. Two examples (Dikaios 1/3, P52) are of RP Philia stroke-burnished fabric (with irregular burnishing marks). The handle on Dikaios 1/3 is set below the midpoint of the body and slants downward. The handle and spout of P52 and P64 are set just above the midpoint of the body; the body of P52 is somewhat more conical. A spout with very slightly flaring end found in Area A, Unit 41, may represent this type in a settlement context, but is too fragmentary to support a certain conclusion. Such deep, straight-spouted bowls occur in the Philia Phase of the settlement at Marki *Alonia* and elsewhere,[51] and represent a morphological continuum from the Chalcolithic period (Dikaios 1953:323; Bolger 1991:30). However, the known Philia Phase examples that are sufficiently preserved either are without any handle or have a vertical lug. A horizontal handle is found at *Vounous* beginning in EC I, where it appears alongside the type with a vertical lug handle, as well as variations with vertical handles and horizontal ledge lugs (cf. Stewart 1962: fig. CXXIV, CXXV:1).

Illustrated examples (fig. 4.3): Dikaios 1/3, P52 (pl. 3.6a), P64.

Spouted Bowl Type B. Probably represented in both cemetery and settlement, although again the settlement examples (P43, P86) are incomplete and therefore cannot be assigned to Type B with absolute

---

[50] P134 also has similarities in both shape and fabric to coarse ware "basins," except that it is better fired: cf. Frankel and Webb 1996b:172–74, fig. 7:24 (e.g., P6846, P6903, P6909).

[51] Webb and Frankel 1999: fig. 6:4–5; Frankel and Webb 1996a: fig.3:P8434; Hennessy et al. 1988: figs. 17:10, 48:S82; Bolger 1983: fig. 3:1; Dikaios 1962: figs. 80:1–4, L:11.

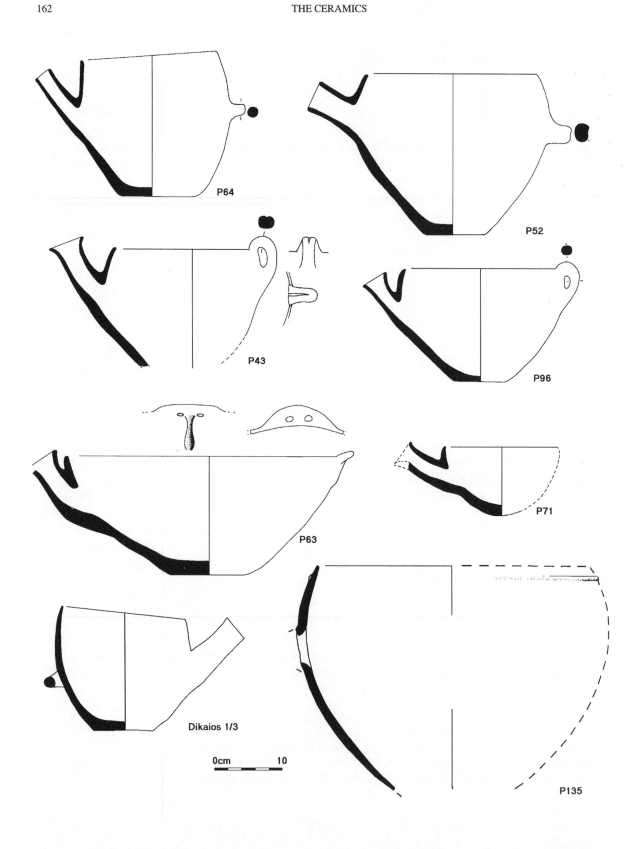

Fig. 4.3. Spouted Bowls Type A (P64, P52, Dikaios 1/3); **Spouted Bowls Type B** (P43, P96); **Spouted Bowl Type C** (P63); **Unclassified Spouted Bowls** (P71, P135).

certainty. The body shape is more globular or piriform than Type A, with a small vertical handle at the rim and a flare to the spout end. It occurs in both RP and RP Mottled fabrics. The settlement examples appear to be slightly larger than those from the cemetery. The handle on P43, from Area A, has a single vertical incision on the upper part of the handle. A stratified fragmentary spout that may come from a bowl of this type was found in Area A Unit 6. Another fragmentary spout, from Unit 28, in a trial trench between Areas A and B, may belong to the same vessel as a very slightly flattened (almost round) base. This appears to be the common spouted bowl on the south coast in the EC III period.[52]

> Illustrated examples (fig. 4.3): P43, P96 (and pl. 3.6c).
> Additional catalogued examples: P42, P86 (?).

Spouted Bowl Type C. A large bowl with flat base and wide conical or hemispherical body, spout with flared end rising from below rim, and a ledge lug opposite the spout. In fragmentary form, this type would not necessarily be distinguishable from some large bowls without spouts, such as Type B. While the only nearly complete example (P63) comes from the cemetery, a ledge lug of the same distinctive type was found in Unit 3 of Area A, suggesting that Type C occurred in the settlement as well. The settlement example appears to be of a more developed RP Mottled fabric. Comparable bowls are known from north coast sites, frequently with relief decoration and usually with round bases; the form of the horizontal lug also varies.[53]

> Illustrated example (fig. 4.3): P63.

Spouted Bowl Type D. Attested only from the settlement and in incomplete form, Type D is a globular jar-like vessel with small flat base, flaring rim and horizontal handle at mid-body opposite the spout (the shape of the spout end is indeterminate), of RP Mottled fabric. The handle is incised with simple linear decoration. The only example of the type complete enough to be certain (P49) comes from Area A, but fragments from the other parts of the settlement suggest it may be represented there as well. From Area B came an incised horizontal handle, very closely similar in shape, fabric and decoration, and from Area C came a similar, although slightly smaller, rim sherd (however, this rim also might be from a small amphora).

This uncommon type of spouted jar with horizontal handle is apparently distinctive of southern Cyprus, with variations in Drab Polished ware known from the west of the island.[54] The earliest examples date to EC III, and the shape has a long history thereafter, continuing into the Late Bronze Age.

> Illustrated example (fig. 4.4): P49.

---

[52] For similar bowls elsewhere, see: Todd 1985: fig. 7:2; Todd 1986: fig. 28:4; Weinberg 1956: fig. 9. Similar vessels from *Vounous* date to EC III, but have the standard north coast round-pointed base: Dikaios 1940: pl. XLIV:5; Stewart 1962: fig. CXXV:13; Stewart and Stewart 1950: pl. XXXb:35.

[53] Cf. Stewart 1962: fig. CXXVI:4, 5. An example from Alambra is incomplete, but has a closely similar spout and rim: Coleman et al. 1996: fig. 70:F608. A similar bowl with a slightly different lug comes from Larnaca *Ayios Prodromos*: Herscher 1988: fig. 2:1.

[54] Cf. Flourentzos 1991: pl. XVIII:57. For discussion, see Herscher and Fox 1993:72. An elaborately decorated MC double-spouted vessel from Marki may also be related to this type: Frankel and Webb 1996b:146, fig. 7:19 (P296). A variation with upright handle on the rim appears at Lapithos at the end of EC III: Grace 1940: pl. II:11. Similar spouted vessels but with vertical handles at the side or basket handles appear in Anatolia in EB and MB: cf., e.g., Goldman 1956:149 (#570), pls. 246:229, 273:571; Joukowsky 1986: fig. 326:2.

Unclassified Spouted Bowls. Several additional examples from stratified contexts differ from the types discussed above, but are too fragmentary for classification. P135 is a large vessel, possibly related to Spouted Bowl Type C, although the shape of its body may be deeper (so little of this vessel is preserved that the body profile is quite uncertain). Its main feature of significance is a relief band below the rim. This plain band differs from the impressed bands more common in northern Cyprus, and may be a feature characteristic of the south.[55]

Another fragmentary bowl, P71, and two additional uncatalogued fragments, all from Area C, resemble smaller versions of Spouted Bowl Type B. While the base of P71 was judged to be round, this is not absolutely certain. Since the body was not preserved opposite the spout, it is also uncertain what kind of handle (if any) the bowl had. The other pieces, both of RP Mottled fabric, one from Unit 8 and the other from Unit 23, consist of a small vertical handle like those of Type B spouted bowls and a fragment consisting of rim section and spout similar to those of P71.

Also worthy of mention are three uncatalogued spouts from a single lot in Area A Unit 30. All are similar in shape—tubular with only very slightly flaring ends (cf. Type A)—but made of three very distinctly different fabrics: RP Mottled, a variety of RP, and the third resembling Red-and-Black Stroke Burnished.

Illustrated examples (fig. 4.3): P71, P135.

DIPPERS

A "dipper" is defined as a small bowl with a high vertical loop handle. Unless the handle is present, the type is indistinguishable in sherd form. None was identified in the *Kaminoudhia* cemetery. The classified examples are undecorated and are of RP Mottled fabric.

Dipper Type A. Related to Bowl Type E, this dipper has a round base and hemispherical body. Only P62 from Area A Unit 6 was sufficiently preserved to be identified. It occurs widely in Cyprus, becoming particularly common in EC IIIB-MC I.[56]

Illustrated example (fig. 4.4): P62.

Dipper Type B is related to Bowl Type A, with flat base and deep ovoid body. The better-preserved example (P18), from Area B, was unstratified. Even without a handle, the example (P38) from the second phase of Area A Unit 3—where it was originally sitting on a bench along with an amphora (Type C, P24: see Chapter 2)—appears clearly to belong to the type. It is an unusual shape for a dipper, seemingly superseded by the more functional Type A form.

Illustrated example (fig. 4.4): P18.
Additional catalogued example: P38.

---

[55] Cf. Karageorghis 1940–1948: fig. 7, upper burial 3; Åström and Biers 1979:12, 45 (No. 16); contrast with, e.g., Dikaios 1940: pls. X:e, XI:b, d, f; Schaeffer 1936: pl. XV:1–2.

[56] E.g., Frankel and Webb 1996b:126–27, fig. 7.6; Todd 1986:114 (K-PC 398), fig. 22.4; Hennessy et al. 1988: fig. 30:1; Dikaios 1940: pl. XLVI:7b; Stewart 1962: fig CXLIX:10; similar dippers but with small flat bases, reflecting south coast styles and perhaps an early EC III date, come from Evdhimou (Herscher 1976: pl. III:3), Paramali (Herscher and Swiny 1992: pl. IX:5), and from Kalavasos Tomb 46 (Todd 1986:114 [K-PC 398]). Similar dippers with flat bases occur in Anatolia throughout the Early Bronze Age: cf., e.g., Lloyd and Mellaart 1962: figs. P.14:3, 9; P.22:9, P.24:11; Goldman 1956: pls. 276:449, 354: 705.

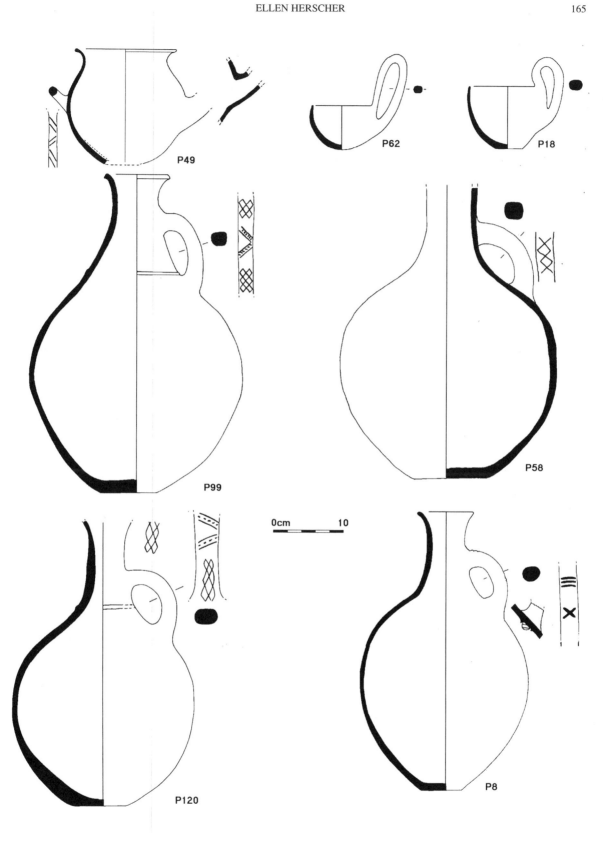

Fig. 4.4. Spouted Bowl Type D (P49); **Dipper Type A** (P62); **Dipper Type B** (P18); **Jugs Type A** (P99, P58, P120); **Jug Type B** (P8).

Unclassified Dippers*.* Two additional fragments, from Areas A and B, preserve portions of bowl rims with loop handles, and are thus certainly dippers, but since neither base is preserved they could not be classified further. Both are undecorated.

CONICAL BOWL

Only one example (P31) of a conical bowl (called "tulip bowl" by Stewart) was found at *Kaminoudhia*, in Tomb 7. Made in RPSC ware, it was fired to create a black-bottomed effect. Its small rounded shape with hooked projections is typical of EC I *Vounous*, although several of the closest parallels are without provenience and many examples are larger than this one.[57] From the south coast came two examples from Psematismenos (Todd 1985: pl. IX:8). The shape and linear style of decoration may also be compared to that of a White Painted IA (Philia) bowl from *Ayia Paraskevi* (Stewart 1962: fig. CLV:3).

Illustrated example (fig. 4.8, pl. 3.6b): P31.

JUGS

Large jugs are the second most frequent shape (after small bowls) at *Kaminoudhia*. They range in height from about 38 to 45 centimeters. With one exception (P106), all have flat bases. Since jugs are difficult to identify in sherd form, it is very likely that they were more common in the settlement than indicated by the sherd count statistics. Types A and F definitely occurred in both settlement and cemetery. Nevertheless, it appears that large jugs were much less common in tombs at *Kaminoudhia* than they were in contemporary tombs on the north coast, perhaps suggesting a significant difference in burial practices.

Jug Type A is a large round-spouted Red Polished ware jug with distinctive incised handle decoration, about 40-45 cm in height, which appears to have been very common at *Kaminoudhia*. The neck is generally conical with flattened rim edge, the handle squarish in section, and there is frequently a horizontal relief band at the neckline, as can be seen on P99, the best-preserved example. The type is well attested in both cemetery and settlement (Areas A and C), although the settlement examples are very poorly preserved. The handle decoration from the settlement is sometimes more carelessly executed (e.g., P120, P70), although that on P136 from the settlement is just as neatly incised as that on P99. Two examples from the settlement (P120, P136) have additional decoration on the neck above the handle, still forming part of the same basic scheme. The handles of P136 and P70 are also notable for their variation on the normal attachment method, with both ends inserted through the pot wall rather than the lower one alone: on P70 the ends were then smoothed down on the interior, but on P136 they were not (fig. 4.5). The base of P120 displays an unusual construction technique, flat on the exterior but round on the interior, so that the section becomes very thin at the center of the base.

Additional uncatalogued handle fragments provide further evidence for the type. Unit 6, in addition to P120, produced a second similar jug in very fragmentary condition. Also from Area A came another handle fragment, this from Unit 42, very similar in shape and decoration to that of P120. Two

---

[57] Cf. Stewart 1962: figs. CXXXIII:16, CXXXIV:21, CXXXV:11; for the shape, cf. Stewart 1962: fig. CXXXIII:2; Karageorghis 1991: pl. CXXX:1; Schaeffer 1936: pl. XVI:1; Dikaios 1940: pl. XLVI:8; for the linear and punctured style of decoration, cf. Stewart 1962: fig. CXLII:20, without provenience.

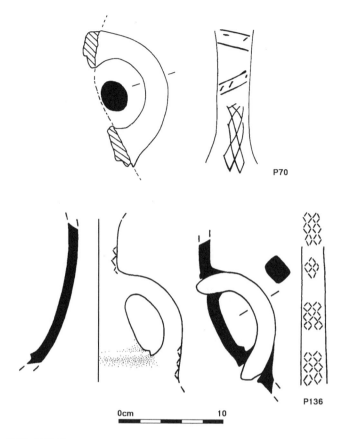

Fig. 4.5. Jugs Type A (P70, P136).

additional handle fragments of the same type, very worn, were found unstratified, one each in Areas B and C. A base fragment (P69) from Area C, likely from this type of jug, also displayed significant wear on its bottom (pl. 4.1a).

The inclusion of P58 with this type is somewhat uncertain, although the jug does at least seem to be closely related to Type A. It has a wider body and base and straighter neck than the standard examples of the type, and its handle decoration is a simplified version of the normal scheme. It may represent an "imitation" of the distinctive type.

Several other examples of the very distinctive Jug Type A, with its extremely uniform shape and highly standardized decoration, are known from looted cemeteries in the nearby Paramali Valley. Some of the Paramali jugs appear to have been decorated by the same meticulous hand as P99 (Herscher and Swiny 1992:75, figs 1:5, 6; pls. X:3, XI:2, XII:1, 4, 5).

Illustrated examples (fig. 4.4): P58, P99 (and pl. 3.6c), P120; (fig. 4.5): P70, P136.

Jug Type B is similar to Type A, but somewhat smaller, with smaller base and a rounded rim edge. The handle is also incised, but on the one preserved example, P8, from Tomb 4, the scheme is different from that typical of Type A: the group of three transverse lines and cross should perhaps be considered a potmark rather than pure decoration. An uncatalogued handle fragment from Area C Unit 21 appears to have the same combination of marks preserved, only there are four instead of three transverse lines in the group.

This type of jug and those of Type D (below) appear to have been important on the south coast, and are particularly notable for often being incised with potmarks.[58] The type has some general similarity to RP I and II jugs from *Vounous*, but its base differs from the smaller raised or pointed base typical of the north coast and the *Vounous* handles are generally plain (cf. Stewart 1962: figs. LXXIV:10, LXXV:14, LXXVI:1).

Illustrated example (fig. 4.4): P8.

Jug Type C. A large RP jug, about 40 cm high, attested only in the cemetery (Tomb 14). Compared to Type A, it has a taller and more ovoid body, wider and straighter neck, and a less flaring rim. The only preserved example, P118, is undecorated except for a single conical knob to the right of the lower handle attachment, perhaps to be regarded as a potmark. A close parallel comes from Psematismenos *Trelloukkas*; it is comparable to a jug from Philia *Vasiliko*, and to RP I jugs from *Ayia Paraskevi* and *Vounous*, although a raised base is more common at the latter site.[59]

Illustrated example (fig. 4.6, pl. 3.7a): P118.

Jug Type D is characterized by a taller, narrower neck and a wider base than the previous types. It is similar in size to Types B and C. Like Type B, it appears to be a south coast type frequently associated with potmarks (above, n. 58).[60] The only preserved example from *Kaminoudhia*, P57, is undecorated. It was found in Tomb 11, associated with Type A jug P58, an indication that various types of large jugs were in use at the same time. This type appears to be the south coast version of the RP III narrow necked jug that is common on the north coast, which generally has a more articulated neck, a round-pointed base, and simple relief decoration (cf., e.g., Stewart 1962: fig. LXXX:9; Stewart and Stewart 1950: pl. XXXIIb:2).

Illustrated example (fig. 4.6): P57.

Jug Type E is known only in fragmentary form (P103), from Tomb 15, but is distinct from the other jugs because its handle is attached at the rim rather than mid-neck. The neck is short and wide, with only slightly flaring rim. Its base is flat, although the body shape is uncertain. This is probably a late Philia Phase shape.

Illustrated example (fig. 4.6): P103.

---

[58] A slightly larger example from Evdhimou is marked with two horizontal and seven vertical lines below; a jug more like Type D has an identical potmark (i.e., three horizontal lines with an "X" beneath): Vavouranakis and Manginis 1995:80, figs. 4:1, 6:12. A handle with an identical potmark was found at Evdhimou *Beyouk Tarla* by the Kent State University survey (unpublished; for site, see Swiny 1981:73–74). At Psematismenos *Trelloukkas* a jug like Type D was found with the same potmark, but with the elements reversed; a jug like Type B bore a potmark of three horizontal lines with a depression at the top of the handle: Todd 1985: figs. 7:3, 7:7.

[59] Dikaios 1962: fig. 81:7; Todd 1985: fig. 8:6; Hennessy et al. 1988: fig. 19:2; e.g., Stewart 1962: fig. LXXIII:9; Stewart 1988: 61, fig. 15:1; cf., e.g., Stewart and Stewart 1950: pl. VIa:1; Stewart 1962: fig LXXIV:3.

[60] Stewart 1962: fig. LXXIII:4 (with potmark); Stewart 1988:60, pl. XIII:4; Todd 1985: fig.7:3, 24 (one with potmark); Vavouranakis and Manginis 1995: fig. 6:12 (with potmark). Stewart's two examples are—significantly—without provenience, but he connected the shape to RPSC ware and dated them to EC II.

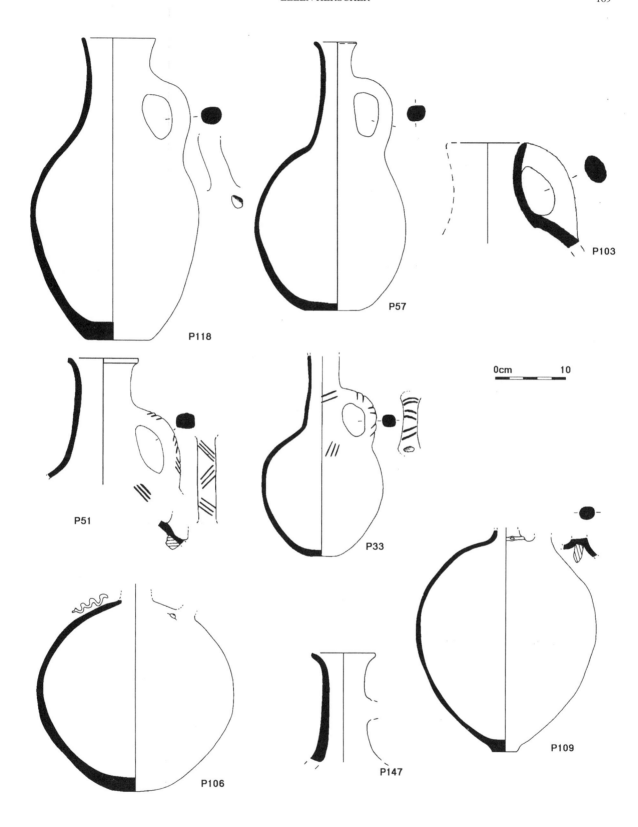

Fig. 4.6. Jug Type C (P118); **Jug Type D** (P57); **Jug Type E** (P103); **Jug Type G** (P51, P33); **Unclassified Jugs** (P106, P147, P109).

Jug Type F has a cutaway spout. Sherds of the type were found in both the cemetery and the settlement, but no examples were large enough to be restored, drawn or catalogued. Nevertheless, it is listed as a type because of the significance of the cutaway spouted jug in the earlier part of the Early Cypriot period. From the cemetery, Dikaios 1/2 is a probable example. In Tomb 6 four different examples of the type may be represented by fragments of trough spouts, to one of which an upper handle attachment seems to belong. The fabrics vary, but two have clear indications of stroke burnishing, as typical during the Philia Phase.[61]

Three spout fragments were found stratified in the settlement, two from Area A (Units 4 and 20) and one from Area C Unit 23. The one from Unit 4 is plain, but the other two have relief knobs ("eyes") attached at the edge of the spout (pls. 4.5c, 4.5d). The one from Unit 20 appears to be the flaring end of a relief band, with two punctures in the flat end next to the spout opening, forming a "snake" motif. The sherd from Unit 23, in irregularly burnished RP ware, has a disk-shaped knob with an "X" incised on it. Both these motifs have parallels on RP I cutaway spouted jugs from *Vounous* and from south coast sites.[62]

Catalogued example: Dikaios1/2.
Illustrated fragments: pls. 4.5c, 4.5d.

Jug Type G. The jugs included in this group, found only in the settlement, have cylindrical necks, round spouts and distinctive incised decoration. This consists of groups of two or three short oblique lines on the body near the lower handle attachment and/or on the neck near the upper handle attachment. On the handle are three similar groups placed in alternating directions (also seen on the handle of spouted bowl Type D, P49). All the examples found, however, are fragmentary, so it is uncertain to what extent they all conform to a single type beyond the similarity in decoration.

The preserved neck of P51, from Unit 16, is similar in shape to that of Type A jugs, but made of RP Mottled fabric. Additional fragments from Area A include another similar RP Mottled large jug neck from Unit 3, but with rounded rim edge and incisions on the neck, and a smaller body fragment from Unit 18 with flat base and incisions on the shoulder. From Area C came the somewhat smaller rimless jug, P33, decorated on both neck (two lines) and shoulder (three lines), and with finger impressions at both ends of the handle. A second, uncatalogued, Type G jug neck came from the same unit (8), similar in size, but of different RP fabric and with three oblique lines on the neck; a rounded flaring rim is preserved on this fragment. From Unit 10 came a handle fragment similar to that of P33 (two groups of two oblique lines preserved).

Illustrated examples (fig. 4.6): P33, P51.

Unclassified Jugs. Several large jugs are too incomplete for classification. However, they still present significant features.

Only the body of the DPBC large jug P109 (fig. 4.6), from Unit 6 in Area A, is preserved but the vessel would almost certainly have had a beaked spout. Its small flat articulated base differs from the pointed base most typical of DPBC ware (cf. Åström 1972: fig. XXIII:3–5). (A similar but slightly

[61] Cf. e.g., Bolger 1983:70–71, figs. 2:1–3, 3:3–9; Dikaios 1962: figs. 80:18–28, 81:1–6; Hennessy et al. 1988: figs. 10, 14, 20.1 and 8; Stewart 1988: fig. 1, pl. 1.

[62] Cf. Stewart 1962: fig. LVIII:1; Todd 1985: fig. 7:5 (undecorated); Herscher and Swiny 1992: fig. 1:2; Vavouranakis and Manginis 1995: fig. 4:2. These decorative elements also occur on round-spouted jugs: Herscher and Swiny 1992: fig. 1:4, pls. XI:1, XIV:5; Todd 1985: fig. 7:3, pl. VIII:5.

larger base was found in Area C Unit 9.) The impressed relief band decoration is one of the few examples of this common EC IIIB-MC I motif from *Kaminoudhia*. A small fragment of a beaked spout from another large DPBC jug, along with a typical DPBC pointed base from a large vessel, was found in a trial trench in Area A, west of the main settlement: they appear to represent two separate vessels. Finally, a somewhat different round-pointed base of a large DPBC vessel was found in Pit B in Area A Unit 1, Phase I. The interior of this base is reinforced with extra clay, forming almost a peg base.

The very globular RP jug body P106 (fig. 4.6), from Unit 8 in Area C, is the only large vessel from *Kaminoudhia* with a round base. Although the neck is not preserved, it clearly was very narrow. The relief "snake" decoration on the body is also unusual. Both shape and decoration appear to be at home in southeastern Cyprus.[63] Also from Area C is a comparable jug body, P117, from Unit 9, with very narrow neck and globular body, although no decoration is preserved. This vessel is slightly smaller than P106 and has a very small flat base, which is very close to a round one. Both P106 and P117 were among the latest material from the *Kaminoudhia* settlement (see also Juglet Type E, below).

Only the neck is preserved of jug P147 (fig. 4.6), from a trial trench (Unit 28) between Areas A and B, but both its fabric and method of manufacture are unusual. While similar in size and shape to Type A jugs, the neck is more cylindrical and the neckline more clearly articulated. The upper end of the handle has been attached by insertion through the neck and flattening on the interior (pl. 4.4b); also clearly visible is the way the neck has been inserted into the body and secured by clay applied to the exterior of the join (pl. 4.4a; cf. Todd 1986: pl. XVI:1B, for similar attachment on a juglet with cutaway spout). The fabric displays characteristics of both RP Mottled and DPBC: in another context, this jug could well be classified as "Proto Base Ring ware." A close parallel, including the method of attachment, has been recorded at Kalavasos.[64]

Additional identifiable but unclassified large jug fragments were also found in Area A, the first phase of Unit 3, and in Area C Units 2 and 8.

JUGLETS

Juglets are defined as jugs with heights of about twenty-five centimeters or less. The four examples of juglets from the cemetery are all different types (Types A-D), two round-spouted and two cutaway-spouted, all with flat bases. Unfortunately the two round-spouted examples were not found in good contexts, but seem to have been deposited outside a funerary context in Cemetery B (see Chapter 3). The settlement too produced a wide variety of juglet types, many in a fragmentary state.

Juglet Type A. The single complete example of this type, P3, in RP fabric, relates closely to P58 (a variation of Jug Type A) because of the distinct incised decoration on the handle. Like Jug Type A, it has a flat base, round spout and squarish handle section.

Illustrated example (fig. 4.7): P3.

Juglet Type B. Represented only by the most elaborately decorated vessel found at *Kaminoudhia*, P2, this RP juglet has a wide flat base, globular body, conical neck with round spout and slightly flaring

---

[63] Todd 1986: figs. 20:4, 22:1, 2; Karageorghis 1989: fig. 9; Coleman et al. 1996: fig. 54:F1; smaller examples: Herscher 1988: fig 2:6, 7. For jug shape, cf. Flourentzos 1995: fig. 1; Herscher 1997: fig.5. For decoration, cf. Todd 1986: fig. 21:5, 6, 8, 10.

[64] Todd 1986: fig. 20:7, from *Panayia Church* Tomb 41, of uncertain date (an incised DPBC sherd dates to MC II-III, but the other RP Mottled vessels appear earlier; several had relief "snake" decoration like that on jug P106).

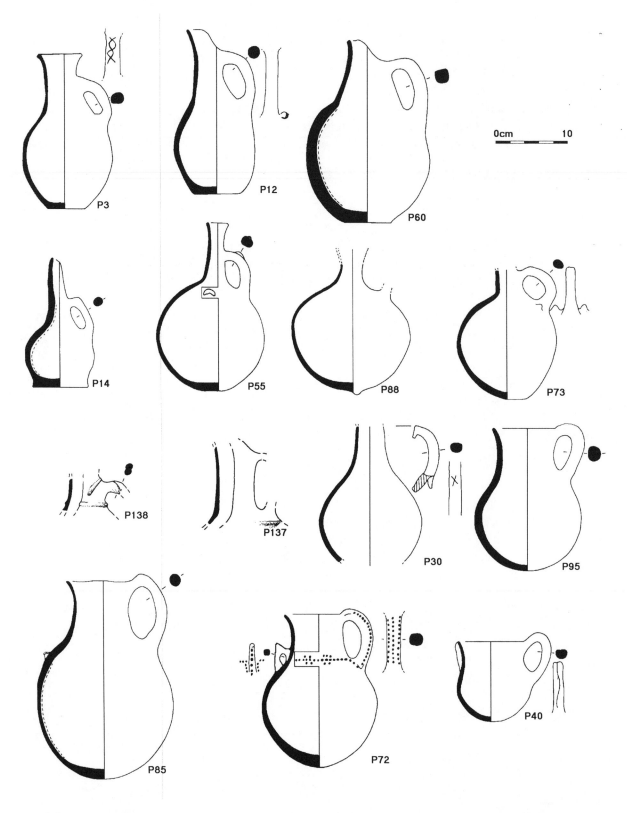

Fig. 4.7. Juglet Type A (P3); **Juglets Type C** (P12, P60); **Juglet Type D** (P14); **Juglet Type E** (P55); **Unclassified Juglets** (P88, P73, P138, P137, P30); **Tankards Type A** (P95, P85); **Tankard Type B** (P72); **Tankard Type C** (P40).

rim. It is also unusual for its slightly angular handle that is attached at the rim. The incised decoration includes a wider variety of elements than is typical of RPSC ware, but instead echoes the pattern of joined lozenges found on the necks and handles of Type A jugs (cf. P99, fig. 4.4). The only other comparable decoration is on the fragmentary amphora, P82 (cf. fig. 4.13). This juglet appears to imitate the EC III incised gourd juglet so common on the north coast,[65] echoing the angular handle of many of them. However, its neck is more conical and body more globular, while its flat base ties it to its south coast traditions.

Illustrated example (fig. 4.10): P2.

Juglet Type C. This is the only juglet type found in both the *Kaminoudhia* cemetery (Tomb 7) and the settlement (Area C Unit 8), although the two examples are not extremely close parallels. Both are of RP Mottled fabric, with wide flat base and short cutaway spout. The cemetery example, P12, has a conical knob to the right of the lower handle attachment, like that on the round-spouted jug P118 (fig. 4.6), also from the cemetery. The juglet from the settlement, P60, has a shorter, wider neck and spout, and is completely undecorated. Similar juglets are known elsewhere on the south coast.[66]

Illustrated examples (fig. 4.7): P12 (and pl. 3.6b), P60.

Juglet Type D. Juglet P14 is from Tomb 6, which also produced fragments of four jugs with cutaway spouts (Type F). It is somewhat crudely formed, and is the only preserved vessel from *Kaminoudhia* resembling the long tapering beak-spouted jugs characteristic of the Philia Phase (cf., e.g., Stewart 1962: fig. LIII). The form of the base, however, is distinctive, with a flared, unfinished-appearing edge around the very wide bottom, as though the vessel was pressed downward to flatten the base. This form of base and crudely formed juglet are also represented in the Philia Phase at Marki *Alonia*, Khrysiliou *Ammos*, and a few other sites, and has also been found at Kissonerga *Mosphilia*.[67] This type of base occurs on other types of small Philia Phase vessels as well (e.g., Stewart 1988: pl. XXVIII:5).

Illustrated example (fig. 4.7; pl. 3.6a): P14.

Juglet Type E. Attested only in the settlement, by P55, this juglet resembles the unclassified jug P106 (fig. 4.6), also from Area C, in its very globular body, very narrow neck, and simple relief decoration. While the base of P55 is slightly flattened, it is still very close to the round base of P106.[68] The southeastern connections of this type have been noted above.[69]

Illustrated example (fig. 4.7): P55.

---

[65] Cf., e.g., Stewart 1962: figs. XC-XCIV, cf. especially XC:7, 19; XCIII:5, with shorter necks.

[66] Karageorghis 1940–1948: fig 7 (second burial: 7, 1); Herscher and Swiny 1992: fig. 1:1. Georghiou 2000: fig. 3:8. Comparable juglets from *Vounous* have round bases: cf., e.g., Stewart 1962: fig. LXVIII:6, 7.

[67] Webb and Frankel 1999:15, fig. 6:23–26; Frankel and Webb 1996a: fig. 3:P7713; Frankel and Webb 1997:96, fig. 9:P8803; Bolger 1983: fig. 3:10; cf. Peltenburg 1998: fig. 76:3; Nicolaou and Nicolaou 1988: fig. 17:16; Webb 1997: Nos. 337, 338, 347; Stewart 1962: fig. LXVII:5; Stewart 1988: fig. 6:1, 3.

[68] There may also be related significance to the crescent motif on P55 and the snake motif on P106, examples of the very rare occurrence of representational relief decoration at *Kaminoudhia*: see Herscher 1997.

[69] Karageorghis 1940–1948: fig. 7 (upper burial: 13, 14); Herscher 1988: fig. 2:7; for similar crescent decoration, cf. Todd 1986: fig. 21:1, 6, 7, 8; Belgiorno 1997: fig. 5:28.

Unclassified juglets. From the settlement came a number of stratified fragments of DPBC juglets, again displaying a wide variety of features. The most complete of these was P137 (fig. 4.7), with "dimple" base (not illustrated), beak or cutaway spout and relief decoration. Also from Area C was another large fragment, P88 (fig. 4.7), with nipple base and globular body. A few smaller fragments came from Area A, Unit 1 in particular, from which came a handle of a beak-spouted juglet and another beak spout with body sherd probably from a second vessel. From Unit 5 came a large body sherd with lower part of handle (pushed through), probably from a juglet. Finally, a handle fragment, round in section, from a very small vessel was found in the hearth (Feature 2) in Unit 30; it displayed no signs of burning however. Comparable beak-spouted juglets begin to appear outside the western DPBC homeland at a number of sites in southern and central Cyprus in EC III.[70]

A few fragmentary RP juglets from the settlement are characterized by their round bases. The most complete of these is P73 (fig. 4.7) from Area B, with irregular ovoid body, narrow cylindrical neck, and the beginning of a cutaway or beak spout (not preserved); two conical knobs were added next to the handle base. From Area A came P123, a small vessel with globular body and round base (neck and rim not preserved). A similar fragmentary juglet came from Area C, with round base, globular body, conical neck, but again no spout preserved.

From Area C came the fragmentary juglet P30 (fig. 4.7), with a small flat base. Like P2 (Juglet Type B, fig. 4.10), it has a vertical handle attached at the rim, but P30 is larger and has no decoration except for a crudely incised "X" on the handle, presumably a potmark.

Several RP juglets, of which only the neck survives, are notable for a variety of decoration in excess of what is common at *Kaminoudhia*. A tapering neck, with handle attached at the midpoint and apparently with round spout (rim not preserved), from Area A Unit 6 is similar to Jug Type G, especially P33 (fig. 4.6). It has groups of three oblique lines on either side, above the handle attachment; at the neckline is a relief band incised with a zigzag. From Unit 7 in Area A comes another juglet neck with relief band at the neckline (which otherwise is not clearly articulated), this one punctured, and a similar band across the upper handle. This neck is conical, and may have had a beaked or cutaway spout. A similar unarticulated conical neck, P138 (fig. 4.7), comes from Area C, this with a two-strand twisted handle.[71] In this case the relief band at the neckline is plain, and there is another band partly encircling the handle attachment.

TANKARDS

This type of vessel has been called either a wide-mouthed juglet or a dipper amphora, but the term "tankard" has been chosen here to stress the fact that the shape of the *Kaminoudhia* examples appears to be a clear precursor of the Middle Cypriot tankard.[72] The developed MC and LC tankard is closely related to the amphora, frequently indistinguishable except for the absence of the second handle. The true tankard is characterized by a globular or rather squat body, a wide cylindrical neck, a handle from rim to upper body (usually with a projecting "thumb-grip" at the top), and frequently a stringhole projection at the neckline opposite the handle.[73] The *Kaminoudhia* "proto-tankards," in comparison to

---

[70] Karageorghis 1940–1948: fig. 23:CVII; Frankel and Webb 1996b:157, fig. 7.22 (P1857, P3733, P6297, P4348); of early MC date: Coleman et al. 1996: fig. 66:F389, F390.

[71] For similar handle, with relief decoration, cf. Coleman et al. 1996: fig. 54:F1.

[72] Stewart used both terms, but recognized the difficulties of always making a distinction: Stewart 1988:129; Stewart 1992:157. For the shape's development into the tankard, see Stewart 1992:160; Herscher 1972:28–29.

[73] It is attested in virtually all Middle Cypriot fabrics, e.g., Åström 1972: figs. VIII:4, XI:12, XV:10, XVII:4–8, XX:6, XXVIII:5–11, XXIX:1–2, XXXIV:9–10, XXXVI:8; Herscher 1976: pls. III:6, V:3.

the later versions, have more concave and somewhat narrower necks. The "thumb-grip" has not yet appeared, but in all examples the handle rises at least slightly above the rim. Most have a projection of some sort opposite the handle. All have round bases. Tankard P95 is one of the very rare vessels from the cemetery with a round rather than a flat base (and is the only DPBC vessel found in the cemetery). The most tankard-like vessels (Types A and B) are in Drab Polished Blue Core ware, perhaps another indication that this ware is a more technologically "advanced" fabric and that it is not local to *Kaminoudhia*. In fact, of the six complete or nearly complete DPBC vessels from *Kaminoudhia*, three are tankards.[74] The examples from the settlement (P72 and P85) may be somewhat later than P95, as they have some additional "tankard-like" features—the body projection, a more angular and oval-sectioned handle, and P72 has fairly extensive (for *Kaminoudhia*) decoration. On the other hand, P95 is almost identical to P72 in shape and size, with a slightly different fabric.

Tankard Type A. There are two examples of this type, P85 from the settlement (Area C) and P95 from Tomb 12. They have a round base, short wide slightly concave neck, and handle rising slightly above the rim; the size range is 21–29 cm. The settlement example has a somewhat narrower neck, a more angular handle, and originally had some kind of a projection on the upper body opposite the handle. Both are undecorated.[75]

Illustrated examples (fig. 4.7): P85, P95 (and pl.3.6c).

Tankard Type B is very similar to Type A (especially P95), with the addition of a very small sharply angular lug-handle at the neckline opposite the handle and fairly complex punctured decoration. The single example (P72) comes from the settlement (Area A). Comparable shapes are attested in RP ware from EC III through MC II.[76]

Illustrated example (fig. 4.7): P72.

Tankard Type C has a shorter, more squat shape, with a wider and shorter neck and more globular body. With its high incised handle, it resembles a cooking pot; a large vertical lug takes the place of the second handle.[77] The single example, P40 (from the settlement, Area B) occurs in Red Polished Mottled fabric. Comparable RP III "cooking dippers" from the north coast have more articulated necks and different kinds of lugs, showing conservative connections to RP I examples.[78] (See also Unclassified Cooking Pot, P128).

Illustrated example (fig. 4.7): P40.

---

[74] Several DPBC fragments of small closed vessels from Marki could have been tankards rather than amphorae: Frankel and Webb 1996b:157–59, e.g., fig. 7.22 (P3187, P3598, P4317).

[75] For a similar shape in RP ware, see Coleman 1996: fig. 56:F33.

[76] Coleman et al. 1996: fig 56:F32; Hennessy et al. 1988: fig. 22:23; Dikaios 1940: pls. XLIX:8, L:2.

[77] Cf. the unclassified cooking pot, P128, which is closely similar but made of coarser fabric and has a flat base.

[78] E.g., Stewart 1962: fig. CXXIII:1–2, 7 (RP III); cf. fig CXXII:18 (RP I). From the south coast, cf. Belgiorno 1997: fig. 5:17–18. A similar "ear handled cup" is a common form in the Anatolian Early Bronze Age: cf., e.g., Joukowsky 1986:396, fig. 332; Lloyd and Mellaart 1962: fig. P.50:45; Goldman 1956: pl. 358:454, 459.

FLASKS

Flasks are handleless small vessels with a narrow neck, a shape that goes back to the Philia Phase in Cyprus.[79] Those from *Kaminoudhia* were all found in the cemetery[80] and, except for P101 (see below), occur in Red Polished South Coast fabric (actually most are black to brown in color) with the elaborate incised and punctured decoration characteristic of this ware. As a group, they are the most highly decorated vessels found at *Kaminoudhia*. They range in height from 14 to 20 cm. All that are preserved sufficiently for a determination to be made have flat bases and two pairs of holes opposed just below the rim.[81] They vary in the proportion of the base, which can be either quite small or rather wide, and the proportions of the neck, which can be short and wide or taller and narrower. These differences appear to have no chronological significance, since both a wide-necked (P76) and a narrow-necked (P80) example were found together in Tomb 7.

The shape of P80, however, is particularly close to that of Philia Phase flasks and its decoration also appears to echo the Philia style (cf. Hennessy et al. 1988: fig. 18:2), with its rows of punctures adjoining groups of parallel lines. This suggests that P80, and perhaps P61, may represent early stages of the type. Several other vessels were too fragmentary to be identified with certainty as flasks, but they are included here and illustrated as examples of Red Polished South Coast decoration (fig. 4.9): P34, P26.

Flasks are well represented at *Vounous* in EC I–II, but their shapes and proportions differ markedly from the *Kaminoudhia* examples (Stewart 1962: figs. XCIX, C). In particular, the necklines of the *Vounous* examples are more articulated, and their bases are round even from the earliest stage. The *Kaminoudhia* flasks are more similar to a smaller group of vessels with flat bases from *Vounous*, Arpera and *Ayia Paraskevi* (called "pots" by Stewart), for which he and Dikaios emphasized both the Philia and south coast connections.[82]

Illustrated examples (fig. 4.8): P32, P61 (and pl. 3.7c), P76 (and pl. 3.6b), P80 (and pl. 3.6b); (fig. 4.9): P28.

Red Polished Philia Flasks. One flask, P101 (fig. 4.8), unfortunately without secure context but found in Cemetery A, has a wider neck and incised decoration of a style more characteristic of the Philia Phase.[83] Two additional fragmentary vessels from Cemetery A and without secure context, P9 and P35 (fig. 4.9), also appear to preserve remnants of Philia style decoration and may represent flasks (cf.

---

[79] Cf. Dikaios 1962: fig. 82.2; Bolger 1983: figs. 2:4, 3:2; Hennessy et al. 1988: figs. 11:11+15, 6; 46. For Late Chalcolithic antecedents, cf. Peltenburg 1987a:59, ill. 1:4–5.

[80] Flask P101 was not found in a secure tomb context, but came from the topsoil above Tomb 4 in the Cemetery A area. Other fragments that may be flasks (P9, P34, P35) were also found in the topsoil in the Cemetery A area.

[81] Cf. Bottles, below, which have round bases and only single opposed holes at the rim.

[82] Stewart 1992:82, 87, pl. XI:2, 3; Stewart 1962: figs. CII:1–4, CIII:1–6; Dikaios 1940:160-162, pl. XXXVIIb (second and third from left). A similar flask, found in the Archaic altar at the Sanctuary of Apollo Hylates at Kourion, may come originally from the nearby cemetery of Episkopi *Phaneromeni*: Buitron-Oliver 1996:41, fig. 45:A1. Two such flasks, one with a side spout, have recently been found at Psematismenos *Trelloukkas*: Georghiou 2000: fig. 3:4, 12. For similar RPSC flasks, unfortunately without provenience, see Lubsen-Admiraal 1999: figs 19, 21, 23, 27, 28, 30.

[83] Cf. Dikaios 1962: fig. 82:7, from Philia *Vasiliko*, a smaller vessel but which displays the distinctive paired holes of the flask classification.

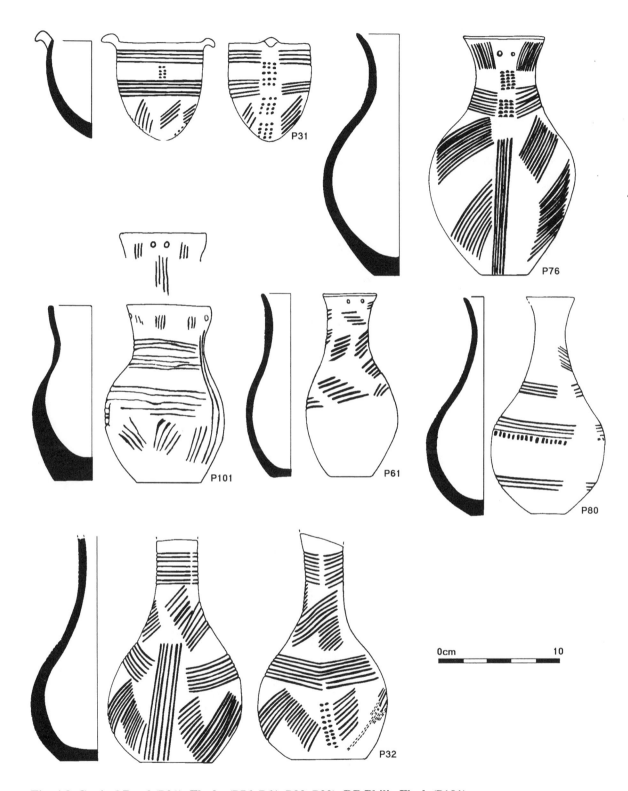

Fig. 4.8. Conical Bowl (P31); **Flasks** (P76, P61, P80, P32); **RP Philia Flask** (P101).

Hennessy et al. 1988: fig. 18:Tomb 12.2). In particular, P9 seems to resemble closely the unusual type of flask termed a "feeding bottle" by Stewart.[84]

BOTTLES

Bottles are also handleless small vessels with narrow necks. At *Kaminoudhia* they are smaller than flasks (14 cm or less) and the neck and rim are more articulated; the bases (where preserved) are round. When the rim is preserved, it is pierced by two opposed holes. (This suggests that they were closed by a different method than were the flasks, which have two opposed *pairs* of holes at the rim.) All have elaborate finely incised decoration. Most come from the cemetery, but the type is also attested in the settlement.

Bottle Type A is the standard Brown Polished bottle, as known from other south coast sites.[85] The two best-preserved examples, P27 and P29 (fig. 4.10), are both from Tomb 4 and probably made by the same potter, with very similar decoration. Additional fragments from the same tomb seem to represent a third vessel, by a different potter. They have a piriform shaped body and a tall narrow cylindrical neck, and are elaborately decorated in fine incision. Fragments of at least three similar bottles came from the stratified deposits of the *Kaminoudhia* settlement (Area A Units 16 and 30; Area C Unit 23). These were the only Brown Polished bottles identified from the settlement, but the fragile nature of this fabric could have affected preservation. The traces of decoration preserved suggest that they are Type A bottles, but this is uncertain.

Illustrated examples (fig. 4.10): P27, P29.

Bottle Type B is also Brown Polished, very similar to Type A, but with a more globular body and a shorter, slightly conical neck. It is also decorated with fine incision, but in a somewhat different style. The two recorded examples come from Tombs 12 and 8.

Illustrated example (fig. 4.10, pl. 3.6c): P98.
Additional catalogued example: P79.

Bottle Type C is represented by only one, incomplete, example, P105 from Tomb 19. It is extremely worn, but appears to be of Brown Polished fabric. Its neck is shorter and slightly wider than Type A, and its body is squatter (or perhaps piriform) with a more flattened (although still rounded) base. Its decorative style is also different from that of Types A or B, more similar to the styles characteristic of north coast black-topped bottles, suggesting that it may be the latest of the Brown Polished bottle types.

Illustrated example (fig. 4.10): P105.

---

[84] Hennessy et al. 1988: fig. 12:13; Stewart 1992:62; Stewart 1962: fig CII:7; cf. Morris 1985: pl. 8b (without a stringhole).
[85] Herscher 1991:47 (with references), fig. 5.3; Todd 1986:132, fig. 36:8–10; Karageorghis 1940–1948: fig. 12:7; probably Coleman et al. 1996: fig. 72:F643.

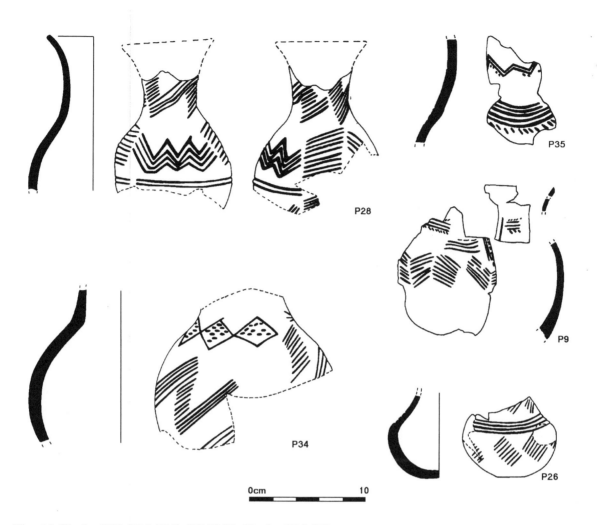

Fig. 4.9. Flasks (P28, P34, P26); **RP Philia Flasks** (P35, P9).

Bottle Type D is a Red Polished Philia small bottle, a type represented at most Philia Phase sites.[86] This seems to be the only known Philia shape with a round base. The two examples identified at *Kaminoudhia* are extremely fragmentary, but are distinctive by virtue of their squatter body, thicker walls, and typical Philia Phase fabric and incised decoration. Both are from tombs.

       Illustrated example (fig. 4.10): P75.
       Additional catalogued example: Dikaios 1/5.

North coast Bottle. Apart from the Brown Polished fragments mentioned above, the only bottle found in the *Kaminoudhia* settlement is P74 (fig. 4.11), a fragmentary Red Polished III black-topped vessel of the kind typical of sites (particularly *Vounous*) on the north coast of Cyprus that are dated

---

[86] Cf. Stewart 1962: fig. XCVIII:10–12; Dikaios 1962: fig. 82:7–8; Hennessy et al. 1988: figs. 11:24, 12:40, 15:14, 48:S80; Bolger 1983: figs. 2:7–8; Nicolaou and Nicolaou 1988: pl. XIX:8; Webb 1997: No. 345; Brown and Catling 1980: fig. 2; Morris 1985: pl. 8c.

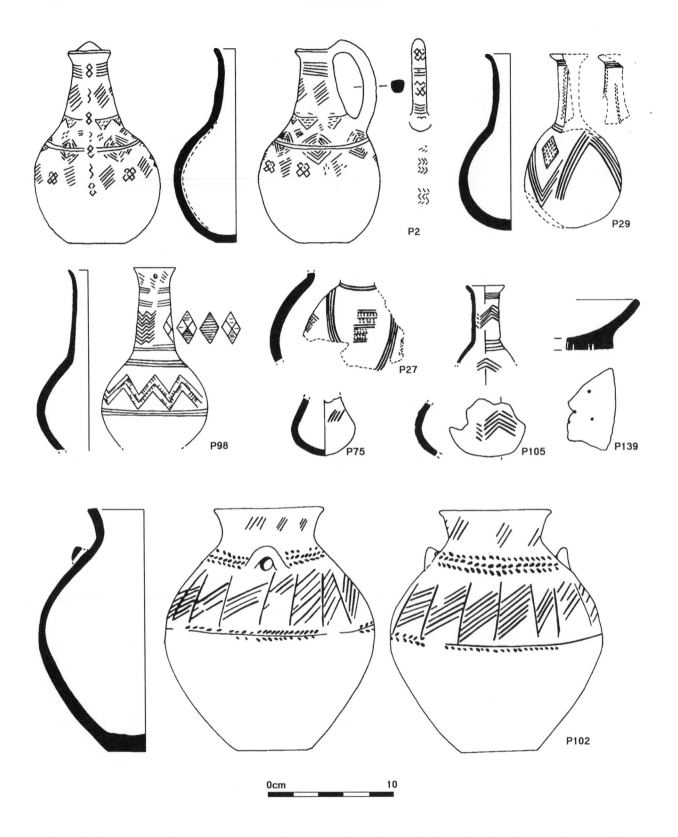

Fig. 4.10. Juglet Type B (P2); **Bottles Type A** (P29, P27); **Bottle Type B** (P98); **Bottle Type C** (P105); **Bottle Type D** (P75); **Griddle** (P139); **Ear-lug Pot Type B** (P102).

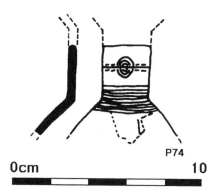

Fig. 4.11. North coast Bottle (P74).

to EC III.[87] It should be considered an import to *Kaminoudhia*. This distinctive type of small closed vessel was widely exported—perhaps for its contents—from the north coast to numerous sites in southern and central Cyprus, including Alassa, *Phaneromeni*, Kalavasos, Marki, and *Ayia Paraskevi*.[88]

EAR-LUG POTS

An ear-lug pot is a type of amphora with pierced lugs (or very small handles) instead of handles on the upper body (Stewart 1992: 84–85). All of the examples that could be identified with certainty came from the cemetery, had flat bases and occur in Red Polished Philia fabric.[89]

Ear-lug Pot Type A is an amphora-shaped vessel with lugs placed vertically on the shoulder. The larger example, P7 (unfortunately not found in a secure context), displays stroke-burnished surface treatment but is otherwise undecorated except for a few lines of incision on the preserved lug. The smaller example, P41, is decorated in Philia Phase style.[90] Comparable pots, both plain and decorated, are known from Philia and other Philia Phase sites.[91]

Illustrated examples (fig. 4.12): P7, P41.

---

[87] Cf. Stewart 1962: fig CI:2–5; Dikaios 1940: pl. LIII:2; for comparable decoration, cf. Stewart 1962: fig. LXXI.4. The closest parallel is from *Vounous* Tomb 133 (ibid., fig. CI:5), unfortunately a very disturbed tomb. For general discussion of the type: Stewart 1992:68–69. For a color illustration of the type, see Morris 1985: pl. 13d. For further discussion of date of P74, see Chapter 17, "Chronology."

[88] Flourentzos 1991:10, pls. XIV:4, XV:21; Karageorghis 1940-1948: figs. 12:9, 24; Todd 1986: fig. 36:1–4; Herscher 1991:46, cf. fig. 5.1; Carpenter 1981:60–61, fig. 3–5; Frankel and Webb 1997: fig. 11:P9; Flourentzos 1988:124, pl. XXVI:8; Hennessy et al 1988: fig. 27:3; Stewart 1962: fig. CI:9.

[89] However, two pointed lugs found in the settlement area, one in the topsoil and the other stratified (Area C Unit 2), may have come from ear-lug pots (such as Stewart 1962: fig. CIII:8), although the type with pointed lugs is not attested among the cemetery examples.

[90] These examples support Stewart's observation (1962:84) that the undecorated ear-lug pot types tend to be larger and heavier, and his suggestion that the incised ones may be exclusively funerary vessels.

[91] Cf. Dikaios 1962: figs. 81:12, 14, 82:29; Stewart 1992: fig. 10:7; Frankel and Webb 1997: fig. 8:P23 (incomplete, no lugs preserved).

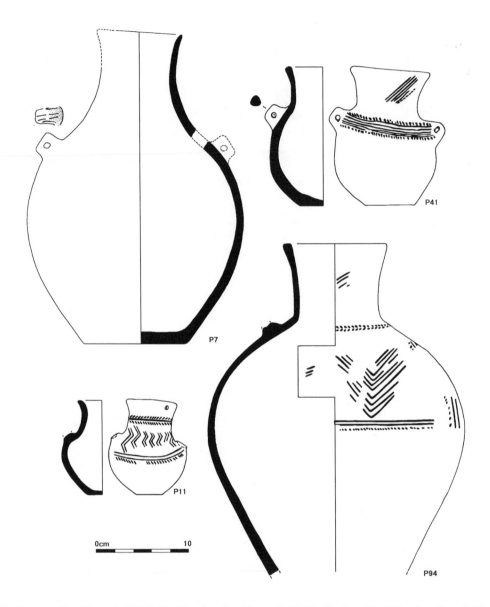

Fig. 4.12. Ear-lug Pot Type A (P7, P41); **Ear-lug Pot Type C** (P94); **Unclassified Ear-lug Pot** (P11).

Ear-lug Pot Type B is represented by a single example, the highly decorated P102. It has a more jar-like shape, with a shorter neck than Types A or C, and like Type C, has lugs set horizontally. A larger example decorated in similar style is known from Philia (Dikaios 1962: fig. 81:17). A smaller fragmentary jar from Kissonerga *Mosphilia*, displaying less developed irregular herringbone decoration, may be similar as well, although no lugs or handles were preserved (Peltenburg 1998: fig. 76.10). Similar jars, but without decoration, are attested from *Ayia Paraskevi* and Khrysiliou *Ammos* (Bolger 1983: figs. 2:11; 3:12, 13).

Illustrated example (fig. 4.10, pl. 4.5a): P102.

Ear-lug Pot Type C is the form fancifully christened "mosque lamp" by Stewart (1962:320, 371; 1992: 149). It is similar to Type A, but has a more conical and more articulated neck, an everted rim, a more piriform body, and the lugs on the shoulder are set horizontally. The type is decorated in the characteristic Philia Phase herringbone style. The examples identified at *Kaminoudhia* were very poorly preserved, but the form and decoration are so distinctive that the attribution seems quite secure. One of the most diagnostic Philia types, mosque lamps are found at Philia Phase sites throughout the island.[92]

>   Illustrated example (fig. 4.12, pl. 3.6a): P94.
>   Additional catalogued (probable) example: P65.

Unclassified Ear-lug pots. The small jar P11 (fig. 4.12, pl. 3.6a) is quite similar to Ear-lug pot Type A, but the lugs (or whatever was attached to the shoulders) are not preserved so the type is uncertain. It also differs from other ear-lug pots in having opposed holes below the rim, as is attested on handleless jars (cf. Dikaios 1962: fig. 82:10). The fabric of P11 is harder and darker than normal RP Philia wares.

A large pointed lug incised with parallel lines found in Tomb 4 appears to come from a Red Polished South Coast ear-lug pot such as one without provenience in the Cyprus Museum (Stewart 1962: fig. CII:5; Stewart 1992:82, pl. XI:4).

AMPHORAE

The amphora is one of the most common shapes at *Kaminoudhia*. All the cemetery examples have flat bases and are undecorated; most settlement examples also have flat bases. Most are quite small, between 20 and 30 cm in height.

Amphora Type A has a wide flat base, globular body, wide unarticulated neck, rounded slightly flaring rim, and vertical handles from mid-neck to upper body. The handles on P90 are very slightly angular. The type occurs in early Red Polished fabrics, and P100 has clearly visible irregular burnishing strokes.[93] These vessels relate to a type with slightly angular handles known in Cyprus throughout the EC. Early north coast examples usually have flat articulated bases, which change to round by EC II or III, while the flat base remains in vogue in the south.[94]

One fragmentary amphora, P82 (fig. 4.13) from the settlement, Area A, has been included with this type, although only a portion of the neck and one handle is preserved. Its shape and size are closely similar to P100 and its fabric is very similar to P90. Its complex incised decoration appears to be related to that of juglet P2 (fig. 4.10).[95]

>   Illustrated examples (fig. 4.14): P90 (and pl. 3.7a), P100 (and pl. 3.6c); (fig. 4.13): P82.

---

[92] Cf. Frankel and Webb 1997:97, fig. 8:P22, P24, with references; Dikaios 1962: fig. 81:15; Bolger 1983: fig. 2:14; Hennessy et al. 1988: figs. 15:S15, 17, 41:28, 3: 48:S3, S17; des Gagniers and Karageorghis 1976: pl. II:2.
[93] For amphorae and an indeterminate vessel in similar fabric, see Todd 1986: pl. XVIII:3; Herscher 1988: pl. XXX:7; Coleman et al. 1996:319:F630.
[94] Cf. Stewart 1962: figs. CIX:18, CXIII:1, 7; Todd 1985: fig. 7:10; Georghiou 2000: fig. 3:20. Also from the south coast is an example found deposited in a Cypro-Geometric tomb at Amathus: Gjerstad et al. 1935:93-94 (#45), pl. XXIII.1 (row 3, no. 7 from right). The type is dated EC IC and EC II by Stewart 1992:116. For another example of Early Bronze Age south coast pottery in a later context, see Buitron-Oliver 1996:3, 41.
[95] For another Type A amphora from the south coast with elaborate incised decoration (although not in exactly the same style as P82), cf. Herscher and Swiny 1992: fig. 2:2.

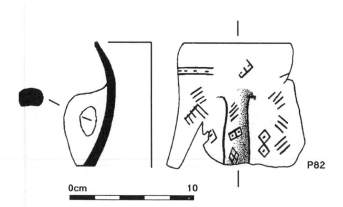

Fig. 4.13. Amphora Type A (P82).

Amphora Type B has a thinner more ovoid body than Type A and sharply angular handles. The single example identified, P68, was found in the same tomb as Type A amphora P90, suggesting a close relationship between the two.

       Illustrated example (fig. 4.14, pl. 3.7a): P68.

Amphora Type C is a small vessel (the example, P24, is less than 20 cm in height) with flat base, everted rim, and small angular handles. It is attested in Area A of the *Kaminoudhia* settlement, where it was found along with a dipper (P38) on a bench dating to the later phase in Unit 3. The neck is straighter and more articulated than that of Types A and B, and the Red Polished fabric has fewer mineral inclusions, more organic temper and a thinner slip.[96]

       Illustrated example (fig. 4.14): P24.

Amphora Type D was found in the *Kaminoudhia* settlement. The neck is taller and narrower than that of Types A and B, but is also not articulated. No base was preserved, but it is likely that it was round. The preserved example, P83, is decorated with a relief crescent on the upper body. Two other distinctive features are the groove around the interior of the rim (perhaps to support a lid) and the fully slipped interior (pls. 4.2a, 4.1b). This is quite a distinctive type, and is known elsewhere on the south coast.[97]

       Illustrated example (fig. 4.14; pls. 4.1b, 4.2a-b): P83.

Amphora Type E. Another incomplete amphora, P127 (fig. 4.14), from Area C of the settlement, appears to be related to Type D, although it is too fragmentary to be certain about its form. In this case the neck is not preserved, but the lower body, with round base, is complete. Although slightly smaller, the body shape is similar to P83, with the addition of a side spout from the upper body. It is also slipped on the interior. The nature of the handles is particularly uncertain: the preserved stumps suggest two vertical handles as Amphora Type D, but the original position of an additional handle stump found

---

[96] For a similar amphora, but with *round* base, cf. Coleman et al. 1996: fig. 70:F633 (from Alambra Tomb 105).
[97] Cf. Todd 1986: pl. XXVIII:2: slightly smaller and with no decoration, but also slipped on interior. A comparable north coast type has a round-pointed base: Dikaios 1940: pl. L:5.

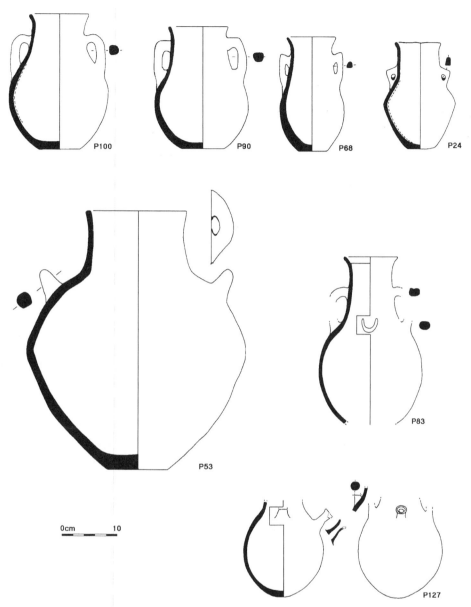

Fig. 4.14. Amphorae Type A (P100, P90); **Amphora Type B** (P68); **Amphora Type C** (P24); **Storage Vessel Type A** (P53); **Amphora Type D** (P83); **Amphora Type E** (P127).

among the sherds (and seemingly belonging to the same vessel) is unclear.[98] A spout from another amphora of this type was found in Area A Unit 6. Its fabric, shape and size are closely similar to P127, but it does not appear to have been slipped on the interior. This Red Polished side-spouted amphora appears to be a distinctly south coast type.[99]

Illustrated example (fig. 4.14): P127.

[98] An additional horizontal handle opposite the spout is one possibility: cf. Stewart 1962: fig. CXV:7, from Lapithos 322E (MC I), which also has a relief crescent like P83.

[99] The parallel from Kalavasos Tomb 46 (see n. 97 above) was incomplete and could originally have had a spout, although none was preserved among the sherds from the tomb.

Unclassified Amphorae. Several Red Polished rim sherds, most of them from the *Kaminoudhia* settlement, appear to belong to amphorae (they represent the rim sherds that had sufficient diameter preserved to distinguish them from a jug rim). These include a very slightly flaring rim with a rounded edge (from Tomb 6 and Area C Unit 8), slightly flaring rims with a flat edge from Area A Unit 3, and unstratified on the surface. One sherd (from Area A Unit 4) with a flaring rim similar to that of Amphora Type C also had the upper handle attachment preserved, which had a finger impression at the top.

COOKING POTS

The cooking pots from the cemetery, Types A and B, have wide flat bases, fairly globular bodies, and two opposed handles that are quite similar in size, although one is usually more angular than the other. The wide flat bases of these types are distinctly different from the early flat-based cooking pots found at *Vounous*, where the bases are smaller and clearly articulated ("raised") from the body of the vessel.[100] All except the unclassified example P128 are made in coarse versions of RP or RP Mottled fabric. None of the examples from the cemetery are made of the very hard fabric typical of later cooking pots and as found in those from the settlement. The later examples are distinctive for their handles of differing sizes.

Cooking Pot Type A. The single complete example of a Type A cooking pot, P23 from Tomb 7, is a small vessel, with a slightly ovoid body continuing directly into a flaring rim, without an articulated neck between them; the pair of handles is uniform in size.

Illustrated example (fig. 4.15, pl. 3.6b): P23.

Cooking Pot Type B. This is the standard cooking pot of the Philia Phase, represented in Tomb 15 (P91) and Dikaios Tomb 1. This type of jar, with two opposed vertical handles, is rare in Philia contexts and appears to be one of the new shapes introduced at this time (cf. Dikaios 1962: fig. 83:21). Its shape is squatter and more globular than the later Type A. While the fabric remains relatively soft in comparison to later cooking pots, the presence of a large amount of inclusions suggests modifications to meet the thermal requirements. Another cooking pot, P66 from Tomb 10, is fragmentary, but has similar fabric and probably represents the same type.

Illustrated examples (fig. 4.15): P91; (pl. 4.6a): Dikaios 1/1.
Additional catalogued example: P66 (?).

Cooking Pot Type C. Found in the settlement, this type is characterized by a small flat base and one handle that is considerably larger than the other.[101] These examples are smaller than most of the other cooking pots, and have a squat, rather globular body; both are made of hard cooking ware fabric. On one example, P50 (fig. 4.15), a vertical incised line is preserved on the smaller handle. Both classified examples come from Area A, but an uncatalogued rim sherd of a vessel very closely similar to P107

[100] For example, the cooking pot from *Vounous* Tomb 164B, dated to later EC IC: Stewart 1962: fig. CXXI:7. By EC II, the bases of *Vounous* examples have become almost rounded or pointed bases.

[101] Stewart considered handles of unequal size to be a regional variation (1992:168), but *Kaminoudhia* does not support this hypothesis.

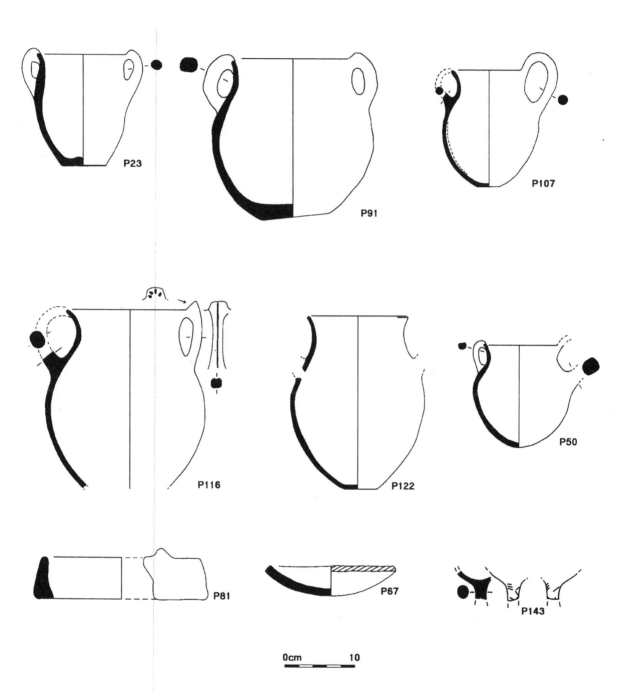

Fig. 4.15. Cooking Pot Type A (P23); **Cooking Pot Type B** (P91); **Cooking Pots Type C** (P107, P50); **Cooking Pots Type D** (P116, P122); **Hob** (P81); **Pot Support/Mold** (P67); **Tripod Legs** (P143).

was also found in Area C. The type appears to have been widely distributed in central and southern Cyprus in EC III–MC I.[102]

Illustrated examples (fig. 4.15): P50, P107.

Cooking Pot Type D. Also found in Areas A and C of the settlement, Type D cooking pots are somewhat larger, with taller proportions and more ovoid bodies than those of Type C, but like Type C, have handles significantly different in size. The fabric is harder and has finer inclusions than that of Type B cooking pots. The single handle that is preserved (which is angular), on P116, has incised and punctured decoration. A handle fragment with section of rim attached, from Area A Unit 35, appears to be from the same type of cooking pot.

Illustrated examples (fig. 4.15): P116, P122.

Unclassified Cooking Pots. A number of fragmentary cooking vessels from the settlement are made of a coarse unslipped fabric. The most complete of these is P128, which is very similar to Tankard Type C, but has a flat base. As preserved, P128 appears to have only a single handle, like a tankard, but since the rim and part of the upper body opposite the existing handle is not preserved, the vessel may have originally had a second, very small handle (or possibly a large lug, again like a tankard). P128 is also decorated with a crude vertical incision on the handle. An undecorated vertical handle in the same fabric came from Area C Unit 22, and other slightly flaring rim fragments in the same fabric came from Area A Unit 16, and two from Area C Unit 10. Another unclassified cooking pot is P92, from Tomb 11, of an unusual very crumbly fabric and with a finger impression at the lower handle attachment.

Griddles. Several fragments belong to a class of objects with Anatolian prototypes that has also been referred to as "pans" or "platters."[103] At least sometimes they are supported by tripod legs, although none of the *Kaminoudhia* examples provides evidence for legs.[104] P139 from the topsoil of Area B exhibits the typical lustrous black interior and pierced bottom that suggest exposure to fire. A second fragment from the topsoil in Area B is very similar to P139, but in addition displays the impression of matting on the exterior of its sides (pl. 4.5b);[105] no holes are preserved in the base of this fragment, but

---

[102] Cf. Karageorghis 1940–1948: fig. 14:2; Todd 1986: fig. 23:6, 7; Coleman et al. 1996: fig. 61:F134.

[103] For a full discussion with references, see Frankel and Webb 1996b:130–33; for analysis and discussion of the thermal qualities of these objects (called therein "*satzes*"), and excellent color illustrations of their distinctive features, see Taramides 1999:47–97. The shape is also well represented at Alambra: cf. Stewart 1962: fig. CXLVIII:6; Coleman et al. 1996:293–95, figs 65:F210, 66:F220 (shallower shape, but with holes). The *Kaminoudhia* examples belong to Frankel and Webb's higher-walled type a, which they suggest may have functioned as a portable brazier (although Taramides argues that cooking was done on the upper surface).

[104] Cf. Taramides 1999: pls. 27a–36, 42; Herscher and Swiny 1992: fig. 2:3. An unstratified leg from Area A probably comes from this type of tripod "griddle," which is known from a few other sites in southern Cyprus. This leg is made of unusual coarse fabric resembling Red-and-Black-Stroke-Burnished ware, although no slip was preserved; it showed no signs of burning. Cf. Frankel and Webb 1996b:131–32, fig. 7.10 (P6627, P6923). For a similar fabric identified in western Cyprus, see G. Philip in Peltenburg 1983:48 ("Degenerate Red and Black Stroke Burnished Ware").

[105] For other examples of mat impressions, with discussion, see Frankel and Webb 1996b:131–32, fig. 7.10, pl. 28o; Ohnefalsch-Richter 1893: pl. XXXV:9.

its interior too is a well-burnished black. At Marki the type appears to be most common in EC III, but elsewhere it is attested as late as MC III.[106]

Illustrated example (fig. 4.10): P139.

STORAGE VESSELS

Early Cypriot storage vessels are poorly attested, perhaps partly as a result of the lack of information about settlements of this period, although larger economic factors may be responsible as well (Stewart 1992:98; Pilides 1996). Those that are known are about a half-meter in height. Large storage vessels of about one meter in height (a highly significant increase in size), that might properly be called "pithoi," seem to appear around the end of the Early Cypriot or early in the Middle Cypriot period.[107] While none of the storage vessels from the *Kaminoudhia* settlement could be fully restored, they provide sufficient evidence of their size and characteristics to indicate that they are among the earliest pithoi so far known in Cyprus. The storage vessel from the cemetery, P53 from Tomb 6, represents important evidence for the existence of such vessels in the Philia Phase. Considerable evidence for wear was noted on the handle P141, the base P142, and overall on P53.

Storage Vessel Type A. Nearly a half meter in height, P53 is considerably larger than similar jars previously known from the Philia Phase (cf. Dikaios 1962: fig. 82:28; Bolger 1983: fig. 2:11). Its characteristic features are a flat base, squat globular body, only slightly flaring rim, and two opposed horizontal handles on the shoulders (in contrast to the vertical handles from neck to shoulder which are common on amphorae and storage vessels of the later EC); there is very little articulation at the neckline. Somewhat comparable jars from Vasilia Tomb 103 have three horizontal handles on the shoulder but distinctly different necks; the few other storage vessels of similar size known from Philia Phase contexts are entirely different from this type.[108] A very close parallel, however, is a jar without provenience in the Cyprus Museum, thus confirming Stewart's tentative attribution of the type to the Philia Phase (1992:128, pl. XVIII:7).

Illustrated example (fig. 4.14; pl. 3.6a): P53.

Storage Vessel Type B. From Area C of the settlement, P140 is a fragmentary vessel reconstructed from scattered sherds; only the upper part could be restored. It has a short wide neck with very straight rim. Preserved on one shoulder is a small horizontal handle with part of an incised motif preserved below it; the preservation of the opposite shoulder was not sufficient to determine the possible existence of a second handle. A pithos of about the same size with a similar short wide neck and straight rim was found at Marki *Alonia*, containing a Philia Phase child burial, but its handles were vertical (Frankel and Webb 2000: fig. 4 [P14040]). Also similar is a pithos from Vasilia T. 103, but it apparently had a

---

[106] Du Plat Taylor 1957: fig. 23:327. Although the *Kaminoudhia* examples were unstratified, the co-existence of the two types at the site provides no support for Taramides' (1999:54) suggestion that the type with a mat-impressed bottom is earlier than the type with punctured bottom.
[107] Frankel and Webb 1996b:146–47; Coleman et al. 1996:282; Pilides 1996:107; Stewart 1992:104–5, fig. 13:1; Stewart 1962: fig. CX:9.
[108] Hennessey et al. 1988: fig. 47: S59, S78; Stewart 1992:164, with references; Frankel and Webb 2000: fig. 4 (P14040).

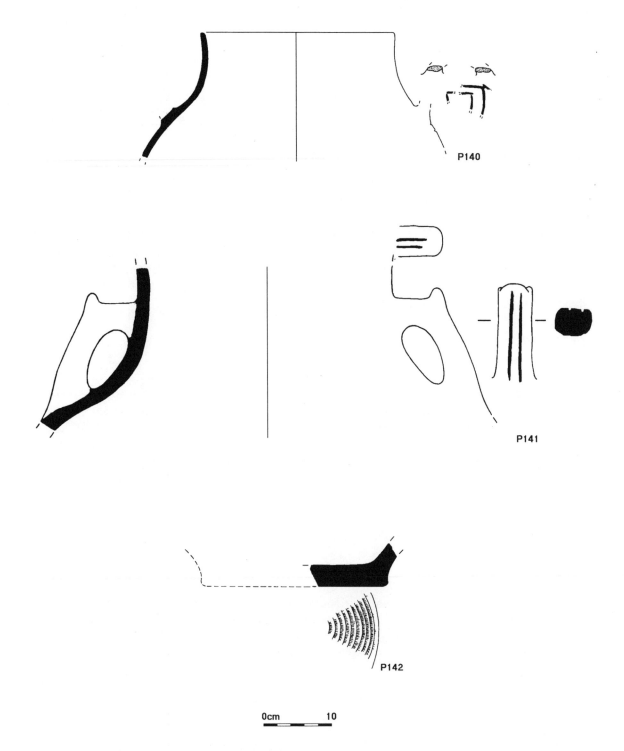

Fig. 4.16. Storage Vessel Type B (P140); **Unclassified Storage Vessels** (P141, P142).

lug of uncertain type rather than handles (Hennessy et al. 1988: fig. 48:2; Stewart 1992:164). It is worth noting that this Vasilia pithos had an incised "X" inside the rim above the lug, perhaps another resemblance to P140 with its incised motif (potmark?) below its handle. A similar but smaller jar was found at Kalavasos (Karageorghis 1940-1948: fig. 7 [upper burial: 2]; fig. 20:AII). Horizontal handles occur on a somewhat smaller jar from Alambra Tomb 101, but this vessel had relief decoration and a more flaring rim (Coleman et al. 1996: fig. 68:F592; cf. Belgiorno 1997: fig. 4.5). The roughly incised decoration is vaguely reminiscent of that on a smaller amphora from Lapithos (Stewart 1962: fig. CXVIII:4).

        Illustrated example (fig. 4.16): P140.

Unclassified Storage Vessels. The incised angular vertical handle attached to a large neck sherd, P141 (fig. 4.16), from Area C, appears to come from a storage vessel generally similar to types known from Marki, Alambra, Kalavasos and other sites in late EC or early MC.[109] However, it showed no evidence for relief decoration, which is common elsewhere; on the other hand, incision at these sites is rare. Similar incised handles occur on a smaller amphora from Larnaca *Ayios Prodromos* (Herscher 1988: fig. 4:1). The interior of this vessel's shoulder shows that the lower end of the handle was pushed through the pot wall and then smoothed (pl. 4.4c). The lower stump of what appears to be a similar handle, from Area A Unit 31, had the ends of three parallel vertical lines incised to its right, perhaps to be interpreted as a potmark. The original height of P141 would have been a meter or more, making it the largest vessel found at *Kaminoudhia*.

        While none of the *Kaminoudhia* pithoi could be fully restored, three fragments of bases were found that probably came from this type of vessel. All are flat, slightly articulated, approximately 30 cm in diameter and 1.5 to 2 cm in thickness. Two of them, from Area C Unit 2, and from a trial trench in Area A (P142, fig. 4.16), had the impressions of coiled mats on the bottom; the third base, from Area A Unit 3, Phase II, was plain (cf. Frankel and Webb 2000: fig. 4 [P14472]). Mat-impressed storage vessel bases are well attested at several other late EC/early MC sites.[110]

MISCELLANEOUS SHAPES

Hob. One fragment of a pot support (or "hob"), P81 (fig. 4.15), was identified at *Kaminoudhia*, from Area A Unit 1, Phase I. These important objects with Anatolian and Levantine connections were identified for the first time in Cyprus at Marki, where they are well attested in all phases of the excavated settlement.[111] While the discovery of one hob fragment at *Kaminoudhia* refutes the supposed absence of such pot stands elsewhere in Cyprus (Webb and Frankel 1999:35, 42; Frankel and Webb 1996b:183), the curious fact remains that they seem to be extremely rare outside of Marki.

        Like the Marki hobs, P81 is very low fired with many large inclusions, and its size is comparable to the smaller examples from Marki. However, it was slipped, which is rare at Marki, and the small fragment preserved did not show evidence for burning. The preserved fragment did not include

---

[109] E.g., Frankel and Webb 1996b:146–47; cf. especially fig. 7.20 (P2430); Coleman et al. 1996:282–83, especially fig. 60: F121; Stewart 1962: fig. CX:9; Merrillees 1984: figs 7–8; Karageorghis 1940–1948: figs 7 (upper burial: 1), 20:AI.

[110] Stewart 1992:112, pl. XV:5; Frankel and Webb 1996b:146–47, fig. 7.19 (P3255); Coleman et al. 1996:282, 324–25, pl. 51.

[111] Frankel and Webb 1996b:181–86, with full discussion and references; Frankel and Webb 1997:99–100, figs. 9:P10000, 10; pl. VI:3, 5.

a terminal, so there is no evidence for what the ends of the object were like, but the small projection on the undecorated ring is extremely modest in comparison to the elaborate form and decoration that is typical of the Marki hobs.

While Frankel and Webb have conclusively traced the Anatolian antecedents of the hob type, the context of this example at *Kaminoudhia* does not suggest that it was part of the Philia Phase assemblage (although it does come from the earlier phase of settlement occupation).

Pot Support/Mold (?). One modified sherd P67 (fig. 4.15), from *Kaminoudhia* Area C Unit 10, differs from the usual modified sherds found at *Kaminoudhia* (see below, Chapter 9) and other prehistoric sites in Cyprus and elsewhere. These are normally flat and no larger than 10 cm in diameter. P67, however, was reworked from a distinctly convex body sherd of a closed vessel to form a shallow bowl about 20 cm in diameter.

While it is possible that P67 was used as a pot lid, as has frequently been suggested for the flatter modified sherds, its size and shape suggest that it may instead have been a support for pottery vessels during the manufacturing process. The reuse of sherds in this way for hand-building pottery is well attested ethnographically: a bowl or the base of a pot under construction can be molded and secured in the concave sherd interior and the potter can easily turn the pot as she works on all sides of it (cf. Rye 1981: 63, figs. 42b, 57; Shepard 1968:60–63). Such a tool would have been useful to produce the round-bottomed pottery that was beginning to replace the traditional flat-based types. Other finds from Unit 10 (which may have been an open space with a bench, located on the edge of the settlement), such as stone pounders, stone and terracotta burnishers (?) or polishers, and large ceramic vessels (e.g., large bowl P121, spouted bowl P135) and basins suggesting the processing of liquids, may provide additional support for the interpretation that pottery manufacturing was associated with this area (cf. Chapter 2).

Bracket from Composite Vessel (?). An uncatalogued fragment from Area C Unit 2 may be part of a composite vessel. This piece is a short (L. pres. 3.9) straight rod, broken at both ends, nearly square or slightly trapezoidal in section and tapering very slightly toward the preserved ends (Th. max. 2.2). It is made of soft RPSC fabric with traces of dark red-brown slip, undecorated. Similar brackets are known from RPSC two-necked jugs, on which they appear horizontally in pairs connecting the two necks (e.g., Stewart 1962: fig. LXXIII:1–3), or joining parts of other types of composite vessels.[112] Such composite RPSC vessels are otherwise unattested at *Kaminoudhia*, however. A similar form also appears in the handle of an unusual type of ladle (des Gagniers and Karageorghis 1976: pl. XXXIX:1).

MISCELLANEOUS BASES

A number of ceramic fragments found at *Kaminoudhia* were too incomplete to be identified with a specific type of vessel, but provided significant supplementary information about the variety of base types represented at the site.

Tripod Legs. Four different detached legs were found at *Kaminoudhia*. They came originally from four different types of vessels, and they occur in a variety of fabrics.[113]

---

[112] E.g., des Gagniers and Karageorghis 1976: pl. XXXIX:2; Karageorghis 1976: fig. 68; Dikaios 1940: pl. XXXII.b; Flourentzos 1991: pl. XV:15.

[113] For the fourth one, see "Griddles," above.

From Area A, a small fragment, P143 (fig. 4.15), is most likely a leg from a small fine ware vessel. It is uncertain whether the pot was an open or closed vessel, but most known decorated tripod vessels are small amphorae, and have been found on north coast sites (cf. Stewart 1962: fig. CXIX:3; Stewart 1992:155).

An uncatalogued tripod leg fragment in RP Mottled ware comes from the hearth, Feature 38 in Area A Unit 30. Only the attachment stump of the leg was preserved, but the vessel to which it belonged appears to be a small thick-walled open vessel: the interior was well smoothed and considerably blackened by fire. An open tripod cooking vessel would be unparalleled in known ceramics from prehistoric Cyprus: this fragment is too small and inconclusive to warrant radical new interpretations, but it is worth noting for future reference.

An unstratified leg, from the cemetery area above Tomb 6, of very hard RP Mottled fabric, is short (H: 3.5) and rather conical in shape. It probably belonged to a tripod jar like those that have been found at the nearby site of Evdhimou (cf. Herscher 1976: pls. III:2, IV:6, V:1).

"Dimple" Base. A fragmentary small vessel from Area A Unit 18 (P77) has an impression (dimple?) in the center of its otherwise round base, similar to those of Type F bowls P13 and P20 (above). While P77 is clearly a closed vessel and not a bowl, its fabric is the same as these bowls: perhaps this distinctive base feature was the idiosyncrasy of a single potter.

CONCLUSIONS

The ceramics from Sotira *Kaminoudhia* display great diversity in fabrics and shapes. Yet several persistent features can be emphasized, most notably the continuity of the wide flat base through the long period of time represented in aggregate by the settlement and cemetery. Also significant is the continuing importance of bottles and flasks (the former with its unusual round base) at the site, probably representing the import of valued substance(s) from elsewhere in Cyprus. *Kaminoudhia* provides important evidence for the early appearance of the large storage vessel (pithos), and produced several examples of a distinctively marked large jug (Type A), perhaps of local manufacture, that has interesting implications for a regional trade network. Apart from the special classes of Red Polished South Coast flasks and Brown Polished bottles, the decoration on Red Polished ware is very limited, mostly occurring on handles and lugs: much of it should probably be considered to be potmarks.

Several recent discussions have focused on the theory that new drinking and eating customs were introduced to Cyprus at the beginning of the Bronze Age (e.g., Webb and Frankel 1999:39: Herscher 1997; Manning 1993:45). While the *Kaminoudhia* ceramic repertoire is very much in keeping with such a hypothesis, and the distribution of the finds in the settlement provides further support (see Chapter 2), the evidence is less apparent that such practices would have centered on an "elite" class at the site.

The strong connections to be seen between the Philia Phase ceramics and those of EC I/II (particularly RPSC) suggest that the standard Red Polished ware of the north coast (best represented at *Vounous*) is really the anomaly of the sequence (cf. Webb and Frankel 1999:42). Although the Early Bronze Age in many areas of the island still needs systematic examination, and full stratigraphic evidence is still lacking, the typological development of EC ceramics elsewhere seems more continuous than that of the north coast.

While the continuous development of the *Kaminoudhia* ceramics is stressed, it should also be noted that the final phase there (EC III), as represented by the settlement and the latest tombs, sees the introduction of several new pottery types that have a long continuing history thereafter, such as the tankard, the deep spouted bowl Type D (e.g., P49), dippers, and the large krater-like bowl. Drab Polished Blue Core ware also appeared here at the same time. This period seems to mark the beginning of more island-wide contact but—at least in the south—the contact does not seem to intensify particularly in the earlier stages of the Middle Cypriot period.

In the preceding discussion, Anatolian antecedents have been suggested for the hob and the griddle types, although it is likely that such influences were exerted on the Cypriot repertoire at some time long before their appearance at *Kaminoudhia*: that is, these types are not to be considered as evidence for contemporaneous direct contact between the Sotira area and Anatolia. The bottle P74 is clearly imported from the north coast of the island, north coastal influence was suggested above in regard to bottle P105 (Type C) and the juglet P2 (Type B), and some connections may be drawn between the RPSC flasks and a few examples from *Vounous* and a few other sites. Yet overall the links are few and only serve to reinforce the sense that the north was largely isolated from the rest of the island.

On the other hand, the diversity of the ceramics found at *Kaminoudhia* seems to be greater than would be expected from just the vagaries of local domestic production. While no firm conclusions can be drawn without undertaking a large-scale analytical program, the suggestion can be made that Sotira *Kaminoudhia* may have been a regional center of transit and exchange, perhaps related to a role in the picrolite trade, for which its location is eminently suited.[114]

---

[114] Cf. Webb and Frankel 1999:40–41. The evidence for *Kaminoudhia* as a center of picrolite production is discussed in Chapter 6.

Table 4.1. List of catalogued pottery.

The catalogued pottery retains the original catalogue numbers given in the field, with which the pieces are marked. (They are currently stored in the Kourion Museum, Episkopi Village.) Some vessels were eliminated from publication ("canceled") because of insufficient preservation. Identification numbers preceded by a * indicate that the vessel was stratified.

Full catalogue descriptions for cemetery pottery appear in Chapter 3, arranged according to tomb group. Settlement pottery is catalogued at the end of Chapter 4, arranged by area.

P1. RP Mottled bowl (Cemetery B)

P2. RP juglet (Cemetery B)

P3. RP juglet (Cemetery B)

P4. RP Mottled bowl (Cemetery A)

P5. RP Mottled bowl (Cemetery B)

P6. RP Mottled bowl (Cemetery B)

P7. RP Philia ear-lug pot (Cemetery A)

*P8. RP jug (T4)

P9. RP Philia flask (Cemetery A)

P10. RP Mottled bowl (Cemetery A)

*P11. RP Philia ear-lug pot (T6)

*P12. RP Mottled juglet (T7)

*P13. RP Mottled bowl (Area A, Unit 5)

*P14. RP juglet (T6)

*P15. RP small bowl (Area A, Unit 7)

*P16. RP bowl (Area A, Unit 5)

*P17. RP bowl (T9)

*P18. RP Mottled dipper (Area B, Unit 12)

*P19. RP Mottled bowl (T13)

*P20. RP Mottled bowl (Area A, Unit 5)

*P21. RP bowl (T7)

*P22. RP bowl (T6)

*P23. RP cooking pot (T7)

*P24. RP amphora (Area A, Unit 3, Phase II)

*P25. RP Mottled bowl (Area A, Unit 7)

*P26. RPSC flask (T4)

*P27. Brown Polished bottle (T4)

*P28. RPSC flask (T4)

*P29. Brown Polished bottle (T4)

*P30. RP juglet (Area C, Unit 10)

*P31. RPSC conical bowl (T7)

*P32. RPSC flask (T9)

*P33. RP jug (Area C, Unit 8)

P34. RPSC flask (Cemetery A)

P35. RP Philia flask (Cemetery A)

*P36. RP Mottled bowl (Area C, Unit 21)

P37. Canceled

*P38. RP Mottled dipper (Area A, Unit 3, Phase II)

*P39. RP miniature bowl (Area C, Unit 2)

*P40. RP Mottled tankard or dipper (Area B, Unit 12)

P41. RP Philia ear-lug pot (Cemetery A)

P42. RP spouted bowl (Cemetery A)

*P43. RP spouted bowl (Area A, Unit 15)

*P44. RP bowl (Area A, Unit 15)

*P45. RP bowl (T11)

*P46. RP Mottled bowl (T19)

*P47. RP bowl (T11)

*P48. RP Mottled bowl (T18)

*P49. RP Mottled deep spouted bowl (Area A, Unit 32)

*P50. RP Mottled cooking pot (Area A, Unit 5)

*P51. RP Mottled jug (Area A, Unit 16)

*P52. RP Philia spouted bowl (T6)

*P53. RP Philia storage vessel (T6)

P54. RP Philia bowl (Cemetery A)

*P55. RP juglet (Area C, Unit 2)

*P56. RP bowl (T11)

*P57. RP jug (T11)

*P58. RP jug (T11)

*P59. RP bowl (T18)

*P60. RP juglet (Area C, Unit 8)

*P61. RPSC flask (T18)

*P62. RP Mottled dipper (Area A, Unit 6)

*P63. RP spouted bowl (T11)

*P64. RP Philia spouted bowl (T10)

*P65. RP Philia ear-lug pot (T10)

*P66. RP cooking pot (T10)

*P67. RP Mottled pot support or mold (Area C, Unit 10)

*P68. RP small amphora (T14)

*P69. RP base (Area C, Unit 8)

*P70. RP jug handle (Area C, Unit 8)

*P71. RP spouted bowl (Area C, Unit 22)

*P72. DPBC tankard (Area A, Unit 6)

*P73. RP juglet (Area B, Unit 14)

*P74. RP III bottle (Area A, Unit 5)

*P75. RP Philia bottle (T15)

*P76. RPSC flask (T7)

*P77. RP Mottled jar (Area A, Unit 18)

*P78. RP bowl (T18)

*P79. Brown Polished bottle (T8)

*P80. RPSC flask (T7)

*P81. RP pot stand (Area A, Unit 1, Phase I)

*P82. RP amphora (Area A, Unit 5)

*P83. RP amphora (Area B, Unit 12)

*P84. RP Mottled bowl (T12)

*P85. DPBC tankard (Area C, Unit 2)

*P86. RP Mottled spouted bowl (Area C, Unit 2)

*P87. RP Mottled composite vessel (?) (Area C, Unit 21)

*P88. DPBC juglet (Area C, Unit 2)

*P89. RP bowl (T17)

*P90. RP amphora (T14)

*P91. RP cooking pot (T15)

*P92. RP cooking pot (T11)

*P93. RP bowl (T14)

*P94. RP Philia ear-lug pot (T6)

*P95. DPBC tankard (T12)

*P96. RP Mottled spouted bowl (T12)

*P97. RP Mottled bowl (T12)

*P98. Brown Polished bottle (T12)

*P99. RP jug (T12)

*P100. RP amphora (T12)

P101. RP Philia flask (Cemetery A)

*P102. RP Philia ear-lug pot (T15)

*P103. RP jug (T15)

*P104. RP Mottled large bowl (T17)

*P105. Brown Polished bottle (T19)

*P106. RP jug (Area C, Unit 8)

*P107. RP Mottled cooking pot (Area A, Unit 32)

*P108. RP Mottled bowl (Area C, Unit 22)

*P109. DPBC jug (Area A, Unit 6)

*P110. RP large bowl (Area C, Unit 22)

P111. Canceled

P112. Canceled

*P113. RP Mottled bowl (Area A, Unit 3, Phase II)

*P114. RP Mottled bowl (Area A, Unit 19)

*P115. RP Mottled bowl (Area C, Unit 23)

*P116. RP Mottled cooking pot (Area C, Unit 2)

*P117. RP jug (Area C, Unit 9)

*P118. RP jug (T14)

P119. Canceled

*P120. RP jug (Area A, Unit 6)

*P121. Coarse RP Mottled large basin (Area C, Unit 10)

*P122. RP Mottled cooking pot (Area A, Unit 4, Phase I)

*P123. RP juglet (Area A, Unit 30)

*P124. RP Mottled bowl (Area A, Unit 20)

*P125. RP bowl (Area A, Unit 3, Phase II)

P126. RP bowl (Area A, Unit 15)

*P127. RP spouted amphora (Area C, Unit 2)

P128. Coarse dipper (Area A, Unit 43)

*P129. RP bowl (Area C, Unit 8)

*P130. RP bowl (Area C, Unit 23)

*P131. RP Mottled bowl (Area C, Unit 2)

*P132. RP bowl (Area C, Unit 23)

P133. RP large bowl (Area C, Unit 8)

*P134. RP coarse basin (Area A, Unit 4, Phase I)

*P135. RP Mottled spouted bowl (Area C, Unit 10)

*P136. RP jug (Area C, Unit 22)

*P137. DPBC juglet (Area C, Unit 21)

*P138. RP juglet (Area C, Unit 8)

P139. RP Mottled griddle (Area B, topsoil)

*P140. RP Mottled storage vessel (Area C, Unit 8)

*P141. RP Mottled storage vessel (Area C, Unit 10)

P142. Coarse RP Mottled base (Area A, Trial Trench 1)

*P143. RP Mottled tripod leg (Area A, Unit 42)

*P144. RP bowl (Area A, Unit 1, Phase II)

*P145. RP Mottled bowl (Area C, Unit 2)

*P146. RP Mottled large bowl (Area A, Unit 4, Phase II)

*P147. RP Mottled jug (Area A, Unit 28)

SETTLEMENT POTTERY CATALOGUE

* Indicates vessel was stratified. All measurements in centimenters.

AREA A

*P13. Red Polished Mottled bowl. (Unit 5) Fig. 4.1; Swiny 1991: fig. 4.3. H:10.0; D:15.1. Round base with circular impression in center, ovoid body, slightly incurving rim, slight thickening on rim in one place. Three transverse impressions on thickened rim, otherwise undecorated. Fairly hard brown to red-brown clay with many small black and white inclusions; moderately thick lustrous slip, dark red-brown with large dark gray and small brown areas, somewhat worn. Bowl Type F.

*P15. Red Polished small bowl. (Unit 7) Fig. 4.1. H:4.9; D:7.2. Very crudely shaped; very thick round base, hemispherical body, plain rim; pointed vertical lug at rim. Undecorated. Hard gray-brown to dark gray clay with many small black and white inclusions; traces of brown and black slip; misfired or burned? Bowl Type H. Cf. Coleman et al. 1996: fig. 64:F202.

*P16. Red Polished bowl. (Unit 5) Fig. 4.1; Swiny 1991: fig. 4.3. H:7.5; D:12.1. Round base, hemispherical body, plain rim; small vertical lug, unpierced, slightly below rim. Undecorated. Rather soft bright orange clay with many black, white and gray inclusions; fairly thick lustrous dark red-brown slip (mostly dark gray on interior), much worn. Bowl Type E.

*P20. Red Polished Mottled bowl. (Unit 5) Swiny 1991: fig. 4.3. H:8.5; D:13.9. Shape, fabric and slip as P13, but slightly smaller. Two transverse impressions on thickened rim. Bowl Type F.

*P24. Red Polished amphora. (Unit 3 Phase II) Fig. 4.14. H:19.4; D:ca.14. Flat base, inverted piriform body, cylindrical neck, everted rim; two opposed vertical handles, only one preserved, small angular, rectangular in section, from lower neck to upper body. Undecorated. Soft thick fine light brown clay with a few small black and white inclusions, some fine organic temper; thin light red-brown slip, probably originally lustrous, very worn and poorly preserved, surface much damaged. Amphora Type C.

*P25. Red Polished Mottled bowl. (Unit 7) Fig. 4.1. H:10.5; D:ca.14.9. Round base, globular body, plain rim; pointed vertical lug at rim. Incised line on top of lug, otherwise undecorated. Hard light orange clay with many fine white and some black inclusions; rather thin somewhat lustrous red-orange slip with some mottled dark gray and light brown areas. Bowl Type D.

*P38. Red Polished Mottled dipper. (Unit 3 Phase II) H (rim pres.):8.9; D (rim):ca.14. Fragmentary, incomplete; flat base, ovoid body, plain rim; vertical (probably loop) handle (not preserved) rising from rim to upper body. Undecorated. Hard quite thick red-brown clay with many small black and white inclusions; thick lustrous dark red-brown slip mottled with dark gray. Dipper Type B.

*P43. Red Polished spouted bowl. (Unit 15) Fig. 4.3. H (pres.):ca.19; D:26.9. Broken, incomplete; base not preserved, globular body, slightly incurving rim; tubular spout with flaring end rising diagonally from below rim; vertical handle, thick oval in section, rising from rim to upper body opposite spout. Deep vertical incised line on handle top, otherwise undecorated. Fairly hard dark red-brown clay with many black inclusions; thick lustrous dark red-brown slip, very worn in some large areas. Spouted Bowl Type B.

*P44. Red Polished bowl. (Unit 15) H:7.5; D:14.5. Round base, hemispherical body, plain rim; small vertical lug below rim (unpierced). Undecorated. Fairly soft orange-brown to pinkish-brown clay with many black, white and gray inclusions; traces of thick dark gray slip with some luster, most slip not preserved. Bowl Type E.

*P49. Red Polished Mottled deep spouted bowl. (Unit 32) Fig. 4.4. Fragmentary, incomplete; small flat base, globular body, short wide concave, neck, flaring rim; tubular spout rising diagonally from mid-body, not preserved; horizontal handle, round in section, rising diagonally from mid-body opposite spout. Incised decoration: double broken zigzag on handle. Fairly soft orange-brown clay with many small black and white inclusions; thick lustrous dark red-brown slip with several black and dark gray areas. Spouted Bowl Type D.

*P50. Red Polished Mottled cooking pot. (Unit 5) Fig. 4.15; Swiny 1991: fig. 4.3. H (to rim):14.9; D:14.7. Small flat base, globular body, short wide slightly concave neck, flaring rim; two opposed vertical handles, one small and round in section, from rim to upper body; other handle larger, not preserved. Decoration: deep vertical incision on preserved handle. Hard red-brown clay with many small black and white inclusions; thick lustrous red-brown slip, mottled with black. Cooking Pot Type C.

*P51. Red Polished Mottled jug. (Unit 16) Fig. 4.6. H (neck):15.0; D (rim):ca.9. Incomplete; base and body not preserved; inverted conical neck, flaring rim with flattened edge; vertical handle, oval in section, from mid-neck to upper body.

Incised decoration (pres.): on upper body, group of three parallel oblique lines; on handle, three groups of three parallel oblique lines in alternating directions. Thick hard red-brown clay with dark gray interior, many small black and white inclusions; thick lustrous dark red-brown slip, poorly preserved. Jug Type G.

*P62. Red Polished Mottled dipper. (Unit 6) Fig. 4.4. H (pres.):13.5; H (rim):6.5; D:9.9. Round base, hemispherical body, plain rim; high vertical loop handle, round in section, rising from rim to mid-body. Undecorated. Fairly hard orange-brown clay with a moderate amount of small black and white inclusions; fairly thick lustrous red-brown slip with a few small dark gray areas. Dipper Type A.

*P72. Drab Polished Blue Core tankard. (Unit 6) Fig. 4.7. H:22.1; D:16.5. Round base, globular body, wide cylindrical neck, flaring rim; two opposed vertical handles, one large and round in section, from rim to upper body, and the other small and hook-shaped, oval in section, from lower neck to upper body. Punctured decoration: row of circular punctures encircling neckline and lower handle attachments; vertical row on each handle. Very hard pinkish-orange clay with many white and dark red inclusions (interior not visible); traces of lustrous pinkish-brown slip, burnish marks visible, surface poorly preserved and flaking off. Tankard Type B. Cf. P95 (Tomb 12).

*P74. Red Polished III bottle. (Unit 5) Fig. 4.11. H (pres.):ca.5. Very fragmentary; round base, body not restored, inverted conical neck, rim not preserved. Incised decoration (preserved): group of horizontal lines on upper body, below neckline and on neck above neckline; at mid-neck (?), a horizontal band of straight and broken lines dividing concentric circles. Black-topped: very soft light brown clay at base, with gray exterior at neck and upper body; thin (?) lustrous dark red-brown slip on base, black on neck and upper body. See North Coast Bottle.

*P77. Red Polished Mottled jar (?). (Unit 18) H (pres.):12.6; D:12.1. Broken, repaired, incomplete; small concave base, globular body, flaring rim; rim edge not preserved, no evidence of handle(s) preserved. Undecorated. Moderately hard dark red-orange clay with many small black and white inclusions; fairly thick lustrous slip, dark red-brown mottled with black, dark gray, etc.; poorly preserved. See Miscellaneous Bases.

*P81. Red Polished pot stand ("hob"). (Unit 1 Phase I) Fig. 4.15. H:7.5; D (est.):19. Small fragment of apparently ring- or horseshoe-shaped vessel, roughly triangular in section, curving inward slightly at base of interior; a triangular projection preserved at top. No decoration preserved. Soft clay with many large black, white and gray inclusions, mostly dark gray with a light orange surface; traces of thick dark red-brown slip, no luster preserved, more slip preserved on interior. See Miscellaneous Shapes.

*P82. Red Polished amphora. (Unit 5) Fig. 4.13; Swiny 1991: fig. 4.3. H (pres.):ca.9.8; D (rim): ca.11. Only about half of neck preserved; wide inverted conical neck, flaring rim; vertical handle (one preserved), oval in section, from mid-neck to upper body. Incised decoration: elaborate pattern of squares and groups of short oblique lines on neck and handle. Fairly soft light brown clay with a small amount of black, white and gray inclusions, some of them large; thick lustrous dark red-brown slip, worn. Amphora Type A.

*P107. Red Polished Mottled cooking pot. (Unit 32) Fig. 4.15. H:19.3; D:ca.14.2. Small flat base, globular body, wide short slightly concave neck, flaring rim; two opposed vertical handles from rim to upper body, one larger and rising above rim, other not preserved. Undecorated. Quite hard brown clay with many small black and white inclusions; fairly thick lustrous slip, mottled black and dark brown. Cooking Pot Type C.

*P109. Drab Polished Blue Core jug. (Unit 6) Fig. 4.6. H (pres.):ca.30; D:ca.27. Broken, repaired, only about half of body preserved; small raised flat base, globular body; handle attachment (pushed through) at upper body. Decoration (pres.): small segment of horizontal impressed relief band preserved at neckline. Medium hard gray clay with pinkish-orange exterior surface, many white and dark red inclusions; thin light orange slip with vertical burnishing marks, flaking off and poorly preserved. See Unclassified Jugs.

*P113. Red Polished Mottled bowl. (Unit 3 Phase II) H (pres.):10.3; D:ca.14. Fragmentary, about half preserved; flat base, deep ovoid body, slightly incurving rim; vertical lug, at or below rim (top of lug not preserved). Undecorated. Moderately hard dark red-orange clay with many black, white and gray inclusions, some of them large; fairly thick slip with some luster preserved, dark red-orange with some dark gray and brown areas. Bowl Type A.

*P114. Red Polished Mottled bowl. (Unit 19) H:9.6; D:ca.14. Broken, incomplete; flat base, ovoid body, plain rim; no evidence of lugs, handle or decoration preserved. Very hard light red-brown clay with many small black and white inclusions; fairly thin matt slip, mostly dark gray with some red-brown areas; worn, especially on base. Bowl Type A.

*P120. Red Polished jug. (Unit 6) Fig. 4.4. H (handle pres.):12.5; D (base):ca.7.5. Fragmentary, incomplete, very poorly preserved, partially restored. Flat base, body not restored, cylindrical neck, flaring rim (edge not preserved); vertical handle, oval in section, from mid-neck to upper body. Decoration (pres.): relief band at neckline, incised joined lozenge group motif on neck above handle; on handle, two incised oblique antithetical dotted bands with incised joined lozenge group motif below. Very soft light brown clay with light gray interior, many white and gray inclusions; lustrous dark red-brown slip, worn and poorly preserved, surface flaking. Jug Type A.

*P122. Red Polished Mottled cooking pot. (Unit 4 Phase I) Fig. 4.15, pl. 2.3a. H:23.5; D:19.8. Incomplete; small flat base, irregular ovoid body, short slightly concave neck, slightly flaring rim; two opposed vertical handles (not preserved) from rim to upper body. Undecorated. Fairly hard dark red-brown clay with many fine black and some white inclusions; fairly thick lustrous slip, mottled dark red-brown, brown and very dark gray, somewhat worn. Cooking Pot Type D.

*P123. Red Polished juglet. (Unit 30) H (pres.):13.9; D:9.9. Broken, incomplete; round base, globular body, neck and rim not preserved; vertical handle, round in section, from (?)mid-neck to upper body. Undecorated. Fairly soft orange-brown clay with thin dark gray interior, many small black, white and gray inclusions; thin slip, poorly preserved, with some luster preserved, mottled from dark red-brown to dark gray. See Unclassified Juglets.

*P124. Red Polished Mottled bowl. (Unit 20) Fig. 4.1. H:10.2; D (rim):ca.14. Broken, incomplete; flat base, ovoid body, plain rim; pointed lug at rim. Undecorated. Hard red-brown clay with many small black and white inclusions, thick gray core; thick lustrous dark red-brown slip, mottled with gray. Bowl Type A.

*P125. Red Polished bowl. (Unit 3 Phase II) H:8.3; D (rim):ca.13. Half preserved; flat base, ovoid body, plain rim; no lug or decoration preserved. Very hard brown clay with a small amount of fine white inclusions, thick dark gray core; thin matt slip, mostly brown with red-brown areas. Bowl Type A.

P126. Red Polished bowl. (Unit 15) Fig. 4.1. H:9.1; D:15.2. Broken, repaired, incomplete; round base, ovoid body, plain rim; convex vertical lug below rim, pierced. Undecorated. Soft bright pinkish-orange clay with many small inclusions; surface very damaged and little preserved; thin lustrous red-brown slip. Bowl Type E.

P128. Coarse dipper. (Unit 43) H:17.2; D:15.6. Broken, incomplete; thick-walled; flat base, globular body, plain slightly flaring rim with slightly flaring edge; vertical handle (apparently only one), oval in section, from rim to upper body. Decoration: deep vertical groove on upper half of handle. Fairly soft dark brown, red-brown, and mostly black clay with large amount of sand inclusions, some fine organic temper; surface smoothed, with very little luster, mottled black to dark red-brown; base worn. Unclassified cooking pot.

*P134. Red Polished coarse basin. (Unit 4 Phase I) Fig. 4.2. D (est.):ca. 50. Fragmentary, rim only preserved; crudely and irregularly-shaped; plain slightly incurving rim of large vessel. Quite hard light brown clay with light red-brown core, very large white and gray inclusions; fairly thick matt dark red-brown slip on interior, traces of brown slip on exterior. Large Bowl Type C.

P142. Coarse Red Polished Mottled base. (Trial Trench 1) Fig. 4.16. D:ca. 30. Fragmentary, approximately one-fourth of base preserved with small portion of pot wall; flat slightly articulated base of very large vessel (pithos?); worn impression of coiled mat on bottom. Coarse fabric with very large sand inclusions, thick black core; traces of dark red-brown slip on exterior, including bottom of base. See Unclassified Storage Vessels.

*P143. Red Polished Mottled tripod leg. (Unit 42) Fig. 4.15. H (pres):ca. 2.3. Small part of leg with attachment to body of a small vessel; round in section (D: ca. 1.6). Incised decoration: short oblique lines in groups or alternating, on all sides of leg. Medium hard clay with many small black and white inclusions, almost entirely very dark gray; traces of thin lustrous brown slip, perhaps also on vessel interior, but this is very worn and encrusted. See Miscellaneous Bases.

*P144. Red Polished bowl. (Unit 1 Phase II) D (rim):ca. 14. Fragmentary; base not preserved, hemispherical body, plain, pointed rim; thin pointed vertical lug at rim. Deep incised line on top of lug. Hard red-brown clay with thick dark gray core, many small black and white inclusions; rather thin lustrous dark red-brown slip with a dark gray area, burnishing marks visible; worn, especially on the interior. Bowl Type D.

*P146. Red Polished Mottled large bowl. (Unit 4 Phase II) Fig. 4.2. D:ca. 46. Fragmentary; no base preserved, body not restored, plain rim; horizontal semicircular ledge lug at mid(?) body. Undecorated. Large Bowl Type A.

*P147. Red Polished Mottled jug. (Unit 28) Fig. 4.6; pls. 4.4a-b. H (pres.): 15; D (rim):9.3. Incomplete, neck only preserved; slightly tapering neck of large jug, round spout, flaring rim; vertical handle from mid-neck, not preserved. Undecorated. Very hard very dark gray clay with a small amount of black and white inclusions, some large, dark red to brown where oxidized (very little oxidation on surface or interior); thin matt slip. See Unclassified Jugs.

AREA B

*P18. Red Polished Mottled dipper. (Unit 12) Fig. 4.4. H:13.2; H (rim):8.6; D:ca.11.6. Broken, incomplete; flat base, ovoid body, plain rim; vertical loop handle, thick oval in section, rising from rim to mid-body. Undecorated. Moderately hard brown clay with many small black and white inclusions; thick lustrous dark red-brown slip, one medium gray area; worn. Dipper Type B.

*P40. Red Polished Mottled tankard or dipper. (Unit 12) Fig. 4.7. H:12.2; H (rim):10.2; D:11.2. Broken, repaired, incomplete; round base, globular body, slightly flaring rim; high vertical handle, oval in section, rising from rim to upper body; large vertical lug opposite handle. Incised decoration: vertical line on handle. Fairly hard brown clay with many small black and white inclusions; traces of thick lustrous slip, some dark red, mostly gray to black. Tankard Type C.

*P73. Red Polished juglet. (Unit 14) Fig. 4.7. H (pres.):ca.19.4; D:14.1. Broken, repaired, incomplete; round base, irregular ovoid body, narrow cylindrical neck, beginning of cutaway or beak spout (not preserved); vertical handle, round in section, from rim to upper body. Relief decoration: conical knob on upper body at either side of lower handle attachment. Thick soft orange-brown clay with light gray interior, small amount of black, white and gray inclusions, some large; rather thin dark red-orange slip, worn and poorly preserved, perhaps once some luster. See Unclassified Juglets.

*P83. Red Polished amphora. (Unit 12) Fig. 4.14; pls. 4.1b, 4.2a-b. H (pres.):32.5; D:ca.21. Broken, repaired, incomplete; base not preserved, ovoid body, cylindrical neck, flaring rim; two opposed vertical handles, oval in section, from mid-neck to upper body; upper handle has been inserted through neck and smoothed on interior. Decoration (preserved): wide shallow vertical groove at top of each handle; horizontal groove below rim on interior; part of relief crescent preserved at the middle of the upper body. Rather soft orange-brown clay with light gray core, many small black and white inclusions; thick lustrous dark red-brown slip, also on interior of pot. Amphora Type D.

P139. Red Polished Mottled griddle. Topsoil. Fig. 4.10. H: 4.3; D (base):ca. 30. Small fragment only preserved. Flat articulated base pierced by numerous holes from bottom (holes do not extend all the way through the base and stop about 0.1–0.2 cm from the interior surface); short, straight flaring sides, plain, rounded rim. Undecorated. Thick fabric with lustrous red-brown slip, especially well-burnished on the interior, with burnishing marks visible; bottom of interior is black.

AREA C

*P30. Red Polished juglet. (Unit 10) Fig. 4.7. H (pres.):19.0. Fragmentary, incomplete; small flat base, body shape indeterminate, conical neck, rim not preserved; vertical handle, oval in section, from rim to upper body. Incised decoration: cross on handle. Soft light brown clay with light gray core in thicker areas, many small black, white and gray inclusions and some fine organic temper; rather thin slip, worn and poorly preserved, a little luster preserved, light brown to red-brown. See Unclassified Juglets.

*P33. Red Polished jug. (Unit 8) Fig. 4.6; Swiny 1991: fig. 4.4. H (pres.):ca.28; D:17.8. Broken, incomplete; slightly flattened base, ovoid body, inverted conical neck, rim not preserved; vertical handle, oval in section, from mid-neck to upper body. Incised decoration: on upper body, three groups of three short vertical lines; on neck, two parallel short oblique lines either side of upper handle attachment; on handle, three pairs of short oblique lines, finger impression at upper and lower handle attachments. Rather soft thick dark orange-brown clay with many small black inclusions; thick lustrous dark orange-brown slip with a dark gray area on body. Jug Type G.

*P36. Red Polished Mottled bowl. (Unit 21) Fig. 4.1. H:7.2; D:19.4. Broken, incomplete; flat base, shallow inverted conical body, plain rim; slightly horned horizontal ledge lug at rim (rim opposite lug not preserved). Undecorated. Hard brown clay with many small black and white inclusions; thick lustrous dark red-brown slip with some black areas, somewhat worn. Bowl Type C.

*P39. Red Polished (?) miniature bowl/composite vessel. (Unit 2) Fig. 4.1. H:2.5; D:3.1. Fragmentary, incomplete, perhaps broken from larger vessel; very crudely formed and irregular; flat base, deep ovoid body, possibly very small portion of plain rim preserved. Undecorated. Soft light brown clay with a large dark gray area, many black, white and gray inclusions and a small amount of fine organic temper; traces of dark red-brown slip on interior and exterior, black on area of dark gray clay. See Composite Vessels.

*P55. Red Polished juglet. (Unit 2) Fig. 4.7. H:23.7; D:15.6. Slightly flattened base, irregular ovoid body, narrow slightly concave neck, slightly flaring rim; vertical handle, oval in section, from mid-neck to upper body. Relief decoration: crescent on one side of upper body, short vertical line on handle. Quite hard brown clay with small black and white inclusions; thick lustrous dark red-orange slip, slightly worn. Juglet Type E.

*P60. Red Polished juglet. (Unit 8) Fig. 4.7; Swiny 1991: fig. 4.4. H:25.7; D:17.7. Flat base, globular body, short inverted conical neck, short cutaway spout; vertical handle, oval in section, from rim to upper body. Undecorated. Hard dark red-brown clay with many small black and white inclusions; thick somewhat lustrous dark red-orange slip with a few small brown areas. Juglet Type C.

*P67. Red Polished Mottled pot support or mold(?). (Unit 10) Fig. 4.15. H:5.0; D:ca.19.3 (irregular). Body sherd from a large closed vessel, broken evenly in a circle to form a shallow hemispherical shape. Undecorated. Very hard dark orange clay with many small black and white inclusions; fairly thick dark red-brown slip, on exterior only. See Miscellaneous Shapes.

*P69. Red Polished base. (Unit 8) Pl. 4.1a. D (base):ca. 9.5. Fragmentary, flat base and small part of body only preserved; from large closed vessel. Evidence for considerable wear on bottom of base. See Jug Type A.

*P70. Red Polished handle from large jug. (Unit 8) Fig. 4.5; Swiny 1991: fig. 4.4. L (pres.): ca. 15. Large vertical handle, oval in section, both ends inserted through wall of pot and smoothed on interior. Incised decoration: shallow and rather carelessly executed; two incised oblique antithetical hatched bands with incised joined lozenge group motif below (cf. P120). Fairly hard brown clay with very thick dark gray interior, moderate amount of black, white, and gray inclusions; fairly thick dark red-brown slip, worn. Jug Type A.

*P71. Red Polished spouted bowl. (Unit 22) Fig. 4.3. H (pres.):ca.11; D(rim):ca.17. Broken, incomplete; round(?) base, ovoid body, plain rim; tubular spout with flaring end rising diagonally from below rim; body and rim opposite spout not preserved, no evidence for handle, etc., preserved. No decoration preserved. Thick quite soft orange-brown clay with many small black and white inclusions; thick lustrous red-brown slip with a few small dark gray areas. See Unclassified Spouted Bowls.

*P85. Drab Polished Blue Core tankard. (Unit 2) Fig. 4.7. H:29.0; D(est.):ca.21. Broken, incomplete; round base, globular body, wide conical neck, flaring rim; vertical handle, oval in section, rising slightly from rim to upper body; projection (not preserved) on upper body opposite handle. Undecorated. Fairly hard blue-gray clay with thin matt light pinkish-orange slip, many small white inclusions. Tankard Type A.

*P86. Red Polished Mottled spouted bowl. (Unit 2) Pl. 2.7a. H (pres.):26.5; D:ca.36.5. Broken, incomplete; flat base, ovoid body, slightly incurving rim; tubular spout with flaring end rising diagonally from below rim; end of spout chipped, no handle preserved (body opposite spout missing). Undecorated. Quite hard dark red-brown clay with dark gray core, many small black and white inclusions; thick lustrous dark red-brown slip, some black and dark gray areas, especially on interior. Spouted Bowl Type B(?).

*P87. Red Polished Mottled composite vessel (?). (Unit 21) Fig. 4.1. H (pres.):6.5; D:15.1. Broken, incomplete; round base, hemispherical body, plain rim; two handle attachments(?) on top of rim, thin oval in section, not opposed but 120 degrees apart; horizontal semicircular lug at rim 120 degrees from handle attachments; rim broken between handle attachments (could have been attached to another vessel). Undecorated. Dark brown clay with thick dark gray core, many small black and white inclusions; thick lustrous dark brown slip with black areas; appears burned. See Composite Vessels.

*P88. Drab Polished Blue Core juglet. (Unit 2) Fig. 4.7. H:ca.21; D:17.0. Broken, incomplete; nipple base, squat ovoid body, narrow neck (incomplete), rim not preserved; vertical handle (not preserved) to upper body. Undecorated. Quite hard gray clay with light pink surface, many small black, white and dark red inclusions; surface worn and damaged, traces of light red-orange slip. See Unclassified Juglets.

*P106. Red Polished jug. (Unit 8) Fig. 4.6; Swiny 1991: fig. 4.4. H (pres.): ca.27; D:27.1. Fragmentary, incomplete; round base, globular body, neck and rim not preserved; vertical handle (not preserved) to upper body. Relief decoration (pres.): on upper body, conical knobs with punctured center at either side of lower handle attachment, vertical wavy line opposite handle. Fairly soft red-brown clay with many small black and white inclusions; thin lustrous dark red slip, worn. See Unclassified Jugs.

*P108. Red Polished Mottled bowl. (Unit 22) H:ca.11.5; D:ca.12. Incomplete; round base, ovoid(?) body, plain slightly incurving rim; no handle, etc., preserved. No decoration preserved. Hard red-brown clay with thick dark gray core, many small black and white inclusions; fairly thin lustrous dark red-brown slip with small brown and black areas. Bowl Type D.

*P110. Red Polished large bowl. (Unit 22) Fig. 4.2; pl. 4.3a. H:17.1; D:ca.42. Flat base, wide inverted conical body, plain rim; two opposed horizontal handles, round in section, on upper body; two opposed narrow horizontal ledge lugs above handles; three pairs of ancient mending holes. Incised decoration: on each ledge lug, three groups of three transverse lines. Rather soft red-orange clay with many small black and white inclusions; thick lustrous dark red-brown slip with black areas, somewhat worn, especially on base. Large Bowl Type B.

*P115. Red Polished Mottled bowl. (Unit 23) H:ca.9; D:12.6. Broken, incomplete; round base, globular body, plain rim; no handle or lugs preserved (perhaps trace of lug). Undecorated. Quite soft brown clay with many small black and white inclusions, some fine organic temper; thick lustrous dark red-brown slip. Bowl Type D.

*P116. Red Polished Mottled cooking pot. (Unit 2) Fig. 4.15. H (pres.):ca.26; D:22.0. Fragmentary, incomplete; base not preserved, ovoid body, short wide concave neck, flaring rim; two opposed vertical handles, one larger (not preserved) than the other, from rim to upper body, smaller handle thick oval in section with a flat angular top. Incised decoration (pres.): on handle, a vertical line, semicircular pattern of five punctures on inside face of handle top. Hard dark orange-brown clay with many small black and white inclusions, some dark gray areas; fairly thick lustrous dark brown slip with considerable black area. Cooking Pot Type D.

*P117. Red Polished jug. (Unit 9) H (pres.):ca.25; D:25.1. Broken, incomplete; very small flat base, globular body, neck and rim not preserved; vertical handle, not preserved, to upper body. No decoration preserved. Fairly soft brown clay with gray interior, many small black, white and gray inclusions; thick lustrous dark red-brown slip. See Unclassified Jugs.

*P121. Coarse Red Polished Mottled large bowl. (Unit 10) Fig. 4.2; pl. 2.7b; Swiny 1986a: fig. 2:7. H (est.):29; H(pres.):24; D(rim):48. Fragmentary, incomplete; flat base, low wide conical body, plain rim with flattened edge; two opposed horizontal handles, round in section, above mid-body. Undecorated. Fairly hard dark gray clay with red-brown surfaces, heavily tempered with gravel; worn dark brown slip, with traces of luster, on interior and exterior; surface on lower interior completely destroyed. Large Bowl Type C.

*P127. Red Polished spouted amphora. (Unit 2) Fig. 4.14. H (pres.): 18; D: ca. 16. Fragmentary, incomplete; round base, globular body, short vertical neck(?), rim not preserved; small conical spout with flaring end from upper body; vertical(?) handles (not preserved), round in section, from upper body (a third handle stump appears to be from same vessel but does not join). Undecorated. Soft light brown clay with thin very light gray core in thicker areas, a few small white inclusions, fine organic temper, straw impression; fairly lustrous red-brown slip on interior and exterior, worn in places. Amphora Type E.

*P129. Red Polished bowl. (Unit 8) Fig. 4.1. H:ca.5.0; D:ca.16. Fragmentary, incomplete; round base with circular impression in center, shallow hemispherical body, plain, rounded rim; two opposed narrow rectangular horizontal ledge lugs at rim; two holes through wall of vessel below one lug. Incised decoration: two pairs of transverse lines on each lug. Fairly hard fine red-brown clay with many fine black and white inclusions, some fine organic temper; fairly thin red-brown slip, quite lustrous, rather worn. Bowl Type G.

*P130. Red Polished bowl. (Unit 23) Fig. 4.1. H:ca.2.5; D:ca.9.0. Broken, incomplete; crudely and irregularly formed; shallow saucer-like vessel with thick curving base, short plain slightly flaring rim. No decoration preserved. Dark gray clay with very large inclusions; fairly thick dark red-brown slip, now matt, on interior and rim exterior; bottom exterior dark gray. Bowl Type H.

*P131. Red Polished Mottled bowl. (Unit 2) Fig. 4.1. H:ca.4.3; D:ca.10.5. Fragmentary, incomplete; round base, shallow hemispherical body, plain rim; pair of pointed vertical lugs at rim; something similar, but not identical, opposite (damaged), with a hole between the lugs. Undecorated. Quite soft dark red-brown clay with many fine black and white inclusions and some fine organic temper, gray core in thickest parts; thick dark red-brown slip, mottled with brown and dark gray. Bowl Type G.

*P132. Red Polished bowl. (Unit 23) Fig. 4.1. D (rim):est. 18. Fragmentary, incomplete; flat base, hemispherical body, plain, pointed incurving rim; pointed vertical lug at rim. Deep incised line on top of lug. Quite hard clay, mostly dark gray with bright red-orange surfaces where oxidized, many moderately-sized black, white and gray inclusions; thin very lustrous slip, very dark gray on the lower exterior and dark red-brown on interior and exterior rim; burnishing strokes visible. Bowl Type B.

P133. Red Polished large bowl. (Unit 8) Fig. 4.2. D (rim):ca. 36. Fragmentary, incomplete; base and most of body not preserved, plain rim with flat edge; small horizontal handle (stumps of one only preserved), round in section, below rim; narrow horizontal horned lug at rim (one only preserved). Decoration: top of lug incised with broken double zigzag, short vertical relief bands below lug extending toward handle. Moderately hard dark red-orange clay with many black, white and gray inclusions, some large, some fine organic temper, medium gray interior; lustrous dark red-brown slip. Large Bowl Type B.

*P135. Red Polished Mottled spouted bowl. (Unit 10) Fig. 4.3. H (pres.):ca. 30; D(est.):ca. 40. Fragmentary; base not preserved, deep ovoid body (?), plain rim; beginning of spout attachment below rim; no handle preserved. Relief decoration (pres.): horizontal band ca. 1.2 cm. below rim. Medium hard red-orange clay with many small inclusions; mottled slip with some luster, heavily encrusted. See Unclassified Spouted Bowls.

*P136. Red Polished jug. (Unit 22) Fig. 4.5. H (pres.):13.5. Fragmentary, incomplete, neck only preserved; tapering neck of medium-sized jug with round spout, rim not preserved; vertical handle, rectangular in section, from mid-neck to upper body, both ends pushed through pot wall. Decoration: sharp horizontal relief band at neckline; incised chevron pattern on handle and on neck above handle. Soft, mostly light gray clay; thin worn lustrous red-brown slip. Jug Type A.

*P137. Drab Polished Blue Core juglet. (Unit 21) Fig. 4.7. H (neck pres.):10.7. Fragmentary, incomplete; round base with finger impression in center ("dimple"), body not restored, narrow cylindrical neck, beak or cutaway spout, end not preserved; vertical handle, round in section, from rim to upper body (not preserved), lower attachment pushed through pot wall. Decoration: parts of horizontal low relief band on upper body either side of lower handle attachment (could be ends of a single band curving around below handle). Hard clay with many white and gray and some red inclusions, mostly dark gray with light red-brown surface in some areas, much of surface gray, core more gray than "blue;" traces of thin light red slip. See Unclassified Juglets.

*P138. Red Polished juglet. (Unit 8) Fig. 4.7. H (pres.):6.0. Fragmentary, incomplete, neck only preserved; conical neck of juglet, rim not preserved; twisted vertical handle from mid-neck, upper part only preserved. Relief decoration: horizontal band at neckline; curved diagonal band at side of neck, extending across neck above handle attachment and down either side. Quite soft brown clay with gray interior, many small white and black inclusions and some fine organic temper; traces of fairly thick dark red-brown slip, worn. See Unclassified Juglets.

*P140. Red Polished Mottled storage vessel. (Unit 8) Fig. 4.16; Swiny 1986a: fig. 2:8. H (pres.):ca. 37; max. pres. D. (body): 61; D(rim): ca. 30. Fragmentary, incomplete, neck and shoulder only preserved; short wide cylindrical neck, plain vertical rim; attachment for small horizontal handle preserved on shoulder (uncertain whether a second handle existed). Deep, rather crudely incised decoration: below the handle, incomplete; preserved portion appears to be two concentric rectilinear motifs. Coarse mottled fabric with large inclusions; thick, crackled, dark red fairly lustrous slip; some fragments burned after broken. Storage Vessel Type B.

*P141. Red Polished Mottled storage vessel. (Unit 10) Fig. 4.16; pl. 4.4c; Swiny 1986a: fig. 2:9. H (pres.):ca. 30; D (neck pres.):ca. 40; H (handle):16.5. Fragmentary, neck and one handle only preserved; short wide cylindrical neck; angular vertical handle, oval in section, from mid-neck to upper body, semicircular vertical projection on top of handle, rim not preserved; shoulder shows cracking where the lower handle end was pushed through and smoothed on interior. Incised decoration: two vertical lines on handle exterior and top. Coarse mottled fabric with many large black, white and gray inclusions; thick fairly lustrous dark red-brown slip, dark brown to dark gray slip on neck interior; handle especially quite worn. See Unclassified Storage Vessels.

*P145. Red Polished Mottled bowl. (Unit 2) Fig. 4.1. D (rim):ca. 14. Fragmentary, incomplete; base not preserved, hemispherical body, plain, incurving rim; small vertical lug, unpierced, below rim. Undecorated. Hard brittle pinkish clay with many small black, white and gray inclusions and fine organic temper; thin light red-brown slip with many dark gray areas, including a dark gray band at the exterior rim and extending about 6 cm down the side of the bowl; traces of luster preserved. See Small Bowls: Lugs, above.

APPENDIX 4.1

POTTERY IN THE CHALCOLITHIC
TRADITION

by Clark A. Walz
edited by Ellen Herscher

The pottery presented in this report includes wares commonly classified as Chalcolithic (i.e., Red on White, Red Monochrome Painted, and Red and Black Lustrous wares), as well as two wares frequently associated with the Philia Phase (Red and Black Stroke Burnished and Red Polished Pattern Burnished wares). In addition, a few sherds of a painted ware, the identity of which remains uncertain, are described. The significance of all these ceramics and the reason for their presence in the Early Bronze Age settlement at *Kaminoudhia* remain unclear (see Chapter 2): the problem is one that would warrant further investigation.

Chalcolithic pottery, most commonly Red on White ware, was found in small amounts in all portions of the site. Only in Area A, however, did the Chalcolithic pottery constitute any significant portion of the total sherds from any specific lot (see Tables 2.1c, 2.1f). The largest concentration was found in Unit 16, with approximately 11% of the total sherds classified as Chalcolithic. Next in significance were Units 3 (Phase I), 6 and 33, which all produced approximately 5% Chalcolithic wares. In Unit 18 approximately 3% of the total sherds were classified as Chalcolithic, while the proportion in all other units of Area A was negligible.

The most common Chalcolithic wares identified in these units were Red on White and Red Monochrome Painted (often difficult to distinguish in sherd form). Where two phases of occupation could be distinguished in Area A, the Chalcolithic sherds from Phase II were considerably fewer, and were in a much poorer state of preservation, being on the whole smaller and more eroded than the sherds from Phase I. Additionally, a far higher proportion of diagnostic sherds occurred in the earlier phase.

DISCUSSION OF WARES

RED ON WHITE WARE (RW)

All of the RW ware from Sotira *Kaminoudhia* was manufactured using a red (10R 5/6 - 2.5YR 6/4) clay of friable texture and exhibiting an irregular fracture. The clay was tempered with heavy concentrations (+30%) of fine (1 mm) to very coarse (10 mm) chaff temper with smaller concentrations of fine (-.33) to coarse (1 mm) white or black grits. Very rarely, pebble (+2 mm) inclusions were employed. The use of heavy chaff temper was common in RW, BL, RBL, and RMP fabrics at *Kaminoudhia,* and was often the only diagnostic feature of heavily eroded sherds.

The RW wares are usually completely oxidized. Where unoxidized cores were noted, they tend to be thin, less than one-quarter the thickness of the vessel wall, and black in color. A few sherds of both RW and RMP exhibit layered cores, with bright purple, orange and crimson layers over central black core.

The slip commonly employed on RW was thick (1.0–1.5 mm), white, chalky, cracked and friable, easy to flake off with a fingernail. Less often the slip is thinner, harder and less friable: these sherds also exhibit the finer painting. On two examples, Cat. Nos. 6 and 10 (see "Catalogue of Selected Sherds" on p. 204), the slip has a definite gray surface over the main white slip. This is probably the result of firing in a partially reducing atmosphere.

The repertoire of shapes in RW at *Kaminoudhia* is extremely limited (see fig. 4.17). In open shapes, only small bowls with plain sloping rims (Nos. 1 and 7) and large bowls with plain vertical rims (No. 2) are attested. For closed shapes, only what appear to be rims of bottles or flasks and deep bowls with unslipped interiors (Nos. 8, 9, and 10), and the flat base of a similar vessel (No.13) were recovered. In the absence of complete shapes, it is difficult to make comparisons, but in general the few shapes known at *Kaminoudhia* are not out of place in the general scheme of Late Erimi Culture RW. The bowls are all straight or sloping sided, common in the later levels at Erimi, but lacking the convex sides sometimes found on deep bowls at Erimi *Pamboula* (Dikaios 1962:118, fig. 59, Nos. 14, 15, 17; 1939:28ff.). The closed shapes find parallels at Kissonerga *Mosphilia* and other Lemba Archaeological Project sites where both flasks and bowls are found (Stewart in Peltenburg et al. 1983: fig. 4, No. 10).

It is difficult to generalize regarding the style of painting employed on the *Kaminoudhia* RW since the fragments are small and there are very few examples of distinguishable decorative schemes or even motifs. Broad horizontal lines in tight groups were employed, often creating a "reserved slip" effect, as on Nos. 6, 10, and 14. Only the hatched bands and pendant diagonal lines (e.g., Nos. 4 and 8) suggest any resemblance to the elaborate precise patterns common to the Erimi Culture RW (Dikaios 1939:28ff.; J.D. Stewart in Peltenburg 1985:262ff.); in no cases are curvilinear designs apparent.

RED MONOCHROME PAINTED WARE (RMP)

The fabric used for RMP is indistinguishable from that of RW, having a similar red to dark red color and very heavy chaff temper. The diagnostic features of this ware are a thin red slip, often with visible brush or cloth marks, applied over a buff slip that is both darker and thinner than that used on RW. The color of this "buff" slip ranges from reddish-brown to reddish-yellow and light red. When sherds are heavily eroded, it is usually impossible to differentiate between RW and RMP.

The range of shapes is similar to that of RW but even more limited. Bowls with plain sloping, vertical or slightly inverted rims, including a version with a lug handle, were the only diagnostic shapes noted, although body sherds from closed vessels were also recovered.

Three sherds of typical RW fabric and exterior surface treatment were found to have a thin black highly lustrous burnished slip on the interior surface. The interior slip is of similar hardness and thickness to that of RP black-topped bowls. No diagnostic sherds of this type of ware were recovered.

RED AND BLACK LUSTROUS WARES (RL, BL, RBL)

The fabric of the Chalcolithic Lustrous wares can be distinguished from RW and RMP on the basis of the consistently fine chaff temper employed. Generally, the Lustrous wares are incompletely oxidized, resulting in gray or black cores which sometimes make up most of the vessel walls. The slips are thin and adhere well. Colors range from light red /reddish-brown on RL and RBL, to dark gray and black on BL. Mottling is common to all sherds, thus blurring the distinction between the categories. The shapes are, again, extremely limited, consisting of a deep bowl with convex body and slightly flaring rim, bowls with sloping plain rims, and a few jars.

RED AND BLACK STROKE BURNISHED WARE (RB/B)

The fabric employed for RB/B is quite distinctive, having a brick red color with obvious blue/gray grit temper. This fabric is easily distinguishable from all others at *Kaminoudhia*, even when the sherds are heavily eroded. A distinctive surface treatment—consisting of burnishing marks which are mottled a dark gray or black—is also sometimes apparent.

This ware was quite rare at *Kaminoudhia* and the sherds recovered were consistently small, eroded, and non-diagnostic. Only two open shapes are attested: a small bowl of uncertain diameter and a larger vertical (steep) sided bowl.

RED POLISHED PATTERN BURNISHED WARE (RPPB)

This ware was not common in the *Kaminoudhia* settlement, with less than one dozen sherds being reported. Like the other Chalcolithic wares, the distribution was primarily in Area A.

The slips are reddish-brown to red (2.5YR 4/4 - 5/8), with the pattern burnishing marks invariably reading one chroma darker than the slip. Catalogue No. 28 is an exception, fired to a dark gray in a reducing atmosphere. Of special interest is Catalogue No. 30, which is a composite of Pattern Burnished ware with a RMP interior surface. This sherd, along with RW/RMP sherds with one RW/BT surface, such as Catalogue No. 21, may indicate experimentation or a lack of standardization among the Chalcolithic fabrics at the site.

UNCLASSIFIED PAINTED WARE

Several sherds of an unclassified painted ware were found at *Kaminoudhia*, three of which have been catalogued and described for this report. Most came from Area A, although single examples appeared in Areas B and C respectively. Initially this pottery was regarded as White Painted IA (Philia) ware, to which it bears some resemblance (although the diagnostic features used to identify WP IA [Philia] at other sites have differed widely among various scholars, further complicating characterizations of this ware). However, the extreme scarcity of other identifiable Philia Phase ceramics in the settlement, and the total absence of WP I (Philia) ware in the excavated Philia Phase tombs at *Kaminoudhia*, cast substantial doubt on this identification. The possibility that this pottery may be Neolithic Red on White ware, connected to the adjacent Ceramic Neolithic settlement at Sotira *Teppes*, is an alternative which must be seriously entertained. Until further study can elucidate the many questions remaining in regard to the occurrence of pre-Bronze Age pottery in general in the *Kaminoudhia* settlement, no firm conclusions can be proposed.

Two sherds, Catalogue Nos. 31 and 32, have lustrous red paint applied directly to the surface of the vessel. One of these is decorated with two parallel bands of red paint; the other is more elaborately decorated with a close group of two straight parallel bands and two zigzag bands. The paint is so precisely applied that it was thought at first that the pattern was combed. However, microscopic examination revealed no trace of scratching on the surface of the sherd. The third group of sherds (Catalogue No. 33) from a single closed vessel, appears to have a very thin layer of slip beneath the lustrous paint; the identifiable motifs from this example include straight and wavy bands.

CATALOGUE OF SELECTED SHERDS

(All diameters estimated and approximate)

RED ON WHITE WARE (RW)

Open Shapes

1. Rim fragment of small bowl or cup with sloping plain rim. (Unit 3, Phase II) Fig. 4.17. D: 13 cm. Red (2.5YR 5/6) fabric with medium to fine chaff temper; cracked chalky white slip, 1.5 mm thick; scant traces of red paint preserved.

2. Rim fragments of large bowl with vertical plain rim. (Unit 1) D: 28 cm. Red (2.5YR 5/6) fabric with heavy and coarse chaff temper, black core; thin cracked chalky white slip; traces of three horizontal lines in red (2.5YR 5/8) paint.

3. Body sherd of large bowl. (Unit 3, Phase I) Fig. 4.17. Red (10R 5/6) fabric with fine chaff and fine black and white grit temper, thin (2 mm) black core; hard chalky white slip, 1.5 mm thick; four bands (approximately 7 mm wide) of lustrous red (2.5YR 4/8) paint on interior, traces of paint on exterior; marks from burnishing visible where paint has flaked off.

4. Body sherd of large bowl. (Unit 3, Phase I) Fig. 4.17. Red (10R 5/6) fabric with heavy fine chaff temper; cracked chalky white slip, 1 mm thick; two broad bands of red (2.5YR 4/6) paint, separated by narrow band, with pendant bands.

5. Body sherd of large bowl. (Unit 3) Swiny 1991: fig. 4.2. Red (10R 4/6) fabric with heavy medium chaff and coarse white grit temper; seven bands of reddish-yellow (5YR 6/8) paint in tightly grouped pattern (1-2 mm apart), creating reserved slip effect on exterior; interior done in Red Monochrome Painted technique.

6. Body sherd of large bowl. (Unit 3, Phase I) Fig. 4.17. Reddish-brown (2.5YR 5/4) fabric, heavy fine chaff temper; very thin hard white slip with gray (2.5YR N5/) surface; six bands of lustrous reddish-yellow (5YR 6/8) paint in a tightly grouped pattern creating reserved slip effect.

7. Rim fragment of a small bowl with plain sloping rim. (Unit 4, Phase I) Fig. 4.17. D: 14 cm. Red (2.5YR 5/6) fabric, light, fine chaff temper, black core; thin white slip; red (2.5YR 4/8) paint in two horizontal hands on exterior, solid band on interior.

Closed Shapes

8. Rim fragment of deep bowl or hole mouth jar with slightly flaring plain rim. (Unit 3, Phase I) Fig. 4.17. Light reddish-

brown (2.5YR 6/4) fabric with light, fine chaff and light, coarse black grit temper; thin hard chalky white slip on exterior only; six horizontal hands of reddish-brown (5YR 4/3) paint, the lower two groups joined by hatching, narrow diagonal hands pendant from the lowest horizontal band.

9. Rim fragment of deep bowl or hole mouth jar with slightly inverted plain rim. (Unstratified) Fig. 4.17. Red (2.5YR 4/6) fabric with light fine chaff temper; thin cracked white chalky slip; dusky red (10R 3/4) paint in a broad band below rim.

10. Rim fragment of deep bowl or hole mouth jar with slightly inverted plain rim. (Unit 1, Phase I) Fig. 4.17. Light red (2.5YR 6/9) fabric with heavy fine chaff and light fine white grit temper; thick cracked chalky white slip, fired with gray undertone; reddish-brown (5YR 4/3) paint in five closely grouped horizontal bands creating reserved slip effect.

11. Rim fragment of flask with slightly flaring rim. (Unit 3, Phase I) Fig. 4.17. Reddish-brown (5YR 5/4) fabric with light fine chaff and white grit temper; thin white slip; highly lustrous reddish-brown (2.5YR 4/4) paint in band around entire rim.

12. Rim fragment of flask with flaring rim. (Unit 3, Phase I) Light red (2.5YR 6/6) fabric with heavy, fine chaff temper; thin chalky white slip; red (10R 4/8) painted band at rim.

13. Base fragment of deep bowl or hole mouth jar with flat base and incurving sides. (Unit 3, Phase I) Fig. 4.17. Base D: 24 cm. Red (10R 4/8) fabric with heavy medium chaff temper and layered core of purple, gray, and black; cracked thin white to pink (5YR 7/4) slip; no paint visible.

14. Body sherd of closed vessel. (Unit 3, Phase I) Fig. 4.17. Red (2.5YR 5/8) fabric with fine chaff and coarse white grit temper; thin chalky white slip, 1 mm thick; reddish-brown (3YR 5/4) paint in four vertical bands with eleven horizontal bands to left, in close grouping creating reserved slip effect.

RED MONOCHROME PAINTED (RMP)

Open Shapes

15. Rim fragment of large deep bowl with plain vertical rim. (Unit 4, Phase I) D: 36 cm. Dark red (2.5YR 3/6) fabric with heavy, fine chaff temper; thin reddish-yellow (5YR 7/6) paint.

16. Rim fragment of small deep bowl with plain slightly in-

verted rim. (Unit 3) D: 20 cm. Red (2.5YR 5/8) fabric with medium coarse chaff and gray grit temper, black core; light red (2.5YR 6/8) slip; no paint preserved.

17. Rim fragment of small deep bowl with plain vertical rim. (Unit 1) Fig. 4.17. D: 37 cm. Red (2.5YR 5/6) fabric with light fine chaff and heavy fine white grit temper, thick black core (constitutes three-fifths of vessel wall); reddish-ycllow (5YR 6/6) slip; red (2.5YR 5/6) paint.

18. Rim fragment of small bowl with plain sloping rim. (Unit 3, Phase I) D: 13 cm. Light reddish-brown (2.5YR 6/4) fabric with light, fine chaff temper, black core (constituting four-fifths of vessel wall); light reddish-brown (2.5YR 6/4) slip; dark red (2.5YR 3/6) paint.

19. Rim fragment of small bowl with plain vertical rim. (Unit 3, Phase I) Fig. 4.17. D: 20 cm. Reddish-yellow (5YR 6/6) fabric with light fine chaff temper, thin black core (constituting one-fifth of vessel wall); reddish-yellow (5YR 6/6) slip; yellowish-red (5YR 5/6) lustrous paint.

20. Lug handle of deep bowl. (Unit 3, Phase I) Reddish-gray (5YR 4/2) fabric with light, fine chaff temper, thick black core (constituting four-fifths of vessel wall); reddish-brown (2.5YR 3/4) paint; surface blackened.

RED ON WHITE/BLACK TOPPED BOWL COMPOSITE

21. Body sherd of Red on White Bowl. (Unit 5) Red (10YR 4/8) fabric with light coarse chaff temper, black core (constituting inner half of vessel wall); cracked chalky white slip; no paint preserved; black interior surface highly burnished in manner of Red Polished black-topped bowls.

CHALCOLITHIC LUSTROUS WARES
(RL, BL, RBL)

22. Rim and body of deep RL bowl with slightly flared rim and convex body. (Unit 16) D: 20 cm.; profile reconstructed from three sherds. Reddish-brown (2.5YR 5/4) fabric with heavy white and black fine grit and very light fine chaff temper, black core constituting almost entire vessel wall; dark reddish-brown (2.5YR 3/4) slip, mottled to black at bottom.

23. Rim of deep RBL bowl with plain sloping rim. (Unit 3, Phase I) Fig. 4.17. D: 18 cm. Red (2.5YR) fabric with me-

dium fine chaff, and a little fine white grit temper, black core; light red (10R 6/6) slip, mottled dusky red (10R 3/4) and black.

24. Rim fragment of BL jar with slightly flaring rim. (Unit 3, Phase I) Fig. 4.17. D: 14 cm. Gray (2.5YR N5/) fabric with light, fine chaff and light coarse gray grit temper; very dark gray (2.5R N3) slip.

25. Rim fragment of BL jar with flaring rim. (Unit 3, Phase I) Fig. 4.17. D: 7 cm. Gray (2.5YR N6/) fabric with very fine chaff and grit temper; very dark gray (2.5YR 3/N3/) slip.

RED AND BLACK STROKE BURNISHED WARE
(RB/B)

26. Rim fragment of vessel with plain vertical rim. (Unit 3, Phase I) Fig. 4.17. D: 16 cm. Red (10R 5/8) fabric with light, medium blue grit temper; light red (2.5YR 6/8) slip, mottled to reddish-gray (5YR 5/2) on exterior; horizontal stroke burnishing visible on interior.

27. Body sherd of small open vessel. (Unit 16) Red (10R 5/8) fabric with light blue grit temper; red (2.5YR 5/8) slip with black diagonal stroke burnishing marks.

RED POLISHED PATTERN BURNISHED WARE
(RPPB)

28. Rim fragment of small shallow bowl with plain sloping rim. (Cemetery A) Fig. 4.17. D: 14 cm. Gray (5YR 5/1) fabric with fine white grit temper; very dark gray (2.5YR N3) slip; black pattern burnished rim band with pendant diagonal band.

29. Body sherd of small bowl with pierced vertical lug handle. (Unit 4) Fig. 4.17. Red (2.5 YR 4/6) sandy fabric with fine white grit temper; red (2.5YR 4/8) slip with red (2.5YR 4/6) pattern burnishing marks.

RP PATTERN BURNISHED/RED MONOCHROME
PAINTED COMPOSITE WARE

30. Body sherd of open vessel. (Unit 2) Fig. 4.17. Red (2.5YR 5/6) fabric with medium coarse gray grit temper; red (2.5YR 4/6) slip with irregular reddish-brown (2.5YR 4/4) pattern burnishing marks on exterior; medium thick (1 mm) reddish-black (5YR 6/6) slip with traces of red (10R 4/6) paint on interior.

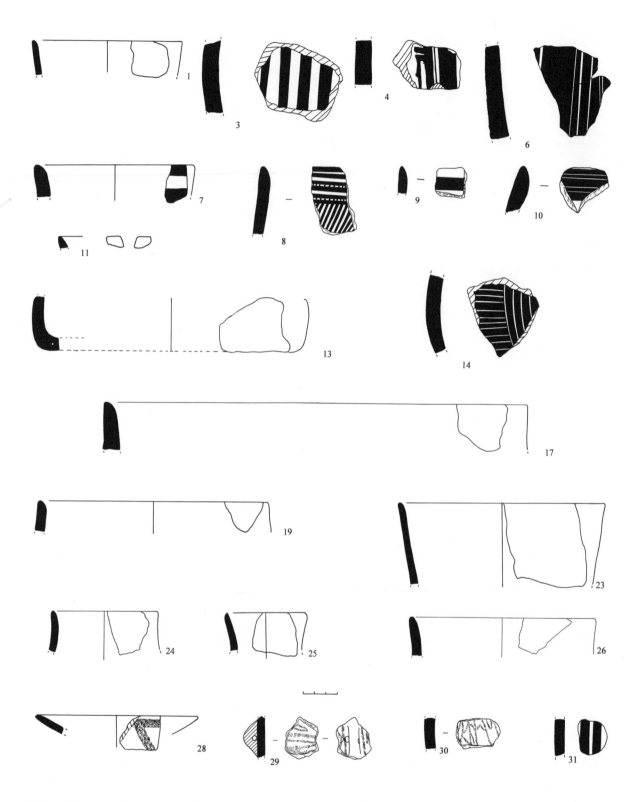

Fig. 4.17. Selected examples of pre-Bronze Age pottery: Chalcolithic Red on White (Cat. nos. 1, 3, 4, 6, 7, 8, 9, 10, 11, 13, 14); Red Monochrome Painted (Cat. nos. 17, 19); Chalcolithic Lustrous (Cat. nos. 23, 24, 25); Red and Black Stroke Burnished (Cat. no. 26); Red Polished Pattern Burnished (Cat. nos. 28, 29); RP Pattern Burnished/Red Monochrome Painted composite (Cat. no. 30); unclassified painted ware (Cat. no. 31).

5

PETROGRAPHIC ANALYSIS OF POTTERY FROM SOTIRA

By Sarah Vaughan

INTRODUCTION

Prehistoric pottery from three localities associated with the site of Sotira in southwestern Cyprus was analyzed petrographically for purposes of establishing a profile of the raw materials represented by the wares, and for use in refining archaeological classifications of the wares at Sotira *Kaminoudhia* and its environs and their correlations with specific pottery fabrics. The three sample localities studied are Sotira *Kaminoudhia*, Sotira *Teppes* and Sotira *Troulli tou Nikola*, reflecting a chronological span from the Neolithic (*Teppes*) to the Early (*Kaminoudhia*) and Middle (*Troulli tou Nikola*) Bronze Ages. Table 5.1 presents the range of wares and numbers of samples analyzed from each locality. The study addresses several questions relating to the ceramics, the main queries being whether regional varieties of Red Polished ware were being produced, how the various wares found in some abundance at the sites were related in material and technological terms to one another, and whether patterns of material exploitation or technological developments were responsible for the appearance of the distinctive pottery called "Drab Polished Blue Core" ware. DPBC represents a southwest ware found (and probably manufactured) at many sites. Its wide distribution and relative abundance at many sites in southwest Cyprus suggests that it was a ware common to many localities, although it is a rare fabric at Sotira *Kaminoudhia*.

Table 5.1. Pottery Sample Numbers from Sotira Sites

WARE CATEGORY	Sotira *Kaminoudhia*	Sotira *Teppes*	Sotira *Troulli tou Nikola*
Red Polished	3, 4, 7, 22, 24, 26, 27, 28		
Red Polished Punctured			51, 53
Red Polished Mottled			52, 54, 55
Red on White	6, 18, 19		
Red Monochrome Painted	21		
Red and Black Lustrous	20		
Red Lustrous		40, 41	
Red and Black Stroke Burnished	8		
Combed		38, 39	
Red Polished IV			56
Red Polished/Drab Polished Blue Core	23		
Drab Polished Blue Core	1, 2, 25		57, 58, 59, 60

METHODOLOGY

Samples

A limited number of pottery samples (32) was selected by the excavator, consistent with the scope of the project, reflecting both well-known typological categories of pottery as well as examples of more problematic fabrics at the sites. Petrographic analysis was selected for the study as it is a technique well suited to the characterization of relatively coarse pottery fabrics (Freestone 1995:111–15; Vaughan 1995:115–17), it is an effective technique to apply to materials reflecting a range of geologic deposits (such as the Neogene sediments at Sotira and the Troodos Ophiolite within 20 km north of the site), and previous comparable analyses of Cypriot artifacts have established the value of this approach (Courtois 1971; Elliot et al. 1986; Vaughan 1991).

Sample Preparation

Centimeter sub-samples were cut from the samples by convention vertical to vessel profile wherever possible (but including some horizontal sections) for preparation as thin sections. These sections were lapped on one side with water and silicone carbide abrasive (50μm), cleaned in an ultrasonic bath, dried and impregnated with epoxy resin @ 180°C to minimize plucking during subsequent preparation steps. The prepared sample surfaces were then lapped on a glass plate with a 30μm abrasive slurry, re-cleaned by ultrasonication, and mounted on glass slides with the resin @ 85°C. The exposed sample surface was then ground on a lapping wheel to approximately 100μm with water and abrasive series to 50μm, and finished by hand to the standard section dimension of 30μm on a glass plate using 25μm abrasive slurry, with the finished section covered with a glass cover slip.

ANALYTICAL RESULTS

Fabric Groups

Seven fabric categories are defined as a result of the petrographic analysis. Two main igneous fabrics are distinguished, one volcanic group reflecting altered Upper Pillow Lava deposits and the other dominated by constituents of the Gabbro and Pyroxenite formations of the Troodos Plutonic Complex. The other main fabrics are a calcareous group distinguished by abundant microfossils, and a category characterized by clasts of siltstone and radiolarian shale. Grain and mineral sizes are given in millimeters to reflect the greatest dimension of the inclusion viewed in thin section, with grain size categories referring to the Wentworth Scale. Munsell colors (when cited) were taken from thin-sectioned ceramics as sherds are no longer available, and percentages of inclusions cited refer to visual percentage estimation (VPE) charts commonly used in petrography.

1. Volcanic (UPL) Group Fabric (pls. 5.1 and 5.2)

SAMPLES	WARE GROUP	FIND SITE
26, 27	Red Polished	Sotira *Kaminoudhia*
6	Red on White	Sotira *Kaminoudhia*
51	Red Polished Punctured	Sotira *Troulli tou Nikola*
54	Red Polished Mottled	Sotira *Troulli tou Nikola*
56	Red Polished IV	Sotira *Troulli tou Nikola*

The groundmass of the fabric contains abundant (10–20%) fine amphiboles and biotites, with varying percentages (5–20%) of subround to subangular quartz grains. Voids are oval to ovoid, with some vugs, in 3–5%, with parallel orientation and dimensions to 0.60 mm in length. In samples 26 and 27 elongated voids and cracks are very abundant and the groundmass clay particles appear isotropic, features consistent with a more vitrified fabric. In the remaining samples the groundmass clay particles exhibit some birefringence, consistent with firing temperatures generally below 850°C.

The constituents reflect sediments derived from altered Upper Pillow lavas in the Volcanic Complex and the diabase of the Troodos Ophiolite on Cyprus. Discrete minerals (silt-sized to 1.00 mm) include clinopyroxene (diopside, though some strongly pleochroic green or fibrous examples occur), occasional orthopyroxene, amphibole, alkali and plagioclase (labradorite to albite) feldspars and biotite, with olivine common, and rare carbonate or marl impurities. Common iron oxide minerals occur as opaque to dark red-brown inclusions or irregular concentrations. Lithic fragments (0.80–1.80 mm) reflect basic Upper Pillow lava sources, with relict intersertal or interstitial texture noted in some clasts, and epidote or very altered red-brown groundmass material in others (ferruginous clay material—possibly iddingsite, see Elliott et al. 1986:88). Sample 56 contains a fragment of polycrystalline metamorphic quartz. Feldspars (Carlsbad and lamellar twinning present) are generally cloudy, and one fragment of silicified (radiolarian) shale is noted in sample 26.

2. Volcanic (UPL) Group Fabric with Carbonates (pl. 5.3)

SAMPLES	WARE GROUP	FIND SITE
2	Drab Polished Blue Core	Sotira *Kaminoudhia*
3	Red Polished	Sotira *Kaminoudhia*
19	Red on White	Sotira *Kaminoudhia*
20	Red on Black Lustrous	Sotira *Kaminoudhia*

The distinguishing feature of this igneous fabric group is the abundant presence of round marly clasts (0.10–0.75 mm) throughout the fabric in concentrations of 15–20%. The igneous constituents of the fabric are as for Fabric 1 above, and calcareous clasts are generally more rounded than the igneous rock fragments and minerals (possibly due to differential weathering properties of the two materials, or to a detrital origin for the carbonates in an igneous clay). Fine grains of epidote are common throughout the groundmass, and detrital volcanic rock fragments appear very weathered, with chlorite and iron minerals replacing most constituents. The presence of the carbonate material in this fabric may represent the addition of a plastic temper, but may also reflect impurities incorporated into the altered lavas from the overlying Neogene sediments. Similar impurities occur in a few Fabric 1 samples, though only very rarely. It is possible that these clays simply were quarried at a slightly different location than those in Fabric 1, perhaps in closer proximity to the overlying calcareous sediments or at the contact zone of the Pakhna Formation and the Upper Pillow lavas along the Kouris River valley, approximately 20 km from Sotira. The greater alteration of the constituents would be consistent with this proposal.

3. Gabbro and Pyroxenite Group

SAMPLES	WARE GROUP	FIND SITE
4, 24	Red Polished	Sotira *Kaminoudhia*
18	Red on White	Sotira *Kaminoudhia*
53	Red Polished Punctured	Sotira *Troulli tou Nikola*
52, 55	Red Polished Mottled	Sotira *Troulli tou Nikola*

The groundmass of the samples in this group is a paler brown (7.5YR 5/6 or 4/2) than that characterizing the darker red volcanic samples (10R 3-4/6, 2.5YR 4/6). Inclusions are relatively abundant (20–30%), with common angular to subangular quartz silt, fine chlorite, amphiboles and iron minerals (possibly magnetite or ilmenite) characterizing the clay matrix. Vugs and vesicles are moderately frequent (15%), elongate and oriented parallel to the sherd surfaces.

Frequent angular to subangular rock fragments (0.50–2.50 mm) from the Plutonic Complex of the Troodos Ophiolite distinguish this group of samples, and are larger and coarser-grained than the lithic clasts in Fabrics 1 and 2. Some gabbroic examples exhibit subhedral granular texture, but the dominant mineral is pyroxene, occurring commonly throughout the matrix and in the lithic clasts from which it was no doubt disaggregated. Some diopside is identified, but more often the pyroxenes are altered, strongly pleochroic (red to yellow), fibrous, or occasionally green (uralite, see also Weisman 1994:32). Calcium-rich plagioclase feldspars with polysynthetic and Carlsbad twins are present, as is a subordinate percentage of quartz. Olivine grains are rare. A few fragments resembling plagiogranite occur, with granophyric texture preserved. Sample 18 is distinguished by notable percentages of carbonate (small marly clasts and micrite aggregates) throughout the groundmass, giving it the appearance of a poorly homogenized mixture of two *plastic* clays.

4. Bioclastic Calcareous Fabric (pl. 5.4)

SAMPLES	WARE GROUP	FIND SITE
7, 22	Red Polished	Sotira *Kaminoudhia*
23	Red Polished/DPBC	Sotira *Kaminoudhia*
38, 39	Combed	Sotira *Teppes*
40	Red Lustrous	Sotira *Teppes*

The groundmass of the samples of this group is well-homogenized, birefringent and pale brown under crossed polars, with uniformly fine-grained constituents, only infrequent angular quartz silt grains, fine biotites and dark brown iron minerals. Vugs and vesicles (0.05–1.00 mm) oriented parallel to the sherd surfaces occur throughout the fabric in concentrations of 3–5%, and are notably less elongate than voids in the igneous fabrics. This feature is consistent with optical properties observed for marl-rich ceramic fabrics and fired samples of calcareous Cypriot clays, which are less plastic (due to relatively lower percentages of montmorillonite) than igneous-derived bentonitic clays. The different percentages of montmorillonite produce fired clay microstructures with significant variations in optical features.

Larger inclusions occur, but are less common than in the igneous fabrics, while abundant discrete microfossils characterize this category. These microfossils are predominantly multi-chambered foraminifera (especially *Globigerina*), though fragments of ostracods, nummulites and possible algal fragments also occur. The test walls are micritic and well preserved, and the majority are filled with microspar. Irregular-shaped marly concretions (oxide-stained, or gray under crossed polars if altered to calcium oxide) and calcareous clasts exhibiting uneven neomorphic spar are common, along with fragments of detrital chert (0.10–0.50 mm), and radiolarian chert in sample 39. Rare diopside, biotite and epidote occur along with occasional uralitic pyroxene (subhedral, 0.20 mm) or fibrous amphibole (sample 7). Sample 22 contains a subrounded basic rock fragment (1.00 mm) with completely altered (red-brown) groundmass and cloudy plagioclase glomerocrysts, and more quartz silt in the matrix than the other examples, but these variations could be due to larger vessel size and related differential refining procedures. Most inclusions were silt-sized, and larger clasts (some 3.25 mm) generally reflect an origin in the local bioclastic limestone and chalk formations. The constituent profile of this fabric probably represents clays derived from the Miocene marls of the Pakhna Formation, which dominates the local landscape around Sotira.

5. Bioclastic Calcareous Fabric with Igneous Constituents

SAMPLES	WARE GROUP	FIND SITE
28	Red Polished	Sotira *Kaminoudhia*
41	Red Lustrous	Sotira *Teppes*

The groundmass and calcareous inclusions of this fabric are as for Fabric 3. The igneous constituents are present in concentrations of 10–15%. Those rock fragments in sample 28 are consistent with a source such as that for Fabric 3. The igneous-derived mineral and lithic clasts are distributed evenly throughout the groundmass in relatively uniform sizes (0.50–1.00 mm) in percentages of approximately 15%, and strongly suggest an aplastic temper. The altered UPL sources for Fabrics 1 and 2 appear to be the origin for the igneous constituents in sample 41, and as they occur more randomly and with less uniformity of size it is not possible to speculate on whether they represent a temper. It is possible they represent transported material present as impurities in younger calcareous sediments.

6. Radiolarian Shale and Siltstone Fabric (pls. 5.5 and 5.6)

SAMPLES	WARE GROUP	FIND SITE
1, 25	Drab Polished Blue Core	Sotira *Kaminoudhia*
21	Red Monochrome Painted	Sotira *Kaminoudhia*
57, 58, 59, 60	Drab Polished Blue Core	Sotira *Troulli tou Nikola*

The groundmass of this fabric is gray and isotropic under crossed polars, with 5–10% elongated voids and vesicles oriented parallel to the sherd surfaces, 0.80–1.00 mm in length. Quartz silt and fine epidote are evenly distributed throughout the groundmass, with larger inclusions present in concentrations of 10–15% (in sample 25 up to 20%). Micrite impurities occur in random concentrations in some sherds (e.g., sample 25), as do fine chlorites (e.g., sample 21). Occasional biotite altering to chlorite, altered amphiboles, subround micritic clasts (0.10–1.00 mm), and detrital chert (0.20–0.50 mm) are present as well. One very altered basaltic fragment was noted in sample 21.

The fabric is distinguished by subangular to subround fragments (0.40–1.00 mm) of argillaceous rock fragments (ARF's), mostly shale, and siltstone. The ARF's vary in color and optical density from pale brown to very dark gray brown, the latter consistently exhibiting fine polygonal cracking in plane polarized light. The presence of shrink rims surrounding many of these clasts, combined with the distinctive cracking pattern, suggests they were hard *on incorporation into the clay* and reflect thermal (firing) features of material with a different (possibly illitic) composition and therefore a different coefficient of expansion to that of the surrounding clay groundmass (Cuomo di Caprio and Vaughan 1993: 30, 32). The sherd exterior surface is extremely flat, with irregular deposits (0.05–0.30 mm) of microfossiliferous carbonate adhering from burial sediments. This fabric is consistent with material and technical data reported by Courtois for a sample of Drab Polished Blue Core Ware from Episkopi *Phaneromeni* (1984:3).

7. Fine Red Sedimentary Fabric

SAMPLES	WARE GROUP	FIND SITE
8	Red and Black Stroke Burnished	Sotira *Kaminoudhia*

This fabric is distinguished by the uniformity of its intensely oxidized red color (Munsell 10R 4-5/8). The groundmass is fine-grained with scarce quartz silt and fine biotites altering to chlorite. Larger inclusions are represented primarily by subangular to subround ARF's (some red, some gray with oxidized rims under crossed polars) in concentrations of approximately 10% and between 0.40–1.50 mm in size. These fragments exhibit the same polygonal cracking described for similar fragments in Fabric 5 above. One fragment is distinguished by abundant fine mica inclusions (chlorite or sericite?) exhibiting parallel alignment, possibly with (shale?) bedding planes. Another feature distinguishing this sample are clusters (20% concentrations) of fine round pores (0.02 in diameter), possibly related to differential wedging of the unfired paste, or to drafts around the vessel during firing resulting in differential baking of the clay fabric.

MATERIALS DISCUSSION

Sources

The vast majority of the igneous-derived fabrics appear to reflect the exploitation by potters at Sotira of raw materials which had undergone low-grade metamorphic alteration in nature, thereby improving their manufacturing properties. With the exception of samples 26 and 54–55, which contain mineral and lithic fragments of a relatively fresh appearance, the materials of Fabrics 1, 2 and 3 exhibit evidence of varying degrees of alteration and weathering of constituents, in composition and in grain morphology. Samples 26 (RP) and 54–55 (RP Mottled) may have been made from clays quarried closer to primary clay deposits in the Troodos foothills. Sample 3 may represent the use of an igneous-derived clay which developed over calcareous terrain, incorporating detrital carbonate material. The percentages of quartz silt throughout the groundmass of the samples varies considerably, exhibiting no correlations to raw material type or ware group, though characterizing all the samples from Sotira *Troulli tou Nikola*. This may simply reflect different clay quarrying locations used by the potters, as some samples of marls collected by the author near Pissouri and in the lower Kouris River valley also show increased percentages of quartz silt. Samples of the Pakhna marl clays collected by the author are consistent with the materials of Fabrics 4 and 5.

Correlations with Wares

While the majority of wares examined in this study are finished with an oxidized exterior surface or slip layer, they were manufactured both from igneous-derived clays as well as from calcareous materials. These data are consistent with those from a previous study by Courtois (1971), who also found a range of materials were used to manufacture Cypriot Red Polished wares. Examples of wares with black or gray exterior finishes (e.g., Drab Polished wares), however, were manufactured from the volcanic or shale-rich clays, which can be made to fire to darker colors more easily than calcareous clays (Vaughan 1991:344, 366).

Fabric 6, with radiolarian shale and siltstone inclusions, was exploited almost exclusively for production of the wares with less reflective luster to their surfaces, such as Drab Polished Blue Core ware. This might suggest that while the Red Polished wares were being manufactured widely and in a range of stylistic variations, Drab Polished Blue Core ware (probably a regional alternative to Red Polished traditions) ultimately became a more specialized product with discrete material traditions perhaps more suited to its unique blue-gray appearance and higher firing temperature. Whittingham described samples of "Proto Drab Polished Blue Core" ware from Erimi *Pamboula* as having "many white limestone inclusions" in hand specimen (1981:38–39), which would be consistent with sample 2 of Fabric 2 in this study, and a possible early material origin with Red Polished wares.

A sample of flysch clay collected by the author in the Kannavious Formation of the Mamonia Complex, west of Sotira, is seen to include ARF's and carbonate impurities comparable to those characterizing Fabric 6 in this study (Vaughan 1991:351–52, 357–58). It is perhaps not insignificant that such flysch clays were also consistent with the materials commonly identified with the later Cypriot Base Ring wares (*ibid*). Sample 23 however, designated as a Red Polished *or possibly a Drab Polished Blue Core sherd*, may be misclassified as Red Polished ware due to exterior surface mottling, as Drab Polished Blue Core ware does not appear to have had any manufacturing association with calcareous clays, probably for reasons associated with its physical appearance.

The calcareous sediments and clays common to Fabrics 4 and 5 must reflect the use by local potters of the abundant marls and calcareous clays of the Circum-Troodos Sedimentary Succession in which Sotira is located. The fact that these clays dominate the small sample from *Teppes* may reflect only limited sample numbers, as would their absence from the Sotira *Troulli tou Nikola* sample. The larger number of samples from *Kaminoudhia* indicates potters were able to exploit a wide range of raw ceramic materials to produce a variety of wares.

TECHNOLOGICAL DISCUSSION

Raw Materials Preparation

In general there was no evidence of the use of fine sieving or settling in water as preparation techniques for the clays of these samples. The grain size of constituents varies sufficiently *within* samples to preclude the use of sieves, while settling the clay in water would have resulted in the consistent absence in the ceramic samples of the heavier rock fragments and minerals. Preparing the clay pastes then may have been accomplished primarily by means of rough hand sorting and crushing, though the latter procedure must have been limited in its application as there is little evidence of consistent angular morphology of constituents (with the exception of sample 24), and the tests of microfossils are largely intact.

Temper (see Table 5.2 below)

There are several exceptions to this norm however, where it may be suggested that aplastic tempering materials were added to a clay paste to improve manufacturing and possibly post-firing functional properties of the pots. Fragments of altered igneous rocks (lavas and/or diabase) in samples 19, 20, 22, 28 and 41 are consistently coarser-grained and more angular than matrix constituents and/ or carbonate impurities, giving them the appearance of an added temper. In sample 18 the appearance and percentages of different materials may even suggest a mixture of two *clays* (e.g., a calcareous and a plutonic source clay). An example of a similar fabric with a comparable mineralogical profile has been identified by the author from Tomb 75 at Kalavasos, Cinema Area, where the material proportions suggested calcareous clay deliberately tempered with igneous material (Barlow and Vaughan 1999). In this study only samples 28 and 41 are calcareous clays possibly tempered with igneous material, the former being the more convincing occurrence. As the six examples of possible material mixtures in this study represent igneous *and* calcareous groundmass clays however, the evidence for the technique is uncorrelated to base clay type. In the absence of more sample data it is impossible to investigate correlation of lithic temper with vessel type or size, which are the most common explanations for the use of this technique.

Further evidence of tempering is noted for samples 6 and 18–20 (Red on White sherds), where patterns of abundant, very fine, elongated voids occur parallel to vessel surfaces. These distinctive voids are strongly reminiscent of the use of vegetal temper (Gibson and Woods 1990:210), and it may be significant that samples 6, 18–20 are all made from igneous clays. The evidence for tempering in these samples is summarized in Table 5.2 below.

Table 5.2. Samples with Evidence of Tempering

SAMPLES AND WARES	VOLC. RF's	MARLY CLAY	VEGETAL
2 Drab Polished Blue Core		?	
3 Red Polished		?	
6 Red on White			√
18 Red on White		√	√
19 Red on White		?	√
20 Red on Black Lustrous		?	√
22 Red Polished	√		
28 Red Polished	√		√
41 Red Lustrous	√		

Firing Temperatures

With few exceptions, the majority of samples in this study are characterized by groundmass particles exhibiting some degree of birefringence, and many carbonate inclusions appear unaffected by firing temperatures, which would appear to have remained below 800°C. The presence of a dark brown or gray core in the majority of sample walls also suggests firing procedures were relatively rapid, generally inhibiting full oxidation of the inner portion of the vessel walls.

There are several exceptions to this pattern. Two samples with the vegetal temper voids (19, 20) are amongst samples exhibiting optical features consistent with firing temperatures higher than 830°C (isotropic matrix, round bloating pores and vesicular microfabric, transformation of calcite to calcium oxide or incipient dissociation of carbonates). Other sherds which appeared to have been fired to such temperatures also were members of the Upper Pillow lava fabrics (samples 2, 26 and 27) or the radiolarian shale and siltstone Fabric 6 Group (samples 1, 21, 25, 57–60). This pattern would suggest that the non-calcareous clays were more routinely exposed to firing temperatures higher than those used for the calcareous clays. This evidence also implies that Sotira potters were well aware of the dangers of spalling associated with firing calcareous clays over 830°C, particularly those as unrefined as the examples in this study. The use of higher firing temperatures (and/or perhaps firing atmospheres less oxygen-rich) for the Drab Polished Blue Core samples in Fabric 6 may be technologically significant, as it has been suggested that the development of this unique regional ware anticipated the wider development of the later Base Ring ware, known to have been made with similar materials and firing procedures (Vaughan 1991).

Surface Finish and Slips

Red (oxidized) slips were preserved as thin layers (0.04–0.10 mm) on a number of samples, occasionally incorporating microfossils or quartz silt. Sample 3, a small hemispherical Red Polished bowl with pinched rim, has a red slip layer with occasional quartz silt inclusions, covered by a crust of micritic to marly carbonate. Sample 7 (Red Polished) has a red slip layer on both sherd surfaces, underlain by a brown-gray layer (0.30 mm) composed of extremely fine constituents above the paler calcareous body (pl. 5.4). Compaction of the surface of the vessel during smoothing and finishing procedures, combined with the presence of a slip layer, may have been responsible for inhibiting oxidation of this region of the vessel wall, while normal oxidation would have proceeded from the interior toward the center. Samples 26 (Red Polished, pl. 5.1), 39 (Combed), 53 (Red Polished Punctured) and 40 (Red Lustrous) also have slip adhering, while sample 41 (Red Lustrous) has what appears to be a thin self-slip layer differentially compacted by skilled smoothing of the exterior surface. Fine-grained carbonate material was noted adhering to the exterior surfaces of samples 1 (Drab Polished Blue Core), 3 (Red Polished), 6 and 19 (Red on White) and 56 (Red Polished IV), the latter example being unusually uniform and thick (0.80 mm), though probably not a deliberate coat as the sample is Red Polished IV.

CONCLUSIONS

The materials of the Volcanic Group Fabrics 1 and 2 outcrop 15 km to the north and east of Sotira, with the sources for the Plutonic clays occurring approximately another 5 km further north and east of the site. Fabric 6 reflects the use of clays commonly found within the Mamonia Complex sediments, again some 20 km from the site, but to the west this time, beginning in the Dhiarrizos River valley. The range of materials exploited to produce the pottery in this study, which spans the Neolithic to Middle Bronze Age periods in Cyprus, may imply either a robust pattern of regional exchange of ceramic vessels (as products, or for the commodities they may have contained) between the inhabitants of Sotira and settlements to the east, west and north. Of course it is also possible that the raw materials reflected in these ceramics represent a familiarity by potters with clays over a wide geographical distance, possibly the result of seasonal population movements associated with food harvests or flock management. However, given the strong and understandable conservatism of traditional potters with regard to choice of manufacturing materials, it would appear that the results of the current study point to the existence of some regional variations in production of particular wares over time and space, or perhaps to the existence of contemporary workshops with different material traditions. Within the limited scope of the current sample however, further interpretation would only breach the boundaries of informed speculation.

ACKNOWLEDGMENTS

The author wishes to express gratitude for support from the National Endowment for the Humanities grant for the Sotira Project, permitting some fieldwork and analyses to be undertaken in Cyprus, and for the many contributions made to the ceramic research by Stuart Swiny.

6

THE GROUND STONE

by Stuart Swiny

INTRODUCTION

The ground stone assemblage of 663 artifacts from the settlement at Sotira *Kaminoudhia* is the largest to be published from an Early or Middle Bronze Age site in Cyprus. To this number may be added the 68 items recovered by the 1978 surface survey (Swiny 1981:65, Table 2) and the 55 objects left in situ, thereby bringing the site total to 786. In general terms, the excavated settlements at Alambra *Mouttes* and Marki *Alonia*, respectively yielding 233 and 206 ground stone artifacts from exposures similar to those at *Kaminoudhia*,[1] would appear to have been less rich in ground stone, unless it is argued that the discard patterns were quite different.

Up-to-date comparanda for most of the types recorded at *Kaminoudhia* may be found in the recent publications of Alambra *Mouttes* and especially Marki *Alonia,* which in turn refer to the Episkopi *Phaneromeni* ground stone corpus covering—with the exception of the gaming stones—material published up to 1983 (Swiny 1986:2, n. 4). The ground stone assemblage from *Kaminoudhia* is broadly speaking very similar to that from *Phaneromeni, Mouttes* and *Alonia*. The most notable exception is the complete lack of perforated stone hammers, 21 of which were recorded at *Phaneromeni* with 29 coming from *Mouttes* and eight—or nine if a 'Perforated Stone' is included—from *Alonia*. It would seem that the type was very rare in the Chalcolithic, with a single unstratified piece described as a 'cupped stone' from Lemba *Lakkous* (Elliott 1985:88, fig. 67:3) and a 'spindle-whorl' from Erimi *Pamboula* which does nevertheless fit the *Phaneromeni* criteria for perforated stone hammers (Dikaios 1962: fig. 61:26). In view of the size of the *Kaminoudhia* assemblage it would seem that the absence of perforated stone hammers could hardly be fortuitous if this tool type had been in use at the site.

Another difference is an absence of the *Phaneromeni* type of 'grinder-pounder" (Swiny 1986:8), which was represented by thirty examples at that site. Since the same criteria for the classification of ground stones were applied at *Kaminoudhia* and the same person (Swiny) was responsible for the attributions, the absence of grinder pounders, like that of the perforated hammers, may have a cultural explanation.

Several changes or improvements have been made to the *Phaneromeni* taxonomy—notably in connection with Saddle querns Type 2 and Rubbers—and they are all discussed within the body of the text. In this report the more general term 'igneous' has been preferred to those found in the *Phaneromeni*

---

[1] The areas of settlement and depths of deposit excavated at Alambra *Mouttes* and *Kaminoudhia* are roughly comparable. Although the overall surface of the excavation is smaller at Marki *Alonia* the presence of several phases of occupation should make up for the disparity if the density of ground stone lithics was similar to that at *Kaminoudhia*. The reports of the seasons after 1996 at Marki *Alonia* (Frankel and Webb 1997, 1999, 2000) were received after completion of this chapter.

report such as 'gabbro,' 'diabase' etc. This decision was brought about by the fact that it remains difficult for geologists to agree on which term to use for the many subtle varieties of igneous rocks commonly found on Cypriot sites. All these igneous rocks were available in the nearby Kouris river-bed and the only visible criterion was the choice of finer grained specimens for items—specifically axes and adzes—requiring the greatest hardness and resistance to fracture. Many of the rubbing stones are shaped from very coarse-grained igneous boulders.

Finally, I wish to acknowledge the work by Frankel and Webb (1996b) in the Marki *Alonia* publication that has taken the study of ground stone artifacts one step further by introducing the notion of 'curation' and 'expediency.' Their division of the assemblage into 'Curated Tools' comprising axes, adzes, mace heads, querns, rubbers, some pestles, dishes, and mortars and, 'Expedient Tools' comprising rubbing stones, rubber-pounders, pounders, some pestles, hammerstones, pecking stones, perforated stones, palettes, lids, and grooved stones is quite correct. Although I had raised the issue of expediency versus curation in connection with the *Phaneromeni* taxonomy,[2] Frankel and Webb are the first to have approached it in a systematic and sophisticated manner.

The numbering on all plates progresses from left to right.

Some of the ground stone utensils, gaming stones and ornaments have been published in Swiny 1985a (figs. 3, 5 and 6), Swiny 1989:186 and Swiny 1995:35 (right). Because the same drawings and photographs are reproduced here, most of these references will not be repeated for the individual items.

AXE

Type 1: **Wedge-shaped**

Sample: 19. (1 questionable). (Fig. 6.1; pls. 6.1a, b). 14 stratified: S9, 128, 132, 159, 238, 254, 278, 327, 389, 521, 524, 549, 671, 698. 6 unstratified: S81, 538, 566, 593, 618, 679.

Material: Mostly fine-grained igneous.

Description: Usually with convex sides, faces and cutting edges. The butt is usually convex with a slightly flattened end. The length of stratified examples ranges from 4.1 to 17.5 cm.

Fourteen stratified Type 1 stone axes are recorded at Alambra *Mouttes* where the classification has been refined to include several sub-types.[3] The unexpected lack of stratified examples from Marki *Alonia* was noted by the authors (Frankel and Webb 1996b:80). How many of the *Kaminoudhia* axes were actually manufactured at the settlement is impossible to determine, but since all the types represented are also recorded at nearby Sotira *Teppes* it is likely that many of them were gleaned from that site during the Bronze Age. A similar scenario was suggested for the presence of axes at LC I Episkopi *Phaneromeni* (Swiny 1986:2).

With the appearance of copper base flat axes in the EC period it is likely that the thick and thus inefficient stone axes of the preceding periods would have been quickly replaced with metal, a process that had already begun during the Chalcolithic (Peltenburg 1991; Gale 1991:44).

[2] Swiny 1986:1 and elsewhere; see, for example, the frequent use of the term 'unaltered riverstone' in the description of artifact types, p. 5, 6, 7 etc.
[3] Mogelonsky 1996:147 ff. One might argue that there are insufficient diagnostic reasons for subdividing the basic Type 1 wedge-shaped axes into three sub-types.

Type 2: *Crude wedge-shaped or roughly oval*

Sample: 10. (Fig. 6.1; pl. 6.1b). 7 stratified: S123, 186, 272?, 326, 369, 416, 680. 3 unstratified: 193, 615, 629. (1 recorded by the surface survey).

Material: Mostly fine-grained igneous.

Description: All the *Kaminoudhia* examples correspond to Dikaios' category of "flaked celts" or Elliott's "flaked tools" (Dikaios 1962:193, pl. 95; Elliott 1985: fig. 70:12–17) in that they are crudely flaked, laterally and frontally on one face only, leaving the other smooth.

The crude wedge-shaped Type 2 axes recorded at Episkopi *Phaneromeni* and Alambra *Mouttes* are not found at *Kaminoudhia* (Swiny 1986:3; Mogelonsky 1996:150). Conversely, neither of the first two mentioned sites yielded any "flaked celts," thus it could be argued that the *Kaminoudhia* examples were, once again, collected at Sotira *Teppes*. A single flaked tool was excavated at Marki *Alonia* (Frankel and Webb 1996b:81).

ADZE

Sample: 5. (S518 questionable). (Fig. 6.1; pl. 6.1b). 4 stratified: S177, 418, 450, 518?. 1 unstratified: S539. All fragmentary (1 recorded by the surface survey).

Material: Mostly fine-grained igneous.

Description: Due to the fragmentary nature of all the *Kaminoudhia* adzes little can be said about their original shape. Only S518 appears to have the angular features of S257a and 440 from Episkopi *Phaneromeni,* a feature typical of Chalcolithic stone adzes (Swiny 1986:4, fig. 5; Elliott 1985: fig 70:1–8).

The availability of copper in the EC would certainly have made the use of stone adzes for wood working redundant. This may have resulted in their disappearance from the EC toolkit, which would explain their rarity at EC and MC sites, a point also mentioned by Frankel and Webb (1996b:81).

RUBBING STONE

In the Episkopi *Phaneromeni* publication rubbing stones were subdivided into two types, *elongated* and *discoidal* (Swiny 1986:5–6). After studying the *Kaminoudhia* assemblage the writer concluded that the morphological division was too arbitrary and not based on any diagnostic difference in use wear. Furthermore, the rarity of the discoidal type—two examples at Episkopi *Phaneromeni* and one at *Kaminoudhia*—further reduced the necessity for retaining the sub-types.

Sample: 32. (Fig. 6.1). 27 stratified: S15, 59, 76, 97 117, 138, 181, 183, 184, 191, 204?, 214?, 220? 225, 228, 233, 240, 248, 267, 282, 291, 399, 405, 447, 487, 572, 588, 690. 5 unstratified: 7, 86, 93, 480, 604.

Material: Igneous and limestone.

Description: Elongated, unaltered river stones, usually oval in transverse section with one or both faces worn smooth and often slightly polished from rubbing. The stratified examples range from 5.3 to 22.5 cm in length, the average ranging from 10 to 15 cm. S117, a uniform, elongated beach pebble, 18.6 cm long, may have served as a rubbing stone but it also exhibits a wear pattern suggestive of use as a whetstone: i.e. well-smoothed depressions on one face (Swiny 1986:12, "Whetstone").

Frankel and Webb (1996b:83) note that the use wear characteristic of rubbing stones argues against their use on saddle querns, as was incorrectly suggested for the Episkopi *Phaneromeni* assemblage. These artifacts were not subjected to heavy use and could well have been used on fibers, leather, or wood.

This tool type was not common at Alambra *Mouttes* or Marki *Alonia,* with only three examples published from each site (Mogelonsky 1996:154; Frankel and Webb 1996b:83).

RUBBER – POUNDER

Sample: 68. 55 stratified. (Figs. 6.2, 6.3, 6.4; pl. 6.1c). See catalogue for numbers. (6 recorded by the surface survey).

Material: Fine to coarse grained igneous.

Description: Rubber-pounders are usually unaltered riverstones, either elongated (31%, fig. 6.2) or discoidal (62%, figs. 6.3, 6.4) in shape. One side or more is smooth and flat from rubbing and one or both extremities are pitted from pounding. Sometimes the rubbing surfaces exhibit discrete areas of pitting from tertiary use as a hammerstone.

Rubber-pounders were slightly more common than pounders at Episkopi *Phaneromeni* (Swiny 1986:65, Table 1), whereas at *Kaminoudhia* the ratio is one to four in favor of pounders. This disparity could be either chronological or functional.

Alambra *Mouttes* (Mogelonsky 1996:155. 32 recorded) mirrors *Kaminoudhia* in that rubber-pounders form the second most common tool type; three were also recorded at Marki *Alonia* (Frankel and Webb 1996b:83).

POUNDER

Sample: 248. 178 stratified. (Figs. 6.5, 6.6, 6.7, 6.8, 6.9; pl. 6.d). See catalogue for numbers. (11 pounders and 4 grinder-pounders—now reclassified as pounders—were recorded by the surface survey).

Material: Fine to coarse-grained igneous.

Description: Pounders form the largest single type of expedient tools, 225 or 91% of which consist of unaltered riverstones with at least one surface pitted from pounding. The remaining 21 pieces or 15% are curated tools, namely fragments of quern rubbers reused as pounders (for an example see fig. 6.6:S116). Depending on how long the tool was utilized, the use wear may vary from light pitting to faceting from repeated pounding. The *Kaminoudhia* pounders fall into three categories based on shape and size: 42% are elongated (from 8 to 27.5 cm long, figs. 6.5, 6.6), 16% are flattened triangular or discoidal (around 10 cm in length or diameter, fig. 6.7, fig. 6.8, top two rows) and the remaining 42% are irregular, quadrangular or spherical (from 3.7 to 8 cm in length, fig. 6.8, bottom two rows, fig. 6.9, top three rows. The bottom two rows are elongated).

Pounders are the most common tool type found at *Kaminoudhia,* representing 58% of the total tool assemblage and 33% of all the ground stone recorded at the settlement. In general they display less use wear than those at Episkopi *Phaneromeni,* where many pounders are multi-faceted, a feature rare at *Kaminoudhia.* Whereas the main source of raw material—the Kouris riverbed—was adjacent to the *Phaneromeni* settlement, at *Kaminoudhia* the tool blanks had to be carried up from the same riverbed, almost 200 m and five kilometers away, therefore greater utilization of individual tools should be expected at this site. This idiosyncrasy is balanced, however, by the fact that 10% of all pounders were reused (curated) rubbers, a practice only rarely encountered at *Phaneromeni.*

Most pounders show secondary use as hammerstones, in which case they have discrete pitted areas on one or several surfaces from having hit (or being hit by) a hard material, such as chert or chalcedony. It is very likely that many pounders were used for flint knapping, as suggested by Kingsnorth (Chapter 7 infra), especially in connection with Unit 21 where 6 pounders and 2 hammerstones were found along with evidence for a knapping station.

At the settlements of Alambra *Mouttes* and Marki *Alonia,* in the center of the island, where the ground stone assemblages were classified following a typology similar to that in use at *Kaminoudhia,* pounders were also the best represented tool type.[4]

PESTLE

Sample: 5. (Fig. 6.4; pl. 6.2a). Stratified: S31, 39?, 178, 199, 392.

Material: Igneous.

Description: S31, 178, 199 are intentionally shaped, elongated, triangular or round in section, with a slightly flaring end. S39 is an unaltered elongated river stone. All have a smooth polished area on one extremity, perhaps from grinding and pounding in a smooth mortar.

The identification of these objects as pestles remains tentative. In the case of S31, which initially served as a pounder/pestle of common Chalcolithic type,[5] the smooth polished area on its larger end post-dates its use as a pounder. Three pestles with smooth or polished extremities were recorded at Episkopi *Phaneromeni* (Swiny 1986:10).

HAMMERSTONE

Sample: 22. (Fig. 6.10 top row). 19 stratified: S58, 62, 65, 68, 92, 133, 137, 227, 299, 366, 401, 437, 438, 562, 571, 582, 642, 647, 650. 3 unstratified: S230, 580, 584.

Material: Igneous.

Description: Unaltered river stones of various shapes with an average length (for the stratified examples) of 8.6 cm. Size suitable to fit comfortably into one hand. Signs of wear may be found on all surfaces with emphasis on the ends of elongated specimens; many were used to hit a small hard object such as, for example, a chert core.

---

[4] Mogelonsky 1996:158–61 (63 pounders divided into 3 types); Frankel and Webb 1996b:82 (10 pounders classified as at *Kaminoudhia* as one type).

[5] Elliott 1985:175, fig. 72, here described as "pestles." They do not, however, have the polished areas on the extremities which are diagnostic of the Episkopi *Phaneromeni* and *Kaminoudhia* pestles.

Although the use wear is more random than that of pounders, borderline examples do exist and some of the attributions are, as noted in connection with the Episkopi *Phaneromeni* material and by Frankel and Webb (Swiny 1986:11; Frankel and Webb 1996b:85), relatively arbitrary. Twenty-three hammerstones were recorded at Alambra *Mouttes* and seven from Marki *Alonia* (Mogelonsky 1996:164; Frankel and Webb 1996b:85), all of which were classified according to the same criteria as at *Kaminoudhia*.

PECKING STONE

Sample: 36. (Fig. 6.10, bottom 3 rows; pl. 6.2b). 30 stratified: S53, 84, 99, 126, 154, 169, 198, 229, 271, 279, 290, 303, 390, 391, 403, 407, 409, 436, 483, 484, 528, 536, 555, 600, 601, 627, 665, 666, 670, 684. 6 unstratified: S26, 27, 44, 341, 394, 512. (5 pecking stones recorded by the surface survey).

Material: chert, chalcedony, quartz.

Description: Cuboid or spheroid. Average diameter of the stratified examples 5.5 cm.

The *Kaminoudhia* assemblage is identical to that from Episkopi *Phaneromeni* (Swiny 1986:11–12) and calls for little additional comment. Frankel and Webb (1996b:85–86) mention instances where pecking stones have been found in association with flintworking installations, suggesting that, at least in the early prehistoric period, these tools were associated with this industry as well as for shaping other stones. This was probably the case at *Kaminoudhia* too, particularly in Unit 21, where Kingsnorth (see Chapter 7 infra) believes that she has isolated a knapping station which included part of a pecking stone along with six pounders and two hammerstones.

Mogelonsky (1996:166) publishes six pecking stones from Alambra *Mouttes* and Frankel and Webb (1996b:85) publish five chert pecking stones from Marki *Alonia*.

WHETSTONE

Two questionable whetstones were recorded. S117 (fig. 6.4) also served as a rubbing stone and it was classified as such. S466 was attributed with greater confidence to this category. Elongated in shape, it is hard crystalline limestone and shows some wear typical of that on the whetstones recorded at Episkopi *Phaneromeni*, namely "well-smoothed depressions on one or both faces" (Swiny 1986:12, fig. 15).

MACE – HEAD ?

Sample: 1. (Fig. 6.10; pl. 6.2c). S275, stratified.

Material: Limestone.

Description: Slightly flattened ovoid, 8 cm long with two diametrically opposed drill holes 1.6 cm deep on the short axis.

This object closely resembles a limestone mace-head with drilled perforation from Episkopi *Phaneromeni*.[6] Mace-heads have not been recorded at Alambra *Mouttes* or Marki *Alonia*.

---

[6] Swiny 1986:13, fig. 16, 49:b. See also this reference for relevant comparanda.

PERFORATED STONE

Sample: 7. (Fig. 6.11). Stratified: S79, 306, 491, 497, 499, 502, 506.

Material: Limestone.

Description: Irregular shaped, usually with pecked hour-glass perforation(s) near edge or in one instance in the middle (S306). S79, 491 and 497 have two perforations, one larger than the other. All weigh between 5 and 7 kg.

Similar stones with perforations from Episkopi *Phaneromeni* were classified as stone weights with suspension holes, although only one (S79) out of 12 showed a wear pattern which suggested it had been suspended (Swiny 1985:19). Since no diagnostic wear marks were recorded on the *Kaminoudhia* examples they are classified by inference to the *Phaneromeni* material. S506 is perhaps large enough to have served as a tethering stone. None of the large and heavy tethering stones recorded at Episkopi *Phaneromeni* and elsewhere were found at *Kaminoudhia* (Swiny 1985:19).

Similar perforated stones are recorded at Alambra *Mouttes,* where they are described as "Weight, Tethering stone" (Mogelonsky 1996:169). None appear to have been excavated at Marki *Alonia.*

DISH

Sample: 3. (Fig. 6.11, bottom row; pl. 6.2d). Stratified: S268, 393, 446.

Material: Igneous, limestone.

Description: Carefully shaped, shallow, circular or slightly oval dish. Diameters range from 16 cm to ca. 25 cm to 25–30 cm. Depth of pecked and pitted depressions range from 3.3 to 4.6 cm.

No close parallels for this shape have been recorded from other pre-LBA sites in Cyprus. A dish published from Marki *Alonia* is a smaller version of the type (Frankel and Webb 1996b:79, fig. 6.7:S4).

MORTAR

Sample: 20. (Fig. 6.11, top row; pls. 6.2e, f, g, h). 19 stratified: S207, 232, 239, 280, 308, 331, 427, 503, 513, 525, 548, 550, 554, 556, 565, 620, 674, 688, 693. 1 unstratified: 525.

Material: Limestone, igneous (S620 only).

Description: Mortars[7] are cobbles or boulders of irregular shape with a pecked depression in one face. Few show evidence of actual use as mortars, namely a small bowl-shaped vessel or rock depression in which substances are pounded or rubbed with a pestle. This action smoothes and polishes the inner surface of the mortar. At *Kaminoudhia* three mortars (S280, 427 and 556) have evidence of this polish-

---

[7] I now consider the typology adopted for the publication of the Episkopi *Phaneromeni* mortars unnecessarily elaborate, therefore it has been abandoned.

ing, which suggests that they were indeed used to pound a substance. S620, a small circular, carefully shaped mortar with a shallow depression 0.8 cm deep, is the only example of a slightly different type. Other mortars from *Kaminoudhia,* which could also be described as troughs, are unaltered riverstones with shallow (S207, 232, 239, 308, 331, 513, 554, 674, 688) or deep (S565) roughly pecked circular or oval cavities. S503 has a cavity on both faces. Three mortars (S548, 550 and 693) are carefully shaped thin-walled, deep basins, up to 30 cm from rim to base. S448 and 550 are unique in that they have rectangular trunnions protruding from the vessel wall, a feature characteristic of many mortars from Late Antiquity onwards.

A range of mortars, basins and troughs was recorded at Alambra *Mouttes* and Marki *Alonia* (Mogelonsky 1996:170 ff.; Frankel and Webb 1996b:77 ff.), demonstrating the popularity of these objects commonly recorded from the Neolithic onwards in Cyprus (Swiny 1986:21).

PALETTE

Sample: 3. (Fig. 6.14). Stratified: S52, 105, 119.

Material: Igneous, limestone.

Description: Cobbles with a flattened work-smoothed area on one face.

Although no (red ochre) staining or any other discoloration is visible on the flattened areas of these stones, they do resemble the palettes published by Elliott from Lemba *Lakkous* (Elliott 1985:192, fig. 76:1).

WORK SURFACE

Sample: 6. (Fig. 6.11). Stratified: S6, 196, 293, 510. Unstratified S535. Questionable S259.

Material: Igneous, limestone.

Description: Flattened igneous cobble, boulder or tabular slab of limestone, up to 36 x 20 cm, with one face differentiated from the other by use wear perhaps from grinding or light pounding.

Episkopi *Phaneromeni* has provided the best parallels for these objects (Swiny 1986:25, fig. 30), although work surfaces with more substantial evidence for use wear are published from Alambra *Mouttes* (Mogelonsky 1996:172, pl. 24).

LID

Sample: 2. (Fig. 6.11). Stratified: S110, 619.

Material: Limestone.

Description: Discoidal slabs of limestone with approximate diameters of 9 and 32 cm with more or less rounded edges.

If the identification of these objects is correct, S110 could have covered the mouth of a storage jar of the type found at *Kaminoudhia*. Parallels for the smaller disks are recorded at Episkopi

Phaneromeni, Alambra *Mouttes* and Marki *Alonia* (Frankel and Webb 1996b:86 for references); the large slab has LC parallels at Kalavasos *Ayios Dhimitrios*.

QUERN

When the ground stone assemblage from Episkopi *Phaneromeni* was classified in the 1970s and prepared for publication in the early 1980s, I made a clear distinction between "saddle querns" and "rubbing stones" (Swiny 1986:5, 23). The descriptive term of saddle quern was applied to all large artifacts with concave work surfaces used for grinding, despite the fact that the smaller Type 2 saddle querns were often described in the literature as "rubbing stones" or "rubbers" on the larger Type 1 querns. The reason for this decision was my failure to detect any evidence for use wear in the form of transverse scratches on the concave surface of Type 2 querns, suggesting that they had indeed functioned on top of Type 1 querns (Swiny 1986:24). In the course of preparing the *Kaminoudhia* ground stone for publication, the work-surfaces of Type 2 querns from both sites were studied under 10x magnification and transverse scratch marks were noted on several examples, thereby requiring a reassessment of the Episkopi *Phaneromeni* quern classification.[8]

Sample: 31. (Fig. 6.12; pl. 6.2i). 14 stratified: S38, 151, 152, 256, 307, 309, 310, 426, 428, 495, 500, 508, 699, 700. IS (left in situ) 1, 6, 8, 12, 13, 19, 25, 26, 37, 38, 39, 41, 42, 43, 46, 53. 1 unstratified: S195. (3 recorded by the surface survey).

Material: Limestone.

Description: Elongated oval in shape, upper face longitudinally concave and transversally flat or slightly convex. The base is flat or uneven. The 6 intact examples measure up to 58 cm in length to 34 cm in width, the average size being 48.8 x 27 cm. The work-surface of non-weathered examples is pitted, yet smooth.

The *Kaminoudhia* querns form a more homogenous group than at Episkopi *Phaneromeni*, where many of the so-called Type 1 querns were igneous. The different choice of material at *Kaminoudhia* is to be expected, since large igneous rocks had to be transported from the distant Kouris riverbed.

All of the Alambra *Mouttes* querns appear to be igneous (Mogelonsky 1996:166), whereas over half the Marki *Alonia* examples are of calcarenite (Frankel and Webb 1996b:74).

RUBBER

In this report the term "rubber" refers to objects described as "Type 2 saddle querns" at Episkopi *Phaneromeni* (Swiny 1986:23) for the reasons stated above in connection with the *Kaminoudhia* querns.

Sample: 64. (Fig.6.12; pls. 6.2j, k). 60 stratified: S5, 32, 61, 101, 107, 112, 118, 121, 160, 188, 206, 236, 261, 266, 298, 318, 324, 359, 361, 372, 384, 386, 387, 396, 419, 422, 430, 453, 476, 490, 493, 494, 498, 504, 505, 507, 526, 581, 614, 632, 672, 692, 694, 695, 696, 697, 701, 702, 703, 704. IS (left in situ) 2, 3, 5, 9, 17, 24, 30, 31, 32, 33. 4 unstratified: S153, 176, 258, 631. (33 recorded by the surface survey). Rubber blank? S509.

[8] Of the Type 2 saddle querns listed in Swiny 1986:23, S77, 273, 274 and 406 did have transverse striations, indicating that they had served as rubbers.

Material: Approximately two-thirds igneous and one-third limestone.

Description: Elongated with rounded ends and concave work surface and chipped edges. The 13 intact rubbers varied in length from 20.8 to 43 cm in length, from 15 to 20.5 cm in width and from 3.4 to11.9 cm in thickness. The preferred size appears to have been around 40 x 16 x 4 or 5 cm.

A comparative study of the Episkopi *Phaneromeni* and *Kaminoudhia* rubbers highlighted several differences. The transverse section of the work surface at *Kaminoudhia* is always convex, whereas at *Phaneromeni* it was often flat. The longitudinal section of the work surface of a sample of 24 *Kaminoudhia* rubbers was flat in four cases, convex in six and concave in 14. Well-polished areas, along the edges especially, revealed at 10x magnification fine scratches at right angles to the main axis on about half of the igneous rubbers. A few examples show scoring, either in both directions (S236) or only longitudinally (S206), which proves that on occasion they also served as querns, perhaps with rubbing stones.

By comparison with the numbers of rubbers recorded at Alambra *Mouttes* (46) and Marki *Alonia* (73), the percentage at *Kaminoudhia* is lower in relation to the overall size of the ground stone assemblage (Mogelonsky 1996:166; Frankel and Webb 1996b:74).

GROOVED STONE

Sample: 3. (Fig. 6.14). S73, 547 stratified; S285 unstratified.

Material: Igneous and limestone.

Description: Oval cobbles from 11.5 to 23 cm in length with a groove pecked around their circumference.

Stones of this size and shape, usually interpreted as weights, have been recorded at Chalcolithic and MC sites.[9]

FUNCTION UNCERTAIN

Sample: 17. (Fig. 6.16). S90, 103, 354, 429, 470, 474, 479, 492, 496, 501, 531, 541, 583, 585, 664, 667, 676.

Material: Igneous, limestone, sandstone.

Discussion: Some objects of uncertain function may have served as burnishers (S90, 470, 541). Others are characterized by a groove or knob at one end (S479, 531) rendering them vaguely phallic or anthropomorphic. Two (S664, 676) of imported sandstone may have been used for sharpening or grinding. Some slabs of tabular limestone (S492, 496, 501) have small, shallow pecked depressions. IS55, a roughly circular perforated limestone disk 60 cm in diameter, must have had a specific function which now completely eludes us: no parallels seem to exist in the Cypriot literature. S585 is a flattened discoid, ca. 3 cm in diameter, with a carefully ground circumference. S474 (fig. 6.16) is a carefully worked perforated disk, ca. 3 cm in diameter, with two concentric circles of drilled indentations sur-

---

[9] See Frankel and Webb 1996b:82 for references and a short discussion of their possible function(s).

rounding the central perforation. It may have been a personal ornament. S667 is another well-shaped limestone disk with a central perforation.

The grooved stones (S479, 531) could also have served as weights with a fiber or leather thong attached around the groove. S479, the stone with a groove near one extremity, finds a good parallel in a figurine(?) from Lemba *Lakkous* (Elliott 1985:281, fig. 82:8).

S103 may have been a blank.

Miscellaneous unidentified objects are recorded at most recently published excavations, with nine coming from Alambra *Mouttes,* one from Marki *Alonia,* and two from Episkopi *Phaneromeni* (Mogelonsky 1996:173; Frankel and Webb 1996b:88; Swiny 1986:28).

GAMING STONE

Stones with a 10 x 3 arrangement of shallow depressions pecked into one or both faces, or with a random number of depressions forming a spiral pecked onto one face, have been the subject of detailed studies in the Episkopi *Phaneromeni* publication and elsewhere (Swiny 1986:32 ff.; Swiny 1980; Buchholz 1981, 1982). Significant additions to the corpus were provided by the publication of eight stones from Alambra *Mouttes* and 15 from Marki *Alonia,* accompanied by a general discussion (Mogelonsky 1996:174 ff.; Frankel and Webb 1996b:86 ff.). Since the new material has not forced a revision of the conclusions reached in the 1986 Kent State University Expedition to Episkopi *Phaneromeni* publication, where the *Kaminoudhia* games were already included (Swiny 1986:34) but without registration numbers or specifications, an in-depth commentary would be both repetitive and unnecessary. The only substantive change is that the original division of the games into Types 1 and 2 based on the size of the 10 x 3 pattern now seems redundant, although in southern Cyprus a "pocket" version is recorded with some frequency (15 out of 92 games from the region were of this type: Swiny 1986:65, Table 1). Elsewhere on the island the pattern ranges from large to small with no noticeable clustering by size.

10 x 3 type (Senet)

Sample: 35. (Figs. 6.13, 6.14; pls. 6.3a–e). 27 stratified: 71, 72, 77, 78, 80, 102, 109, 114, 163, 234, 235, 281, 325, 330, 424, 425, 467, 475, 530, 532, 533, 546, 609, 611, 612, 613, 705. 7 unstratified: 120, 161, 167, 168, 608, 610, 633. In situ, cut into the bedrock: 1 (Unit 22).

Material: limestone.

Description: Tabular fragments of limestone, sub-rectangular or eroded, oval in shape with three roughly parallel rows of ten depressions each pecked into one or both faces. S425 has a crude spiral (Mehen) on the other face. The number of depressions and basic arrangement may vary a little or may be incomplete, usually due to damage or weathering, but the diagnostic pattern can always be extrapolated. The average length and width of the 10 x 3 motif is 16 x 6 cm. Note, however, that the playing surface of 26 examples averaged 20 x 8 cm, and that of six others averaged 12 x 3.5 cm, or almost half the size. Many of the games have one or two larger, circular depressions to one side of the 10 x 3 motif. These secondary troughs, equally common at other sites, were presumably for storing the gaming pieces (Swiny 1986: 48).

Stones with similar arrangements of depressions have been found on Bronze Age sites throughout the island and with the addition of examples published since 1985, number well over 200 (Swiny

1986:32–49, fig. 43a). Of note was the chance discovery of several 10 x 3 patterns pecked into the flat bedrock surface among the dromoi of the vast Dhenia *Kafkalla* cemetery (Herscher 1998:320, fig. 7). This is not the only funerary connection with the game in Cyprus: indeed, a terracotta board from the Hadjiprodromou Collection was the first 10 x 3 motif from the island to be published. It almost certainly came from a tomb (Swiny 1986:33, fig. 55:c). Two other lithic examples are also considered to have come from burial chambers, one from the cemetery at Paramali *Mandra tou Pouppou* (Swiny 1981: Table 2)[10] and the other from Marki *Kappara* (Frankel and Webb 1996b:86).

Spiral type (Mehen)

Sample: 3. (Fig. 6.13; pl. 6.3f). S425, stratified, has a Senet on its other face (see fig. 6.13, bottom right). S530 unstratified. One in situ pecked into the bedrock to the east of Area C in the alignment of the present road.

Material: Limestone.

Description: Tabular fragments of limestone with from 20 to 37 pecked depressions preserved in a spiral running clockwise. The original number of depressions would have been greater. The spiral cut into the bedrock is intact, and consists of 15 elongated depressions surrounding a larger circular one in its center.

Interestingly, no spiral games were excavated at Alambra *Mouttes,*[11] whereas four come from Marki *Alonia* (Frankel and Webb 1996b:86).

It is noteworthy that both stones with spirals from *Kaminoudhia* had Senets cut into the reverse face and that both came from Area B. S425 and the in situ spirals have elongated and not circular depressions, similar to S281 from *Phaneromeni* and SY-AP S19 from Anoyira *Peralijithias.*[12]

Since the detailed discussion of Cypriot gaming stones appeared in the Episkopi *Phaneromeni* publication, no argument in favor of altering the original interpretation of these stones as rustic versions of two well known Egyptian games has been proposed. The 10 x 3 arrangement of depressions would have been suitable for playing Senet or the game of "passing," and Mehen, meaning "large snake" or "coiled one," could have been played on the stones with random numbers of cavities arranged in spirals.

The religious and funerary connections of the Cypriot Mehens discussed in the *Phaneromeni* publication (Swiny 1986:59 ff.) are strengthened by the discovery of a spiral pecked into the bedrock at Dhenia *Kafkalla* with the above mentioned Senets. It is probably a coincidence that the only examples of both games to have been cut into the bedrock should come from *Kaminoudhia* in the south and Dhenia *Kafkalla* in the center of the island.

The above mentioned religious connection especially noted at Kition is further emphasized by the discovery of two slabs with "cupulae" from acropolis at Amathus, one from the temple of Aphrodite

---

[10] Table 2 does not specify the find spot of the single game from this site, but the present writer's detailed notes refer to its discovery in the spoil heap from a looted tomb.

[11] The arrangement of depressions described as a possible spiral on one side of B317 is too damaged to allocate to either category. In the present writer's opinion it does not look like part of a spiral. See Mogelonsky 1996:176, fig. 43, pl. 25.

[12] Swiny 1986:figs. 40–41. For information on Anoyira *Peralijithias* see Swiny 1981:77.

and the other associated with a tomb (Aupert 1997:20, fig. 3). They appear to be fragmentary Senet game boards that were either of Iron Age date or were carried to the acropolis (presumably as ex votos) from a Bronze Age site. This last explanation seems unlikely since there are no known settlements of this period in the vicinity. It would seem , thus, that the games of Senet and presumably Mehen, if the Kition example saw use after the Bronze Age, were still practiced at major Cypriot Iron Age cult centers.

How these games, or at least the general concept thereof, reached Cyprus remains to be satisfactorily elucidated, but it should be noted that the earliest recorded occurrence of depressions arranged into a spiral in Cyprus is at Lemba *Lakkous*.[13] Early Levantine or Egyptian connections have been suggested at the nearby site of Kissonerga *Mosphilia*, Period 4, by the presence of blue faience at the site (Peltenburg 1989:30). If the suggestion of mainland contacts is correct, it is preferable to view these games as being introduced directly from the Levant or preferably Egypt in the Old Kingdom, rather than via some circuitous route later in the Bronze Age.

PERSONAL ORNAMENTS

PENDANT

Sample: 11. (Fig. 6.15; pls. 6.3g, 6.3i). 10 stratified: S140, 143, 150, 165, 340, 468, 469, 542, 545, 551; unstratified: S660.

Material: Picrolite.

Description: The category of personal ornaments commonly described as "pendants" is the most frequently represented type at *Kaminoudhia*. They are carefully worked plaques of picrolite, carved in a range of shapes, from figures of eight to ovals and lozenges, or else are left in the form of the original river pebble. The majority are perforated towards one extremity, either by drilling or gouging, though some (S143) have a large perforation in their center. The bottle-shaped, fragmentary S140 has no perforation preserved, but in shape and size is identical to the perforated pendant from a Philia Phase burial at Nicosia *Ayia Paraskevi* (Hennessy et al. 1988:14, fig. 12:1).

The general type of flattened discoidal pendant made from picrolite is well recorded at Episkopi *Phaneromeni* and elsewhere in the southern half of Cyprus.[14] Picrolite in the EC and MC is very rare in the center of the island, with a single surface find of a "possibly worked nodule" from Marki *Alonia* (Frankel and Webb 1996b:89) and a mere three objects—none of which are stratified or readily identifiable, except for B308 which may be part of a pendant—from Alambra *Mouttes* (Mogelonsky 1996:174). The implications of these discoveries, or the lack thereof, for the understanding of EC and MC exchange networks are notable if the abundance (47 pieces) of picrolite in two Philia Phase burial chambers at Nicosia *Ayia Paraskevi* is also taken into account.[15]

The figure of eight (S150) and lozenge (S468) shaped pendants are the most unusual shapes found at *Kaminoudhia*. S140, the fragmentary bottle-shaped piece, has good Chalcolithic anteced-

---

[13] Swiny 1982:53; Peltenburg 1985:289, fig. 86:3, described as a "cup-marked stone;" Swiny 1986:51.

[14] See Swiny 1986:28 ff. for those from *Phaneromeni* and elsewhere in Cyprus.

[15] Hennessy et al. 1988:14–17, from Tombs 4 (41 items) and 12 (6 items).

ents[16] and exact Philia Phase counterparts as noted above. The piece from *Ayia Paraskevi* could well have been made at *Kaminoudhia*.

BEAD

Sample: 3. (Fig. 6.15; pls. 6.3g, h). Stratified: S338, 460, 461. Questionable S472.

Material: Picrolite.

Description: S338, cylindrical in shape, is the only true bead and even it has an unusually large perforation for the type. S460 and 461 may also be described as tubes, respectively 2.8 and 3.6 cm long, with one or two perforations near one end. The two perforations of S461 display wear patterns suggesting that a filament had been passed through them for suspension purposes. S673 is a miniature bead (diameter 3.3 mm, Th. 1 mm), with central hourglass perforation identical to those from necklaces associated with burials.

The picrolite beads from Lemba *Lakkous* (Peltenburg 1985:285, fig. 84) provide a good parallel for S338. The tubular beads S460 and 461, with secondary suspension(?) holes, have a generic resemblance to an object allegedly from Souskiou *Vathyrkakas* consisting of a picrolite tube, 3.3 cm long with a diameter of 1.8 cm, decorated with shallow drill holes.[17] From the wear pattern visible around the lateral perforation in the published photograph, it too seems to have been suspended. Vagnetti casts doubt on the Souskiou provenance, preferring a Bronze Age date, which is supported by the finds from *Kaminoudhia* and an excellent parallel from a MC tomb in Limassol (Karageorghis 1978:888, fig. 25). Although the latter at 4.8 cm is slightly longer and perhaps more "bead like" than the *Kaminoudhia* examples, it certainly belongs to the same class. A tube identical to the *Kaminoudhia* pieces in shape, size and well-worn lateral perforation—unfortunately without provenance—belongs to the Leto Severis Collection.[18] The only difference is that her piece is decorated with rows of lightly drilled concentric dots and circles. Perhaps these objects did serve as personal ornaments, but could equally well have had another function, serving as some kind of holder or decorative band on a wooden shaft.

BEAD (MINIATURE)

Sample: 857 (minimum count). (Fig. 6.16; pl. 6.4b). Stratified: S208 (646 beads; Swiny 1995:35 on right), S543 (132 beads), S673 (1 bead), S710 (80 beads).

Material: Quartz (black, Cairngorm variety), calcite (white), jasper (red/brown).

Description: Small, cylindrical or disc-shaped, from 2.8 to 3.6 mm in diameter (av. D. about 3 mm) and 0.8 to 3 mm thick. Biconical or cylindrical perforations, depending on thickness of bead. Average D. of perforation 0.5 mm.

---

[16] Peltenburg 1985: fig. 83: 3 and especially 5 and perhaps 17.

[17] Vagnetti 1980:64, pl. XIX:I.3 described as a "tubular object."

[18] I thank the late Mrs. Leto Severis for showing me this object, and others in her collection (see Herscher and Swiny 1992: 80 ff.).

Miniature beads strung into necklaces appear for the first time in Philia Phase burials (Stewart 1962:260, fig. 105:1–5; Hennessy et al. 1988:15, 17, figs. 17:26, 25:39) and become increasingly common as the period progresses. The EC and MC tombs at Episkopi *Phaneromeni* produced six necklaces with a total of 1,676 beads (Swiny 1986:30, with references to other sites; see also Todd 1986:117, 119, 166–67) made from the same materials as those from *Kaminoudhia*. Although almost all miniature beads come from funerary contexts—none have been recorded from the settlements at Marki *Alonia*, Alambra *Mouttes* or Episkopi *Phaneromeni*—they were probably also worn by the living, since a single jasper bead, S673, came from Unit 7 in Area A at *Kaminoudhia*. Unless large quantities of occupational debris are water sieved, there is little chance of detecting such small objects.

NECKLACE SPACER

Sample: 9. (Fig. 6.16; pl. 6.3h). Stratified: S208 (6 pieces; Swiny 1995:35 on right), 473, 662, 663.

Material: Picrolite, quartz (black).

Description:
Type 1: Elongated with rounded ends and 3 perforations. Av. L: 1.2 cm, W: 0.3 cm, Th: 0.15 cm.

Type 1 spacers, always associated with miniature beads, first appear in Philia Phase burials (Stewart 1962:263, fig. 105:6) and remain in use throughout the EC and MC periods (Swiny 1986:30, fig. 21:60, for spacer drawn with the necklace). It is interesting to note that six spacers were found with the necklace S208, the largest number to be found associated with a single necklace.

Type 2: Thin elongated plaque of picrolite with straight or rounded ends and two perforations, one near each extremity.

Whether or not these objects were used as spacers cannot at present be proven, since they have not been found in association with beads, but S662 does have wear marks (see catalogue description) suggesting that a filament had been passed through one hole and then the other as if to keep both strands apart.

The best parallel for these perforated plaques was recovered from a looter's spoil heap at the EC cemetery of Paramali *Pharkonia*, 6.5 km due west of Sotira (Herscher and Swiny 1992:77, fig. 3:8). Although smaller than these pieces, it clearly belongs to the same class and could have served a similar function.

PIERCED DISK

Sample: 1. (Fig. 6.15). S661 unstratified.

Material: Picrolite.

Description: Small disk with central perforation, closely resembling a button.

No meaningful parallels have been noted for this object.

CRUCIFORM FIGURINE

Sample: 1. (Fig. 6.15; Swiny 1985a: fig. 5.9; Swiny 1985: fig. 3:23). S144 stratified.

Material: Picrolite.

Description: Head, neck and one arm of a small cruciform figurine with suspension hole through the head (see catalogue description).

Cruciform anthropormophic pendants (i.e. with suspension holes) carved from picrolite are common in the Cypriot Chalcolithic.[19] This piece is unusual in that it has breasts, whereas most of the smaller cruciform pendants are devoid of anatomical features. The pointed arms and the oval flattened head are similar to figurines from Souskiou *Vathyrkakas*.[20] S144 was probably an heirloom contemporary with the Chalcolithic pottery found at the site.

ANTHROPOMORPHIC FIGURINE

Sample: 8. (Fig. 6.16; pl. 6.4a). S465 (fragmentary), 471 (necklace with 1 shell [S471 #7] and 6 picrolite [S471 # 1–6] pendants. S471 #3 fragmentary).

Material: Picrolite.

Description: Highly stylized anthropomorphic outline with a perforated flattened oval "head" (7 examples), or without head (1 example), round belly with large central perforation and well defined splaying feet. With the exception of the shell example (not counted with the stone pieces), which has vestigial arm stubs, no arms are represented. The intact pieces range in height from 1.8 to 2.8 cm, with thickness ranging from 0.13 to 0.2 cm. All perforations are drilled, hourglass in section, with striations visible. Several bear scratches on their surfaces. S465 from Unit 16 in Area A is similar, though smaller than the others with "heads." Its head has been broken off. No signs of wear are visible in any of the suspension holes, so these pendants must have been made especially as a funerary offering, or had only seen little use prior to burial.

Identical pendants have been recorded in Philia Phase burials at Nicosia *Ayia Paraskevi* (Stewart 1962:261, fig. 105:10–12; Hennessy et al.1988:15, 17, figs. 17, 25). They appear to come from the same workshop as those excavated at *Kaminoudhia*. Only one of the *Ayia Paraskevi* pieces has a head (Stewart 1962: fig. 105:12) and Stewart describes them as "fish amulets," a term also followed by Hennessey et al. (1988). They do indeed resemble fish when viewed from the side, but since they were clearly intended to be suspended through the smaller perforation they are more anthropomorphic in appearance, an impression reinforced by the pieces with "heads," or the shell example with arm stubs from *Kaminoudhia*. Pendants of similar type were excavated at Philia *Vasiliko* (Dikaios 1962: fig. 84:18–24, fig. LII), made of shell and stone. This type of ornament is not, with the exception of S465 perhaps an heirloom, known to predate or post-date the Philia Phase.

---

[19] Vagnetti 1980; Peltenburg 1985: fig. 80; Morris 1985: figs. 128–131, 136–147, 152–56, 162, 167; Crouwel 1978: pl. IV.
[20] Vagnetti 1980; Morris 1985: figs. 133, 154.

BURNISHER ?

Sample: 1. (Fig. 6.16). S148 stratified.

Material: Picrolite.

Description: Elongated pebble with one very smooth, flat, highly polished area (see object description).

Under 10x magnification faint striations are visible running diagonally across the main axis of the object.

WORKED PICROLITE

Sample: 28. (Figs. 6.15, 6.16; pls. 6.3h, i). 24 stratified: S141, 142, 146, 145, 147, 148, 149, 209, 224, 332, 333, 334, 335, 336, 337, 339, 457, 458, 459, 462, 463, 464, 707, 708, 709. 3 unstratified: 544, 628, 706.

Material: Picrolite.

Description: To this category belong pieces of picrolite, varying in shape and size from small carefully worked fragments of larger items (S334, 551 for example), to intentionally shaped but unidentifiable objects (S142, 333, 339 for example). Some pieces show only very faint signs of working and are only one step removed from blanks (S149). S209 has no signs of working at all, but exhibits too high a polish for a normal river pebble and must have been subjected to some specific activity. The handling of picrolite over an extended period of time can produce a similar polish.[21]

The 12 unidentified picrolite objects from Episkopi *Phaneromeni* (Type 1e) all belong to the category of worked picrolite (Swiny 1986:31). That so few pieces were found at *Phaneromeni* suggests that the manufacture of picrolite items was on a smaller scale at the later site, even though it was located immediately next to the island's main source of the raw material. A possible explanation for this change is that picrolite was no longer so desirable for the manufacture of ornaments, especially as other more exotic materials were becoming available through exchange in the burgeoning LC period.

The range of shapes and abundance of pieces of worked picrolite suggest that one of the on-site activities at Sotira *Kaminoudhia* was the manufacture of artifacts from pebbles collected in the Kouris riverbed. Although no caches were located, many such pebble blanks were scattered throughout the excavation. In all, 47 pieces of altered or worked picrolite[22]—excluding the blanks—were recovered from the excavation, a greater number in relation to the size of the area investigated than at any other site of Chalcolithic or Bronze Age date.

Convincing evidence for this activity was the discovery at Nicosia *Ayia Paraskevi* Tomb 4 (Hennessy et al. 1988: fig. 25:21, 23, 25 etc.) of a necklace with pendants identical to the "headless"

---

[21] Contemporary jewelry and trinkets such as key rings made from picrolite acquire a similar polish after being worn or handled for several weeks. Personal observation.

[22] This total is made up of the 28 pieces listed in the category of "Worked Picrolite" and an additional 20 uncatalogued small fragments with some signs of working.

example (S471/3) from Tomb 15 at *Kaminoudhia*. The similarity is such, both in shape and size, that they are surely the product of the same workshop, if not the same hand. In light of the preceding discussion and our present knowledge of the period, it is not unreasonable to suggest that the Nicosia *Ayia Paraskevi* pendants are most likely to have been manufactured at Sotira *Kaminoudhia*.

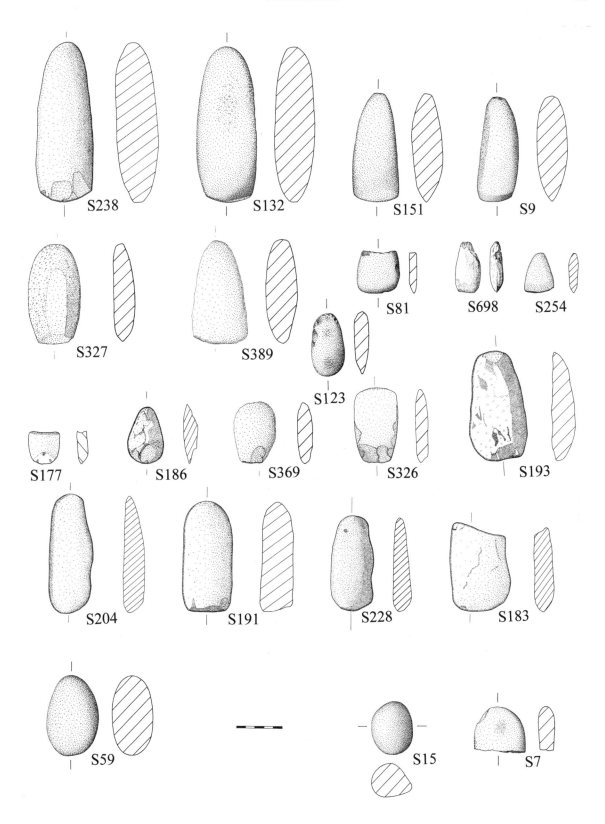

Fig. 6.1. Axes Type 1, rows 1 and 2. Row 3, Adze S177; Axes Type 2, S186, 369, 326, 193 and 123 above. Rubbing stones, rows 4 and 5.

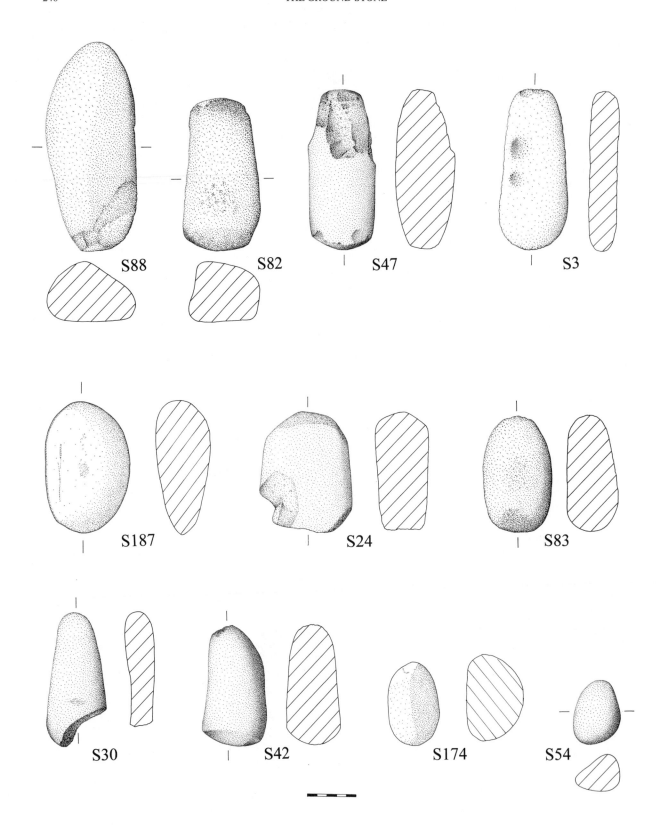

Fig. 6.2. Rubber-pounders.

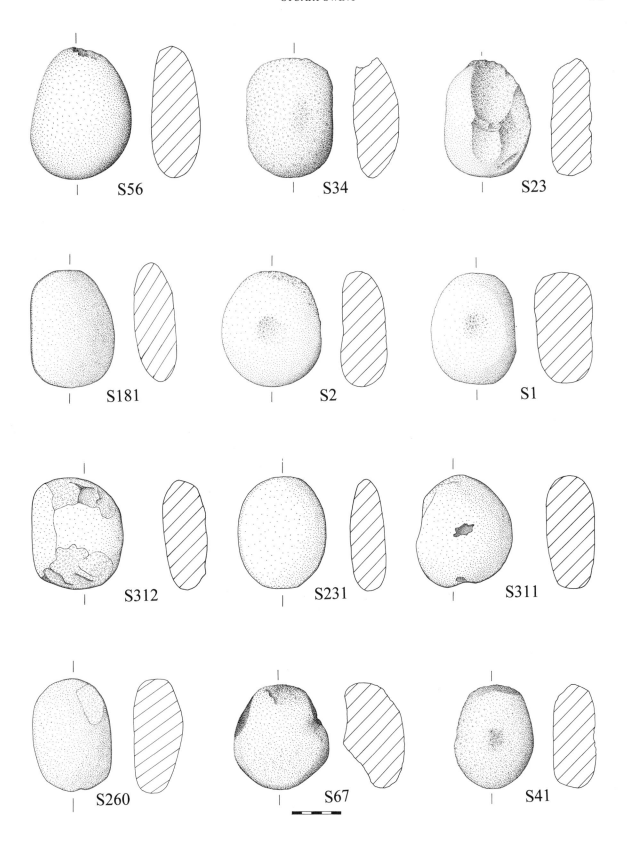

Fig. 6.3. Rubber-pounders.

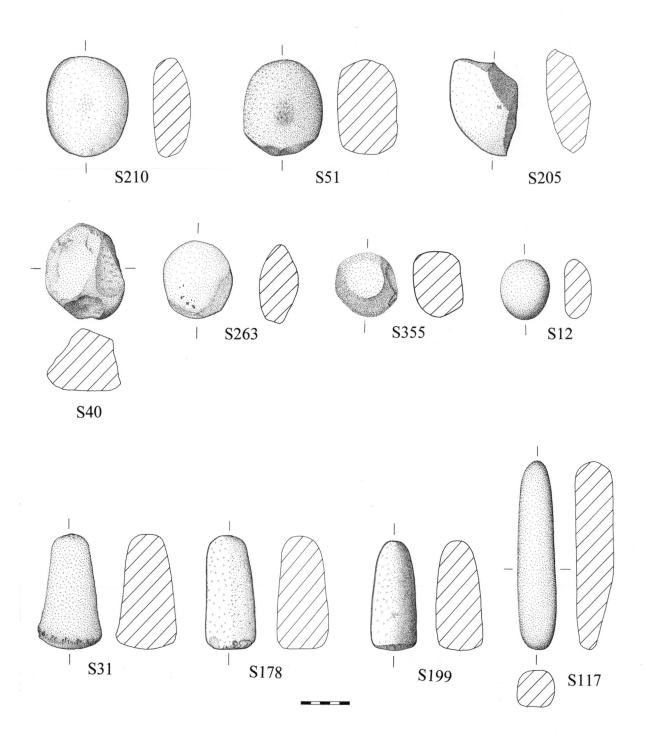

Fig. 6.4. Rubber-pounders, rows 1 and 2. Pestles S31, 178, 199. Whetstone S117.

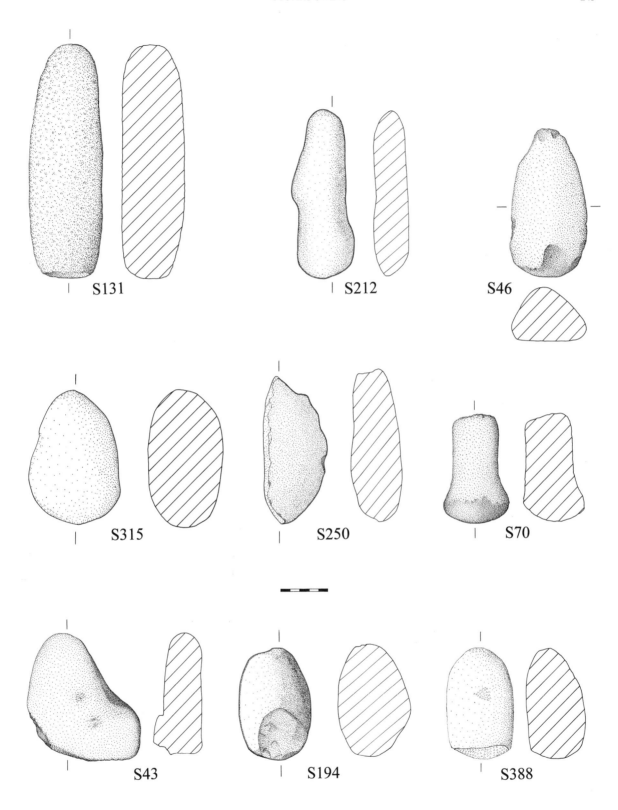

Fig. 6.5. Pounders (elongated).

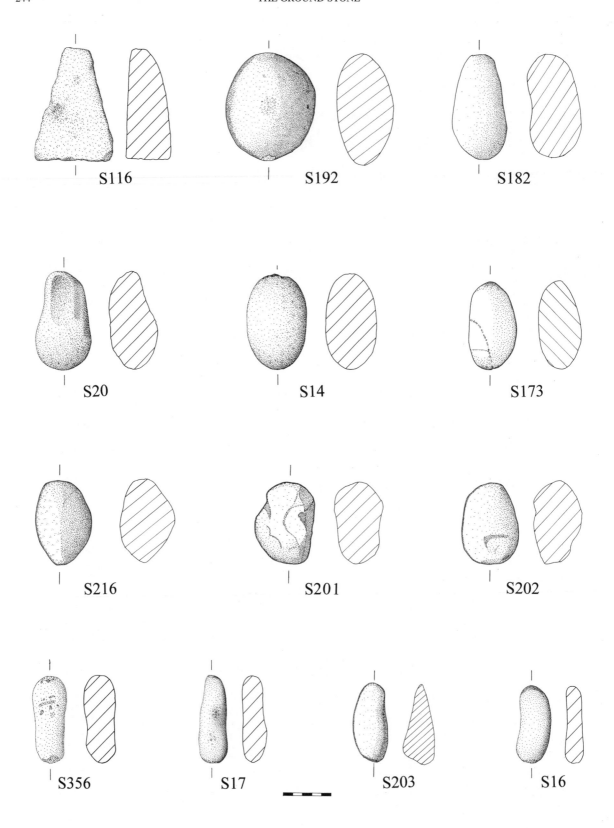

Fig. 6.6. Pounders (elongated).

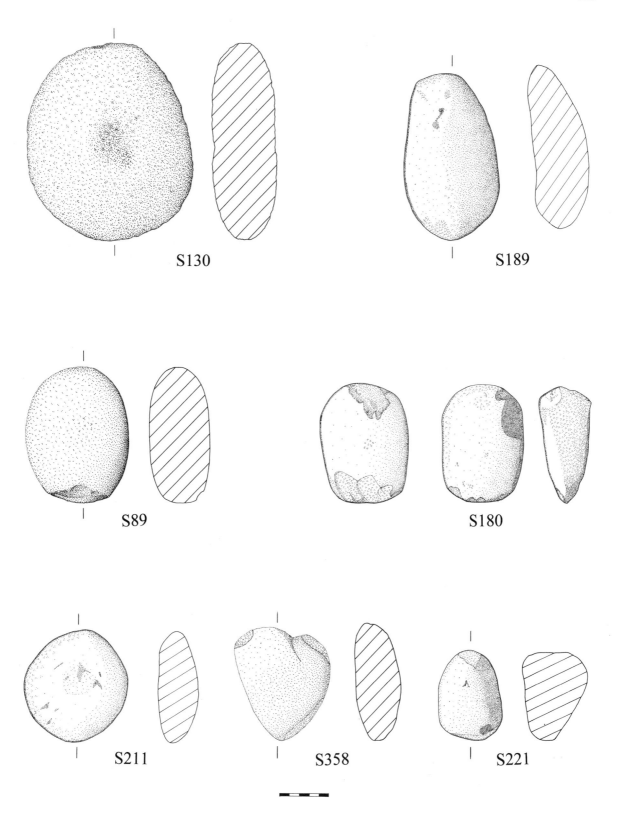

Fig. 6.7. Pounders (flattened, discoidal or triangular).

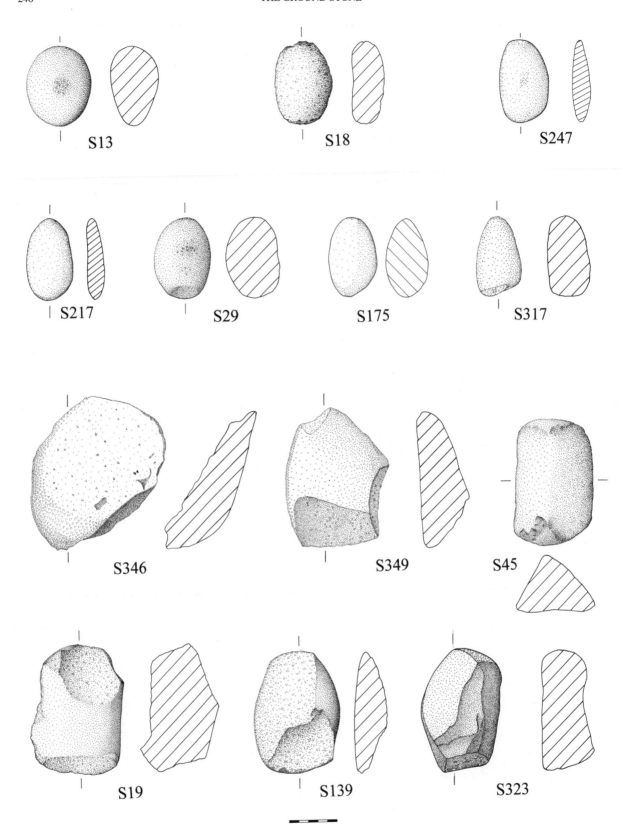

Fig. 6.8. Pounders (flattened, discoidal, rows 1 and 2); (irregular, quadrangular, spherical, rows 3 and 4).

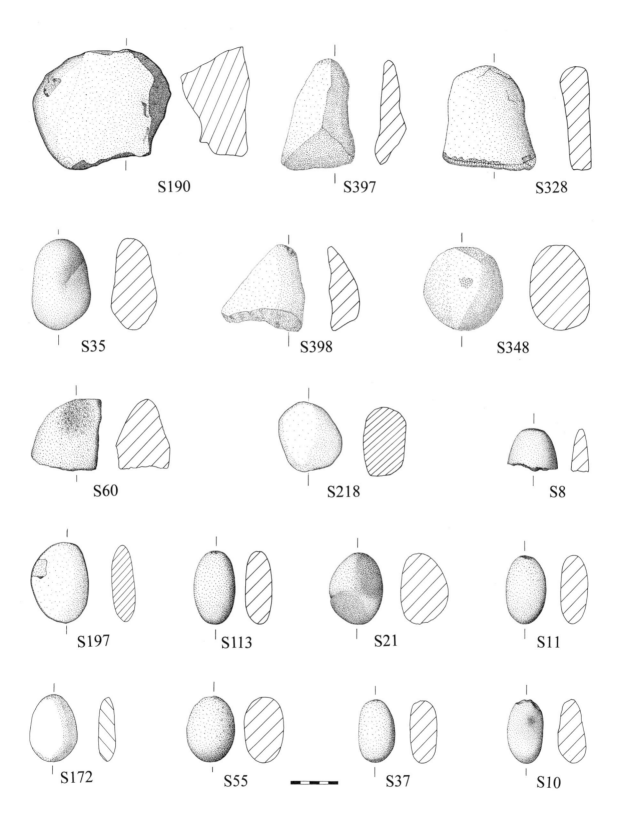

Fig. 6.9. Pounders (irregular, quadrangular, spherical, rows 1–3); (elongated, rows 4 and 5).

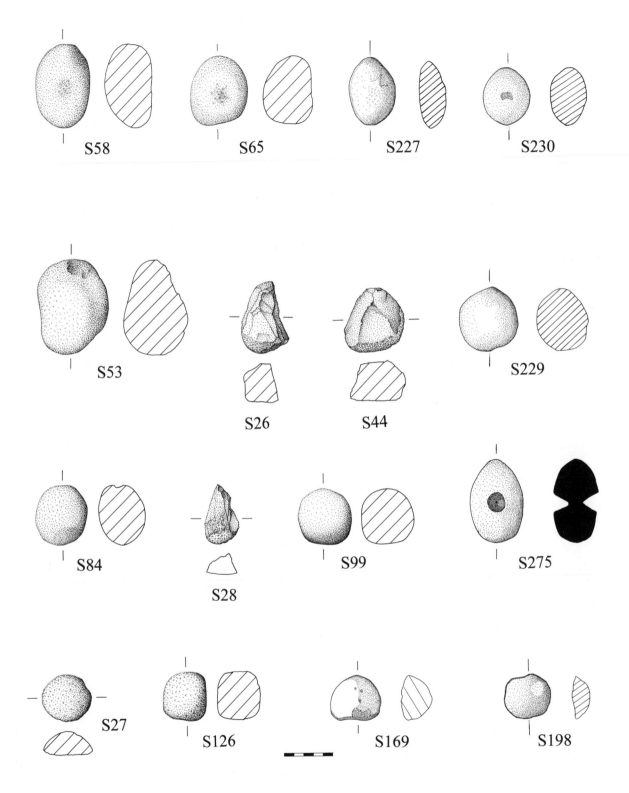

Fig. 6.10. Hammerstones, row 1. Pecking Stones, rows 2–4, excluding the Macehead(?) S275.

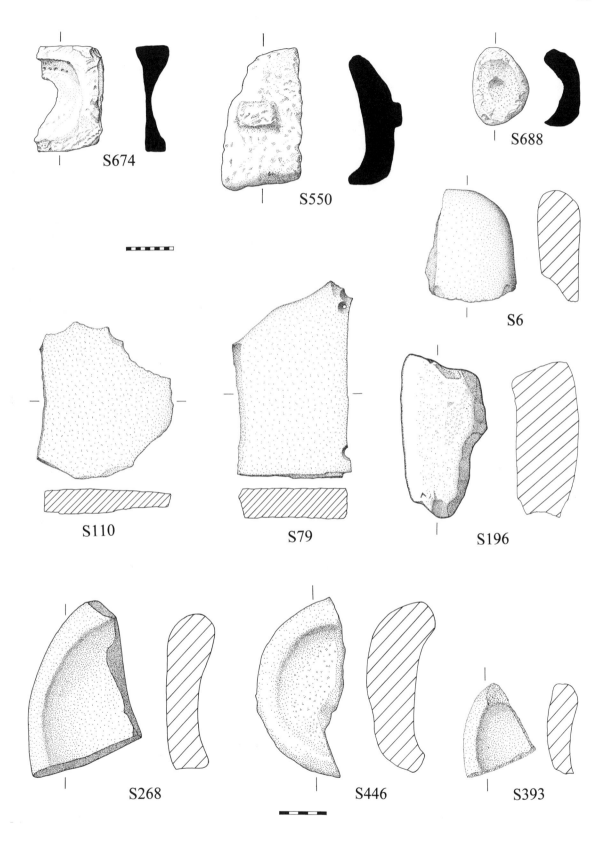

Fig. 6.11. Mortars, row 1; Lid S110. Work Surfaces S6, 196. Perforated Stone S79. Dishes, bottom row.

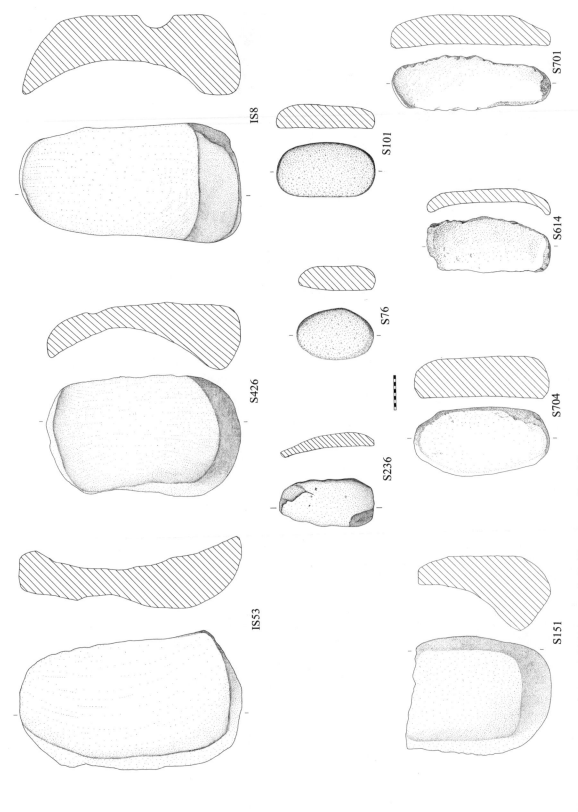

IS8

S701

S101

S614

S76

S426

S704

S236

IS53

S151

Fig. 6.12. Querns, row 1 and S151 in row 3. Rubbers, rows 2 and 3.

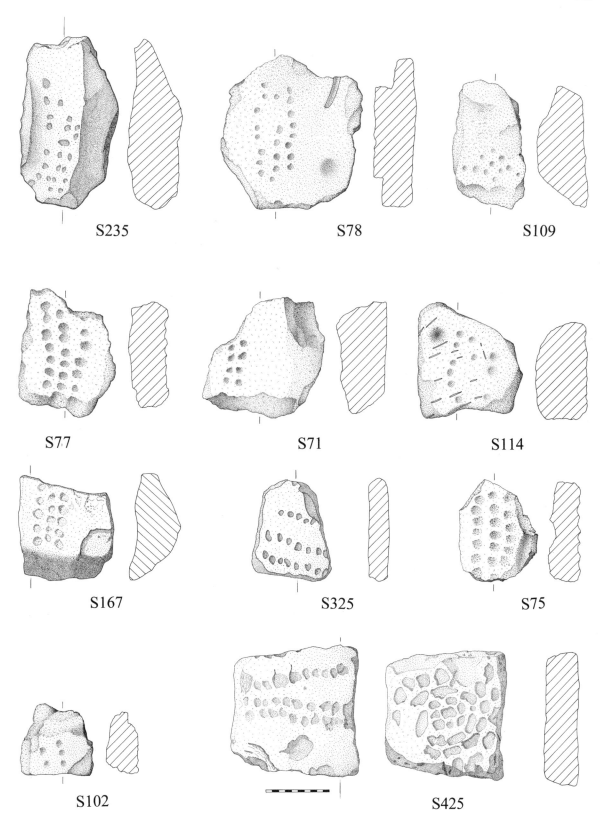

S235   S78   S109

S77   S71   S114

S167   S325   S75

S102   S425

Fig. 6.13. Gaming stones, Senet, except for one face of S425 on row 4, which is a Mehen.

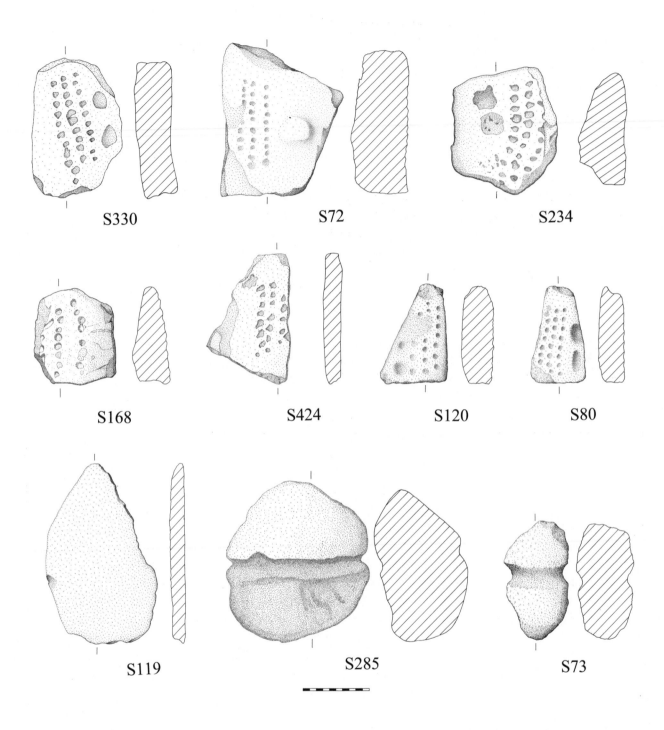

Fig. 6.14. Gaming stones, Senet, rows 1 and 2. Row 3, Palette S119, Grooved Stones S73, 285.

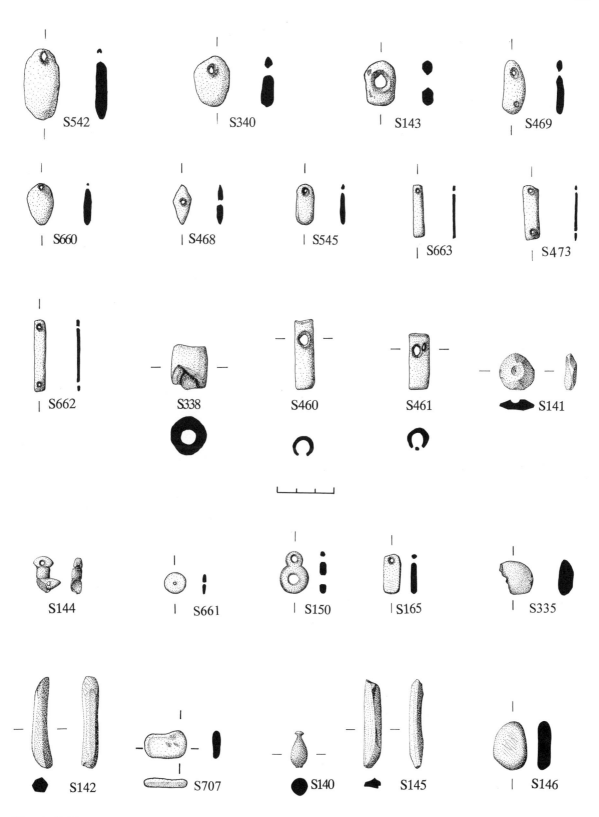

Fig. 6.15. Picrolite. Personal Ornaments and Worked Picrolite. Pendants S542, 340, 143, 469, 660, 468, 545, 150, 165, 140; Beads S338, 460, 461. Cruciform Figurine S144. Pierced Disk S661. Worked Picrolite S141, 335, 142, 707, 145, 146. Spacers S663, 473, 662.

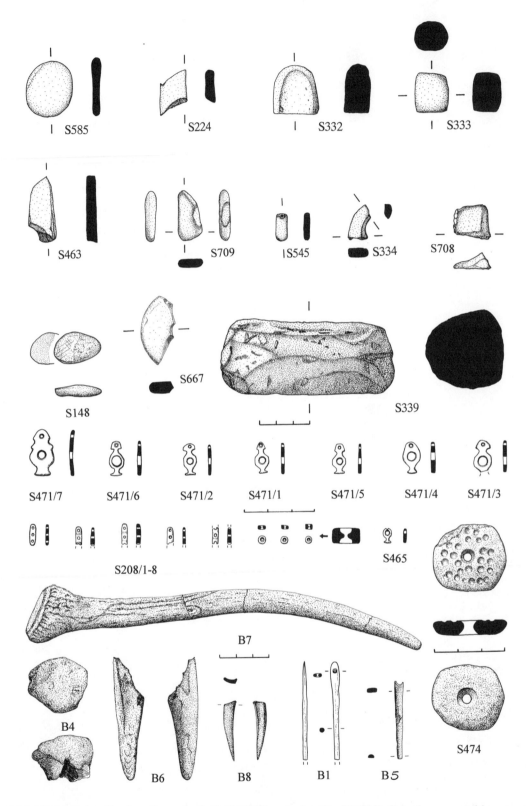

Fig. 6.16. Worked picrolite (top 3 rows), shell (S471/7) and picrolite (S471/1-6) anthropomorphic ornaments, stone spacers and beads (S208/1-8), antler hammers (B4, B7) and bone points (B6, B8) and needles (B1, B5). Unidentified perforated stone (S474). Note that S471/1–7 and S474 are reproduced at a different (larger) scale.

GROUND STONE CATALOGUE

All measurements are in centimeters. The IS (in situ) artifacts are listed at end of the catalogue. Unless indicated as coming from Phase I in Units 1 and 4, all stratified finds belong to Phase II

S1. Rubber-pounder. Area A. Unit 1. Igneous. Intact. L: 10, W: 5.6, Th: 8.6. Elongated discoidal. Both ends flattened. Fine-grained, blue/gray. Both faces slightly smoothed from use as a rubbing stone and pitted from use as a hammerstone. Sides and ends slightly pitted from pounding.

S2. Rubber-pounder. Area A. Unit 1. Igneous. Intact. L: 10.9, W: 9.4, Th: 5.0. Discoidal. One face convex, the other flattened. Fine-grained, green/gray. One face smooth from use as a rubbing stone: use on the convex face questionable. Circumference pitted from use as a pounder. Both faces slightly pitted from tertiary use as a hammerstone.

S3. Rubber-pounder. Area A. Unit 1. Limestone. Intact. L: 10.6, W: 5.7, Th: 2.7. Elongated, one end round, the other flat. Fine-grained, off-white. Both faces well smoothed, probably from rubbing. The narrow extremity heavily pitted from use as a pounder. One face with two shallow pecked depressions of unknown function.

S4. Pounder. Area A. Unit 1. Igneous. Intact. L: 9.2, W: 7.4, Th: 3.2. Roughly discoidal. Coarse-grained, yellow to dark yellow. Both ends pitted, one more obviously so, from pounding. The tool is so badly weathered, it is difficult to distinguish the markings with certainty.

S5. Rubber. Area A. Unit 1. Igneous. Fragmentary. L: 15.7, W: 15.4, Th: 4.7. Roughly quadrangular. Both ends missing. Coarse-grained, gray/green. Work face slightly concave, with worn edges, other face convex.

S6. Work surface. Area A. Unit 1. Igneous. Fragmentary. L: 11.0, W: 9.9, Th: 4.4. Two straight edges with broken rounded corners, edges broken. Fine-grained, blue/gray. One face worn smooth, the other partially pecked, as well as the corner. Work surface perhaps used for grinding.

S7. Rubbing stone. Area A. I17C 2. Igneous. Fragmentary. L: 5.0, W: 5.5, Th: 2.3. Rounded end of what was probably an elongated flattened tool. Fine-grained, green/gray. Both faces very smooth, with faint signs of localized pitting. Edges rounded, perhaps with signs of pitting.

S8. Pounder. Area A. I17C 3. Igneous. Fragmentary. L: 4.0, W: 5.2, Th: 4.2. Roughly semi-circular, flattened, with rounded end. Fine-grained, blue/gray. Both faces smooth, but not necessarily from rubbing. End flattened and pitted.

S9. Axe, Type 1. Area A. Unit 1. Igneous. Intact. L: 10.5, W: 4.2, Th: 3.3. Crudely shaped axe, with well-sharpened cutting edge. Fine-grained, greenish. One side convex, the other flat. Butt slightly pointed.

S10. Pounder. Area A. Unit 4. Igneous. Intact. L: 6.1, W: 3.5, Th: 2.5. Small oblong, with rounded ends. Medium-grained, gray/green. One end pitted.

S11. Pounder. Area A. Unit 1. Igneous. Intact. L: 6.5, W: 4.0, Th: 2.6. Elongated with rounded ends. Medium-grained, gray/green. Both ends pitted, one end only slightly.

S12. Rubber-pounder. Area A. Unit 1. Igneous. Intact. L: 5.5, W: 4.5, Th: 2.8. Discoidal. Fine-grained, gray/green. One face smoothed and flattened from rubbing. Both ends slightly pitted, together with both sides, from use as a pounder.

S13. Pounder. Area A. Unit 1. Igneous. Intact. L: 7.6, W: 5.8, Th: 4.6. Thick discoidal with rounded ends. Fine-grained, blue/gray. Faint signs of pitting on extremity, one side and both faces.

S14. Pounder. Area A. Unit 1. Igneous. Intact. L: 9.6, W: 6.0, Th: 4.7. Elongated ovoid. Fine-grained, gray/green. Both ends rounded, one end well pitted, the other only slightly.

S15. Rubbing stone. Area A. Unit 1. Igneous. Intact. L: 5.3, W: 4.4, Th: 3.3. Roughly discoidal. Fine-grained, gray. One face slightly smoothed from rubbing, the other face convex. Faint pitting on one end from secondary use as a pounder.

S16. Pounder. Field 40/1. Surface. Igneous. Intact. L: 7.5, W: 3.2, Th: 2.1. Elongated, kidney bean-shaped, with rounded ends. Fine-grained, gray/green. Both ends pitted from pounding.

S17. Pounder. Field 40/1. Surface. Igneous. Intact. L: 8.5, W: 3.4, Th: 2.4. Elongated with rounded ends. Fine-grained, gray/green. Both ends pitted from use as a pounder. Both faces pitted from secondary use as a hammerstone.

S18. Pounder. Field 40/1. Surface. Igneous. Intact. L: 8.0, W: 6.0, Th: 3.4. Roughly discoidal. Coarse-grained, gray/green. Both ends pitted, one end more heavily so.

S19. Pounder. Field 40/1. Surface. Igneous. Fragmentary. L: 6.4, W: 2.1, Th: 7.5. Roughly quadrangular. Medium-grained, gray/green. Heavily chipped before use as a pounder. One end smoothed from pounding, the other only faintly so. Very faint signs of rubbing on the most fragmentary face.

S20. Pounder. Field 40/1. Surface. Igneous. Intact. L: 9.4, W: 5.8, Th: 4.6. Roughly piriform. Fine-grained, reddish-brown, possibly discolored by fire. One end well pitted, the other, smaller, end only slightly pitted. Two adjacent faces pitted from use as a hammerstone.

S21. Pounder. Field 40/1. Surface. Igneous. Intact. L: 7.0, W: 5.4, Th: 4.5. Ovoid. Fine-grained, gray/blue. One face convex, the other quite flat with an area of pitting from secondary use as a hammerstone. Both ends pitted from use as a pounder.

S23. Rubber-pounder. Field 40/1. Surface. Igneous. Fragmentary. L: 9.0, W: 11.2, Th: 4.1. Discoidal. Medium-grained, gray/green. Damaged before use. One face shows faint signs of rubbing. Both extremities and broken edge pitted from pounding.

S24. Rubber-pounder. Field 40/1. Surface. Igneous. Fragmentary. L: 9.8, W: 8.4, Th: 5.0. Roughly quadrangular. Fine-grained, gray/green. One face slightly smooth from rubbing. One end faceted and pitted from pounding. One edge and the other extremity pitted from pounding.

S25. Pounder. Area C. Unit 34. Igneous. Intact. L: 5.4, W: 5.2, Th: 3.0. Irregular shape, roughly piriform. Fine-grained, gray/green. Pointed end slightly pitted, as well as a small area on the side. One area smooth, perhaps from secondary use as a rubbing stone.

S26. Pecking stone. Field 40/1. Surface. Quartz. Fragmentary. L: 6.2, W: 4.6, Th: 3.8. Irregular spheroid. Off-white. Signs of use at both ends and along one face.

S27. Pecking stone. Field 40/1. Surface. Quartz. Fragmentary. L: 4.5, W: 4.3, Th: 2.4. Spherical. Off-white. Surface smoothed and micro-faceted from pecking.

S29. Pounder. Area A. Unit 1. Igneous. Intact. L: 8.0, W: 5.5, Th: 4.4. Ovoid. Fine-grained, gray/green. One face convex and pitted. One area on opposing face and both ends, well pitted.

S30. Rubber-pounder. Area A. Unit 1. Igneous. Fragmentary, unaltered river stone. L: 13.0, W: 6.0, Th: 3.0. Elongated, with one rounded end, the other missing. Fine-grained, gray. One end and a small area on the side pitted from use as a pounder. Along one side there is a smooth area, perhaps from use as a rubbing stone.

S31. Pestle? Area A. Unit 1. Igneous. Intact. L: 11.5, W: 6.7. Elongated, triangular transverse section. Intentionally

shaped. Fine-grained, gray. Large end pitted and faceted from pounding. One small area worn smooth and slightly polished. Small end heavily pitted and fractured from pounding.

S32. Rubber. Area C. Unit 2. Igneous. Fragmentary. L: 4.5, W: 4.1, Th: 2.2. Roughly quadrangular. Coarse-grained, gray/green. One side convex, the other missing. Well-defined flattened surface on edge.

S33. Rubber-pounder. Area A. Unit 1. Igneous. Intact. Th: 6.5. Thick discoidal. Fine-grained, gray. One face and edges worn smooth from rubbing. Circumference pitted from use as a pounder.

S34. Rubber-pounder. Area A. Unit 1. Igneous. Fragmentary. L: 11.7, W: 8.4, Th: 4.6. Roughly discoidal or "tortoise shell"-shaped. Fine-grained, gray. One face convex, the other missing. All edges faceted from use as a pounder. Very faint signs of rubbing on convex face.

S35. Pounder. Area A. I17C 6. Igneous. Intact. L: 9.0, W: 6.4, Th: 4.5. Roughly quadrangular. Fine-grained, gray/green. One face convex, the other flatter with an area missing near the edge. Both ends and an area on one side pitted. Very faint signs of rubbing on the flattened face.

S36. Rubber-pounder. Area A. Unit 1. Igneous. Intact. L: 10.0, W: 10.4, Th: 5.3. Discoidal. Coarse-grained, green/blue. One face very weathered. Heavily pitted on both faces and circumference. Smooth on one face from rubbing.

S37. Pounder. Area C. I24C 8. Igneous. Intact. L: 6.1, W: 3.4, Th: 2.8. Elongated with rounded ends. Fine-grain, gray/green. One end and small area on side pitted from use as a pounder.

S38. Quern. Area A. Unit 1. Igneous. Intact. W: 49.2, L: 25.8, Th: 11.5. Large, elongated with rounded ends. Fine-grained, blue/gray. Heavily calcified. Working surface concave in lateral and transverse section. Underside convex in lateral section, transverse section also convex. Edges worn.

S39. Pestle? Area A. Unit 1. Igneous. Intact. L: 13.5, W: 4.3, Th: 3.0. Elongated. Triangular in transverse and longitudinal sections. Fine-grained, blue/gray. Very faint signs of wear on large end.

S40. Rubber-pounder. Area A. Unit 1. Igneous. Intact. L: 9.8, W: 8.5, Th: 6.4. Roughly spherical in longitudinal section, lateral section irregular. Fine-grained, gray/green. Circumference and other angles used for pounding. Faint signs of wear from rubbing on face.

S41. Rubber-pounder. Area A. Unit 1. Igneous. Intact. L: 9.9, W: 8.9, Th: 3.8. Discoidal. Medium-grained, blue/gray. Both ends and one side faceted from pounding. Smooth area on one side from use as a rubbing stone. One face pitted from tertiary use as a hammerstone.

S42. Rubber-pounder. Area A. Unit 1. Igneous. Intact. L: 11.2, W: 6.2, Th: 5.5. Elongated, square in transverse section. Fine-grained, gray/blue. One round and one slightly pointed end. Pitting on both ends from use as a pounder. Faint signs of rubbing on one side. One face pitted from tertiary use as a hammerstone.

S43. Pounder. Area A. Unit 1. Igneous. Fragmentary. L: 12.5, W: 13.2, Th: 5.5. Elongated. Fine-grained, gray/black. One end rounded, the other missing. Regular pitting on one end and all other edges.

S44. Pecking stone. Area C. I24C 9. Quartz. Intact. L: 5.5, W: 5.3, Th: 4.2. Roughly triangular. Brown/white. Signs of use along the side and bottom. Preserved circumference micro-faceted from pecking.

S45. Pounder. Area A. Unit 1. Igneous. Fragmentary. L: 13.0, W: 11.5, Th: 7.6. Quadrangular in transverse section. Fine-grained, gray/black. Pitting on both ends. Some traces of pitting on one face from secondary use as a hammerstone.

S46. Pounder. Area A. Unit 1. Igneous. Intact. L: 15.2, W: 7.7, Th: 7.1. Elongated, triangular in section. Fine-grained, green. Well pitted on apex and both edges. Deep grooves around the base.

S47. Rubber-pounder. Area A. Unit 1. Igneous. Fragmentary. L: 15.3, W: 6.8, Th: 5.1. Elongated. Fine-grained, blue/gray. Both ends flattened. Transverse section oval. Several large chips missing prior to use as a pounder. Regular shape probably indicating original use as a Type 1 axe. Narrowing of both faces towards cutting edge and rounded butt. Re-used as a pounder. Cutting edge flattened in typical manner.

S48. Pounder. Area A. Unit 1. Igneous. Fragmentary. L: 5.1, W: 7.1, Th: 12.3. Small irregular fragment. One edge rounded, the other missing. Medium-grained, gray/green. Pitting on both ends. One face flat from previous use as a rubber.

S49. Pounder. Area A. Unit 1. Igneous. Intact. L: 6.0, W: 4.7, Th: 1.9. Ovoid, rounded at both ends. Fine-grained, gray/green. Pitting at the more pointed end.

S50. Pounder. Area C. Unit 10. Igneous. Intact. L: 5.2, W: 3.7, Th: 2.7. Roughly oval, one end pointed, the other rounded. Fine-grained, gray/green. Pitting on the pointed end from use as a pounder.

S51. Rubber-pounder. Area A. Unit 1. Igneous. Intact. L: 9.3, W: 8.4, Th: 4.9. Discoidal, rounded at both ends. Fine-grained, gray. Both ends and sides well pitted from use as a pounder. One surface smoothed and flattened from use as a rubbing stone. Edges of flattened surface also worn smooth. Area of faceting in center of convex face from tertiary use as a hammerstone. One end flattened from pounding.

S52. Palette. Area A. Unit 1. Limestone. Intact. L: 8.5, W: 8.3, Th: 1.6. Spheroid. Fine-grained, gray. Faint signs of pitting in small central area of one face smoothed from some form of activity.

S53. Pecking stone. Area A. Unit 1. Chalcedony. Intact. L: 9.1, W: 7.0, Th: 6.6. Irregular. White/blue-yellow. Narrow end pecked.

S54. Rubber-pounder. Area C. Unit 10. Igneous. Intact. L: 6.4, W: 4.6, Th: 2.6. Irregular, with rounded ends. Fine-grained, gray/green. Pitting on both ends and along broad side from pounding. One face smooth from secondary use as a rubbing stone.

S55. Pounder. Area A. Unit 1. Igneous. Intact. L: 6.7, W: 5.2, Th: 3.7. Ovoid, with rounded ends. Fine-grained, green. Slight pitting on both ends.

S56. Rubber-pounder. Area A. Unit 1. Igneous. Intact. L: 12.8, W: 10.0, Th: 3.2. Discoidal. Fine-grained, green. Well pitted on one rounded end from use as pounder. Faint signs of pitting on one side. One face slightly smooth from use as a rubbing stone.

S57. Pounder. Area C. Unit 10. Igneous. Fragmentary. L: 9.0, W: 11.5, Th: 4.2. Small irregular fragment of a quern. Medium-grained, green/gray. One face rounded, the other missing. Irregular pitting on edges of both faces.

S58. Hammerstone. Area A. Unit 1. Igneous. Intact. L: 8.5, W: 5.8, Th: 4.8. Elongated, with rounded ends. Fine-grained, gray/green. Both faces faceted from use as a hammerstone.

S59. Rubbing stone. Area A. Unit 1. Igneous. Intact. L: 8.5, W: 5.3, Th: 3.3. Ovoid, with rounded ends. Fine-grained, gray/green. One face smoothed from rubbing.

S60. Pounder. Area A. Unit 15. Igneous. Fragmentary. L: 5.8, W: 6.9, Th: 4.9. Quadrangular in lateral and transverse sections. Fine-grained, gray/green. One edge and the extremity of one face well pitted.

S61. Rubber. Area C. Unit 2. Igneous. Fragmentary. L: 12.0, W: 14.3, Th: 3.9. Roughly quadrangular, with both ends missing. Medium-grained, gray/green. Working surface cracked. Long section flat, transverse section convex. Convex face shows faint signs of smoothing from use as a rubbing stone.

S62. Hammerstone. Area A. Unit 1. Igneous. Intact. L: 9.2, W: 6.1, Th: 6.1. Ovoid, with rounded ends. Fine-grained, gray/blue. Very faint signs of pitting on one face.

S63. Rubber-pounder. Area A. Unit 1. Igneous. Intact. L: 11.5, W: 8.6, Th: 6.4. Triangular. Quadrangular in section. Fine-grained, gray/green. Pitting on apex and along one edge from use as a pounder. One side smooth from rubbing. Signs of irregular pitting on base from tertiary use as a hammerstone.

S64. Pounder. Area A. Unit 1. Igneous. Intact. L: 14.9, W: 8.7, Th: 3.0. Elongated, triangular. One end pointed, the other long and rounded. Fine-grained, gray/green. Faint signs of pitting on the pointed end.

S65. Hammerstone. Area A. I17C 5. Igneous. Intact. L: 6.7, W: 6.9, Th: 5.0. Ovoid. Fine-grained, green. One end rounded, the other flattened. Heavy pitting on the flat face, the rounded end and side of the convex face.

S66. Pounder. Area A. Unit 1. Igneous. Intact. L: 8.2, W: 5.9, Th: 6.1. Ovoid. Fine-grained, blue/gray. One end rounded, the other flattened. One face convex, the other flat. Flattened end pitted.

S67. Rubber-pounder. Area A. Unit 1. Igneous. Intact. L:10.0, W:9.7, Th:5.9. Roughly discoidal. Medium-grained, gray/green. Well faceted around the circumference. One face smooth from use as a rubbing stone.

S68. Hammerstone. Area A. Unit 1. Igneous. Intact. L: 5.4, W: 4.2, Th: 3.4. Ovoid. Fine-grained, green/gray. Slightly pitted on one face, with random pitting on the other and along one side from hammering.

S69. Pounder. Area C. I24C 9. Igneous. Fragmentary. L: 4.4, W: 13.0, Th: 2.9. Elongated. Small irregular quern fragment. Medium-grained, green/black. One edge rounded, the other missing. Heavily pitted on edges.

S70. Pounder. Area A. Unit 1. Igneous. Intact. L: 11.4, W: 7.5, Th: 4.4. Mushroom-shaped, triangular in transverse section. Medium-grained, gray/green. Small area missing at the extremity of one face. Small rounded end flattened and well pitted from pounding as well as edges. Larger end heavily pitted.

S71. Gaming stone, Senet. Area C. Unit 2. Limestone. Fragmentary. L: 17.7, W: 18.1, Th: 7.8. Sub-rectangular fragment of tabular limestone. One face pecked with two parallel rows of four irregular depressions.

S72. Gaming stone, Senet. Area C. Unit 2. Limestone. Intact. L: 23.3, W: 1.9, Th: 8.8. Sub-rectangular fragment of tabular limestone. Two intact parallel rows of 10 shallow pecked depressions. Third row damaged. Length of row of ten depressions=12 cm, width=4.2 cm.

S73. Grooved stone. Area A. Unit 1. Limestone. Intact. L: 17.5, W: 9.6, Th: 4.4. Elongated, irregular shaped coarse limestone with many small inclusions. Deep regular pecked groove around center, approximately 2.7 cm wide with maximum depth of 1 cm. No obvious signs of wear at either end.

S74. Pounder. Area A. Unit 1. Igneous. Intact. L: 22.8, W: 10.5, Th: 8.4. Elongated, quadrangular in transverse section. Fine-grained, gray/green. Well pitted on convex face, apex, and all angles. Very heavy pounding on edges.

S75. Gaming stone, Senet. Cemetery B. Surface. Fragmentary and weathered. L: 16.5, W: 13.0, Th: 5.9. Fragment of tabular limestone. 3 parallel rows of 7, 7, and 6 depressions. Extrapolated L of 3 x 10 design = 21 cm, W =7 cm.

S76. Rubbing stone. Area A. Unit 1. Igneous. Intact. L: 22.5, W: 14.7, Th: 4.6. Elongated, with rounded ends. Medium-grained, gray/green. One side convex. Work surface flat and smooth from rubbing. Edges of work surface worn. Work surface convex both in transverse and longitudinal section. Transverse striations from use as a rubbing stone.

S77. Gaming stone, Senet. Area C. Unit 10. Fragmentary. L: 19.4, W: 15.3, Th: 6.0. Extrapolated L of 3 x 10 design = 21 cm, W of 3 x 10 = 7.5 cm. Fragment of tabular limestone. Three rows of 5, 6 and 7 shallow depressions.

S78. Gaming stone, Senet. Area C. Unit 10. Intact. L: 23.5, W: 21.5, Th: 7.7. Badly weathered. Secondary depression to one side. Extrapolated L of 3 x 10 motif = 18 cm, W = 6 cm. Rounded piece of tabular limestone. Three rows of parallel depressions.

S79. Perforated stone. Area A. Unit 1. Limestone. Fragmentary. L: 41.7, W: 24.8, Th: 7.1. Quadrangular, the two long sides parallel. One end at right angles, the other diagonal. One face very smooth, the other rough and weathered. Diagonal edge also smooth, the others irregular. The slab apparently broken along both sides. The longest of these has a drilled perforation 3.5 cm from base; max. depth of perf. = 3.4 cm; min. D of perf. = 2.1 cm. Other end has remains of similar drilled perforation, probably of same dimensions. Another drilled hole, entirely preserved, 1.7 cm from this perforation, max. D = 9 cm, min. D = 3 cm. Usage unknown.

S80. Gaming stone, Senet. Area C. Unit 10. Fragmentary. L: 14.2, W: 8.5, Th: 4.5. Extrapolated L of gaming area = 12 cm, W = 3.3 cm, av. depth of depression = 0.7 cm. Sub-rectangular fragment of tabular limestone. Two well preserved parallel rows of 8 and 9 depressions. The third row is badly damaged.

S81. Axe, Type 1. Area A. Surface. Igneous. Fragmentary. L: 4.3, W: 4.6, Th: 1.0. Sub-rectangular. Fine-grained, gray/green. One end missing. Convex faces and edges. Cutting edge tapered and blunt.

S82. Rubber-pounder. Area A. Unit 1. Igneous. Intact apart from one chip near apex. L: 14.8, W: 7.5, Th: 6.1. Elongated, quadrangular in transverse section. Fine-grained, gray/green. One side smooth from use as a rubbing stone. Pitting on both ends and angles from use as a pounder. Traces of pitting on one face from tertiary use as a hammerstone.

S83. Rubber-pounder. Area A. Unit 1. Igneous. Intact. L: 11.3, W: 6.1, Th: 4.5. Elongated, with rounded ends. Medium-grained, gray/green. One face flat and smooth from use as a rubbing stone. Both ends pitted and flattened from pounding. Traces of pitting on convex face from tertiary use as a hammerstone.

S84. Pecking stone. Area A. Unit 1. Chalcedony. Intact. L: 5.3, W: 5.4, Th: 3.9. Spheroid. Blue/gray. Traces of use on two faces.

S85. Pounder, Type 1. Cemetery A. I6D 3. Igneous. Fragmentary. L: 11.9, W: 6.1, Th: 4.4. Fragment of a saddle quern. Fine-grained, gray/green. One end rounded, the other missing. One face concave, the other flat. There are traces of pitting at the extremity of both faces.

S86. Rubbing stone. Area A. I17A 3. Igneous. Intact. L: 5.1, W: 4.6, Th: 2.4. Spheroid. Medium-grained, brown/red. One face smooth from use as a rubbing stone.

S87. Pounder. Area A. Unit 1. Phase I. Igneous. Intact. L: 5.2, W: 4.0, Th: 2.5. Elongated, with rounded ends. Fine-grained, blue/gray. Pitting on one end.

S88. Rubber-pounder. Area A. Unit 1. Igneous. Intact. L: 19.8, W: 7.5, Th: 5.5. Elongated, triangular in transverse section. Fine-grained, blue/gray. Pitting on both ends and along one edge from use as a pounder. Deep indentations at one extremity. One face worn from use as a rubbing stone.

S89. Pounder, Type 2. Cemetery A. I6D 5. Igneous. Intact. L: 13.1, W: 10.6, Th: 4.9. Discoidal. Fine-grained, gray/green. One end flattened and pitted, the other also slightly pitted.

S90. Function uncertain. Area C. Unit 10. Igneous. Intact. L: 5.6, W: 4.0, Th: 3.0. Irregular-shaped. Fine-grained, blue/gray. One face with high polish. Usage unknown, burnisher?

S91. Pounder, Type 1. Cemetery A. I6D 8. Igneous. Intact. L: 12.7, W: 6.1, Th: 5.0. Elongated, triangular in transverse section. Fine-grained, gray/green. Pitting on both extremities. Marks of pitting on one face from secondary use as a hammerstone.

S92. Hammerstone. Area A. Unit 1. Igneous. Intact. L: 8.4, W: 5.6, Th: 3.5. Roughly quadrangular. Fine-grained, gray. Pitting on one face from use as a hammerstone.

S93. Rubbing stone. Area C. Unit 2. Limestone. Intact. L: 11.8, W: 6.4, Th: 2.5. Quadrangular. Fine-grained, buff-colored. The edges rounded and worn. One face calcified, therefore impossible to detect use wear. The opposite face smooth from use as a rubbing stone.

S94. Rubber-pounder. Area C. Unit 2. Igneous. Intact. L: 6.5, W: 6.4, Th: 3.3. Roughly discoidal. Fine-grained, gray/blue. One face smooth from use as a rubbing stone. Traces of pitting on two edges from secondary use as a pounder.

S95. Rubber-pounder. Area C. Unit 17. Igneous. Intact. L: 9.1, W: 5.2, Th: 4.0. Elongated, square in lateral section. Medium-grained, dark gray. Light pounding on one end and rubbing on one face.

S96. Rubber-pounder. Area A. Unit 1. Igneous. Intact. L: 10.8, W: 10.4, Th: 4.5. Discoidal. Fine-grained, blue/gray. One face slightly convex. Pitting on all edges from use as a pounder. One face slightly flattened towards one edge and smoothed from rubbing. Irregular pitting of both faces from tertiary use as a hammerstone.

S97. Rubbing stone. Area C. Unit 10. Igneous. Fragmentary. L: 13.7, W: 17.9, Th: 6.0. Hemispherical. Edges rounded except for broken section. Medium-grained, gray/green. The original longitudinal section was flat to slightly concave. Transverse section convex, indicating use as a rubbing stone.

S99. Pecking stone. Area A. Unit 1. Quartz. Intact. L: 5.4, W: 5.3. Cuboid/spheroid. White. Two faces rather smooth, other surfaces micro-faceted.

S100. Pounder. Area C. Unit 10. Igneous. Fragmentary. L: 9.1, W: 5.7, Th: 4.0. Quadrangular in longitudinal section, triangular in transverse section. Fine-grained, gray/blue. One end rounded, the other missing. Pitting on one end from use as a pounder. Traces of abrasion on one edge and the extremities of one face.

S101. Rubber. Area A. Unit 1. Igneous. Intact. L: 29.1, W: 15.8, Th: 3.9. Elongated, with rounded ends. Fine-grained, gray/green. Working surface is convex both in longitudinal and transverse sections. The underside is convex and flattened in middle. Some areas highly polished, with distinct scratch marks at right angles to longitudinal axis.

S102. Gaming stone, Senet. Area C. Unit 10. Limestone. Fragmentary. L: 11.4, W: 11.6, Th: 5.0. Roughly quadrangular. Small fragment of a Senet gaming stone with one row of 2 and one row of 3 pecked depressions.

S103. Function uncertain. Stone tool blank? Area C. Unit 10. Igneous. Intact. L: 7.5, W: 5.2, Th: 3.1. Ovoid. Fine-grained, white/gray. Usage uncertain as there is no pitting or smooth surfaces. Its almost perfect shape and size suggest it was intended for some specific function.

S104. Pounder. Area A. Unit 20. Igneous. Intact. L: 8.4, W: 7.0, Th: 3.2. Roughly piriform. Fine-grained, gray/green. Apex and one edge pitted.

S105. Palette. Area A. Unit 1. Limestone. Fragmentary. L: 13.6, W: 10.1, Th: 2.4. Roughly discoidal. Fine-grained, white/gray. Circular area on one face depressed and smooth.

S106. Rubber-pounder. Area A. Unit 1. Phase I. Igneous. Intact. L: 8.5, W: 6.4, Th: 3.1. Oval in lateral section. Medium-grained, gray/green. One face smooth from use as a rubbing stone. Traces of pitting on the edges and both ends from use as a pounder.

S107. Rubber. Area C. Unit 10. Igneous. Fragmentary. L: 13.6, W: 15.6, Th: 3.9. Elongated with one rounded end, the other missing. One side convex, the other slightly concave. Transverse section of work face slightly concave with worn edges.

S109. Gaming stone, Senet. Area C. Unit 10. Fragmentary. L: 19.8, W: 11.2, Th: 8.0. Roughly quadrangular piece of tabular limestone. Fine-grained, off-white. Badly chipped and weathered. One face has 3 irregular rows of small (av. D = 1.0 cm) depressions, 5, 3, 3. Attribution slightly questionable due to weathered pitted surface of stone.

S110. Lid? Area C. Unit 2. Limestone. Fragmentary. L: 32.1, W: 28.4, Th: 4.9. Approximately discoidal. Off-white. One end missing and a section broken away from other end. One face almost flat with small central indentation, other face slightly convex. Some shaping at one end.

S111. Stone with depression. Area C. Unit 2. Limestone. Intact. L: 12.6, W: 10.0, Th: 4.7. Roughly rectangular in plan. Off-white. Central concave pecked area with rough surface, D of concave area = 7 cm, max. D = 1.4 cm.

S112. Rubber. Area C. Unit 10. Igneous. Fragmentary. L: 22.6, W: 19.5, Th: 3.8. Elongated. One end rounded, the other missing. Underside flattened. Work surface slightly concave in longitudinal section, convex in transverse section. Edges well worn.

S113. Pounder. Area C. Unit 10. Igneous. Intact. L: 7.6, W: 4.5, Th: 2.7. Elongated. Fine-grained, blue/gray. Small pitted area on one extremity.

S114. Gaming stone, Senet. Area C. Unit 10. Fragmentary. L: 17.8, W: 17.1, Th: 8.8. Extrapolated L of 3 x 10 motif = 20 cm, W = 7 cm. Tabular fragment of limestone. Three roughly parallel rows of 6, 4, and 3 pecked depressions.

S115. Pounder. Area C. Unit 10. Igneous. Intact. L: 7.6, W: 7.4, Th: 4.8. Irregularly shaped, triangular in transverse section. One end rounded, the other more pointed and flat. Faint signs of pitting on both ends from use as a pounder. Irregular pitting on flat face from secondary use as a hammerstone.

S116. Pounder. Area C. Unit 10. Igneous. Fragmentary. L: 11.5, W: 8.3, Th: 4.8. Triangular in transverse section. Fine-grained, gray/green. One face convex, the other (the working surface) flat. Both ends missing. On the apex and edges of

convex face originally used as a rubber, there is now pitting from use as a pounder. On convex face, abrasions from secondary use as a hammerstone. Numerous deep indentations on base of the stone.

S117. Rubbing stone/whetstone? Area C. Unit 10. Limestone. Intact. L: 18.6, W: 4.0, Th: 3.8. Elongated, with rounded ends. Off-white. One face flat and smooth from rubbing or sharpening, the other concave and tapering to the extremity.

S118. Rubber. Area C. Unit 10. Igneous. Fragmentary. L: 5.8, W: 5.6, Th: 2.9. Irregularly shaped, quadrangular in transverse section. Medium-grained, green/gray. Both faces flat, edges very worn. No signs of secondary use. Very weathered.

S119. Palette. Area A. Unit 1. Igneous. Fragmentary. L: 26.5, W: 17.3, Th: 2.2. Roughly triangular. Fine-grained, gray. One face rough and irregular, the other (used as a work surface) is flat and smooth.

S120. Gaming stone, Senet. Area C. I24A Surface. Limestone. Fragmentary. L: 15.2, W: 9.8, Th: 4.6. Roughly triangular in shape. Fine-grained, gray. Face with depressions flat, the reverse has a large sliver missing. Sides flat. Obverse is reddened by fire? A well-preserved row of 8 small depressions next to less well preserved row of 4. Third row of 3 depressions which are slightly larger. Average diameter of well preserved depressions 1.0., depth, 0.3. Two larger depressions to one side, 1.9 D. Extrapolated L of depressions = 12 cm, W = 3.5 cm.

S121. Rubber. Area A. Unit 1. Igneous. Fragmentary. L: 26.6, W: 17.1, Th: 6.3. Elongated, with rounded ends. Fine-grained, dark gray. One end and the side of one face missing. Underside flattened. Work surface slightly concave in lateral section and convex in transverse section.

S122. Rubber-pounder. Area A. Unit 3. Igneous. Intact. L:7.3, W:5.9, Th:4.1. Ovoid. Fine-grained, gray/green. One end slightly flattened and pitted. Other end shows faint traces of pitting as does a small area on one edge, from use as a pounder. One face smooth from rubbing.

S123. Axe, Type 2. Area A. Unit 1. Igneous. Intact. L: 6.7, W: 3.6, Th: 1.2. Roughly oval. Fine-grained, gray/green. One side well flattened and smooth, the other crudely shaped. Butt and cutting edge crudely flaked. Signs of light pitting on smooth face.

S124. Rubber-pounder. Area A. Unit 3. Igneous. Intact. L: 9.6, W: 8.5, Th: 5.2. Discoidal. Fine-grained, gray/green. One face convex, the other flat. Both ends rounded. Pitting on both ends and edges from use as a rubber. One face smooth and flattened from use as a pounder. The opposing convex face shows marks of pitting from tertiary use as a hammerstone.

S125. Pounder. Area A. Unit 3. Igneous. Intact. L: 12.5, W: 4.6, Th: 3.6. Elongated, with rounded ends. Fine-grained, gray/ black. Quadrangular in transverse section. One face flat, the other convex. Faint traces of pitting on one end. Irregular pitting along edge of one face from secondary use as a hammerstone.

S126. Pecking stone. Area A. Unit 1. Chalcedony. Intact. L: 4.7, W: 4.6. Cuboid. White/brown. Whole surface micro-faceted.

S127. Rubber-pounder. Area A. Unit 1. Phase I. Igneous. Intact. L: 11.3, W: 8.8, Th: 3.9. Discoidal. Medium-grained. Gray/green. One face flattened and fairly smooth from use as a rubbing stone. Pitting on both ends and along edges from use as a pounder. Irregular pitting on convex face from tertiary use as a hammerstone.

S128. Axe, Type 1. Area A. Unit 1. Igneous. Intact. L: 13.5, W: 6.4, Th: 3.2. Triangular. Fine-grained, blue/gray. One end pointed, the other square and flattened. Pitting on pointed end from secondary use as a pounder. Heavily pitted on both faces and along one edge from secondary use as a hammerstone.

S129. Pounder. Area C. Unit 2. Igneous. Intact. L: 8.6, W: 5.4, Th: 4.0. Elongated, with rounded ends. Fine-grained, gray/green. Well pitted on one end, slightly pitted on other from use as a pounder.

S130. Pounder. Area A. Unit 1. Igneous. Intact. L: 18.6, W: 16.6, Th: 4.4. Large discoidal. Fine-grained, gray/green. Well pitted on each end and around circumference. Heavy irregular pitting on each face from secondary use as a hammerstone.

S131. Pounder. Area C. Unit 2. Igneous. Intact. L: 24.6, W: 7.7, Th: 6.3. Elongated. Fine-grained, green. One end rounded, the other square and flat. Rectangular in transverse section. Both ends and edges well pitted from use as a pounder. Entire stone pitted, probably intentionally for purpose of shaping.

S132. Axe, Type 1. Area A. Unit 1. Igneous. Intact. L: 16.3, W: 6.4, Th: 3.2. Elongated. Fine-grained, gray/green. Irregular rounded butt. One face flattened, the other convex. Cutting edge convex, flattened and blunt. Probably in process of manufacture since original chips and irregularities not yet ground away. Signs of pecking on one edge, probably from shaping process and not from pounding: this edge most badly chipped. No signs of shaping on convex face. Well smoothed towards cutting edge. Blunt edge either part of shaping process or from secondary use.

S133. Hammerstone. Area A. Unit 1. Igneous. Intact. L: 8.2, W: 5.8, Th: 3.4. Ovoid. Pitting on one face from use.

S135. Pounder. Area C. Unit 10. Igneous. Fragmentary. L: 7.1, W: 8.9, Th: 1.0. Triangular in transverse section. Fine-grained, gray/green. Traces of pounding on apex from use as a pounder.

S136. Rubber-pounder. Area A. Unit 1. Phase I. Igneous. Intact. L: 7.4, W: 6.5, Th: 3.4. Irregularly shaped. Medium-grained, dark green. Signs of burnishing on both faces from use. Elongated, with rounded ends. Rectangular in transverse section. Well pitted, flattened area in center of one face from use as a hammerstone. One end flattened and slightly pitted from secondary use as a pounder.

S137. Hammerstone. Area A. Unit 3. Igneous. Intact. L: 7.0, W: 5.0, Th: 3.8. Elongated, with rounded ends. Fine-grained, gray. Rectangular in transverse section. Well pitted, flattened area in center of one face from use as a hammerstone. One end also flattened and slightly pitted from secondary use as a pounder.

S138. Rubbing stone. Area C. Unit 10. Igneous. Fragmentary. L: 6.4, W: 4.2, Th: 4.1. Roughly rectangular, both ends missing. Fine-grained, gray/green. One face slightly convex, other face flattened. Roughly rectangular in transverse section. Smooth, slightly depressed area near edge from rubbing.

S139. Pounder. Area A. Unit 1. Igneous. Intact. L: 12.1, W: 9.9, Th: 3.4. Roughly quadrangular. Fine-grained, gray/white. Part of one face missing prior to use as a pounder. Signs of pounding on all edges, especially those previously damaged.

S140. Pendant. Area C. Unit 10. Picrolite. Fragmentary. L: 1.8, Th: 0.4. Bottle-shaped. Dark and light green.

S141. Worked picrolite. Area C. Unit 10. Fragmentary. L: 1.9, W: 1.9. Spheroid. Light green. Partially drilled button, toggle, or spindle whorl.

S142. Worked picrolite. Area A. Unit 1. Intact. L: 4.7, W: 8.0, Th: 0.7. Elongated. Light green. Scratch marks clearly visible on all faces. Function uncertain.

S143. Pendant. Area A. Unit 1. Picrolite. Intact. L: 2.3, W: 1.6, Th: 0.7. Sub-rectangular. Light green. Central perforation with rounded corners. D of inner perforation = 6 mm.

S144. Figurine. Area A. Unit 1. Picrolite. Fragmentary. L: 1.7, W: 1.4, Th: 0.4. Cruciform type. Dark green. Triangular head, flattened at the back, with perforation. No facial features. Medium length neck. Left arm outstretched, pointed at the end. Right arm missing. Left breast visible on body. Lower body missing. Tool marks visible on both sides of head, neck, and body.

S145. Worked picrolite. Area C. Unit 10. Fragmentary. L: 4.5, W: 0.9, Th: 0.5. Elongated, quadrangular in section. Light green. One end missing. Clear signs of having been cut and shaped. Function uncertain.

S146. Worked picrolite. Area C. Unit 2. Altered pebble. Picrolite. Intact. L: 2.4, W: 1.8, Th: 0.9. Roughly rectangular. Mottled, light green/white. Scratch and polishing marks visible. Intended to be a pendant?

S147. Worked picrolite. Area C. Unit 10. Intact. L: 2.9, W: 1.7, Th: 0.4. Oval in shape. Mottled, dark gray/green. Some evidence of shaping around the edges. Usage uncertain.

S148. Worked picrolite. Burnisher?. Area C. Unit 10. Intact. L: 2.9, W: 1.7, Th: 0.7. Elongated: oval in section. Mottled, white/green/brown. High shine on surface. Possible signs of shaping. Probably used as a burnisher. Highly burnished area towards larger extremity with a few diagonal, very faint striations visible. The edges of the burnishing surface are angular and sharp from wear of the burnishing area. Fits nicely between thumb and index finger. Appears to have served as a burnisher.

S149. Worked Picrolite. Area A. Unit 16. Altered pebble. Picrolite. Intact. L: 1.9, W: 1.8, Th: 1.0. Ovoid. Light green/white. Very smooth surface. Little evidence of shaping. Function uncertain.

S150. Pendant. Area A. Unit 1. Picrolite. Intact. "Figure-8" shaped. Light green. Biconical drilled perforations. D of small perforation = 3 mm, D of large perforation = 5 mm.

S151. Quern. Area A. Unit 3. Limestone. Fragmentary. L: 40.0, W: 30.5, Th: 4.2-21. Roughly rectilinear. Preserved end flattened, thickening towards end. Work surface curved at preserved end, sloping down and thinning at broken end. Underside flattened and pecked for initial shaping and steadying. Peck marks visible on work surface and above work area. Concave in lateral and transverse sections. Max. thickness of grinding surface = 16.5 cm.

S152. Quern. Area A. Unit 3. Limestone. Intact. L: 49.5, W: 22.5 min., Th: 5.2 min. Ovoid. Both ends curved, tapering to one end. Very concave work surface, base only slightly flattened. Large peck marks on underside. Work surface well smoothed, especially toward lower, narrower end. Work surface concave in lateral section.

S153. Rubber. K21D 1. Igneous. Fragmentary. L: 7.3, W: 3.1, Th: 2.8. Triangular in transverse section. Medium-grained, green/black. Differentiation between work surface and underside not clearly defined, due to size of fragment. One face slightly concave, opposing face flat. Edges worn, though not apparently from reuse as a tool.

S154. Pecking stone. Area A. Unit 1. Chalcedony. Fragmentary. D: 5.4. Spheroid. White/buff. Micro-faceted.

S155. Rubber-pounder. Area A. Unit 1. Igneous. Intact. L: 13.0, W: 9.1, Th: 3.1. Discoidal. Fine-grained, gray/green. Quadrangular in transverse and lateral sections. Both ends flattened and heavily pitted. Extended flattened areas at center

of edges pitted from use as a pounder. One face flattened and smoothed from rubbing. On opposing, slightly convex, face irregular pitting from tertiary use as a hammerstone.

S156. Pounder. Area B. C20A 2. Igneous. Intact. L: 5.8, W: 4.3, Th: 2.3. Elongated, with rounded ends. Quadrangular in transverse and lateral sections. Medium-grained, gray/green. Traces of pitting on both ends from use as a pounder. Pitting on center of one face from secondary use as a hammerstone.

S157. Pounder. Area A. Unit 1. Phase I. Igneous. Intact. L: 9.2, W: 7.2, Th: 5.3. Roughly discoidal. Medium-grained, gray/green. Triangular in transverse section. Both ends rounded. Traces of pitting on both ends and at the edge of one face.

S158. Pounder. Area A. Unit 1. Igneous. Intact. L: 6.9, W: 3.1. Spheroid. Medium-grained, gray/green. Traces of pitting on edges and one end.

S159. Axe, Type 1. Area A. Unit 1. Igneous. Intact. L: 11.6, W: 5.2, Th: 2.9. Elongated, irregular rounded butt. Fine-grained, gray/green. One face flattened, the other convex. Cutting edge square, flattened and blunt. Traces of chip marks on both edges and flat face. Flattened face smooth, tapering towards rounded end, which shows signs of pitting. Convex face darker than rest of tool and very highly burnished.

S160. Rubber. Area A. Unit 1. Igneous. Intact. L: 42.8, W: 20.2, Th: 3.4. Elongated, with rounded ends. Medium-grained, gray/green. One edge chipped before use as a quern. Work surface convex in transverse section and concave in lateral section, especially at one end. All edges well worn. L of work surface = 40.2 cm, W = 20 cm. Transverse striations prove it served as a rubber.

S161. Gaming stone, Senet. K21D Surface. Limestone. L: 20, W: 11, Th: 7.3. Roughly rectangular piece of tabular limestone. 3 parallel rows of 6, 4, and 3 depressions run diagonally across one face.

S162. Pounder. Area C. I24C 1. Igneous. Intact. D: 4.3. Cuboid, quadrangular in transverse and lateral sections. Medium-grained, gray/green. One face smooth from use as a rubbing stone (?). Traces of pitting on all other faces and edges from pounding (?). Signs of wear may also have been from shaping process.

S163. Gaming stone, Senet. Area A. Unit 4. Limestone. Fragmentary. L: 32.0, W: 21.0, Th: 11.5. L of 3 x 10 motif = ca. 20 cm, W = ca. 8 cm. Sub-rectangular fragment of tabular limestone, both faces smooth. Off-white. Three parallel rows of 10 well preserved shallow depressions each.

S164. Rubber-pounder. Area A. Unit 1. Phase I. Igneous. Intact. L: 13.0, W: 9.9, Th: 3.6. Discoidal, quadrangular in lateral section. Fine-grained, gray. Both ends and edges well pitted from pounding. One face flattened and smoothed from rubbing.

S165. Pendant. Area C. Unit 17. Picrolite. Intact. L: 2.0, W: 0.9, Th: 0.35. Rectangular. Light green. Both faces parallel, well smoothed with some scratch marks. Ends slightly rounded, edges straight. Perforation perhaps drilled, biconical in section and piercing pendant diagonally. Signs of wear on upper edge of perforation, indicating prolonged use/wear. Max. D of perf. = 0.35 cm, min. D = 0.2 cm.

S167. Gaming stone, Senet. Area A. H17C. Limestone. Fragmentary. L: 17.3, W: 14.6, Th: 7.0. Longitudinal section roughly rectangular, transverse section triangular. On a smooth area, 15 x 11 cm, three rows of five shallow depressions have been pecked. W of playing area = 5.5 cm, extrapolated L = 20 cm, av. D = 1.1 cm, depth = 2 mm. A large shallow depression pecked to one side.

S168. Gaming stone, Senet. Field 40. Surface. Limestone. Fragmentary. L: 14.6, W: 12.5, Th: 5.4. Sub-rectangular fragment of tabular limestone. One face smooth, the other irregular convex. Unbroken edges uneven. Smooth face is pecked with two irregular lines of eight or nine shallow depressions. Av. D = 1 cm, av. depth = 2.5 mm.

S169. Pecking stone. Area A. Unit 1. Chalcedony. Fragmentary. L: 5.0, W: 4.3, Th: 3.4. Spheroid. Gray/brown translucent. Work surface abraded.

S170. Pounder. Area A. Unit 1. Igneous. Intact. L: 5.7, W: 4.4, Th: 3.2. Flattened ovoid. Fine-grained, light gray. One end very slightly pitted.

S171. Pounder. Area A. Unit 1. Phase I. Igneous. Intact. L: 9.2, W: 8.2, Th: 6.1. Flattened ovoid. Fine-grained, light gray. One end slightly pitted. Faint signs of pitting on both faces.

S172. Pounder. Area A. Unit 1. Igneous. Intact. L: 6.7, W: 5.0, Th: 2.0. Flattened oval/discoidal. Fine-grained, gray. Slightly pitted on both ends.

S173. Pounder. Area C. Unit 17. Igneous. Intact. L: 8.8, W: 5.0, Th: 4.1. Ovoid. Fine-grained, light gray. Very faint signs of pounding.

S174. Rubber-pounder. Area A. H17D 1. Igneous. Intact. L: 8.3, W: 5.3, Th: 5.1. Ovoid. Medium-grained, light gray. Black vein around diameter. Very smooth with traces of pounding on the more rounded end. One face slightly flattened from rubbing or grinding. Signs of pounding on rubbing surface.

S175. Pounder. Area A. Unit 5. Igneous. Intact. L: 8.1, W: 5.4, Th: 4.8. Ovoid, transverse section quadrangular. Medium-grained, gray/black/white. Smooth on all surfaces. Signs of pounding in various areas.

S176. Rubber. Area A. H18B. Surface. Igneous. Fragmentary. L: 13.1, W: 6.7, Th: 4.7. Sub-rectangular. Coarse-grained, gray to black/blue/green. Work surface well smoothed but slightly pitted. Original would have had slightly convex transverse section. Weathered. Underside unusually well smoothed.

S177. Adze. Area C. Unit 2. Igneous. Fragmentary. L: 3.2, W: 3.3, Th: 1.4. Oval in transverse section. Very fine-grained, light gray/red. Butt not preserved. Very smooth surfaces, sharpened on one side. Cutting edge well beveled. One face ground, the other only slightly so.

S178. Pestle. Area A. Unit 6. Igneous. Intact. L: 11.1, W: 5.3, Th: 5.3. Elongated, one end rounded. Fine-grained, light gray. Round in transverse section, truncated conical (?) in longitudinal section. One end flattened from use as a pestle. Surface pitted from possible secondary use as a pounder. Shaped to produce a symmetrical tool.

S180. Pounder. Area B. Unit 14. Igneous. Intact. L: 11.3, W: 8.6, Th: 5.2. Sub-rectangular. Fine-grained, light gray. Ovoid in transverse section, slightly wedge-shaped in longitudinal section. Both faces very smooth. One end pitted and faceted from use as a pounder, other end heavily abraded and chipped from use as a chopper. Possible secondary use as a hammerstone. This tool may be the cutting edge of an unusually large axe, as indicated by the striations on the sides left from the original shaping of the tool.

S181. Rubbing stone. Area A. Unit 3. Igneous. Intact. L: 11.8, W: 8.6, Th: 4.3. Discoidal, oval in both sections. Fine-grained, gray/blue. White vein around the diameter. Faint traces of pounding on one end and one side. Unusual faint transverse striations adjacent to lateral pitting.

S182. Pounder. Area A. Unit 3. Igneous. Intact. L: 10.8, W: 6.1, Th: 5.6. Elongated, ovoid in transverse section, round in lateral section. Fine-grained, light gray. All surfaces pitted from shaping? Only one small area preserved. One end pitted from use as a pounder. Similar to original smoothness of a river-worn pebble.

S183. Rubbing stone. Area B. Unit 14. Limestone. Fragmentary. L: 9.4, W: 6.5, Th: 2.4. Sub-rectangular. White. Ovoid in transverse section and sub-rectangular in longitudinal section. One face flattened, the other convex. One face smooth, the other slightly pitted from rubbing.

S184. Rubbing stone. Area B. Unit 14. Limestone. Fragmentary. L: 4.5, W: 3.7, Th: 3.0. Roughly rectangular, ovoid in transverse section. White. Both ends flat, both faces convex. One face smooth from rubbing.

S186. Axe, Type 2. Area A. Unit 7. Igneous. Intact. L: 5.9, W: 3.8, Th: 1.1. Ovoid, one face flat, the other heavily flaked. Very fine-grained, light gray. No signs of wear on cutting edge. Morphologically identical to Dikaios' "flaked celts."

Either this is a surface find collected in the vicinity of *Teppes* or it is an archaizing tool type.

S187. Rubber-pounder. Area A. Unit 3. Igneous. Intact. L: 13.1, W: 9.1, Th: 5.8. Ovoid, oval in transverse section, slightly wedge-shaped in longitudinal section. Coarse-grained, gray/white. Pitted on one end and one side from use as a pounder. One face smooth from rubbing.

S188. Rubber. Area A. Unit 3. Igneous. Intact. L: 42.0, W: 15.6, Th: 3.6. Elongated oval. Coarse-grained, gray/white/black. Work surface concave in longitudinal section, convex in transverse section. Underside irregular and flat. Both sides abraded. Work surface pitted and smooth from use as quern. Transverse striations from use as a rubbing stone.

S189. Pounder. Area A. Unit 3. Igneous. Fragmentary. L: 16.6, W: 9.8, Th: 5.3. Sub-rectangular. Medium-grained, gray/white/green. One side flat, the other convex. Pitted on narrow end from use as a pounder. Broken in antiquity and re-used as such.

S190. Pounder. Area A. Unit 32. Igneous. Intact. L: 15.4, W: 11.6, Th: 7.3. Sub-rectangular, irregular. Sub-rectangular in section. Medium-grained, gray. Signs of pitting on one side from use as a pounder.

S191. Rubber-pounder. Area B. Unit 13. Limestone. Fragmentary. L: 11.6, W: 5.4, Th: 3.9. Elongated. White. One face flat, the other convex. One end rounded, the other faceted. Rounded end pitted from pounding, the other missing.

S192. Pounder. Area A. Unit 36. Igneous. Intact. L: 11.5, W: 10.2, Th: 6.9. Circular, oval in both sections. Fine-grained, light gray. Pitted on both ends. Pitting in the center of both faces from secondary use as a hammerstone.

S193. Axe, Type 2. Area A. G17D Surface. Igneous. Intact. L: 11.6, W: 6.1, Th: 2.7. Sub-rectangular. Medium-grained, gray. One face flat, the other convex. One face very smooth, the other abraded. Possibly used for rubbing?

S194. Pounder. Area A. Unit 6. Igneous. Intact. L: 11.9, W: 8.3, Th: 7.9. Cylindrical, oval in both sections. Coarse-grained, gray/white. Narrow end faceted from use as a pounder. Other end broken.

S195. Quern. Area A. G17B 2. Limestone. Fragmentary. L: 25.5, W: 12.2, Th: 6.4. Triangular. Coarse-grained, white limestone. One face concave, the other flat.

S196. Work surface. Area A. Unit 3. Igneous. Fragmentary. L: 18.0, W: 8.9, Th: 7.8. Irregular shape. Medium-grained, gray/blue. Surface pitted from pounding.

S197. Pounder. Area A. Unit 35. Igneous. Intact. L: 8.2, W: 5.8, Th: 2.8. Oval in both sections. Coarse-grained, gray/white. Pitting on both ends. Abrading on one side.

S198. Pecking stone. Area A. Unit 6. Chalcedony. Fragmentary. L: 4.7, W: 4.2, Th: 2.2. Ovoid. White. One face flat, the other convex. Surface rough from use as a pecking stone.

S199. Rubbing stone. Area B. Unit 14. Igneous. Intact. L: 11.0, W: 5.2, Th: 5.2. Elongated, truncated conical in longitudinal section, round in transverse section. Fine-grained, gray. One end rounded. One end flattened from use as a pestle. All surfaces pitted from shaping.

S200. Pounder. Area A. Unit 3. Igneous. Fragmentary. L: 9.7, W: 8.6, Th: 3.6. Discoidal, somewhat irregular. Medium-grained, gray/black/white. Signs of pitting from secondary use as a hammerstone.

S201. Pounder. Area A. Unit 1. Phase I. Igneous. Fragmentary. L: 8.6, W: 6.7, Th: 5.0. Roughly ovoid. Fine-grained, light gray. Signs of pitting on both ends.

S202. Pounder. Area A. Unit 3. Igneous. Intact. L: 8.6, W: 6.2, Th: 5.7. Roughly ovoid. Medium-grained, gray. Pitted and slightly faceted on both ends from use as a pounder.

S203. Pounder. Area A. G17D Surface. Igneous. Intact. L: 8.4, W: 3.5, Th: 3.5. Elongated ovoid. Coarse-grained, gray/yellow. Pitted on both ends from use as a pounder.

S204. Rubbing stone? Area B. Unit 14. Limestone. Intact. L: 12.8, W: 4.9, Th: 2.7. Elongated. Gray. One face flat, the other convex. Slight pitting on both ends and on one surface.

S205. Rubber-pounder. Area A. Unit 1. Phase I. Igneous. Fragmentary. L: 10.6, W: 7.4, Th: 4.2. Discoidal. Fine-grained, light green. Signs of pitting on edge from pounding.

S206. Rubber. Area A. Unit 1. Phase I. Igneous. Fragmentary. L: 30.0, W: 21.0, Th: 6.5. Roughly rectangular. Coarse-grained, gray/white/blue. One face flat, the other convex. One end rounded, the other broken. Pitting on flat face from use. Underside very rough. Work surface concave in longitudinal section and convex in transverse section. Edges of work surface chipped. Longitudinal scratches from use on a quern.

S207. Mortar. Area A. Unit 7. Limestone. Intact. L: 9.1, W: 6.3, Th: 4.8. Roughly quadrangular. Off-white. Deep depression and rounded underside revealed in transverse section. Cavity rough and pitted. Max L of depression = 6.3; Depth = 1.4 cm.

S208. Beads and spacers. Cemetery A. Tomb 6. Jasper, white limestone, siltstone and picrolite. Approximately 646 beads with single perforations and 6 spacers, the latter with 3 perforations each. Av. D of cylindrical beads = 0.3. Av. Th of most beads 0.2. One intact and 4 fragmentary 3-hole black quartz spacers. One fragmentary 3-hole picrolite spacer.

S209. Worked picrolite. Area A. Unit 16. Intact. L: 3.2, W: 1.9, Th: 1.4. Irregular ovoid. Light green/white. One face flat, the other slightly convex. No evidence of intentional shaping, but polished surface suggests it might have been a trinket.

S210. Rubber-pounder. Area A. Unit 1. Phase I. Igneous. Intact. L: 10.0, W: 8.3, Th: 4.2. Discoidal. Fine-grained, gray. Both faces smoothed from rubbing. Circumference pitted from pounding. One face pitted from tertiary use as a hammerstone.

S211. Pounder. Area A. Unit 7. Igneous. Intact. L: 10.6, W: 10.4, Th: 4.5. Circular. Medium-grained, gray/green. Both faces flat. Slightly faceted area on circumference, whole circumference pitted from pounding. Both faces smooth, perhaps from rubbing. Shallow, smooth depression in center of each face, ca. 2 mm deep. This pounder is unique.

S212. Pounder. Area A. Unit 1. Phase I. Igneous. Intact. L: 17.5, W: 5.7, Th: 4.1. Elongated, roughly rectangular in transverse section. Fine-grained, dark gray. Both faces almost flattened, rounded ends. Both ends slightly pitted.

S213. Pounder. Area B. Unit 14. Igneous. Intact. L: 6.1, W: 4.8, Th: 3.2. Ovoid. Medium-grained, gray/white. One face flat, the other convex. Slight pitting along the two ends.

S214. Rubbing stone? Area B. C20A 19. Limestone. Fragmentary. L: 6.8, W: 4.3, Th: 2.4. Elongated. White. Oval in transverse section. Both faces smooth from use as a rubbing stone? Small area of pitting on one face.

S215. Pounder. F20A 1. Surface. Igneous. Intact. L: 5.5, W: 3.3, Th: 1. Oval flattened. Fine-grained, gray. Slight pitting along the two rounded ends.

S216. Pounder. Area A. Unit 5. Igneous. Intact. L: 8.5, W: 5.9, Th: 5.9. Roughly ovoid. Coarse-grained, gray/blue. Multi-faced. One end pitted.

S217. Pounder. Area A. Unit 5. Igneous. Intact. L: 8.3, W: 4.7, Th: 2.1. Ovoid. Medium-grained, gray/white/blue. One face flat, the other convex. Faint signs of pitting along rounded ends and on one edge.

S218. Pounder. Area B. Unit 14. Igneous. Fragmentary. L: 7.3, W: 6.6, Th: 4.8. Roughly circular. Fine-grained, light gray. Irregular, multi-faced. Two areas pitted.

S219. Pounder. Area A. H18B 1. Igneous. Intact. L: 6.0, W: 3.8, Th: 0.3. Sub-rectangular. Coarse-grained, gray/brown. One face flat, the other convex. Slight pitting on the narrow rounded end.

S220. Rubbing stone? Area C. Unit 34. Limestone. Fragmentary. L: 8.3, W: 5.5, Th: 2.9. Sub-rectangular. Gray/brown. One face almost flat. Convex in transverse section.

Both faces smooth from use as a rubbing stone. Pitting on both faces.

S221. Pounder. Area B. Unit 13. Igneous. Fragmentary. L: 9.0, W: 6.6. Triangular, sub-rectangular in longitudinal section. Medium-grained, gray/blue. Signs of pitting and faceting on rounded end, other end and third angle pitted.

S222. Pounder. Area C. Unit 17. Limestone. Intact. L: 10.2, W: 7.5, Th: 4.9. Discoidal. Cream-colored limestone. One face mostly flattened, the other convex. Possible signs of pitting at one end and one side.

S223. Pounder. Area A. Unit 3. Igneous. Fragmentary. L: 4.9, W: 3.9, Th: 3.0. Sub-rectangular. Medium-grained, black. Three broken, almost flat, faces, one face convex. Burned and badly damaged. Signs of pitting and faceting on one side from pounding. Another area very smooth, perhaps from rubbing.

S224. Worked picrolite. Area B. Unit 14. Fragmentary. L: 1.8, W: 1.6, Th: 0.5. Lozenge shaped. Rectangular in transverse section with slightly rounded ends. Gray green with brown inclusions. Both faces very smooth. Sides ground into shape: one with transverse, the other with longitudinal striations. Original function and shape unknown.

S225. Rubbing stone. Area A. Unit 16. Igneous. Fragmentary. L: 6.6, W: 4.8, Th: 3.1. Two broken, almost flat, faces; one curved side. Coarse-grained, dark gray/brown. Surface smooth from rubbing.

S226. Pounder? F20A 1. Igneous. Fragmentary. L: 4.3, W: 4.0, Th: 1.2. Round in longitudinal section. One face flat, the other convex. Medium-grained, gray/green/blue/white. The flat work area is the result of pounding.

S227. Hammerstone. Area A. Unit 5. Igneous. Intact. L: 6.9, W: 5.1, Th: 3.2. Ovoid. Fine-grained, maroon/gray. One face slightly pitted from hammering a broad but narrow object (chert?). Pitting over other face and slightly deeper in center.

S228. Rubbing stone. Area C. Unit 10. Limestone. Intact. L: 10.2, W: 7.2, Th: 2.5. Elongated. Sub-rectangular. White. One face flat, convex in transverse section and narrows towards narrow end. Both faces smooth from rubbing, with one worn completely flat from this activity.

S229. Pecking stone. Area A. Unit 7. Chalcedony. Intact. L: 6.0, W: 5.6, Th: 5.3. Spherical, slightly faceted, resembling a cuboid with rounded angles. White. Most of surface rough and micro-faceted. Large smooth surface at one end, and two small ones at other end.

S230. Hammerstone. Area A. H17D 5. Igneous. Intact. L: 5.7, W: 5.1, Th: 3.5. Ovoid. Convex in both sections. Fine-grained, gray/green/white/yellow/brown. Deep pitting on both faces from use as a hammerstone. All surfaces rough. Slight pitting on one side.

S231. Rubber-pounder, type 2. Cemetery A. Tomb 6. Igneous. Intact. L: 11.3, W: 9.0, Th: 4.2. Discoidal. Fine-grained dark gray. Both faces smooth from rubbing. Both ends and circumference pitted and faceted from pounding.

S232. Mortar. Area C. Unit 10. Limestone. Fragmentary. L: 13.8, W: 7.9, Th: 7.4. Half circle, with one corner missing. White. Deep depression and rounded underside in transverse section. Cavity smooth and uneven. L of cavity = 7 cm, max. Depth = 4.5 cm.

S233. Rubbing stone. Area B. Unit 14. Limestone. Fragmentary. L: 5.0, W: 3.7, Th: 2.0. Sub-rectangular. Oval in transverse section. White. One face flat from rubbing.

S234. Gaming stone, Senet. Area C. Unit 10. Limestone. Fragmentary. L: 19.5, W: 16.0, Th: 7.7. Sub-rectangular. One face flat, the other irregular. Fine-grained, white soft limestone. Fragmentary 3 x 10 arrangement of depressions with 2 larger depressions at the side. Max. L of motif = 15 cm; max. W = 6 cm; Av. D of depressions = 1.2 cm; max. Depth = 0.4 cm; D of larger depressions = 2.9 cm; max. D = 1 cm.

S235. Gaming stone, Senet. Area B. Unit 13. Limestone. Intact. L: 26.0, W: 15.5, Th: 7.8. Roughly sub-rectangular. One face flat, the other uneven. Coarse-grained, calcareous. Three irregular rows of shallow depressions: row one, 8 preserved; row two, 7 preserved; row three, 7 preserved. One longer depression at one end. Max. L of depression = ca.17 cm; max. W = ca. 5 cm.

S236. Rubber. Area B. Unit 12. Igneous. Intact. L: 28.5, W: 16.0, Th: 5.5. Elongated. One face flat, the other concave. Rounded ends, convex in transverse section. Medium-grained, gray/white/blue. Flat face pitted from use on a quern. Chipped around the edges. Striations in both directions indicate it was used both as a rubbing stone and as a quern.

S237. Pounder. Area C. Unit 22. Igneous. Fragmentary. L: 10.0, W: 6.2, Th: 5.0. Elongated. One end rounded, the other broken. Ovoid in transverse section. Medium-grained, gray/white. Very slight signs of pitting on one face and on the rounded end.

S238. Axe, Type 1. Area B. Unit 12. Igneous. Intact. L: 17.5, W: 6.2, Th: 5.2. Elongated. Oval in both sections, narrowing towards one end. Fine-grained, light gray. Pitting and faceting on one end from use as a pounder. Chipping around the broader end, probably from attempt to shape it into an axe. Alternatively, this might have been a large axe that saw secondary use as a pounder. Both faces toward cutting edge show clear signs of abrasion, as a result of intentional shaping. The butt was perhaps left intentionally rough.

S239. Mortar. Area B. Unit 12. Limestone. Intact. L: 10.1, W: 8.8, Th: 3.2. Irregular, sub-rectangular. Cream-colored, rough cavity in the middle. L of cavity = 7.3 cm; W = 5.1 cm; max. Depth = 1.7 cm.

S240. Rubbing stone? Area C. H23D 1. Igneous. Fragmentary. L: 8.2, W: 7.0, Th: 4.8. One end broken, the other rounded. One face flat, the other convex. Medium-grained, gray/brown. Flat face slightly smooth from rubbing.

S241. Pounder. F20A 2. Igneous. Intact. L: 7.5, W: 7.3, Th: 4.4. Sub-rectangular in longitudinal section, triangular in transverse section. Medium-grained, gray/blue. Some signs of pounding on pointed end.

S242. Pounder. Area B. Unit 12. Igneous. Intact. L: 10.0, W: 8.1, Th: 7.7. Irregular, multi-faceted. Fine-grained, light gray/blue. One end pitted and faceted, the other slightly flattened.

S243. Pounder. Area A. Unit 7. Igneous. Intact. L: 9.4, W: 7.8, Th: 3.4. Sub-rectangular. Fine-grained, dark gray. One end broken before use as a pounder. Faint signs of pounding at both ends.

S244. Pounder. Area C. Unit 10. Igneous. Fragmentary. L: 6.6, W: 5.2, Th: 4.7. Irregular, one end rounded, the other broken. Coarse-grained, gray/brown. All surfaces rough. Rounded end pitted.

S245. Pounder. Area B. Unit 12. Igneous. Fragmentary. L: 8.0, W: 7.3, Th: 5.3. Discoidal. Medium-grained, gray/brown. One end broken. Apex pitted from use as a pounder.

S246. Rubber-pounder. Area B. Unit 12. Igneous. Intact. L: 8.5, W: 7.4, Th: 7.4. Roughly spherical, one face flattened. Coarse-grained, gray/brown. Faint signs on flat surface of use as a rubbing stone. Some pitting on one end.

S247. Pounder. Area B. Unit 12. Igneous. Intact. L: 8.2, W: 5.0, Th: 2.3. Ovoid. Fine-grained, gray. Both ends flattened from use as a pounder. Some pounding also on edges. Both faces slightly pitted from use as a hammerstone. Borderline between Types 1 and 2.

S248. Rubbing stone. Area A. Unit 39. Igneous. Fragmentary. L: 5.3, W: 4.4, Th: 2.7. Ovoid. One face flat, the other convex. Medium-grained, dark gray/brown. One area worn smooth from rubbing.

S249. Pounder. Area A. Unit 7. Igneous. Intact. L: 11.4, W: 7.0, Th: 7.5. Oval in longitudinal section, triangular in transverse section. Medium-grained, gray/light blue. Edges abraded from use as a pounder.

S250. Pounder. Area A. H14D 7. Igneous. Fragmentary. L: 15.7, W: 8.1, Th: 6.0. Almost half-circular. Oval in longitudinal section. Fine-grained, light gray. Same wear pattern as S249, only slightly more pronounced on both ends.

S251. Pounder. Area C. Unit 10. Igneous. Fragmentary. L: 3.7, W: 3.7, Th: 3.4. Conical, broken face very uneven. Fine-grained, light gray. Rounded end pitted from shaping.

S252. Pounder. Area C. Unit 10. Igneous. Fragmentary. L: 7.4, W: 7.6, Th: 6.0. Broken face roughly flat, rounded end. Oval in longitudinal section. Medium-grained, dark gray/green/white. Rounded end pitted and faceted from pounding. Some evidence for secondary use as a hammerstone.
S253. Pounder. Area C. Unit 10. Igneous. Intact. L: 7.7, W: 5.6, Th: 4.3. Irregular, multi-faceted. Medium-grained, gray/white. One end slightly pitted.

S254. Axe, Type 1. Area C. Unit 10. Igneous. Intact. L: 4.1, W: 3.2, Th: 1.1. Rounded narrow butt. Fine-grained, dark gray. Sharp, well-defined cutting edge. Oval in transverse section. Butt and edges flattened. All surfaces carefully ground smooth. Manufacturing scratches clearly visible. Transverse striations on cutting edge from re-shaping. No wear pattern visible.

S256. Quern. Cemetery A. I5B 2. Limestone. Fragmentary. L: 21.5, W: 19.5, Th: 10.8. Work face concave in both sections, other face rough and irregular. Coarse-grained, cream-colored limestone. Work surface pitted from use as a saddle quern. NB-this belongs to the hollow, mortar-like class of saddle quern.

S258. Rubber. Area B. C20B 5. Limestone. Fragmentary. L: 19.5, W: 16.5, Th: 7.0. Sub-rectangular. Coarse-grained, cream-colored. Underside carefully cut with 6 notches. Usage unknown.

S259. Work surface? Area C. Unit 34. Limestone. Intact. L: 25.0, W: 23.5, Th: 3.0. Rectangular. One face flat, the other slightly convex and rough. White. Flat face smooth, the other very rough. Possible evidence of shaping on two sides.

S260. Rubber-pounder. Area C. Unit 22. Igneous. Intact. L: 11.2, W: 8.4, Th: 5.5. Ovoid. One face flattened. Coarse-grained, gray/blue/brown. Pitting on both ends from pounding. Evidence of rubbing on one face.

S261. Rubber. Area B. Unit 12. Igneous. Fragmentary. L: 8.1, W: 6.5, Th: 2.4. Irregular. Fine-grained, gray. All faces rough. One face very smooth from use on quern. Perhaps lightly used as a pounder?

S262. Pounder. Area A. H18B 1. Igneous. Intact. L: 5.0, W: 3.1, Th: 3.0. Ovoid. Medium-grained, gray/brown. Slight pitting and faceting on one end.

S263. Rubber-pounder. Area A. Unit 7. Igneous. Intact. L: 7.7, W: 7.6, Th: 4.5. Discoidal. Both faces irregular. Coarse-grained, gray/brown/blue. Most of circumference faceted and pitted. One face slightly smoothed from rubbing.

S264. Rubber-pounder. Area A. Unit 16. Igneous. Intact. L: 5.8, W: 5.0, Th: 3.1. Ovoid. One face flattened. Fine-grained, gray/green. Pitting on one end from pounding. Slight evidence on one face of rubbing.

S265. Pounder. Area A. Unit 5. Igneous. Intact. L: 6.8, W: 5.3, Th: 4.5. Ovoid. Fine-grained, light gray. Pitting on one end.

S266. Rubber. Area C. Unit 8. Igneous. Fragmentary. L: 12.8, W: 11.7, Th: 5.0. Sub-rectangular: only one corner rounded. One face slightly convex, the other concave. Medium-grained, gray/brown/blue. Pitted and smoothed on concave face from use on a quern. Definite evidence for secondary use as a pounder.

S267. Rubbing stone. Area B. Unit 13. Limestone. Fragmentary. L: 8.0, W: 5.5, Th: 2.6. Sub-rectangular, ovoid in transverse section. One rounded end. White. One face smooth from rubbing.

S268. Dish. Area A. Unit 7. Igneous. Fragmentary. L: 18.5, W: 12.0, Th: 4.9. Shape of a pie slice. Small fragment of a large, shallow dish between 25-30 cm in diameter. Concave in transverse section. Fine-grained, light gray. Concave face pitted. Max. depth of depression = 4 cm.

S269. Rubber-pounder. Area B. C20B 8. Igneous. Intact. L: 15.7, W: 6.6, Th: 5.9. Elongated. One face flat, the other convex, narrowing towards one end. Both ends rounded. Fine-grained, light gray/white. Flat face smooth in certain areas from rubbing. Pitting on one end from pounding.

S270. Pounder. Area A. Unit 15. Igneous. Fragmentary. L: 7.3, W: 5.3, Th: 3.5. One rounded end, one side badly damaged. Ovoid in transverse section. Medium-grained, dark gray/brown. Pitting along rounded end.

S271. Pecking stone. Area A. Unit 7. Chalcedony. Fragmentary. L: 5.6, W: 5.2, Th: 5.1. Roughly cuboid, multi-faced. White.

S272. Axe, Type 2? Area A. Unit 5. Igneous. Intact. L: 7.6, W: 4.3, Th: 1.3. Elongated ovoid, oval in transverse section. One face convex, the other slightly concave. Narrow, rounded, slightly flattened butt. Flattens towards "cutting edge." Fine-grained, light gray/dark gray. Area along cutting edge damaged, perhaps in preparation for use as a tool. Intentional shaping on butt.

S273. Pounder. Area C. Unit 22. Igneous. Intact. L: 8.3, W: 6.5, Th: 5.0. Irregular, multi-faced. Sub-rectangular in longitudinal section. Fine-grained, gray/brown. Narrow end pitted from pounding, other end pitted and faceted from pounding. Secondary use as a hammerstone.

S274. Rubber-pounder. Area B. Unit 13. Igneous. Intact. L: 11.3, W: 8.6, Th: 4.5. Discoidal. Oval in both sections.

Medium-grained, gray/blue/brown. Both ends pitted and one slightly faceted from pounding. One face smooth from rubbing.

S275. Unfinished mace head. Area A. Unit 16. Limestone. Intact. L: 8.0, W: 5.4, Th: 4.7. Ovoid. White. Two conical holes symmetrically placed on either face. Striation marks clearly visible in perforation. Depth of holes = 1.6 cm; max. D = 1.5 cm.

S276. Pounder. Area B. Unit 12. Igneous. Intact. L: 6.4, W: 3.5, Th: 2.7. Elongated ovoid. Fine-grained, light gray. Deep pitting on one face and one side from pounding.

S277. Pounder. Area B. Unit 12. Igneous. Intact. L: 8.0, W: 5.6, Th: 4.8. Ovoid. One end narrower than the other. Medium-grained, light gray/light blue. Pitting on both faces from pounding. Slight pitting on the two ends.

S278. Axe, Type 1. Area B. Unit 13. Igneous. Fragmentary. L: 5.2, W: 4.6, Th: 2.2. Sub-rectangular. Rounded cutting edge. Oval in transverse section. Fine-grained, very light gray. Sharp cutting edge. One face badly damaged.

S279. Pecking stone. Area A. Unit 16. Chalcedony. Intact. L: 4.8, W: 4.8, Th: 4.1. Roughly spherical. Cream-colored. Most of surface rough and multi-faceted. Two large smooth areas.

S280. Mortar. Area C. Unit 2. Limestone. Intact. L: 20.5, W: 14.3, Th: 12.1. Bowl-shaped. Underside oval. Cavity roughly in middle. Max. L of cavity = 11.2 cm; max. W = 11.9 cm; max. Depth = 5.2 cm. Very smooth inner face. Used as a true mortar, probably in conjunction with a pestle.

S281. Gaming stone, Senet. Area C. H23D Surface. Limestone. Fragmentary. L: 17.5, W: 17.8, Th: 6.8. Roughly sub-rectangular. Both faces uneven. Three rows of depressions badly preserved. Row One, six preserved; row two, 7 preserved; row three, 3 preserved. Av. L of depressions = 1.7 cm; av. W = 1.5 cm; av. Depth = 0.4 cm; W of scheme = 7.8 cm.

S282. Rubbing stone. Area A. Unit 16. Limestone. Fragmentary. L: 12.9, W: 9.1, Th: 3.8. Sub-rectangular, both ends broken, one unevenly so. Oval in transverse section. Cream/brown limestone. One face smooth from rubbing.

S283. Pounder. Area A. Unit 16. Igneous. Intact. L: 7.2, W: 5.7, Th: 4.3. Ovoid. Fine-grained, light gray/blue. Pitting on both faces and ends. Pitting on one side from hammering.

S284. Pounder. Area C. Unit 34. Igneous. Intact. L: 6.0, W: 4.6, Th: 2.0. Ovoid. Medium-grained, gray/brown/blue. Pitting on both ends from pounding. Slight pitting on both faces from hammering.

S285. Grooved stone. Surface. Limestone. Intact. L: 23.0, W: 22.5, Th: 13.9. Circular, uneven surface. Cream/brown with areas of darker brown. Line of av. W 2.3 cm, Depth 0.9 cm, cut around circumference.

S286. Pounder. Area A. Unit 7. Igneous. Intact. L: 8.0, W: 5.7, Th: 4.0. Ovoid, one face flattened, the other irregular. Fine-grained, gray/dark gray. Deep pitting on both faces from hammering. Pitting on both ends.

S287. Pounder. Area B. Unit 12. Igneous. Intact. L: 7.5, W: 6.2, Th: 5.6. Ovoid. Fine-grained, light gray. Faint pitting on ends.

S289. Pounder. Area B. Unit 12. Igneous. Intact. L: 7.6, W: 6.3, Th: 5.4. Ovoid. Medium-grained, light gray/blue. Slight pitting on one end from pounding. Pitting on one face from hammering.

S290. Pecking stone. Area B. Unit 12. Quartz. Fragmentary. L: 8.8, W: 6.8, Th: 5.8. Irregular, multi-faced.

S291. Rubbing stone. Area C. Unit 10. Limestone. Fragmentary. L: 6.6, W: 4.5, Th: 1.7. Discoidal, oval in transverse section. White. One face smooth.

S292. Pounder. Area C. Unit 10. Igneous. Intact. L: 10.2, W: 5.8, Th: 2.7. Elongated ovoid. One face damaged. Fine-grained, light gray. Slight pitting on both ends. Pitting on one face from use as a hammerstone.

S293. Work surface. Area A. Unit 16. Limestone. Fragmentary. L: 8.8, W: 5.5, Th: 2.5. Rectangular in shape and sections. Gray. One face very smooth and irregularly pitted from use as a work surface?

S294. Pounder. Area C. Unit 10. Igneous. Fragmentary. L: 5.0, W: 3.3, Th: 1.8. Sub-rectangular. One rounded end, the other broken off. Oval in transverse section. Coarse-grained, gray/blue. Slight pitting on rounded end.

S295. Pounder. Area B. Unit 12. Igneous. Fragmentary. L: 7.0, W: 5.6, Th: 4.8. As preserved, irregular. Fine-grained, light gray. Very regular, fine pitting on end.

S296. Pounder. Area A. Unit 7. Igneous. Fragmentary. L: 10.9, W: 8.5, Th: 4.8. As preserved, irregular. Sub-rectangular in longitudinal section. Medium-grained, gray/brown. One edge pitted.

S297. Quern fragment. Cemetery A. Tomb 15. Igneous. Fragmentary. L: 6.3, W: 6.0, Th: 5.9. As preserved, irregular and multi-faced. Coarse-grained, gray/brown. One face pitted and smoothed from use as a saddle quern.

S298. Rubber. Area A. Unit 7. Igneous. Fragmentary. L: 5.1, W: 4.4, Th: 3.4. As preserved, irregular. Work face very smooth. Medium-grained, dark gray/brown.

S299. Hammerstone. Area B. Unit 12. Igneous. Intact. L: 8.7, W: 5.0, Th: 3.7. Ovoid. Coarse-grained, gray/brown. Pitting on one face from hammering.

S300. Pounder. Area B. Unit 13. Igneous. Fragmentary. L: 10.0, W: 9.8, Th: 5.3. Irregular, multi-faced. Fine-grained, very light gray/blue. Pitted on the curved edge from pounding.

S302. Pounder. Area B. C20B 3. Igneous. Fragmentary. L: 8.7, W: 2.5, Th: 2.5. Elongated, oval in longitudinal section. One side curved, the other broken. Fine-grained, light gray. Pitting along edge and on end.

S303. Pecking stone. Area A. Unit 7. Quartz. Intact. L: 6.0, W: 5.9, Th: 4.3. Cuboid. Four large smooth areas on four faces. Other surfaces rough.

S304. Pounder. F20A 2. Igneous. Intact. L: 7.4, W: 2.8, Th: 1.8. Ovoid. Coarse-grained, dark gray/brown. Slight pitting on both ends from pounding.

S305. Pounder. Area B. C20B 5. Igneous. Intact. L: 14.7, W: 10.3, Th: 5.1. Irregular, resembling a hexagon. Narrows toward one side. Coarse-grained, dark gray/brown. Pitting from pounding.

S306. Perforated stone. Area A. Unit 15. Limestone. Intact. L: 28.0, W: 27.8, Th: 7.3. Irregular, with two roughly flat faces. One large perforated hole in center, four smaller holes. Unclear whether holes are natural or intentional.

S307. Quern. Area B. Unit 14. Limestone. Fragmentary. L: 31.8, W: 26.4, Th: 12.6. Sub-rectangular. Work surface concave, underside convex. White. Work surface pitted and smoothed from use as a quern.

S308. Mortar. Area C. Unit 25. Limestone. Intact. L: 10.5, W: 7.9, Th: 3.7. Ovoid. Cavity in middle. Cavity measures 6.1 x 5.9 cm, Depth=1.7 cm. White.

S309. Quern. Area A. Unit 16. Limestone. Fragmentary. L: 34.0, W: 31.3, Th: 10.6. Sub-rectangular. One face flat. Work surface concave. One end rounded. White. Work surface pitted and smoothed from use as a saddle quern.

S310. Quern. Area A. Unit 16. Limestone. Intact. L: 49.8, W: 33.9, Th: 15.0. Oval. Underside concave, bowl-shaped work surface concave. White. Work surface pitted and smoothed from use as a saddle quern.

S311. Rubber-pounder. Area A. Unit 5. Igneous. Intact. L: 11.0, W: 10.0, Th: 4.7. Discoidal. D-shaped. Oval in sections. Fine-grained, dark gray. Both ends deeply pitted from pounding. Smooth areas on both faces from rubbing. Deep pitting on both faces from tertiary use as a hammerstone.

S312. Rubber-pounder. Area A. Unit 5. Igneous. Intact. L: 10.8, W: 9.2, Th: 4.8. Discoidal. D-shaped. One face flat, the other irregular. Fine-grained, light gray on one face, dark gray on the other. One side flattened and smoothed from rubbing. Circumference pitted from pounding. Small smooth area on one face from rubbing. Beveled face on this piece is so far unique.

S313. Rubber-pounder. Area B. Unit 12. Igneous. Intact. L: 9.1, W: 8.4, Th: 5.4. Discoidal. Oval in section. Medium-grained, light gray/green. Pitting on one end and on one side from pounding. One face slightly smooth from rubbing.

S314. Pounder. Area A. Unit 5. Igneous. Intact. L: 14.0, W: 9.6, Th: 3.6. Sub-rectangular. Oval in longitudinal section. Fine-grained, gray. Pitting on circumference.

S315. Pounder. Area A. Unit 5. Igneous. Intact. L: 13.7, W: 10.3, Th: 7.7. Irregular, multi-faced. One narrow end, the other much broader. Fine-grained, light gray. Pitting on one face from secondary use as a hammerstone. Deep pitting on ends.

S316. Pounder. Area A. Unit 18. Igneous. Fragmentary. L: 4.8, W: 3.7, Th: 2.0. Elongated. One end rounded, the other broken off. Oval in transverse section. Fine-grained, light gray/brown. Pitting on the rounded end from pounding.

S317. Pounder. Area A. Unit 5. Igneous. Intact. L: 8.0, W: 4.7, Th: 4.9. Elongated. Conical. Quadrangular in transverse section. Fine-grained, light gray/dark gray. Area on broad end pitted and faceted from pounding. All other surfaces very smooth. Borderline between Type 1 and Type 2.

S318. Rubber. Area B. Unit 14. Igneous. Fragmentary. L: 9.2, W: 8.0, Th: 4.0. Irregular. One face flat, the other damaged. Coarse-grained, gray/white/brown/ blue. One face smooth and flat from use on a saddle quern. Pitting along rounded end from secondary use as a pounder.

S319. Pounder. Area A. Unit 7. Igneous. Intact. L: 9.1, W: 5.9, Th: 4.3. Ovoid. Fine-grained, gray. Evidence for pounding on one edge. Pitting on both faces from use as a hammerstone.

S321. Pounder. Area C. Unit 34. Igneous. Intact. L: 6.3, W: 3.8, Th: 2.9. Ovoid. Fine-grained, light gray/dark gray. Pitting on both faces.

S322. Pounder. Area A. Unit 7. Igneous. Intact. L: 10.0, W: 6.0, Th: 4.7. Elongated. Ovoid. Medium-grained, gray/blue/ dark gray. Pitting on both ends from pounding. Pitting on both faces from secondary use as a hammerstone.

S323. Pounder. Area A. Unit 19. Igneous. Intact. L: 12.3, W: 8.2, Th: 4.9. Irregular, multi-faced. Fine-grained, gray. One end and half of one side faceted from pounding.

S324. Rubber. Area A. Unit 5. Igneous. Fragmentary. L: 13.1, W: 9.0, Th: 4.6. Triangular, one face flat, the other convex. Coarse-grained, gray/brown/green/dark gray. One face very smooth from use on a quern.

S325. Gaming stone, Senet. Area B. Unit 12. Limestone. Fragmentary. L: 15.3, W: 12.7, Th: 3.5. Sub-rectangular in shape and sections. Three rows of depressions on both faces, partially preserved: Row 1: eight preserved; row 2: seven preserved; row 3: five preserved. W of scheme = 8.6 cm; av. D of depressions = 1 cm. Side two, three rows of five, six and seven depressions with additional larger cavity at the side; W of gaming area = ca. 6.5 cm; av. D of depressions = 1.3 cm.

S326. Axe, Type 2. Area A. Unit 5. Igneous. Intact. L: 7.9, W: 4.8, Th: 1.8. Sub-rectangular. Oval in both sections. Fine-grained, light gray. Well flattened in transverse section. Edges pitted and flat. Broad butt heavily chipped and convex cutting edge flattened from secondary use as a pounder. The flattened profile would suggest that this object might have been an adze.

S327. Axe, Type 1. Area C. Unit 10. Igneous. Intact. L: 10.3, W: 5.7, Th: 2.7. Elongated, ovoid. Slightly flattened butt. Well-defined cutting edge. Both faces convex with flattened areas in the middle. Medium-grained, gray/blue/light gray. Butt pitted from secondary use as a pounder. Distinct flat bevel on both faces of cutting edge. Either unfinished or saw secondary use as a pounder.

S328. Pounder. Area A. Unit 5. Igneous. Intact. L: 10.2, W: 10.1, Th: 3.6. Irregular. Oval in transverse section. One end rounded, broken end flat. Fine-grained, light gray. Pitting on the rounded end.

S329. Pounder. Area B. Unit 13. Igneous. Fragmentary. L: 11.2, W: 7.2, Th: 6.4. Irregular, multi-faced. Fine-grained, light gray. Pitting on both ends and circumference.

S330. Gaming stone, Senet. Area A. Unit 39. Limestone. Intact. L: 20.7, W: 14.0, Th: 4.7. Sub-rectangular. One face flat, the other convex. Three rows of depressions, and two bigger holes to one side. Row 1: 11 depressions, the eleventh depression being natural. Row 2: 10 depressions. Row 3: 10 depressions. Width of gaming area: 5.6 cm. Average D of each depression 9 x 7 mm. L of 3 x 10 area = 14.0 cm. Depth of depression = 0.5 cm. (NB: The depressions are unusually deep).

S331. Mortar. Area C. Unit 17. Limestone. Fragmentary. L: 17.8, W: 14.7, Th: 7.5. Ovoid. Underside uneven. Cream-colored. Pitted cavity. W of cavity = 12.8 cm; max. depth = 3.6 cm.

S332. Worked picrolite. Cemetery A. Tomb 9. Fragment. L: 2.8, W: 2.6, Th: 1.5. Sub-rectangular. Light green/white. One end flat, the other rounded. Oval in transverse section.

S333. Worked picrolite. Area B. Unit 13. Fragmentary. L: 2.3, W: 1.9, Th: 1.7. Carefully ground barrel-shaped or cylindrical. Brown/cream.

S334. Worked picrolite. Area A. Unit 19. Fragmentary. L: 2.1, W: 1.0, Th: 0.5. Sub-rectangular, both sides curved. Sub-rectangular in sections. Light green.

S335. Worked picrolite. Area C. Unit 8. Fragmentary. L: 1.8, W: 1.6, Th: 0.8. Sub-rectangular, narrowing and sharpening towards one end. Light purple/white. Perhaps arm fragment of a cruciform figurine.

S336. Worked picrolite. Area C. Unit 10. Fragmentary. L: 2.6, W: 2.5, Th: 1.8. Sub-rectangular. Oval in transverse section. Light green/white.

S337. Worked picrolite. Area A. Unit 5. Fragmentary. L: 1.8, W: 1.0, Th: 0.5. Sub-rectangular. One face concave, the other convex. Light green.

S338. Bead. Picrolite. Area A. Unit 7. Fragmentary. L: 2.3, W: 2.1, Th: 2.1. Cylindrical, perforated. Light green/white.

S339. Worked picrolite. Area A. Unit 5. Fragmentary. L: 10.1, W: 4.6, Th: 4.2. Elongated ovoid. Uneven surfaces. Light green/white/brown/ dark green.

S340. Pendant. Area B. Unit 12. Picrolite. Intact. L: 2.5, W: 1.9, Th: 0.7. Sub-rectangular, oval in sections, narrowing towards one end. One end perforated and broader than the other. One face green, the rest light green with white flecks.

S341. Pecking stone. Area A. Surface. Chalcedony. Fragmentary. L: 5.5, W: 3.6, Th: 5.1. As preserved, half of a sphere. Broken face, smooth areas on one side. Pitted and micro-faceted.

S342. Rubber-pounder. Area A. Unit 5. Igneous. Intact. L: 10.8, W: 9.7, Th: 4.5. Discoidal, oval in section. Coarse-grained, dark gray/light gray. Pitting on the face, one end and circumference from pounding. Both faces smooth from rubbing.

S343. Pounder. Area B. Unit 12. Limestone. Fragmentary. L: 10.7, W: 9.2, Th: 9.1. Cylindrical, one end rounded, the other broken. Circular in transverse section. Rounded end slightly flattened from pounding. Distinct ring before break on other end suggests this was a bottle-shaped pounder. (NB-unusual rare use of limestone for this function).

S344. Rubber-pounder. Area C. Unit 10. Igneous. Intact. L: 12.6, W: 11.0, Th: 4.5. Discoidal, oval in section. Fine-grained, light gray/blue. Pitting along circumference from pounding. One face smooth from rubbing with striations clearly visible.

S345. Pounder. Area A. Unit 5. Igneous. Intact. L: 5.0, W: 3.8, Th: 2.1. Ovoid. Medium-grained, gray/light gray. Both ends pitted and slightly flattened.

S346. Pounder. Area C. Unit 10. Igneous. Fragmentary. L: 16.5, W: 12.7, Th: 4.7. Irregular. Coarse-grained, light gray/blue. Circumference slightly abraded from casual use as a pounder.

S347. Rubber-pounder. Area B. Unit 12. Igneous. Intact. L: 9.4, W: 8.1, Th: 5.2. Ovoid. Fine-grained, light gray. One end pitted and faceted from pounding. Both faces pitted from tertiary use as a hammerstone. One face smoothed and darkened from rubbing.

S348. Pounder. Area C. Unit 22. Igneous. Intact. L: 8.6, W: 7.9, Th: 6.2. Ovoid, multi-faced. Medium-grained, gray/white/brown. Four areas on one side pitted and well faceted from pounding. Pitting on one face from secondary use as a hammerstone.

S349. Pounder. Area C. Unit 22. Igneous. Fragmentary. L: 13.8, W: 10.6, Th: 5.1. Irregular, one face flat. Fine-grained, light gray. Faint signs of pounding along irregular circumference.

S350. Pounder. Area C. Unit 22. Igneous. Intact. L: 7.0, W: 3.9, Th: 3.0. Elongated, narrowing towards one end. One face flat, the other convex. Fine-grained, light gray. Pitting on both ends from pounding.

S351. Pounder. Area B. Unit 11. Igneous. Intact. L: 5.2, W: 5.5, Th: 5.0. Roughly spherical. One area pitted and flattened.

S352. Pounder. Area C. Unit 23. Igneous. Intact. L: 10.7, W: 9.1, Th: 4.7. Ovoid. Coarse-grained, black. Burnt. Areas on both ends pitted and faceted from pounding. Both faces pitted from secondary use as a hammerstone.

S353. Pounder. Area A. Unit 16. Igneous. Fragmentary. L: 12.7, W: 9.8, Th: 5.8. Sub-rectangular. One end rounded, the other broken and irregular. Wedge-shaped. Medium-grained, light gray/brown. Pitting along rounded end.

S354. Function uncertain. Area C. Unit 17. Limestone. Fragmentary. L: 11.5, W: 7.3, Th: 1.8. Oval, sub-rectangular in section. Both faces flat. Brown.. One end rounded, the other heavily chipped.

S355. Rubber-pounder. Area B. Unit 12. Igneous. Intact. L: 6.3, W: 5.9, Th: 4.5. Roughly cubical, multi-faced. Fine-grained, light gray. One face smooth from rubbing. Pitting along all other areas from pounding.

S356. Pounder. Area B. Unit 11. Igneous. Intact. L: 8.7, W: 3.5, Th: 3.0. Elongated, ovoid. Oval in section. Fine-grained, light gray. Deep pitting on one face from hammering on a sharp object. Pitting on other face also from hammering. Pitting on both ends.

S357. Pounder. Area A. Unit 5. Igneous. Fragmentary. L: 8.7, W: 7.4, Th: 4.3. One face flat, the other convex, sides uneven. Medium-grained, light gray/brown. One face very smooth from original use as a rubber. Some evidence along edges of use as a pounder.

S358. Pounder. Area A. Unit 16. Igneous. Intact. L: 11.2, W: 10.5, Th: 4.7. Heart-shaped, oval in section. Fine-grained, light gray. Pitting on all three angles.

S359. Rubber. Area B. Unit 12. Igneous. Fragmentary. L: 10.1, W: 9.9, Th: 4.0. As preserved, irregular. One face flat, the other convex. Medium-grained, gray. Work surface flat and smooth.

S360. Pounder. Area A. Unit 5. Igneous. Fragmentary. L: 7.3, W: 6.3, Th: 5.0. Irregular shaped, multi-faceted. Roughly semi-circular in section. Fine-grained, very light gray. Pitting and faceting on preserved end.

S361. Rubber. Area B. Unit 12. Igneous. Fragmentary. L: 9.3, W: 5.7, Th: 4.1. As preserved, irregular. Coarse-grained, gray/brown. Work surface flat and smooth.

S362. Pounder. Area B. Unit 12. Igneous. Intact. L: 5.8, W: 3.9, Th: 2.9. Irregular, multi-faced. One end narrow, the other broad. Medium-grained, gray/blue. Pitting on the narrow end.

S363. Pounder. Area A. Unit 32. Igneous. Fragmentary. L: 14.0, W: 8.7, Th: 4.7. One face flat, the other convex. Oval in transverse section, almost triangular in longitudinal section. Fine-grained, light gray/green. One face flat and smooth from use as a rubber. Deep pitting along rounded end from secondary use as a pounder.

S364. Pounder. Area C. Unit 34. Igneous. Intact. L: 5.4, W: 4.0, Th: 4.5. Flattened ovoid. Fine-grained, light gray. Pitting on both ends from pounding.

S365. Rubber-pounder. Area B. C20B 7. Igneous. Intact. L: 13.0, W: 10.0, Th: 4.8. Discoidal, oval in section. Fine-grained, light gray. Pitting along sides from pounding. One face smooth from rubbing.

S366. Hammerstone. Area A. Unit 7. Igneous. Intact. L: 11.3, W: 6.3, Th: 3.7. Ovoid. Medium-grained, dark gray/brown/white. Slight pitting on both faces from hammering.

S367. Pounder. Area B. Unit 13. Igneous. Intact. L: 9.3, W: 5.5, Th: 2.0. Elongated, irregular, flattened. Fine-grained, light gray. Very slight pitting on one face from secondary use as a hammerstone. Pitting on narrow end.

S368. Pounder. Area B. Unit 12. Igneous. Fragmentary. L: 8.4, W: 6.9, Th: 5.5. Ovoid. One face flat, the other damaged. Medium-grained, light gray. Part of side pitted and slightly flattened from pounding.

S369. Axe, Type 2. Area C. Unit 22. Igneous. Fragmentary. L: 6.5, W: 4.3, Th: 1.8. Roughly oval in shape and transverse section. Intact areas very smooth. Fine-grained gray. Both cutting edge and butt damaged and heavily flaked, either from use or as part of the manufacturing process of a Type 2 axe.

S370. Pounder. Area B. Unit 14. Igneous. Intact. L: 1.1, W: 9.3, Th: 4.4. Irregular, multi-faced. Triangular in transverse section, sub-rectangular in longitudinal section. Medium-grained, gray. All angles pitted.

S371. Pounder. Area C. H23/24 2. Igneous. Intact. L: 7.5, W: 6.7, Th: 5.9. Ovoid. Coarse-grained, gray/white. Pitting along circumference from pounding.

S372. Rubber. Area C. Unit 22. Igneous. Intact. L: 6.9, W: 6.2, Th: 5.6. Irregular, one face concave, the other convex. Coarse-grained, gray. Concave face smooth from original use as a rubber on a quern. One end pitted from pounding.

S373. Pounder. Area B. C19D 8. Igneous. Fragmentary. L: 10.9, W: 8.3, Th: 4.8. Irregular, one face concave, the other convex. Coarse-grained, gray. Concave face smooth from original use as a rubber. One end pitted.

S374. Pounder. Area A. Unit 5. Igneous. Intact. L: 6.9, W: 5.5, Th: 4.2. Ovoid. Coarse-grained, dark gray/ light gray. Pitting on both ends.

S375. Pounder. Area C. Unit 2. Igneous. Intact. L: 14.3, W: 8.0, Th: 7.7. Elongated, cylindrical. Almost circular in transverse section, one end smaller. Fine-grained, light gray/ green. Pitting on both ends.

S376. Rubber-pounder. Area A. Unit 18. Igneous. Intact. L: 12.8, W: 7.5, Th: 6.6. Elongated, cylindrical. Oval in section. One end more narrow than the other. Fine-grained, light gray/ green. One side well smoothed from use as a rubbing stone. Fine pitting on narrow end from pounding or intentional shaping. Other end pitted and chipped from use as a pounder. Deep pitting on one face from tertiary use as a hammerstone.

S377. Rubber-pounder. Area A. Unit 6. Igneous. Intact. L: 11.6, W: 10.0, Th: 5.8. Discoidal, oval in section. Medium-grained, gray/light gray. Slight pitting along circumference from pounding. Faces smoothed from rubbing. Slight pitting on both faces from tertiary use as a hammerstone.

S378. Pounder. Area A. Unit 39. Igneous. Fragmentary. L: 14.1, W: 10.2, Th: 5.6. As preserved, irregular. Oval in longitudinal section. One face flat, the other convex. Medium-grained, gray. Flat face smooth from original use as a rubber. Rounded end pitted from secondary use as a pounder.

S379. Pounder. Area A. Unit 38. Igneous. Intact. L: 12.4, W: 7.0, Th: 4.1. D-shaped. Oval in longitudinal section.

One face smooth from original use as a rubber, the other rough. Fine-grained, gray. One end flattened from use as a pounder.

S380. Pounder. Area A. Unit 6. Igneous. Intact. L: 12.9, W: 7.5, Th: 5.4. Elongated, multi-faced. Triangular in transverse section. Oval in longitudinal section. Fine-grained, light gray. Pitting and faceting on both ends from pounding. Pitting on two faces from secondary use as a hammerstone.

S381. Pounder. Area B. Unit 12. Igneous. Fragmentary. L: 10.0, W: 8.5, Th: 6.8. Irregular, multi-faced. One end rounded. Fine-grained, light gray. Pitting and slight faceting on one end and on edges.

S382. Pounder. Area A. Unit 18. Igneous. Intact. L: 11.4, W: 5.0, Th: 3.6. Elongated. Triangular in transverse section. Both ends rounded. Oval in longitudinal section. Fine-grained, gray. Pitting on both ends from pounding.

S383. Pounder. Area A. Unit 6. Igneous. Intact. L: 7.5, W: 4.9, Th: 4.3. Ovoid. Medium-grained, light gray. Pitting on both faces from secondary use as a hammerstone. One end pitted.

S384. Rubber. Area C. Unit 2. Igneous. Fragmentary. L: 10.5, W: 9.9, Th: 3.7. Sub-rectangular. One face flat, the other convex. One end rounded, two badly damaged sides. Coarse-grained, black/green/blue.

S385. Pounder. Area B. Unit 12. Igneous. Intact. L: 8.2, W: 5.1, Th: 4.9. Ovoid. Fine-grained, light gray. Pitting on both faces from secondary use as a hammerstone. Ends pitted. Borderline between Type 1 and Type 4.

S386. Rubber. Area A. Unit 5. Igneous. Fragmentary. L: 10.5, W: 6.8, Th: 4.4. One face flat, the other convex. Oval in longitudinal section. Coarse-grained, gray/white/green.

S387. Rubber. Area B. Unit 12. Igneous. Fragmentary. L: 17.3, W: 17.0, Th: 5.9. Sub-rectangular. Both faces concave, one end rounded, the other broken off. Medium-grained, light gray/brown/white.

S388. Pounder. Area A. Unit 18. Igneous. Intact. L: 11.2, W: 7.0, Th: 6.4. Elongated, oval in both sections. Medium-grained, light gray. Pitted and faceted at one end from use as a pounder. Pitting on faces from secondary use as a hammerstone.

S389. Axe, Type 1. Area A. Unit 18. Igneous. Intact. L: 11.0, W: 5.8, Th: 3.6. Triangular. Narrow rounded butt. Well-defined cutting edge. Medium-grained, light gray. Cutting edge pitted and blunt from use as a pounder.

S390. Pecking stone. Area C. Unit 21. Chalcedony. Fragmentary. L: 5.3, W: 4.8, Th: 4.8. As preserved, irregular. Purple/white. Broken faces have smooth areas; remaining surfaces pitted and micro-faceted.

S391. Pecking stone. Area C. Unit 10. Chalcedony. Intact. L: 5.3, W: 5.1, Th: 4.6. Spherical. Cream/gray. One smooth area, remaining surface pitted and micro-faceted.

S392. Pestle. Area A. Unit 18. Igneous. Fragmentary. L: 6.7, W: 4.1, Th: 3.3. Elongated, triangular in transverse section. Sub-rectangular in longitudinal section. One end rounded, the other broken. Medium-grained, gray/brown. Rounded end smoothed and polished from use as a pestle, which is diagnostic of this category.

S393. Dish. Area C. Unit 21. Limestone. Fragmentary. L: 10.4, W: 8.3, Th: 2.1. Triangular. Brown/gray limestone. D of cavity = 4.5 cm, max. Th of side = 2.5 cm, min. Th of base = 1.7 cm.

S394. Pecking stone. Area B. C19A 1. Chalcedony. Fragmentary. L: 7.8, W: 5.2, Th: 3.3. Roughly ovoid in shape and longitudinal section. Brown/gray. Smooth, broken face; greater part of surface pitted and micro-faceted.

S395. Pounder. Area A. Unit 15. Igneous. Intact. L: 5.8, W: 4.4, Th: 3.8. Ovoid. Coarse-grained, gray/brown/blue. Pitting and faceting on one end.

S396. Rubber. Area B. Unit 13. Igneous. Fragmentary. L: 17.8, W: 14.2, Th: 5.5. Sub-rectangular. One end rounded, the other broken. Work face concave. Medium-grained, light gray/white.

S397. Pounder. Area A. Unit 5. Igneous. Intact. L: 11.3, W: 7.4, Th: 4.1. Elongated but irregular. Medium-grained, light gray/white. Triangular in transverse and longitudinal sections. One rounded end. Pitting on rounded end and edges.

S398. Pounder. Area B. Unit 13. Igneous. Intact. L: 9.8, W: 8.4, Th: 3.1. Triangular. One face flat, the other convex. One rounded end. Coarse-grained, gray/light gray. Apexes pitted from pounding. This piece and preceding (S397) are re-used fragments of igneous river stones and appear to have had a specific function, i.e. a small pointed area required for pounding.

S399. Rubbing stone. Area A. Unit 5. Limestone. Fragmentary. L: 7.8, W: 3.8, Th: 2.4. Elongated, oval in transverse section. One flat face, the other convex. Brown/gray. One face smooth from rubbing.

S400. Pounder. Area B. Unit 12. Igneous. Intact. L: 15.6, W: 9.2, Th: 5.1. Elongated, oval in plan and sections. Medium-grained, gray. Pitting on both ends and one side.

S401. Hammerstone. Area B. Unit 12. Igneous. Intact. L: 7.3, W: 6.3, Th: 2.5. Discoidal, flattened. Oval in sections. Fine-grained, light gray. Pitting on one face.

S402. Pounder. Area C. Unit 17. Igneous. Intact. L: 7.1, W: 5.8, Th: 4.5. Elongated ovoid. Fine-grained, light gray. One end pitted and slightly flattened from pounding.

S403. Pecking stone. Area C. Unit 9. Chalcedony. Fragmentary. L: 4.6, W: 4.4, Th: 3.2. As preserved, four (?) roughly flat faces and one curved. Roughly spherical. Brown/cream. Curved face pitted and micro-faceted.

S404. Pounder. Area B. C20B 7. Igneous. Fragmentary. L: 7.5, W: 6.3, Th: 2.7. Ovoid. One face flattened. Coarse-grained, gray/white/brown. Pitting on circumference.

S405. Rubbing stone. Area A. Unit 6. Igneous. Intact. L: 10.4, W: 9.1, Th: 5.0. Discoidal, oval in sections. Coarse-grained, dark gray/light gray. Slight pitting along circumference from pounding. Both faces smooth from use as a rubbing stone.

S407. Pecking stone. Area B. Unit 12. Chalcedony. Intact. L: 6.1, W: 6.0, Th: 4.5. Spherical. Two smooth areas, remaining surface pitted and micro-faceted. Cream/gray.

S408. Pounder. Area C. Unit 21. Igneous. Intact. L: 8.2, W: 6.0, Th: 5.2. Irregular. Fine-grained, light gray. Pitting on one end and side.

S409. Pecking stone. Area A. Unit 6. Chalcedony. Intact. L: 5.1, W: 5.0, Th: 4.9. Spherical. Brown/cream. Pitted and micro-faceted over entire surface.

S410. Pounder. Area A. Unit 6. Igneous. Intact. L: 9.1, W: 5.9, Th: 4.7. Ovoid. Fine-grained, light gray. Pitting on one end from pounding. Striations and pitting on both faces from secondary use as a hammerstone.

S411. Pounder. Area A. Unit 18. Igneous. Intact. L: 9.0, W: 5.8, Th: 5.2. Ovoid. Medium-grained, light gray/dark gray. Pitting on one end.

S412. Pounder. Area B. Unit 12. Igneous. Fragmentary. L: 11.5, W: 7.1, Th: 5.4. Elongated, oval in transverse section, narrowing towards the rounded end. Other end broken. Fine-grained, light gray. Pitting on rounded end.

S413. Pounder, Type 3. Area C. Unit 10. Igneous. Intact. L: 13.0, W: 9.8, Th: 6.4. Irregular, sub-rectangular in plan. Multi-faced. Medium-grained, gray/brown/ light gray. Pitting along one edge and one side.

S414. Pounder. Area A. Unit 32. Igneous. Intact. L: 27.5, W: 10.5, Th: 8.9. Elongated, two faces flat, the other convex, narrowing towards one end. Coarse-grained, dark gray/light gray. Some evidence for pounding or shaping (?) along one edge.

S415. Pounder. Area C. Unit 10. Igneous. Fragmentary. L: 5.0, W: 3.0, Th: 2.0. Elongated, oval in transverse section. One end rounded, the other broken. Medium-grained, gray.

Pitting and flattening on rounded end and one side from pounding.

S416. Axe, Type 2. Area C. Unit 2. Igneous. Intact. L: 5.8, W: 3.5, Th: 1.4. Elongated, flattened, with rounded butt and cutting edge. Roughly oval in transverse section. Cutting edge and part of one side flaked. Fine-grained, gray. This is a crude tool, briefly used for "chopping" or pounding, or it is an unfinished Type 2 axe.

S417. Pounder. Area A. Unit 6. Igneous. Intact. L: 8.7, W: 5.8, Th: 4.9. Ovoid. Medium-grained, gray/brown/blue. Pitting on both ends.

S418. Adze. Area B. Unit 12. Igneous. Fragmentary. L: 3.6, W: 2.0, Th: 1.1. Triangular, oval in transverse section, one end pointed. Medium-grained, gray/dark gray. From the cutting edge of an adze. One side perfectly smooth and flat, the other beveled and rounded. Edge damaged.

S419. Rubber. Area B. Unit 13. Igneous. Fragmentary. L: 11.1, W: 8.8, Th: 4.2. As preserved, irregular. One face flat, the other convex. Coarse-grained, gray.

S420. Pounder. Area C. Unit 10. Igneous. Intact. L: 12.8, W: 6.3, Th: 4.8. Elongated, oval in longitudinal section. One face flat. Coarse-grained, light gray/white. Pitting along curved side from pounding.

S421. Pounder. Area A. Unit 16. Igneous. Fragmentary. L: 7.3, W: 4.1, Th: 2.6. Elongated, oval in transverse section. One rounded end, the other broken. Medium-grained, gray/light blue. Pitting on rounded end.

S422. Rubber. Area B. Unit 13. Igneous. Fragmentary. L: 4.4, W: 3.1, Th: 3.1. As preserved, irregular. Coarse-grained, light gray. One small area smooth from use on a quern.

S424. Gaming stone, Senet. Area B. Unit 12. Limestone. Fragmentary. L: 17.9, W: 13.3, Th: 2.6. Sub-rectangular. Three rows of depressions preserved. Row one: 4 large, 3 very small and unfinished; row two: 8, perhaps 9 preserved; row three: 8 preserved. Av. D of depressions = 0.8 cm; max. Depth = 0.15 cm; av. W of gaming area = 4.5 cm. Possibly a secondary, larger depression at one side.

S425. Gaming stone, Mehen-Senet. Area B. Unit 12. Limestone. Intact. L: 22.0, W: 20.0, Th: 5.4. Two-faced gaming stone. Face A, three rows of depressions: rows 1, 2, 3: ten depressions preserved for each. One large depression beneath gaming area, D = 4.0 cm. Max. W of 3 x 10 area = 9.3 cm. Av. D of depressions = 1.4 cm; av. Depth = 0.2 cm. Face B, depressions form a spiral of 37 preserved depressions.

S426. Quern. Area B. Unit 12. Limestone. Intact. L: 57.0, W: 22.0, Th: 34.0. Ovoid. Underside surface uneven. White. One face pitted and smoothed from use as a saddle quern. Part of original work surface preserved at broad end.

S427. Mortar. Area C. Unit 22. Limestone. Intact. L: 44.5, W: 39.0, Th: 18.0. D-shaped, underside convex, upper face concave with hole in middle. One side rounded. D of hole = 14.0 cm; Depth = 5 cm. Deep mortar depression packed tight with large fragment of an igneous rubber as well as many small chinks.

S428. Quern. Area C. Unit 2. Limestone. Fragmentary. L: 36.5, W: 32.0, Th: 23.5. Both faces convex, underside uneven. Sub-rectangular. White. One face pitted and smoothed from use as a saddle quern.

S429. Function uncertain. Area A. Unit 3. Igneous. Fragmentary. L: 24.0, W: 20.0, Th: 11.0. Sub-rectangular, oval in transverse section. One end broken. Fine-grained, light gray. Intentionally shaped.

S430. Rubber. Area A. Unit 18. Igneous. Intact. L: 29.0, W: 20.0, Th: 14.5. Ovoid. Fine-grained, light gray. Slightly flattened face used as a rubbing stone.

S431. Pounder. Area B. C19A 1. Igneous. Fragmentary. L: 7.1, W: 5.2, Th: 4.1. Elongated, sub-rectangular in plan and in longitudinal section. Medium-grained, gray. Pitting on one end.

S432. Pounder. Area B. Unit 12. Igneous. Intact. L: 13.2, W: 11.2, Th: 5.6. Discoidal, oval in sections. Fine-grained, gray. Pitting on circumference from pounding. Slight pitting on both faces from secondary use as a hammerstone.

S433. Pounder. Area B. Unit 12. Igneous. Intact. L: 8.6, W: 6.2, Th: 4.5. Ovoid. Medium-grained, gray. Deep pitting on both faces from use as a hammerstone and on circumference.

S434. Rubber-pounder. Area B. C19A 1. Igneous. Intact. L: 7.3, W: 7.3, Th: 5.1. Spherical in plan. Oval in transverse section, sub-rectangular in longitudinal section. Fine-grained, light gray. One face smooth from rubbing. Three-fourths of circumference pitted from pounding. Both faces pitted from tertiary use as a hammerstone.

S435. Pounder. Area B. C19A 1. Igneous. Intact. L: 8.5, W: 5.7, Th: 4.8. Irregular, multi-faced, oval in plan. Medium-grained, gray/blue/white. Pitting on one end.

S436. Pecking stone. Area A. Unit 5. Chalcedony. Fragmentary. L: 8.5, W: 8.3, Th: 5.6. Spherical in plan. As preserved, roughly half a sphere. Larger than the average pecking stones. Brown. Apart from broken face, two smooth areas. Rest of surface pitted and micro-faceted.

S437. Hammerstone. Area B. Unit 12. Igneous. Intact. L: 7.5, W: 6.0, Th: 4.3. Ovoid. Medium-grained, dark gray/light gray. Pitting on one face from use as a hammerstone. Wear marks consist of series of parallel striations.

S438. Hammerstone. Area C. Unit 22. Igneous. Intact. L: 7.5, W: 7.1, Th: 6.0. Roughly triangular, very rounded ends. Oval in sections. Fine-grained, light gray. Pitting on faces from use as a hammerstone.

S439. Pounder. Area C. Unit 22. Igneous. Intact. L: 8.7, W: 6.5, Th: 4.8. Ovoid. Medium-grained, black/light gray. Both ends pitted from pounding.

S440. Pounder. Area B. C19A 1. Igneous. Intact. L: 7.0, W: 5.8, Th: 2.3. Triangular, very rounded ends. Oval in sections. Medium-grained, dark gray/brown. Narrow end faceted from use as a pounder. The faceting may have been the first step in the preparation of a small adze(?). Perhaps some evidence of pitting and shaping on the other angles as well.

S441. Pounder. Area C. Unit 22. Igneous. Intact. L: 12.0, W: 4.7, Th: 3.9. Elongated, oval in section. Fine-grained, gray. Deep pitting on both faces from use as a hammerstone. Pitting on both ends.

S442. Pounder. Area A. Unit 4 Phase I. Igneous. Intact. L: 8.0, W: 8.0, Th: 4.1. Triangular, uneven surfaces. Fine-grained, dark gray. Pitting on all ends from pounding. Burnt.

S443. Pounder. Area C. Unit 22. Igneous. Fragmentary. L: 5.7, W: 4.9, Th: 3.8. As preserved, conical, but with rounded end. Oval in longitudinal section. Coarse-grained, dark gray/blue/brown. Pitting on rounded end.

S444. Pounder. Area B. Unit 12. Igneous. Intact. L: 8.7, W: 5.7, Th: 3.0. Sub-rectangular, two sides flat. Wedge-shaped. Fine-grained, gray. Pitting on one end and edges.

S445. Pounder. Area B. C19A 1. Igneous. Intact. L: 8.4, W: 7.5, Th: 5.7. Irregular, multi-faced. Fine-grained, light gray. Two faces smooth and flat from rubbing.

S446. Dish. Area A. Unit 35. Igneous. Fragmentary. L: 18.5, W: 9.9, Th: 4.1. As preserved, part of a circle. Large cavity, D = 3.3 cm. Av. Th = 4 cm. Fine-grained, light gray. Cavity smoothed and pitted from use as a mortar.

S447. Rubbing stone. Area A. Unit 7. Limestone. Fragmentary. L: 11.1, W: 6.4, Th: 2.8. Elongated, one end broken, the other rounded. Oval in transverse section. White/gray limestone. One face worn smooth from rubbing.

S448. Rubber-pounder. Area C. Unit 9. Igneous. Intact. L: 10.1, W: 5.8, Th: 4.8. Elongated ovoid. Coarse-grained, dark gray/brown/ light gray. One face worn smooth from rubbing. Both ends pitted.

S449. Rubber-pounder. Area A. Unit 43. Igneous. Intact. L: 11.9, W: 7.1, Th: 4.5. Elongated, sub-rectangular in sections. One end narrower and more rounded. Medium-grained, gray/dark gray/brown. Both faces and area of one side worn smooth from rubbing. Both ends pitted.

S450. Adze. Area A. Unit 6. Igneous. Fragmentary. L: 3.6, W: 2.9, Th: 1.1. Sub-rectangular, oval in transverse section. Cutting edge preserved, butt missing. Fine-grained, gray. Cutting edge slightly chipped from use as an adze.

S451. Pounder. Area A. Unit 19. Igneous. Fragmentary. L: 9.9, W: 9.0, Th: 5.0. Sub-rectangular in plan and in longitudinal section. One face flat, the other convex. Coarse-grained, black. One end pitted.

S453. Rubber. Area A. Unit 16. Igneous. Fragmentary. L: 16.0, W: 8.9, Th: 5.8. Elongated, sub-rectangular. Two roughly straight sides, one curved. One face flat, the other convex and broken. Medium-grained, light gray.

S454. Pounder. Area A. Unit 38. Igneous. Intact. L: 10.8, W: 8.9, Th: 5.4. Sub-rectangular in plan and longitudinal section. Triangular in transverse section. One face flat, the other convex. Medium-grained, gray/white. Flat face smoothed from original use as a rubber. All angles pitted from subsequent use as a pounder.

S455. Rubber-pounder. Area A. Unit 16. Igneous. Intact. L: 14.8, W: 9.0, Th: 6.0. Elongated, irregular and multi-faced. Fine-grained, gray. Pitting on both ends from pounding. One face well-smoothed and pitted from tertiary use as a hammerstone.

S456. Stone weight. Area B. Unit 12. Limestone. Intact. L: 23.5, W: 18.0, Th: 6.0. Irregular shape with rounded angles. Flat. Circular pecked hourglass perforation. Max. D = 6.1; min. D = 3.5

S457. Worked picrolite. Area C. Unit 17. Fragmentary. L: 2.4, W: 1.6, Th: 0.7. Triangular, with one side curved and the other two flat. Light green/white.

S458. Worked picrolite. Area A. Unit 7. Fragmentary. L:4.2, W: 3.0, Th:1.6. Flattened, irregular shape. One face roughly flat, the other convex. Blue/white.

S459. Worked picrolite. Area C. Unit 21. Fragmentary. L: 4.7, W: 1.4, Th: 1.2. Elongated. Sub-rectangular, two rounded angles. Light gray/green/white.

S460. Bead, tublar object. Area A. Unit 16. Picrolite. Fragmentary. L: 3.6, W: 1.1, Th: 1.1. Cylindrical. Central perforation. Another perforation near one end, measuring 0.5 x 0.4.

S461. Bead, tubular object. Area A. Unit 16. Picrolite. Fragmentary. L: 2.8, W: 1.3, Th: 1.3. Cylindrical, with central perforation. Two more perforations near one end. One measures 0.6 x 0.5, the other 0.5 x 0.4. Light gray/green.

S462. Worked picrolite. Area B. Unit 12. Fragmentary. L: 2.4, W: 1.8, Th: 1.0. Triangular in plan. Sub-rectangular in sections. Very light green.

S463. Worked picrolite. Area C. Unit 2. Fragmentary. L: 3.8, W: 1.5, Th: 0.6. Sub-rectangular in plan, with one side curved and a corner missing. Sub-rectangular in sections. Light gray/green/white.

S464. Worked picrolite. Area B. Unit 12. Fragmentary. L: 2.4, W: 1.5, Th: 1.5. Cylindrical. Broken flat face, the other rounded. Light gray/green/white brown.

S465. Anthropomorphic figurine. Area A. Unit 16. Picrolite. Fragmentary, head missing. L: 0.6, W: 0.4, Th: 0.15. Anthropomorphic pendant, of the same type as S471, only smaller in size. Both faces show shallow scratches and the perforation has been drilled.

S466. Whetstone? Area A. Unit 18. Limestone. Fragmentary. L: 2.9, W: 1.5, Th: 1.3. Elongated, roughly square with rounded corners in transverse section. Fine-grained, gray. All faces well-smoothed. One face flat from prolonged use as a whetstone(?). Preserved end also well smoothed.

S467. Gaming stone, Senet. Area B. Unit 12. Limestone. Intact. L: 28.0, W: 24.2, Th: 0.7. Irregular-shaped. Gaming area face roughly flat, the other uneven. Three rows of ten depressions each. Av. D of depressions = 1.5; av. Depth = 0.2; W of gaming area = 6.1; L = 19.5.

S468. Pendant. Area C. Unit 9. Picrolite. Intact. L: 2.0, W: 0.9, Th: 0.3. Rhomboid. Flattened. Perforation roughly in middle. Light gray/green/white. D of perforation = 0.3 cm.

S469. Anthropomorphic figurine (pendant). Area A. Unit 7. Picrolite. Intact. L: 2.7, W: 1.3, Th: 0.4. Ovoid. Light green/ white. Perforation near narrower end. Small puncture near broader end, D = 0.3. D of perforation = 0.5.

S470. Function uncertain. Area A. Unit 40. Igneous. Intact. L: 4.3, W: 1.5, Th: 1.3. Elongated. Sub-triangular in plan and in longitudinal section. Oval in transverse section. Wedge-shaped. Medium-grained, gray/light blue. One end highly burnished.

S471. Anthropomorphic figurines (pendants). Cemetery A. Tomb 15. Seven made of picrolite, one of shell. Mostly intact. Seven pieces from a necklace and a foot of a pendant, plus one found water sieving. L: between 1.3 and 1.9. Drilled perforations. Hourglass in section with horizontal striations.
#1. Surface gray and polished. Both faces show diagonal scratch marks from original manufacturing process. L: 1.28, Th: 0.15.
#2. Same surface treatment as #1 only slightly broader head.
#3. Same surface treatment and color as #1. Where the foot has been broken off the light green picrolite is visible. H (pres): 1.26, Th: 0.15.
#4. Light green. Same surface treatment. Without a shaped head. If there had once been a head that broke off during manufacture, the "broken" edge was left in a well-rounded and symmetrical state. H: 1.28, Th: 0.2.

#5. Light gray and smaller, otherwise identical to the others. H: 1.24, Th: 0.13.
#6. Same color as #5. Foot is slightly rounder, instead of flat like others, and the "head" is slightly damaged. H: 1.46, Th: 0.15.
#7. White shell, matte on one face, lustrous on the other. Slightly convex on the matte (outer) surface. The shape is different with the addition of the "arm stubs." The horizontal striations of the drill holes are very visible on this piece. Note the lack of signs of wear on this rather soft shell. H: 1.9, Th: 0.17.
#8. Dark gray picrolite, otherwise identical to #1. H: 1.3, Th.: 0.17.

S472. Bead? F20A 4. Limestone. Fragmentary. L: 2.0, W: 1.0, Th: 1.2. Semi-circular in plan and longitudinal section. Oval in transverse section. White.

S473. Necklace spacer. Area A. Unit 6. Picrolite. Intact. L: 2.7, W: 0.9, Th: 0.2. Rectangular in shape and sections. Two small perforations at either end. Light green. Restored. D of perforations = 0.2 cm.

S474. Perforated disc. Area C. Unit 2. Limestone (siltstone). Intact. L: 3.1, W: 2.6, Th: 0.6. Irregular ovoid. One face flattened with ca. 24 shallow depressions. Av. D = 0.3 cm. Perforation in the middle. D of perforation = 3.7 cm. Fine-grained, gray. Mostly intact, some chipping on one edge. Shallow drilled depressions are arranged in an irregular circle around the central perforation. Function unknown.

S475. Gaming stone, Senet. Area A. Unit 18. Limestone. Fragmentary. L: 14.3, W: 11.6, Th: 4.6. Irregular. Three rows of depressions: Row one, five preserved; row two, six preserved; row three, eight preserved. Av. dimensions of depressions = 1.2 x 0.8 cm. W of gaming area = 5.1 cm. One large depression below gaming area, D = 3.1; W = 1.9; Depth = 0.6.

S476. Rubber. Area A. Unit 38. Igneous. Fragmentary. L: 9.4, W: 9.1, Th: 8.2. As preserved, irregular. Sub-rectangular in plan. Two convex faces. Coarse-grained, gray/white/ brown. One face flat from use.

S477. Pounder. Area A. Unit 38. Igneous. Intact. L: 7.9, W: 7.4, Th: 7.0. Spheroid. Medium-grained, gray. Signs of faceting over whole surface.

S478. Pounder. Area C. Unit 22. Igneous. Intact. L: 13.0, W: 9.8, Th: 6.3. Elongated, oval in transverse section. Fine-grained, light gray. One end pitted and flattened from pounding. One face pitted, the other has a deep depression from secondary use as a hammerstone. Signs of hammering on sides.

S479. Function uncertain. Stone with groove. Area A. Unit 7. Limestone. Intact. L: 15.5, W: 6.8, Th: 6.0. Slightly phallic, bottle-shaped. Elongated, oval in transverse section. In longitudinal section, one end rounded near groove, the other flattened. Chip missing on grooved area. Broad groove 3 cm from rounded end, W = ca. 2 cm, av. Depth = 3 mm, circumventing stone. Groove crudely pecked. Other end, flattened and damaged, possibly used as a pounder. Function unknown.

S480. Rubbing stone.   Area B.   C19A <u>1</u>. Limestone. Fragmentary. L: 14.2, W: 5.6, Th: 5.0. Elongated: oval in transverse section.   One end rounded, the other broken. Brown. One face smooth from rubbing.

S481. Pounder. Area C. Unit 22. Igneous. Intact. L: 7.7, W: 7.8, Th: 5.5.   Roughly circular.   Oval in transverse section. Fine-grained, gray.   Pitting along circumference from pounding. Both ends faceted. Pitting on faces from secondary use as a hammerstone.

S482. Pounder. Area A. Unit 37. Igneous. Intact. L: 8.9, W: 9.4, Th: 6.9. D-shaped in plan and sections. Two flat faces, one convex.   Medium-grained, gray/white.   Pitting on one face and all edges.

S483. Pecking stone. Area A. Unit 38. Chalcedony. Intact. L: 5.8, W: 5.8, Th: 4.4.   Spherical.   Brown.   Three smooth areas. Remaining surface pitted and micro-faceted.

S484. Pecking stone.   Area A.   Unit 18. Chalcedony. Fragmentary. L: 5.5, W: 3.7, Th: 4.0. As preserved, irregular. Many smooth faces. One small area pitted and micro-faceted. Gray/white.

S485. Pounder. Area B. C19A <u>1</u>. Igneous. Intact. L: 9.5, W: 4.9, Th: 4.1. Elongated. Ovoid. Medium-grained, gray. Faint pitting on both ends from pounding. Pitting on one side from secondary use as a hammerstone.

S486. Pounder. Area C. H23/24 <u>2</u>. Igneous. Intact. L: 8.0, W: 6.1, Th: 5.4.   Ovoid.   Coarse-grained, dark gray/blue. Pitting on both ends from pounding. Pitting on both faces from secondary use as a hammerstone.

S487. Rubbing stone. Area A. Unit 35. Igneous. Intact. L: 11.4, W: 10.3, Th: 6.5. Discoidal, oval in section. Medium-grained, gray/blue. One face smooth from rubbing. Pitting on one face from secondary use as a hammerstone.

S488. Pounder. Area A. I17A <u>6</u>. Igneous. Fragmentary. L: 11.2, W: 10.8, Th: 7.5.   D-shaped.   One side narrower than the other. One end rounded, the other flat and broken. Fine-grained, light gray. Pitting on one face from secondary use as a hammerstone. Pitting on both ends.

S489. Stone with natural perforation. Area A. G17C <u>1</u>. Limestone. Fragmentary. L: 10.5, W: 8.0, Th: 6.4. Ovoid. From side view, a parallelogram with unequal sides. Two sides asymmetrically perforated. D of larger side = 2 x 1.9;

of smaller side = 1.5 x 1.8.   Cream-colored.   This object is not an artifact but might have served as some kind of weight.

S490. Rubber. Area B. Unit 12. Limestone. Fragmentary. L: 28.0, W: 27.5, Th: 23.0. Irregular. One face smooth with two holes, the other uneven.

S491. Perforated stone (weight). Area A. Unit 18. Limestone. Intact. L: 22.5, W: 18.8, Th: 18.0. Irregular. Two perforations: first measures 2.3 x 1.9 at one end and 1.8 x 1.8 cm at the other, second measures 3.7 x 2.9 at one end and 2.3 x 2.3 at the other.

S492. Function uncertain.   Stone with depression.   Area C. Unit 9. Limestone.   Intact.   L: 21.5, W: 15.5, Th: 9.8. Rectangular, with one corner missing. Rectangular in sections. Depression near one side, D = 3.7 cm, Depth = 1.7 cm.

S493. Rubber. Area B. Unit 12. Limestone. Fragmentary. L: 20.5, W: 17.4, Th: 6.5. D-shaped. Work face smooth and convex. Underside uneven. White. Work face smooth from use on a quern.

S494. Rubber. Area B. Unit 12. Limestone. Fragmentary. L: 23.5, W: 16.5, Th: 8.8. D-shaped. Work face convex. Underside convex, but uneven. White. Work face pitted and smoothed from use on a quern.

S495. Quern. Area A. Unit 16. Limestone. Intact. L: 30.0, W: 25.0, Th: 10.0. Irregular-shaped. One face flat, the other uneven.

S496. Function uncertain.   Stone with depressions.   Area C. Unit 9. Limestone. Intact. L: 27.0, W: 20.0, Th: 6.0. Irregular. One face flat, the other uneven. One depression on uneven face: D = 5.6 cm, Depth = 2.3 cm. Second depression: D = 3 cm, Depth = 1 cm.

S497. Perforated stone (weight?). Area C. Unit 2. Limestone. Intact. L: 24.5, W: 15.7, Th: 11.4. Natural piece of limestone. Uneven shape and surfaces. Two perforations. One measures 7.3 x 4.3. The second measures 4.2 x 4. They unite on the other face where the perforation measures 6.7 x 5.6 cm.

S498. Rubber. Area A. Unit 37. Limestone. Fragmentary. L: 26.0, W: 24.4, Th: 11.1. Sub-rectangular. Longitudinal section concave. Transverse flat, the underside uneven. One side narrower than the other. Work surface pitted and smooth from use on a quern.

S499. Perforated stone. Area A. Unit 18. Limestone. Intact. L: 30.0, W: 25.5, Th: 9.0.   Ovoid.   Uneven circumference. One face flat, underside uneven. Two perforations on one side joining on the other. Two perforations: 6.6 x 6 cm and 3.3 x 2.9 cm. One on other face: 10.5 x 6.7 cm.

S500. Quern. Area B. Unit 12. Limestone. Fragmentary. L: 26.0, W: 18.5, Th: 11.2.   Sub-rectangular.   One face smooth and concave, the other uneven and convex. Work face pitted from use as a quern.

S501. Function uncertain. Stone with depression. Area A. Unit 32. Limestone. Intact. L: 28.0, W: 18.5, Th: 8.0. Sub-rectangular. Irregular and uneven sides. Depression near one end: 7.2 x 5.6cm, Depth = 1.4 cm.

S502. Perforated stone (weight). Area C. Unit 2. Limestone. Intact. L: 29.2, W: 21.8, Th: 9.2. D-shaped, oval in section. One face quite smooth, the other very rough. Perforation near one side: 4.5 x 4.5 on one face and 4.5 x 4 on the other.

S503. Double mortar. Area C. Unit 9. Limestone. Fragmentary. L: 25.0, W: 23.5, Th: 13.0. Originally sub-rectangular. Cavities on both faces. First: L = 13.1 cm, Depth = 4.6 cm. Second: L = 15 cm, Depth = 4.2 cm.

S504. Rubbing stone. Area A. Unit 18. Igneous. Fragmentary. L: 26.0, W: 21.3, Th: 7.5. D-shaped. Both faces convex. Convex in transverse section. Coarse-grained, dark gray/white/blue. This is an unusually large Type 3 rubbing stone. No transverse striations visible, but convex transverse section of work surface proves use as a rubbing stone.

S505. Rubber. Area B. Unit 12. Igneous. Intact. L: 43.0, W: 15.3, Th: 11.5. Elongated. Ovoid. Both faces concave in longitudinal section, convex in transverse section. Medium-grained, gray/green/blue. Both ends rise toward the original work surface which was ground down from rubbing on a quern. Transverse striations clearly visible.

S506. Perforated stone (weight?)/tethering stone? Area B. Unit 12. Limestone. Intact. L: 36.0, W: 28.5, Th: 23.0. Irregular. Uneven surfaces. Perforation at one end: 9 x 7cm on one face, 8.5 x 5 cm on the other.

S507. Rubber. Area C. Unit 23. Igneous. Intact. L: 40.0, W: 20.0, Th: 9.2. Ovoid. One rounded end narrower and thicker than the other. Large convex area on one face, work face. Coarse-grained, dark gray/light blue. Work face smooth.

S508. Quern. Area B. Unit 12. Limestone. Fragmentary. L: 37.3, W: 28.5, Th: 25.0. Irregular. One face smooth, the underside rough. White. Only a small portion of an unusually large quern.

S509. Rubber blank(?) Area A. Unit 5. Igneous. Intact. L: 36.0, W: 20.0, Th: 13.0. Ovoid. Sub-rectangular in transverse section. Medium-grained, gray. All surfaces flat and smooth.

S510. Work surface. Area C. Unit 21. Igneous. Fragmentary. L: 32.0, W: 21.0, Th: 8.0. Ovoid. Coarse-grained, black. One face altered from use as a work surface. Burnt.

S511. Pounder. Area B. C19A 2. Igneous. Fragmentary. L: 8.3, W: 4.7, Th: 4.5. Part of a discoidal pounder, oval in longitudinal section. One end rounded, the other broken. Fine-grained, light gray. Pitting on rounded end.

S512. Pecking stone. Area B. C19A 1. White chalcedony. Fragmentary. L: 5.3, W: 4.6, Th: 3.0. Spheroid-cuboid. Two smooth areas, the rest pitted and micro-faceted.

S513. Mortar. Area C. Unit 9. Limestone. Fragmentary. L: 11.6, W: 7.4, Th: 4.7. Sub-rectangular. Underside convex but irregular. Cavity in middle: 6 x 4.7 cm, Depth = 1.7 cm. Cavity pitted.

S514. Rubber-pounder. Area B. C19A 1. Igneous. Fragmentary. L: 7.1, W: 5.1, Th: 2.8. Elongated, oval in transverse section. One end rounded, the other broken. Fine-grained, gray. Slight pitting on rounded end from pounding. One face well flattened and very smooth with very fine transverse scratches, result of prolonged use as a rubbing stone. Evidence of shaping on back towards broken end.

S515. Rubber-pounder. Area A. Unit 38. Igneous. Intact. L: 9.5, W: 6.4, Th: 3.0. Discoidal. One face flat, the other convex. Fine-grained, light gray. Pitting on the circumference from pounding. One face smooth from rubbing. Pitting on both faces from tertiary use as a hammerstone.

S516. Pounder. Area A. Unit 38. Igneous. Intact. L: 12.6, W: 10.9, Th: 4.7. Triangular, with one side curved. One face flat, the other convex. Coarse-grained, light gray/green/blue. Pitting on the rounded side and all angles. This object was first used as a rubber.

S517. Rubber-pounder. Area A. Unit 38. Igneous. Intact. L: 6.5, W: 6.0, Th: 3.3. Almost circular in plan. One face flat, the other wedge-shaped. Sub-rectangular in sections. Fine-grained, gray. Circumference pitted and flattened from pounding or intentional shaping. One face smooth and flat from rubbing. Signs of flattening from rubbing on other face. (Closest parallel to an Episkopi *Phaneromeni* grinder pounder).

S518. Adze? Area A. Unit 35. Igneous. Fragmentary. L: 11.7, W: 8.0, Th: 1.9. Truncated conical. Cutting edge missing, butt badly damaged. Fine-grained, gray. Both faces ground smooth. Transverse striations from this operation clearly visible. Edges flattened.

S519. Pounder. Area B. C19A 1. Igneous. Intact. L: 10.7, W: 9.3, Th: 3.0. Irregular. One face flat, the other convex. Medium-grained, dark gray/green/ blue. All angles pitted from pounding. Faceting and pitting on one side from pounding. Prior use as a rubber.

S520. Pounder. Area B. C19A 1. Igneous. Intact. L: 9.1, W: 6.8, Th: 6.7. Roughly oval in plan and sections. Multi-faced. Coarse-grained, dark gray/ brown/blue. Pitting on the rounded ends from pounding.

S521. Axe, Type 1. Area A. Unit 1 Phase I. Igneous. Intact. L: 10.2, W: 5.5, Th: 2.9. Elongated, with narrow butt. Both faces convex. Rounded end damaged. Fine-grained, gray. Cutting edge ground smooth on both faces prior to secondary use as a pounder.

S522. Pounder. Area A. Unit 38. Igneous. Intact. L: 9.4, W: 6.8, Th: 4.0. Irregular. One face flat, the other convex. Three flat sides, one curved. Medium-grained, gray/brown. Pitting along one end and one side from pounding. Previously used as a rubber.

S523. Rubber-pounder. Area C. H24A 1. Igneous. Fragmentary. L: 7.7, W: 7.4, Th: 3.4. One face flat, the other convex. One end rounded, the other broken. Medium-grained, gray/brown/blue. Pitting along intact sides from pounding. One face smooth from rubbing. Pitting from tertiary use as a hammerstone.

S524. Axe, Type 1. Area C. Unit 22. Igneous. Intact. L: 6.5, W: 3.9, Th: 1.1. Elongated, with narrow butt and broad, rounded cutting edge. Fine-grained, gray. Both faces very smooth, sides flat and smooth, somewhat faceted. Butt either damaged or unfinished. Cutting edge still very sharp and well polished. Clearly an axe and not an adze.

S525. Mortar. Area B. C19A 1. Limestone. Fragmentary. L: 6.1, W: 4.4, Th: 3.3. Ovoid. Cavity in middle: 4.2 x 3.3cm, Depth = 1.3 cm.

S526. Rubber. Area A. Unit 19. Igneous. Fragmentary. L: 7.5, W: 6.0, Th: 4.4. Irregular. One face flat, the other convex. Coarse-grained, dark gray/brown/ white/blue. One face pitted and flat from use on quern.

S527. Rubber-pounder. Area A. Unit 19. Igneous. Fragmentary. L: 12.5, W: 8.7, Th: 5.3. Sub-rectangular, with one corner missing. Elongated, sub-rectangular in both sections. Medium-grained, gray/blue. Two ends pitted from pounding. Pitting on one face from tertiary use as a hammerstone. Both faces smoothed from rubbing.

S528. Pecking stone. Area A. Unit 19. Chalcedony. Intact. L: 4.8, W: 4.1, Th: 4.0. Spherical, slightly cuboid. Gray/ white. Pitted and micro-faceted all over.

S529. Pounder. Area A. H17B. Surface. Igneous. Fragmentary. L: 11.6, W: 9.3, Th: 7.1. Elongated, sub-rectangular. Irregular in transverse section. One end rounded. Fine-grained, light gray. Pitting and faceting on rounded end and on both sides. Pitting on other side. Evidence of secondary use as a hammerstone.

S530. Gaming stone, Mehen-Senet. Area B. C19A 1. Limestone. Fragmentary. L: 12.0, W: 11.2, Th: 3.5. Irregular. Uneven surfaces. Depressions seem to form a spiral. Av. D of depressions = 1.3 cm, Depth = 0.2 cm. Cream/brown. Ca.

20 depressions. Mehen well preserved. Possible Senet on other face.

S531. Function uncertain. Stone with groove. Area A. Unit 4. Limestone. Intact. L: 7.4, W: 4.4, Th: 3.2. Sub-rectangular in plan and section. One end flattened, the other rounded. Groove 2 cm from flattened end circumvents stone: W = 1 cm, Depth = 0.4 cm. Function uncertain, but is vaguely phallic in appearance. Is there a connection with S479 (which is also somewhat phallic)?

S532. Gaming stone, Senet. Area A. Unit 37. Limestone. Fragmentary. L: 18.0, W: 16.0, Th: 5.8. Sub-rectangular. Three rows of very shallow worn depressions: row one, six depressions; row two, five depressions; row three, six depressions. Av. D = 1 cm; W of playing area = 5.5 cm; D of large depression = ca .2.5 cm, Depth = 0.4 cm.

S533. Gaming stone, Senet. Area C. H24C 1. Surface. Limestone. Fragmentary. L: 19.2, W: 13.0, Th: 6.8. Sub-rectangular. Face of gaming area flat, underside uneven. Row 1: four depressions preserved, row; 2: 9 depressions.

S534. Pounder. Area C. Unit 22. Igneous. Intact. L: 10.4, W: 8.2, Th: 4.6. Irregular in plan. One face flat. Triangular in transverse section. Medium-grained, gray/brown. Pitting on angles from pounding.

S535. Work surface. Area A. G17D 1. Limestone. Fragmentary. L: 11.7, W: 7.9, Th: 2.3. D-shaped. One face flat and smooth face, the other irregular. Brown. Work face flat and smooth.

S536. Pecking stone. Area C. Unit 22. Chert. Intact. L: 9.7, W: 8.4, Th: 7.0. Multi-faced and angular. All surfaces faceted from use as a pounder, some areas micro-faceted. Light to dark brown chert, with some buff veins.

S537. Pounder. Area B. C19A 1. Igneous. Intact. L: 5.7, W: 3.4, Th: 1.5. Ovoid. One rounded end narrower than the other. Fine-grained, gray/green. Both ends pitted.

S538. Axe, Type 1? Area B. C19A 1. Igneous. Fragmentary. L: 5.7, W: 2.8, Th: 3.1. Roughly conical in plan. Oval in longitudinal section. Part of cutting edge preserved. Fine-grained, gray. Probably fragment of a Type 1 axe.

S539. Adze. Area B. C19A 1. Igneous. Fragmentary. L: 5.5, W: 3.0, Th: 1.3. Ovoid, with one large chip missing. Rounded broad butt. Cutting edge damaged. Less than half preserved. Fine-grained, light gray.

S540. Pounder. Area A. I17A 1. Igneous. Fragmentary. L: 6.9, W: 4.9, Th: 3.0. Elongated, sub-rectangular. Sub-triangular in transverse section. Coarse-grained, gray/white/ brown. One end pitted.

S541. Function uncertain. Area A. I17A 1. Igneous. Fragmentary. L: 5.3, W: 4.1, Th: 3.3. Ovoid in plan, roughly conical in section. One face flat, the other convex. Intact surfaces very smooth. Fine-grained, gray/green/white.

S542. Pendant. Area C. Unit 10. Picrolite. Intact. L: 3.7, W: 1.9, Th: 0.6. Ovoid, flattened. Flattened sides. Slightly chipped on one face. Perforation near one end: dimensions = 0.4 x 0.4 cm. Blue gray/white.

S543. Beads. Cemetery A. Tomb 15. Stone. Intact. 132 beads. Small, cylindrical, drilled, made from various materials. See S208 for dimensions and materials used.

S544. Worked picrolite. Area C. H24C. Unstratified. Fragmentary. L: 3.6, W: 1.6, Th: 0.9. Elongated. One end rounded, the other flat and broken. Ovoid in transverse section. Light green/gray/white.

S545. Pendant. Area A. Unit 5. Picrolite. Intact. L: 1.5, W: 0.6, Th: 0.3. Sub-rectangular, two sides slightly curved. Perforation near one end. Light gray/green.

S546. Gaming stone, Senet. Area C. Unit 21. Limestone. Intact. L: 33.0, W: 25.5, Th: 7.8. Sub-rectangular. Three rows of ten depressions each. W of gaming area = ca.7.1 cm. Av. dimensions of depressions = 1.6 x 1.4 cm, Depth = 0.2 cm. Large puncture near one side = 3.6 x 3.6 cm.

S547. Grooved stone. Area A. Unit 5. Igneous. Intact. L: 11.6, W: 8.0, Th: 8.0. Ovoid. Brown ultra mafic stone. Very rare at *Kaminoudhia*. Groove on one flattened face, roughly in middle. Shallow groove: L=2.6 cm, Depth = 0.6 m.

S548. Mortar. Area B. Unit 12. Limestone. Fragmentary. L: 50.0, W: 44.0, H: ca. 31, Th of side wall: 4, Depth of cavity: 27. Oval in plan. Straight, slightly convex sides, carefully shaped. Flat base. Broken in antiquity. Two opposing rectangular trunnions close to the base.

S549. Axe, Type 1. Area C. Unit 22. Igneous. Intact. L:11.5, W:6.2, Th:4.6. Elongated. Oval in transverse section. Rounded narrow butt. Narrows toward straight, cutting edge. Medium-grained, gray.

S550. Mortar. Area C. Unit 22. Limestone. Fragmentary. L: 32.0, W: 13.0, Th: 7.0. Small fragment, wedge-shaped, of side of deep mortar. One face concave, the other convex. Medium-grained, off-white. Fragment comprises entire profile, from rim to base, part of which is missing. Outer edge has a small rectangular trunnion, 8 x 5.5 cm, protruding 2 cm from surface.

S551. Pendant? Area A. Unit 5. Picrolite. Fragmentary. L: 2.0, W: 1.2, Th: 0.3. Roughly lozenge-shaped. Dark gray through burning. One side well smoothed and rounded, the other broken. Hourglass drill hole in one corner. This might have been a pendant.

S553. Pounder. Area A. Unit 7. Igneous. Intact. L: 8.7, W: 7.8, Th: 5.7. Roughly quadrangular. Medium-grained, blue/gray. Unaltered river stone with both ends pitted.

S554. Mortar. Area C. Unit 25. Limestone. Fragmentary. L: 9.7, W: 3.5, Fine-grained, off-white. Shallow, well pecked depression clearly visible. The depression would probably have been oval.

S555. Pecking stone. Area C. Unit 25. Quartz. Intact. L: 5.3, W: 5.3. Brown veined with white. Roughly cuboid. All sides abraded from pecking.

S556. Mortar. Area C. Unit 8. Limestone. Intact. L: 27.2, W: 17.3, Th: 14.0. Sub-rectangular with deep oval depression in one face. Medium-grained, buff. Well-shaped and smoothed on all surfaces. Hollow (20 x 11 x 8.8 cm), carefully shaped and quite smooth, especially on bottom.

S557. Pounder. Area C. Unit 10. Igneous. Intact. L: 12.9, W: 6.4, Th: 4.9. Elongated ovoid. Fine-grained, gray. One end rounded, the other flattened from pounding. Signs of pounding on rounded end.

S558. Pounder. Area C. Unit 10. Igneous. Intact. L: 9.4, W: 5.8, Th: 5.3. Roughly ovoid. Medium-grained, light gray. Signs of random pounding on circumference and both faces.

S559. Pounder. Area C. Unit 23. Igneous. Intact. L: 11.7, W: 7.0, Th: 6.2. Roughly triangular. Quadrangular in section. Medium-grained, gray. All apexes and one angle used for pounding.

S560. Pounder. Area C. Unit 23. Igneous. Intact. L: 7.9, W: 4.9, Roughly ovoid. Fine-grained, dark gray. Both ends and one area of circumference with faint signs of pounding.

S561. Pounder. Area C. Unit 23. Limestone. Intact. L:11.3, W:6.7, Th:5.2. Elongated ovoid. Fine-grained, off-white. Faint signs of pounding at one end.

S562. Hammerstone-anvil. Area A. Unit 3. Igneous. Intact. L: 10.8, W: 4.5. Quadrangular in plan, triangular in section. Fine-grained, gray. Two faces have scratch marks, probably from use as an anvil during flint knapping.

S563. Slab. Cemetery A. Tomb 17. Limestone. Fragmentary. L: 24.5, W: 16.5, Th: 1.2. Three side of a square or rectangle preserved. Fourth side irregular and broken. Fine-grained, white. Before breakage, this was a well-squared slab of tabular limestone. Apparent signs of burning on one side, the other shows no sign of discoloration. Note that the missing fragments were not recovered from the tomb. Usage uncertain.

S564. Pounder. Area C. Stratified. Igneous. Intact. Roughly discoidal. Medium grained, dark gray. Circumference pitted.

S565. Mortar. Area C. Unit 21. Limestone. Intact. L: 33.5, W: 30.0, Th: 17.0. Roughly ovoid. Outer surface irregular convex, inner surface quite smooth and concave. Medium-grained, off-white. Carefully hollowed depression, the bottom of which is concave not flat. Pecking marks clearly visible. This piece could be classified either as a mortar or a trough. Size of depression = 26.5 x 22.5 x 8 cm.

S566. Axe, Type 1. Southeast trial trench. Surface. Igneous. Fragmentary. L: 6.2, W: 5.8, Th: 3.8. Elongated, hemispherical. Medium-grained, gray. Blade end of an axe. Both faces taper sharply towards the cutting edge, which has been abraded by secondary use as a pounder.

S567. Stone basin. Area C. Unit 21. Limestone. Fragmentary. L: 23.1, W: 13.0, Th: 13.3. Irregular fragment. One surface flat (base), one convex (outside), one concave (inside). Medium-grained, buff. Fragment of a large, circular shallow mortar with a rough inner surface.

S568. Stone basin. Area C. Unit 21. Limestone. Fragmentary. L: 36.0, W: 22.0, Th: 13.0. Irregular fragment. One surface flat (base), one convex (outside), one concave (inside). Medium-grained, buff. Fragment of a large circular basin with straight edges and a flat bottom, quite well smoothed.

S569. Rubber-pounder. Area C. Unit 21. Igneous. Fragmentary. L: 9.5, W: 6.3, Th: 5.4. Elongated ovoid. Medium-grained, light green/gray. One face smooth from rubbing and the preserved end pitted from pounding.

S570. Pounder. Area C. Unit 21. Igneous. Intact. L: 8.5, W: 5.0, Th: 4.2. Elongated ellipsoid, oval in section. Medium-grained, gray. Both ends slightly pitted from pounding.

S571. Hammerstone. Area C. Unit 21. Igneous. Intact. L: 13.5, W: 10.0, Th: 6.5. Roughly triangular. Fine-grained, light gray with olivine inclusions. Some evidence for heavy hammering on both faces.

S572. Rubbing stone. Area C. Unit 21. Limestone. Fragmentary. L: 8.0, W: 4.1, W: 3.5. Sub rectangular, square in section.

S573. Pounder. Area A. F18 2. Igneous. Intact. L: 10.0, W: 7.3, Th: 1.8. Roughly triangular in plan. Very flat. Fine-grained, green/gray. Slight evidence for pounding on all three angles.

S574. Pounder. East-west trial trench. Igneous. Intact. L: 9.1, W: 8.3, Th: 6.2. Irregular spheroid, multi-faced. Roughly triangular in transverse section. Medium-grained, gray/green. Both ends and much of the circumference pitted and faceted.

S575. Pounder. East-west trial trench. Igneous. Fragmentary. L: 5.9, W: 5.8, Th: 2.3. Elongated discoidal, with transverse break. Fine-grained, gray. Very faint signs of pounding at one end. One face slightly pitted from use as a hammerstone.

S576. Pounder. East-west trial trench. Igneous. Intact. L: 8.8, W: 5.4, Th: 3.8. Quadrangular in longitudinal and transverse sections. Fine-grained, gray. Both ends chipped from heavy pounding. Both faces and one side show striations, probably caused by hitting flint cores. Damage on both ends probably associated with knapping.

S577. Pounder. East-west trial trench. Igneous. Intact. L: 14.5, W: 6.5, Th: 5.4. Rectangular in longitudinal section, both faces convex. Medium-grained, gray/gray. Both ends flattened from pounding. Reused rubber fragment.

S578. Pounder. East-west trial trench. Igneous. Intact. L: 6.2, W: 4.2, Th: 2.3. Discoidal/ovoid. One face flat, the other convex. Medium-grained, gray. Narrow extremity slightly pitted.

S579. Pounder. Area C. I24B 7. Igneous. Intact. L: 12.8, W: 8.3, Th: 4.3. Elongated discoidal. One face convex, the other flat. Medium-grained, gray/green. One extremity pitted and flattened.

S580. Hammerstone. Area B. C19/20 11. Igneous. Intact. L: 6.8, W: 5.5, Th: 4.8. Ovoid. Very fine texture, dark brown/gray. Both faces show evidence of use as a hammerstone/anvil for the bipolar reduction of flakes.

S581. Rubber. Area A. Unit 4. Igneous. Fragmentary. L: 5.3, W: 1.8. Small sub-rectangular fragment. Medium-grained, green/gray. Both faces very flat from use on a quern. Only a small fragment of the edge preserved.

S582. Hammerstone. Area A. Unit 5. Igneous. Intact. L: 7.7, W: 6.2, Th: 4.8. Ovoid. Medium-grained, gray. Both faces slightly abraded from use as a hammerstone, perhaps associated with knapping.

S583. Function uncertain. Area A. G18A 1. Limestone. Intact. L: 7.7, W: 6.2, Th: 4.8. Elongated, axe-shaped. One extremity rounded, the other chipped and straight. Oval in transverse section. Fine-grained, white limestone. The chipped end has been subjected to some form of pounding or cutting. Scraper?

S584. Hammerstone. Area B. C19/20 11. Igneous. Intact. L: 7.4, W: 6.2, Th: 4.6. Flattened ovoid. Fine-grained, gray. Both faces have some pitting from use as a hammerstone.

S585. Disc. Area B. C20A 29. Limestone. Intact. L: 3.3, W: 2.8, Th: 0.5. Flattened discoid. Fine-grained, off-white. The slightly irregular oval pebble has been carefully flattened on the edges. Usage uncertain.

S586. Pounder. Area A. Unit 4. Igneous. Intact. L: 7.0, W: 4.6. Roughly triangular. Apex rounded, opposing side broken. Medium-grained, gray. The broken end has some signs of pounding.

S587. Pounder. Area A. G17A <u>3</u>. Igneous. Intact. L: 11.2, W: 8.4, Th: 7.6. Roughly conical, transverse section almost square. Coarse-grained, dark gray/green. Both ends pitted from heavy pounding. Re-used rubber.

S588. Rubbing stone. Area C. Unit 2. Limestone. Fragmentary. L: 9.0, W: 5.3, Th: 3.5. Trapezoidal in longitudinal section, sub-rectangular in transverse section. Fine-grained, off-white. One face very smooth from use as a rubbing stone.

S589. Pounder. Area B. C19A <u>1</u>. Igneous. Intact. L: 6.0, W: 4.0, Th: 1.5. Elongated discoid. Fine-grained, gray. Both ends slightly abraded from pounding. One face scratched and pitted from use as a hammerstone, perhaps in connection with knapping.

S590. Pounder. Area B. Unit 14. Igneous. Intact. L: 8.5, W: 5.5, Th: 2.9. Roughly sub-rectangular in longitudinal section, triangular in transverse section. Fine-grained, gray. One end with slight evidence for pounding. Re-used fragment of a rubber.

S591. Pounder. East-west trial trench. Unit 29. Igneous. Intact. Elongated, multi-faced. Transverse section roughly triangular. Fine-grained, dark gray. Both ends show evidence of pounding.

S592. Pounder. Operation F18. Igneous. Intact. L: 10.0, W: 9.5, Th: 8.5. Multi-faced. Fine-grained, gray. All angles worn, pitted and sometimes faceted from pounding.

S593. Axe, Type 1. East-west trial trench. Surface. Igneous. Fragmentary. L: 8.5, W: 5.4, Th: 2.8. Roughly sub-rectangular, one end straight, the other convex. Both faces well flattened, edges well-defined and rounded. Fine-grained, green/gray. Blade and general configuration typical of Type 1 axes. Butt missing. Appears to have been broken in antiquity.

S594. Pounder. Area A. I17A <u>6</u>. Igneous. Intact. L: 9.0, W: 7.8, Th: 5.1. Multi-faced. Fragment of a rounded river stone. Fine-grained, gray. Some evidence for pounding on all edges.

S595. Pounder. Area A. I17A <u>6</u>. Igneous. Intact. L: 10.6, W: 9.0, Th: 4.6. Multi-faced, roughly triangular. Fine-grained, gray. Some evidence for pounding on all edges.

S596. Pounder. Area A. I17A <u>6</u>. Igneous. Intact. L: 4.7, W: 6.2, Th: 4.9. Roughly ovoid, slightly flattened. Medium-grained, light gray. Some evidence for pounding on both extremities.

S597. Pounder. Area A. I17A <u>6</u>. Igneous. Intact. L: 9.2, W: 6.6, Th: 4.1. Flattened ovoid. Medium-grained, green/gray. Some evidence for pounding on both extremities.

S598. Pounder. Area A. I17A <u>6</u>. Igneous. Intact. L: 14.2, W: 9.0, Th: 3.6. Elongated, flattened irregular shape. Fragment of a large river pebble. Coarse-grained, dark gray. Both ends pitted from pounding, edges also show some signs of pounding.

S599. Pounder. Area C. H24C <u>3</u>. Igneous. Intact. L: 12.8, W: 10.5, Th: 5.7. Multi-faced, flattened. Fragment of a large river pebble. Fine-grained, dark gray. Three angles well worn and sometimes faceted from use as a pounder.

S600. Pecking stone. Area A. Unit 5. Quartz. Intact. L: 4.4, W: 4.4. Roughly quadrangular. Light brown. Micro-faceted on all faces.

S601. Pecking stone. Area A. Stratified (found in dump from Units 6, 18, 32 and 33). Chalcedony. Intact. L: 4.8, W: 4.4. Roughly quadrangular. Light brown to buff. Micro-faceted on all faces.

S602. Pounder. Area C. Unit 8. Igneous. Fragmentary. L: 8.0, W: 5.1, Th: 3.4. Section of a discoidal river stone. One side broken. Fine-grained, gray/green. Some pitting along one broken edge and on the preserved sections of the circumference. Possible secondary use as a hammerstone.

S603. Pounder. Area C. Unit 8. Igneous. Intact. L: 9.6, W: 3.8, Th: 2.8. Elongated, transverse section triangular. One end rounded, the other pointed. Fine-grained, gray. Both ends pitted from use as a pounder.

S604. Rubbing stone. East-west trial trench. Limestone. Fragmentary. L: 11.0, W: 5.4, Th: 2.3. Sub-rectangular in basic shape. One side straight, the others chipped and irregular. Fine-grained, off-white. Both faces very smooth, presumably from rubbing.

S605. Pounder. East-west trial trench. Igneous. Intact. L: 9.5, W: 9.0, Th: 4.5. Trapezoidal in longitudinal section. One face flat (from use as a rubber), the other convex. Coarse-grained, brown/gray. All angles abraded from use as a pounder. The flat face has a shallow, regular depression caused by hammering.

S608. Gaming stone, Senet. East-west trial trench. Fragmentary. L: 14.2, W: 12.3, Th: 8.4. Trapezoidal. Reddish, coarse (burnt grained). One face with three rows of depressions: two rows of 8, one row of 6. Extrapolated length of gaming area 12 cm; width 4.5 cm; Av. D of holes 1 cm.

S609. Gaming stone, Senet. Area C. Stratified (from dump of Units 8 and 21). Limestone. Intact. L: 22.5, W: 17, Th: 11. Surface very weathered. One face pecked with a series of depressions.

S610. Gaming stone, Senet. Area A. G17C <u>5</u>. Limestone. Fragmentary. L: 15.5, W: 11.4, Th: 4.8. Very weathered. One face pecked with a series of depressions.

S611. Gaming stone, Senet. Area C. Stratified (from dump of Units 8 and 21). Limestone. Fragmentary. L: 22.5, W: 13.5, Th: 5.6. Weathered. One face pecked with a series of depressions.

S612. Gaming stone, Senet.. Area C. Stratified (from dump of Units 8 and 21). Limestone. Fragmentary. L: 18.5, W: 13, Th: 4.8. Roughly hemispherical. Medium-grained, off-white. Badly weathered. One row of 5, one row of 6 shallow depressions.

S613. Gaming stone, Senet. Area C. Unit 21. Limestone. Intact. L: 22, W: 22.5, Th: 7.5. Almost square. Sides as well as one face rough. The other face smooth and bears a varied arrangement of depressions. The main central motif: three rows of 10 depressions with an additional row of 7 to one side. Also three rows of undetermined depressions to one side.

S614. Rubber. East-west trial trench. Igneous. Intact. L: 36.5, W: 16, Th: 3.5. Elongated, both ends rounded. Coarse-grained, gray. Work face concave in longitudinal section, slightly convex in transverse section. Underside flattened. Both ends rise toward the original work surface. Transverse striations clearly visible.

S615. Axe, Type 2. East-west trial trench. Igneous. Intact. L: 16.0, W: 6.5, Th: 3.8. Elongated, with narrowing, flattened butt. Cutting edge heavily flaked. One face convex, the other almost flat. Sides slightly rounded. Fine-grained, green. Strictly speaking, this tool should be considered an adze because the cutting edge is beveled. This might be an unfinished Type 1 axe because no signs of wear are visible on the cutting edge.

S616. Pounder. East-west trial trench. Igneous. Intact. L: 9.6, W: 4.5, Th: 5.5. Ovoid, flattened on one side. Medium-grained, light gray. One end flattened and pitted from pounding.

S617. Pounder. Unit 28. Limestone. Fragmentary. L: 6.7, W: 5.6, Th: 2.7. Originally square with rounded corners, now ca. one-third missing. Elongated oval in section. Veined off-white. Abraded around the circumference from use as a pounder.

S618. Axe, Type 1. Southeast trial trench. Surface. Igneous. Fragmentary. L: 6.2, W: 5.4, Th: 3.5. Sub-rectangular in longitudinal section, oval in transverse section. Fine-grained, gray/green. Cutting end of a Type 1 axe, badly flaked on one face and at cutting edge.

S619. Lid? Area A. Unit 18. Limestone. Intact. L: 9.0, W: 8.0, Th: 2.4. Discoidal. Circumference quite smooth and rounded. Soft, laminated limestone. Both faces quite smooth, edges intentionally shaped.

S620. Mortar. East-west trial trench. Unit 29. Igneous. Intact. L: 9.6, W: 8.6, Th: 6.2. Thick discoidal river stone. Fine-grained, gray. All surfaces carefully shaped. Sides rounded, small flattened area on base. Upper surface flattened with a shallow regular, circular depression in its center. D = 4.8 cm, Depth = 0.8 cm.

S621. Pounder. Area C. H24C 3. Igneous. Intact. L: 11.8, W: 10.1, Th: 7.4. Multi-faced, irregular. Roughly pyramidal in transverse section. Medium-grained with a white vein running diagonally through the object. Light gray. The sharp angles are all flattened from use as a pounder.

S622. Pounder. East-west trial trench. Unit 29. Igneous. Intact. L: 8.3, W: 6.3, Th: 5.8. Longitudinal section roughly oval, transverse section circular. Medium-grained, green/gray. Both ends pitted from use as a pounder, the larger end well-faceted. Two faces show secondary use as a hammerstone.

S623. Pounder. East-west trial trench. Unit 28. Igneous. Intact. L: 1.3, W: 8.5, Th: 2.0. Triangular in plan with rounded angles. Both faces rather uneven. Fragment of a large river stone. Fine-grained, dark gray. All three angles pitted and rounded from use as a pounder.

S624. Pounder. East-west trial trench. Unit 28. Igneous. Intact. L: 14.2, W: 8.3, Th: 5.0. Trapezoidal in plan, sub-rectangular in transverse section. Coarse-grained, gray/green. Some evidence for pounding at narrow end. Fragment of a rubber.

S625. Pounder. East-west trial trench. Unit 28. Igneous. Fragmentary. L: 13.3, W: 8.8, Th: 5.3. Trapezoidal in plan:, sub-rectangular in section. Coarse-grained, green/black. Two angles well rounded and pitted from use as a pounder.

S626. Pounder. East-west trial trench. Unit 28. Igneous. Fragmentary. L: 8.4, W: 5.7, Th: 5.2. Discoidal with flattened ends. Fine-grained, green/gray. Both ends flattened and pitted from use as a pounder. One face pitted from use as a hammerstone.

S627. Pecking stone. East-west trial trench. Unit 28. Chalcedony. Intact. L: 4.7, W: 4.8. Rough cuboid with rounded angles. White. Most areas micro-faceted, others rough and only faceted on periphery.

S628. Worked picrolite. East-west trial trench. Unit 28. Fragmentary. L: 4.2, W: 1.9, Th: 1.3. Fragment of a discoidal or elongated pebble. Light green. Evidence of shaping in the form of long scratch marks along the edges.

S629. Axe, Type 2. Area A. Unstratified. Igneous. Fragmentary. L: 7.8, W: 6.8, Th: 3.8. Irregular in longitudinal section, two sides roughly parallel, diagonal break and a semi-circular cutting edge. Transverse section roughly oval. One face smooth, the other flaked. Fine-grained, gray. Blade end of an unusually large "flaked celt."

S630. Rubber-pounder. Area A. G17A. Igneous. Intact. L: 16.5, W: 6.6, Th: 5.9. Elongated, both ends rounded, roughly triangular in transverse section. Medium-grained, gray/green. Both ends slightly pitted from use as a pounder. All three faces slightly pitted from use as a hammerstone.

S631. Rubber. Area C. H24C 2. Igneous. Fragmentary. L: 28, W: 17, Th: 6.0. Elongated, one end rounded, the other missing. Medium-grained, gray. Work surface concave in longitudinal section. Convex in transverse section. Underside convex. No wear marks visible on work surface.

S632. Rubber. Area A. Unit 7. Igneous. Fragmentary. L: 28.5, W: 16, Th: 9.0. Elongated, one end rounded. The broken work face slightly convex in the longitudinal and transverse section. Underside uneven but smooth. Fine-grained, light gray. Probably used as a rubbing stone on a quern.

S633. Gaming stone, Senet. East-west trial trench. Surface. Limestone. Fragmentary. L: 16.5, W: 13, Th: 9.0. One face pecked with a series of depressions forming three incomplete parallel rows.

S639. Pounder. Area A. Unit 1. Phase I. Igneous. Intact. L: 12.0, W: 10.0, Th: 5.4. Discoidal. Secondary use as a hammerstone.

S641. Pounder. Area A. Unit 16. Igneous. Intact. L: 7.6, W: 5.8, Th: 4.6. Some light pounding on edges.

S642. Hammerstone. Area A. Unit 7. Igneous. Intact. L: 9.7, W: 7.8, Th: 4. Pitting on both faces.

S645. Pounder. Area A. Unit 3. Igneous. Intact. L: 13.2, W: 7.0. Th: 3.7. Re-used rubber.

S646. Pounder. Area A. G18B/D 1. Igneous. Fragmentary. L: 6.8, W: 6.8, Th: 3.9. Secondary use as a hammerstone.

S647. Hammerstone. Area A. Unit 3. Igneous. Intact. L: 9.2, W: 9.1. Discoidal. Pitting on one face.

S650. Hammerstone. Area A. Unit 3. Igneous. Intact. L: 8.8, W: 5.4, Th: 5.6.

S651. Pounder. Area C. Unit 10. Igneous. Intact. L: 10.2, W: 9.8, Th: 5.6. Secondary use as a hammerstone.

S653. Pounder. Area C. Unit 10. Igneous. Fragmentary. L: 7.4, W: 5.9, Th: 3.0. Originally an ovoid, but one half now missing. Medium-grained, gray. One end pitted and faceted.

S654. Pounder. Area C. Unit 10. Igneous. Intact. L: 9.4, W: 5.3, Th: 4.3. Elongated triangular, quadrangular in section. Very fine-grained, dark gray. Both extremities show faint signs of pounding.

S655. Pounder. Area A. Unit 7. Igneous. Intact. L: 11.1, W: 7.9, Th: 3.1. Elongated discoidal. Coarse-grained, gray/white. Flake from a large river stone used as a pounder. Circumference slightly pitted.

S656. Pounder. Area A. Unit 7. Igneous. Intact. L: 11.3, W: 9.4, Th: 4.4. Discoidal. Fine-grained, gray. Circumference pitted from pounding. Both faces pitted from secondary use as a hammerstone.

S657. Pounder. Area A. Unit 7. Igneous. Intact. L: 7.6, W: 6.1, Th: 2.8. Roughly discoidal, slightly concave in section. Fine-grained, gray. Two areas of circumference pitted from pounding. Both faces pitted and scratched from use as a hammerstone and anvil?

S658. Pounder. Area A. Unit 7. Igneous. Intact. L: 8.2, W: 5.5, Th: 4.2. Ellipsoidal, oval in transverse section. Fine-grained, dark gray. Both ends pitted from pounding. Both faces pitted and scratched from secondary use as a hammerstone and anvil for knapping.

S659. Pounder. Area A. Unit 7. Igneous. Intact. L: 12.2, W: 11.4, Th: 4.4. Roughly discoidal. Fine-grained, gray. Both faces quite smooth with a heavily abraded and chipped circumference before use as a pounder.

S660. Pendant. East-west trial trench. Surface. Picrolite. Intact. L: 2.2, W: 1.5, Th: 0.5. Irregular ovoid. Edges well-rounded. Very smooth. Green with some white flecks. Irregular hourglass drilled perforation at one end. Under 10 x magnification striations clearly visible. Some signs of wear on upper circumference of perforation.

S661. Pierced disk. East–west trial trench. Unstratified. Picrolite. Intact. L: 1.1, W: 1.4. Small button-like disc with central perforation, perhaps used as a bead. Scratch marks visible on both sides, running in different directions. Two edges have been ground smooth and are slightly faceted in places.

S662. Necklace spacer. Area C. Unit 10. Picrolite. Intact. L: 3.1, W: 0.6, Th: 0.15. Sub-rectangular plaque with slightly rounded ends and convex sides. Both faces are very smooth and parallel. The sides and ends have been ground smooth and the faces, though smooth and polished, show deep scratch marks, probably resulting from the method of manufacture. At 3.5 mm from both ends, there are two gouged hourglass perforations. On one face, both have wear marks facing each other as if a piece of thread had been passed through the holes. The other side shows no wear marks.

S663. Necklace spacer? Area C. Unit 10. Picrolite. Fragment. Probably 2/3 preserved. L: 2.5, W: 0.65. Th: 0.15. Sub-rectangular plaque, broken at one end, with a gouged perforation. What remains of S663 is identical in every respect to S662, next to which it was found

S664. Function uncertain. Area C. Unit 21. Sandstone. Fragmentary. L: 8.6, W: 7, Th: 1.5. Quadrangular fragment of tabular sandstone. Fine-grained, brown/gray. One face very smooth from some activity, probably grinding or sharpening. Other face rough and unworked. Edges probably broken. Shows sign of burning. Perhaps used as a grinding surface. Probably imported to the site.

S665. Pecking stone. Area C. Unit 10. Chalcedony. Intact. L: 6.2, W: 5.7. Quadrangular with rounded angles. Gray/blue. All faces micro-faceted from use as a pecking stone.

S666. Pecking stone. Area C. Unit 2. Chalcedony. Intact. L: 4.7, W: 4.9. Spherical with several chipped areas. Light brown. Micro-faceted from use as a pecking stone.

S667. Perforated disk. Area A. Unit 7. Limestone. Fragmentary, 1/3 preserved. D: 4.6, Th: 0.7, D hole 0.6. About 1/3 of a well-cut disk, with both faces smooth, edges smooth and rounded, and a central hourglass perforation. Fine grained, white. Function uncertain.

S668. Pounder. Area A. Unit 1. Phase I. Igneous. Intact. L: 10.8, W: 5.9, Th: 5.4. Roughly conical with flat sides. Broad end chipped and uneven. Fine-grained, gray/green. Broad end faceted from use as a pounder.

S669. Pounder. Area A. Unit 7. Igneous. Intact. L: 8.3, W: 6.7. Th: 5.4. Elongated cuboid. Course-grained, gray/brown. Reused rubber. One end flat from initial use as a quern, the other pitted from pounding. Some evidence of pounding on the circumference of the smooth edge. Sides very irregular.

S670. Pecking stone. Area A. Unit 7. Chalcedony. Intact. L: 6.3, W: 5.3, Th: 3.7. Discoidal. Circumference and one face micro-faceted from use as a pecking stone. Light gray.

S671. Axe (?), Type 1. Area A. Unit 1. Phase I. Igneous. Intact. L: 6.8, W: 4.2, Th: 2.2. Wedge-shaped. Cutting edge slightly convex and well smoothed back from the edge. Fine-grained, blue/gray. Both sides rough and pecked but very regular. Both faces near butt smooth with areas of scratching as if used as an anvil. Butt is broad and broken, was perhaps used as an axe. Cutting edge slightly damaged.

S672. Rubber. Area A. Unit 38. Igneous. Fragment. L: 7.9, W: 8.4, Th: 3.9. Irregular quadrangular, one face flat in both transverse and longitudinal sections, the other convex. Edges irregular. Medium grained, gray/brown.

S673. Bead. Area A. Unit 7. Jasper? Intact. D: 0.33, H: 0.1. Miniature discoid with central perforation. Identical to those found in large numbers in the tombs. Note hourglass drilled perforation ca.0.05 (0.5 mm) in diameter.

S674. Mortar. Area A. Unit 37. Limestone. Fragmentary. L: 11.8, W: 7.6, Th: 42. Approximately rectangular in plan, three outer sides preserved, damaged fourth side concave.

Soft white limestone. Inner surface that served as a mortar slightly, pecked, 1.2 cm deep. Underside damaged.

S675. Pounder. Area A. Unit 7. Igneous. Intact. L: 8.2, W: 4.5, Th: 2.8. Elongated oval. One end rounded, the other flattened from pounding. Oval in transverse section. Fine grained, blue/gray. Flat end chipped and faceted from pounding. Round end also faceted from pounding. Both faces scoured from use as an anvil.

S676. Function uncertain. Area A. Unstratified. Sandstone. Fragmentary. L: 10.9, W: 7.8, Th: 1.8. Irregular parallelogram. One face perfectly flat, the other uneven. Sides quite straight. Fine grained brown/gray. Identical to S664.

S677. Pounder. Area A. Unit 6. Igneous. Damaged. L: 17.5, W: 7.3, Th: 5.1. Flattened conical. Oval in transverse section. Fine-grained, blue/gray. Butt heavily flaked after having been faceted from use as a pounder. Apex also worn from pounding. Both faces and sides show some pitting from use as a hammerstone. The whole surface is weathered and pitted, probably from initial shaping. Large Type 1 axe reused as a pounder.

S678. Rubber-pounder. Area A. Unit 5. Igneous. Intact. L: 12.6, W: 7.8, Th: 4.1. Elongated discoid. Oval in longitudinal and transverse sections. Fine-grained, light gray. Both ends and sides pitted from use as pounder. Both faces pitted from tertiary use as a hammerstone.

S679. Axe, Type 1. Area A. Unit 33. Igneous. Intact. L: 6.3, W: 4.2, Th: 1.6. Wedge-shaped, broad butt, one side straight the other convex. Cutting edge rounded and chipped. Both faces very smooth, with signs of intentional shaping. Blade in process of being re-ground when discarded. Sides also ground.

S680. Axe, Type 2. Area A. Unit 33. Intact. Igneous. L: 5.5, W: 4, Th: 1.5. Oval in plan, ellipsoid in section, with pointed ends. One face smooth, the other mostly flaked according to the diagnostic pattern first recognized by Dikaios.

S681. Pounder. Area A. Unit 6. Intact. Igneous. L: 9.8, W: 7.5, Th: 6.4. Irregular cuboid. One face very flat from use as a rubber. Several angles faceted and pitted from use as a pounder.

S682. Pounder. Area A. Unit 7. Intact. Igneous. L: 11.6, W: 8.4, Th: 5.5. Discoidal. Oval in both sections. One end flattened. Fine-grained, blue/gray. Flattened end pitted and faceted from use as a pounder, other end and sides pitted from pounding. Both faces pitted from use as a hammerstone.

S684. Pecking stone. Area A. Unit 7. Intact. Chalcedony. D: 6.2. Roughly cuboid with rounded angles. White. All surfaces micro-faceted from use as a pecking stone.

S685. Rubber-pounder. Area A. Unit 7. Intact. Igneous. L:

10.4, Q: 7.5, Th: 4.4. Rectangular in plan. One face flat from use as rubbing stone, the other convex. Sides flat and chipped. Medium-grained, blue/gray. Two angles pitted from use as a pounder.

S686. Pounder. Area A. Unit 1 Phase I. Intact. Igneous. L: 12.3, W: 7.6, Th: 5.1. Irregular parallelogram. Both ends rounded, one face flat, the other convex. Sides quite flat. Fine-grained, dark gray. Both ends and one edge slightly pitted from use as pounder.

S687. Pounder. Area A. Unit 7. Intact. Igneous. L: 12.5, W: 9.5, Th: 7.4. Irregular shaped, elongated. One flat side. Triangular in transverse section. Fine-grained, light gray. Both ends faceted from use as a pounder. One edge pitted from use as a pounder.

S688. Mortar. Area A. Unit 42. Intact. Limestone. L: 8, W: 4.6 Depth (max.) 2.1. Roughly oval in plan. White, fine-grained. Sides and rim rounded, base slightly flattened. Roughened inner cavity.

S689. Pounder. Type 1. Settlement. Unstratified. Intact (Chipped). Igneous. L: 9.4, W: 5.4, Th: 2.4. Irregular, triangular in plan with rounded corners. Both faces flattened, one with a large flake missing. Fine-grained, blue/gray. Broad end and both sides pitted from use as a pounder. Secondary use as an anvil as shown by scratches on one face.

S690. Rubbing stone. Area A. Unit 6. Fragmentary. Limestone. L: 11.5, W: 7.5, Th: 3.9. Two parallel sides and both extremities broken. Edges rounded. Both faces flat. Fine, off-white. Transverse striations clearly visible on both faces: this proves it was used a rubbing stone. Also a few deep longitudinal scratches.

S691. Pounder. Area A. Unit 7. Intact. Igneous. L: 5, W: 2.2, Th: 0.7. Flattened ellipse in plan and section. Fine-grained, blue/gray. One end very slightly pitted from use as a pounder.

S692. Rubber. Area A. Unit 6. Fragmentary. Igneous. L: (pres.) 17.5, W: 19, Th: 6. Ca. 1/2 preserved. Stone very weathered and soft. Preserved extremity rounded or oval, straight transverse break. Longitudinal section concave, other convex. Reverse convex. Fine-grained, green/brown.

S693. Mortar. Area A. Unit 7. Fragmentary. Limestone. H (pres.): 19, L: 29, Th: 5.5. Roughly sub-rectangular fragment from the side of a large stone mortar. Irregular rounded rim. Inside uneven and pitted, more so than the outside. Medium-grained.

S694. Rubber. Area A. Unit 6. Fragmentary. Igneous. L (pres.) 16, W: 16, Th: 5.5. Quadrangular, irregular. Two sides broken. Work surface concave in longitudinal section, convex in transverse section. Fine-grained, gray/green. Some evidence of secondary use as a pounder.

S695. Rubber. Area A. Unit 6. Intact. Igneous. L: 32, W: 18.5, Th: 6. Elongated, roughly triangular with rounded angles. Work surface very slightly concave in longitudinal section. Transverse section convex. Medium-grained, gray/green. Transverse striation indicates use as a rubbing stone.

S696. Rubber. Area A. Unit 1. Phase I. Fragmentary. Igneous. L: 14, W: 9, Th: 4.8. Rectangular in plan and longitudinal section. One side flat, the other convex. Medium-grained, gray/green. Work surface flat in longitudinal and very slightly convex in transverse section.

S697. Rubber. Area A. Unit 1 Phase I. Intact. Igneous. L: 20.8, W: 15.4, Th: 5. One end damaged. Original shape oval. Work face convex in longitudinal and transverse section. Reverse, convex. Some signs of chipping on perimeter, one long side has signs of secondary use as a hammerstone. Longitudinal work surface has an 8 mm convexity. Transverse convexity is 6 mm. No work striations visible.

S698. Axe, Type 1. Area A. Unit 1. Phase I. Intact. Igneous. L: 5.3, W: 2.9, Th: 1.5. Wedge-shape. Both faces convex. Almost straight cutting edge. Flattened and chipped butt. One face has a large ground depression. Generally crudely shaped. Very fine-grained, light green. Cutting edge sharp with some evidence of use/wear, but no longitudinal striations from prolonged cutting of a hard substance.

S699. Quern. Area A. Unit 7. Fragmentary. Igneous. L: 36, W: 26, Th: 5. About 1/3 missing. Roughly quadrangular with rounded sides. Work face concave, other side convex. Three edges damaged and chipped. One end missing. Medium-grained, dark gray. Transverse section of work surface flat, no work striations visible.

S700. Quern. Area C. Unit 21. Intact. Limestone. L: 58, W: 32, Th: 21.3. Rectangular in plan. Work surface very concave in longitudinal section (11 cm deep). Flat in transverse section. Reverse flat in longitudinal section, convex in transverse section. Course-grained, yellow. No wear marks visible.

S701. Rubber. Area C. Unit 21. Intact. Igneous. L: 48, W: 16, Th: 7.2. Elongated, both ends rounded, sides almost parallel and irregularly chipped. Work surface concave in longitudinal section, convex in transverse. Reverse flat in longitudinal section, triangular in transverse. Coarse-grained, gray/white/black. The narrow end is more upturned than the other broader end. Transverse striations prove this stone was used as a rubbing stone.

S702. Rubber. Area A. Unit 7. Intact. Igneous. L: 34, W: 22, Th: 6. Elongated lozenge with rounded corners. Work face slightly convex in both sections. Reverse convex. Work surface identical to S697. Medium-grained, gray/green. A few small patches are well polished and show transverse striations from use as a rubbing stone.

S703. Rubber. Area C. Unit 21. Intact. Igneous. L: 33.5, W: 18, Th: 11.9. Sub-rectangular, one end beveled. Work face slightly concave in longitudinal section, convex in transverse. Other face rough and irregular. Course-grained, gray/green. The larger crystals at 10x magnification show parallel scratches at right angles to the main section: this proves that S699 was used as a rubbing stone.

S704. Rubber. Area C. Unit 8. Intact. Igneous. L: 40.5, W: 20.2, Th: 11.1. Elongated oval. Work surface concave (6 mm concavity) in longitudinal section, convex in transverse section. Reverse flat in longitudinal section and rounded in transverse section. Medium grained, light gray. Clearly visible transverse striations from use as a rubbing stone on a Type 1 quern.

S705. Gaming stone, Senet. Area A. Unit 30. Fragmentary. Limestone. L: 49.5, W: 16.2, Th: 7. Three fragments. Three parallel rows of depressions. Row near upper edge has 9 depressions. Middle row has 2 small followed by 2 large and then 2 small depressions. Bottom row has 7-plus poorly pecked depressions. Overall impression is that of an incomplete gaming stone made by an inept craftsman.

S706. Worked picrolite. Area A. Surface. Intact. L: 2.3, W: 0.8, Th: 0.2. Thin, carefully shaped sliver. Both faces flat, sides slightly rounded and one end rounded, the other almost flat. Well polished, light blue. The ends are ground or cut to shape and are faceted. Function unknown.

S707. Worked picrolite. Area A. Unit 33. L: 2.2, W: 1.4, Th: 0.5. Rectangular pebble with rounded corners, some evidence for shaping.

S708. Worked picrolite. Area A. Unit 20. L: 2.1, W: 2.0, Th: 1.0. Almost square with rounded corners. Triangular in section. Flaked on all edges.

S709. Worked picrolite. Area B. Unit 12. L: 2.9, Th: 1.5, W: 0.8. Roughly triangular pebble with rounded corners. Some evidence for shaping.

S710. Beads. Cemetery A. Tomb 18. Stone. Mostly intact. 80 miniature beads. Cylindrical drilled, made from jasper, quartzite and limestone. See S208 for dimensions and additional comments.

IS1. Quern. Area A. Unit 32/33.

IS2. Rubber. Area A. Unit 32/33.

IS3. Rubber. Area A. Unit 32/33.

IS5. Rubber. Area A. Unit 18.

IS6. Quern. Area A. Unit 6.

IS8. Quern. Area A. Unit 30.

IS9. Rubber. .Area A. Unit 7.

IS10. Post support. Area A. Unit 7.

IS12. Quern. Area A. Unit 3.

IS13. Quern. Area A. Unit 3.

IS14. Pounder. Area A. Unit 1.

IS15. Pounder. Area A. Unit 3.

IS17. Rubber. Area A. Unit 7.

IS19. Quern. Area C. Unit 21.

IS24. Rubber. Area C. Unit 22.

IS25. Quern. Area C. Unit 22.

IS26. Quern. Area C. Unit 10.

IS30. Rubber. Area C. Unit 22.

IS31. Rubber. Area C. Unit 8.

IS32. Rubber. Area C. Unit 8.

IS33. Rubber. Area C. Unit 8.

IS34. Rectangular slab of limestone. Area C. Unit 8.

IS35. Mortar. Area A. Unit 6.

IS37. Quern. Area A. Unit 15.

IS38. Quern. Area A. Unit 15.

IS39. Quern. Area A. Unit 15.

IS41. Quern. Area A. Unit 1.

IS42. Quern. Area A. Unit 1.

IS43. Quern. Area A. Unit 1.

IS46. Quern. Area A. Unit 3.

IS53. Quern. Area A. Unit 3.

IS54. Mortar. Area C. Unit 9.

IS55. Roughly circular slab of limestone with a pecked perforation in its center. From below wall tumble in East West Trial Trench. D ca. 60 cm, Th ca. 5 cm. Perhaps intact, though possibly chipped on circumference.

7

THE KNAPPED STONE

by Alice Kingsnorth

INTRODUCTION

For the reader with only a cursory interest in the knapped stone study Part I highlights a series of topics that involve other areas of archaeology. It also mentions some matters regularly discussed in chipped stone reports by the general Cypriot archeological community, for example whether or not obsidian was found. What is more important, it considers problematic misunderstandings among all kinds of archeologists concerning stone tools, which commonly prompt imaginative inferences about the functions of specific sites. Part II describes the Sotira *Kaminoudhia* collection. Part III considers the *Kaminoudhia* knapped stone collection within the larger prehistoric and theoretical framework.

We hope to broaden appreciation both of stone tool manufacture studies in Cypriot archaeology and of production sequence identification, a basic orientation to artifact analysis. It is our premise that determining production sequences is useful for the analysis of most archaeological finds.[1] Accordingly, the knapped stone from Sotira *Kaminoudhia* excavations published here is written primarily for the general archaeologist.[2] In order to be of interest to many readers, the text explains a few concepts and techniques familiar to the specialist.

PART I: SOME OBSERVATIONS OF GENERAL INTEREST

OBSIDIAN

Obsidian has always been an important find in Cypriot collections because of its exotic nature. However, no obsidian is known from Sotira *Kaminoudhia*. However, the sources, times of acquisition, distribution, and uses of *every* kind of lithic raw material are equally telling. This chapter looks at evidence for preferences in raw materials and their implications.

ARROWHEADS

"Arrowhead" is a word that problematically merges a use, a shape, popular mythic associations, and other distinct attributes. Scenarios elaborated out of a purported absence of "arrowheads" in the Cypriot archaeological record have continued to be tolerated.

---

[1] In Cyprus, Cluzan (1984) on ground stone vessels from *Khirokitia*, (Guilaine et al. 1998, 1995) at Parekklisha *Shillourokambos*, Kingsnorth (n.d.) on ground stone from Kholetria *Ortos* have taken similar approaches.
[2] Analysis of quantitative data results is planned for a separate venue.

Prehistoric Cypriots used stone tipped projectiles. We hypothesize that functional equivalents to so-called "arrowheads" are very common in Cypriot archaeological knapped stone collections, including that from Sotira *Kaminoudhia*. The morphological and manufacturing differences between non-Cypriot *"arrowheads"* and the possible Cypriot functional equivalents are temporal, practical, and consistent with the already known picture of knapping practices on Cyprus. It is time to abandon the expression "arrowhead" because it confuses physical attributes, possible modes of use, purposes, social roles, as well as temporal and cultural connotations. Following a well-established practice, we advocate the term "projectile point" or simply "point."

TOOLS

Traditional tool names and tool typing may be misleading. To many, terms such as "knife," "axe," "pick," and "sickle segments" automatically equate with identifiable tasks such as cutting, chopping, stabbing, felling, picking, mining, and harvesting. This should not always be the case.

During the last two hundred years, specialists needing standardized taxonomies to simplify discussion have often labeled a stone tool based on a loose similarity between a stone artifact's shape or edge and a contemporary metal tool. Moreover, accurate assignment of functions based on experimental replication, microwear analysis, or controlled ethnographic comparison is time consuming, uncommon, and frequently reveals a different use from that of the literal tool name. Unfortunately, both non-lithic specialists and experienced lithic scholars have too readily adduced the functions of a deposit or of a site based on the presence or absence of labels initially adopted generations ago as a convenience for archaeologists sorting finds.

Throughout the world the most common, versatile, utilized and reutilized stone implements have been unmodified flakes, chunks of so-called "debris," and unmodified rock. Ethnography and microwear analysis rarely corroborate archaeological extrapolations from named categories of retouched "tools" at the expense of equally weighted investigations of unretouched nodules, chunks, chips, blades, and flakes.

For both reasons this chapter generally avoids classic tool typing, tool nomenclature, and unexamined functional attribution. Instead, it emphasizes observations of stone modification and discard combined with hypotheses about their temporal, economic, social, and cultural correlates. We believe a well-seriated typology of flaked stone production methodologies and their output will be helpful to Cypriot archaeology for dating, field survey, and analysis of stray and similarly weakly contextualized finds. Such a typology would comprise both "tools" and the byproducts of manufacturing activities, use, and refurbishment. Appreciation of the difficulties associated with realizing this goal has guided our choice of figures and catalogue entries.

THE "CHALCOLITHIC SCRAPER": A HALLMARK OF THE CYPRIOT CHALCOLITHIC?

An exception to the above is the informally nicknamed "Erimi Scraper" or "Chalcolithic Scraper," which is well represented at Sotira *Kaminoudhia*. Prehistoric, ethnographic, and experimental replication research outside Cyprus partially favors interpreting parallels to this artifact as a scraping instrument, possibly associated with preparation of leather. However, one study on analogous Levantine "tabular scrapers" conjectures that they are ceremonial knives. Experimental and microwear tests of these retouched, ovoid flake tools are needed for Cypriot specimens.

Discussion of the economic and social connotations of "scrapers" or their functions in Cyprus is almost nonexistent, which strongly contrasts with the interest generated by "arrowheads" and "sickle blades." This study compares ovoid, so-called "scrapers" from different periods. Although variants occur as early as the Aceramic, at present they are most commonly found on Cypriot Chalcolithic through Middle Bronze Age sites, including Sotira *Kaminoudhia* (Kingsnorth 1996a). A similar situation occurs in the Levant. We explore possible reasons for their increase.

STOCKS OF LARGE FLAKES

In common with three Chalcolithic assemblages, very large flakes of non-local materials were found at *Kaminoudhia*. We tentatively interpret these as stores of knapping supplies from well-known sources that were intentionally collected and saved or exchanged. They may also have enjoyed an ideological function. It is possible that small scale stocking of grand lithics constitutes a behavioral trait of the culture(s) of the late Early Prehistoric (EP) period. Nevertheless, with so few examples caution is necessary.

SMALLNESS OF SOTIRA *KAMINOUDHIA* KNAPPED STONE

This assemblage is small whether gauged by numbers of artifacts, weight, capacity, or in relationship to volume of the archaeological deposit.[3] For the non-specialist or the regional specialist, specific meanings and implications of not necessarily related concepts such as "micro-burin," "micro-flake." and "bladelet," some of which are discussed later in this report, can be problematically entangled with the term microlith. This is in contrast with most other collections now known in Cyprus. The knapped stone collection also contains several examples of miniature cores not published from other sites in Cyprus. *Kaminoudhia* flaked stone as a whole is similar to that from other sites. (D'Annibale 1993, 1992; Hordynsky and Kingsnorth 1979; Kingsnorth 1996b; Lehavy 1989).

We attribute the seeming "plainness" of Cypriot industries (a constant through the millennia in the face of enormous changes in other cultural variables) to continual, repeated adaptations of several factors. Raw materials were abundant throughout the island. This abundance presented an array of choices in fabric characteristics, permitting selection to meet different needs rather than requiring elaborate retouch strategies. The knappers' knowledge of materials and methodology made intellectual investment in strategic planning more beneficial than investment in complicated retouches. Cypriot industries evince neither a lack of skill, stagnation, nor sectarian, retrograde isolationism as some claim, but rather a pragmatic and knowledgeable capitalization on excellent local conditions.

---

[3] The term "microlith" has several implications. Although the collection contains some bladelets, small implements, and minuscule cores, the industry is not microlithic as usually understood by specialists. Currently in Cyprus, the term "microlithic" can be correctly applied only to epi-Paleolithic Akrotiri *Aetokremnos*, at which site all knapped materials are tiny.

"Microlithic industries" throughout Southwest Asia, North Africa, Europe, and Archaic North America correlate with densely settled foraging, frequently dependent on fish and fowl, and associated with lacustrine or coastal settings; variously designated by such terms as Mesolithic, epi-Paleolithic, pre-Clovis. Akrotiri *Aetokremnos* matches the setting and period usually identified with microlithic industries. Sotira *Kaminoudhia* does not.

For the specialist, the term 'microlith' frequently connotes not merely a size, but a distinct manufacturing technique. It entails planned snapping of parallel-sided blades to produce small, regularly shaped, usually retouched segments intended for composite tools (Crabtree 1982:43, 44; 1972:75, 78). For some, size alone suffices for tools, for example Addington (1986:107) or Gramly (1992:37), for whom a length of less than 3.0 cm. qualifies.

Elaborate retouch and attractive shaping of lithics either correlate with marking social relations or are the result of material conservation activities. Lithic artifacts, retouch, or figurative flints and obsidian that evoke animals, people, or metal tools are not indices of intellectual or cultural sophistication, superiority, or advance. The former are subjective, ethnocentric concepts most meaningful to latent unilinear evolutionist explanations, but are counterproductive to the goal of objectively explaining social change.

Lithic retouch is most frequently either the expression of social difference or the result of reestablishing an implement attribute that has become worn (for example the resharpening of a dulled or nicked edge, notch, or point, or the strengthening of a part to be hafted by thickening of proportions). To confuse the supposed simplicity of Cypriot industries with inadequacy and entrenchment is to misunderstand both Cypriot lithic technology and methodology as well as cultural processes.

SOCIOECONOMIC SPECIALIZATION

The uneven distribution of chipped stone from *Kaminoudhia* offers a hint of possible socioeconomic specialization or spatial differentiation within the site. Possibly, not all parts of the site were used for knapping, an important source of microchippage. Moreover, some walled areas imply knapping stations. These areas contrast with others that contain intensely repaired tools or with the unique set of knapped stone finds associated with the human skeleton found in Unit 21. Different activities may have taken place in separate parts of the site either routinely or just prior to its abandonment. Alternatively, knapping may not have been an activity in which all members of the community participated.

Social scientists seeking early evidence of occupational specialization should be reminded that ethnological evidence indicates that the knapping profession tends not to be characterized by prestige or power. The evolution of knapping from a universal skill to a low-status profession would imply a concomitant development of high-status positions. Inequalities in the wealth of sites during the late Chalcolithic through Middle Bronze Age in Cyprus are apparent in knapped stone, both in raw materials and products.

EXCHANGE

We suggest that during the late EP and Bronze Age in Cyprus preferred knapping materials from particular regions passed to sites at significant distances from their sources.[4] Although distances on the island may not be far, we posit that these distances often mandated a heavy commitment of time and probably entailed negotiating the crossing of socially defined boundaries. Our reasoning is based both in ethnologic analogy and the prehistoric distribution of raw materials, large sites, and small scatters.

---

[4] We are not persuaded by the habit of naming prehistoric phases after a particular site, (e.g., Erimi Culture, Philia Culture). It generalizes too much on the basis of one site, usually the longest-known site or the most alluring site of the era explored by a particularly famous researcher. It also biases understanding of the time period heavily towards what that is believed to typify. Unlike widespread regional or universal terms, it conveys nothing to newcomers. The device arguably served a helpful mnemonic purpose in Cyprus in Dikaios' and the Swedish Cyprus Expedition's day. They conducted a major excavation on a particularly promising site from each of the key EP periods which they hypothesized existed in a country that was virtually a *tabula rasa* when they began. However, now that we have dozens of extensively surveyed and excavated sites the practice begins to pose the danger of underestimating the role of any one of the sites.

SPECIALIZATION IN MATERIALS

We propose that throughout the Cypriot EP and beyond preferences for certain kinds of raw material to produce specific flaked artifacts were the norm. The *Kaminoudhia* collection also shows a high degree of selectivity and matching of materials to reduction techniques and products.

RELATIONSHIP OF KNAPPING TO ARTIFACTS OF GROUND STONE, ANTLER, BONE, SHELL, TEETH, AND WOOD

Previous Cypriot reports have not considered the universal role of antler in stone extraction or reduction. Two studies acknowledge the likelihood of stone for chopping antler and bone and of burin extraction of needle and awl blanks, while several works identify antler hafting. Similarly, there is hardly any mention in Cypriot archaeology of wood or ground stone as components of the knapper's tool kit. Ethnographically, bone and shell are usually less popular for flakers than other materials. Some literature on knapping experiments attributes this to their slipperiness. However, teeth, including tusks and ivory, do have a role.[5] We identify prehistoric ground stone and antler artifacts from *Kaminoudhia* and other Cypriot sites that could have made suitable stone extractors and fabricators.[6] We theorize that decreasing availability of antler and changing roles of deer hunting by the late EP may have stimulated developments noted in the flaked stone industry and in the knapper's tool kit.

MODELING THE RELATIONSHIP BETWEEN STONE TECHNOLOGY AND EARLY METALLURGY

The transition from beating to heating and casting copper is ranked as a major technological innovation. Non-specialists do not generally know that heating prior to knapping is excellent preparation for many kinds of stones. Although heat treatment experiments on Cypriot knapped raw materials have not been attempted, we believe they need to be undertaken. The stone-worker's methodology may have furnished the knowledge prerequisite to the initiation of annealing, roasting, or smelting ores. Indeed, what was copper during the advent of metallurgy, if not another stone to be hit, heated and hit, or heated and processed further by an artisan who handled and explored the properties of diverse rocks?

---

[5] Teeth (including those in the mouth of living humans), tusks, and ivory appear to a limited extent in the ethnographic and experimental literature on pressure flaking and on punched blades. Tixier et al. (1980:101, fig. 43) depicted a hafted ivory pressure flaker. Donald Crabtree, an inveterate experimenter, was particularly enthusiastic about ivory. He ranked those he studied by age of animal, environment, and genus (for example, contrasting ivory from elephants from different parts of Africa, walrus, and fossilized mammoth—apologizing for his inability to obtain narwhal samples). Crabtree noted: "Ivory from the hippopotamus is ideal for the tip of the chest crutch, such as that used for the removal of blades from the polyhedral cores. It appears to be harder than that of elephant, mammoth, or walrus, and it also resists slipping. Apparently this is due to a lack of natural oils" (1971:69). While we have not considered the use of ivory at Sotira *Kaminoudhia*, the comment suggests avenues for future Cypriot research.

[6] A worthwhile follow-up might be microscopic investigation of possible antler and fabricators for micro-traces of chert from hypothetical working surfaces. Trace analyses of collagen, amino acids, and phytoliths on the knapped products would be less efficient since they require a prohibitively large database to distinguish between manufacturing and use patterns. Lauriston Sharp's (1952) "Steel axes for stone age Australians" is an ethnological example of this phenomenon.

According to modern avocational knappers, copper constitutes the ideal pressure flaking bit fabric. Ideally it should be drawn cold and hafted. However, both traditional and hobbyist knappers have employed metal picks as well as sharpened iron nails and awls for flaking and retouch. In antiquity, something similar might also have been the case on copper-rich Cyprus. Morphologically suitable copper "awl" and "chisel" fragments occur at Cypriot Chalcolithic and later sites and are found at *Kaminoudhia*. The connection between lithic manufacturing and metallurgy in the eastern Mediterranean may have been more closely associated than previously recognized.

We believe development of copper and bronze metallurgy would have had almost no direct impact for the majority of people at *Kaminoudhia*. Knapped implements probably served the same general mechanical ends as they had throughout all of prehistory. The need for knapped products continued throughout the EP and beyond the later Bronze Age, particularly in communities with low population density. However, major changes in social status relationships, as well as inequalities in population density and occupation, probably were eventually enacted around focal-point metal objects.[7] In this chapter we have formulated a simple model of societal incorporation of copper metallurgy in relation to knapped stone.

HIERARCHY OF KNOWLEDGE

Late EP–MC society depended directly or indirectly on knowledge of certain stone sources and strategies for maximizing investment in knapping. This understanding was as critical as knowledge of other natural resources and of domesticates. Proficiency with stones that slice and chop was required to butcher animals and to cut vegetation efficiently. Overlooking or underrating the place of knapping resources and their manufacturing and exchange strategies has been a serious oversight in Cypriot archaeology.[8]

Until recently archaeologists and lithic specialists have undervalued Cypriot flaked stone industries because of their limited aesthetic component and supposed scarcity of classic tools. Indifference has been especially pronounced for later periods. Much of the following chapter urges that we treat the de facto hierarchy of formal tools and their status with extreme caution. It is our premise that the beauty, complexity, or ease of recognition of certain lithics has overly dominated the specialist literature at the expense of an understanding of the whole.[9]

---

[7] Excavation and survey project directors should save and record everything—including unworked raw material. However, it is far better to bring in a lithics specialist while formulating goals and strategies and to follow that person's recommendations on sampling and on what to archive. Eye-catching finds alone are insufficient. We need to know about the unworked material as with microscopic chippage from flotation. This is as true in chert-rich Cyprus for sites from all periods. Without a specialist, we cannot discriminate between techniques that were unique to a prehistoric period and those that continued through long phases of rural history.

[8] In the field and lab, the sorting, weighing, and measuring, describing and latterly, data entry of knapped products need to keep pace with acquisition and evaluation of the largest body of finds such as pottery. Chipped stone studies can, if allocated time for description, data entry and analysis of virtually every specimen found including unmodified raw materials, reveal where people were walking, with whom they were in contact, off what they were living, how they were processing their basic foods, what their relationship to the environment was, and what percentage of the population was left-handed, but this takes time. Preliminary reports serve their purpose, but if a full-scale report is to be done on architecture and pottery then to relegate the category of artifact that can be identified by use to an aside is unwise.

[9] The problem extends to nineteenth and twentieth century knapped production in Cyprus (see Given and Coleman 1998; McCartney 1993; Pearlman 1984; Ronen n.d; Whittaker 1994, 1996), specifically *dhoukani*/threshing

PART II: STUDY BACKGROUND,
APPROACH AND GOALS

The reconstruction of manufacturing methodology and techniques for a vast array of crafts including lithic research has become a standard topic for short professional papers, (e.g., Bordes 1968; Bordes and Crabtree 1969; Bordaz 1970; Crabtree and Butler 1964—all of which cite earlier research). For well over a generation artifact research has explored technological, experimental, ethnoarchaeological, and theoretical problems.[10]

Lithic research is one of the many branches of archaeology that has benefited from the contributions of hobbyists and late arrivals to archaeology. We regard avocational knapping as an invaluable neo-ethnographic and experimental data set to be consulted consistently.[11]

With the *Kaminoudhia* flaked stone, our aim has been to incorporate topical research results without forsaking the needs of archaeologists looking for typological information. Our guiding analytical and descriptive principles have been to emphasize not only well-made or highly distinctive items but also the mundane that forms the bulk of knapped stone at the majority of sites and elucidates manufacturing stages and cultural strategies (cf. Perlès 1992).

While interest in the subject of techniques and methodology may change in the future, a body of published knapped stone figures will continue to be useful despite any inherent limitations. A major aim of this contribution is to produce a substantial corpus of flaked stone figures for comparative use.

As recently as the mid 1990s, specialist knowledge of the knapped stone industries in Cyprus was predominantly informal, based on visits to excavations and surveys in progress, museum collections, and personal communications. Although publication of knapped stone has become more common, many references in this report are to materials described in unpublished manuscripts or familiar to the author firsthand and not yet in print. By promulgating these sources it is our hope they may become more accessible.[12]

---

sledge knapped products. So far no one has launched anything comparable on other uses of knapped stone in agriculture or industry (e.g., firearm and lighter flints).

[10] Exemplified for knapped stone in Cyprus by: Coqueugniot (1984), on the microwear and reconstructions of samples from Khirokitia *Vouni*, by Finlayson (1987) on *Mosphilia* microwear, by Hordynsky on Kalavasos *Tenta*, (in preparation 1997), Alambra *Mouttes* excavated specimens, (referenced in Kingsnorth 1996b), as well as Vasilikos Valley survey materials (Hordynsky, in preparation), by Kardulias for Malloura Valley sites; (Toumazou et al. 1992), by Lehavy (1989) on Dhali *Agridhi*, interviews of former knappers by Fasnacht (1996 and 1980), Fox (1984), Fox and Pearlman (1987), Ronen (n.d) and Whittaker (1996); by Kardulias and Yerkes (1998), McCartney (1993) and Pearlman (1984) on *dhoukhani* sled flake manufacture, metric attribute and use wear analysis; by Morris (1977) on taphonomy, replication and microwear, amino acid trace analysis on Akrotiri *Aetokremnos* tools (Simmons, personal communication). McCartney (personal communication) has successfully undertaken replication research. Smith (personal communication and 1996) and Debney (1997 and 1996) have been working on use-wear analysis.

[11] Avocational knapping, particularly in the United States and Canada, ranges from meticulous, controlled experimental replication of all stages of stone tool manufacture and its by-products to imaginative exploration techniques and material production of artifacts. Projectile points are the most popular with knives a close second. Discussion, newsletters, pamphlets, self-published booklets, "how-to" videos, workshops, seminars, advertisements for supplies marketed in different states of readiness and, more recently, web pages constitute excellent first hand sources on knapping technology with inbuilt experimental replication cross-checks. For the reader needing to check informal information on knapping technology alluded to in our report see Crabtree (1982, 1972a, 1972b, 1967), Hellweg (1984), and Whittaker (1996, 1994).

[12] The author has had the good fortune to handle knapped stone extensively in excavated and surveyed Aceramic through Classical sites as far west as the Paphos district to as far east as the Kyrenia district, and as a visitor has

At the time of the original study, publications of chipped stone collections were rare. Late Prehistoric site reports have frequently published flaked stone as a brief list of "tool" types, accompanied by one or two discussion pages. Consequently, scholars concerned with Chalcolithic and EC–MC Cyprus have not been able to incorporate chipped stone into their syntheses (see for example, Bolger 1985; Croft 1981; Heywood et al. 1981; Karageorghis 1985; Knapp 1994; Peltenburg 1996, 1989; Swiny 1981; Thomas 1988; Vermeule and Wolsky 1990).

Until the mid 1990s, no inter site comparison of dated knapped stone within a region had been published. Publication of the Lemba Archaeological Project collections will make it possible to begin contrasting chipped stone from sites within a circumscribed region (Peltenburg 1998; Peltenburg 1985). The *Kaminoudhia* data similarly permits comparison between lithics of different dates nearby and within the same drainage.

The report notes some discard clustering and rejoining, pointing to a few places where stone may have been knapped, utilized, or disposed. However, ethnoarchaeology and taphonomy underscore the speculative nature of this evidence. Equations between discard and last use are most accurate among small archaeological specimens (Clark 1986; Metcalfe and Heath 1990), and knapped stone at *Kaminoudhia* is rather small.

The knapped stone from the *Kaminoudhia* excavations comprises an immediately recognizable Cypriot late EP–Bronze Age assemblage. Our description and discussion evaluate its distinctive attributes as an adaptation to the site's location and to the manufacturers' and users' needs, constraints, and cultural norms through choice of materials, size, and production methods.

STUDY METHOD

From the start of excavation, all worked stone and all potentially knappable lithic material was kept. All stratified deposits were screened through 0.5 cm mesh, and flotation residue was scrutinized for lithic and bone microchippage. The completeness of the collection makes it exemplary for the study of all stages of manufacturing processes and of discard patterns.

Specimens were cleaned by soaking; scrubbing was entirely avoided. A few items with ostensible postdepositional, calcareous adhesions that interfered with examination required immersion in dilute hydrochloric acid.[13] All lots excavated prior to 1984 were weighed, and the number of specimens was counted. The entire collection was spread out in one place by lot location, so that the overall visible pattern could be observed. Sorting itself took place within this grid. It was through this direct visual means that distinctive clustering patterns became apparent, refitting was attempted, and possible specific reduction trajectories were considered.[14]

---

been generously permitted to examine in progress and past excavation and survey project and museum samples, all over the island, from all archaeological periods for more than twenty years. Despite some hesitation, we counter tradition by including several documents on Cypriot lithics in the bibliography that we have not actually seen but which are cited in other works. We do not know if they are in progress works or if unpublished drafts exist. Identifying them should allow other researchers who may be unaware of them to follow up.

[13] The collection has great potential for microwear analysis, although such was beyond the scope of the initial study.

[14] The small size of the assemblage and the availability of a spacious, well-protected area available for spreading out the entire collection (covered as needed) made this kind of work possible. It has become common practice in processing lithics to code one or a few lots as rapidly as possible, bag and label them, and immediately get on to the next one, driven by the overwhelming pressures of having to put sufficient quantities of data into the computer to make the statistical analysis of the data meaningful. On the basis of the Sotira *Kaminoudhia* experience, we recommend also spreading out as many adjacent lots as possible and contrasting them, both early in the

The author looked at most items saved through 1991. Those acquired after 1984 or discovered in the heavy quotient were not examined among the 1984 gridded materials. Extensive quantitative data on half a dozen to several dozen variables were collected. A small initial test sample of 180 specimens was evaluated quantitatively by area, deposit, product, and attribute.[15] Each lot was recorded both by sorting category and as a unit, and specimens were selected for illustration.

PRODUCTION SEQUENCE SORTING

In converting naturally occurring stone into an artifact, one must locate a source of raw material, acquire it, and modify it through various techniques. For the most part, modification entails removing portions of the original stone. Stone products result at each stage of the transformation from raw material to implement, and sometimes afterwards. In practice, some products are abandoned and some are worked further. Some results may constitute an intended or accidental product, while others may be an expected or expedient way station which the knapper intends to modify further, but for one reason or another it does not occur. Products may also be reworked or altered by use, specialized discard, or disturbance. This may be planned or occur by mistake or chance. Archaeologically, the nature of the reduction sequence products recovered and the presence or absence of products and their location can be a clue to 1) the sequence of physical steps originally taken, 2) where they were taken, and 3) a hint of why a particular trajectory was followed. How best to translate the above, with its branching continua of intentions, actions, and results, into the practicalities of sorting archaeological finds is a major interest of middle range theory. It is difficult to lump and to split lithics so that their groupings correspond to their original position in the chain of alterations when they became discards. The problems inherent in classifying are arbitrariness, subjectivity, modern cultural bias, and replicability. Definitional issues are also a concern (for example, distinguishing a step from a stage). Broader theory centers on the importance of the knapper's original intention, whether the agent is the individual or society, and what is style and meaning—the spectrum of philosophical issues familiar to archaeology and many branches of the social sciences. At the highest levels of late twentieth century theorizing, affinities entwine between lithic paths, transformational grammar, neural networks, and for some, even the scaffolding of DNA (Matsuzawa 1996; Pinker 1995).

For *Kaminoudhia* sorting categories and their parameters, we adapted groupings familiar in Cyprus in various guises (Morris 1977: Hordynsky and Kingsnorth 1979; Kingsnorth 1996a, 1996b, initially delineated by Collins 1975).[16] Results can be compared both to research elsewhere grounded in traditional tool typologies and to scholarship that avoids them.[17] Both genres of investigation exist for Cyprus.

---

project and later on as a descriptive and analytical tool for the specialist, and for all interested parties, especially with unfamiliar collections, if time, space, collection size, and project goals permit.

[15] The sample size resulted in cells too small to be statistically significant, but we expect to follow this study with data entry and analysis of the remainder. At the time of the original study, resources for data entry and packaged statistical programs were less accessible to the independent scholar than currently, in the era of affordable computers and extremely user-friendly statistical packages. Nevertheless, we collected quantitative data in the expectation of improved research conditions or financing.

[16] Formalized in print for example by Bordes 1961; Crabtree 1982; Gramly 1992; Mortensen 1970; Neuville 1934; Rosen 1997; de Sonneville-Bordes and Perrot 1954-1956; Tixier 1974 and 1963; Tixier et al. 1980.

[17] Logical and self-evident, these facts are typically underrated, neglected, forgotten, or ignored in analysis of archaeological collections. Although works by Richard A. Gould, (1980, 1978, 1969, 1968; Gould et al. 1971), illustrating the sovereignty of the least modified of lithics are almost de rigueur bibliographically, his most cited

We tried to discover possible modification routes through the production stages at *Kaminoudhia* using four major divisions. Similarities and differences were noted in morphology, edge, and edge modification of surviving specimens in sequential product groups. The results suggested possible alternative manufacturing trajectories, provided an index of the range of variation for the collection, and furnished a basis for comparison with other collections.

PRODUCT GROUPS (PG)

The basic groups used for sorting *Kaminoudhia* lithics were:

PG1. **Raw material**.

PG2. **Initial reduction products**, such as cores, unmodified flakes/blades, and chunks.

PG3. **Results of one subsequent action**. This group was identified by an additional individual or continuous step (e.g., retouch on one edge on one face, or a single notch).

PG4. **Results of more knapping**. This group was identified by additional steps (e.g., pressure flaking at a second location, or shoulder thinning combined with point narrowing).

PG5 Lithics with traces of refurbishing.

Product groups 1–4 are sequential. For example, retouch converts a PG2 item into PG3, and a PG4 item must previously have been PG3, PG2, and PG1. Product Groups 1–4 roughly correspond to phases of reduction. Earlier researchers would have proposed these groups also corresponded to mental categories of the knapper. Within these stages a lithic may be a "blank," with the potential to be transformed in different directions, or a "preform," offering a much narrower range of options, practically, physically, or within the norms of the collection. We looked for similarities and differences between blanks, preforms, and other lithics.

To critics of this application of the production sequence model we argue that limiting product group analysis to classic tools or bifaces offers an incomplete and seriously biased picture of the role of lithics in society. Since flakes and blades, their edges, their edge configurations, dorsal presentation, and extremities are crucial to the tasks performed, so-called "opportunistic tools," or so-called "ad hoc tools," require attributes and attribute combinations appropriate to the job for which they have been chosen. Even if the demeanor with which lithics are chosen may be casual, to function they cannot be selected capriciously. They must be oriented sensibly and knowledgeably to work. Variations in edge, end, back, thickness, and width—as well as traces of prior knapping events (often evident on flaked lithics)—illuminate modes of planning and scope of methodology.[18]

We have found one additional product grouping helpful. Product Group 5 (PG5) brings together specimens showing traces of conservation. Unlike others, items of this category may have been created out of any previously modified stone from any product group. A summary of the refurbishing category follows.

---

pertinent ethnological results do not shape research design. Over-familiarity, or cultural habits which reward the innovative, the eye catching, the distinctive, the traditional, or the diagnostic have taken precedence, latterly justified by the hat in societies in which bifaces and retouched projectile points et cetera are a signal component, more quotidian lithics playing "very minor roles in the general circulation and reiteration of social relationships" (Gero 1989:103). For the sake of the argument, accepting the conception of social relations implied in the previous quote (predicated on inequality?), it may follow that the more significant unmodified and barely modified lithics are in a culture's assemblages the less socially differentiated the society is. If accurate, this in itself is important information about a given society. However, here we suggest other reasons for prominence of unretouched tools in Cypriot collections (see also Kingsnorth 1996b).

[18] See especially Tixier 1963 and 1974.

Category PG5 designates lithics with traces of refurbishing. The term "rejuvenation" is here applied exclusively to techniques and their resulting byproducts used to tidy up a core that has become very difficult to flake. Rejuvenation removes obtruding bumps and ridges from the core formed by previous detachments.

Curation. Curation refers to actions undertaken to extend the working life of an implement or tool, such as retouching or polishing an edge blunted by use, or grinding a dulled point. Identifying curation without microwear analysis and distinguishing it from PG 3 and PG4 are only occasionally feasible.

Recycling. Recycling refers to rearranging a formerly reduced item (usually already PG3 or PG4), to create a new tool or turn it into a core and/or the discard from the process. Newer retouch and/or edges intersect prior ones. The retouch or edge is often of a different kind and is the easiest to discern.

Other Modifications. This category includes damage, break, snap, truncation, shearing, and burin blow scars. We coded breaks within product groups, distinguished by fresh looking surfaces, or abrupt interruptions of profiles, edges, or ends (and not by deviation from an expected PG2 configuration). We classed as snaps breaks accompanied by one or two very small adjacent conchoidal scars at one or both ends of the break and traversing the lithic from lateral to lateral, rather than axially. Truncation refers only to shortening of a lithic associated with retouch on a transverse edge.

We identify burin blow reduction on a flake, blade, or bladelet face by an angular or shear edge at right angles or an oblique angle to a face. The scar must originate after PG2 detachment from the core and must exhibit a minuscule negative bulb. This conservative set of criteria is meant to avoid prejudicing interpretation of shear scars in favor of deliberate knapping practice and should be considered when examining our figures and making inter site comparisons. At one end of the spectrum, we avoid the term "burin" as a formal tool name and at the other end try to differentiate between burin blow manufacturing techniques and oblique to the face scars caused by other means.

Angular faces (rather than edges) that do not meet the previous criteria are most commonly attributes of chunks, especially if dominating more than one adjacent surface and/or edge, or are an indicator of shearing, smashing, breaking, or of heat fracturing, depending on the angularity, presence, or quality of conchoidal ripples. We noted these criteria in written comments rather than numerical codes.

Striking a flake, blade, or bladelet against an anvil, or striking the lithic itself at a right or oblique angle to its faces, constitutes the burin blow technique. One result is a faceted relationship of new edges, which to early researchers evoked a chisel ("burin"). Experimentally, some "burins" are favored for incising bone and antler, especially for excising little wedges for awl and needle blanks. However, calling any lithic with a burin blow scar a "burin" elevates the scar to the dominant feature at the expense of other attributes and functions.

Many so-called "burins" may have been created to function as chisels, but the classification based on one attribute obscures their role as cores for bladelets and spalls, items that are implements in their own right, and as blanks for celebrated tool industries in some parts of the world.[19] The bladelet, microflake, or spall removed by a burin blow has a dorsal composed of the faces of flake or blade from which it was removed. In the case of a "burin plat" it may seem to have an entire dorsal face, which is a ventral. A further hazard is that in practice the "burin" designation seems to be predicated on a vague or arbitrary size-based distinction in technique and resultant scars. Only rarely do "burins" encompass

---

[19] For further discussion see Pitzer's 1997 introduction and reprint of three classic twentieth century articles on the classifications of burins and Vaughan (1985).

large flakes and blades patently altered by oblique force or the consequent scars. Furthermore, the purpose of the burin strike may have been to thin or narrow a lithic for hafting, to thicken it to strengthen or haft it, or to create a long, narrow flat surface for scraping or slotting. Hence, we are comfortable with the expressions "burin blow" and "burin scar," but rarely with "burin" alone. We prefer using this term for a specific reduction technique rather than for a tool type.[20]

Other Alterations and Their Speculative Causes. We coded other evidence of modification that could affect any specimen or that is not reductive within the Product Groups. This included signs of core preparation, platform preparation, and technique of detachment. Indicators of combining of lithics into composite utensils or hafting fall were handled within PG categories. It is likely that all these were deliberate processes.

Indicators of alteration that involved changes in immediate local conditions were also recorded within PG categories. These were dominated by evidence of burning or intense heating (recognized by potlidding or crazing), thermofracture, and alteration in calcareous cortex color and texture. Patination (possibly caused by weathering) was also noted. We distinguished between glow, sheen, and gloss.

Defining Use, Implements, and Tools for this Chapter. Use can alter lithics in any product group. Although it is usually reductive, this is not always the case. Visual inspection and use of a five or ten power hand lens magnification alone, the means available to us at the time of original research, was not considered a sound means of determining the function of a knapped stone item (Coqueugniot 1984; Finlayson 1987; Hordynsky 1996; Keeley 1980 and 1974; Keeley and Newcomer 1977; Morris 1977; Newcomer 1976; Vaughan 1985). We recorded smeary, scalar, stepped, battered, smashed, and similar scars. We also noted nicks on edges, crests (ridge/aris), and/or terminals but did not consider these attributes to be reliable evidence of use. Discard, contextual, and postdepositional disturbance is an additional source of damage.

For the reader unfamiliar with the specifics of microwear research, we emphasize that it is extraordinarily time consuming. Microwear studies of stone tools recovered from archaeological contexts must be compared with microwear studies of modern, experimental duplicates ideally of identical materials (i.e., preferably from the same beds), and utilized in known ways. Creating the comparative material takes innumerable hours. Examples must experience different actions such as sawing, scraping, piercing, and chopping. The control specimens should be used only once, a few times, and many times. They need to be tried out at different angles and on different materials. Work with single actions and combined tasks is important.

Coqueugniot alludes to the time constraints imposed by high power magnification microwear analysis: "Examination of an implement requires at least two hours of observation under the microscope, which cannot be continuous. Furthermore, [creating] the experimental control [groups] also requires a lot of time" (1984; 89, footnote 5. Translation this author).[21] In contrast, after conquering the learning curve, with low-level magnification it may be possible to average five to twenty specimens per hour, depending on nature of fabric, specimen, microscope, and lighting. This method is not a form of analysis that can be undertaken for many hours at a time.

---

[20] Subsequent work in Cyprus by Debney (1997, 1996) and Smith (1996) has been more courageous about visual identification of use wear. We look forward to description of details of the method. If tested against microwear and non-use damage controls on replications in regional materials, they will have opened a very fruitful avenue for Cypriot research.

[21] "A l'examen d'un outil demande au moins deux heures d'observation microscopique, or cette dernière ne peut pas être effectuée de manière continuée et les contrôles experimentaux demandent eux aussi beaucoup de temps."

Visible sheen and gloss are frequently thought of as reliable indices of use. However, we suspect some cherts in Cyprus take on an overall sheen through exposure to sun, heating, or wind.[22] Certain fine, dark Moni formation cherts common in the western part of the island have mirror-like patches, which most specialists consider not to be anthropogenic. We documented shininess, noting density and location. Metaphorically, sheen gives the impression of being something between a patina and an inherent quality of the stone. Whereas sheen is diffuse and thin, gloss is so shiny that it looks like poured lacquer. A few lithics had surfaces with a dull glow. Despite a common equation in the general literature between visible sheen and gloss and grain harvesting, precisely what kind of materials and what kind of activities produce them is unclear.

This writer continues to apply the term "tool" to lithics evincing a high degree of planning and purpose, whether or not actually used, (cf. Hordynsky and Kingsnorth 1979; Kingsnorth 1996a, 1996b). The definition includes gloss pieces, retouched lithics, and morphologically identical specimens lacking retouch or gloss. We have found the term "implement" valuable for knapped products suited to a task, but which are not tools by the criteria defined above (see Hordynsky and Kingsnorth 1979; Kingsnorth 1996a, 1996b). We assert that "implement" is preferable to "debitage," a term specialists trained in French lithic analysis traditions apply to unretouched flakes, blades, and bladelets, but which other archaeologists use synonymously with "debris" (our chunks and chips). We find "waste," a common equivalent, inappropriate because of its erroneous connotations. Its widespread, unexamined application may help explain why unmodified flake use is seen as "ad hoc," "opportunistic," or "expedient," when 90% of lithics are classified as "waste."

Production Technology Versus Production Methodology. "Technology" in the present study pertains to the physical aspects of manufacturing, and "methodology" to the cognitive. A knapper knows a method but applies a technique. Our goal has been to look for insights into both technology and methodology at *Kaminoudhia*.

THE COLLECTION

SIZE AND WEIGHT

The knapped and knappable stone excavated through 1984 from *Kaminoudhia* amounts to 3,570 items. The total weight of the collection was 11.285 kg, and individual specimens averaged 3.16g. Fine-grained cherts[23] as well as suitable coarser grained materials are ubiquitous, index of the smallness of the collection and of its components.[24] All but 1% show signs of knapping.[25]

[22] Similarly, Swiny (1988:10) reports "high gloss, probably [due to] wind-blown sand ..." on a surface lithic from the Akrotiri Peninsula.

[23] Debate over the terms "flint," "chert," "chalcedony," "quartz," "quartzite," and "jasper" is rife. We follow Luedtke (1992) and others in using "chert" as the generic term and in avoiding the word "jasper." The problem is compounded by "psycholinguistic" differences of lumping and splitting habits across language boundaries. Therefore, we continue to describe texture, color, knappable qualities first and foremost. Concordance lists issued by each archaeological project and tied to a national type collection could be helpful. The beginnings of a small, named one assembled by the Tremithos project, housed in Nicosia, at the Cyprus American Archaeological Research Institute has proven valuable to some researchers. The reference collection of materials from other sites at Cyprus American Archaeological Research Institute has been expanded greatly by the former Director, S. Swiny.

[24] In contrast at the later quarry site of Alambra *Mouttes*, approximately one third as many specimens (approximately 5,000), added up to more than three times this weight (more than 35 kilos), equaling an average of about seven grams (Kingsnorth 1996b).

[25] This proportion is unlike that of slightly later Alambra *Mouttes,* seated directly on usable chert outcrops but

RAW MATERIALS: (PG1) LOCATION OF SOTIRA *KAMINOUDHIA* IN RELATIONSHIP TO RAW MATERIALS AND THE ISSUE OF PREFERRED SOURCES

Even-grained, siliceous, and cryptocrystalline stone that consistently and predictably distributes the force of blows received is the globally preferred substance for flaking. In Cyprus relatively fine-grained cherts and suitable coarser grained materials are ubiquitous, and knapped goods are scattered over most excavated Early Prehistoric sites. Nevertheless, although chert deposits occur all over the island, and worked chert is commonplace on prehistoric and later sites in Cyprus, not every archaeological site is located within rapid walking distance of preferred sources.

For several years we have argued that prehistoric knappers in Cyprus favored certain raw materials and deposits over others (Kingsnorth 1996b, and an earlier draft of this report, 1991). This preference was confirmed historically and ethnographically for Cyprus (Pearlman 1984; Whittaker 1996). For example, Pearlman's (1984) interviews of fourteen retired Cypriot manufacturers of *dhoukania* (threshing sledges) reveal that some twentieth century flint knappers (*athkiakadhes*, alternate transliteration in the singular, *athkiajas*) gathered cherts twenty-five kilometers away from their village of residence, despite its being located within a kilometer of "excellent chert supplies" (Pearlman 1984:124). Grigoris Hadjiagathangelou, a professional Cypriot knapper, judged that, " acquiring a supply of good cherts is one of the most important aspects of the work. It takes a special skill not only to knap the chert, but also to select the proper material in the first place" (Pearlman 1984: Appendix 4, Interview #1, p. 216–17). Some of Pearlman's consultants journeyed two hundred kilometers to stock favored materials. Northern *athkiakadhes* crossed the island, leaving home for several weeks or months, to collect and work materials from targeted sources in the south (Pearlman 1984; Andreou, reported in Whittaker 1996). To do so they had to confront major sociopolitical boundaries.

We contend proximity of sources has not been the most important influence on material choice for knappers of any period. Knapping quality, suitability of a stone's traits to manufacture the intended artifact, aesthetics (in some examples), and prestige value of exotics have been important. The social and economic need to nurture intergroup relationships through exchange and through cultivating of symbols influenced desirability of particular sources. Procuring river cobbles depended on seasonal increases in supply and seasonal variations in physical accessibility. Social control would also have influenced the degree of availability of sources. All these factors have played a role around the world through time, and we believe they are evident in prehistoric Cyprus lithic selection.

Few systematic archaeological surveys in Cyprus have successfully sought, recorded, evaluated, and published the distribution of likely lithic raw material sources.[26] Moreover, site gazetteers have not incorporated available geoarchaeologic data. Although overshadowed by interest in specialized, easily identified commodities, the documentation of changing access to lithic raw materials for the prehistoric period in Cyprus may be as important to students of culture as documenting changing access to water, fauna and flora, and other primary and secondary resources. Since archaeology attempts to recognize changes in resource bases and to identify adaptations to them to help explain social change, this has to include the basic materials of tools for daily living.

The work of the Canadian Palaiopaphos Survey Project and its successor, the Western Cyprus Project, stand out as particularly successful exceptions. They conscientiously set out to discover sources,

---

very similar to Episkopi *Phaneromeni*, nearby in place if not in time.

[26] In the late 1990s this has begun to change rapidly. See Guilaine et al. 1997–1998; Toumazou et al. (1998), who have identified Middle Lapithos Formation chalk sources; Kingsnorth 1996a; McCartney personal communication; Stewart personal communication.

engaging specialists with both the appropriate geologic and knapping knowledge (D'Annibale 1993, 1992; Rupp 1987a; Rupp 1987b; Rupp et al. 1994, 1993, 1992, 1987, 1984; Rupp and D'Annibale 1995; Stewart 1992, 1987 and 1985).[27] Informally, geologists, geoarchaeologists, and archaeologists working on early metallurgy issues have often been extremely helpful. Smith (1996) described the genesis and knapping properties of chalcedony,[28] two Lefkara cherts, and a few of the Troodos-associated cryptocrystallines, (umber, "jasper," hematitic chert, and reheated basalt)[29] used on archaeological sites and identified sources for all but one material used at EC–MC Marki *Alonia* within one and a half km of the site. These studies independently corroborated the work of the Canadian Palaiopaphos Survey Project, the Western Cyprus Project, and other surveys.

Guilaine et al. (1995) located a source they believe provided the majority of the fabric at Parekklisha *Shillourokambos* one kilometer south of the site. The Sydney Cyprus Survey Project (Knapp and Given 1996; Knapp et al. 1994, 1992) investigated changing uses of both lithic and copper resources within its project area on a limited, systematic sampling and combined intuitive basis. They identified a few probable extraction sites, including one for hematitic chert/"jasper" (Kingsnorth 1996b; Coleman, personal communication). Pearlman and Betts (Betts 1987) identified a bed for one distinctive, fine dark material at Kissonerga *Mosphilia*. Betts (1987, 1979a) proposed that seven other categories known at Lemba *Lakkous* and Kissonerga *Mosphilia* were most likely acquired from nearby Troodos streams. McCartney (personal communications) developed hypotheses about knapped stone sources used during the EP at Lemba area sites. Obsidian sourcing is standard procedure.[30]

Some projects have assembled carefully labeled and identified type collections of raw material, although precise sourcing has not necessarily been a feature.[31] Unfortunately, these collections comprise "in-house" holdings that are generally unknown and underutilized. Moreover, concordances cross-referencing different projects' lithic nomenclature are informal and not well circulated. Until recently, unlike the situation with obsidian, copper ores, and picrolite, geologists and geoarchaeologists

---

[27] It is probably their work more than any other that familiarized archaeologists with Moni formation cherts. Their term "Mamonia cherts," however has not been widely accepted.

[28] Here we use "chalcedony" for a chert variant recognized as distinctive by all archaeologists interested in the subject but designated variously as "quartzitic," "quartz," "clear quartz," and "milky quartz." The stone is tough, elastic, and homogenous. Colors range from clear to white (frequently with a bluish cast), translucent orange, to translucent brown. It sometimes grades into or abruptly borders the common opaque, fine- to medium-grained (lower/basal) Lefkaras. In Cyprus, it is only rarely retouched. Nevertheless, many collections possess a very small percentage of flaked chalcedony, almost invariably represented by one or more of the following: hammerstones, simple flaked bifaces, and small rounded flakes.

[29] The terms jasper, hematitic chert, and vitrified or naturally reheated igneous stones can refer to different materials but have often been informally confused. Their colors and, to a superficial extent, their textures overlap. All can fracture conchoidally and, therefore, have theoretical use for a knapper. Red and yellow cherts, hematitic cherts, and revitrified igneous stone, found in the Troodos and Troodos foothills related deposits are often called jasper (or occasionally prase).

[30] Obsidian's cachet has merited at least two articles entirely independent of their project reports in general archaeology journals sourcing a few pieces of obsidian from two different Cypriot sites (Briois et al 1997; Gomez et al. 1995). We believe that the two contributions are important and well justified, but we suggest that other knappable materials should stimulate just as much scholarly prestige.

[31] Among others, the Canadian Palaiopaphos Survey Project, the Cornell University Alambra investigations, the Lemba Archaeological Project, the Marki *Alonia* Project, the Sydney Cyprus Survey Project, the Tremithos Valley Project, the Vasilikos Valley Project, and their follow up projects in more recent years compiled sample collections of materials for flaked stone.

in Cyprus have rarely made sourcing of knapped lithics a priority. Relating chert sources to the evolving cultural landscape remains an important area of investigation in Cyprus.

In Cyprus chert occurs as field, stream, and beach cobbles, as either visible or subsurface boulders, in bedded seams, or as eroding outcrops.[32] Both natural and anthropogenic topographic change has often altered the availability and exposure of cherts. In the case of *Kaminoudhia*, the closest prehistoric sources were probably lithics scavenged from neighboring Neolithic Sotira *Teppes* and perhaps Kouris River gravels. To reach the nearest point of the river from *Kaminoudhia* is now a brisk fifty-minute walk and about twice that time for the uphill return hike (Swiny, personal communication).

We posit that riverbed cherts have fluctuated in availability along the river's course by season, by year, and by location. Wet years and months bring a heavy wash of stones. However, these may not be easily collectible until the river recedes or dries up, yet cherts are most visible when not completely cortex-coated and when slightly damp. Dry months and drought years contribute their own impediments. There is less new material, and all nodules look the same after days or months in the sun with their uniform, pale exteriors, and blanketing of dust. Hot, dry periods require more time to test the caliber of chert by removing a few exterior flakes by smashing or to listen to its ring.[33]

Athkiakades who worked with river cobbles mentioned that spring was the best time of year to collect chert because of its visibility (Pearlman 1984). On the other hand, the professional *dhoukani* maker Grigoris Hadjiagathangelou and Pearlman successfully collected chert from the mouth of the Vasilikos River in September by testing stones with a small metal pick (Pearlman 1984). Both believed that selection of suitable nodules took more work than it would have at another time of year because of a unifying silt coating that obscured visual selection, forcing individualized hammer contact with rocks that proved unsuitable.

Our own visits along the lower reaches of the Kouris River to appraise the accessibility of cherts attractive to knappers revealed that this zone was not ideal for chert procurement in midsummer of different years when water tables are extremely low. The chert encountered was very grainy and bore little relationship to even the poorest nodules and reduction products at any archaeological site in Cyprus with which the author is familiar.[34] In 1977, H. Morris and geologist John Gifford compared cobbles from the Kouris River with worked materials from Episkopi *Phaneromeni* and came to similar conclusions. Morris states, "it seems reasonable to suggest that the Kouris River was not the main source for the highest quality chert, and was perhaps only one source for the poorer quality chert. It seems likely that the chalcedony and siliceous limestone were taken from the Kouris riverbed and used to supplement the chert supply. The main source of chert for *Phaneromeni* remains a problem" (Morris 1977:2–3).

Other positions on the river or other times may have been more profitable. Waldorf (1984), a respected avocational knapper, believes certain materials knap best when they are wet or are partially set in damp clays. Thus, a damper season for collection may also have suited other production stages. If the Kouris River were a source as is usually assumed, it would have been a variable one, demanding knowledge of and adaptations to its irregularities.[35]

---

[32] Umber and revitrified basalt are known to the author as stratified seams and as redeposited cobbles. Obsidian is not endemic.

[33] For citations on the "sound" of desired cherts see, Crabtree 1967, 1972a; Pearlman 1984; Waldorf 1984; author's own experience and avocational knappers' personal communications.

[34] Throughout the text material "quality" refers to the knapper's perspective, primarily a combination of evenness, elasticity, predictability.

[35] McCartney (personal communication) has observed differential seasonal availability of suitable cherts in riverbeds and streams of Western Cyprus.

In 1997, the Sotira Archaeological Project (Swiny and Mavromatis 2000) systematically surveyed twelve square kilometers around the Sotira sites paying close attention to lithics, including looking for possible chert sources. Stretching from foothills to sea and from Evdhimou on the west to the Kouris River valley on the east, this survey reconfirmed the absence of other nearby exposed field, boulder, or stratified chert for any prehistoric group of knappers except one extremely unlikely source (Swiny, personal communication).[36]

We are unable to determine if the fine cherts of *Kaminoudhia* might have been acquired from the bed approximately 30 km to the east near Parekklisha *Shillourokambos* in person or through exchange (Guilaine et al. 1995). On the other hand, several south coast beaches now sport a broad array of instantly perceptible chert nodules even in midsummer (not to mention calcareous and igneous blocks and semiprecious pebbles). Prehistoric islanders may have utilized this coastal rim asset and selected the fine lithics from marine beaches at the early Akrotiri sites, Sotira *Teppes*, Sotira *Kaminoudhia*, and Episkopi *Phaneromeni*.[37]

Kaminoudhia does not seem to have the abundance of easily handled nearby materials found at many published Cypriot prehistoric sites.[38] In contrast, our site seems similar to Episkopi *Phaneromeni*, within the same drainage as *Kaminoudhia* (Morris 1977). In both collections there is strong evidence for conservation of materials, although the strategies are different. The difference in method may reflect temporal and social differences.

---

[36] Morris' description explains the reasoning: "a small number of exposed veins of coarse gray chert have been found near the path to the sea, about one and one-half kilometer from the site [of Episkopi *Phaneromeni*], just below the Roman site of Curium. This appears to have been exposed as a result of the limestone quarrying which occurred during Roman times. A survey of the area showed no evidence of any core preparation signs of chert working. Its seems likely that this was not a chert source in Bronze Age times" (Morris 1977:2. Brackets this author). Nor, by extension, we would assume for *Kaminoudhia*, especially given the kind of raw material, PG1, that dominates the *Kaminoudhia* excavated assemblage.

[37] The author is not the first to whom the idea of beach collection of fines has occurred. LeBrun (1981:31) notes regarding aceramic Neolithic Cape Andreas *Kastros* flaked stone: "Des silex de meilleure qualité ont également été employés, ils sont de couleurs varieés blond, brun et bèige, brun, rouge, gris ou vert. Les galéts apportes par la mer presentent la même varieté de qualité et de couleur." "Likewise, better quality cherts had been used. They were of various colors: creamy, brown and beige, brown, red, gray or green. Pebbles brought in by the sea display the same range of quality and color." (Loose trans. this author.)

In a related vein, see Peltenburg 1982:100, re: "jasper nuggets." Also, Elliot's (1991) investigation of likely igneous ground stone points for Lemba area EP sites considers nearby beaches to be crucial sources for those materials. She even comments on the presence of "red jasper" and chert on one of the beaches. Although she does not discuss the collection of chert, all the others she lists (e.g., serpentinite), are ones discussed in her text on ground stone. By implication it seems to have occurred to her also that beaches may be a source for knapping materials.

Beach formation, perpetuation, redeposition, burial, re-exposure, disintegration, and dispersion, are mutable. Therefore, it is too much to hope that present or former beach collection sites might be identified directly.

[38] Ayios Epiktitos *Vrysi* is implied by its excavator to have enjoyed the convenience of supplies from the Kyrenia lowlands, and perhaps also "jasper nuggets," "readily available along the littoral near Vrysi" (Peltenburg 1982:100). By extension, Troulli might have employed the same or similar sources. Other well-positioned sites are those high in the foothills, Marki *Alonia* and the Alambra area, those in the Dhiarizos and Vasilikos Valleys, and Parekklisha *Shillourokambos*, as well as Kholetria *Ortos* and Dhali *Agridhi* with their cobble-rich Pleistocene river terrace emplacements.

RANGE OF MATERIALS

Very fine-grained, semi-translucent cherts dominate the industry at *Kaminoudhia*. These are the finest of the Lefkara formation cherts. They are easy to flake and are among the most responsive, indigenous siliceous stones on the island.[39] Products can be repeatedly resharpened or refashioned, since they permit extremely delicate retouch. When very thin, the material is friable (a disadvantage shared with obsidian).[40] At *Kaminoudhia*, the substance was worked to the nub; knappers reduced some stock into tiny cores.

Judging by the dorsal convexity of exterior flakes, we think that the material at *Kaminoudhia* was obtained most frequently as cobbles, sometimes coated with a calcareous cortex, rather than quarried from seams or extracted from exposed blocks or boulders. It would have taken concerted effort to amass the fine-grained translucent lithics of *Kaminoudhia*. Prehistoric peoples may have visited sources that we missed. They may have carefully tested and selected many nodules, or were discriminating in their retention of reduced products.[41] When viewed in its entirety, the appearance of the Sotira *Kaminoudhia* assemblage inspired our perception that in prehistoric accumulation of materials ease of reduction, looks, or tolerance of conservation outweighed proximity of sources.

Minority materials bolster this picture. They amount to a handful of items. Most are high-quality versions of more ordinary materials abundant at other sites, such as medium-grained gray or orange translucent Lefkara cherts with calcareous inclusions or bands. They are mostly restricted to objects characterized elsewhere in Cyprus by the same material. Raw materials included chalcedony for bifaces, "hammerstones," and a few short thick flakes, three short roundish igneous flakes; banded gray parallel-sided blades with natural cortex backing; two very dark very fine-grained articulated parallel-sided linear flakes, with some calcareous cortex, and two translucent, orange-banded tabular chert megaflakes, probably awaiting further reduction. Expertise in the properties of Cypriot materials and a common mode of handling them and/or discriminating acquisition of a few deliberate products may explain the assortment.

SPECIFIC EXAMPLES

Unless otherwise indicated, lithics depicted in the knapped stone plates and described in the catalogue are of fine, frequently translucent Lefkara chert. Lot 6, in G 17 B, Unit 5 in Area A, contained 30 pieces of worked fine chert. These translucent, very fine-grained cherts vary in color from light through medium green and pale yellow variegated with orange. Green and orange were the most common colors.[42] Some are of a uniform color and some are variegated or mottled with pale gray and white flecks. A harder, grainier gray, occasionally with white speckling, is represented regularly (Munsell 7.5R–2.5YR 6/0). Hard, darkish reds (Munsell 10R 3.5/6–6.5), which frequently show heat crazing, were also found with equal regularity. We theorize they acquired their color through deliberate or unintentional heating. Various fine-grained, very pale grays, as well as rather dark, opaque grays and

---

[39] Very dark, opaque, fine-grained, Moni formation cherts plentiful on sites further west may actually be comparably impressive although a little less elastic.

[40] At the site of Agrokipia *Palaiokamina*, even mere fragments of broken thin, flat tools in the fabric were so valued that they were recycled as small utilizable segments (Kingsnorth 1996a).

[41] Perhaps this is support of our suggestion that collection may have taken place at seaside beaches. Beach pebble spreads can be diverse and colorful, especially when wet, and consequently easy to select among

[42] Munsell 2.5Y 4.5/1 "Dark gray/grayish/dark grayish brown" - 2.5Y 5.5/2 "Light brown gray" –l0 YR 4/4 "Dark yellowish brown" - 10YR 5/3 "brown" - 5YR 5/4 - 4/6 "Yellowish red."

whites were stratified within units in Area A. Some grays are speckled or mottled, and some whites are chalky or gritty in texture. The range of colors and textures may be due to 1) the variegated properties of a single mass of chert, 2) the number of nodules, 3) unequal heating and burning, or 4) procurement from different sources.

In Area C, Unit 17, Lot 7 chipped stone specimen 18 is argillaceous and gritty. Crabtree (1972) observed that these are sought-after traits for sawing antler, wood, and soft stone. Such desired attributes may explain the existence of three igneous flakes (fig 7.6, 173–76), although it is possible that they constitute byproducts from initial ground stone reduction. Examples of igneous flakes are common on Lemba area late prehistoric sites (McCartney, personal communication).[43] There is a tiny component at aceramic Kholetria *Ortos* (author's familiarity with the collection), but not generally reported elsewhere. It is possible that archaeologists accustomed to Cypriot knapped products in more common materials have not recorded igneous flakes.[44]

The latter impression is supported by the presence of 1) a worked piece in umber (Munsell 5YR 5-6/6-8 "Reddish-brown/yellowish-red") with small calcareous inclusions, 2) milky quartz (Deposit 2 in G 17 D in area A, two out of the fourteen specimens saved) and 3) chalcedony. There are also rare, exceptionally dark, fine-grained brown or black specimens found in stratified deposits (see Unit 18, Lot 5, specimen # 12 and one from each of the overlying deposits in the Unit). Among the finds from the 1986 excavations in Area C, was a light, opaque, pinkish-buff (Munsell 5YR 6.25/2.5), medium-fine textured basal Lefkara chert. This specimen is of the standard Alambra *Mouttes* assemblage fabric in color, opacity, and texture.

Lithics in these materials are common at some Sydney Cyprus Survey Project sites and in threshing sledges in the area (Kingsnorth 1996a, material 2). They are a minority component of Troodos and Troodos foothill sites with which we are familiar and may be found at Dhali *Agridhi* (Lehavy 1989, "red agate?" or "green prase chert?") as well as in the Alambra survey lithics (Kingsnorth 1996b). The "brick red" specimens of the Lemba *Lakkous* cache may refer to one of these materials (Betts 1979b). The one hematitic flake tool, together with two other minority lithics found in association with the excavated human skeleton at *Kaminoudhia*, hints at its being an individual exotic possession (see Chapter 2, Unit 22).

The most common chipped stone material in the Vasilikos and Maroni Valley sites from the Aceramic through the twentieth century is a blocky semi-translucent gray or orange chert (with pale variants). It contains calcareous inclusions that sometimes give the impression that the white grains are actively amassing toward flake exteriors.[45]

This chert intercalated with calcareous bands occurs *in situ* as exposed seams and field blocks and cobbles. The tabular morphology and calcareous strata readily lend to the production of linear flakes/blades with natural cortex backing. Gray Lefkara chert is extremely common at the excavated Neolithic sites and the one LC site. It is also noted in neighboring fields. However, polygonal blade cores do not seem to be a feature of the best-known excavated EP sites in the area (Betts n.d.; Cauvin

---

[43] Previously often referred to generically as "basalt." During the last decade specialists have moved from "basalt" to "andesite" to "diorite" and distinguished the latter from gabbro and other utilized igneous fabrics.
[44] Before discounting use of igneous flake implements, it is worth remembering that in other parts of the world complete, flaked igneous assemblages are not unusual, and that igneous flakes and cores comprise humanity's earliest surviving implements.
[45] The author has seen this material referred to as mottled, quartzitic, sugary, granular chert with (calcareous) inclusions or impurities, laminated, banded, bedded, tabular, blocky Lefkara, Middle Lefkara or a combination of these terms. One researcher calls the coloring "gray/brown /olive."

1984; Hordynsky and Kingsnorth 1979; Stekelis 1953). This may change with more analysis. The volume of knapped material from the Kalavasos *Tenta* and Khirokitia *Vouni* excavations is overwhelming, and the published data are not based on systematic sampling (Hordynsky and Todd 1987; Le Brun 1984a, 1984b; Todd 1987; author familiarity with collections). It is possible that blade production was more complex than it at first appears or that it took place elsewhere.

At Sotira *Kaminoudhia* the material appeared in two forms. The rarer version is as pale orange flakes. The other form is the occasional parallel-sided, naturally backed gray blade-like flake or blade fragment (e.g., one out of fourteen specimens saved in Lot 2 in G 17 D in Area A, and f90). Its form but not its quantity is consistent with earlier and later sites from the Vasilikos and Maroni Valleys, but not with the most studied site closest in time to *Kaminoudhia,* Kalavasos *Ayious,* since flakes are more common than blades there (Betts n.d.). We conjecture that the *Kaminoudhia* result is either due to sampling bias, or that we are seeing preservation of fragments of earlier or specialized forms. It is unclear if the latter form was present at Sotira *Teppes.* Stekelis (1961) mentions gray chert and blades, but not cortex backed gray blades. His figures do not illustrate anything with a cortex.

The *Kaminoudhia* assemblage is not similar to either Chalcolithic or Bronze Age sites where the material is endemic. It also differs from contemporary Marki *Alonia.* At that site blocks were imported early and manufactured into blades (Debney 1997). According to Debney (1996) by the MC those blades alone were imported as preforms to gloss blades. Additionally, we suggest that at Marki *Alonia* EC blades may have been salvaged, heavily curated, and recycled in the MC. Either way, the heavy curation of this material as blades is comparable to what we see at *Kaminoudhia.* For example, f90 is a heavily weathered medial section with pronounced scarring.

Gray banded cherts are in the Lemba *Lakkous* cache of grand lithics (Betts, personal communication and 1979b). We concur chert was imported at each of these sites and suggest that it may have originated artifactually within the Vasilikos and Maroni Valleys.

The range of fabrics at *Kaminoudhia* may reflect the diversity offered by riparian or maritime accretions or individual procurement from scattered sources. If the latter, the presence of one specimen in hematitic cherts ("jasper" in the vocabulary of some archaeologists) and two Moni formation cherts imply import or exchange scenarios deeper into the mountains.

UNWORKED RAW MATERIAL: PRODUCT GROUP 1 (PG1)

It is significant that, of the specimens excavated, unworked chert makes up less than 1% by raw count.[46] Therefore, unlike the case of igneous pebbles, hoarding of unworked cherts is not evident (see Chapter 6, The Ground Stone). The largest flakes at *Kaminoudhia* are f99, f100, f143 and f144. F99 and f100 are of Lefkara chert, which is a little coarser texture than the majority of Lefkara lithics at the site. Furthermore, their blocky proportions do not correspond well to the more common, smaller chalcedony flakes (f143 and f144). These four may be the sole surviving examples of material stocked in relative quantity for later use. Whatever their role, it is notable that they are at the site in a partially reduced state and not as unmodified raw material.

Since excavations in Cyprus have rarely saved or commented on unmodified raw materials (PG1), there are very few projects with which a confident comparison can be made. An exception is Alambra *Mouttes. Kaminoudhia's* dearth of raw material strongly contrasts with *Mouttes,* located within a veritable natural emporium. At that site both worked and unworked chert is so abundant that it even

---

[46] Given the care taken with lithics by the *Kaminoudhia* archaeological team, we consider the dearth of raw materials significant. It is unusual for projects to keep raw material, but in this case there was a strong commitment from the start to do so.

appears as a medium of wall construction (Kingsnorth 1996b), whereas in the *Kaminoudhia* excavations it is barely present in any form. Stone brought to the site for knapping may have been worked on another part of the site, altered so quickly after reaching the site that stores did not endure, or may have come to the site already partially reduced as in the two examples cited above (fig.7.9: f99 and f100).

Preparation of Materials and Reduction Techniques. Knappers obtaining raw material (PG1) as rounded cobbles must break into the nodules to access chert within and form the first platforms. This may be done with force, by hurling or banging a rock against another, or tossing it up into the air to crash upon other blocks as it lands. Occasional pieces found at *Kaminoudhia* that are extremely angular, usually with a disproportionate, original cortex may show evidence of smashing (fig. 7: f47). Similarly, fig. 7.2: f15 (specimen on the left) shows the compressed, virtually invisible rings characteristic of shearing.

Archeologists usually assume that if a large percentage of the cortex flakes at a site are entirely, or almost entirely, of dorsal cortex, then initial reduction has been carried out at the site. If cortex lithics are relatively small and possess cortex only on a platform and/or on a lateral, they probably testify to a later stage of core reduction. At *Kaminoudhia*, the author recorded the ratio of cortex surfaces on PG2s (platform or platform scars, dorsal or dorsal scars, ventral, laterals, or lateral scars). Specimens with limestone cortex or other skin and entirely coated dorsals are rare. If decortification was necessary, it was usually carried out elsewhere on the site, on the way back from, or at the collection point. Hauling home only the essential is a strategy common to knappers who harvest materials at some distance.

Alternatively, *Kaminoudhia* knappers may have sought cobbles without a limestone cortex, expending time on the selection of individual cobbles or in choice of source rather than in decortification. It is possible that the knappers sought very large stones (PG1), whose ratios of cortex/skin to inner material would be much lower than in small nodules (Skinner, Fagan and Ainsworth 1989). The four largest flakes at *Kaminoudhia* may support either or both explanations. It is possible that the excavators might not have recognized heavily calcareous knapped products. However, given the small size of the majority of the knapped stone at *Kaminoudhia*, this seems unlikely.

A few anomalous chunks with what seemed to be very thick limestone cortex were found among the 1986 excavation lithics. Closer inspection revealed that the limestone was a thin outer coating, less than 0.2 cm thick, and that what appeared to be calcareous was similarly colored and similarly textured off-white chert. Evidently the original stone workers had ascertained the high ratio of very fine chert to cortex before transporting it. Either they removed one or more exterior test flakes and by look, sound, or sample knapping selected only the most useful material, or their extraction locales so clearly displayed their wares that no testing was needed. Both the range of materials and traces of initial reduction steps suggest that material selection strategies played an important role in the *Kaminoudhia* methodology.

Heating. Since the 1930s lithic researchers have understood that in some parts of the world careful heating and cooling were routine for many kinds of stone (Crabtree and Butler 1964). Regulated roasting promotes homogeneity and elasticity that facilitate flaking, particularly pressure flaking. Modern avocational knappers resort either to small pits, layered with wood charcoal and sand, fired in dry, warm weather, preferably with a slight wind (Hellweg 1984; Waldorf 1984), or to commercial ovens and kilns (Native Way n.d.; Waldorf 1984). Prolonging the firing and cooling from twelve hours to two or three days secures the most satisfactory results. Preliminary firing of the pit and reruns may be helpful. The changes wrought by baking may be obvious, may be subtle ones—darkening the color, changing the luster, or conferring a slightly glossy, greasy, or waxy quality—or may not be visually discernible at all (Crabtree 1972a). At some point in the future evaluating the *Kaminoudhia* collection for heat treatment using the characteristics of sheen or glow may be possible.

A database of controlled experiments on raw materials is mandatory to detect thermal treatment archaeologically. Unfortunately, none existed for Cyprus at the time of the analysis for this report. Therefore, hypotheses about Cypriot thermal strategies cannot yet be verified. Scorched lithics can derive from several sources. Planned agricultural field burns and wild fires endemic in recent centuries have compounded the problem. We propose a few speculations and the following testable hypothesis that must await verification or refutation by future experimental studies.

Since we know from ceramic analysis that Chalcolithic and Bronze Age populations fired pottery, we submit that the use or non-use of heat preparation on lithics during these cultural periods in Cyprus would have been a matter of strategic choice. Baking initial reduction products (PG2s) at 400–900°EC, depending on fabric and on size, confers extra vitreousness. This result guarantees the sharp edge desired for many tasks such as cutting, scraping, or deep piercing of soft substances like vines, reeds, grasses, furs, flesh, skins, or very small animals (Crabtree 1972a; Waldorf 1984). On the other hand, the procedure does not benefit lithics requiring durability. Tasks such as boring, picking, battering, and heavy butchering exert too heavy a toll (Crabtree 1972a).

We hypothesize that different factors based on urgency or destined tasks as well as availability and kind of materials would have directed the choice of whether to heat and cool lithics (Gero 1989). Where material for knapping was abundant, tolerating the imperfection of rapidly prepared and rapidly replaceable implements may have been simpler or more economical than expending time and energy on fuel, on controlling temperatures, and on waiting. Sites in Cyprus to which this might apply are Chalcolithic Prastio *Ayios Savvas tis Karonos* Monastery (D'Annibale 1993; Rupp et al. 1995, 1993), the lower Vasilikos Valley and nearby sites (Betts n.d.; Hordynsky and Todd 1987; Hordynsky and Kingsnorth 1979), or at later Marki *Alonia* (Debney 1997; Frankel and Webb 1992; Smith1996) and Alambra *Mouttes* (Kingsnorth 1996b). Products likely to be curated such as hafted blades and "scrapers" may have been prime candidates for thermal preparation, since retouching them while still in their housing would have been more convenient than creating replacements and then rehafting them. Initial heating would have permitted frequent resharpening, reducing the frequency of replacements.

On the other hand, the laminated, tough, coarser-grained Lefkara cherts, chalcedony, hematitic cherts, and igneous stones may have been consistently appreciated for their toughness, so the pliancy caused by baking would have been omitted. At *Kaminoudhia* all of the hardy fabrics are rare and are used for a narrow range of implements. Both observations endorse the notion that they may have been chosen for their inherent ruggedness. Given that knappers at *Kaminoudhia* were used to the ease of flaking fine-grained chert, the presence of more demanding materials was probably due to their function or social significance. The same holds for the adjacent, earlier site of Sotira *Teppes* (personal inspection of materials on the site and in collections) and the later site of Episkopi *Phaneromeni* (Morris 1977). Both sites are in the same valley and used the same resources. We would not be surprised to learn that the fine-grained cherts at these three sites had been deliberately heated, especially those most employed for tools likely to be retouched, but probably also small cores, blade cores, and recycled items.

Many items in the *Kaminoudhia* flaked stone collection manifest unmistakable evidence of heating such as internal coloring and degree of graininess distinctly different from the outer surface, crazing, or "potlidding" (semicircular pitting caused by small rounded cones exploding off the surface). The few specimens that retain calcareous cortex do not routinely show these characteristics. We find this interesting, since at least one avocational knapper strongly urges that only cores and flakes should be heated and not raw nodules (Hellweg 1984). In some cases at *Kaminoudhia* where heating effects are obvious, products are brittle or chipped. Contrary to automatic assumptions, even extreme fire-damage does not necessarily render a fabric or reduction products completely unworkable or unusable. At *Kaminoudhia* severely heated items are most frequently associated with ashy deposits. These deposits strongly suggest that at least some heating occurred accidentally, late in the specimens' histories and not as a preliminary, deliberate method.

Over half the specimens inspected from lots excavated in 1986 were burnt. In several lots almost three-quarters were burnt, but in each there were also pristine-looking lithics that were apparently unaffected. This is perhaps explained by the fact that most of the lots excavated were habitation surfaces covered with ash, perhaps from the final destruction of the site.

At present in Cyprus we are unable to distinguish between weathering, accidental heating or overheating, and a routine step of lithic transformation. For an archaeological era consumed by concerns with copper production, ceramic firing habits, fuel consumption needs, and deforestation, it is important that we establish to what degree and how knappers may have used fire. There is a need for controlled comparison heating experiments of Cypriot raw materials.

Whatever their outcome, we suggest that students of early metallurgy evaluate the relationship between the heating of hammered stone to 'soften' it and the heating (annealing) of beaten copper to make it less brittle. An initial move from heating stone for knapping to heating stone that is copper ore might have been a minor one. With this knowledge, a change from the beating of copper to annealing is not a momentous one. Roasting or smelting a lump of copper ore may have been a variation on treatment of stone selected for other purposes. Because of their subsequent development, metallurgical processes seem worlds apart from knapped stone manufacture, but for prehistoric craftspeople this may have been far less true.

The shared identity of copper and knappable stone may have been both conceptual and practical. In this framework transforming copper into artifacts is almost the same as transforming chert into artifacts. Both are stones that are hit—"beaten" for copper, "struck" for chert. Both are stones that are hit, heated, and hit—"annealed" for copper, "detached," "heat-treated," and "flaked" for chert. Both are stones that are heated—"roasted" or "smelted" for copper, and "heat-treated" for chert. Both raw materials are then processed further. The terms in quotations are conventional, technical ones applied to copper working. Take them away and we have described knapped stone manufacture Alternatively, we could change the terminology for chert processing making it identical to that for copper processing. The difference is a convention of language and archaeological practice, not of gross manufacturing technology and possibly not of a prehistoric mental construct. Like so many innovations, the initial change may have been small, almost unnoticed, or merely an oddity, although the impact of its long-term history is ineradicable.

Abrading and Platform Preparation. To remove a flake or blade the surface struck must not be so slippery that the fabricator slides off, which is a hazard with siliceous materials. Preparing the platform often involves one or more of the following steps, not necessarily in the following order. Each is found at *Kaminoudhia*. 1) Abrading or battering the intended point(s) of contact may improve purchase. Abrading can occur accidentally. Without microwear analyses of platforms contrasted with other parts of lithic objects, we cannot be confident that it was deliberate. Objects sufficiently coarse-grained to suit this action occur within the *Kaminoudhia* ground stone collections, such as S18, "Coarse-grained" Pounder, one of thirty-one of the type (see Chapter 6, Pounder, Rubber-pounder and Hammerstone). 2) The sides of antler billets and pressure flakers may roughen or smooth flake edges. Antler items with appropriately smoothed surfaces are reported in the Cypriot EP literature and here (Croft, Chapter 11). 3) Taking off small flakes adjacent to the expected point of contact isolates the contact region turning it into a small projection that increases the chance of it being struck as intended. Removing part of the crest of the flake, blade, bladelet, or spall to be detached is a variant that is most likely when forming a blank or preform on the core itself. The blades in fig. 7.16: f21, f22, f24 are examples of crest thinning.

Detachment. Specialists customarily make a distinction between 1) detaching products with a wood, bone, or antler percussor ("soft hammer"), 2) striking stone with stone or steel ("hard hammer"), 3) percussion utilizing another intermediary implement ("punch technique"), and 4) pressing microflakes off an edge, frequently with the point of an awl-like implement ("pressure flaking"). Pressure flaking requires the knapper, often seated, to coordinate action of his hands, upper body, and frequently his legs. There is disagreement about how distinguishable each technique is in archaeological products.

Fabricator hardness and softness grade along a continuum. In practice the terms "hard hammer" and "soft hammer" pertain far more to the specific percussion's density or hardness rather than to whether it is of stone. Speed, force, and dimensions of contact area are just as important as fabricator material (see especially Hayden 1989; Speth 1985). The terms refer far more to differences in technique than to the flaker itself. Ascriptions of blades to punch removal have been equally subject to criticism. Even simple retouch scars can be highly suspect. Nevertheless, the majority of technological descriptions of collections, including those in Cyprus, have adhered to some, or all, of the four distinctions listed above (e.g., Betts n.d.; Debney 1997; Hordynsky and Kingsnorth 1979; Morris 1977; Smith 1996; cf. also Rosen on late Levantine knapped stone: 1997).

Since soft hammer flaking is at its most effective on fine-grained, even-textured raw materials, it is predictable that this would be a common technique at *Kaminoudhia*, with its preponderance of fine cherts. For most of the collection's PG2–5 products, the scale of bulbs, the relative gentleness of ripple marks, and the absence of fissures support this hypothesis. However, the quality of the scarring makes us suspect that in using a "soft hammer" technique either the billet itself or the technique may have been fairly hard (i.e., toward the middle of the spectrum from soft wood to hard stone). Hard, dense wood or antler, gently handled stone, or copper may have been used.

Hayden (1989) observed that soft-hammer flaking can disengage more flakes and more edge per volume of raw material than hard-hammer flaking. He noted that although the soft-hammer technique usually requires a specially formed billet, unlike hard-hammer reduction, its desirability rests in the decrease of shattered products and in greater productivity. At *Kaminoudhia*, we see a strategy adapted to maximizing quantity of implements produced while minimizing quantity of raw stone material used, a strategy based on clear understanding of the value of small, high quality materials. At *Kaminoudhia*, it seems to have made more sense to aim for more secondary products per cobble of high quality raw material than to expend the energy on stockpiling larger quantities. The approach avoided depending on rougher, more damaging, less productive percussion techniques and on tougher raw materials.

THE KNAPPING TOOL KIT, "HAMMERSTONES," BILLETS, AND PRESSURE FLAKERS

Today, the skilled knapper's tool kit commonly includes an assortment of abraders, percussors, and pressure flakers (and often specialized bits and jigs for shearing, burinating, and fluting) of different sizes and in different materials. Artisans normally alternate fabricators in accordance with the size and texture of the lithic being reduced and the step in the reduction process. Stone percussors are usually rounded or elongated and are often rough textured to avoid slippage on contact. Some double as abraders.

Replacement of kit components and their rejuvenation are ongoing necessities. Stone flakers become increasingly "softened" through use. After a while, striking renders them too brittle, nicked, battered, or flake-scarred to be satisfactory. Some may even shear apart. This hazard is especially likely with hammers composed of easily knapped materials like chert. In response to the same kind of deterioration, relatively soft billets such as wood, antler, bone, shell, or soft metal routinely need to be reground or discarded when too splintery or too "shattered." Stone pressure flakers dull rapidly. Continual regrinding of the points for resharpening eventually shortens them so much that they become no longer serviceable. Finally, aging delimits the life span of any organic fabricator. Although seasoning initially benefits a few materials, for most, the passage of time brought excessive loss of oils, moisture, flexibility, and commensurate decreased responsiveness, increased hardness, and brittleness. In antler—normally the most desired material for knapping tools among modern avocational knappers—unshed, green antler is usually preferable, since it is usually denser, heavier, more elastic, and less brittle than either shed or older antler in most species.

PERCUSSORS

Hammerstones. For the knapped stone specialist, the term "hammerstone" is used in at least two related ways. It can be generically applied to any elongated or ovoid stone known or thought to have served to mine raw materials (PG1) or to knap (PG 2–5) by direct percussion (Gramly 1992; Rosen 1992; Waldorf 1984). In this identification, it is frequently an igneous or hard, gritty material, and it may be pitted. Like many other prehistoric Cypriot ground stone publications, the *Kaminoudhia* catalogue exemplifies numerous feasible percussors. Some noticed by the author are S16, "Type 1 Pounder"; S68 "Hammerstone"; S113 "Small Pounder."

A second, narrower application of the term "hammerstone" by knapped stone specialists is as a formal tool type designating faceted cobbles of cryptocrystalline materials lacking platforms and is usually battered (Gramly 1992; Rosen 1997; Seton-Williams 1936). For *Kaminoudhia*, Chapter 6 records 36 of them as "Pecking Stones," of which 30 are stratified (e.g., S126 and S154).

Experimental work abroad (Crabtree 1967) and in Cyprus (Fox, personal communication; Hordynsky, personal communication; author's own experience) supports the identification of faceted ovoids as actual hammerstones, that is to say as tools for flaking lithics in practice and not just in name. This kind of hammerstone in chalcedony is known from aceramic Neolithic Koletria *Ortos* (author's familiarity with collection and Fox 1988), Alambra *Mouttes* surface (Kingsnorth 1996b), and Marki *Alonia* (Frankel and Webb 1996b). Seton-Williams describes hammerstones of the same morphology and dimensions at Erimi *Pamboula*, identifying the fabrics as "quartzite" and "quartzitic sandstone." The same tool in hematitic chert ("jasper"), occasionally sheared in half, is known from Agrokipia *Palaiokamina* (Kingsnorth 1996a) and a few other smaller Sydney Cyprus Survey Project sites (author's familiarity). The spherical, faceted hammerstone may be a universal tool that may be of little value as a temporal diagnostic. This is true outside Cyprus (Gramly 1992; Rosen 1997).

In Cyprus, hammerstones are reported mostly from stratified prehistoric sites and one site surface collection dating from the late aceramic Neolithic to well into the Bronze Age: Koletria *Ortos*, Erimi *Pamboula*, Sotira *Kaminoudhia*, and Episkopi *Phaneromeni*. The most likely explanation of the association between this tool type and EP–LCA sites is probably one of reporting. We cannot eliminate temporal associations. It is possible hammerstones lost favor among knappers within a few centuries of the end of the LC when soft iron tools became generally available, although when available earlier specimens were doubtless reused. According to interviews, twentieth century Cypriot professional knappers used iron or steel fabricators rather than stone (Pearlman 1984; Whittaker 1996).

Antler Billets. Croft (1983: C251, pl. IV, figs. 7 and 8) illustrates a severed antler base from the nodal Early Chalcolithic site of Kissonerga *Mylouthkia* that, although somewhat stubby, also has potential as a percussor. It could be a billet in the making. Although the distal has been hacked, possibly to snap it initially (as Croft suggests, from the published photo), a combination of initial sawing, followed by flake scarring, may have been employed. Nevertheless, modern knappers favor the bulkier, denser, and weightier burr/rosette end as the working surface. While not essential, grinding would turn either surviving end into a well-rounded, more consistent percussor. This kind of billet can be either swung to remove lithic flakes or tapped against the stone for flaking or retouching.

Three antler segments illustrated from Sotira *Teppes* retain burr and basal tine (Dikaios 1961: pl. 106:199, 203, 679). This makes them look like picks, but it is possible that they shared the function of a billet, pressure flaker, or punch. Even more likely billets are illustrated on (op. cit.) pl. 106: 108, 181, 198, 245, and 299. Drawings of the antler found in the *Kaminoudhia* excavations reveal a potential, excellent flaker, adequate proximally for detaching PG2s, unretouched flakes, and blades (fig. 7.18). Its length of 23.8 cm is well within the range of modern billets, and its smoothed rosette end is typical. Croft (Chapter 11) makes the same observation, and comments on a shed base fragment from Unit 21 in this capacity.

PRESSURE FLAKERS AND PUNCHES

Tusks. Site reports usually only mention tusks if they are perforated or modified in other ways. Tusks are usually considered ornaments, but they can be employed in pressure flaking. The increase of percentages of suids throughout the late Early Prehistoric and well into the Bronze Age confirms accessibility of boar tusks, even if domestication sometimes selects for reduction in tusk sizes.

Antler and Copper. *Several* published Early Prehistoric antler artifacts could have made excellent pressure flakers. Dikaios' site report on nearby Neolithic Sotira *Teppes* illustrates tines that qualify in this respect (Dikaios 1961: pl. 106; 163, 164, 648, 680, 531). For *Kaminoudhia*, Croft (Chapter 11) mentions ten pieces of antler, four of which are not bases. The tines could have worked well as pressure flaking styli.

A distally modified fallow deer antler with rosette from Unit 1 at *Kaminoudhia* would make a satisfactory, although dull, punch (fig. 7.18 and referenced by Croft, Chapter 11). Although we cannot unequivocally verify indirect percussion in the *Kaminoudhia* lithic assemblage, we strongly suspect it was used for detaching certain small flakes. The method has been the subject of debate over many years regarding Cypriot blade production in all periods, (Crew 1978, personal communication; Debney 1996; Hordynsky and Kingsnorth 1979; Odell 1980, personal communication; Smith 1994, personal communication). Therefore identifying feasible punches is significant.

The disadvantages of making pressure flakers and punches out of antler are 1) brittleness and loss of responsiveness with age, 2) incessant need for resharpening, and 3) complexities of accessibility. Copper has the responsiveness and flexibility of fresh antler but mitigates the problems. Many modern knappers use copper for pressure flaking and indirect percussion rather than antler. Copper reduces the time and energy needed to resharpen and is more readily available. This raises the possibility that Cypriot prehistoric knappers may have chosen the same route. If, as we have argued elsewhere (Kingsnorth 1982; Simmons and Kingsnorth 1996a), the passage of the Chalcolithic saw a decrease in forest and in deer (Croft 1991), at the time there may have been more than one impetus to knappers to employ copper.

Because they become smaller through continual resharpening, copper flakers are not likely to be preserved in the archaeological record. Small copper items oxidize and deteriorate readily when abandoned. Their softness and slenderness make them particularly vulnerable. If hammered during manufacture and maintenance, as recommended by some modern knappers, they may be particularly brittle by the time of discard. Furthermore, copper is frequently recycled. Since a narrow, pointed, or a flattened copper stylus is such a generic item, even when found its function may not be identified correctly. The Cypriot EC–MC repertoire of surviving copper artifacts includes so-called awls, nails, pins, and strips that morphologically evoke knapping bits. The softness of the Episkopi *Phaneromeni* ones, at a time when alloyed harder forms were possible, drew comment from their publisher (Swiny 1986; Tylecote 1986). We suggest non-alloyed awls met a well-understood need.

At present, the earliest known copper artifacts on Cyprus are from Kissonerga *Mylouthkia,* Erimi *Pamboula,* Lemba *Lakkous,* and Kissonerga *Mosphilia* (Bolger 1985; Gale 1991; Peltenburg 1991). The *Lakkous* "chisel" in illustration and description would make an excellent pressure flaker or shearing/burinating bit. Other illustrations and brief descriptions seem to include the kind of item that could be used similarly. The so-called copper "(fish) hooks" from *Mylouthkia* and *Pamboula* appear to have consisted of drawn copper, the medium preferred by many today for copper pressure flaker points. Croft (1981) suggested that a small antler haft from *Mylouthkia,* hollowed out at one end, might have been designed to hold a copper awl. If correct, it could have been a knapping tool. A review of the catalogue of metal finds from Sotira *Kaminoudhia* (Chapter 8) includes "awls" and "chisels" of appropriate shape and dimensions to constitute remnants of pressure flakers or punch bits.

FEET, ANVILS, AND BIPOLAR TECHNOLOGY

It can be helpful to stabilize small nodules (PG1) and small cores (PG2) with the knapper's feet. Nodules may also be set in depressions in the ground or in suitably rough wood or stone. Among the ground stone found at *Kaminoudhia,* almost any object with depressions or with a pecked, scratched, flat surface could have served as an anvil. So-called "rubbing stones," "rubber-pounders," "pounders," "hammerstones," and various kinds of ground stone with "secondary" or "tertiary" use could have been employed to hold a core in place.

When an anvil is used as the base for a nodule being struck by direct or indirect percussion, the force is likely to ricochet back into the stone being reduced, hence the term bipolar reduction. Battering marks may result at the end of the lithic that is set in the anvil. Also, the conchoidal rings on the newly exposed surfaces may appear jammed or effaced. At *Kaminoudhia* bipolar reduction is not most evident in the larger specimens, which would probably have been removed early in the reduction process. Instead it is seen on the cores that are almost completely exhausted and on flakes that are correspondingly small. Bipolar reduction seems to have been another strategy for maximizing the amount a nodule produced.

CORES: PRODUCT GROUP 2 (PG2)

For the sake of replicability, we recognize cores as possessing negative scars only, or as having at least one negative ventral scar. Scarring that extends into a flake interior must have occurred after the flake's detachment from a core, thus turning the flake itself into a core. The definition recognizes only cores from which PG2s have already been removed and bypasses potential cores as well as ignoring intent and tool function.

Except for one very large flake, f99, that has a single abrupt ventral removal, practically the only common trait of *Kaminoudhia* cores is small size (see figs. 7.1 to 7.4). Negative scars cover the very small cores so comprehensively that platforms are obscured. Nevertheless, completely wasted cores are extremely rare in this collection (see: f17, f104, f141). Many cores have some cortex: f195 has a substantial amount, while f103, f140, f171, f193, f250, f252 have a small amount. All of the foregoing may be indices of material conservation.

Kaminoudhia cores vary by inherent properties of the material, shape, size, type of scar(s) and scar directionality, core preparation, and amount and kind of platform preparation. They also vary by the number and kinds of options for further reduction. These variations are illustrated in figs. 7.2–7.4, and additional examples are scattered throughout the figures.

CORE MORPHOLOGY

Cobble and Blocky. The most recurrent classically typed cores at *Kaminoudhia* are small, multidirectionally flaked, and blocky (see f101, f103, f141, f142, f177, f198, f211, f217, f252). The faceted, squarish core, f66, is a fine, but slightly larger example of the type. Given the number of flakes at the site that correspond in size and dorsal scarring to what could still be removed from this core, we suggest that knappers most frequently prepared cores of this general size and degree of flaking. Possibly this work was done closer to the sources. Since the industry is generally composed of small flakes and blades (and most of the cores found are correspondingly small), it seems likely that much of the material brought to the site to knap was either small or that knappers used materials almost to their limits.

The most common cores in less represented materials are modified chalcedony cobbles, and these range greatly in size (from the very small f142 and f211 to f144). Chalcedony cores retain the most skin. The convexity of chalcedony cores, f171 and f102, suggests derivation from rounded cobbles, although the size of the very large flake, f144, implies either very large cobbles or block sourcing. Chalcedony cobble cores f102 and f171 with bold flaking evoke classic "chopper" tools. To what extent cores were brought to the site already altered to suit the most common tool or blank to be produced and the degree to which reduction strategies were adapted to the attributes of each kind of material remains a matter of conjecture.

Cores on Flakes. Strictly defined, only a few *Kaminoudhia* cores are large flakes (cf. f99). However, determining lithic function may be problematic even in the matter of what was used as a core. Ventral scars may be accidental, produced by use or damage, or a blank or preform prepared for further modification into a retouched tool (f11, f17, f22, f28, f99, f140, f179, f186, f189, f250). Some blocky cores at *Kaminoudhia* are highly reduced, and the last flakes removed from them must have been very small. Thus, deliberate, miniature flake production from cores on small flakes should not be automatically dismissed. It may be significant that some possible cores on flakes are exterior (dorsally cortex covered) "primary" flakes (f6, f196, f201).

Dorsal scarring raises a similar issue. Large flake tools with substantial flake scars on either the dorsal or ventral face, many at almost right angles to an edge, may have furnished implements (f50, f52, f55, f71, f99, f140, f143, f154, f187, f218). The dorsal face of f145 is enigmatic. The pronounced scar could be the result of inadvertent damage, a mistake in its manufacture, or intended to provide a staggered proximal. The flake is large enough, and the scarring on its dorsal face and sides big enough that it may represent a core on a flake. The specimen appears slightly burnt and is associated with a small flake from the same deposit. The issue becomes even more abstruse for bladelet cores and burin blow modifications. Evidence for crest thinning, end or edge damage or modification, and bladelet production is problematical. The similarities and differences between f1, f48, f67, f88, f192, f207 illustrate the concern. A few flakes may be detachments from ventrals. Their dorsals look like a ventral surface (e.g., f55, f183, f188, f246), which lends credence to the suggestion that some flakes served as cores for flakes removed from their ventral face.

CORE SCARS

Blade, Bladelet, and Other Linear Scars. Consistent with most documented late Cypriot EP knapped collections, large navicular cores and symmetrical, polyhedral, prismatic blade and bladelet cores (except for f67) which are capable of providing blade after blade in succession have not been found at *Kaminoudhia*. This contrasts at one end of the spectrum with aceramic Neolithic sites and at the other end with Alambra *Mouttes* (Kingsnorth 1996b). At *Kaminoudhia*, several cores and flakes have a single linear scar superimposed, or more commonly underlying flake scars (e.g., f70, f99, f103, f140, f166, f172). If industrialized blade production occurred at *Kaminoudhia*, the evidence does not survive.

Pyramidal and similar blade cores were possibly recycled into flake cores to maximize PG2 production. Voluminous blade production may have taken place outside Areas A, B, or C, or nearby off site. Perhaps it did not happen at all, which would be consistent with Debney's analysis of temporal changes in blade production at EC–MC Marki *Alonia* (Debney 1996). Reports on Marki *Alonia* lithics by Debney (1997 and 1996) do not identify core types, but the discussion on changes in blade technology strongly implies cores designed for repetitive production of parallel-sided blades. In a study of the same collection Smith (1996) refers to single and double platform cores and to crested core rejuvenation blades, so it is possible that navicular and pyramidal blade cores are in the collection.

Debney's evidence suggests that gray-banded blades were imported to Marki *Alonia* in the MC. This is interesting, since the one Late Early Prehistoric–Early Cypriot site where a specialist has reported single and double opposing platform blade cores is Kalavasos *Ayious*, in the Vasilikos Valley, where there is a long tradition of gray-banded blade production (Betts n.d.). Perhaps by the early Chalcolithic, the Vasilikos Valley or adjacent regions were furnishing blades for consumption beyond that area, occasionally including *Kaminoudhia*. Similarly, in the west of the island, Betts implies that blades in "fine grained gray/black banded flint were created at least a day's walk from the middle Chalcolithic site of Kissonerga *Mosphilia*" (1987:10).

The pattern that is emerging differs from that of the Neolithic. Repetitive, "true" blade production in the late Early Prehistoric–MC and onwards may have developed into a localized, specialized process dominated by certain materials (gray-banded and Moni cherts). It is possible that these blades were items of exchange emanating from distinct manufacturing zones. If so, for what were they exchanged along the way? Also, what had altered in the economics of production and in the political geography of the period that explains the change? Our report on blades and our discussion of the relationship of the *Kaminoudhia* knapped stone collection to the era consider possible answers.

Multi-Directionality. Several *Kaminoudhia* core scars and flake dorsal scars run in opposite directions. For example, knappers must have turned the core of f241 upside down before removing it. Two blade-like flakes, f16 and f17, in a minority dark, fine material, one of which has dorsal cortex on both edges to the ridges, fit together with their platforms in opposite directions. Opposed dual platform blade cores are reported from the aceramic Neolithic onward (see Guilaine et al. 1997, 1995a and 1995b for Parekklisha *Shillourokambos*; Cauvin 1984 for Khirokitia; Le Brun 1981 for Cape Andreas *Kastros*) but are rare during the late EP (Betts n.d.). Opposed platform flake scar cores also appear by the Aceramic Neolithic, but unlike opposed platform blade cores they continue to appear in collections at least up to the time of Episkopi *Phaneromeni*.

At Sotira *Kaminoudhia*, there also seems to have been a tendency to take flakes off at right angles to each other. The scars can be on the same face or on opposite faces. Cores were rotated ninety degrees between detachments, and sometimes the core was flipped over between moves. Removals at right angles to each other are especially apparent on smaller cores and chunks (For pertinent illustrations, see figs. 7.1–7.4: f70, f71, f99, f103, f166, f177, f193, f195, f196, f198, f201, f214. See also f6). Each technique suggests a habit of removing as much flake surface as possible from small stones.

SPECIALIZED CORE REDUCTION EVIDENCE

One of the most interesting impressions provided by both cores and flake dorsals is the amount of preparation undertaken prior to detachment of PG2s. Preplanning affected flakes, blades, and bladelets in different ways. Core preparation and deliberate orientation prior to flake or blade removal has already been commented on for other Cypriot industries. The particular variants described below differ in degree and in kind from what has previously been published.

"Levallois"-Like Cores and Products. Flake dorsals at *Kaminoudhia* consistently show all-over flaking evocative of the Paleolithic technique called "Levallois." Researchers generically apply this term to late industries. "Levallois" refers to cores and blanks that are flaked all around one surface. The designation also refers to implements and tools derived from this surface when detached. Examples at *Kaminoudhia* are f14, f72–75, f81–5, f109, f135, f154, f197 and possibly f3, f69, f97, f251, f253; blade (f12); cores with ventral flaking or no obvious distinction between ventral and dorsal (f81, f83, f154, f177, f182 and possibly f250–253); chunky cores (f85, f103, f134, f140, f198, possibly f166, which might be a bifacial core blank for the type of core in question, possibly f151–153).

It is possible that the all-around flake scars result from the use of flakes as cores for microflakes. Alternatively, the flaked detachments could be rejuvenation flakes from platform preparation for cores (even polyhedral blade core variants), which have been reduced or recycled beyond recognition. Sharpening (curation) or recycling by secondary flaking may account for the morphology. In some cases the "Levallois"-like products seem to be implements (f250), blanks (f75 to f74 or f73; f82 to f81), or even tools (f85, small, rounded "scraper"). The diversity may indicate that the technique was not employed with a specific product as its object. It may have been another means of getting as much surface to edge as possible from a given piece of raw material. A small bladelet negative scar (f140) reveals that a blow from almost any platform would furnish the prepared core flakes listed above. Qualitatively, it suggests deliberate organization of the flaking sequence. The bifacial squarish core with step scarring and retouch (f166) is similarly suggestive.

From the aceramic Neolithic on, a few other prehistoric Cypriot sites record hints of a "Levallois" or "Levallois"-like techniques (Cauvin 1984; Guilaine et al. 1997 and 1995; Kingsnorth 1996b; Le Brun 1981; Perrot, cited in Le Brun 1981). Comparisons are problematic because most have not described the attributes prompting the term. Some authors appear to share our reluctance about a straightforward application of the designation, "Levallois." Le Brun (1981:31) with regard to Cape Andreas *Kastros* circumlocutes thus, "… des traces de technique *apparement* levallois." This hesitation contrasts with his forthright pronouncement in the same sentence on the presence of Clactonian products. Smith (1996) describes but does not name the hypothetical process for Marki *Alonia* ventrally flaked cortex, exterior nodular flake cores. The cautions exhibited by the above researchers are perhaps because their most "Levallois"-like preparation flake and core examples, by number of flake scars and evenness of their disposition, are far from textbook representations of the process.

At Alambra *Mouttes* the most distinctive "Levallois"-like indicators are flakes that are bigger, thicker, more convex, and more rounded than comparable *Kaminoudhia* ones (Kingsnorth 1996b). Furthermore, the Alambra *Mouttes* dorsal scars are fewer and larger. The rounded, medium-sized, plano-convex flakes in question may have been core preparation or ovoid "scraper" blanks. Smith (personal communication, and 1996) did not find these kinds of flakes in the contemporary and slightly later Marki *Alonia* lithics. On the other hand, several published "convex scrapers" in illustration (Smith 1996: pl. 27c. and fig 6.18, especially specimens, f212, f217, and f265) look almost identical to the Alambra *Mouttes* specimens, but they are edge-scarred or retouched (PG3s and PG4s). This suggests that the rounded, medium-sized, plano-convex flakes at the three sites may be not only implements but preforms and core preparation products as well. We cannot yet say whether each community pursued the whole process, or if only certain settlements created the specialized flakes and then exchanged them. The latter is a possibility, since Marki *Alonia* is the only collection in which possible cores for their manufacture have been noticed (Smith 1996:105, fig. 6.19).

If there is a temporal correlation in changing uses of the "Levallois" genre of reduction, it is one of decreasing number and increasing size of the flake scars and flakes themselves over time. The *Kaminoudhia* products are more elaborate than the Marki *Alonia* and Alambra *Mouttes* examples. Moreover, at *Kaminoudhia* the technique appears not only on early core preparation flakes and smaller implements but also on small cores. Proximity and abundance of raw material may be factors in the number of preparatory steps taken at the source. It is not surprising that exterior flakes and core preparation flakes are found at Alambra *Mouttes*, which is located on an extraction site. Similarly, at Marki *Alonia*, which is near its sources initial preparation may have taken place in the field, whereas prepared cores and their in-use products were found essentially in place (Debney 1997, 1996; Frankel and Webb 1992; Smith 1996). At the other extreme, *Kaminoudhia* cores are repeatedly reestablished by means of a "Levallois"-like technique as is revealed in surviving core preparation flakes and many small flakes with dorsal scarring.

DISTINCTIVE ALMOST EXHAUSTED, MINIATURE CORES: POSSIBLE METHOD OF FURTHER REDUCTION

Evidence for particularly forceful detaching of small flakes and blades from very small, almost exhausted cores of a distinctive, pyramidal shape is of note (e.g., f134, f198, f214, f252). These mini cores are all of the prepared type, discussed above. An important additional attribute is that usually only one major negative scar stretching the length of one face remains. The scar normally evinces the jammed look of bipolar reduction. The pyramidal shape of the core formed by the surfaces opposite the negative scar may have afforded a projection that could be gripped either with particularly strong fingertips or some type of vice. Tipping the core obliquely would have given a strong, pointed percussor a sufficient platform that, combined with carefully directed force and possibly also a slight moving of the core in tandem against the blow, a small flake or blade could still be stripped off the otherwise depleted core. F101 has a series of small overlapping scars that could be part of this type of preparation. In shape, size, and scarring it is reminiscent of flake f84. If the procedure described above is a correct interpretation of the evidence, devising miniature prepared cores is an ingenious development that affected serial production of little blade-like flakes from "remainders."

While we realize that it is extremely difficult to identify the products of indirect percussion, it may have been the technique used here. The process just described might have involved a punch. A single antler branch with all but one distal or proximal tine removed or dense wood would have been adequate. The antler artifacts reviewed earlier in this chapter are suggestive, and cold drawn copper may also have worked.

The Akrotiri *Aetokremnos* and Kholetria *Ortos* excavations yielded small cores. The same is true of the Lemba area prehistoric sites (McCartney, personal communication). One Bronze Age miniature prismatic bladelet core comes from excavations at Alambra *Mouttes*. However, none are like the *Kaminoudhia* tiny pyramidal, complete platform cores. At this point, we cannot say whether these constitute a diagnostic type or have merely not been commented on elsewhere.

CHUNKS AND CHIPS (PG2)

Depending on size and configuration, we classify items that exhibit the rippling of conchoidal fracture but lack platforms, bulbs, and negative scars as chunks or chippage. These parameters encompass some lithics that other approaches would classify as flakes or flake fragments. It is notable that chunks and chips are sparse at *Kaminoudhia* despite an inclusive definition. In any deposit, less than 20% of the material by count regularly qualifies. The range of small flakes (f157 and f163), chunks (f159 and f161), and chips (f158 and f164), from one lot (Unit 1, Lot 9) is illustrated in fig. 7.7. Chippage and chunks are scarce even in Unit 3, which contains a complete sequence of reduction elements from raw material through blanks/preforms and tools in materials so similar that one suspects they originated in the same block.

Although the paucity could reflect vagaries of preservation, it may indicate little early stage reduction activity in the areas excavated or the maximum utilization of available materials. The contrast with sites such in the Dhiarizos and Vasilikos Valley, the Lemba area, Khirokitia *Vouni*, Kholetria *Ortos*, and Iambra *Mouttes* that yield abundant lithic material and complete reduction sequences is profound. The similarity to Episkopi *Phaneromeni* is noteworthy.

FLAKES, BLADES, AND BLADELETS

Researchers have described Cypriot prehistoric knapped assemblages as "flake industries," both informally and in print, implying a contrast to collections with an impressive bifacially worked, retouched, blade tool, or microlith component, regarded as the goal of the knappers' productivity. Hordynsky (1996) investigating microwear traces from Kalavasos *Tenta*, and D'Annibale (1993) analyzing quantitative data from Prastio *Ayios Savvas tis Karonos* Monastery, empirically confirm the salient role of flakes, flake edge angle, and flake edge configurations at these sites. *Kaminoudhia* patterns of flake production support their thesis.

SOME FLAKE EXAMPLES. The range of amorphous flakes and chunks with extensive calcareous cortex at *Kaminoudhia* is depicted in fig. 7.1. They are a clue to original cobble and core sizes. Additionally, they confirm habits of core rotation in flake production (see supra). An array of interior flakes illustrating common flake sizes and dorsal scarring is shown in figs. 7.4, 7.5, and 7.7. As stated previously, the pattern is one of small flakes and of dorsal faceting. Six small flakes on the bottom of fig. 7.8 illustrate the versatility of flake reduction sequences. The thick blade-like flake f79 is the kind of item that constitutes a core preform with the potential for detachment of blade-like flakes (f43, f97, f169, f170). F43 is a point created through distal bladelet/burin removal and shoulder narrowing and thinning. F97 is a lunate and a "backed" lunate. Basal thinning and distal snapping of a flake similar to f29 (fig. 7.9) may be the model for the small flake adjacent to f202.

OFF-CENTER BULBS. Many blade-like flakes and blades in the assemblage have bulbs that are "off-center" (see for example, f16, f17, f23, f27, f36, f48). A similar phenomenon is visible in the figures from Cape Andreas *Kastros* (LeBrun 1981: fig. 18:1, 9, 10; fig 19:1; fig 20:1; fig 21:1; fig. 22:3, 8). The reason for this pattern is not obvious. At *Kaminoudhia* this may have been a method for getting the longest flakes possible off small cores while retaining breadth and may have constituted another core/material conservation technique. It is consistent with the avoidance of blade, bladelet, and blade core technology and the preference for flake proportions in the late EP.

MINIATURE FLAKES. Very small flakes are common in the *Kaminoudhia* collection. The smallness of exterior flakes, flake scars on possible cores on flakes, tiny, blocky and pyramidal cores, and the tidiness of some extremely small flakes, including a few examples with basal, ventral scarring, suggest that some manufacturing was scaled to the production of miniature flakes. Although microflakes and flaked chunks are usually considered the results of discard, spalling, core preparation, core rejuvenation, retouch, trimming, thinning, curation, or recycling and are often classified as "debris," one should not discount their deliberate manufacture in a material conserving industry.

BLADES. The *Kaminoudhia* research used the term "blade" in its strictest definition. This required that a blade be at least twice as long as it is wide, parallel-sided, and showed dorsal scarring which verified prior removal of linear scars from a core oriented in the same direction. We found less than half a dozen "true" blades at *Kaminoudhia*, all of which are damaged, broken, intensely retouched, curated, or recycled (i.e., exclusively PG4s and PG5s).

There are no complete, parallel-sided, dorsally elongated flakes, conclusively exemplifying original PG2 blade configurations. However, specimens f27, f35, f36, and f38 (and quite possibly several others on figs. 7.12–15) when originally detached as PG2s might have matched the most exacting definition. We cannot ascertain removal technique since their original platforms are missing. They must have come from cores bigger than any found. If these probable blade products had been manufactured in quantity, they would have come from cores of a different type than those found.

Blade paucity, along with their heavily conserved, intensely worn state, is consistent with the absence of "true" prismatic blade cores. We are unsure of the reason for this situation. They may have been individual, specialized local products not produced through a traditional true blade core technique. Alternatively, manufacturing "byproducts" may have been modified beyond our recognition. Perhaps different segments of the population had differential access to renewal of this commodity. Blade production may have taken place elsewhere on the site; blades may have been salvaged from earlier collections or were exceptional imports. In all events their condition is consistent with the intense conservation for all classes of knapped products at *Kaminoudhia*.

A more common, looser definition of a blade requires only that it be a linear flake that is twice as long as it is wide. Even by this standard the *Kaminoudhia* collection contains very few blades. Several tools look like blades, but by either definition they are not. The most common blade-like tool is a parallel-sided or sub-parallel-sided flake or fragment with gloss. All examples have been illustrated.

BLADELETS AND BURIN SPALLS. Bladelets (blades less than 1.2 cm wide and conforming to any of the blade definitions above) and burin spalls are rare at *Kaminoudhia* (see f57 and f67). They are reported in Cypriot collections exclusively from excavations with considerable knapped stone and where sieving or meticulous, slow digging was practiced. Contrasting the excavation and survey collections from the same sites substantiates the hypothesis. At both Kholetria *Ortos* (author's familiarity with collection, and Fox, personal communication) and Alambra *Mouttes* (Kingsnorth 1996b), bladelets and spalls were recorded from the excavations but not in the survey data. The two sites are separated by time and place. What they share most in common is an abundance of local raw materials and knapped products. Therefore, the few bladelets and burin percussion spalls observed at *Kaminoudhia* may reflect the smallness of the collection and the high standard of archaeological recovery.

At *Kaminoudhia* the absence is consistent with other reduction practice evidence from the site. Furthermore, no transverse or long burin removal spalls, curved bladelets, or snaps were found, all of which are very different from blade-rich aceramic Neolithic sites, Alambra *Mouttes,* Akrotiri *Aetokremnos*, and Episkopi *Phaneromeni*. It seems likely that despite the huge temporal and cultural differences, these sites in the same general area using similarly small amounts of predominantly cobble materials, share this set of technological traits as a common solution to conserve fine material.

Blade/blade-like Flake Platform and Ridge Preparation. Blade and blade-like flake platforms are either natural or slightly flaked. Dorsal platform edge angles are slightly acute, and the ventral ones are correspondingly slightly oblique (i.e., neither is far off a right angle), which is consistent with the usual broad proportions of this blade/blade-like flake industry. Removal of a short portion of the basal ridge is common. Occasional longer, narrow ridge scars occur, particularly on longer, narrower specimens.

Both types of removal may have been easiest to achieve before separation from the core. (See parallel-sided bladelets, f57, f67; PG4 bifacially retouched blade, f54; blade-like flake, burin blow edge, f27, f32, f35, f38a, f38b, f68, f76.)

Prepared Shoulders and Thinned Proximals. Similarly, prior removal of flakes and blades resulted in a significant number of blades and blade-like flakes that had an "automatically" narrowed or thinned proximal. This effect may have been inadvertent, the inevitable result of blade core preparation and sequential flake/blade production from the same core. However, we are inclined to believe that it was deliberate, because slight shouldering is a common feature of several assemblages on the island, although not always achieved through the same process. Despite almost no comment on shoulder narrowing and thinning in Cypriot archaeology texts, these attributes are visible in innumerable figures and of concern to lithics research for its hafting implications (e.g., Nishiaki 1990).

Published illustrations of the plates from Dikaios' excavations at Sotira *Teppes* show many blades that have proximals narrowed and thinned by retouch. It is possible that a heavily refurbished piece, *Kaminoudhia* f39 with its two basal linear scars, may be an example of reuse of a Sotira *Teppes* product (see especially Dikaios 1961: pl. 116:390a with its two tiny right dorsal linear scars).

Core Preparation, Trimming and Rejuvenation Blades. Differences in researcher perceptions, terminology, and prior experience complicate inter-site comparisons between core preparation, core trimming, and blade core rejuvenation. Seton-Williams lists nine "lames de dégagement" from Erimi *Pamboula*, which she describes as "… long flakes of brown flint with squared sides, rather battered on the upper surface. The best specimen is 9 cm long and triangular in cross-section" (1936:52). We wonder what Seton-Williams' "lames de dégagement" share in common with "… des lames de préparation, parfois très soignées …" ("… preparation blades, sometimes very carefully made …" loose translation, this author) from a small sounding at aceramic Neolithic Parekklisha *Shillourokambos*, which imply local blade manufacturing (Guilaine et al. 1993:716). Later publications from the site recognize a range of blade core preparation, trimming, and rejuvenation blades (Guilaine et al. 1997 and 1995). Another "lame de dégagement" is referenced by Stekelis (1953:410, fig. 109) from Khirokitia. In the *Kaminoudhia* collection, nothing equitable to the Erimi *Pamboula* "lame de dégagement" illustrated in Seton-Williams (1936: pl. 27, 11) was observed. At *Kaminoudhia*, one of the few "true" blades, f17, retains a strip of dorsal cortex, indicative of an early stage detachment product.

At Prastio *Ayios Savvas tis Karonos* Monastery, D'Annibale (1993) encountered 25 "crested blade flakes" in a collection of 4,215 analyzed specimens of chipped stone, which he considered "quite similar to lames à crête" and to be predominantly unused "waste." Similar blades were not seen at *Kaminoudhia*.

Betts (n.d. and 1987) reports "core trimming elements" at Kalavasos *Ayious* and Kissonerga *Mosphilia*. We are not sure if these are the same kind of lithic, since we have seen neither accompanying descriptions nor illustrations. Some researchers expect "core trimming elements" to be long, narrow, jagged examples of the strict definition of a blade, that are also high ridged, steeply triangular in cross-section. They associate them with core rejuvenation, not initial preparation. These have not been observed in the *Kaminoudhia* collections.

COMPARISON WITH BLADE PRODUCTION TECHNOLOGIES IN PUBLISHED CYPRIOT LITERATURE. Parallel-sided blades with a dorsal ridge formed by flake scars originating all along the ridge at right angles to it (i.e., not created after PG2 detachment) have not been observed in the *Kaminoudhia* assemblage. Fox (1988) noticed two from Kholetria *Ortos* and one from the Krittou Marottou *Ais Yorkis* 1980s survey collections. Following Bordes and Crabtree (1969), he calls them lames à crête and states that, "These indicate that the Ortos knappers used the Corbiac technique of *blade core preparation...* " (Fox: 1988: 31. Italics, this author).

The interpretation raises several issues. The blade production method reconstructed in Bordes and Crabtree (1969) was based on analysis of an estimated 100,000 blades and 1,000 cores classed as five different types in many different phases of reduction. The replication also relied on many damaged and discarded byproducts. The technique consisted of a long interconnected sequence of production attributes: alternation between direct percussors in different materials, indirect punches, position of cores on wooden anvils, knapper body position, action of feet, core preformation, platform angles, shape and size, blade shape and curvature, and bulb location and size. Which and how many of these interrelated practices does the "Corbiac core preparation technique" appellation encompass when applying it to Cypriot prehistory? Was it only the crested blade creation or all the steps leading to it?

If none, then using the term is problematic; if only a few, which ones are employed? If all, do any other elements in prehistoric Cypriot assemblages support the chain of operations subsumed under by the term "Corbiac blade technique," abridged from the Bordes and Crabtree article? The Khirokitia *Vouni* "lame de dégagement" looks very much like the kind of backed blade retaining a little natural cortex that would be removed immediately after a "lame à crête" in many blade core reduction systems, including the Corbiac. Ridge bladelet scars noted above and at Alambra *Mouttes*, and other ridge modifications, are consistent with a straightening of the Corbiac prepared core-crested ridge, prior to "lame à crête" removal. The straight profile of the vast majority of blades on Cypriot sites is also consistent with Corbiac technique products. These alone are not sufficient to equate blade production method in Cyprus for any period with the entire Corbiac sequence. The answer to the opening questions would involve more research on Cypriot industries than has so far been attempted for almost any site.

Judging by the corpus of blades illustrated or referenced in EP literature to date, the "lame à crête" in Cyprus is exclusively an aceramic Neolithic form (Guilaine et al. 1997 and 1995; Fox 1988; LeBrun 1981; author's familiarity with 1990s Kholetria *Ortos* excavations collection). At Cape Andreas *Kastros* and Parekklisha *Shillourokambos*, retouched "lames à crête" raise the unlikely possibility that the flaked crest is integral to tool design, rather than a reduction method or an addition to it (Guilaine et al. 1997; 1995: fig. 4:2; LeBrun 1981:31). However, D'Annibale (1993) reports Chalcolithic variants at Prastio *Ayios Savvas tis Karonos* Monastery. It is possible that the gracile blades described for Marki *Alonia* (Debney 1997 and 1996), the conical, prismatic blade and bladelet cores from Alambra *Mouttes* (Kingsnorth 1996b), or the bladelet, blades, and blade-like flakes of *Kaminoudhia* may have passed through a crested blade producing step. The flaked dorsal on triangular cross-section blades may have been overlooked or interpreted as a kind of blade backing, prepared prior to detachment, and not have been linked to core preparation. Similarly, researchers may have interpreted the products of other steps in the "Corbiac technique" differently.

Attempting to recognize the steps and products of different blade production methods in Cyprus and to place them chronologically and geographically is highly desirable. For example, the discovery of opposing platform blade cores at Parekklisha *Shillourokambos* (Guilaine et al. 1995; 1997) corroborates and expands upon knowledge of already documented opposing blade cores at Cape Andreas *Kastros* (LeBrun 1981). Through detailed analysis of more than 30,000 specimens, Guilaine and his colleagues have successfully worked out a complete blade/bladelet reduction sequence from location and acquisition of raw material, to production of artifacts, one of which includes crested pieces. Several blade production sequences use a crested blade step. Conversely, lack of crested blades in archaeological collections, especially small ones or arbitrarily sampled ones, do not demonstrate the absence of the step. At *Kaminoudhia*, the absence of crested blades (or crested blade-like flakes), blade core "trimming" blades, unidirectional, unifacial, single platform, conical blade cores, and opposing-direction, dual-platform blade cores, contrasts to the situation at many Neolithic and Bronze Age sites.

Comparison of Blade Production Technologies in Published Cypriot Literature of Naturally Backed Blades, Punch Technique, Blanks and Preforms. Only one example at *Kaminoudhia*, a blade-like flake illustrated on fig. 7.14, represents naturally backed blades common in the Vasilikos Valley and neighboring vicinities from the Aceramic through late Bronze Age. In that part of the island retention of a steep calcareous edge on gray and orange-banded Lefkara cherts with inclusions is an adaptation repeated over the millennia. It is an efficient use of the natural properties of the locally abundant, accessible, tough chert, which because of its blockiness lends itself to linear flake/blade production. The natural backing method in this fabric is not a temporal index, but it might be a regional one.

Debney (1997, 1996) has adduced that narrow, parallel-sided blades found at Marki *Alonia* were more common in earlier levels than in later ones. She suggests they were detached by the punch technique and used for harvesting emmer and einkorn. Investigators believe many blades came to that site unretouched "as blanks" to be further modified. While much of this may be correct, there is insufficient evidence to support or evaluate any of these statements extrapolated to *Kaminoudhia*.

We see little difficulty with the interpretation that blades arrived in the assemblages as PG2s, detached before arrival at the collected parts of the sites. We question the interpretation of the function of the PG3–4 modifications. Blades themselves were probably desired for their long edges and the fact that they tolerated restoration, rather than requiring edge retouch, prior to use. To the extent that unretouched blades or blade-like flakes are "blanks" or preforms for retouched ones, we suggest that the effects of maintenance rather than necessary preliminaries were responsible for the transformations. As previously noted, blade retouch was probably a resharpening of worn edges, rather than a tool manufacturing goal.

LATE PRODUCTION STAGE MODIFICATIONS: PRODUCT GROUPS 3–4 (PG3–PG4)

POST-DETACHMENT SCARRING: FLAKE SCARS, BURIN BLOW SCARS, BLOW SCARS, NICKS, AND BREAKS. Scattered, short, and varied scars characterize the *Kaminoudhia* assemblage. Coupled with debates over the fallacy of deliberate retouch, natural, and use-damage distinctions, ascribing sources is as difficult as pinpointing diagnostic retouch types and tools. The industry forces one to recognize both the importance of flakes per se as implements, and the repetitiveness of core organization and preparation, which produced flakes of a consistent configuration (in shape, size, thickness, number and relationship of dorsal scars, platforms, and edges). This impression is conveyed in figs. 7.7 and 7.8. Also, these lithics make one think about scarring in unconventional ways.

Some of the most confusing modification traces at *Kaminoudhia* are substantial, steep flake scars. They might be the result of severe postdepositional damage. The most egregious are so steep as to be at true right angles and are large and narrow (e.g., f145, f215, and a milder variant on the left distal of f49). Others overshoot steepness, slanting into the ventral (e.g., f17, f28, f99, f154, f186, f187, f246). These alterations suggest considerable force but also containment_perhaps a casing. The left edge scar on the distally broken blade-like flake f231 evokes damage, although it could be a deliberate notch (see also f165, an anomalous piece, open to several interpretations).

Less dramatic flaking is one of the more common PG3 and PG4 modifications. It is quite often invasive (on the ventral, which means struck from the dorsal), and often consists of only one scar, which might be due to damage (e.g., f22, f36) to miniature flake production, or to intended implement formation (f52). Some may have been core preparation (f11, f101, f154, f177, f179, f214, f217, f249, f250). We believe basal flaking to be deliberate thinning and sometimes narrowing, possibly for hafting (e.g., f28, f50, f189, f194, f233, f250; see also f112, with a little smaller scar overlay). Some modifications are less pronounced. They consist of no more than one to three flake removals. Because of their scarcity and crudeness, they would not be classed as retouch in the conventional pressure fabrication sense. They are most common proximally. We suggest they are a technique for bulb and platform thinning. Several examples indicate that flaked basal thinning is usually ventral and characterizes all kinds of flakes and flake sizes, including miniatures, blades, blade-like flakes, and ovate "scrapers" (see especially f36, f38, f42, f55, f78, f80, f124, f128, f148, f194, f225, f249).

Steep, continuous pressure retouch appears in conventional positions on a very few specimens. One is as "backing" on a single blade or blade-like flake lateral margin (e.g., f27, f37, f170, f191, and perhaps f17, f18, f154 is initial, incomplete, or modified versions). Another is responsible for the ovate shape of one so-called tabular "scraper" (f2). Abrupt and semi-abrupt retouch is equally scarce and conventionally placed. F12, f17 proximal, f44, f50, f53, f55, f112, f187 show enough continuous abrupt or semi-abrupt retouch to be classed as "scrapers" in many classic tool typologies. Because the abrupt and semi-abrupt scars are so few, the left edge of f27, and margins of f34, f35, f37, f42, f94, f192 would not qualify in a traditional tool typology. We suggest the continuous retouch reestablishes the bite of the rounded edge and its relationship to the flat ventral. Thus, it is a curation technique as much as an initial tool shaping process. The sporadic small scars in contrast to continuous retouch may be deliberate narrowing or thinning. F59 and f84 exemplify variations on both these interpretations.

Other kinds of retouch are still rarer. Shallow, fine, tidy, semi-parallel, or alternate retouch embellishes a few lithics (see for example, f9, right distal; f233; "scrapers" f50, f53, f74; and many blade and blade-like flakes and fragments with gloss). In most of these, the "cruder" modifications described above coexist. Determining whether the "refined" scars were a first-step curation strategy superseded by "cruder" scars or vice versa is difficult. Since a few tools are only nibbled, some only roughly retouched, and some display finer working, we suggest they may belong to both categories.

Tidy, complex, and even retouch on the small, refurbished blade, f39 (fig. 7.13), a baulk find, is so exceptional in the collection that the lithic may originate in a different industry, such as Sotira *Teppes*. The pseudo-denticulated f165 is equally atypical for *Kaminoudhia*. Other reduction modifications observed at *Kaminoudhia* are nicks, especially on point tips and a point proximal edge, nibbled laterals (particularly on blades), blade-like flakes and segments, battering, burin blow scars, and shearing.

In summary, when retouch occurs it is rarely fine. It is occasionally invasive (on the ventral). The most usual edge changes other than disruptions of edge outline (i.e., breaks, or an unretouched notch) are thinning, sharpening, or thickening. Backing (the blunting or steepening of a long edge that changes proportions to strengthen or to assist hafting) has been effected in different ways. Shearing, burin blows, steep flaking, or steep retouch are common. Retention of natural cortex on medium-grained semi-translucent gray chert with inclusions (e.g., f65), the standard material and method for all prehistoric Vasilikos Valley sites, is very rare at *Kaminoudhia*. The other most common morphological modifications are rounding, basal thinning (for examples, see fig. 7.16), and proximal narrowing. Functionally, PG3 and PG4 alteration predominantly thins and/or narrows proximals. When continuous, alteration reestablishes edge angle sharpness or bluntness, frequently at the expense of length.

PG3 AND PG4 SEQUENCES. We sorted implements and tools that were worked after removal from the core into PG3s and PG4s. If a lithic at *Kaminoudhia* was worked after detachment, it was usually at more than one position. Flakes, blade-like flakes, or blades were generally used without modification. This usage may have occurred because curation and tool making was such a simple process, was so closely tied to original manufacturing goals, or was so urgent, that it was carried immediately further. At *Kaminoudhia*, the distinction was mooted between blank and preform (PG3 and PG4). Preforms on the core or in the mind of the maker characterize the collection, rather than as PG3s and PG4s.

We have already interpolated different sets of modification paths of PG3s and PG4s from small flake blank (PG2s). See also f43, f170, f169, quite possibly modified from blanks like f79; f34 and f38 derived from parallel sided, trapezoidal blade blanks, for a range of PG3 to PG4 reduction routes in blade-like flake implements and tools. F74 may represent another set of scenarios with PG4 dorsal flaking and retouch on small, rounded, prepared core flakes.

F46, a weathered, battered, wing-shaped flake with a steep platform, thinned below the right edge and notched, came from Area C, Unit 9. The flake core with cortex, f45 (fig. 7.1), has several traits evocative of the former. The pale green material of f45 mottled with white is similar to that of the probably wasted, tabular core on a blade in the adjacent Unit 2. Because all items just discussed were either weathered or found in a disturbed deposit it is possible that retouched, notched flakes were not a part of the original assemblage.

REFURBISHING: PRODUCT GROUP 5 (PG5)

We had assumed that because of its proximity Episkopi *Phaneromeni* would share similar resource constraints and solutions (Morris 1977 and author's familiarity with collection). However, very few items at *Kaminoudhia* evince obvious recycling, evident in retouch overlayering on reoriented lithics. As noted in this chapter, at *Kaminoudhia* numerous other forms of conservation prevail.

TOOLS

End "Scrapers" and Nosed "Scrapers." An absence of nosed "scrapers" and paucity of end "scrapers" (see f187), particularly on parallel-sided blades (f38 is the only example), distinguishes the collection at *Kaminoudhia* from many Cypriot EP assemblages. References to end "scrapers" on blades, including parallel-sided blades, are very frequent in the literature on Neolithic Cypriot collections (Cauvin 1984; Fox 1988; Guilaine et al. 1997 and 1995; Stekelis 1953 and 1961; Waechter 1953; and this author's familiarity with several collections). At Erimi *Pamboula* (Seton-Williams 1936), Kalavasos *Ayious*, (Betts n.d.), and the Lemba area (Betts 1979a), end "scrapers," especially on blades, are among the most common tools. The author knows of end "scrapers" on thick blades from Kalavasos *Pamboules* in the Vasilikos Valley. References to nosed "scrapers" or steep end "scrapers" are also prevalent in the literature on Neolithic and mixed Neolithic–Chalcolithic collections.

At *Kaminoudhia* adequate blanks are available, so their rarity cannot be explained in terms of the small representation of blades. It is possible the vagaries of preservation and recovery or different methods of describing collections may account for their scarcity. Reports that emphasize formal tool types might be more prone to itemize end and nose "scrapers" than we have, but we find this explanation unlikely because it is the emphasis that differs, not the powers of observation of retouch form and location. They are rare at Marki *Alonia* (Smith 1996), and neither item is recorded in the material from Episkopi *Phaneromeni* (Morris 1977), nor from Alambra *Mouttes* (Kingsnorth 1996b). It is possible that other artifacts such as the discoidal "scrapers" discussed in the next section supplanted both forms at *Kaminoudhia*, Marki *Alonia*, Alambra *Mouttes*, and Episkopi *Phaneromeni*.

Could the difference be a diagnostic of temporal change, or due to varying environments and their adaptations, or to a difference between denser population agglomerations and smaller ones, a combination of these, or yet another factor? Customarily in archaeology, until demonstrated otherwise, the temporal diagnostic is the default position. Following this practice, based on very few sites, we would have to say tentatively that a decline in presence of end "scrapers" and nosed "scrapers" on blades is associated with the transition from Chalcolithic into the EC–MC.

Relatively Large, Retouched, Discoidal Flakes: "Chalcolithic Scrapers"/"Erimi Scrapers."

Temporal Contexts: Relatively large, well made, rounded, aesthetically pleasing, retouched "scrapers," known from Chalcolithic and other sites with a substantial pre-Late Cypriot (LC) component is an exception to the comments about named tool types above. Variants occur at Lemba *Lakkous,* Kissonerga *Mylouthkia*, Erimi *Pamboula*, Episkopi *Phaneromeni*, Kalavasos *Ayious*, Kalavasos *Kokkinoya*, Kalavasos *Pamboules*, Maroni *Karayannides*, Marki *Alonia*, Alambra *Mouttes*, and Agrokipia *Palaiokamina*.[47] The foregoing sites have substantial Chalcolithic, EC, or MC material culture components, though some are mixed or of uncertain date. Therefore, a rough temporal correlation between the lithic form from the Chalcolithic continuing through to the beginning of LC may exist.

Apart from a few exceptions discussed below, we have not encountered these artifacts in the relevant published literature on pre-Chalcolithic sites, nor on the incompletely published ones. Since the only work on lithics from the LC to the present concerns threshing sledge *dhoukania,* their absence in later site reports does not clarify their temporal correlations.

Stekelis (1961:230) referred to a "fan scraper" in the assemblage from Dikaios' excavations at Sotira *Teppes*. Even if this should be similar, without a closed context one could not rule out its being a stray, later discard from *Kaminoudhia*. Le Brun (1981:37–38, 142–45) records rounded scrapers on flakes from Cape Andreas *Kastros*, some of which are denticulated. Proportions and PG4 modifications, especially the denticulation, of the few illustrated examples distinguish these from the Chalcolithic–MC specimens we have seen.

Two specimens illustrated from Parekklisha *Shillourokambos* (Guilaine et al. 1995: fig. 4.1 and especially fig. 5.2), although not identical to any of the later specimens, merely appear to be variants in a later collection. Moreover, the latter is fan-like retaining the cortex, popular on Levantine tabular scrapers. Simmons illustrates a rounded flake from the early excavations at Akrotiri *Aetokremnos* (Simmons 1988: fig. 5 k). He does not call it a "scraper" or even categorize it as a tool. The figure implies a diameter, some dorsal features, and proximal modifications similar to those of ovoid "Chalcolithic scrapers." Without additional information, we cannot evaluate it.

Until detailed comparative studies of all identified specimens and related forms are undertaken, we conclude that the discoidal scraper is known from the Aceramic but becomes most significant in the Chalcolithic through LC IA. It may even have replaced other forms toward the end of the Chalcolithic. By the late Bronze Age it, in turn, may have been superceded. It is not possible to determine if the longevity represents a continuous tradition, reinvention, or erroneous lumping together of superficially similar lithics without precise attribute analysis.

Attributes. The distinctive features of the discoid "scrapers" (figs. 7.11 and 7.12) are the circular or sub-circular shape (f2, f53, f55 in particular), the flatness or smoothness of the ventral surface (f2, f50, f53, f145), which sometimes gleams slightly, and by Cypriot knapped stone industry norms, the exceptional, controlled quality of the retouch that varies from very abrupt (f2, f53) to very delicate. Specimens from Maroni *Karayannides*, Agrokipia *Palaiokamina*, and aceramic Neolithic Parekklisha *Shillourokambos* are particularly delicately retouched. Betts (1979a) remarks that in the combined

---

[47] For Lemba *Lakkous* and Kissonerga *Mylouthkia*, see Betts 1979a. For Erimi *Pamboula* see Seton-Williams 1936; pl. XXVII, 6. For Episkopi *Phaneromeni* see Morris 1977:L82 and possibly, L89?. For Kalavasos *Ayious* see Betts, n.d.. For Kalavasos *Kokkinoya* and Kalavasos *Pamboules*, see Hordynsky and Ritt 1977. For Maroni *Karayannides* see Manning and Conway 1992. For Marki *Alonia* see Smith 1996. For Alambra *Mouttes* see Kingsnorth 1996b. For Agrokipia *Palaiokamina* see Kingsnorth, 1996a. The author has personally examined the collections at Kalavasos *Ayious*, Kalavasos *Kokkinoya*, Kalavasos *Pamboules*, and Maroni *Karayannides*.

Lemba *Lakkous*/Kissonerga *Mylouthkia* assemblage, the round "scrapers" are among the most finely worked objects. Qualitatively, most are aesthetically attractive.

Without a complete inventory or analysis of all specimens and related forms we have no means of establishing reliable metric parameters. To provide a general idea of their size, we estimate diameters to be in the 3.5–5.0 cm range and thickness, 0.3–1.0 cm, although both much smaller and much larger variants would be included. This is a definitional problem, with temporal implications.

Seton-Williams (1936:51), who recognized 49 discoidal scrapers at Erimi *Pamboula,* stated that absence of retouch distinguished the ventral surface, although the platform may have been removed. In the Lemba *Lakkou*s/Kissonerga *Mylouthkia* collection Betts (1979a) also noted that the striking platform had been removed in some cases. The narrowing and thinning of bases, and in one case of the distal instead (f49), seem to constitute the *Kaminoudhia* equivalent (cf. f50, f52 a variant, f53, f55, f80). Such a modification is consistent with many kinds of lithics in the assemblage. Related forms f82, f145, and f225 may share the latter attributes.

Some specimens (f50, f55, f80) have had their bulbs removed or have a few pronounced, flake scars at one end of the ventral surface (f52, f55). The latter may be the result of recycling, which seems to have occurred with specimen L89 from Episkopi *Phaneromeni*. F50 and f53 are slightly pointed. F2 is the only one with steep, flaked edging. Its dorsal is comprised entirely of cortex and is evocative of Levantine "tabular scrapers," a type also heavily correlated numerically with the Chalcolithic (Rosen 1997).

Reduction. Surviving specimens offer hints of some steps in their reduction histories. All must have left a simple platform on the core from which they were removed, and yet no Cypriot literature reports mirror-image discoidal "scraper" scars on cores. However, two discoidal flakes from Alambra *Mouttes* have rounded scars on their exteriors (Kingsnorth 1996b: pl. 27. C57, C58). These are too small to have produced the kind of discoidal flake in question. However, they imply that the range may have been greater than what survives and offer one idea of the appearance of the core surfaces. Because they were usually of highly desirable chert, cores were probably reduced further, leaving an excellent platform. It is also possible they came from a manufacturing center not yet found. In any case one stage of these forms may have been as core preparation for other lithics.

The dorsals of f49 and f50, and to a lesser extent f52 and f145, exemplify a simplified "Levallois"-like technique of core preparation. The technique is visible in an even more rudimentary form in the two large opposing flake scars on the small f45 core. The probable Marki *Alonia* cortex-coated exterior flake cores for the product have not been observed at *Kaminoudhia*, although the ventral flaking on many *Kaminoudhia* cortex products is unexpected. They could conceivably be fragments of similar kinds of items, reflecting a comparable technique. At *Kaminoudhia* the cores may have been reduced further than at Marki *Alonia*; the ovoids may have been made elsewhere by a different method, or a combination of these conditions was in force.

All the *Kaminoudhia* specimens have been modified in more than one location after removal from the core (PG4). Four particularly fine, virtually classic examples are depicted in fig. 7.11, while fig. 7.12 contains three dissimilar flakes that could have become like the specimens on the previous figure with little modification. F80 is a large expanding flake with basal thinning ventrally and distal trimming. Although it is not completely rounded, it is well on its way to becoming so. F55 came off a core prepared so that the flake is already in an almost perfectly rounded condition. F50 would require heavier flaking than the other two to be transformed into a version of f145, which is remarkable for its solidity and keeled dorsal scar.

Their range of morphology and scars are reminiscent of products from what Tixier et al. (1980:55, fig.11) refer to as "*la methode Kombewa.*" In the absence of a thorough Cypriot-wide study and because of our concern about transferring regional terms, we are not ready to draw conclusions about these suggestive parallels.

Role: The Prominence of Discoidal "Scrapers" in the Era. At present determining what other changes prompted the prominence of discoidal "scrapers" is not possible. Among the factors considered are developments in metallurgy, secondary products, population clustering, techniques of working wood or skin. It is possible something else not yet considered significant may have influenced their importance. Some evidence suggests that the tool, always relatively scarce in the collections that contain it, is represented in proportionally greater numbers at the sites closer to the coast than those slightly more inland. Damage scars on both the dorsal and ventral surfaces of these "scrapers" occasionally are severe and distinctive. The overall form of the tool is reminiscent of a plane. Possibly, its use required it to be hafted. If it were a device for evening timbers, it could have been used for building houses, conveyances or farming equipment. However, it is difficult to believe that this tool would have sustained a long life as a plane and would have been replaced frequently. Numbers of damaged and undamaged specimens do not display good evidence of this having been the case.

Conceivably, "scrapers" were skin-working tools. Ethnographic parallels exist. If late EP "scrapers" were so used, why had they become salient? Why was there a preference for a retouched end instead of using an unmodified flake? Leather preparation does not require retouched knapped scrapers. Other materials or chemical tanning can be used for preparing leather. Were the original employers of the equipment working a new kind of animal skin or one from a species that had previously not been important for its hide? Unlike deer, goat, sheep and pigskin, was the hide particularly thick or hard to work, like cowhide? Might they have been handling a hide in a new way, more intensely, or more frequently? The preceding discussion suggests that a microwear study of the known specimens of this tool is required and to clarify the concept of the history of secondary products.

The greatest difficulty in accepting the Aceramic denticulated "scrapers" as scrapers is as leather preparation tools. The publication on Cape Andreas *Kastros* illustrates and lists three round "scrapers"/"grattoirs" (LeBrun: 1981:37–38, 144–45, fig. 27). In our view these are "scrapers" purely in the classificatory sense and not functionally. Their sharp, pointy edges would shred and not merely defur, defat, and thin skins as required.

Seton-Williams (1936:51) observed that at Erimi *Pamboula* retouch occurs on only one end or nearly all the way around. The rounded shape of most of the *Kaminoudhia* "scrapers" may relate to ongoing resharpening or the whittling down of a longer instrument through curation. The heftiest example, f145, is long. Similarly, in a standard tool typology, f187, might be classed as an end "scraper," or even an end "scraper" on a blade, both of which are common at Lemba area Chalcolithic sites and Erimi *Pamboula*, but almost absent at *Kaminoudhia*. We suggest that the retouched discoidal forms may owe their shape to ongoing use, refurbishment, and reuse. The resultant roundness may not have been so much a goal, as an effect of longevity and ongoing curation. Using this perspective, the fans/ "en eventail" "scrapers" of Erimi *Pamboula* (and the Chalcolithic–Bronze Age Levant) might be lessworn variants. Thus, the high ratio of round to end "scrapers" at *Kaminoudhia* would be another hallmark of intense conservation.

If conservation of hide-scraping tools is the explanation, then why did it occur at this point and not earlier? Might hide preparation have become a specialized economic role rather than a routine subsistence skill enculturated into every family? Had tanning methodology become restricted, making the tools little known, harder to acquire, and more worthwhile to maintain for as long as possible? In reconstructing social evolution it is important to realize that hide preparation cross-culturally is a role low in prestige, power, and wealth in socioeconomically differentiated communities. Ethnologically, it is occasionally a female occupation, and the knapper and flesh-preparer is the same individual (Brandt

1994). On the other hand, in at least one highly stratified subculture more than a dozen different specialists may be involved.

Pointed Flakes, Blade-like Flakes and Blades: Piercers, Drills and Projectile Points.

Piercing. In any collection, almost any two adjacent edges on most flakes and blades can pierce, but determining which did, or were intended to, is problematic. If an unhafted, hand-held point is narrow or has a protruding spur, it is sometimes considered a piercer or an awl. Without use wear analysis, this is unsupported assumption.

When the pointed portion has been resharpened or thickened by retouch on one or more edges, the functionalist nomenclature "piercer"/"awl," "borer," or "drill" are normally ascribed, depending upon whether the same or alternate faces are scarred. This is especially likely if the point projects from a lateral or distal. Unlike most other prehistoric sites in Cyprus, the *Kaminoudhia* collection does not include any examples (unless the slight nibbling on the left distal of f9 qualifies it).

Nonspecialists assume that so-called "piercers," "awls," "borers," or "drills" on a tool type list verify the activities themselves. On the one hand, a "drill" may not have drilled. On the other hand, piercing, boring and drilling do not require retouch and do not necessarily leave macroscopically visible traces. Nonetheless, the absence of the type does not mean absence of perforating at *Kaminoudhia* or anywhere else.

Points and Projectile Points. When a pointed lithic has basal retouch, especially contributing to shoulders and/or tangs, it is usually assumed to have been hafted longitudinally and used as a projectile tip. In formal tool typology, basal tangs seem to be the principal attribute that causes a flake or blade to be designated as an "arrowhead" in Near Eastern archaeology. Failing a tang, a combination of basal pressure retouch and small size qualify for the "arrowhead" label. By extension, small size and pressure flaking alone sometimes suffice (Rosen 1997 on microlithic lunates). Also by extension, transverse flakes and distally truncated flakes with basal and/or lateral pressure flaked retouch are encompassed (Gopher 1994; Rosen 1997). Therefore, the label "arrowhead" in Near Eastern knapped stone tool typing encompasses an array of tools with an unspecified assortment of only partially overlapping attributes of shape, size, and modification.

For years in many parts of the world archaeologists have avoided the term "arrowhead" because of its overly precise launch mechanism implication. Hard tips can reinforce darts, spears, harpoons, and lances also propelled by a bow. Points can enhance instruments that are not released but used for jabbing, for equipment propelled by hand, arm, and shoulder or aided by a throwing stick (frequently called an atlatl in the Americas), or by blowgun, particularly suitable in dense forest. For these reasons we use the term "projectile point" or "point" instead of "arrowhead."

Extremely serviceable projectile points that are neither tanged, tined, nor retouched have been used throughout the world from at least the Upper Paleolithic to the present. Lashing a flake of almost any shape into split wood or onto a stem, with or without the help of adhesives, is not difficult. Moreover, neither missiles nor hand-held jabbing devices require pointed distals. Transverse, blunted, knobby, and chunky tips have all been used as projectile tips. They can also be made of ground stone, antler, bone, shell, wood, reeds, bamboo, or metal, most of which were available to EP and Bronze Age inhabitants of Cyprus. Finally, it is a mistake to assume that projectile points automatically indicate either hunting or conflict. Conversely, their absence from the archaeological record does not mean hunting, raiding, and warfare did not exist prehistorically.

Bearing all this in mind, we nevertheless propose that many triangular flakes that are distally pointed and trapezoidal in cross-section could have been projectile points, not only at *Kaminoudhia* but in many Cypriot collections. Given how rare extensive retouch is in Cypriot tools, we would not predict greater elaboration for this item than for others. Since projectile points are particularly subject to damage or loss in use, they require either continual curation or continual replacement. If the industry follows a continual replacement mode, projectile points are prime candidates for a simple en masse means of production. The "Levallois"-like method noted in flakes at *Kaminoudhia* and other assemblages (see above) is one of several suitable strategies.

Pointed implements and tools are common at *Kaminoudhia*. Most deposits contain at least one flake or blade that is in part triangular. We interpret many as projectile points. They have slightly hollowed proximals created by core flake scars or ridge thinning, which would comfortably cradle the shaft. Others, such as f1 at *Kaminoudhia*, have different possible haft rest arrangements. Many are basally thinned or shouldered, through diverse means (as already discussed under Retouch above), both of which characteristics are helpful in slotting and lashing the haft end. The very frequent, slight damage often midway up one edge may have provided a nick for tying. This process may also have caused it. The tip, which is one of the most vulnerable areas, is often dulled or missing. We suggest that use as a projectile point and not merely the inherent vulnerability of a thin end explain the pattern. Illustrated examples are on the bottom of fig. 7.7 (f1, f9, f48, f18, f77; f108 on fig.7.8, and f26 on fig. 7.17). One possible hafted reconstruction is depicted in fig. 7.18, taking into account hollow crest, shoulder, and lateral nick.

Cypriot Parallels. Identical and variant projectile point flakes, blades, bladelets, and spalls occur throughout prehistoric Cypriot collections. Moving back from *Kaminoudhia*'s time through four EP periods, we cite a few illustrated examples. At Chalcolithic Kissonerga *Mosphilia,* Betts (1987: fig. 3. #6) illustrated a typical small triangular flake. The dorsal is hollowed by core flake scars. A burin blow forms shouldering on the right proximal, and two small scars thin the basal left. There is a mid-left edge nick and blunted tip. At Sotira *Teppes* many illustrated basally thinned and narrowed "knives" are candidates (Stekelis 1961). In the same chapter Stekelis noted that the absence of "pedunculated" points at Sotira *Teppes* distinguished it from *Khirokitia* Vouni. We suggest that the "pedunculated" pointed flakes at *Khirokitia* (Stekelis 1953) are probable projectile points. Therefore, it is not surprising that another set of finds at Sotira *Teppes* corresponds to their vacant niche. Note an earlier proximally narrowed, dorsally thinned, distally pointed flake reported from the first season at Akrotiri *Aetokremnos* (Simmons 1988: fig. 5g).

The writer has perceived an absence of projectile points in Cypriot prehistory. Moreover, a review of Cypriot lithics reports reveals that we are not alone at *Kaminoudhia*. Swiny (1988) describes two projectile points from the Akrotiri Peninsula. Betts (1987) discusses two fragments of biface "projectiles" from Kissonerga *Mosphilia,* although she believes them to be imports from across the sea. Le Brun (1981) lists and illustrates both "armatures de flèches" and "mèches de forêt". At Sotira *Teppes,* Stekelis (1961: pl. 116, fig. 336) called a basally retouched, concave base point with inverse distal retouch and a missing tip an "arrowhead." In the same publication he discussed four "spearheads" from aceramic Neolithic Phrenaros (1961:231).

Although we arrived at our interpretation independently, we are not the only ones to identify the particular genre of projectile points. Cauvin (1984) suggests that "Levallois" flakes at Khirokitia could have served as projectile points. Experimental replication, use trials, and more refined wear analysis are necessary to refute, modify, or support the hypotheses.

SHEEN AND GLOSS

IMPLICATIONS OF LOCATION, RELATION TO RETOUCH, CURATION, AND CONSERVATION. Visible gloss, especially when extensive enough to be quickly noticed by those to whom it is new, and especially if extending along the long edge of elegant blades, has always attracted the attention of lithics specialists working in the Near East. Lithics identical in all ways, but lacking visible gloss, have not engendered a comparable response, although probably produced by the same method and used in the same way, merely not to the same extent. Macroscopically visible gloss is a sign of very heavy use. Tool exploitation severe enough to generate immediately obvious gloss usually dulls the tool's edges. Reactivation requires energy input. From the point of view of prehistoric peoples, gloss may have been a sign of imminent tool fatigue.

At *Kaminoudhia*, gloss appears on blades, blade-like flakes, and fragments (but see also f84, f111 bladelet, and f183, a miniature flake). The amount varies from merest specks, thin edging, edging plus crest skimming, a heavy blanket over one face from one edge to crest, to an unequal bifacial coating. Specimens with gloss are depicted in figs. 7.13–15 and 7.17. Extent and density of the gloss have been recorded. The figures show that retouch overlays gloss and vice-versa, demonstrating that retouch constitutes resharpening or curation. F36 and f47 illuminate clear contrasts. Gloss enters the scars of f47 indicating intense utilization after curation to the point of gloss formation, unlike f36. Especially heavy gloss coating, accompanied by heavy retouch, appears to have transformed f35 from a "true" blade to a severely constricted shape. Retouch is found on most blades and blade-like flakes at *Kaminoudhia* that underwent gloss-creating activity. We conclude that the prehistoric population intensely curated and preserved linear flakes employed in gloss engendering work. Dull sheen, common in other collections with which the author is familiar, was very rare at *Kaminoudhia*. Here as in other areas, heavy use and conservation characterize the *Kaminoudhia* assemblage.

We propose that the urgency and relentlessness of tasks, such as harvesting of grains or reeds and pruning of vines combined with the constraints of hafting, made repeated retouch (curation) preferable in this material conserving industry. It is possible that restrictions on access to blade production in the period may have encouraged their extreme conservation.

Hafting. Bearing in mind the unreliability of suggestions based on discovery location, the in situ row of lithics with gloss (f60–f62, and nearby f156, from Unit 1), raises the possibility of the pieces having been hafted together (see Chapter 2, Unit 1). Antler fragments from *Kaminoudhia* and antler hafts from Sotira *Teppes* have survived. Unless taphonomic differences explain the absence, this tool may have had a wooden casing. Hansen (Chapter 12) noted evidence for pine, almond, olive, pistachio, and unspecified pear angiosperms and gymnosperms. Each of these poses their own set of difficulties as wood for hafting materials, but none is insurmountable. Other more flexible handles are also possible. Elster (1989) and Nishiaki (1990) illustrate simple hypothetical reconstructions of hafts for comparable composite tools from Neolithic Greece and Syria respectively, either of which provides models for the *Kaminoudhia* set.

Alternatives are possible. Stone parts may have occupied different positions over time, since at *Kaminoudhia* there is no clear-cut domination of right or left edge, nor ventral or dorsal gloss, and one specimen, f35, has bilateral gloss. Hafting may not have been backing, but positioned centrally exposing both edges of a lithic. Each gloss item may have been housed in its own handle. Furthermore, alternation between forehand and backhand movements, rotation in the hand between passes, or alternation of the hand holding the haft would account for the lack of differentiation in gloss location. Replication and trial research is needed in this field.

Use. Silica gloss does not necessarily equate to use as a sickle or similar tool. Coqueugniot's (1984) microwear analysis of gloss blades from Neolithic Khirokitia *Vouni* reiterates that implements and tools with gloss may not have harvested grains. He states that sawing soft woods and splitting reeds or rushes yield visible gloss and that collecting or preparing materials for bedding, architecture, and caning, mat, and basketry work (*vannerie*) may be responsible.

Most "sickle" segments examined under a high-powered microscope by Coqueugniot seem to have acquired their macroscopically visible gloss through contact with grains. Debney (1997, 1996) believes the same of MC Marki *Alonia* gloss lithics, suggesting grains harvested by genus and species (barley and emmer). Finlayson (1987) discovered two different gloss patterns microscopically on Kissonerga *Mosphilia* "sickle blades" (quotation marks his), but avoids ascribing sources. The row of gloss blade-like flakes possibly hafted together from Unit 1 at *Kaminoudhia* may also have comprised a sickle without microwear analysis. However, we do not rule out a role in the other crafts itemized by Coqueugniot.

Comparing the model of hafted gloss pieces sketched in Elster (1989) to the image of a bronze tool from LC Hala Sultan Tekke called a "pruning hook" in various publications prompts one to question whether some prehistoric hafted blade and blade-like flake tools of Europe and Southwest Asia, including from *Kaminoudhia*, may have been used for other purposes as well as cutting grains. Clearing away competitor plants, trimming and pruning young branches or shoots of bushes, vines, and "wild" or domestic fruit trees can improve short-term output. From Hansen's list of documented *Kaminoudhia* vegetation, almond, "wild" pear, grape, and *Prunus* sp., could be candidates for pruning. Moreover, there are rarely enough "sickles" at a given archaeological site, including *Kaminoudhia*, to harvest sufficient grain for the population required to construct and maintain the site. Wastage, off-site use and disposal, preservation problems, and longevity of archaeological features relative to tools are partially responsible for the discrepancy. It is also possible that gloss tools may be only a small component of grain acquisition.

FURTHER INDICATORS OF POSSIBLE COMPOSITE EQUIPMENT

ADHESIVES. A thick, sticky, black coating adhered to the parallel-sided, central portion of the dorsal of f112. This small, blocky core on a very thick, intensely weathered flake came from stratified Lot 3 in Unit 10 in Area C. It had semi-abrupt knapping on all edges, becoming narrow and overlain by small scarring on the distal that would qualify it as an "end scraper on a core" in traditional typologies. The coating might be adhesive.

BASAL THINNING AND/OR NARROWING. We have discussed many examples of basal thinning, narrowing and/or shouldering at *Kaminoudhi*a. Some techniques for achieving this distinguish the *Kaminoudhia* collection from others. In most cases at *Kaminoudhia* they involve core preparation or post-detachment removal of one or two flakes on PG2s, particularly on points, blades, and blade-like flakes. Further modified products such as "scrapers" and gloss items are consistently affected. Constricting and/or thinning proximals may have accommodated hafts or overlapping of lithics set in a casing.

MINIATURES. Basal thinning and narrowing appear on miniature flakes (e.g., f127, f128, f220, and f221), which may indicate that they were an intended product. Miniatures may have been components of complex composite tools. This would have entailed combining several miniature flakes in a haft.

DISTINCTIVE ASSOCIATIONS

REFITTED LITHICS. The four largest flakes from *Kaminoudhia* are pairs whose members were found next to each other and fit together closely. They are of two different materials both of which are rare at *Kaminoudhia*. Rectangular flakes, f99 and f100 (fig. 7.4), are of semi-translucent orange-banded Lefkara chert. F100 was still part of the core when f99 was detached. The ventral bulb of f99 fits into the dorsal scar of f100. It is interesting that the more interior of the flakes, f100, has cortex but the more exterior one, f99, does not. This is contrary to standard assumptions about flake and cortex ratios.

They are the second largest cherts recovered from the excavation. They are very fresh in appearance. Their size, shape, unrolled edges, and material imply possible direct extraction from stratified chert beds or blocks rather than from nodular redeposition in fields, rivers, or littorals. Their find location, a pit in Unit 7, might imply safekeeping or special disposal. The only larger flake is f144, which is of chalcedony. F143 fits into its dorsal (see figs. 7.5, 7.6). Their find spot is Unit 10 on bedrock (see fig. 2.11).

These two pairs of very large, meshing flakes may constitute surviving examples of stocking of material. From a *Kaminoudhia* knapper's point of view, they harbor an exceptional amount of good material. Almost any lithic is a potential core, but by the standards of *Kaminoudhia* where even minuscule cores are not exhausted, these two blocks would have been very attractive for someone wanting to stock potential cores of specially imported material.

Their size and the find spot of f99 and f100, a pit, are reminiscent of the in situ reserve of large lithics from Lemba *Lakkous* (Betts 1979b). The Lemba *Lakkous* cache contains more specimens, and they are retouched. However, some chert in the *Lakkous* cache is the gray variant of the banded chert found in our example. Their large size also ties them to huge, well-retouched tools, in many fabrics from the catchment area around Alambra *Mouttes* (Kingsnorth 1996b). Based on analogy to the Lemba *Lakkous* cache, and to large "scraper"-retouched, worked blades reported by Seton-Williams from Erimi *Pamboula,* we suggested that these lithics may be Chalcolithic (Coleman et al. 1996; Kingsnorth 1996b). The two *Kaminoudhia* flakes extend the range of dates for the few very large-scale lithics published in Cyprus.

Except for the Erimi "scraper retouched" blades, we speculate that all are blanks produced and perhaps exchanged for use as potential cores. All are of minority materials in the collections or in the localities in which they were found, and all are specimens of noticeably good quality material. What better way to show off desirable raw materials from beyond the vicinity, whether for exchange, display, banking, or special disposal, than with huge examples? Working them into prototypes of other knapped products, as in the non-*Kaminoudhia* specimens, is even better advertising.

With merely four cases, one of which is dated only by analogy, inferences are very tentative. At present we suggest that stocking large lithics in specialized materials is a Chalcolithic characteristic that continues at *Kaminoudhia* in a diminished way. This may imply continuity in habits of exchange of goods and services.

DISTRIBUTION OF FLOTATION FINDS. In Table 12.1 of this volume, Hansen lists deposits with small chippage found in flotation residues. There has been some controversy in the literature about the precise significance of these kinds of reduction products. It has been proposed that at minimum their presence verifies the actual location of knapping activity within a site, the more visible side products having been removed so as not to cut or hurt people (Clark 1986). Some claim that they correspond to the locus of trimming, as opposed to the coarser work of initial reduction, equated in our schema with PG3–5. One aspect of the discussion seeks to distinguish between the impact of direct percussion and pressure flaking and on the size and ratios of microdebitage. In approximately half the samples with knapped stone from the flotation residue, small pieces of bone, wood, or carbon were also found. Again *if* one accepts the most optimistic results of the literature on taphonomy and the view that automatic sorting by size may identify primary refuse loci, then Chapter 12, Table 1 may reveal where knapped stone tools were being created or used with bone or wood at *Kaminoudhia*. No distinct pattern is obvious.

Significantly, residues were found that lacked chippage. Bearing in mind the standard caveats about discard pattern studies, this would support the view that knapping did not take place throughout the site, and that spaces had separate roles at least temporarily. It could even imply that at this period knapping may not have been a fundamental subsistence technology engaged in equally by all members of society. This view is consistent with an interpretation that distinctions existed in knapping based on age, sex, or part-time occupational specialization.

UNIT 21: A KNAPPING STATION? In Area C, Unit 21 a complete sequence of knapped stone reduction occurred, including raw material, a variety of PG2 items—cores, chunks, flakes and blade-like flakes—as well as some finely retouched PG3/4s (see f117–f134 in figs 7.16 and 7.17). Blanks, implements, and tools are spread throughout the sequence. From the flotation residue at the juncture of the north and west corner walls come chert chippage, bone fragments, lentisc, and an olive pit fragment. The most conservative accounting for such a mixture of finds in this zone would call upon chance, the accident of discovery, differential preservation, or erosion. Another explanation may be that Unit 21 was a waste disposal zone. A still bolder interpretation suggests that this may have been a place to work chert (perhaps with bone and wood) from start to planned objective. Some accompanying ground stone artifacts, six "pounders," a "pecking stone" and a "hammerstone," support the interpretation (Swiny Chapter 6, this volume). These are the kinds of items that might constitute components of the knapper's tool kit, the "percussors," "hammerstones," and "billets" in flaked stone lithic terminology.

DISCOIDAL SCRAPER PRODUCTION, USE, OR CURATION LOCI. Several circular "scrapers" occurred in deposits with flakes that seemed so similar in fabric that they may have come from the same block. Examples include f53 from Area B within the confines of Unit 12. The "scraper" and 19 small chunks and flakes in the same lot share a uniform, fine texture and distinctive dark-green coloring. F55, one of three probably related flakes, also came from Unit 12. Various small fine green flakes, some with cortex, suggest reduction of one continuous nodule within the same built area. If there is any relationship between discovery location and original activity, the least conservative interpretation of Unit 12 would be that chipped stone tool production occurred here, including creation of rounded "scrapers," the period's diagnostic artifact. If this was a reduction locus, the absence of corresponding cores is consistent with our discussion above.

HUMAN SKELETON. Knapped stone found in the deposit around the human skeleton in Unit 22 constitutes an interesting set. Each of the seven pieces (f26, f41 and f42, f86, f87, f89 and unillustrated PG2 flake) is of exceptional fabric. Three specimens (f26, f87, f89) fit our description above of possible projectile points, one (f26) so well that it would make an excellent definitive type specimen.

The only opaque, tough, dark red cryptocrystalline material at *Kaminoudhia* is f89, the largest of the three hypothetical projectile points. It is a striking mix of colors, opaque yellow ("limonite") and dark, opaque-red ("jasper"), that would stand out even in the few known Cypriot assemblages dominated by these materials. The black fabric of f26, the most credible of the three suggested projectile points, is also unique for *Kaminoudhia*, although its coloring is like f108, a specimen similar in size, shape, modifications and possibly function.

F42, f86, and f87 are of excellent, very fine-grained gray-white, or gray-greenish with white, Lefkara chert. They may come from the same nodule. The PG2 blank, f41, might also be derived from the same block, but it is green, lustrous, and possessed of a crisp band of cortex. Uniquely for *Kaminoudhia*, f42 crosses dramatically to banded orange. An expanding PG2 flake distal fragment in an exceptionally pale orange-banded Lefkara chert is not illustrated (d: 1.2 + cm x 2.9 cm x .6 cm). Each of the Lefkara flakes is of exceptional quality, and two have unusual coloring.

Taken as a group the seven stand out, despite the skeletal association. Because of the association, they imply a deliberate constellation, perhaps pertaining to an activity in the locality or to the individual represented by the skeleton. The small assortment here may not be actual burial offerings, but they distinguish Unit 22 from all others.

PART III: SUMMARY OF RELATIONSHIP OF *KAMINOUDHIA* TO OTHER ASSEMBLAGES

RELATIONSHIP OF SOTIRA *KAMINOUDHIA* KNAPPED STONE TO EARLY PREHISTORIC–MIDDLE CYPRIOT ARCHAEOLOGY

Bolger (1985) has observed that "Erimi culture sites are most easily distinguished from their Sotira Culture predecessors on the basis of pottery . . ." (p. 223) and identified "short-distance shifting of Erimi culture settlements" (p. 225) as well as extensive use of picrolite ornament, figurine manufacturing, and distribution as a "mainstay of the economy" (p. 243). Bolger also raised the issue of the role of the olive and its products in the economy of the culture. This author believes that it is appropriate to add several knapped stone attributes to Bolger's list of diagnostic traits. We suggest that it may also be possible to distinguish Chalcolithic knapped stone characteristics from later ones. Some of these are now definite whereas others are hypothetical and need to be confirmed, modified, or rejected by ongoing testing through the collection of empirical data. Other knapped stone traits continue throughout the EP and well into the MC.

The *Kaminoudhia* assemblage is consistent with published late Early Prehistoric–MC Cypriot knapped work. It is heavily flake-based. At this site like many non-ephemeral ones that are also not immediately on top of an extraction site, some preparation takes place before lithics arrive at the site. Much early stage production happens before detachment, and it emphasizes orientation of the core and prior flake locations, obviating the need for careful flaking and retouch after detachment. Most subsequent shaping is proximal and restricted to two or three thinning and narrowing scars that are not delicate. We suggest exceptions are predominantly a reestablishing of attributes, i.e., curation. The repertoire like most others includes a range of serviceable projectile points that are small pointed flakes, which have been thinned and narrowed basally. Formal typed tools, like the discoid "scraper," are not the characteristic that best summarizes the nature of the production method but are familiar from generally contemporary sites. There is a little evidence that knapped stone associations vary within a site.

The assemblage is strikingly different from that of its nearby predecessor, Erimi *Pamboula*. At Erimi knappers did not use the same materials and did not exhaust large cores. They maintained a large blade technique and attractively retouched formal tools, including end "scrapers" on blades. The differences may typify variations between the lithic traditions of the two periods that each site represents. They may be temporal indices that discriminate between the Chalcolithic and Bronze Age knapped stone industries. Confirmation will require comparison with other sites from the same periods within a region. Although we believe the terms "nodal" and "non nodal" to be misleading designations for the relationship between contemporary sites, Erimi *Pamboula* is abundant in knapped stones. The later *Kaminoudhia* is not.

DISTINCTIVE ASPECTS OF *KAMINOUDHIA* KNAPPED STONE. The following subsections summarize the distinctive *Kaminoudhia* features described above concerning materials, reduction techniques, flake to blade ratios, classic tools, other tools, and conservation. In the process we compare *Kaminoudhia* assemblage attributes with earlier and later collections. Some particularities of the assemblage may have temporal significance, but determining which do is not straightforward. Part of our synopsis controls for regional differences by contrasting collections from within the Kouris River drainage and nearby. The final subsection highlights the methods and intensity of *Kaminoudhia*'s knapped stone conserving habits, attempting to relate this aspect of the assemblage to time, place, and social conditions. In the ensuing section, we tie the increasing conservation of Late EP through LC flaked stone industries to standard patterns of social and economic evolution. The last section proposes a model for interrelated changes in the parallel industries of copper and flaked stone.

The *Kaminoudhia* collection strongly suggests that selection between different cherts was a vital step in the manufacturing sequence. As we have shown, this affected choice of sources, choice of individual nodules or spalls, selection of manufacturing tools, knapping techniques, and the kinds of products surviving at the site. We believe this is generally true of Chalcolithic–EC sites, but at present it has not been well documented in Neolithic and earlier Cypriot collections. However, this discrepancy may be merely a matter of reporting.

Alternatively, the differences may accurately reflect prehistoric changes. Over time increasing familiarity with the sources and properties of different cherts throughout the island may have stimulated intensified selectivity. However, changes in availability of tool knapping kit supplies such as antler or in advertising and control of access to preferred raw materials may have had an impact. Additionally, changes may have been a response to an accumulation of ecological alterations, such as changes in river flow, beach access, or decline in deer population or of hardwoods. They may also have had a social component entailing modifications of hunting and food getting practices (see above, and Keswani 1994). Lastly, developments in competitor industries such as metallurgy and evolution of political organization (Keswani 1997) may have played a role.

The fine cherts that dominate *Kaminoudhia* are common to all the other earlier and later Kouris River drainage sites as well as to nearby early EP sites on the Akrotiri Peninsula and at Parekklisha *Shillourokambos* (see Raw Materials PG1). However, Erimi *Pamboula* selected differently or routinely employed other sources than *Kaminoudhia*. Unlike at the other sites, the most frequent cherts at *Pamboula* "… buff or gray coarse granulated chert . . ." (Seton-Williams 1936:51) evoke basal and middle Lefkara cherts. It is possible that *Pamboula* brokered supplies at its optimum. Its decline by the time of *Kaminoudhia* may have made accessibility more difficult, a situation that lasted throughout the Bronze Age.

Finally, in contrasting materials selection in the region it is possible that Seton-Williams' (1936:51) "… close grained dark brown flint, at times exhibiting considerable patination," may refer to Moni formation cherts or to the brown material of the one large (flake) core that Stekelis (1961) recorded at Sotira *Teppes*. Although the specialized fabric and attitudes to cores shown at Sotira *Teppes* and in Erimi *Pamboula* blades may not be unique to a period or place, they are consistent with both sites' prominence in their own eras and contrast with *Kaminoudhia*'s practice. Nevertheless, large scale flakes, blades, and tools may be a temporal marker tentatively associated with the Chalcolithic in Cyprus, having a slight precedent in the Sotira *Teppes* core and continuing in a highly simplified form in two *Kaminoudhia* examples.

SUMMARY OF TEMPORAL CORRELATES. There is some overall unity of knapping techniques crossing time and cultural phases identified by other material and behavioral traits. For example, throughout the EP–MC the distinction between PG3 and PG4 is mooted; PG2 detachments modified in one location are usually modified further. Over all, the current observed temporal pattern of changes in method is one of decreasing use of several techniques during the Neolithic and Early and Middle Chalcolithic, picking up again in the EC. Inversely correlated with this trajectory is the increase in percentage of flakes to blades, which becomes pronounced during the Chalcolithic, peaks in the EC, and begins to ebb in the MC. During the late EP–MC there is some evidence of decreasing snapping and retouch of distal truncations. Possibly, a decrease in linear flakes inevitably results in a decrease in distal breaks, snaps, or other scarring noticed in collections.

Other examples of waves of popularity in techniques include turning the blade core in opposite directions. This appears occasionally in the Neolithic, Chalcolithic, and at *Kaminoudhia*. Repetitive blade production from single or dual, opposed platform cores is both a Neolithic and an MC phenomena. So far this trait has not been observed in the millennia between. "Levallois"-like styles of core preparation follow the same ebb and flow. Reports on Neolithic and late EP–MC collections have documented the technique (see PG2. Cores. General comments on "Levallois"-like core technology during the EP period in Cyprus). Variations in specialist orientations complicate evaluations of burin blows, shearing, and different kinds of retouch and of changes in the rate of use of the above-mentioned styles. Bipolar reduction, important at *Kaminoudhia*, may be in the same category, although we suggested above that it is one of many conservation techniques at this site.

The problems associated with formal tool typologies have been discussed at length in this text. We have implied similar difficulties for core and scarring typologies. Nevertheless, we appreciate the potential value of typologies for relative dating purposes. We have described a few conventional tool types from *Kaminoudhia*. Just as techniques in Cyprus seem to vary by proportional representation over time, the same is true of some classic tool types. Their archaeological history indicates that changes in the frequency of tool types rather than the types themselves are the best temporal indices. This interpretation may change when more collections are published.

The naturally "backed" calcareous cortex blades, so common in the Vasilikos and Maroni Valleys, are found from the aceramic Neolithic through the LC I but are less common in the Chalcolithic than earlier or later. Parallel-sided "true" blades, including gloss ones, follow a similar pattern. The decline correlates inversely with broad blade-like flakes with a retouched edge, sometimes thick enough to be called "backing" and also sometimes with gloss. These are most frequent on late Early Prehistoric–MC sites, although they are known at least as segments as early as Cape Andreas *Kastros*. The same is true of ovoid "scrapers."

On the other hand "borers," rare when they do occur, seem to decline in numbers at the time in question. However, the smallness of the later collections may make them unrepresentative samples. The numerical decline of "borers," like the decline of end "scrapers" and nosed "scrapers" may mark the end of the EP.

An exception to these patterns may be the "end scraper" on a large parallel-sided blade, mentioned above from Erimi *Pamboula*. Seton-Williams endowed it with the title "type tool." It continues to correlate narrowly with that single affluent late Chalcolithic site and not with the late EP generally. Its absence at *Kaminoudhia* is consistent with the dating of *Kaminoudhia* and its economics.

SUMMARY OF OTHER TOOLS: PROJECTILE POINTS. Our interpretation of *Kaminoudhia* and other late Early Prehistoric–MC flakes is that they encompass an assortment of simple points, thinned and narrowed basally through varied means. Popularity of thinning and narrowing techniques may vary temporally.

OTHER MODIFICATIONS. In trying to explain distinctive features of the *Kaminoudhia* assemblage, contrasting collections should theoretically be possible, controlling for time, geography and conservation habits. Filtering out conserving traits from geographic and temporal ones would then be feasible, but in practice differences in reporting currently permit only a limited attempt.

Conservation is an all-pervasive characteristic of the *Kaminoudhia* collection and surfaces under almost every subheading in this. Conservation is also an important feature of other Cypriot assemblages, for the most part within the general vicinity. Table 7.1 lists Cypriot excavated sites and one survey site with flaked stone collections published in suitable detail or well enough known to the author to rank by degree of conservation. It orders them in temporal sequence by loose proximity to the Kouris River drainage and by a rough index of conservation. It includes the two major sites in the area in question that we are unable to evaluate, Sotira *Teppes* and Kandou *Kouphovounos*. The ranking is based on published statements or author familiarity with the collections.

Table 7.1. Cypriot prehistoric knapped stone collections ordered by region and materials. Conservation status.

KOURIS RIVER DRAINAGE		ADJACENT LOCATIONS	OTHER SITES
LC	*Phaneromeni*		
MC		Alambra Mouttes, *Alonia*	
EC (Ch?)*	*Kaminoudhia*		Alambra survey, *Palaiokamina*
LCh		Pamboula	Ayious, Ayios Savvas
LN	*Kouphovounos*, Teppes		
EN		*Aetokremnos*	Ortos, Khirokitia, Tenta, Shillourokambos

Key: For convenience sake except for Khirokitia *Vouni*, Prastio *Ayios Savvas tis Karonos* Monastery, and the two Alambra assemblages, collections are listed alphabetically by site name without village referents. (For sources of information see supra and specific site reports.) *Underlined Bold Italic* = Conserving; *Bold Italic* = Conserving of some material (other than obsidian); *Italic* = Unknown; Plain = Non-Conserving; *Dating speculative.

The table does not contain enough examples to interpret variations with confidence. More data are needed to evaluate if any of the differences are significant or haphazard. Table 7.1 records some conservation at most periods. Nevertheless, it peaks in the Bronze Age. The phenomenon is even more evident if we place the uncertainly dated small collection at Agrokipia *Palaiokamina* in abeyance. Moreover, the basis for including the Akrotiri *Aetokremnos* assemblage is different from the basis for the others (see Morris 1977; Smith 1996). Its smallness and microlithic methodology may have had little to do with avoiding running out of stone for knapping. If we discount it, then conserving may be a Bronze Age trait (observed by three different teams).

Moving from temporal correlations to geographic ones, the Kouris Drainage and nearby sites were particularly prone to conserving. However, this is based on a maximum of three sites, accepting Akrotiri *Aetokremnos* as one of them. It does not take into account two major sites in the drainage that we cannot evaluate and considers Erimi *Pamboula* to be the exception that proves the rule. At present, overall assemblage conservation cannot be taken as a temporal marker alone, but when tied closely to locality it may be useful.

The picture changes if we look at conservation more narrowly by types of materials or differences in conservation strategies. Table 7.2 summarizes references to conservation of particular materials mentioned in or inferred from reports. It lists only sites with specific references to conservation of a particular material or in the case of obsidian known to have only a few small fragments. The table suffers from a shortage of data, possible over interpretation, and differences in analytical interests and styles of researchers. Bearing this in mind it presents a stark contrast between the EP and Bronze Age.

Table 7.2 reveals a clear pattern of change in conservation of particular materials between the early EP and Bronze Age. There is a switch from prizing obsidian to selecting indigenous fine and banded Lefkara cherts. This may be an illusory alteration due to reports. If not, it should probably not be viewed as independent of changes in other variables. The pattern may be associated with alteration in blade manufacturing materials and techniques as well as increasing demand for ovoid "scrapers" (see supra and Debney 1997; Smith 1996). However, it might have archaeological utility as a temporal indicator.

It may also carry further implications about changing control of resources. Comparing Tables 7.1 and 7.2 raises the possibility that non conserving sites in each era, such as Parekklisha *Shillourokambos*, Prastio *Ayios Savvas tis Karonos* Monastery, Kalavasos *Ayious*, Alambra (survey), Erimi *Pamboula*, or Alambra *Mouttes*, played key roles in dominating sources and distribution of the specific materials worth preserving at the time.

Table 7.2. Cypriot prehistoric knapped stone collections: conservation of specific materials.

PERIOD	SITE	FINES	GRAY/ORANGE BANDED	OTHER NON-OBSIDIAN	OBSIDIAN
LC	*Phaneromeni*	+	+	Absent	
EC/MC	*Alonia*		+		Absent
EC	*Kaminoudhia*	+	+	+	Absent
(Ch?)*	*Palaiokamina?*	+			Absent
EN	*Ortos*				+
	Kastros		-		+
	Khirokitia		-	+	
	Tenta		-	+	
PPN	*Aetokremnos*	+			Absent
	Shillourokambos	-		Absent	

Key: Except for Khirokitia *Vouni*, collections are listed by site name without village referents. (For sources of information see supra and collection reports in bibliography.) **Bold = Kouris River Drainage and nearby region**; * = dating speculative; plus = conserving; minus = abundant; Absent = none in the collection; blank space = not possible to evaluate.

In the earlier era this was primarily imported obsidian that was generally replaced with indigenous Lefkara fine and banded cherts by the Bronze Age. However, we hypothesize the change took place long before and affected many more categories of materials. Future research may fill in the picture. Tables 7.1 and 7.2 imply a precedent as early as Akrotiri *Aetokremnos*. We further hypothesize that the categories of conserved knapped stone raw materials changed again in subsequent eras. Moreover, the practice of substituting one material for another, while conserving some classes of items of the older kind, extends to the relationship between knapped stone products and metallurgy.

SUMMARY OF METHODOLOGICAL DIFFERENCES IN CONSERVATION WITHIN A REGION.
Table 7.2 shows that conserving sites in the same region safeguarded the same materials. This is predictable, but what is important is how their conservation strategies differed, even between temporally relatively close sites. The methodological differences form a local temporal index. We suggest that the following collection traits may have been means of conserving materials at *Kaminoudhia*:

1) Discriminating initial selection of materials
2) Substantial preliminary reduction before reaching the site

3) Working most chert brought to the site

4) Preserving very few chunks and chips, which suggests that most were reduced farther

5) Domination of small products

6) Reorienting cores ninety or 180 degrees

7) Employing bipolar reduction for small PG2s

8) Specialized technique for reducing distinctive miniature cores

9) Standard detaching of PG2s through a soft to medium hammer technique

10) Angling of detachments perhaps to maximize width to length ratios

11) A high ratio of round "scrapers" to end "scrapers," which may constitute particularly heavily curated versions of the same tool

12) Intense use and reuse of blades and blade-like flakes

13) Resharpening of most blades that survived gloss-forming actions; reuse of many of these in further gloss-creating tasks; curation so intense of at least one blade that its laterals became concave

14) Intense curation of banded medium-grained semi-translucent Middle Lefkara chert flakes

These traits may occur elsewhere even if not underlined in publications. We suggest that #1 was true of all prehistoric Cypriot collections but believe at *Kaminoudhia* it was particularly aimed at maximizing materials rather than other goals. Number 5 is reported of Episkopi *Phaneromeni* and #4 and #6 at both Akrotiri *Aetokremnos* and Episkopi *Phaneromeni*. The sheer number of combined techniques at *Kaminoudhia* amounts to a large commitment to conserving materials.

Although at *Kaminoudhia* conservation of material affected every aspect of the assemblage, two important methods used by non-contemporary sites in the region are rare. Unlike the very early site of Akrotiri *Aetokremnos,* a strict microlithic technique is absent with the possible exceptions of specimens f233 and f74. Microlithic core tablets, thumbnail scrapers and other formal microlithic tools, such as geometrics severed from true blades or shaped by very small retouch scars, are not featured at *Kaminoudhia*. The microlithic strategy they represent is still currently equitable first and foremost to the earliest aceramic period (Simmons 1996, 1992, 1991a, 1991b, 1989, 1988, Simmons and Rose 1999). *Kaminoudhia's* maximizing of materials took a different form.

Contrary to the later Episkopi *Phaneromeni*, there is very little obvious recycling (reorienting and retouching in new locations) of tools at Sotira *Kaminoudhia*. This too may qualify as a temporal/cultural difference in conservation habits. Additional data are required to discover if the marker is valid beyond the region.

SOTIRA *KAMINOUDHIA* CONSERVATION IN THE LIGHT OF HYPOTHETICAL METHODS FOR COPING WITH SHORTAGES. Without reliable sources, a community in Cyprus that required stone for knapping faced several alternatives. It could improvise with less satisfactory materials. For example, artifacts could be made with inclusions or of coarse grain, such as umber, or hematitic chert ("jasper"). These appear more frequently in assemblages in or near the Troodos, especially at Kataliontas *Kourvellos* (Watkins 1979), and at sites located farther down the valleys.

The population could accept the limitations of widespread but not particularly fine materials and adapt its method of manufacture accordingly. In such a situation we would predict that large amounts of raw material would be found archaeologically. This seems to have been the case in the Vasilikos and Maroni Valleys, where the abundant medium-grained, tabular, banded chert has been used extensively for blades and flakes with natural backing from the earliest aceramic Neolithic sites to at least the Late Bronze Age. These calcareous layers are intercalated between the cherts in the raw material. Comparable patterns may explain conditions at Chalcolithic Prastio *Ayios Savvas tis Karonos* Monastery with its heavy use of basal Lefkara cherts from nearby fields for a large deliberate, unmodified flake industry. Variations on the pattern apply to Alambra *Mouttes* and Marki *Alonia* (see supra).

Obstacles to easy acquisition might encourage people encountering desired quality cherts to minimize long distance hauling by initiating the reduction activity in situ either purposely or on a chance basis. The implements created can then be conveyed to their projected place of use as shaped products either in their final state or in need of only minimal further reduction. Suitable raw materials or chipped stone in any stage of modification can be sought directly from distant collection spots or acquired through exchange with people settled closer to the sources, with or without intermediaries. The consequence of this pattern would be little representation of raw materials (PG1) but a high percentage of later products, probably mixed with a few exotics or imports. This is very much the *Kaminoudhia* picture.

Knappers lacking immediate access to good sources of raw material may strategically conserve what materials they acquire. Stockpiling, sparing use, attempts to extract the maximum amount of working edge possible out of the chunk of stone being reduced, maximum amount of surface per block, or maximum number of products, through application of an appropriate manufacturing technology, careful handling of finished products, reuse and recycling could all accomplish this goal. In varying degrees each of these approaches appears at *Kaminoudhia*. They also occur in select products during some EP sites and at Marki *Alonia* (see Table 7.2).

More radical means of coping with an unsatisfactory supply of a needed resource, include moving closer to the resource, forcibly taking control of those closer to the resource and its distribution, resorting to an alternate technology (such as one previously used, a contemporary borrowed one, or a novel invention that does not rely upon the resource), and finally, facing economic collapse, depending upon exactly how crucial the resource may be. Each of these may be impossible to document archaeologically.

At *Kaminoudhia* the evidence points to the importance of solutions three and four. However, the discussion under the fifth solution raises several issues with implications for the archaeology of the period. These are discussed in the following sections.

IMPORTANCE OF PREHISTORIC SITE LOCATONS TO CHERT SOURCES. To what extent were prehistoric Cypriot so-called settlement sites also extraction and processing sites? More specifically, how important was proximity to preferred chert sources to selection of settlement location, and to its expansion and waning? These factors may be more significant than previously considered. As we have seen above, many major Cypriot EP–MC sites are well placed for either good cherts or abundant usable poorer quality ones. This is especially true of the large aceramic Neolithic settlements but continues as late as the MC (for example at Marki *Alonia* and Alambra *Mouttes)*, which suggests continued importance of knapping or knapped products in the daily life of the time. Sotira *Teppes,* Kantou *Kouphovounos,* Erimi *Pamboula,* Sotira *Kaminoudhia* and Episkopi *Phaneromeni* are more the exceptions than the rule because they are not close to a reliable knapping stone source.

If this observation is accurate, a few specific sites pose intriguing avenues of inquiry. Firstly, what other resources explain the location and development of the sites just mentioned that are not well positioned for preferred cherts? Secondly, determining the nature of both Sotira *Teppes*'s and Erimi *Pamboula*'s sources becomes an even more important matter of inquiry, given the sites' statuses and their consumption of materials unlike those at Sotira *Kaminoudhia* and Episkopi *Phaneromeni.* Thirdly, how and to what extent did Neolithic Kantou *Kouphovounos* and Sotira *Teppes* conserve? If either did not, as the large core from Sotira *Teppes* mentioned previously suggests, why were its needs different from adjacent, later *Kaminoudhia*? What changed? Was it merely a matter of labor being more available for acquisition and replenishment of chert stocks in the earlier period?

The impact on knapped stone of decreasingly land-extensive, increasingly labor-intensive food production is significant. Globally, the evolution of knapped stone technology during the Paleolithic resulted in more and more centimeters of tool edge per lump of raw material. From the earliest core and flake tools, through prepared core tools to prismatic blades, with some increased investment of time and preplanning, we see more edge-produced artifacts. Paradoxically, in Cyprus, from Neolithic to Chalcolithic and continuing through the EC, we note a reversal of this pattern. Why was there a return to less edge and more surface per detachment? One explanation may be that more surface per nodule of material was desired in the Chalcolithic and Bronze Age to serve functional needs. Evaluating tool function and the reasons for the origin of new ones and decrease in previous ones is an ongoing area of research. It should be possible in the future to support, modify, or refute the suggestion that the change from a blade-based to a flake-based and minimally modified flake tool tradition was functionally driven.

A different possibility relates to allocation of time and energy. The cultural and economic changes in the Chalcolithic and EC–MC in Cyprus correspond to an increasingly labor intensive and decreasingly land extensive food acquisition system. Investing time and energy in the routine manufacture of knapped artifacts was probably less expeditious in our period than it had been in the more land extensive economy of the Neolithic. The author would predict that the plateau of the trajectory described will be seen in LC knapped stone collections when they are studied. We believe, at that period of far more intense occupational specialization and concomitant social stratification, the knapper's craft was less of a subsistence skill required of all families and more of a specialist activity in the more densely populated settings of Cypriot heterarchies (Keswani 1997). This last situation has persevered since that time.

IMPLICATIONS AND THEORETICAL CONCERNS FOR PREHISTORIC ARCHAEOLOGY. A MODEL FOR THE EVOLUTION OF COPPER METALLURGY IN RELATION TO KNAPPING.
Explanations for the rise of metallurgy might usefully extend Binfordian ideas about the incentive to control supplies for those at the periphery. Here we describe multi-mode model of copper metallurgy incorporation into society in relation to knapped stone. It combines present understanding of the archaeological record, historical patterns, technical innovation, and anthropological concepts of culture change. Each mode involved diverse products and smaller steps which did not always leave archaeological traces. We show which steps are demonstrable within the Eastern Mediterranean. While our concern here is with the overall process, it might be valid for the relationship of other classes of technological change to society.

We underline that we do not envisage a unilinear path impelled by each stage to the next. Each mode permits maintenance of status quo or movement into the adjacent one(s) in either direction. After describing each mode, we discuss its dating in Cypriot context. We also consider the possible impetus for transformation from one mode to another.

Table 7.3. Model for the evolution of copper metallurgy in relation to knapping.

Mode 0. No utilization of any metal in any way.

Probable lithic impact*	n/a
Probable economic, ecological, and social impact	n/a
Probable archaeological evidence	None

Mode 1. A likely initial exploration of the properties of raw and modified copper was part of working other kinds of stone.

Probable lithic impact	None
Probable economic, ecological, and social impact	None
Probable archaeological evidence	None

Mode 2. We suggest that the first function of worked copper was for novelties such as beaten or wire jewelry, hooks, wire, sheets, and knapping bits. Although the novelty value overlaps and merges with practical uses for some artifacts, this does not change the likelihood that society's interest in small copper objects would have required little commitment of time, energy, or affect and would not have altered routine use of knapped and ground stone products.

      We disagree with Rosen's assertion that the earliest copper goods are specialized religious ritual props ("cult"). However, we believe it is possible that, at some point in this mode in the Cypriot EP, small cast copper figurines that have not survived predate, prefigure, or parallel picrolite and clay Chalcolithic ones. The plaque-like form, minimally elaborated backs, size, coloring, changes in coloring, and polished finish of picrolite bent knee human figurines evoke cast copper techniques and limitations. This might explain the absence of picrolite figurines at Chalcolithic sites in regions that have important bronze working or redistributing sites during the Bronze Age. For example, under this scenario clay variants at Kalavasos *Ayious* would not be a poorer site's imitation of inaccessible picrolite figurines from more lavish sites in the Western part of the island but local variants of local copper ones.

Probable lithic impact	None to slight
Probable economic, ecological, and social impact	None to slight
Probable archaeological evidence	None to slight

Mode 3. Moving an innovation into this stage requires backing. Promoting a new tool into the larger society requires the interest, the wealth, and the power of the endowed segments of society. In ranked, heterarchical, and stratified societies this means the corporate bodies are seeking new techniques, new resources, and new symbols of status inequality. In this mode copper for *objets d'art*, sacred goods, symbols of wealth, weapons, and tools meet a created demand for prestige goods, media of exchange, and all-pervasive symbols of power. This stage is often inaccurately described as "becoming established" or "the first," because it is most visibly documented in graves and at settlement sites. It is also here that the material goods are most likely to be endowed with meta-physical properties by the powerful and used in enactments of their relationships (religious ritual/"cult") as legitimating power inequalities.

      It is in this mode that copper goods sequentially replace stone ones. Copper methodology here includes deliberate, purposeful exploration of new sources and creation of new mining methods, production techniques, consumers, and distribution arrangements. Certain individuals, sodalities, or geographic communities become specialists in copper production and distribution or in component parts of the process on a part or full-time basis. Under these circumstances training or apprenticeship requirements mitigate against the skill becoming a univer-sal one beyond gender and age differentiation. The corollary is that knapping becomes an obscure, or non-affluent individual or sub-community specialization, to which, unlike in Modes 1 or 2, not all members of the community have access. Competing time constraints due to commitment to competing specializations, or to economic impoverishment, mitigate against universality of training in production of and access to products.

      In this mode, a return to Mode 1 or 2 would require an overturning of established social and economic inequalities depending upon the subculture, community, and status of the individuals or political body. Mainte-nance of the status quo is more likely. A new technology (e.g., iron, glass, plastic) would move through variants of modes 1–3 and replace both copper and knapped stone.

Probable lithic impact	Slight to pronounced varying by community and date
Probable economic, ecological, and social impact	Extremely pronounced
Probable archaeological evidence	None to pronounced

Mode 4. This is the current global situation. Knapping has become a forgotten technique, almost inaccessible through living memory. To participate requires reinventing extinct processes. Copper metallurgy is no longer in competition with knapping, even in its most obscure and specialized or long-lasting uses (locally for *dhoukani* and firearms). Other materials have replaced copper's hegemony.

Known lithic impact	Pronounced to devastating
Known economic, ecological, and social impact	Extremely pronounced
Probable archaeological evidence	None to pronouonced

*Impact pertains to effect on society at the height of implementation of the mode in question, relative to the previous mode. n/a = not applicable.

We do not believe the first or early steps in any of the modes can be identified empirically. Copper survives poorly, and the first identification of anything in the archaeological record is an *ante quem* date. Although copper is documented in Cyprus during the Chalcolithic, its use and its being taken up socially may be far earlier.

Although antler for modern knappers is one of the most appreciated tool kit materials for pressure flakers and indirect percussors, it may have given way to other materials in later prehistory. In Cyprus by the late Chalcolithic, pollen, faunal, pedological, hydrological, and shifting settlement patterns record decrease in forest cover, appropriate forage and browse, and deer percentages on settlement sites (Simmons and Kingsnorth 1996a). Alteration of the role of deer during the Chalcolithic and Bronze Age turned deer hunting into a smaller part of the economy than previously and with a new status (Keswani 1994). Fresh antler may have become a less abundant and less acceptable commodity for knapping. Alternative knapping reduction tools and methods may have taken on increasing importance. In the case of percussors these could initially have been "hammerstones." Hard copper points that were perhaps hafted may have been used as pressure flakers or indirect percussion implements. Mode 2 is evident in the Cypriot Chalcolithic. Mode 3 is most evident in the EC–LC.

When Mode 2 supplanted Mode 3, copper products became an alternative to stone. It is possible that expansion of copper metallurgy gained its impetus beyond insiders' craft tool from settlement incursions into areas not located close to suitable cherts. As food getting became more labor intensive, procuring raw material for knapped stone may have become less cost effective than obtaining finished copper products. This could be particularly true if some communities or sectors of society were able to dominate chert sources or product creation through increasing occupational specialization, necessitating exchange of goods and services for survival, in lieu of universal participation in subsistence activities. We have seen indications of both in differences between knapped stone resources and products of Erimi *Pamboula* and Sotira *Kaminoudhia*.

In conclusion, we hypothesize that Mode 0 through Mode 2 are associated with societies in which status distinctions are restricted to age, gender, part-time religious specialization, and cultural/ecological area differences but are otherwise not corporate. Traditional anthropology calls these conditions "egalitarian." Late twentieth century archaeology and anthropology may prefer the term "acephalous." Mode 0 through Mode 2 require only individual or immediate family/friendship participation and not societal investment of time energy, systemic physical, strategic or ideological support. Because there is so little social interest, social value, and social cost, Mode 0 through Mode 2 may have shifted between one and the other many times.

Regarding transformation into and between the other modes, we posit Mode 1 correlates to status diversity beyond that subsumed under "egalitarian" or "acephalous." Mode 2 requires corporate support and/or demand of upper echelon subgroups within society. It either initiates, furthers, or requires status differentiation. Because Modes 3 and 4 entail organic solidarity, to use an old Durkheimian concept, changes from one to the other theoretically require or reflect intense social cost. Because these changes may have occurred as other technologies were developing, both the evidence for change and later interest in the issue may have been lost.

CONCLUSIONS

The rubrics that for us would sum up the unity of Cypriot Early Prehistoric through MC knapped stone would need to move away from the item or object (core, blade, burin, microlith, composite tool) and beyond the technique (stated by prepared core, ground, or polished and implied by, core, blade, or microlith). Instead they would have to emphasize method, which is the cognitive underpinning of knapping techniques in prehistoric Cyprus.

The industries share in common an understanding of the capabilities of the wide range of available materials (including copper), how best to use them in a way that requires little to no retouch, and strategic physical orienting of all products, augmented by a range of core and dorsal preparations. Resource responsivity through preliminary preparation is one essence of EP–MC Cypriot knapping methods. Also, the industries respond to abundance with disregard for economizing but address shortages with numerous conserving stratagems. Many responses minimize secondary and tertiary reduction stages. Enhancements pertain almost exclusively to proximal hafting or conservation rather than to basic tool formation or to social differentiation. The cognitive and technical simplicity of adaptation to resource availability, whether due to location, seasonality, or long-term changes, unifies Cypriot EP–MC industries.

ACKNOWLEDGEMENTS

During the summer of 1984, under the auspices of the American Schools of Oriental Research (ASOR), the author had the good fortune to spend four weeks studying knapped stone from the previous seasons' excavations at Sotira *Kaminoudhia*. In 1991 as a Charles U. and Janet Harris Fellow, the author reviewed materials collected since that time as well as the results of colleagues working on other aspects of the site, and an initial draft of the present report was completed. We wish to express great indebtedness to ASOR, to the Charles U. and Janet Harris Fellowship donors and selection committee and above all to Helena Swiny for their ongoing, enlightened support and invariably friendly assistance. We extend gratitude for their support, insights, and succor to John Coleman, Michael Given, Sylvie Hartmann, Larissa Hordynsky, Ian Humphreys, Douglas K. Beard, Rodney Kingsnorth, Tally Kingsnorth, Frank Koucky, Astero Machliotis, Carole McCartney, Vathoulla Moustoukki, Alan Simmons, Alessandra Swiny, Folly Swiny, Philip Swiny, A. Voll, Marella Webb, Gillian Webster, and Elizabeth Wheeler-Ludlow.

Perlès (1987) recommends that lithics specialists summarize their background, because their experience affects their perceptions and interpretations of materials. The author has probably handled as many Cypriot lithics as all but a handful of other specialists. First hand familiarity with lithics outside of Cyprus is very moderate and based predominantly in Great Britain, France, Mexico and the Western United States. For over twenty years she taught more than twelve different introductory anthropology courses.

OBJECT–FIGURE CONCORDANCE FOR KNAPPED STONE

OBJECT #	FIGURE #	TYPE (*indicates type identification by G. Holdridge)	AREA	OPERATION	UNIT	LOT
F1	7	core on flake/retouch/ triangular +hafted/pos. proj. point	A	I17A	20	2
F2	11	tabular scraper/ circular- abrupt retouching	A	H17C	1	5
F6	1	core on flake/ primary flake	C	H17C	1	15
F9	7	right distal retouched/ left distal pointed impl./pos. proj. point	C	H24C	21	2
F11	15	core on flake/ ret/pointed impl	C	H24A	21	6
F12	11	Blade	C	H24A		4
F13	15	*scraper	C	H24A	21	6
F14	7	Levallois-like core	C	H24A	21	5
F16	9	blade/ off center bulb	C	I24A		
F17	9	blade / off center bulb/core on flake	C	H24A	21	6
F18	8	blade-like flake/pos. proj. point	C	I23C	9	8
F19	7	miniature flake	C	I24A	2	11
F20	13	*scraper	C	H24A	21	6
F22	9	blade/ core on flake/ miniature flake	C	H24A	21	5
F23	13	blade-like flake	C	H24A	21	6
F26	17	proj. point	C	H24B	22	6
F27	13	blade-like flake	C	H24A	21	5
F28	4	core on flake	C	H24A	21	5
F29	9	Pointed impl.	C	H24A	21	5
F34	13	Blade	C	H24A	21	6
F35	13	Blade				
F36	13	Blade	B	C19D/C20A	12	11
F37	13	Scraper				
F38	13	blade/pos. endscraper	A	H17D	15	19
F39	13	blade with thinning	A	I17A	BAULK	
F41	17	Possible projectile point	C	H24B	22	6
F42	17	Possible projectile point	C	H24B	22	6
F43	8	blade-like flake/ pointed end	A	I17A	45	9/7?
F44	1	Scraper	C	H17C	1	15
F45	1	core on flake	C	I24C		
F46	15	flake/ notched impl.	C	I23C	9	12
F47	13	blade/ blade-like flake w/gloss	C	H24C	21	3
F48	7	retouched flake/pos. proj. point	A	H17D	15	15
F49	11	blade like flake with gloss	C	H24B		3
F50	11	Discoid scraper	C	H24D2		
F52	11	core on flake-discoid scraper	A	G17D/C20A		11

F53	11	Discoid scraper	B	C19D	12	5
F54	9	retouched flake	C	H24A	21	5
F55	12	core on flake/retouched/circular scraper		C14D		7
F57	9	miniature flake	A	I17A	20	5
F59	14	Retouched flake	A	H17C	1	9
F60	14	hafted flake with gloss	A	H17C	1	7
F61	14	hafted flake with gloss	A	H17C	1	7
F62	17	hafted flake with gloss	A	H17C	1	7
F63	9	*blade-like flake	A	H17C	1	9
F65	14	Flake	A	H17C	1	24
F66	14	Core	A	H17C		10
F67	9	Bladelet	A	G17D	5	5
F68	8	blade like flake/ burin blow edge	A	G17D	5	5
F69	7	Levallois like core	A	G17D	5	5
F70	1	core on flake	A	G17D	5	15
F71	2	Blade	C	H24C		6
F72	7	Levallois-like core	A	H17C	1	15
F73	7	Levallois- like core		C18		
F74	7	Levallois-like core		A3		
F75	7	Levallois-like core		C8		
F77	8	Pointed impl.	A	G17D	7	4
F78	8	Worked flake	A	G17D	5	8
F79	8	modified blank	C	H24D	8	7
F80	12	Scraper	B	C19D	12	8
F82	12	Scraper				
F83	2	Core	A	G17D	7	4
F84	14	core on flake	A	G17D	7	4
F86	17	Pointed impl.	C	H24B	21	6
F87	17	Pointed impl./ pos. proj. point	C	H24B	22	6
F88	17	Pointed impl.	C	H24B	22	6
F89	17	Pointed impl./ pos. proj. point	C	H24B	21	6
F90	9	blade fragment	C	H24A	21	6
F97	8	Levallois- like core	C	I24A		
F99	4	miniature flake/ detached from 100/stock				
F100	4	flake "core"/ attached to 99/stock				
F101	3	Core	C	G17D	5	5
F102	2	core/ chopper tool	A	G17D	5	8
F103	2	core on flake	A	G17D	5	8
F105	8	Pointed impl./pos. hafted	A	H18A		13
F107	6	miniature flake	A	G17D	5	3
F108	8	miniature flake/pos. proj. point	A	G17D	7	2
F109	7	Core	A	G17D	7	2
F110	8	miniature flake	C	I24B	10	3
F111	14	bladelet/miniature flake	C	I24B	10	3
F112	2	retouched flake	C	I24B	10	3

F114	15	miniature flake	C	H24A	21	6
F115	15	miniature flake	C	H24A	21	6
F116	15	miniature flake	C	H24A	21	6
F117	16	miniature flake	C	H24A	21	6
F118	16	*blade fragment				
F119	16	miniature flake	C	H24A	21	6
F120	16	*blade fragment	C	H24A	21	6
F121	16	*blade fragment	C	H24A	21	6
F122	16	*blade fragment	C	H24A		6
F123	16	*blade fragment	C	H24A	21	6
F124	16	miniature flake	C	H24A	21	6
F125	16	Flake	C	H24A	21	6
F126	16	miniature flake	C	H24A	21	6
F127	26	miniature flake	C	H24A	21	6
F128	16	miniature flake	C	H24A	21	6
F129	16	miniature flake	C	H24A	21	6
F130	16	*flake	C	H24A	21	6
F131	16	*flake	C	H24A	21	6
F132	17	*flake	C	H24A	21	6
F133	17	Chip	C	H24A	21	6
F134	17	Chip	A	G17A		
F136	8	miniature flake/	A	I17C	15	7
F138	8	pointed impl..	A	G18B	6	4
F140	2	Core/for blade or bladelet production	C	H24A		1
F141	3	Core	B	C19D	12	6
F142	3	Core	C	I24B	17	7
F143	6	Large flake/unworked/ stock	C	I24C	10	17
F144	5	Large flake/unworked stock	C	I24C	10	17
F145	12	discoid scraper	A	H17C	1	5
F146	6	*miniature flake	A	H17C	3	10
F147	6	*reused blade fragment	A	H17C	3	10
F148	9	Flake				
F149	6	miniature flake	A	H17	3	10
F150	6	miniature flake	A	H17C	3	10
F154	4	core with impl.				
F155	1	miniature flake		C3		
F156	14	hafted flake	A	H17C	1	7
F157	7	miniature flake	A	H17C	1	9
F158	7	Chip	A	H17C	1	9
F159	7	miniature flake	A	H17C	1	9
F161	7	Core	A	H17C	1	9
F162	7	Chip	A	H17C	1	9
F163	7	miniature flake	A	H17C	1	9
F164	7	Chip	A	H17C	1	9
F165	5	psuedo-denticulated		A2		
F166	3	Core	A	G17D	5	5
F167	1	*pointed impl.	C	H24D	8	7

F169	8	blade-like flake	C	H24D	8	7
F170	8	blade-like flake	A	H17B	3	3
F171	3	core/ chopper tool	A	G17D	5	8
F172	3	Core	C	H24A	21	5
F173	6	*scraper		C1		
F174	6	miniature flake	A	G17D	7	4
F175	6	miniature flake	C	H24A	21	6
F176	6	pointed impl..	A	I17A	20	5
F177	3	miniature flake		A4		
F178	10	*flake		C6		
F179	10	Core on flake-into ret tool		C7		
F180	10	*flake		C16		
F181	5	*pointed impl.	C	H24D	8	7
F183	16	Core on flake		C5		
F185	3	miniature flake	C	H18B	39	7
F186	15	Core on flake/pointed impl.	A	H18B	29	7
F187	12	End scraper	A	H18B		7
F188	6	Core on flake/ miniature flake	A	I17A	19	8
F189	10	hafted flake/core on flake	A	I17A	19	8
F190	15	*bladelet	A	I17A	19	8
F191	14	blade-like flake	C	H23D	22	3
F193	1	Core	A	H17C	1	16
F194	1	hafted flake	A	H17C	1	16
F195	1	Core	A	H17C	1	16
F196	1	Core on flake/primary flake	A	H17C	1	16
F197	10	Levallois-like core	A	H17C	1	16
F198	2	Core	A	H17C	1	16
F199	1	*miniature flake	C	H17C	1	16
F201	1	Core on flake/primary flake	C	H24D	8	7
F202	9	small flake/ pointed impl..	A	H17C	1	15
F203	1	*miniature flake	A	H17C	1	16
F205	8	pointed impl.	A	G17D	7	4
F206	6	miniature flake	A	G17D	5	8
F207	9	Core on flake / bladelet prodiction	A	H17D	15	19
F208	15	pointed impl.	A	H17D	15	19
F209	15	*flake	A	H17D	15	19
F210	15	pointed impl.	A	H17D	15	19
F211	3	Core	C	H18B	39	7
F212	5	scraper	A	H17D		13
F213	4	miniature flake	C	H17D		13
F214	4	miniature flake	C	H17D		13
F215	4	miniature flake	C	G17C	7	3
F217	4	Core on flake/circular scraper	C	G17C	7	3
F218	15	Core on flake	A	G17C	7	3
F219	4	miniature flake	C	G17C	7	3
F220	10	miniature flake	A	G17D	5	3
F221	10	miniature flake	A	G17D	5	3

F222	10	miniature flake	A	G17D	5	3
F223	8	flake	A	G17D	5	3
F224	10	*flake	A	G17D	5	3
F225	12	scraper-thinnd at one end	A	G17D	5	3
F227	10	*core on flake	A	G17D	5	3
F228	15	*knotched impl.	A	G17D	5	3
F231	6	blade-like flake	A	H17D		9
F232	8	flake	A	H17D	16	9
F233	9	core-miniature flake/hafted /scraper /retouched	A	H17D	16	9
F235	15	flake	A	H17C	16	13
F236	15	flake	A	H17C	1	15
F237	15	*miniature flake	A	H17C	1	15
F239	15	*miniature flake	A	H17D	1	15
F241	5	core	C	H18A	16	9
F242	5	core	A	H18B	16	6
F244	15	*pointed impl.	A	H18B	6	6
F245	5	*core on flake	A	I17A	4	6
F246	5	flake	A	I17A		6
F247	5	*flake/ notched impl.	A	I17A		6
F248	5	*miniature flake	A	I17A		6
F249	5	flake/ core preparation	A	I17A		6
F250	3	flake/ core preparation-to become impl. by Levallois technique	A	I17A	4	6
F252	2	core	C	H17C	1	8
F253	6	Levallois-like flake	A	H17C	1	8

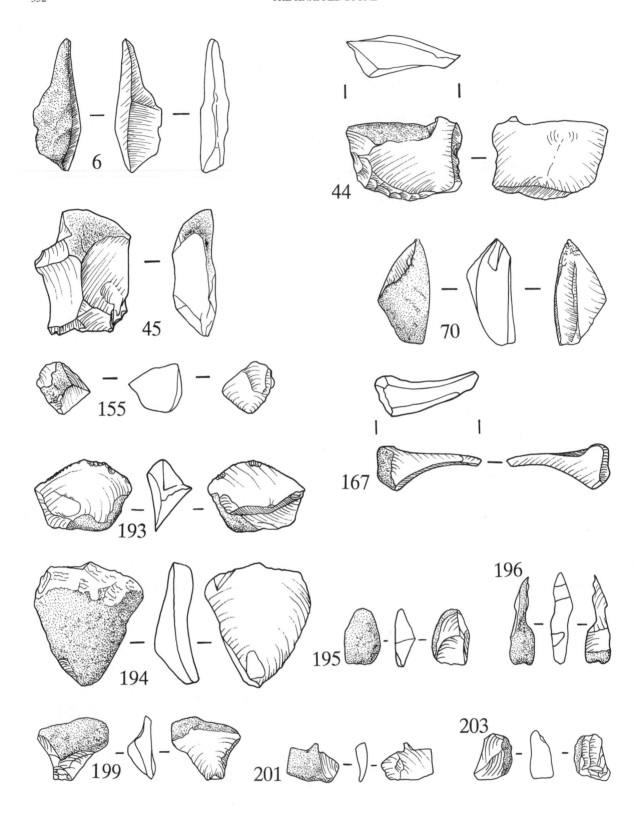

Fig. 7.1

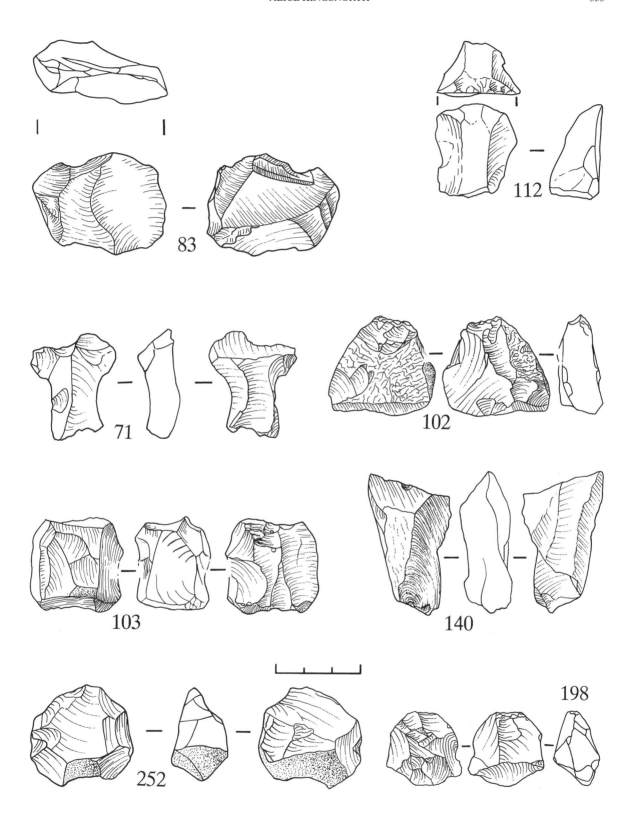

Fig. 7.2

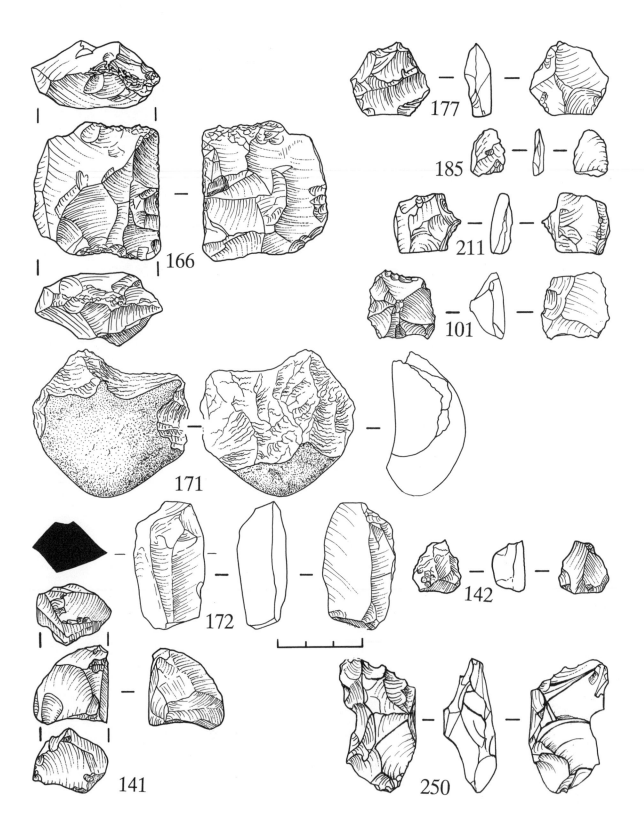

Fig. 7.3

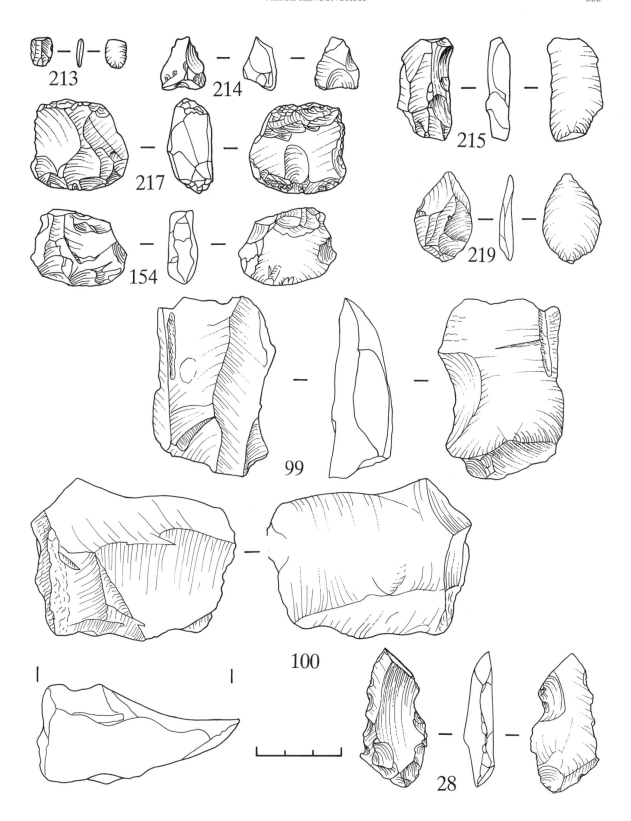

Fig. 7.4

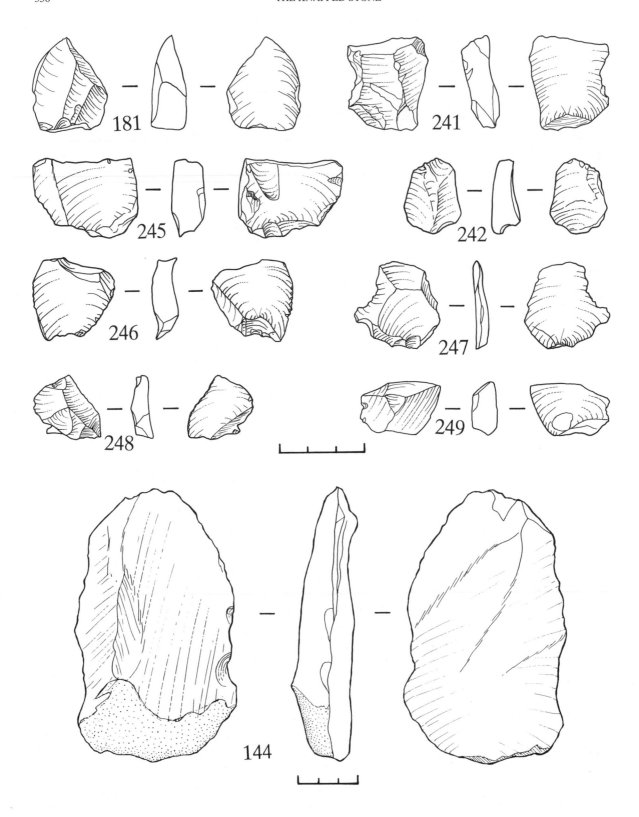

Fig. 7.5

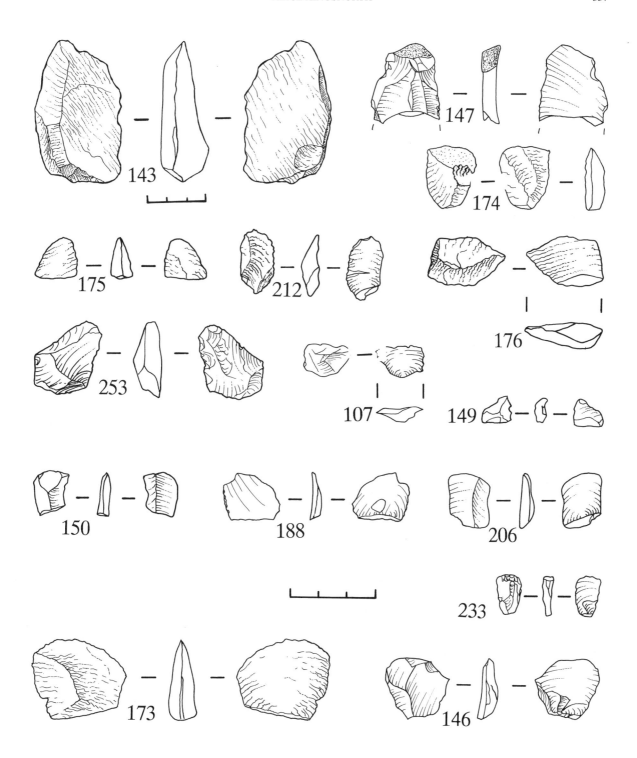

Fig. 7.6

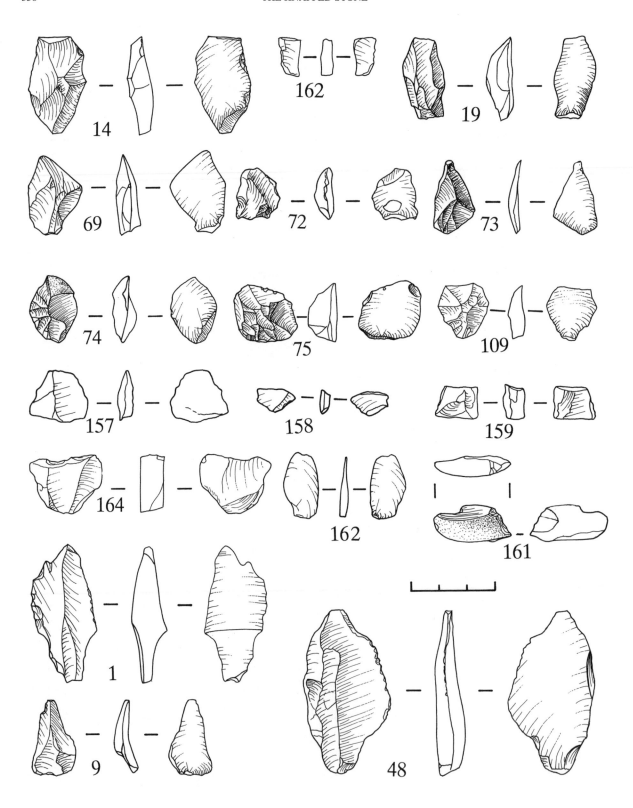

Fig. 7.7

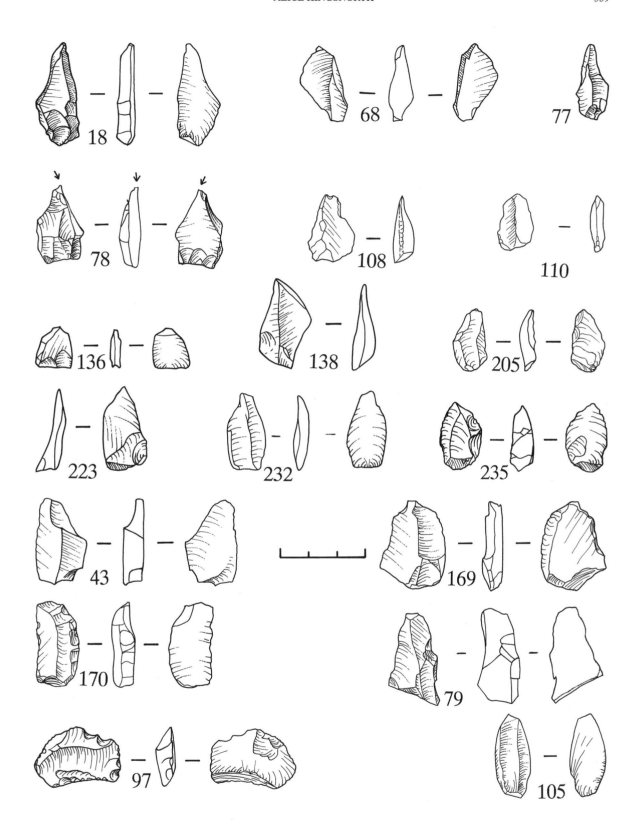

Fig. 7.8

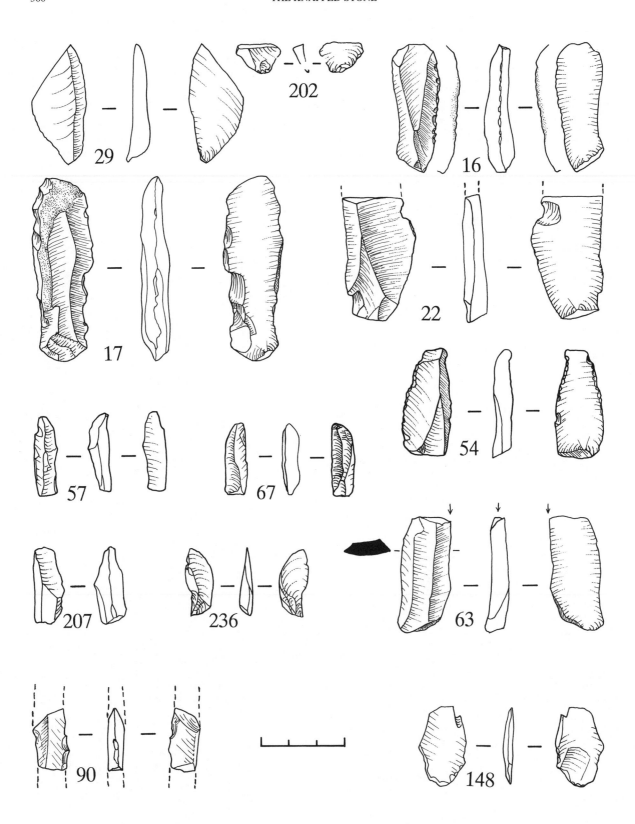

Fig. 7.9

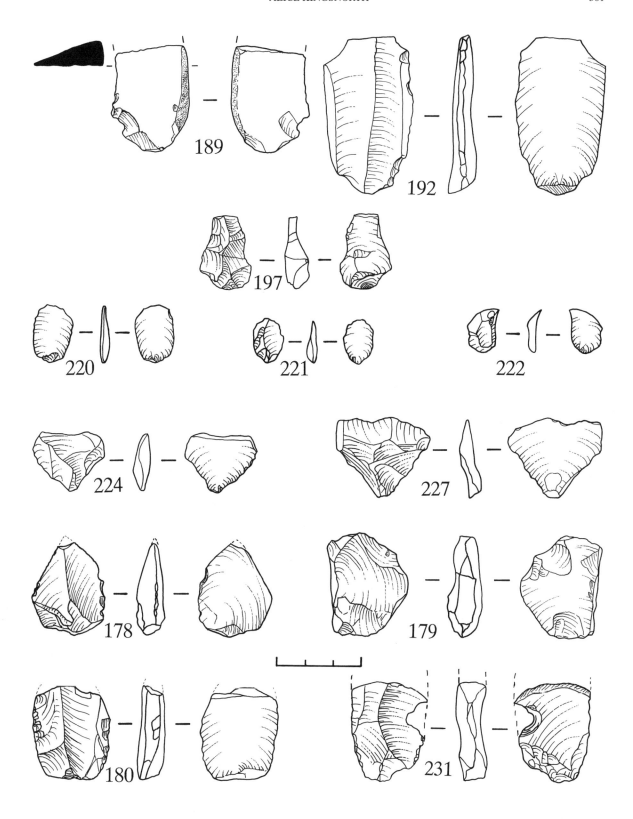

Fig. 7.10

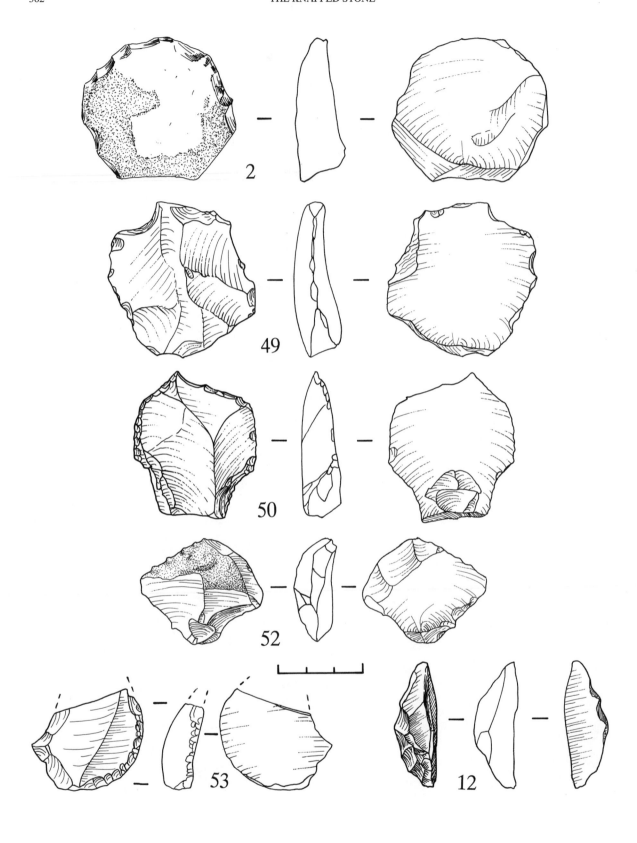

Fig. 7.11

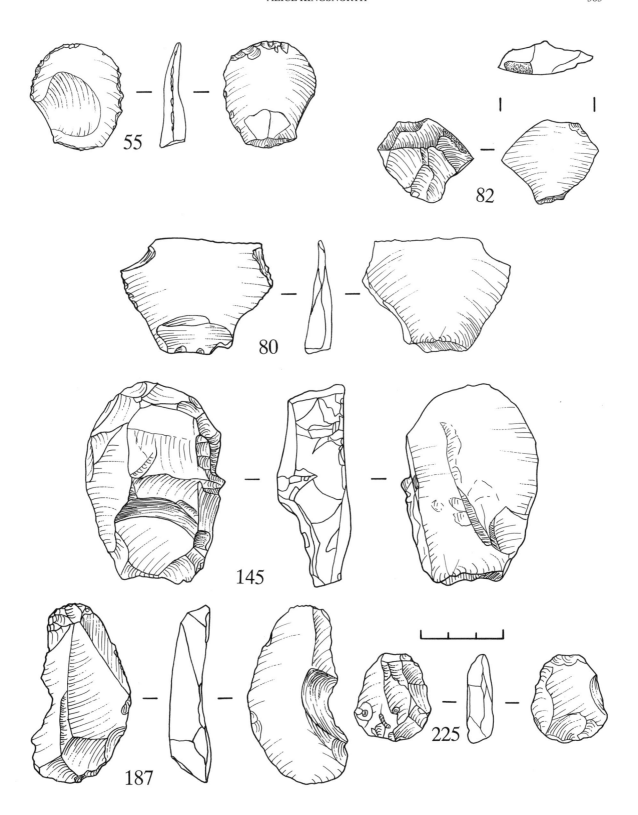

Fig. 7.12

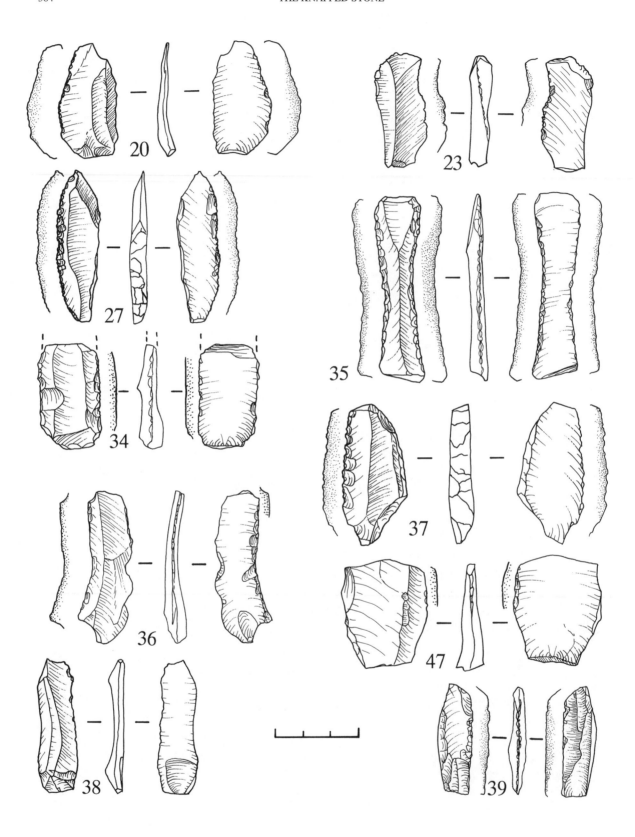

Fig. 7.13

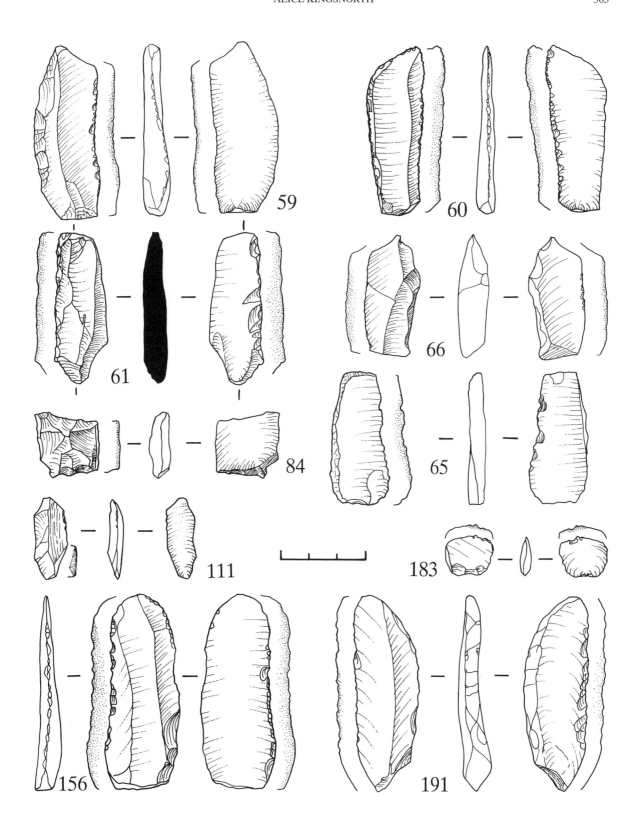

Fig. 7.14

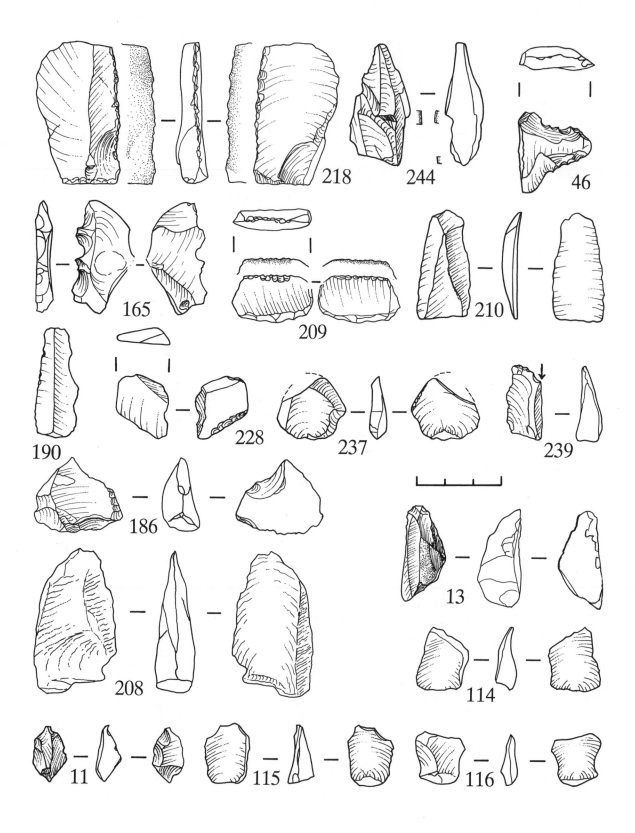

Fig. 7.15

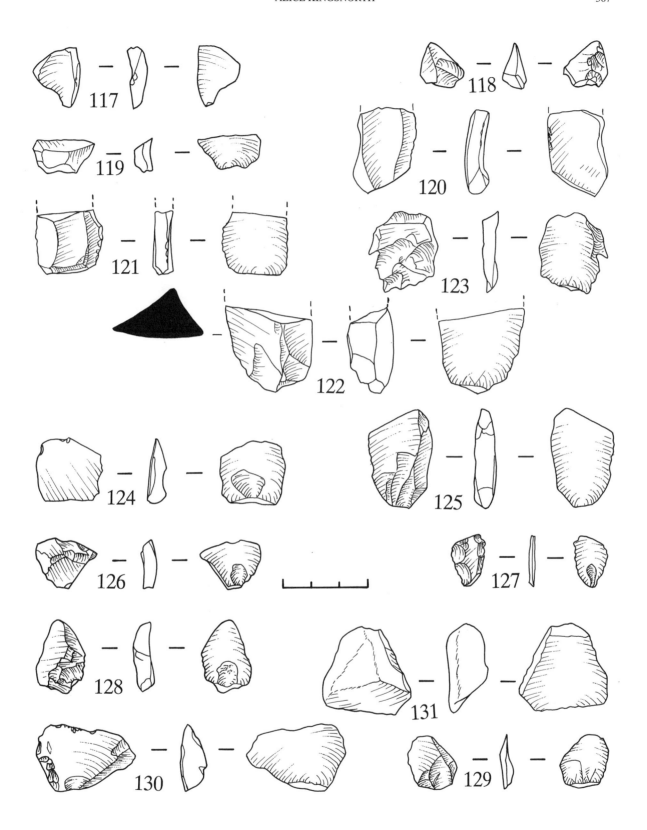

Fig. 7.16

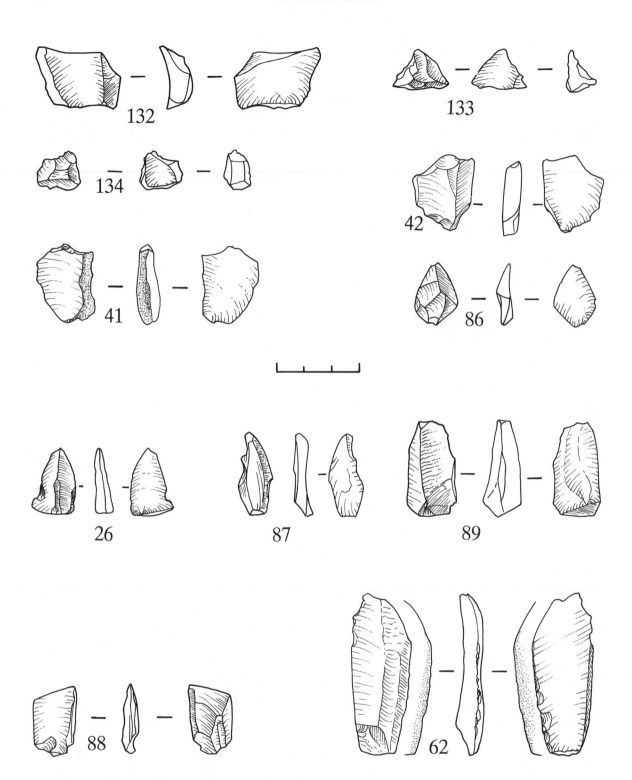

Fig. 7.17

8

THE METAL

by Stuart Swiny

INTRODUCTION

The twenty-five stratified metal finds from Sotira *Kaminoudhia* were evenly distributed between Cemetery A, with twelve items, and the settlement with thirteen (fig. 8.1). All are of copper-based metal unless otherwise stated. They were studied in the same manner as those from Episkopi *Phaneromeni*, which consists of a classification of each object followed by a discussion.

The small size, nature and broken condition of the copper-based objects excavated in the settlement suggest that the use of metal was quite common (cf. Gale et al. 1996:361). They are consistent with the expected assemblage from a settlement belonging to a mature phase of the Early Bronze Age. No evidence for smelting—which would be unlikely in view of *Kaminoudhia*'s distance from the nearest ore body—or even remelting has been recorded. Eleven items (M1, 4, 5, 13, 15, 16, 19, 21, 22, 23, and 24) were subjected to qualitative chemical analyses in 1984 by Mike Wayman and Vanda Vitali, Department of Metallurgy and Materials Science at the University of Toronto. The equipment employed was a Hitachi 520 scanning electron microscope equipped with a Tracor Northern 2000 energy dispersive analysis system. In addition to copper, all samples were found to contain a typical range of elements such as aluminum (Al), arsenic (As), calcium (Ca), iron (Fe), potassium (K), manganese (Mn), lead (Pb), sulfur (S) and silicon (Si) typically recorded in Bronze Age Cypriot metal objects. Much more significant at the time of the study was the detection of appreciable amounts of tin (Sn) in two of the Philia Phase spiral earrings, M13 and M21, which provided the earliest occurrence of tin bronze on the island. The presence of tin was later verified by Neutron Activation Analysis undertaken by Ron Hancock, Slowpoke Reactor Facility at the University of Toronto.

These results were confirmed again in 2000 by C. Giardino, G. Gigante and S. Ridolfi's quantitative X-Ray Fluorescence analyses presented in Appendix 8.1. Giardino sampled all but three (M1, 2 and 4) of the stratified metal finds—including the gold or electrum earrings—from the site, and was thus able to provide the most comprehensive analytical picture of the metal assemblage from any Cypriot Bronze Age site. The three series of analyses mean that every single metal object of significance excavated at Sotira *Kaminoudhia* has been analyzed with the exception of the fragmentary spiral earring, M2, found on bedrock (not in a tomb chamber) in Cemetery A. Note that my remarks below on the use of alloys to produce gold colored or silvery looking earrings were written prior to Giardino's study presented in Appendix 8.1. His comments suggest that there now seems to be general agreement on the use of tin and/or arsenic alloys for aesthetic purposes.

For an up-to-date discussion of Early and Middle Cypriot metal artifacts, see the discussion of the finds from Marki *Alonia* by Frankel and Webb (1996b:213 ff.) and the wide-ranging report on copper and copper working at Alambra *Mouttes* by N. Gale, Z. A. Stos-Gale and W. Fasnacht, in Coleman et al. 1996.

All measurements are in centimeters.

DAGGER

Three daggers[1] were recorded at *Kaminoudhia*, one from the cemetery (M18) and the fragments of two dagger butts with rivets still in place (M1, 27) from the settlement. As noted concerning the Episkopi *Phaneromeni* examples (Swiny 1986:69), the essential criteria for the classification of this class of objects are the shape of the butt followed by the location and number of rivets. Besides the above items, the uncast billet of a fourth dagger came from the cemetery (M12).

M18. Dagger. (Fig. 8:2, pls. 8.1a, 8.1c). Tomb 15. Copper (Cu 99.2%). Intact. L: 16.2, W: 3, Th: 0.4, L of tang: 2.8.

> Flat medium-length tang, rectangular in section with a straight-end, slightly damaged to one side. Asymmetrical straight shoulders. Long tapering blade, heavily corroded for 4 cm below one shoulder. The flattened mid-rib becomes rhomboidal in section toward the rounded point. The thinner cutting edges, especially in the section of the blade with the flattened mid-rib, are the result of work hardening.

The angular outline, straight rivetless tang, and especially the broad flat midrib make this a dagger diagnostic of the Philia Phase (Swiny 1986a:37). Stewart (1962) does not publish any similar knife/daggers, and for some reason did not include the type in his category of tanged daggers (his Type a).[2] All the provenanced Cypriot examples of daggers with this shape of mid-rib and flat tang, with or without a rivet, belong to Philia Phase sites such as Philia *Vasiliko (Laksia tou Kasinou),*[3] Vasilia *Alonia*[4] and Dhenia *Kafkalla* (see figs. 8.2, 8.3).[5] It should be noted that to date not one has been recovered from an EC burial or habitation context. Besides the provenanced pieces listed above there are at least four more examples, two believed to have come from the Vasilia area (fig. 8.2:2/23, 2/22),[6]

---

[1] Bronze Age two-edged cutting implements have been commonly described as "knives" in the Cypriot literature (see especially Åström 1972, Dikaios 1962, Stewart 1962, Swiny 1986), though not by Catling (1964). The term is in fact incorrect since a knife, by definition, has a single edged cutting blade. In order to adhere to the correct definition of the tool/weapon type, in this publication the term "dagger" has been used instead of "knife." Here the use of "dagger" does not imply that its primary function was that of a weapon: on the contrary, the evidence for sharpening in the form of concave cutting edges is quite common (Swiny 1986:69).

[2] Mrs. Eve Stewart kindly sent me a copy of the unpublished manuscript of J. R. Stewart's *Corpus of Metal Artifacts*.

[3] Pl. 8.1c; Dikaios 1962:173, fig. 84:2, 3, 4.

[4] Karageorghis 1966:326 ff., fig. 73; Swiny 1985:24; Swiny 1997:180. A detailed description of this object (illustrated in fig. 8.3:1965/V.3/7) follows: L: 23.8 cm (original overall L: 24.2 cm), Th: (at tang) 0.65 cm; Diam. of rivet hole: 0.5 cm. Weight 118 gr. Straight, slightly asymmetrical shoulders, respectively 1.9 and 2.25 cm wide. Flat tang tapering in thickness from near the shoulders to the tip, where it is 0.2 cm. Flattened barely discernible mid-rib extending from the shoulders to the tip of the blade. The dagger shows clear signs of abuse. At the tip both cutting edges have been hammered. The end of the tang has also been hammered and bent over.

[5] Catling 1964: figs. 3:1, 5:1. The hook-tanged weapon from Vasilia published in Catling 1964: fig. 1:1 is problematic (see Swiny 1985:23). The objects from Dhenia, Philia and Vasilia discussed here have been redrawn for the present publication. The writer remembers seeing a similar, unprovenanced, dagger with a flattened mid-rib in the Morphou Museum, established since 1974.

[6] These pieces, published by Webb (1997:73, nos. 334, 335), were studied, drawn and sampled by the writer in 1985, but never published. The daggers—bought from a private dealer and coming from the so-called "Vasilia

another in the Cesnola Collection of the Semitic Museum at Harvard University (1995.10.1233),[7] and a fourth in the Ligabue Collection in Venice (Karageorghis 1998:88-89). The latter is the only known hafted example: the flat rivetless tang is inserted into a large eroded bone handle. Like most of the other daggers of this class, the blade edges are very slightly concave, or to use a contemporary term, "hollow ground." An interesting feature of the dagger illustrated in fig. 8.2:2/23, not mentioned by Webb or shown in her illustration, is a series of five shallow notches cut into both sides of the tang. I had not noted anything similar in 1985, but the notching now finds a parallel in the dagger belonging to the Semitic Museum (fig. 8.2:1995.10.1233). This is the only Philia Phase object known to me from Cesnola's vast collection now scattered throughout the world, and is thus the earliest item he obtained in Cyprus. One would like to know from where it came! Did his workmen excavate a Philia Phase tomb, or was it sold to him by a villager? The dagger has up to a dozen carefully hammered grooves or indentations on all four edges of the tang, made by hammering with a sharp instrument. On one side, several very shallow grooves extend across the tang from one set of indentations to another. In hindsight, a dagger published by Stewart (1962: fig. 98:5) with several V-shaped marks on one side of the tang, may in fact have been provided with similar notches, an impression strengthened by careful scrutiny of the object's photograph published in 1988 (Hennessy et al.: fig. 61:11). These indentations and grooves seem to be connected with hafting.

Arguably the earliest copper-based dagger excavated on the island is that from Vasilia *Alonia* (redrawn for fig. 8.3:1965/V.3/7),[8] which already displays the distinctive flattened midrib, although less pronounced than on later examples. The ten accessible (i.e., excluding the Ligabue and Morphou Museum specimens) flat-tanged daggers of this type known from Cyprus are published in figs. 8.2 and 8.3.[9] In addition to their characteristic midribs, all—except Vasilia 2/5 with unusually slanting shoulders—have visibly asymmetrical shoulders. In every instance one is closer to the extremity of the tang and displays a more rounded profile; furthermore, it is always slightly broader than the other. The opposing shoulder branches off almost at right angles a few millimeters lower down the tang. Note that T4/14 has a rivet hole in the narrower, more angular shoulder, 1.35 cm wide (the other is 1.5 cm wide). It is interesting that the *Kaminoudhia* casting M12 already displays shoulders that are slightly

---

Deposit 2"—form an eclectic group of items which, in my opinion, are not all contemporary with one another. My original drawings are published here (fig. 8.2).

[7] Thanks are due to the Director of the Semitic Museum for permission to publish this object, catalogue no: 1995.10.1233. It was part of L. P. di Cesnola's original sale of Cypriot objects to the Metropolitan Museum of Art in New York and was purchased by Jane L. Stanford in 1884 in anticipation of the establishment of an art museum in honor of her son. The dagger was not catalogued by the Metropolitan Museum prior to its resale and has thus never been published. In 1995 it came, by exchange, from the Stanford University Art Museum to the Semitic Museum: see H. W. Swiny, *The Cesnola Collection from Ancient Cyprus, the Semitic Museum at Harvard University*. Web publication: www.fas.harvard.edu/~semitic/Cesnola. I thank the latter for bringing this piece to my attention and for the drawing published in fig. 8.2.

[8] For a detailed discussion of the dating of the deposit, see Swiny 1997:180. Note that the dagger was found along with a large, fragmentary flat axe, illustrated in Karageorghis 1966.

[9] The piece from Philia Tomb 1, published by Catling (1964) in fig. 5:1, is described by him as a "razor." I see no reason for this identification on the grounds of the shapes of other Cypriot razors, and in view of the relative thickness of the blade, a point emphasized by comparing the sections of the typical dagger T4/14 (fig. 8.2) and the Philia Tomb 1 piece (fig. 8.3:T1/46), which are both of the same thickness. There may be others of which I am unaware, since no exhaustive search was made of Cypriot metals in collections scattered throughout the world. There are, however, no examples in the Metropolitan Museum of Art collection (pers. obs.). Thanks are due to Joan Mertens, Curator, Department of Greek and Roman Art at the museum for her assistance. The daggers in figs. 8.2 and 8.3 represent all the published provenanced pieces, as well as most of those which are unprovenanced.

asymmetrical in profile (cf. especially the left view in fig. 8.2), suggesting that the mold had the same shape. Is there a reason for this ubiquitous asymmetry or is it an unintentional coincidence? If for some reason molds were difficult to cut with a perfectly symmetrical casting depression, the difference in the cast object is slight enough to have been easily rectified while forging and work hardening the blade, yet this was not done. The asymmetry of these daggers must be quite intentional, as noted in connection with later flat tanged "knives," i.e., daggers (Swiny 1986:71, fig. 65:LM RR619/21).

Daggers and short swords with similar profiles and especially the flattened midribs are common in Anatolia during the Early Bronze Age. The material from the Soli-Pompeipolis hoard in western Cilicia still provides the largest number of close parallels, at least ten of which are illustrated (Bittel 1940: pls. 2 and 3). Some of these pieces, specifically nos. S 3424 (15 cm long) and S 3420 (20 cm long), with their single rivet hole at the end of the flat tang and their asymmetrical straight shoulders in particular, are absolutely identical to Cypriot examples from Philia *Laxia tou Kasinou*[10] and Vasilia *Alonia* (Karageorghis 1966: fig.73). Likewise the daggers of similar shape, but *without* rivet holes in the tang, are equally good parallels, as demonstrated by the examples from Karagach and Soli-Pompeipolis. Stronach illustrates the development of the type in an article, which despite its age, still stands as the best overview of EB Anatolian metal types.[11] Here the blades with flat midribs, classified at Type 2c, are described as having a broad raised flange and are considered to have originated in central Anatolia. Several swords and daggers from central to northeastern Anatolia, dated from middle to late EB, display the same type of midrib (Muscarella 1988:395 ff. nos. 541, 542, 545) as do the daggers and spearheads from Ikiztepe on the Black Sea (Bahadir and Alkim 1988:221, pl. LIX, no. 318).[12] Of note is the fact that the most diagnostic blade from EBII Karataş-Semayük, 450 km west of Tarsus, also belongs to Stronach's Type 2c (Mellink 1969: pl. 74 and especially Bordaz 1978:231 ff.). Bordaz, who studied Karataş-Semayük, suggests that the flat ridge is possibly the result of work hardening. Perhaps so, but most daggers, rhomboidal in section, were equally work hardened (see Tylecote 1986 for a 218 HV work-hardened blade) and were probably easier to hammer. It must be more time consuming to produce a straight-sided midrib rising 2–3 mm proud of the blade, so the style is surely based on aesthetic and not functional considerations. Although only represented by a small dagger or an arrowhead from a late EBII or early EBIII context at Tarsus, the presence of the type is very important to the present discussion.[13] The line of the flattened midrib is clearly discernible in the photograph.

Of note is a hook-tanged spearhead in the Brock University Collection (Robertson 1986:29), which appears to have a flat midrib in the drawing (no. 118) but a rounded one in the photograph (p. 61). The only other hook-tanged spearhead with a flat midrib is said to be from the Vasilia area, but it too is without secure provenance or date and is described by Catling (1964:56) as "an extraordinary weapon, of great weight and clumsiness."[14]

---

[10] Dikaios 1962: fig. 84:2, or for a slightly more accurate drawing (specifically in connection with the manner in which the mid-rib coalesces into the point) see fig. 8.3:T5a/11 in this publication.

[11] Stronach 1957; for good parallels for the raised "flange" (i.e. flat mid-rib type), see fig. 1:11, 3–5, 16, 18; fig. 2:7 (from Soli-Pompeipolis), 10–12, 24; fig. 3:1–3.

[12] No. 318, however, is a surface find, but is considered contemporary with no. 153 from a burial. The spearhead is dated to EB III/MB I (p. 225) and continues an old tradition which originates in EB II.

[13] Goldman 1956:291, fig. 427, no. 77 (38.1595), here classified as EBIII, but it could equally well be of late EBII date.

[14] This piece, along with much of the metal sold by dealers said to be from the Vasilia area, is unique, and poses serious problems of classification and dating.

M12. Billet casting of a dagger blade (fig. 8.2, pl. 8.1b, 8.1c). Tomb 6. Arsenical copper (As 3.2%). L: 16.2, W: 2, Th: 1.

> Elongated wedge-shaped with a distinct flat-ended tang and rounded, slightly asymmetrical shoulders. Obverse is blistered with forty-one "bubbles" distributed all over the surface. On average the blisters are 2–3 mm in diameter and protrude 1–2 mm above the surface. A single pockmark, 2.5 cm from the point, consists of a 1.5 mm protuberance, 7 mm in diameter with a 1 mm hole in its center, through which a bubble of hot gas must have vented. The reverse and sides are uneven but smooth.

M12 had been cast in an open mold and deposited with the burial in an unforged state as a simple billet. The blisters and vent hole would have formed immediately after the molten copper-based metal had been poured into an open mold. Had a double mold been used, both faces would have been identical. The dimensions and proportions of M12 suggest that it could have been forged into a dagger with proportions identical to those of M18, as demonstrated by pl. 8.1c, where both objects are seen side by side. Both also date from the Philia Phase and one may ask whether M18 was a product of the same mold?

Giardino et al. in Appendix 8.1 argue, however, that this object should not be interpreted as a billet, and that it is in fact an ingot. Their reasoning, based on the excessive amount of forging that this thick casting would have required, provides an interesting alternative to my interpretation of M12. I feel that their suggestion is weakened by the "asymmetrical" shoulders of the casting which mirror the asymmetrical shoulders of most daggers of the period. If M12 had not been intended to be forged into a dagger, one would hardly expect it to exhibit this idiosyncratic feature.

No parallels for EC or MC (ingots?) billets of daggers, or any other tool or weapon, are currently known. The six Late Cypriot I "cast-hilted dirks" from Enkomi *Ayios Iakovos* are close parallels (Dikaios 1969:232; 1971:446, pl. 126:20–23, pl. 153:14–17, 27), though they must have been subjected to some smithing, since they lack the characteristic blisters and pock marks noted on M12. Unfortunately the Enkomi castings are not described in any detail in the report. Thus, determining hether they had obverse and reverse faces or whether any subtle evidence of blistering was detectable is impossible (Dikaios 1969:232). They too could be interpreted as miniature ingots.

Evidence for the existence of open molds of MC date comes from Ambelikou *Choma tis Galinis* Site B[15] and Alambra *Mouttes* (Gale et al. 1996:135 ff.). Those from the former site were for casting flat axes and those from the latter were unfortunately too fragmentary to enable the identification of the objects for which they were intended. It has been argued that most—I would hazard to suggest all—EC and MC objects except the tin bronze shaft hole axes[16] were forged from billets cast in open molds (Balthazar 1990:352; Gale et al. 1996:135).

M1. Dagger tang with single rivet in situ (fig. 8.1). Area A Unit 1. Copper. L: 3.5, W: 1.8, Th: 0.15. Rivet: L: 1, D: 0.25.

> Corrosion has distorted the original shape of the tang and shoulders. The tang was shorter and broader than that of M18 and probably belonged to a smaller dagger. There is no evidence for a flattened midrib. The single rivet was bent at right angles.

---

[15] Swiny 1986:67, especially with reference to the date of the site; for the primary reference, see Dikaios 1946.
[16] See Swiny 1986:37 ff. For a discussion of the role of these objects in the Cypriot metal assemblage, see Balthazar 1990:370 ff.

No meaningful parallels may be drawn between this fragmentary, highly corroded blade and other Cypriot daggers. Flat-tanged daggers with a single rivet close to the extremity are most common in the Philia Phase and during the EC period (Dikaios 1962: figs. 74, 84; Stewart 1962: figs. 99, 100). Later daggers usually have butt-tangs with multiple rivets (Swiny 1986:69 ff., figs. 63, 65; Åström 1972:139ff., fig. 10).

M27. Dagger tang with single rivet in situ (fig. 8.1). Area A Unit 6. Copper (tang: Cu 98.7%, Fe 0.7 %; rivet Cu 99%, As 1.0%). L: 3.1, W: 1.9, Th: 0.2. Rivet L: 1.0, D: 0.2-0.4.

Wedge-shaped tang with rounded extremity. Broken toward the blade. Single tapering rivet driven from one side. No midrib visible.

The sharply tapering tang with a rivet set well down from the extremity is without parallel in the corpus of published EC daggers. With little of the blade preserved, not much more can be said about this piece other than that it belonged to a dagger far larger than M1. The relative thinness of the tang in relation to its size hints at a function other than that of a regular dagger.

M29. Dagger blade fragment (fig. 8.1). Area A Unit 6. Copper (Cu 100.0%). L: 4, W: 1.2, Th: 0.2.

Ogival with both edges narrowing to a rounded point. The break appears to have occurred as the result of torsion. No midrib visible.

AXE

M19. Axe fragment (fig. 8.1). Area A Unit 7. Copper-based (Cu 97.9%, As 1.7%, Fe 0.4%). L: 2.6, W: 1.9, Th: 0.4

Sub-rectangular with rounded cutting edge and straight slightly tapering sides.

Flat axes are common throughout the Cypriot Bronze Age (Dikaios 1962: fig. 84; Stewart 1962:49, fig. 100). This piece, however, is unusually small.

M26. Axe butt (fig. 8.1). Area A Unit 7. Copper-based (Cu 98.4%, As 1.6%). L: 3, W: 1.6, Th: 0.35.

Wedge shaped, one end narrow and sharp, the other end is broken. Both sides slightly rounded, especially toward the butt.

This object is the butt of M19 the flat axe. Note that this small 5.7 cm long axe is very similar in shape to an ECI "adze," pointed at both extremities, from Bellapais *Vounous* (Stewart 1962: fig. 100:20). Both pieces are shown joined on fig. 8.1.

CHISEL

M9. Chisel (fig. 8.1). Area B Unit 12. Arsenical copper (Cu 97.3%, As 4.0%). L: 7.1, W: 0.6, Th: 0.5.

Elongated shank, almost square in section; one flat end and the other with a cutting edge.

Although the identification of this piece is questionable, it does resemble a long narrow chisel and is lacking the usual pointed butt common to awls. No contemporary parallels are known from the corpus of EC and MC metal objects.

M5. Chisel? (fig. 8.1). Area C Unit 8. Copper. L: 6.2, W: 0.4, Th: 0.3 (av. Th: 0.2).

Elongated shank, rectangular section. Extremities may be damaged.

This piece may have served as an awl; however most awls are square in section, a fact that suggests that M5 was perhaps a long narrow chisel similar to M9.

M17. Chisel (fig. 8.1). Area A. above Units 6, 18 and 33. Copper-based. Although unstratified this item has been included since it is likely to be contemporary with the settlement. L: 5.6, W: 1.0, Th: 0.4.

Elongated with a narrow butt and rounded cutting edge. Both sides flat.

An EC I chisel of similar size and shape came from Bellapais *Vounous* (Stewart 1962: fig. 100:25).

AWL

M10. Awl (fig. 8.1). Tomb 6. Arsenical copper (Cu 97.3, As. 2.7%). L: 8.5, W: 0.5, Th: 0.4.

Elongated shank, almost square in section, tapering to a point at one end. The tang tapers more rapidly to a flat end.

M11. Awl (fig. 8.1). Tomb 15. Copper-based. L: 9.5, W: 0.5, Th: 0.4.

Elongated shank, almost square in section, tapering to a blunt point at one end. The more sharply tapering tang is bent.

M4. Probable awl fragment (fig. 8.1). Area C Unit 2. Sub-rectangular in section. Copper. Pres. L: 6.1, W: 0.4, Th: 0.4.

M8. Probable awl fragment (fig. 8.1). Area C Unit 2. Rectangular in section. Copper-based. Pres. L: 2.8, W: 0.4, Th: 0.3

M25. Possible awl fragment (fig. 8.1). Tomb 6. Sub-rectangular in section. Copper-based. Pres. L: 1.3, W: 0.35, Th: 0.35.

M4, M8 and M25 are too fragmentary to classify accurately, but their rectangular to sub-rectangular sections suggest that they were fragments of awls and not of needles or pins. The two fragments from Unit 2 are the only examples from the settlement and it is curious that more examples of such utilitarian tools were not found. Despite the utilitarian simplicity of these tools, they occur but rarely in EC burials and never before in Philia Phase burials (Stewart 1962:250, fig. 100:26). These three examples (M10, 11 and 25 from Tombs 6 and 15) are thus highly significant. Cypriot awls of Philia Phase and later date are characterized by a distinct haft, which narrows more rapidly than the working end, which when preserved, is always pointed.[17] A similar dearth of awls was noted at Alambra *Mouttes* and Marki *Alonia*, where needles and pins dominated the assemblage (Gale et al. 1986:129 ff., Frankel and Webb 1996b:213).

NEEDLE

M30. Needle (fig. 8.1). Area A Unit 7. Arsenical copper (Cu 95.7%, As 2.9%, Fe 1.4%). L: 2.5, D: 0.2. Broken through eye and probably the other extremity, since the shank is blunt.

Circular shaft with one extremity flattened and broken with only half of the eye remaining. The other extremity is blunt, perhaps due to an ancient break.

Copper-based needles are recorded from the EC period onward (Swiny 1986:82) and, in view of their common occurrence at the settlements of Marki *Alonia* (seven out of the eleven excavated metal finds were needles) and Alambra *Mouttes* (six out of seven excavated metal finds were needles or pins), it is surprising that only one was found at *Kaminoudhia*.

EARRING

The remains of at least eleven intact or fragmentary arsenical copper, bronze (M13, 14, 21, 22) and electrum (M6 and 7) spiral earrings were excavated from two Philia Phase burial chambers or were found in unstratified contexts within Cemetery A.

M2. Earring (fig. 8.1). Immediately west of Tomb 4 on bedrock. Copper-based. Fragmentary. D: 1.2; Th: 0.09.

M6. Earring (fig. 8.1, pls. 8.1c, 8.1d). Tomb 6. Electrum (Au 77–84%, Ag 15–20%, Cu 1–3%). Intact. D: 1.3, W: 1.0, Th: 0.03.

M7. Earring (pl. 8.1d). Tomb 6. Electrum. (Au 77–84%, Ag 15–20%, Cu 1–3%). Intact. Identical to M6 except that it has been coiled in the opposite direction.

M13. Earring (fig. 8.1). Tomb 6. Tin bronze (Cu 93.7%, Sn 4.8%, As 0.9%, Pb 0.3%, Fe 0.3%). Two fragments of a spiral widening toward one end. D: 1.4. Th: 0.2.

M14. Earring (fig. 8.1). Tomb 6. Tin bronze (Cu 93.7%, Sn.5.8%, As 0.5%). Two fragments of a spiral widening toward one end. D: 1.2, Th: 0.2.

M16. Earring. Tomb 15. Arsenical copper (Cu 90.9%, As 7.0%, Fe 2.1%). Ten fragments of various segments of a spiral widening toward one end.

M20. Earring (fig. 8.1). Tomb 15. Arsenical copper (Cu 97.2%, As 2.8%). Fragment of a spiral widening toward one end. D: 1.1, W: 0.75, Th: 0.1.

---

[17] For a fine example of an MC awl see Åström 1972: fig. 11:15.

M21. Earring (fig. 8.1). Tomb 6. Tin bronze (Cu 87.1%, Sn 10.2%, As 1.7%, Fe 0.7%, Pb 0.3%). Four fragments of a spiral widening toward one end. Largest frag. 1 x 0.65 x 0.13.

M22. Earring. Tomb 6. Tin bronze (Cu 86.4%, Sn 13.1%, As 0.5%). Eight fragments of a spiral widening toward one end. Largest frag. 0.7 x 0.6 x 0.1.

M23. Earring. Tomb 6. Copper-based. Seven fragments of a spiral widening toward one end.

M24. Earring. Tomb 15. Copper with some arsenic (cf. Appendix 8.1 "Arsenical-copper alloys"). Eighteen fragments of a spiral widening toward one end.

M31. Earring. Tomb 6. Copper with some tin (cf. Appendix 8.1 "Tin-copper alloys"). Fragment of the narrow end of a spiral. May have originated from one of the other clusters of spiral fragments.

All the earrings originally consisted of a strip of sheet metal cut either in the shape of a miniature oar or spatula, or as a simple elongated right angle triangle. The long sides are asymmetrical, one being straight or almost straight, the other more curvilinear (compare top and bottom edges in expanded views of M6 and T166/12a on figs. 8.1 and 8.3). The flattened extremity cut at right angles to the long axis is between 1 and 1.4 cm wide, the average being around 1 cm. The narrow end on the best preserved pieces, especially those in electrum, was not pointed, but cut to a width of 1–2 mm. The strips are coiled to form a loop of about 1.5 cm in diameter, with the narrow terminal protruding slightly above the straighter edge when viewed from the side (see figs. 8.1:M2 and M6). The thickness of the sheet metal ranges from 0.3 mm for the electrum pieces to ca. 1 mm for those in copper and bronze (all were corroded to some degree).

Curled strips of copper-based metal with one end pointed and the other expanding to a broad flattened terminal have been variously described as "earrings" (Dikaios 1953:13–18), "hair ornaments" (Stewart 1962:251, fig. 101:4; Karageorghis 1965) or "hair-rings" (Peltenburg 1988:235, fig 3). These spirals of copper, bronze and electrum, which vary little in shape and size, are ubiquitous in Philia Phase contexts. Indeed, not one has been discovered with stratified Chalcolithic material or in an EC context devoid of Philia Phase connections,[18] making them—along with the dagger with a flattened midrib and a number of specific ceramic types—a Philia Phase horizon marker.

Dikaios excavated the first metal spirals in tombs near the Mesaorea villages of Philia[19] and Kyra (fig. 8.3, T1/9, T1/10, T1/11—illustrations of T1/10 and T1/11 are published here for the first time—see Swiny 1985 for references to both sites) and photographs of them first appeared in 1946 (Dikaios 1946). Drawings followed (Dikaios 1962: figs 74 and 84) along with identical pieces excavated at Nicosia *Ayia Paraskevi* (Stewart 1962: fig. 101, see also Hennessy et al. 1988: figs. 17, 25), with different interpretations (see above). A study by Karageorghis (1965) resulted in their classification as "Type a hair ornaments" and there the situation rested until the Sotira *Kaminoudhia* excavations

---

[18] Not a single spiral was discovered at the great EC cemetery at Bellapais *Vounous* despite the wealth of metal from this site (Stewart and Stewart 1950). These spirals should not be confused with the much larger and a little later, (EC) gold "hair ornaments" from Lapithos, Bellapais *Vounous* or similar copper-based ones from Kalavasos and elsewhere (see Stewart 1962:251, 254 for references).

[19] A number of Philia Phase metal objects were redrawn to be illustrated here. Thanks are due to the Director of the Department of Antiquities for permission to restudy and publish selected items from Philia *Laksia tou Kasinou*, Kyra *Kaminia* and Dhenia *Kafkalla*.

produced a similar spiral ring from the cemetery area in 1981 (Karageorghis 1982b:718; Swiny 1985:22, fig. 5:10). The 1983 season yielded the unique pair of electrum spiral rings (Karageorghis 1984:938, fig. 134; Swiny 1995:33) along with more than eleven intact and fragmentary spirals from Cemetery A. This new body of material called for a reassessment of their traditional interpretation as hair ornaments or earrings.

The electrum (described as "gold" in Appendix 8.1) spirals from Tomb 6 were found interlocked at the feet of the single skeleton (see Chapter 3, Tomb 6 "Stratigraphy and finds") along with several bronze examples. Although the bronze spirals both turn in the same direction and thus do not form an antithetical pair like the electrum ones, they may have been paired with other fragmentary earrings from the same area of the tomb chamber.

Since the 1981 season at *Kaminoudhia*, when the first spiral earring was discovered (Karageorghis 1982:718, also for discussion of Anatolian connections), identical spiral earrings have been published from Kissonerga *Mosphilia* (Peltenburg 1988:235, fig. 3), Dhenia *Kafkalla* (Nicolaou and Nicolaou 1988:105, fig. 17),[20] Maa *Palaeokastro* (Karageorghis and Demas 1988:232, pl. LXXXIII),[21] and from the settlement at Marki *Alonia* (Frankel and Webb 1996a:64), which is the only example to have originated from a non funerary Philia Phase context.

After cleaning the electrum spirals M6 and M7, it was noticed that they did not consist of an identical pair with, for example, each loop starting with the narrow end on the left and turning to the right toward the broad terminal. Instead, they formed an antithetical pair with the spirals turning away from each other, i.e. in *opposite* directions. If the spirals had served as some form of ornamental binding for thick strands of hair, experimentation demonstrates that they must have been tied in place with some other material to stop them from slipping down the strand. This function is perfectly plausible. Nevertheless, it does not explain why the spirals run alternatively clockwise and anticlockwise, a refinement that would be virtually undetectable and would serve little purpose if the spirals were meant as hair ornaments. This feature does matter, however, if they were intended for use as earrings, because they would thus present the same appearance when viewed either from the front or the side. If the wearer had pierced ears it would have been easy to insert the narrow extremity through the earlobe and the spiral shape would have kept the earring firmly in place (see pl. 8.1e).[22]

Antithetical spirals are not restricted to Sotira *Kaminoudhia*, as proved by the visual examination of the examples from other sites. Three were recovered from Kyra *Kaminia* Tomb 1 of which No. 9, from the upper burial, is far larger than the others were. In the lower burial two spirals of identical size were found 10 cm apart (Dikaios 1962: fig. 73), close to where the skull must have rested if the long bones and pelvis remained in situ.[23] It is significant that these spirals form an antithetical pair, like the electrum earrings.

---

[20] K. Nicolaou excavated these tombs in 1960. The published drawings in Nicolaou and Nicolaou 1988: fig. 17 are too faint to interpret satisfactorily.

[21] Although no Philia Phase occupation has been excavated at the site, there was earlier Chalcolithic occupation, which may have been followed by a Philia presence as at Kissonerga *Mosphilia* (Peltenburg 1988). It is difficult to tell the exact shape of the object described as a "hair ring" from the illustration (pl. LXXXIII:344), but the authors do draw a parallel with the Philia Phase spirals without commenting on the reasons for the unexpected presence of this object at the Late Cypriot site of Maa.

[22] The electrum earrings from *Kaminoudhia* were copied in gold by the Nicosia jewelers Stephanides and Sons, and have been frequently worn by Helena Swiny since 1983 without ever falling off if properly bent closed.

[23] A skull, some vertebrae and long bones are indicated on the plan near the edge of the chamber. Could they have been moved there at the time of the second burial, or were there in fact three burials in the chamber?

Of all the metal objects from *Kaminoudhia* sampled for qualitative and quantitative chemical analysis, only the spiral earrings contain appreciable amounts of tin. One might ask why were earrings instead of the utilitarian daggers (M1 or M18), axe (M19) or some of the awls made of the copper tin alloy? All other Philia Phase daggers so far analyzed are also of pure copper (Craddock Table 2 in Swiny 1986). I believe that the decision was taken on aesthetic grounds alone, because tin bronze has a light golden color very different from the pinkish red of copper. Exactly the same argument may be made for earrings (M16) with a high percentage of arsenic. The mechanical properties imparted by tin and arsenic would have been quite unnecessary for these personal ornaments, which could equally well have been forged from copper, although none were of this material at *Kaminoudhia*.

New World examples of making artifacts out of bronze for color reasons have been noted (Hosler 1994:228 ff.) and since gold or electrum must have been very rare in Cyprus at the time, a well-polished bronze earring would have been a satisfactory substitute. While studying Philia Phase metal objects in the Cyprus Museum, I noticed that the spiral earring from Philia *Vasiliko* (Tomb 2, no. 17) was the color of bronze and not copper like many other fragmentary earrings. This suggests that the use of copper tin alloy for earrings was not restricted to *Kaminoudhia*. The lead isotope analyses of copper-based rings (arm rings, earrings[?], finger or hair rings) from Alambra *Mouttes*, of which two consisted of tin bronze, corroborate this argument. Gale et al. (1996:379) mention in passing that the bronze has a gold color, making it a luxury item, a conclusion that I first reached when studying the earrings from Sotira and other sites in 1993.

Confirmation of the use of these metal spirals as earrings must await either a graphic representation of such earrings being worn (very unlikely) or the discovery of a pair on either side of a skull (more likely). Still, as the evidence stands, these objects, which seem to have been much appreciated during the Philia Phase, work well as both attractive and functional earrings.

The foreign parallels for the earrings were discussed in Swiny 1986a:38 and remain valid since no new material requiring a revision of the situation has been published. It is significant that the comparisons are consistently described as "earrings" and not hair ornaments. The gold EB II example from Tarsus (Goldman 1956: fig. 434:2) does differ from the later *Kaminoudhia* examples in that its pointed end is a piece of wire, circular in diameter, whereas the Cypriot examples are always (when well-preserved) rectangular and flattened in section.

FRAGMENT

M15. Irregular, elongated fragment (fig. 8.1). Area B Unit 12. Copper-based (99.2%, As 0.6%, Fe 0.2%). L: 2.5, W: 0.8, Th: 0.3.

M28. Wedge-shaped fragment (fig. 8.1). Area A Unit 6. Copper-based (Cu 99.0%, As 0.4%, Fe 0.6%). L: 1.4, W: 0.8, Th: 0.3.

> Fragment of a flat tool-like object, either a dagger or a small flat axe. One possible finished edge, the other rough as if broken. One face smooth and only slightly corroded, the other rough and very corroded.

Nothing more can be said about these small items, other than to note that their existence emphasizes the common occurrence and variety of metal finds from the *Kaminoudhia* settlement.

CONCLUSIONS

The most remarkable aspect of the metal assemblage from Sotira *Kaminoudhia* is the range of shapes and forms recorded in the Philia Phase tombs and the small, apparently isolated EC settlement.

Burials belonging to the Philia Phase are accompanied by a number of metal objects: some of them, such as the spiral earrings and the dagger with a flat midrib, are diagnostic of the period. Of note is the lack of metal from the later tombs, which may either be interpreted as a sign of poverty or, more likely, due to the vagaries of discovery. The range of utilitarian types recorded from the EC III settlement suggests that the use of metal was quite widespread.

The metal finds from *Kaminoudhia* demonstrate that already in this early phase of the Bronze Age the Cypriots made a judicious use of alloys. Tools that were required to retain a good edge or point, such as the chisels and the axe, were made from arsenical copper, as was one of the five awls and the single needle. On the other hand, all three daggers, whether from the cemetery or the settlement, were, surprisingly, made of pure copper. That the majority of analyzed Philia and EC daggers were also made of unalloyed copper (Swiny 1982a:73; Balthazar 1990:324 ff.) somewhat supports Giardino's suggestion that M12 is an ingot and not a billet since it consists of arsenical copper. There are, however, enough arsenical copper daggers to argue that M12 was to be forged into a dagger and thus not intended as an ingot.

METAL CATALOGUE

All measurements in centimeters.

M1. Dagger tang with single rivet in situ. (Fig. 8.1) Area A Unit 1. Copper. L: 3.5, W: 1.8, Th: 0.15, rivet L: 1, D: 0.25.

M2. Earring. (Fig. 8.1) Immediately west of Tomb 4 on bedrock. Copper-based. Fragmentary. D: 1.2, Th: 0.09.

M3. Unstratified fragment of sheet metal.

M4. Probable awl fragment. (Fig. 8.1) Area C Unit 2. Subrectangular in section. Copper. Pres. L: 6.1, W: 0.4, Th: 0.4.

M5. Chisel(?). (Fig. 8.1) Area C Unit 8. Copper. L: 6.2, W: 0.4, Th: 0.3 (av. Th: 0.2).

M6. Earring. (Fig. 8.1, pls. 8.1c, 8.1d) Tomb 6. Electrum. Intact. D: 1.3, W: 1.0, Th: 0.03.

M7. Earring. (Pl. 8.1d) Tomb 6. Electrum. Intact. Identical to M6 except that it has been looped in the opposite direction.

M8. Probable awl fragment. (Fig. 8.1). Area C Unit 2. Rectangular in section. Copper. Pres. L: 2.8, W: 0.4, Th: 0.3.

M9. Chisel. (Fig. 8.1) Area B Unit 12. Arsenical copper. L: 7.1, W: 0.6, Th: 0.5.

M10. Awl. (Fig. 8.1) Tomb 6. Arsenical copper. L: 8.5, W: 0.5, Th: 0.4.

M11. Awl. (Fig. 8.1) Tomb 15. Copper. L: 9.5, W: 0.5, Th: 0.4.

M12. Billet or ingot. (Fig. 8: 2, pls. 8.1b, 8.1c) Tomb 6. Arsenical copper. L: 16.2, W: 2, Th: 1.

M13. Earring. (Fig. 8.1) Tomb 6. Tin bronze. Two fragments of a spiral widening toward one end. D: 1.4. Th: 0.2.

M14. Earring. (Fig 8.1) Tomb 6. Tin bronze. Two fragments of a spiral widening toward one end. D: 1.2, Th: 0.2.

M15. Irregular, elongated fragment. (Fig. 8.1) Area B Unit 12. Copper. L: 2.5, W: 0.8, Th: 0.3.

M16. Earring(s). Tomb 15. Arsenical copper. Ten fragments of various segments of a spiral widening toward one end.

M17. Chisel. (Fig. 8.1) Area A, above Units 6, 18 and 33. Unstratified. Arsenical copper. L: 5.6, W: 1.0, Th: 0.4.

M18. Dagger. (Fig. 8.2, pls. 8.1a, 8.1c) Tomb 15. Copper. Intact. L: 16.2, W: 3, Th: 0.4, L of tang: 2.8.

M19. Axe fragment. (Fig. 8: 1) Area A Unit 7. Copper with some arsenic. L: 2.6, W: 1.9, Th: 0.4.

M20. Earring. (Fig. 8.1) Tomb 15. Arsenical copper. Fragment of a spiral widening toward one end. D: 1.1, W: 0.75, Th: 0.1.

M21. Earring. (Fig. 8.1) Tomb 6. Tin bronze. Four fragments of a spiral widening toward one end. Largest frag. 1 x 0.65 x 0.13.

M22. Earring. Tomb 6. Tin bronze. Eight fragments of a spiral widening toward one end. Largest frag. 0.7 x 0.6 x 0.1.

M23. Earring. Tomb 6. Copper. Seven fragments of a spiral widening toward one end.

M24. Earring. Tomb 15. Arsenical copper. Eighteen fragments of a spiral widening toward one end.

M25. Possible awl fragment. (Fig. 8.1) Tomb 6. Arsenical copper. Sub-rectangular in section. Pres. L: 1.3, W: 0.35, Th: 0.35.

M26. Axe butt. (Fig. 8.1) Area A Unit 7. Arsenical copper. L: 3, W: 1.6, Th: 0.35.

M27. Dagger tang with single rivet in situ. (Fig. 8.1) Area A Unit 6. Copper-based. L: 3.1, W: 1.9, Th: 0.2; rivet L: 1.0, D: 0.2-0.4.

M28. Wedge-shaped fragment. (Fig. 8.1) Area A Unit 6. Copper-based. L: 1.4, W: 0.8, Th: 0.3.

M29. Dagger blade fragment. (Fig. 8.1) Area A Unit 6. Copper. L: 4, W: 1.2, Th: 0.2.

M30. Needle. (Fig. 8.1) Area A Unit 7. Arsenical copper. L: 2.5, D: 0.2; broken through eye and probably the other extremity since the shank is blunt.

M31. Earring fragment. Tomb 6. Tin bronze. Piece of the narrow end of a spiral. May have originated from one of the other clusters of spiral fragments.

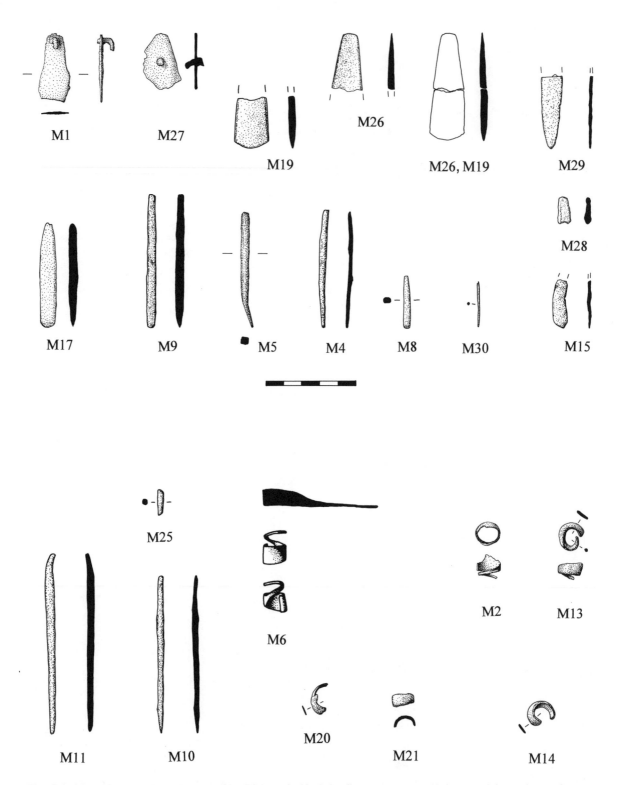

Fig. 8.1. Metal from Sotira *Kaminoudhia*. The top half of the figure presents all the metal from the settlement. Dagger tangs with rivets in situ, M1, M2; fragments of a flat axe M19 and M26 (M19 and M26 are also shown joined); Dagger blade fragment M29; Chisels M17, M9, M5?; Awls M4, M8; Needle M30; unidentified fragments M15, M28. The bottom half of the figure presents metal from the cemetery. Awls M11, M10, M25?; Earrings M6 (electrum), M2, M13, M20, M21, M14.

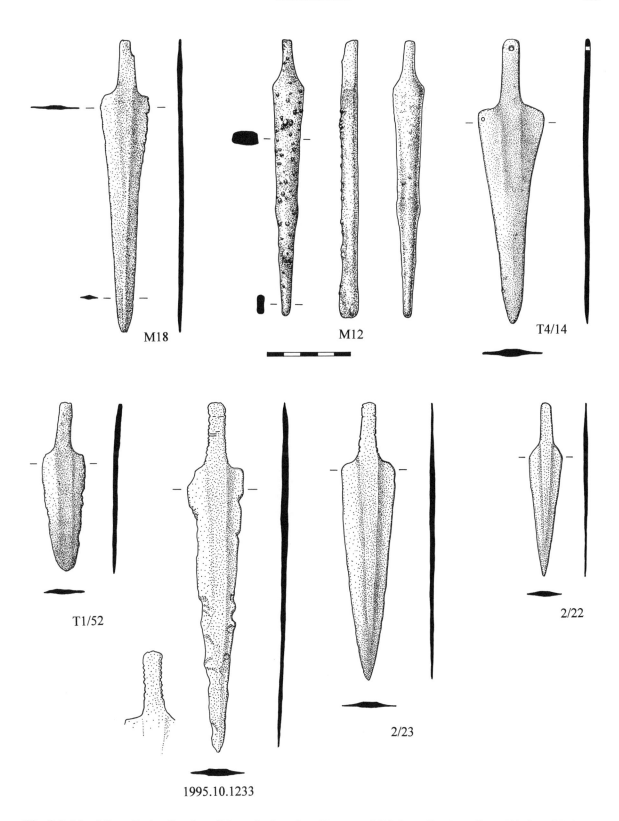

Fig. 8.2. Metal from Sotira *Kaminoudhia* and other sites. Daggers: M18 from *Kaminoudhia*; T4/14, T1/52 from Philia *Vasiliko (Laksia tou Kasinou)*; 1995.10.1233 unprovenanced, now in the Harvard Semitic Museum; 2/22, 2/23 from Vasilia Deposit 2. Billet or ingot M12 from *Kaminoudhia*.

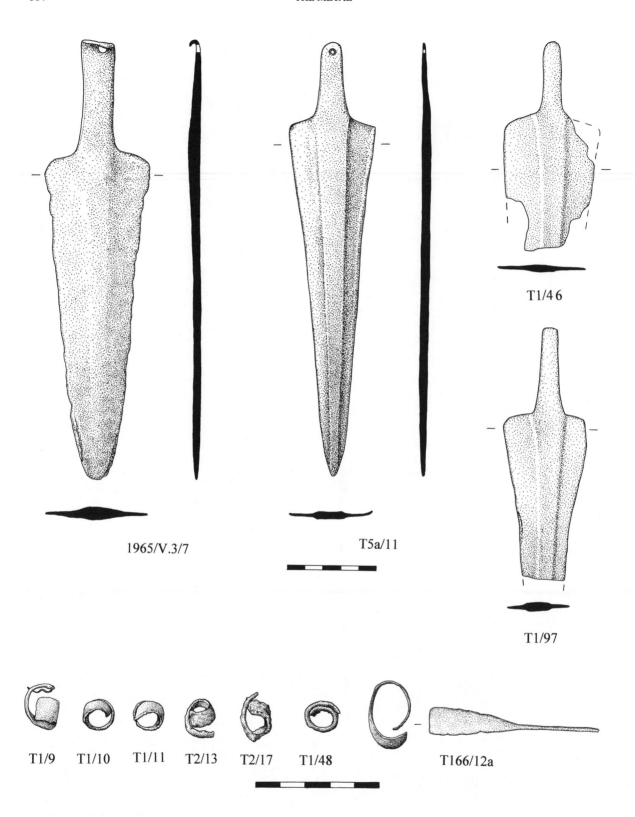

Fig. 8.3. Metal from various sites. Daggers: 1965/V.3/7 from Vasilia *Alonia*; T5a/11 and T1/46 from Philia *Vasiliko (Laksia tou Kasinou)*; T1/97 from Dhenia *Kafkalla*. Earrings: T1/9, T1/10, T1/11, T2/13, T2/17 from Kyra *Kaminia*; T1/48 from Philia *Vasiliko (Laxia tou Kasinou)*; T166/12a from Dhenia *Kafkalla*.

APPENDIX 8.1

ARCHEOMETALLURGICAL STUDIES

*by Claudio Giardino, Giovanni E. Gigante
and Stefano Ridolfi*

INTRODUCTION

Twenty seven metal items from Sotira *Kaminoudhia* were analyzed by Energy Dispersive X-Ray Fluorescence (EDXRF). One of the main advantages of this technique is that it is non-destructive and thus preserves the integrity of the artifacts. A portable EDXRF spectrometer was used to obtain in situ measurements on the objects, which are stored in the Cyprus Museum, Nicosia.

Because EDXRF only analyzes the surface of a metal object, in the case of copper-based artifacts it is necessary to remove a few square millimeters of patina from around the target area. The results in Table 8.1.1 have a precision of 10% for concentrations below 1%; 4% for concentrations between 1% and 4%; 2% for concentrations between 4% and 10%; less than 1% for concentrations higher than 10%. An element is quoted as tr (trace) when it is detected, but not quantified.

METHODOLOGY

EDXRF is a non-destructive multi-elemental analytical technique which consists of irradiating a sample with low energy X-rays and detecting the resulting X-ray fluorescence. The energies of the X-rays emitted are characteristic of the elements present in the sample (as "finger prints") and their intensities are proportional to the concentrations of the elements.

The depth to which the X-rays penetrate the sample varies from a few to several hundred microns, depending on the matrix studied and the element analyzed. This characteristic feature of EDXRF analysis has both advantages and disadvantages. In particular, it is necessary to evaluate whether a surface measurement obtained by EDXRF, as compared with the results from core boring, may be viewed as representative of the overall composition of the material. With reference to this issue it is worth noting the results of an experiment carried out by V.F. Hanson (Herglotz and Birks 1978) in which a non-arsenical bronze alloy was cast and then cut in very thin layers (0.15 mm). The analysis of each layer demonstrated that at different depths the concentrations of the various elements do not undergo important variations and that the composition remains constant throughout.

With optical positioning instruments and a microscope the target area can be accurately identified (Giardino et al. 1996:327). The possibility of analyzing the surface of the artifact in several places offers the ability to characterize the artifact through variations of its essential parameters linked to its composition. Figure 8.1.1 shows the results of a measurement performed with EDXRF on an alloy.

In addition to the non-destructive nature of analyses performed with EDXRF, the equipment is also easily transportable so that the analyses may be undertaken in situ. Carrying the instrument to the sample and not vice versa (if this second solution were possible) overcomes security and bureaucratic issues. The mobility of the analytical equipment (due to a non cryogenic detector, a miniaturised X-ray tube and a laptop computer) even allows us to go beyond the concept of analysis in situ. Such an instrument could be made available to an excavation project, thereby assisting the research of archaeologists and archaeometallurgists in the field.

MEASUREMENT SPECIFICS

The diagram of the measurement system is shown in fig. 8.1.2.
The technical characteristics of the tube used are:
  •Tungsten anode
  •Focus 0.6 mm
  •Inherent filtering 3 mm Al
  •Anode HV max 50kV
  •Anode current max 1 mA
  •Air cooled
  •Dimensions 163(W) x 193(D) x 180(H) mm
  •Weight 7 kg
  •Laser pointer

The tube operates with a voltage of 40 kV and current of 0.35 mA. To maintain the stability of the tube when the environmental temperature is high it, along with the detector and computer, was cooled with portable fans. The whole system tended to rapidly overheat in the high summer temperatures in Cyprus.
The characteristics of the detector are as follow:
  •Si-PIN of AMPTEK with a 300 micrometers Si-diod cooled with a Peltier cell.
  •Resolution 250 eV at 5.9 keV.

The pointing system uses a laser diode, which along with the collimating system of the X-ray beam permits the study of surfaces 5 mm square.
The uncertainties shown on Table 8.1.1 have been calculated with error propagation on the net counts and on the estimated background (Poisson's statistic) as well as by a Monte Carlo method inside the iterative cycle, which is at the basis of the solution of a set of integral equations with common variables.
For silver and zinc the minimum concentrations detectable are 0.8% and 1% respectively. No sample reached these limits of detection.
The strong self-absorption of the radiation emitted in the sample is an intrinsic limit of the method; it produces non-linearity in the response of the measurement system. To avoid this, a physical model of the emission process of characteristic X-rays must be used.
With this technique the non-linear response of the system may be corrected. The "fundamental parameters" model was used, in which some parameters may be fixed using standard samples.
It is opportune to stress that in the method employed here the concentration of the matrix element (copper in this case) is calculated by difference. The presence of any elements detected but not quantified does not affect this calculation. In other words, copper is not measured directly, the sum of the elements concentration is normalized to 100% with the variation of the copper.

DISCUSSION

All the objects from Sotira *Kaminoudhia* were made of copper alloys, with the exception of two earrings made in gold. This same technique was used to analyze metallic traces on a crucible fragment found on the surface of the EC/MC settlement of *Pharkonia* in the Paramali Valley (Swiny 1981:68). The use of X-ray fluorescence, being non-destructive, permitted multiple measurements to be taken from several artifacts (fig. 8.1.5) in order to highlight any differences in the composition of the alloy connected to segregation phenomena, an aspect often mentioned in studies on arsenical alloys.

In this connection, the results from M12, the dagger-ingot (or billet), are significant because the measurements taken on the lower side (A), on the tang (C) and near the tip of the blade (B), gave practically identical values (As 3.2%, As 3.5% and As 3.8%). This is an indication that the metallurgist had good control of the composition of the arsenical alloy. Furthermore, the piece has a relatively high weight (114 g)—therefore a high metal mass—and even the thickness (1.7 cm) and length (16 cm) are comparatively substantial.

Among artifacts made from copper alloys, three groups stand out: 1) those made of nearly pure copper in which other metals are present only as traces, certainly unintentional; 2) those made with arsenical copper; 3) those made of tin bronze.

COPPER-BASED ARTIFACTS

Eight of the metal objects from *Kaminoudhia* (M5, 8, 11, 18, 27A, 27B, 28, 29) are copper, with only small amounts of other elements (see Table 8.1.1). It could be argued they were made of native copper, which does exist in Cyprus, but it is rare. Native copper is extremely pure, impurities occurring only in the parts per million level (Gale 1991:50) which is beyond the detection limits of X-ray fluorescence. In any case most copper-based artifacts from *Kaminoudhia* contain small percentages of arsenic or iron much higher than those recorded in native copper. These data suggest that the objects analyzed were not made from Cypriot native copper and were more likely to have been forged from smelted copper ore.

ARSENICAL-COPPER ALLOYS

Arsenical alloys are the first true form of copper alloying, extensively widespread in the Near East and in Europe. The addition of arsenic to the alloy lowers the melting point of copper; it also acts as a deoxidant and improves both the castability and the mechanical properties of the metal. This considerably increases the ultimate strength of copper and makes it easier to work, whether cold or hot, and finally, it makes it less brittle. Cold hammering considerably hardens Cu-As alloys by comparison with pure copper, and imparts properties quite similar to tin bronzes (Charles 1967:21–24; Tylecote 1976:7–8; Northover 1989:111–15; Giardino 1998:182–83). Arsenic also modifies the color of copper, making it lighter; in sufficiently high concentrations it bestows a silver color to the surface (Eaton and McKerrell 1976:175–76) and tends to concentrate on the surface of objects (surface enrichment). Experimental studies have shown how enrichment can involve surface layers of up to 0.5 mm thickness; this surface concentration occurs during casting in the early stages of solidification (cf. McKerrell and Tylecote 1972; Mohen 1990:99–101). This behavior of arsenic must be kept in mind when comparing the quantitative data obtained by EDXRF with that taken from other types of analysis, even if patina removal before measurement is considered as a corrective precaution.

One of the main issues connected with the study of prehistoric artifacts containing arsenic is to determine whether the alloy was voluntary or the result of the chance use of copper ores rich in arsenic.

A point of controversy is the determination of the minimum value of intentionally added arsenic in a Cu-As alloy (cf. Craddock 1995:287–89). Branigan suggests that in the Early and Middle Bronze Age Aegean the presence of more than 1–2% of arsenic in an artifact is indicative of a deliberately produced alloy (Branigan 1974:71–73); Craddock (1986:153–54) suggests a deliberate alloying level of about 1% of arsenic in the Cypriot Bronze Age. With specific reference to Cyprus, some authors have theorized that the arsenic came from the direct smelting of the arsenical copper-ore (de Jesus et al. 1982:27; cf. also Muhly 1985:278–79); yet according to others it is connected with deliberate alloying with arsenic minerals such as realgar (As4S4) or orpiment (As2S3) (Craddock 1986:154).

The amount of arsenic in Cypriot copper sulfide ores is generally very low. At around 0.02%, it is insufficient to change the mechanical properties of smelted artifacts. The only known areas where the ore contains sufficient values of arsenic (up to 7.6%) are at Laxia tou Mavrou near Dhierona and around Pevkos in the Limassol Forest. There the sulphide and arsenide mineralizations contain arsenic associated with other metals such as iron, nickel and copper (Swiny 1982:71; Thalhammer et al. 1986). Experiments have shown that copper arsenic alloys could have been produced using the arsenical ore available in Cyprus, with an addition of CaO flux. Arsenic could be transferred from the ore to the liquid copper when operating in a reducing atmosphere under a layer of charcoal at 1250°C (Zwicker 1982:64–67).

The data from the analysis has been used to produce a chart (fig. 8.1.3) showing the content of arsenic in the finds from *Kaminoudhia* which have been arranged in categories. The first one, which is quite large, consists of pieces with contents of As less than 1%. The second category, separated from the first by a caesura, exhibits values of between 1.7% and 4%. The third category consists of a single piece with 7% of As. The chart emphasizes how the first caesura actually coincides with the unintentional alloys, while the other samples exhibit a deliberate addition of arsenic.

At least eight of the *Kaminoudhia* artifacts (M9, 10, 12, 16, 17, 20, 25, 30) analyzed have sufficient arsenic to make them deliberate alloys (2.5–7%). In these pieces other elements are normally absent (such as antimony, bismuth or nickel), elements which are generally present in arsenic-rich ore (cf. Craddock 1995:287). The highest values of arsenic have been found in tools used for cutting, carving or sewing (axe [M19+26], awls [M10, 25], needle [M30], chisels [M9, 17]) and in ornamental objects (earrings M16, 20). For the ornaments the silvery effect was clearly sought after by the ancient metallurgist. It should be pointed out that the piece with the highest content of arsenic (7%) is M16, an earring.

Mention should be made that the analysis confirmed that fragments M26 and M19 belong to the same object, a flat axe broken in antiquity. Both pieces show a similar chemical composition. While this axe contained substantial arsenic (1.7%), the amount was below the 2.5% considered to be the minimum threshold to indicate an intentional alloy.

M24 was only qualitatively analyzed; it revealed the presence of copper and arsenic.

TIN-COPPER ALLOYS

The presence of tin in some of the samples examined has aroused considerable interest. This element has been found in four earrings: M13, M14, M21 and M22, all of which were excavated in Tomb 6, which dates to the Philia Phase. The amount of tin is so high (between 5% and 13%) that it cannot be regarded as an accidental alloy.

The presence of tin bronzes at *Kaminoudhia* is significant because these objects provide the first evidence for tin-copper alloys in Cyprus during the Philia Phase. These results strengthen the connection between the Philia Phase and the appearance of technological, economical and social developments and innovations (Webb and Frankel 1999:4).

In the Aegean, tin bronzes appear in Crete and in the Cyclades in the Early Bronze 2 (Early Minoan II and Early Cycladic II), in the second half of the third millennium B.C.E. (Branigan 1974:106–9). Yet in Anatolia the bronze alloy appears much earlier, at the end of the fourth millennium B.C.E., in the southeast at Tell Judeideh in the Amuq.[24] A concentration of bronzes occurs in the Troad during the Early Bronze Age, at Troy and Thermi (de Jesus 1980:150). The earliest, sporadic evidence from Troy and Thermi is dated to the late fourth millennium B.C.E.,[25] but in the Troad tin bronze becomes more common later, in the first half of the third millennium.[26]

On the basis of the few analyses previously undertaken on Philia Phase metal objects, it appeared that most consisted of unalloyed copper and arsenic-copper alloys (Balthazar 1990:97–106). The Sotira earrings now prove that tin bronze was also in use, although it was apparently reserved for prestige objects. Chronological data seem to emphasize the importance of Cyprus in transmitting this new technology by sea from the Anatolian coast across to the Aegean.

The *Kaminoudhia* tin bronzes all belong to the same type of spiral earring with a narrow circular loop broadening to an expanded end, consisting of a strip of metal with one end pointed and the other flattened, a type of artifact peculiar to the Philia Phase (Swiny 1997: fig. 2a:9; Webb and Frankel 1999:31). It is significant that the use of bronze was reserved for delicate ornaments, where the mechanical properties of the alloy found no use. As in the case of similar samples in arsenical copper, the artisan's aim was to make jewellery with a particular chromatic effect, in this case a brilliant tone of yellow similar to gold. Since a pair of gold earrings (M6 and M7) were found on the site, this metal was well known and appreciated by the *Kaminoudhia* community.

Unfortunately all the *Kaminoudhia* bronze artifacts were extremely corroded, so much so that no trace of non-mineralized metal was preserved. The quantitative result of the analysis is therefore purely indicative, since it concerns values measured on patinas, even though the more superficial alteration products had been previously removed. In order to check whether and to what degree the percentage of tin was linked to the core of the artifact, a microstratigraphic analysis was undertaken on the completely mineralized earring M13 by progressively removing the layers of alteration from an area about 5 mm in diameter. At the point examined, the earring had a thickness of little more than 1 mm.

First the outer layer was analyzed, then the deeper ones, proceeding through four layers of patina of various thickness, characterized by different colors, from green to red-brown. Pure metal was never reached, having been completely destroyed during the corrosion process. The percentage of tin remained constant from the surface to the innermost layer, thus proving that the high percentages of tin registered were actually linked to the composition of the object and were not the result of post-depositional surface enrichment.

No known tin deposits exist on Cyprus, nor is any tin present in Cypriot copper ore (Muhly 1985:277), so the tin—or bronze—used for making earrings must have been imported. As previously mentioned, the earrings are of a typical Cypriot type, therefore must have been made on the island. It is impossible to establish how this tin reached Cyprus, whether as a stanniferous mineral to be alloyed with copper or as bronze in the form of ingots or scrap metal that was then remelted as required.

---

[24] Tell Judeideh, level G: a pin (7.79% Sn), an awl (10% Sn) and slag (5% Sn) (Yener et al. 1996:379). The presence of three bronze artifacts from the late Chalcolithic period at Mersin is doubtful; they may be incorrectly attributed to this stratum (see Muhly 1976:89; de Jesus 1980:132–33).

[25] At Troy I a bangle appears with 10% Sn; at Thermi I a pin with 13.1% Sn (Branigan 1974:147).

[26] A dagger from Troy II has 10.62% Sn. Seven bronzes from Troy II g (6 chisels and 1 flat axe) have tin levels of between 2.89% and 8.49% (Branigan 1974:147). On the chronology of the first tin alloys in the Near East, cf. also Pernicka 1990:52.

Tin is certainly one of the less widespread metals on the crust of the earth and there are no geologically verified deposits in the eastern Mediterranean area (Maddin et al. 1977:35). Aside from the deposits in central and western Europe (British Isles, France, Germany, Bohemia, Italy and the Iberian Peninsula), deposits of cassiterite ($SnO2$) have been reported in Egypt, in the Eastern Desert, even though ancient exploitation of them is quite unlikely (Wertime 1978:5; Muhly 1978:45–46; Penhallurick 1986:7–13). In the Taurus region, in central Anatolia, and in Kestel and Göltepe, tin deposits have preserved traces of worked outcrops (Earl and Özbal 1996). Other deposits are in Iran, near Tabriz and in the region of Lake Sistan, as well as in central-south and eastern Afghanistan (Muhly 1973:260–61; Cleuziou and Bertoud 1982:14–20; Pigott 1986:21–23).

Three of the *Kaminoudhia* pieces fail to exhibit the presence of elements other than tin; in one of the pieces, earring M21, 10.2% tin is associated with 1.7% arsenic. Even though the measurement was taken on the patina since the piece was deeply corroded, the substantial presence of arsenic suggests that the tin may have come from melting bronze with arsenical copper scrap metal, a practice that some scholars suggest was in use in the MC period (Balthazar 1990:73).

Earring M31, only qualitatively analyzed, revealed the presence of copper and tin.

SECONDARY ELEMENTS

Iron is a measurable element in nearly all the samples although in variable proportions, sometimes reaching around 2%. On average, however, iron ranged from around 0.5% to 0.6%. It is found as an impurity in unalloyed copper and in the arsenical and tin bronzes. In this respect the *Kaminoudhia* metals do not differ substantially from other previously analyzed Philia Phase and EC objects, for which a variable iron content was observed within a range of between 0.1% and 0.95% (Balthazar 1990:105). The iron content provides information on the smelting process and it is generally connected with the use of iron oxides as fluxes to remove the silica gangue from copper ore. At about 1200°C, iron and silica react to form liquid iron silicate slag. On Cyprus the most common copper mineral is chalcopyrite (Tylecote 1982:81; Constantinou 1982:13–17; Rapp 1982:35) and the preliminary roasting of sulphide ore in order to convert it to an oxide, in which the elimination of iron is difficult, could also explain the presence of iron (Tylecote 1982:97). In the reducing atmosphere of the furnace some iron from the ore and the flux is picked up by the molten copper to form copper-iron alloys (Craddock and Meeks 1987:191–92; Craddock 1995:137–39).

Data regarding the presence of relatively high percentages of iron in Philia Phase and EC artifacts could provide information on the choice of (sulphide) ores and slagging techniques adopted for copper production in Cyprus at this early period. The most recent research tends to move sulphide metallurgy back in time, which was previously thought to begin with the Late Bronze Age (Rapp 1982:35). Archaeometallurgical investigations carried out on the slag from the Pyrgos *Mavroraki* site demonstrates that the use of sulphides for the production of copper dates back at least to the Middle Bronze Age (Giardino 2000). In some areas of prehistoric Europe there is proof of sulphide treatment from cultures of the Early Bronze Age. This is the case of the eastern Alps area, a region rich in copper ore deposits, mainly of chalcopyrite as in Cyprus (Fasani 1988:172–79).

In only one sample, the chisel M17, were nickel and antimony found, both of them in high concentrations, around 2% and 1% respectively. These values were confirmed by repeating the measurement several times, even in the presence of the patina. These percentages make the piece under examination—made of an alloy low in arsenic—unique in the group of *Kaminoudhia* metals. Although M17 is typologically similar to other chisels of EC date (Stewart 1962: fig. 100:25) and most likely originated from the settlement, it was unstratified, having been found above Units 6, 18 and 33. This might explain why the mineral from which the copper was smelted differed in origin from that of all other pieces at the site. Nickel can occur in copper minerals in quantities much greater than 1% and its presence in finished objects may therefore be considered accidental (Branigan 1974:71).

Nickel was usually absent from the EC and MC analyses undertaken to date, although a few remarkable exceptions do show fairly high values.[27]

EVIDENCE FOR METALLURGICAL ACTIVITY IN THE EPISKOPI REGION

The 1997 Sotira Archaeological Project Survey discovered a crucible fragment on the surface of the EC/MC settlement of Paramali *Pharkonia* (Swiny 1981:68; Swiny and Mavromatis 2000:435). The original crucible had been cup-shaped and about 10 cm in diameter. The X-ray fluorescence analysis was undertaken on several points of the inner surface, three of them localized on a lump of slag material adhering to the wall of the crucible.

The results of the investigation clearly show the presence of copper with a high iron content. The presence of arsenic was not significant (0.3 %), so there is no evidence that arsenical copper had been melted in the crucible. The crucible had apparently been used to produce artifacts of almost pure copper with a small unintentional amount of arsenic. The analysis supports the attribution of the fragment to the same chronological and cultural environment as the other finds, bearing in mind the characteristic composition of most metal artifacts from *Kaminoudhia* (fig. 8.1.4).

Although no evidence for metallurgical activity has so far been found at *Kaminoudhia*, the presence of crucibles at Paramali *Pharkonia* and Episkopi *Phaneromeni* (Swiny 1986:67, 87) argues in favor of at least some metal work being carried out at the site. In view of this fact, it is worth mentioning the issues concerning the identification of the dagger-ingot M12. It appears to be a casting produced inside a one-piece mold. The upper surface clearly shows blisters and other casting irregularities, while the lateral and lower sides are nearly smooth.

The considerable thickness of both the blade and the tang (7–12 mm) argues against its interpretation as an unforged dagger preform. Daggers of this period are usually between 2 and 2.5 mm thick, so an inordinate amount of metal would have had to have been removed from the preform in order to produce a dagger of typical Philia or EC proportions. In view of the above we suggest that M12 is an arsenical copper ingot (3.5% of As) weighing 114 g.

Ingots of various metals, with tapered shapes and of sizes similar to the Cypriot piece, are found in the Aegean area in middle third millennium B.C.E. contexts.[28] Ingots shaped as weapons, tools or ornaments are fairly frequent in Aegean prehistory and on the European continent in this early period.[29]

GOLD

The analyses performed on the two gold earrings (M6 and M7, described as "electrum" in Ch. 8) from Tomb 6 at *Kaminoudhia* showed that they were made from an alloy of gold, silver (15–20%) and copper (1–3%). In this case it is not easy to establish if the alloying was deliberate or not: native gold can contain quite high values of silver, much higher than those found in the two earrings (Giardino

---

[27] For example the knife CMRR 18/3 from a tomb at Ephtagonia *Pervolia* had 1% Ni (Swiny 1986:95); the nail M17 from Episkopi *Phaneromeni* 0.62% Ni (Craddock 1986:156); the pin 16 from Tomb 91 at Bellapais *Vounous*, 1% Ni (Desch 1950:371).

[28] Cf. Poliochni, copper alloy, EB 2; Troy II g, silver; Mochlos, copper alloy, EM-MM (Branigan 1974:198).

[29] For example there are two ingots from Mochlos which again show the type of coeval triangular daggers (Branigan 1974: pl. 25:3297A and 3298).

1998:151). Even copper may be combined with gold, though in much lesser amounts. Percentages of Cu above 2% are in fact considered a deliberate addition (cf. Hartmann 1970:9; Stos-Ferner and Gale 1979:306; Pingel 1995:389). It is not possible to determine if the two pieces from *Kaminoudhia* suggest the deliberate addition of copper, perhaps to counterbalance the paler hue imparted to the gold by the silver, because of the relatively wide range in the quantitative evaluation of this element. The sheet of gold from Tomb 164B at Bellapais *Vounous* was a gold alloy with silver and copper as well as some lead (Plenderleith 1950:370).

CONCLUSIONS

The use of X-ray fluorescence permitted the analysis in a substantially non-destructive manner of most of the metal finds from Sotira *Kaminoudhia*. The results demonstrate how Cypriot metallurgy was quite advanced in the Philia Phase and Early Cypriot period.

Along with the arsenical alloys, which show a clear addition of arsenic to obtain an alloy with precise characteristics of hardness and color, tin alloys have also been found. In this latter instance, tin, which was certainly a highly prized and valued metal, appears to have been used for mainly aesthetic purposes, to obtain objects of prestige denoting a particular social rank of the people who possessed them. Gold had a similar function and was used, like tin-bronze, for the manufacture of earrings.

Finally, it must be mentioned how a range of evidence, such as the dagger-ingot and the crucible for melting copper-based metal, suggests the presence of local metallurgic activities, mainly aimed at the casting of artifacts. It is therefore possible to suggest that at least some of the *Kaminoudhia* objects were made directly *in loco*.

ACKNOWLEDGMENTS

The authors wish to thank the Department of Antiquities and the Cyprus Museum for giving permisssion to analyze the metal from Sotira *Kaminoudhia*. Thanks are also due to Dr. Maria Rosaria Belgiorno, who facilitated the import of the instruments to Cyprus. We are grateful to Dr. Angela Cracas Giardino, who prepared the illustrations for the present study. The following authors contributed to the these sections: Introduction: C.G., G.E.G., S.R.; Methodology: G.E.G., S.R; Measurement Specifics: G.E.G., S.R.; Discussion: C.G.

Table 8.1.1. Quantative Energy Dispersive X-Ray Fluorescence analyses of metal objects from Sotira *Kaminoudhia* and a crucible from Paramali *Pharkonia*.

sample name	%							weight
	as	pb	sn	fe	sb	ni	cu	grams
m5 (A)	-	-	-	tr	-	-	100.0	3
m8 (A)	-	-	-	tr	-	-	100.0	2
m9 (A)	4.0	-	-	tr	-	-	96.0	8
m10 (A)	2.7	-	-	tr	-	-	97.3	4
m11 (A)	-	-	-	tr	-	-	100.0	6
m12 (A)	3.2	-	-	0.3	-	-	96.5	114
m12 (B)	3.8	-	-	0.6	-	-	95.6	
m12 (C)	3.5	-	-	tr	-	-	96.5	
m13 (A)	0.9	0.3	4.8	0.3	-	-	93.7	1
m14 (A)	0.5	-	5.8	-	-	-	93.7	1
m15 (A)	0.6	-	-	0.2	-	-	99.2	1
m16 (A)	7.0	-	-	2.1	-	-	90.9	<1
m17 (A)	2.0	0.1	-	tr	0.9	2.1	94.9	10
m18 (A)	0.3	-	-	0.5	-	-	99.2	35
m18 (B)	0.3	-	-	0.5	-	-	99.2	
m19 + m26 (A)	1.7	-	-	0.4	-	-	97.9	20
m19 + m26 (B)	1.6	-	-	tr	-	-	98.4	
m20 (A)	2.8	-	-	tr	-	-	97.2	<1
m21 (A)	1.7	0.3	10.2	0.7	-	-	87.1	<1
m22 (A)	0.5	-	13.1	-	-	-	86.4	<1
m25 (A)	2.9	-	-	0.7	-	-	96.4	<1
m27 (A)	0.6	-	-	0.7	-	-	98.7	4
m27 (B) rivet	1.0	-	-	tr	-	-	99.0	
m28 (A)	0.4	-	-	0.6	-	-	99.0	1
m29 (A)	-	-	-	-	-	-	100.0	4
m30 (A)	2.9	-	-	1.4	-	-	95.7	<1

	cu	ag	au		
m6	1 - 3	15 - 20	77 - 84		
m7	1 - 3	15 - 20	77 - 84		

	as	pb	sn	fe	sb	ni	cu
crucible (A)	0.3	-	-	2.8	-	-	96.9

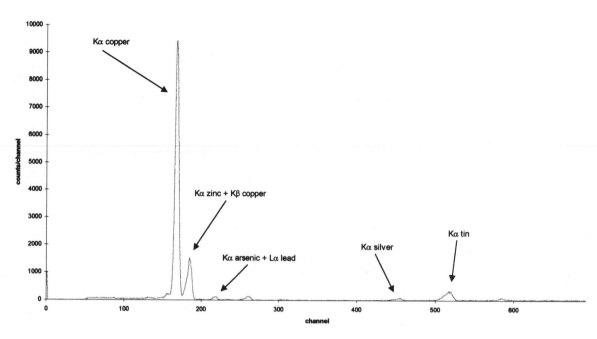

Fig. 8.1.1. Measurement performed by Energy Dispersive X-Ray Fluorescence on an alloy.

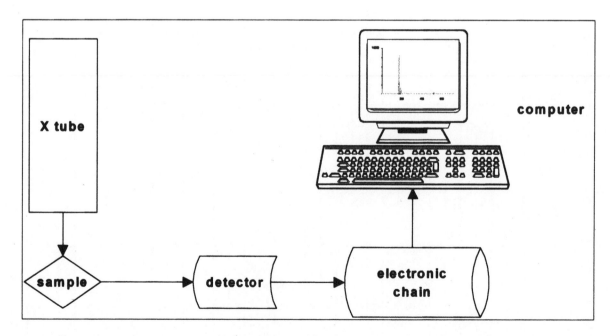

Fig. 8.1.2. Diagram of the equipment used for Energy Dispersive X-Ray Fluorescence Analyses.

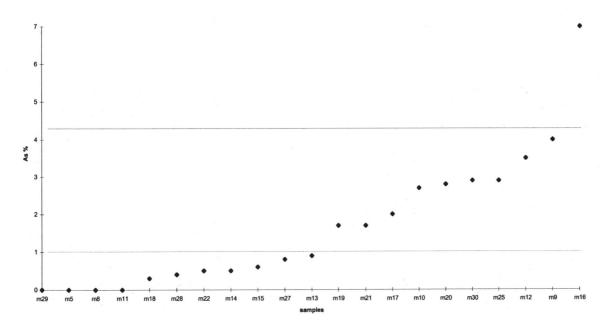

Fig. 8.1.3. Arsenic content of the objects from Sotira *Kaminoudhia*. Objects with less than 1% arsenic are considered as unintentional alloys.

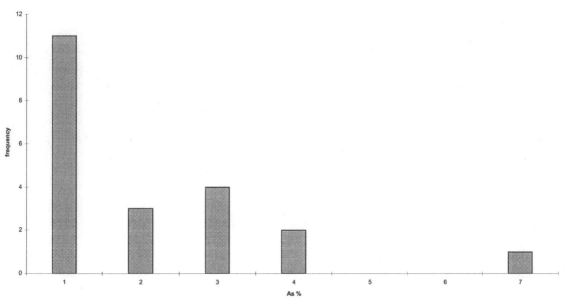

Fig. 8.1.4. Relative percentage of arsenic found in the metal objects from Sotira *Kaminoudhia*.

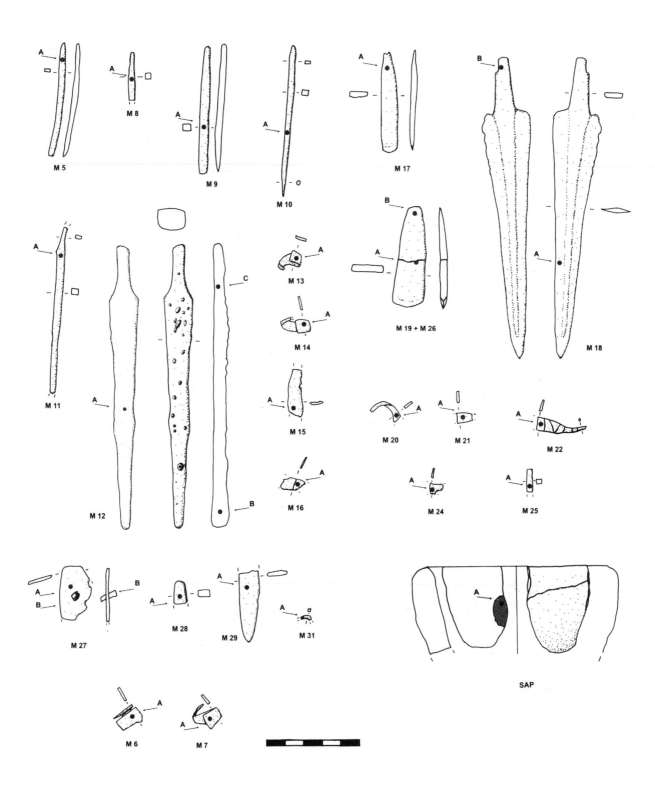

Fig. 8.1.5. Location of samples (A, B, C, etc.) taken from the metal objects from Sotira *Kaminoudhia* and the crucible (SAP) from Paramali *Pharkonia*.

9

THE TERRACOTTAS

by C l a r k A. W a l t z a n d S t u a r t S w i n y[1]

INTRODUCTION

The assemblage of terracotta objects excavated at Sotira *Kaminoudhia* is quite small, but is typical of sites such as Marki *Alonia*, Alambra *Mouttes* and Episkopi *Phaneromeni*, which all belong to the earlier phases of the Cypriot Bronze Age. Of the 54 objects classified in this category, 30 were beads and spindle whorls, two were loom weights and the remainder were modified sherds—such as roundels—or unidentified and questionable pieces like TC22, the figurine arm (?), and TC8 a possible tripod foot.

LOOM WEIGHTS

Loom weights dated to the EC period are uncommon because of the previous emphasis on the excavation of cemetery sites, where such objects were rarely deposited with the dead (Stewart 1962:233). The excavations at Marki *Alonia* have, however, significantly changed the picture with 11 complete, near complete and fragmentary loom weights dated to the EC III-MC I periods (Frankel and Webb 1996b: 197ff.). An additional four fragmentary MC loom weights were recorded at Alambra *Mouttes* (Coleman et al. 1996:234ff.). The two loom weight fragments from Sotira *Kaminoudhia* are, therefore, significant in terms of the total sample. However, their fragmentary state renders them less useful for providing significant information on the typology of the objects or the nature of EC weaving.

TC1 is from a weight similar to Åström's Type 1—or roughly conical—loom weight, which is perhaps better described as pyramidal (Åström 1972:156). The closest parallel for TC1 is found at Episkopi *Phaneromeni*, where TC187 of Type 1b exhibits the same truncated top (Swiny 1986:108, fig. 71). Other similar types are found at Bellapais *Vounous* (Dikaios 1940:79, pl. LIX, 15), Marki *Alonia* (op. cit.), Alambra *Mouttes* (op. cit.) with four examples (E205–208) similar to Type 1b from *Phaneromeni*, and at Kalopsida (Myres 1897:139, figs. 4, 5).

TC2 (fig. 9.2:TC2) is a fragment of a conical loom weight, Åström's Type 1 (Åström 1972:157). It is interesting to note that his MC Types 3 and 4, discoidal in shape, are unattested at *Kaminoudhia*, *Alonia*, *Mouttes*, and *Phaneromeni*. TC2 is not sufficiently preserved to make a definite typological determination. Several parallels were found previously at Alambra (Stewart 1962:233, fig. 96:20) and Kalopsida (Myres 1897: fig. 4: 6, 7).

---

[1] This chapter was written by the first author in 1984 who at that time undertook a detailed study of the Sotira *Kaminoudhia* terracottas. His manuscript was provided with a short introduction, updated and edited for publication in 1997 by the second author.

These terracotta loom weights are among the earliest so far attested in Cyprus. If warp weight looms were in use on the island during the Early Prehistoric period, the weights were certainly of stone. Numerous pierced stones from Neolithic and Chalcolithic sites were weighed and measured by the writer (C.A.W.); of these, two—Khirokitia *Vouni* no. 1096 (Dikaios 1962: fig. 22) and Sotira *Teppes* no. 83 (Dikaios 1961:202, pl. 103) are of sufficient size and weight (425.6 gr and 125 gr respectively) to have served as loom weights. However, comparable artifacts of terracotta are unrecorded until the Bronze Age, a conclusion supported by the extensive excavations at Lemba *Lakkous* (Peltenburg 1985) and Kissonerga *Mosphilia* (Peltenburg 1991).

If, as the fragments from *Kaminoudhia* would suggest, terracotta loom weights made their first appearance on Cyprus during the EC period, they are one of several classes of artifacts to have Anatolian prototypes, as noted by Frankel and Webb (1996b). Both pyramidal (conical) and ovoid terracotta loom weights were found in the Early Bronze II levels of Tarsus (Goldman 1956:323, fig. 411). The *Kaminoudhia* examples are too fragmentary for definite equation with the Tarsus weights, but both chronological and typological considerations support a possible connection.

TC1 and 2 do not shed any light on the relative chronology of Cypriot Bronze Age loom weights. The best parallel for TC1 comes from Alambra *Mouttes* (Coleman et al. 1996:235, fig. 50, pl. 31) and the LC 1A settlement at Episkopi *Phaneromeni*, and this shape is supposedly less common in the early period (Swiny 1986:107, n. 71). MC parallels for both weights from *Mouttes* and Kalopsida have been noted above. It is suggested here that, once introduced during the EC period, terracotta loom weights were subject to the same conservatism that is a general feature of EC and MC pottery on the east and south coasts (Herscher 1976:14).

Both loom weights were recovered from the Phase II level of Unit 1 in Area A, which formed part of a large courtyard. Three spindle whorls (TC3, 6 and 7) were also recovered from this unit, possibly suggesting that textile production was carried out here.

MODIFIED SHERDS

The modified sherds from Alambra *Mouttes* (Coleman et al. 1996:218 ff.) and Marki *Alonia* (Frankel and Webb 1996b:202 ff.) have been the subject of detailed studies, which need not be duplicated, since many parallels may be drawn between the material from these sites and that from *Kaminoudhia*.

TERRACOTTA TRIPOD FOOT? (TC8; fig. 9.2). TC8 is part of a larger object of unknown size and function and is unique at Sotira *Kaminoudhia*. It is most likely to have been the end of a tripod leg from a RP cooking pot. Appropriately enough the tip shows definite signs of abrasion or wear.

SHERD PENDANT (TC34; fig. 9.2; pl. 9.1). Though sherds which have been shaped for secondary use are not uncommon in Cypriot Early Prehistoric contexts—for example at Troulli (Dikaios 1962: fig. 36: 21, 22) and Erimi *Pamboula* (Dikaios 1939: fig. 14:A, B)—their use often has been difficult to interpret accurately. TC34 clearly was used as a pendant. The placement of the perforation opposite the point insures a proper hang and the wear around the perforation is consistent with that noted on indisputable pendants made from stone.

While not as common as pendants fashioned of picrolite or even andesite, terracotta was used for objects of personal adornment in the Chalcolithic. A similar, though more ovoid, example found at Erimi *Pamboula* was made of Red-on-White ware (Dikaios 1939: fig. 16:F). This was originally fashioned as a pendant and not chipped from a sherd. Another example was located among unpublished sherds from Erimi *Pamboula* Level 160–180 m in the Cyprus Museum. This pendant, made from a

Red-on-White sherd, is also in the shape of a pentagram. Drilling of the perforation was not completed, due perhaps to the off-center placement of the hole. Two similar "labels or pendants," one quadrilateral and one hexagonal, were recovered from EB II levels at Tarsus (Goldman 1956:327, pl. 445: 70, 71).

SHERD ROUNDELS (TC29, 30, 31, 32, 37, 42, 43, 44, 45, 46, 47, 48, 49, 50, 51, 52, 53, 54; fig. 9.2; pl. 9.1). Eighteen sherd roundels were found at Sotira *Kaminoudhia*, seventeen from the settlement and one (TC31) unstratified from Cemetery A. All were formed from RP sherds which had been chipped into irregular discs, and no attempt had been made to smooth the edges. Sherds from both open and closed vessels were used. It is perhaps a coincidence—but an unlikely one—that none of the *Kaminoudhia* roundels was pierced (the known repertoire of roundels from other EC and MC sites includes at least some pierced examples).

Comparative material in greater quantities was excavated at Alambra *Mouttes* and Marki *Alonia*. From the former came 125 specimens of varying size and shape (Coleman et al. 1996:219–33), and from the latter 41 pierced, partially pierced and unpierced items were recorded (Frankel and Webb 1996b:207 ff.)

The Episkopi *Phaneromeni* typology for these objects is based on average diameter (Swiny 1986:109). One example from *Kaminoudhia*, TC29, with an average diameter of 2.6 cm, falls into the *Phaneromeni* Type I; diameters between 2.0 and 2.7 cm belong to Type II (three examples, TC30, 31, 32); diameters between 3.4 and 4 cm (TC37) fall between the types as defined by Swiny, with an average of 3.05 cm. It has been included in Type I for convenience as its diameter falls almost exactly midway between the two groups.

Swiny suggested that sherd roundels, especially the unpierced pieces, were used as jar stoppers, an interpretation generally accepted by other researchers. In fact, TC47 fits into the neck of jug P120, with which it was found in Unit 6. However, more recently a strong case has been made for interpreting at least some such objects as counters (Holloway and Lukesh 1995:52).

FIGURINE FRAGMENT?

The identification of TC22 (fig. 9.2) as the arm of a cruciform figurine is problematical. P. Åström (verbal communication to C.A.W., 1983) has suggested that it is a fragment of a hilt-shaped handle of a spouted bowl or a tab handle from a tankard or even an idol projection from a body of a Red Polished vase. These possibilities will be examined first. It should be noted, however, that despite its typically EC fabric, decoration and surface treatment, TC 22 is unstratified

Hilt-shaped handles do not appear in the RP ware of the Philia Phase, where the deep flat-bottomed spouted bowls are invariably handleless, as at Philia *Vasiliko* (Dikaios 1962: fig. 80) or have small lug handles as at Khrysiliou *Ammos* (Bolger 1983:66, pl. VII:1). The spouted bowls from Sotira *Kaminoudhia* have small horizontal or vertical handles (cf. fig. 4.3).

In the EC period hilt-shaped handles first appear on RP spouted bowls, types XA^2a, at Bellapais *Vounous*. They became increasingly common in RP II and III, types XAc_3, XAf_2, XAf_3, XA^2d (Stewart 1962: figs. CXXV:5–8, CXXVI:9). Numerous examples were recovered from Cemetery B at *Vounous* (Dikaios 1940: Tomb 2 n. 29; Tomb 6 no. 101; Tomb 13 nos. 23, 52; Tomb 15 no. 10; Tomb 18 no. 17; Tomb 29 no. 55; Tomb 36 nos. 22, 55). Similar handles also appear on WP IA spouted bowls, as on Tomb 2 no. 166 from *Vounous* (ibid. p. 7, pl. LV:3). These handles are morphologically distinct from TC22. They are all much larger and possess splayed rectangular ends and thicken noticeably toward the bottom. TC22 has a uniformly rounded end and does not thicken perceptibly towards its extremity. It is not incised on both sides as is common at *Vounous*, nor is there any evidence of a relief band.

TC22 is also distinct from the tab handles found on MC tankards (e.g., Åström 1972: fig. 15:10) in that it does not thicken toward the bottom where it would join with the lower handle. In any case, the tankard with tab handle seems to be an exclusively MC–LC form and is not found in the Sotira *Kaminoudhia* repertoire. If TC22 is part of a tab handle, this unstratified object would have to be regarded as intrusive to the site, which is very unlikely given the absence of any known MC settlement nearby and TC22's close similarity to the RP fabric of *Kaminoudhia*.

It might also be suggested that TC22 is an idol projection such as those found on RP III gourd juglets (e.g., Stewart 1962: fig. XCIII:2; fig. XCV:10), but the incised decoration on TC22 bears no resemblance to the anthropomorphic decoration found on such projections, nor is the motif paralleled in the motifs used on RP plank idols (Flourentzos 1973:30, fig. 2). Therefore, it is suggested that TC22 is the arm of a cruciform figurine. Chalcolithic cruciform figurines of picrolite are extremely common (Peltenburg 1985, 1998; Vagnetti 1979). Less favored are examples in terracotta. Two fragments of terracotta figurines with stump arms were found at Erimi *Pamboula* (Dikaios 1939: pl. XXVIII:550, no. 1123 unpublished). These stump arms approach the more fully developed cruciform type. A somewhat later example, in RW ware, was found at Kissonerga *Mosphilia* (Karageorghis 1983:919, fig. 36). A whole series of terracotta figurine fragments, including those of arms, was excavated at Kalavasos *Ayious* (South 1985). The most relevant piece for our discussion is an albeit much larger, but morphologically similar, undecorated arm fragment (South 1985: fig. 2.3). The full cruciform type in terracotta is reached by a steatopygus RP figurine in the Papanicolas Collection (Flourentzos 1982:24, pl. II:3). If our interpretation is correct, TC22 with its incised decoration seems to represent a late variant of the type, marking a transition between Chalcolithic figurines and EC RP plank idols.

An almost exact parallel to TC22 was found at Kissonerga *Mospihilia* (Peltenburg 1979:14, fig. 2, top). It is the left arm of a picrolite figurine with a similar section profile and exactly the same decorative motif, consisting of a vertical band of incisions connected with a diagonal band. The slight difference in the motif may be explained by the different medium.

Both the *Kaminoudhia* and *Mosphilia* fragments bear a marked resemblance to other figurines with segmented diagonal bands on the arms which are interpreted as some kind of ritual garment (Morris 1985:127, 129). The addition of the vertical segmented band is an elaboration of the basic type. One possible interpretation is that the vertical band represents an armlet, because on the *Mosphilia* fragment it continues around the entire arm. It may also be noted that the decoration on TC22, though incomplete, bears some resemblance to that on RP Philia ceramics.

Even though the specific motif employed on TC22 has Cypriot prototypes, the form and technique of decoration are seemingly Anatolian in origin. The Anatolian connections of some Chalcolithic figurines (Vagnetti 1979) and the Bronze Age RP plank idols (Flourentzos 1975:33) are well established. In addition to the connections already known, we may consider idols of the "Çaykenar" type (Thimme 1977, nos. 539–550). Some are similar in shape to the Beycesultan marble idols which have Cypriot picrolite parallels (Vagnetti 1979:112–13), while others may closely resemble Cypriot Early Bronze plank idols (Thimme 1977, nos. 544, 550). More importantly, the incised and punctured decoration with lime fill characteristic of these idols is similar to that employed on TC22 and the EC plank idols. The Çaykenar idols are commonly, if uncertainly, dated to the Early Bronze II (Thimme 1977:179–80). If this is correct, they may be seen as a prototype for the form and decorative technique of the later Cypriot terracotta idols.

These figurines—the Cypriot picrolite idols of the Beycesultan type and Sotira *Kaminoudhia* TC22—are all indicative of a period when native Cypriot elements combined with foreign influences. Despite its unstratified provenance, TC22 fits in well with what might be expected of figurines at this early stage of the Cypriot Bronze Age.

SPINDLE WHORLS AND BEADS

Typology

The artifacts considered here are pierced conical, truncated conical, biconical, hemispherical and discoidal objects of terracotta. The distinction between spindle whorls and beads is problematical and will be discussed below. Both beads and whorls may be classified according to similar typological considerations and will be considered together.

Stewart's (1962:349) classification of spindle whorls was based on shape alone. Åström (1972: 155–57) added ware as a secondary consideration. Swiny (1986:98–107) included decoration as a classifying feature, a system followed by Mogelonsky for the corpus of 65 whorls—including three probable beads—from Alambra *Mouttes* (Mogelonsky in Coleman et al. 1996:205 ff.). The 26 spindle whorls from Marki *Alonia* were classified by shape (Frankel and Webb 1996b:192 ff.).

Shape and decoration have been used as the basis for the classification of the *Kaminoudhia* material, the distinction between a Red Polished and a Brown Polished conical whorl seeming some-what artificial for these basically functional objects. The placement and nature of decoration can, on the other hand, be indicative of function, so it is retained as a criterion.

The whorls and beads from Sotira *Kaminoudhia* may be classified in the following manner:

Type 1: *Biconical* (fig. 9.1)
Sample: 8. Two with asymmetrical decoration (beads TC17, 18), 3 with symmetrical decoration (whorls TC12, 27, bead TC15), 3 undecorated (whorl TC19, beads TC13, 23).

Type 2: *Conical and truncated conical* (fig. 9.1)
Sample: 17. Fourteen decorated (whorls TC 3, 5, 6, 7, 11, 14, 25, 26, 28, 33, 38, 39, 40, 41), 3 undecorated (whorls TC9, 10, 16).

Type 3: *Ovoid* (fig. 9.2)
Sample: 1. Decorated (whorl TC 36).

Type 4: *Hemispherical* (fig. 9.2)
Sample: 2. Undecorated (whorls TC 20, 35).

Type 5: *Discoidal* (fig. 9.1)
Sample: 3. One decorated (bead TC21), 2 undecorated (whorl TC24, bead TC4).

The typological categories are self-explanatory, with the exception of truncated conical types, which have a deliberately flattened platform at the apex of the cone. Morphological variations within a single type are not noted, being irrelevant to the function in an artifact class, which is, on the whole, rather crudely manufactured.

Metrology

The difficulty of distinguishing between small spindle whorls and large beads was alluded to above. This problem has often been remarked upon (Taylor 1957:78; Swiny 1986:98; Coleman 1996:207–8; Frankel and Webb 1996b:191). At Episkopi *Phaneromeni* height was the factor used for differentiating biconical and spherical beads and whorls, any object under 2.4 cm in height being classed as a bead, a criterion which is not entirely satisfactory. To be effective a whorl must weigh over 10 gr and have a diameter of at least 2 cm. The maximum practical weight is around 160 gr (see in general Barber 1991 and Crewe 1998).

If a weight of 10 grams and a diameter of 2 cm are accepted as the smallest *functional* size of a spindle whorl, anything having smaller dimensions should be interpreted as a bead. One cannot assume however that ancient Cypriot weavers were aware of such precise distinctions and it is necessary to examine as large a sample of objects as possible according to a specific criterion in order to determine if any natural categories develop.

At *Kaminoudhia*, an attempt to establish mass/diameter ratios was abandoned as unproductive when the smallest beads and the largest whorls were found to exhibit similar ratios. Weight, therefore, was chosen as the most instructive category because it is equal to diameter as a functional criterion for spinning, and additionally it could be argued that there should have existed an upper limit on the weight of beads which may be worn comfortably (see Table 9.1). The actual or estimated weights of twenty-two beads and whorls from *Kaminoudhia* were noted.

Four distinct groups are apparent: 0–15 grams, 20–35 grams, 40–45 grams and 75–80 grams, with peaks within the groups at 10–15 grams, 20–25 grams and 40–45 grams (Table 9.2). When compared with the known weights of all Bronze Age terracotta beads and whorls available to the writer,[2] the overall groupings expand but peaks occur at the same weights (Table 9.3). This is indicative of functional categories.

How may these data be interpreted? It is suggested that, at *Kaminoudhia*, objects with a weight of 15 grams or below are best seen as beads, especially given the relatively small diameter of these pieces. Overall, 20 grams should be seen as the maximum weight for definite beads. Objects in the next category, 20–35 grams, with diameters of ca. 3 cm and above, are best seen as whorls although some of the smaller may, in fact, be large beads. The other two groups 40–45 grams and 75–80 grams are definitely whorls.

The different weight groups of the whorls may be explained as being intended for the spinning of different fibers. Wool requires a whorl of medium weight, which perhaps corresponds to the *Kaminoudhia* categories of 20–35 grams and 40–50 grams, with lighter whorls being employed for finer sheep's wool and the heavier whorls for coarser goat's hair. The heaviest whorls were undoubtedly used for spinning flax. Linen was used to wrap swords and daggers in Early and MC tombs (Åström 1965; Pieridou 1967).

It also seems possible to correlate shapes and function among the *Kaminoudhia* whorls and beads. The beads, as established by the above criteria, are either biconical or discoidal, whereas spindle whorls are primarily conical or truncated with only one discoidal and two biconical examples. The weights of TC12 and TC19, the biconical pieces, are both ca. 22 grams. With these fairly low weights and given the preponderance of biconical beads at *Kaminoudhia*, these objects may have been intended as large beads. In which case it would seem that at this site, the conical form was used exclusively for spindle whorls.

A similar situation exists at Philia *Vasiliko*, where five of the six "spindle whorls" found by Dikaios (1962:173, fig. 34 nos. 13–17) may be classified as definite beads according to the arguments put forth here. The two discoidal examples, T1.131 and T2.24, have weights of 12.35 and 9.1 grams. Three of the biconical examples, T2.20, T2.22 and T2.29, have weights less than 20 grams and diameters below 3 cm. Only one of the biconicals, T5a.32, has a large enough weight (25.8 grams) and diameter (3.5 cm) to make it a likely candidate for use as a spindle whorl.

---

[2] C.A.W. The total sample is 88 excluding the Alambra *Mouttes* and Marki *Alonia* material.

Table 9.1. The terracotta beads from Sotira *Kaminoudhia* (all measurements in centimeters).

TC NUMBER	WARE	TYPE	HEIGHT	DIAM.	DIAM. OF HOLE TOP BOT.		WEIGHT IN GR.	PROV.
4	RP?	Discoidal Undecorated	1.3	3	0.6	0.6	8.4	Surface
21	RP	Discoidal Decorated	1	2.1	0.4	0.4	3.7	Unit 5
13	RP	Biconical Undecorated	2.2	2.6	0.50	0.55	10.2	Unit 8
23	RP	Biconical Undecorated	1.8	2.7	0.4	0.5	11.	Tomb 15
15	Br P	Biconical Decorated	1.6	2.1	0.5	0.5	5.9	Unit 2
17	?	Biconical Decorated	2.2	2.4	0.5	0.5	12.	Unit 12
18	RP	Biconical Decorated	2.2	3.2	0.5	0.6	14.5	Unit 4
689*	RP ST	Biconical Decorated	2.3	3.75	7.5	7.5	13.4	Area 1 *Teppes*

*689 was excavated in Level III or more likely IV (surface to Floor 1) by P. Dikaios at Sotira *Teppes*. See Dikaios 1961.

Table 9.2. Bar chart with the weights of 22 beads and whorls from Sotira *Kaminoudhia*. Vertical axis represents number of items, horizontal the weight in grams.

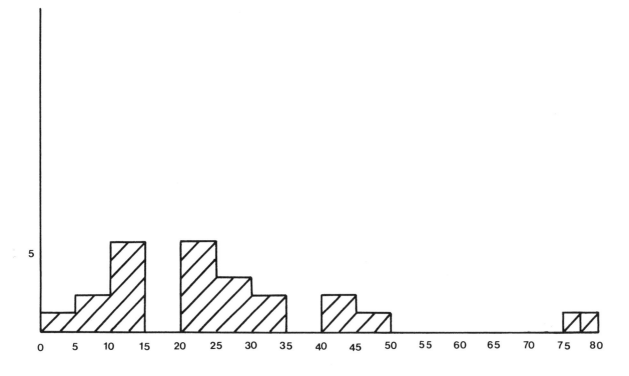

Table 9.3. Bar chart with the weights of 88 Cypriot Bronze Age beads and whorls. Vertical axis represents the number of items, horizontal axis the weight in grams.

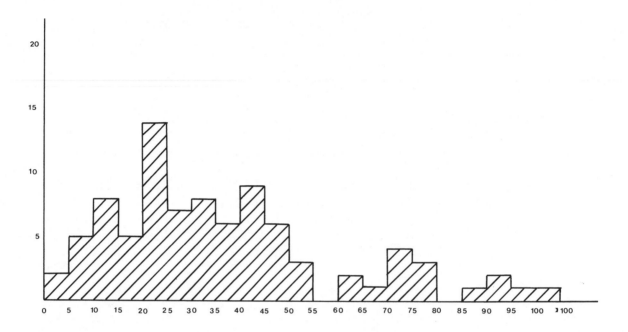

Table 9.4. Decorative motifs used on beads and whorls from Sotira *Kaminoudhia*. The numbers below the individual motifs indicate which whorls display the motif. Note that the motif found on TC3 is also recorded on TC33 and 38; that found on TC14 is also recorded on TC39; that found on TC6, 11 and 35 is also recorded on TC38; that found on TC29 and 38 is also recorded on TC27; the chevrons found on TC5 are also recorded on TC28, and TC38 has a double row of these chevrons; the single diagonal row of dots found on TC25 is also recorded on TC36 (some elements from TC 28 and TC35 not included in this table).

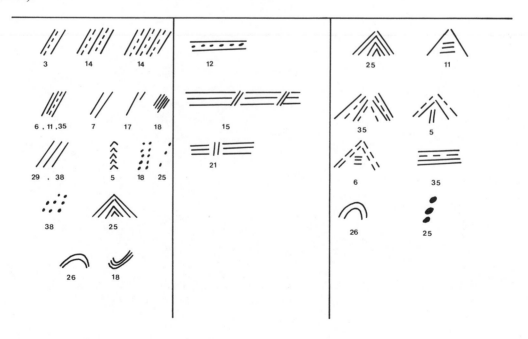

Decoration

The decoration of the *Kaminoudhia* beads and whorls consists of lime filled "incisions" (made with a sharp pointed object, rectangular in section) and "punctures" (pinpricks made with a sharp pointed object, circular in section) arranged in simple linear patterns with a definite emphasis on linear diagonal motifs. Of the 25 distinct patterns employed, only four are horizontal, and two are curvilinear (see Table 9.4). The preferred pattern consists of two or more parallel diagonal lines which often frame a series of incisions or punctures. Chevron patterns are a variation of this basic element which is often employed on the flat surface of conical whorls. All of the patterns are abstract, with the possible exception of what may be a "feather" pattern on TC5 and TC28. Even though only one pattern is repeated in an identical manner more than once, the overall homogeneity of the decoration suggests that the persons who produced the *Kaminoudhia* whorls and beads were cognizant of each others' work and maintained an artistic tradition with little deviation from an accepted norm throughout the life of both settlement and cemetery. The singular lack of variety does suggest that the coroplasts were a tight knit group, perhaps even an extended family.

The motifs employed at *Kaminoudhia* have little in common with the majority of the decorative schemes used on beads and whorls from other published EC sites. Although framed incisions and punctures occur at Marki *Alonia* (Frankel and Webb 1996b: fig. 8.5:P784, 5032, 5899; fig. 8.6:P7141), they are rare by comparison with *Kaminoudhia*. The two parallel curved lines found on TC26 have several comparanda at Bellapais *Vounous* (E. and J. Stewart 1950: pl. C:T92.7, T97.2, T116.25.30, esp.T93.12). The double chevron pattern consisting of one solid line and one line of punctures, found on the base of TC5, is found on the body of another *Vounous* whorl (ibid., T95.1). A row of framed punctures, found on TC12, is also paralleled at *Vounous* (Stewart 1962: fig. 95:13, *Vounous* Dump no. 2) and the "leaf" pattern on TC5 is similar to that on a whorl from Lapithos (ibid., fig. 95:17, Lapithos 314B²:80). The closest parallels for one of the *Kaminoudhia* terracottas come from Philia *Vasiliko*, T2.24 and T1.131 (Dikaios 1962: fig. 84:16,17), which are very close in profile and decoration to *Kaminoudhia* TC21. The framed puncture motif seems to have a relatively long life in the south coast, appearing on several whorls from Episkopi *Phaneromeni* (Swiny 1986: fig. 70: TC10, 11, 19, 24, 25).

Some of the motifs found at *Kaminoudhia* were also used on EB II Anatolian whorls. The framed punctures on TC3 and TC14 are paralleled on a biconical whorl from Level XIII at Beycesultan (Lloyd and Mellaart 1962:274, fig. 5, Level XIII.2). A chevron pattern similar to that used on TC25 is found on a Level XIV whorl (ibid. level XIV.2). Although no parallels are noted from the EB II levels at Tarsus, there is a rough similarity between the leaf and chevron patterns at *Kaminoudhia* and whorls from EB III levels (Goldman 1956: pl. 448:37, 43). Even though the resemblance is clear, the importance of comparisons should not be over-estimated, due to the simplicity of the objects and the designs used on them.

Chronology

The pierced sherd roundels common to early prehistoric sites may have been used as spindle whorls but this is not firmly established. It seems certain that modeled whorls of terracotta were not known in Cyprus prior to the Philia Phase (Swiny 1979:197; Swiny 1986a:38; Peltenburg 1991:31). The biconical bead, TC 23, from Philia Phase Tomb 15 at *Kaminoudhia* thus complements the evidence provided by the biconical whorls from Philia *Vasiliko* (Dikaios 1962:173, figs. 84:13–15, LII:14), Nicosia *Ayia Paraskevi* (Stewart 1962:233, fig. 96:4; Hennessy *et al.* 1988:14, fig. 12), Dhenia *Kafkalla* (Nicolaou and Nicolaou 1988:105, pl. XIX:11) and most recently, Marki *Alonia* (Frankel and Webb 1997:103, fig. 13:P9758, P9572; 1999: fig. 9: P11211, P12238, P11675; 2000: fig. 11: P14222; Webb and Frankel 1999: fig. 22:12–15).

The biconical form was used exclusively for clay whorls in EB I and II Tarsus, Alishar Hüyük and Beycesultan (Goldman 1956:328–29; Lloyd and Mellaart 1962:277). It seems likely that these whorls were inspirations for the biconical terracottas of the Philia Phase. This same shape was used most often, if not exclusively, for Philia Phase beads. Note, however, that biconical stone and shell beads are well known in Cyprus from early prehistoric sites such as Khirokitia *Vouni* (Dikaios 1962: fig. 27:1117) and Kalavasos *Ayious* (South 1985:73, figs. 4, 13, 21), so the shape could also be the continuation of an earlier tradition.

The origin of the conical whorl common at the *Kaminoudhia* settlement probably goes back to the EB III in Anatolia (Goldman 1956:329; Lloyd and Mellaart 1962:277). In Cyprus, its appearance in EC I (Stewart 1962:233, fig. 96) suggests continuing interaction with and influence from the mainland. In any case, the two *Kaminoudhia* whorls from Unit 6 in the settlement, TC19 and TC27—if they are not in fact large beads—may support Stewart's contention that the biconical form remained popular into the later EC period.

The reliance on the conical form continues through the MC in the southern region of the island (Swiny 1986:101, Table 3 p. 103), while the biconical and spherical forms were more popular elsewhere (Åström 1972:155–57; Swiny 1986:102). This reliance on the conical shape extends a previously noted south coast cultural trait well back into the EC period, which confirms both the essential cultural conservatism of southern Cyprus and the general unreliability of spindle whorls as chronological indicators, a point also noted by Frankel and Webb (1996b:195).

Placement of Whorls on the Spindle

Several *Kaminoudhia* whorls have central perforations that are wider at one end, a characteristic interpreted as being intended to prevent slippage down the spindle (Frankel and Webb 1996b:193; Swiny 1986:99). The *Kaminoudhia* examples suggest that the new technology represented by the clay whorls was not fully understood, because seven of the whorls have uniform perforations.

Exactly how the whorls would have been placed on the shaft has been debated (Frankel and Webb 1996b:193–94). Two terracotta spindle models from Bellapais *Vounous* (E. and J. Stewart 1950: pl. C; Stewart 1962: fig. 90:6; Dikaios 1940: pl. LVI) show differing placements. One example, T29.52, shows a conical whorl at the thick end of a tapering spindle while the other, T92.6, has a conical whorl about one-third of the way down the spindle. It has been suggested that these models "must differ from reality in that they show the spindles incorrectly tapered, a feature which would have caused the whorl to work loose and slip down the shaft" (Swiny 1986:99). This statement was based on the contemporary Cypriot practice of placing the whorl at the top of the spindle (Swiny 1986: fig. 32b) and attaching the yarn to a metal hook inserted into this end. It would appear, however, that, as suggested by Frankel and Webb (1996b), in the Bronze Age spindles were employed the other way up.

These models have in fact been viewed upside down and the whorl was placed at or near the bottom of the spindle. Both ancient and modern Greek spindles were employed in this manner, with the widest flat decorated "base" of conical whorls facing up towards the spinner. Such an arrangement would explain the decorated "bases" of the conical whorls, which hardly need to bear ornamentation if placed facing down at the top of the spindle in the manner of contemporary wooden whorls from Cyprus and elsewhere (Swiny 1986:99, fig. 32b).[3]

---

[3] This conclusion was reached independently by Walz prior to the publication of the Marki *Alonia* excavations in 1996, which argues for the same disposition of the whorl. Swiny's comments (1986:99) on the placement and use of conical whorls have thus been proven to be incorrect. The tapering of the central perforation was surely intentional and intended to enable the whorl to fit tightly into the spindle, something especially necessary if the whorl was placed at the bottom of the spindle, as seen in the Bellapais *Vounous* models. The remarks by Frankel and Webb (1996b:194) on wear patterns noted on whorls add further weight to their interpretation.

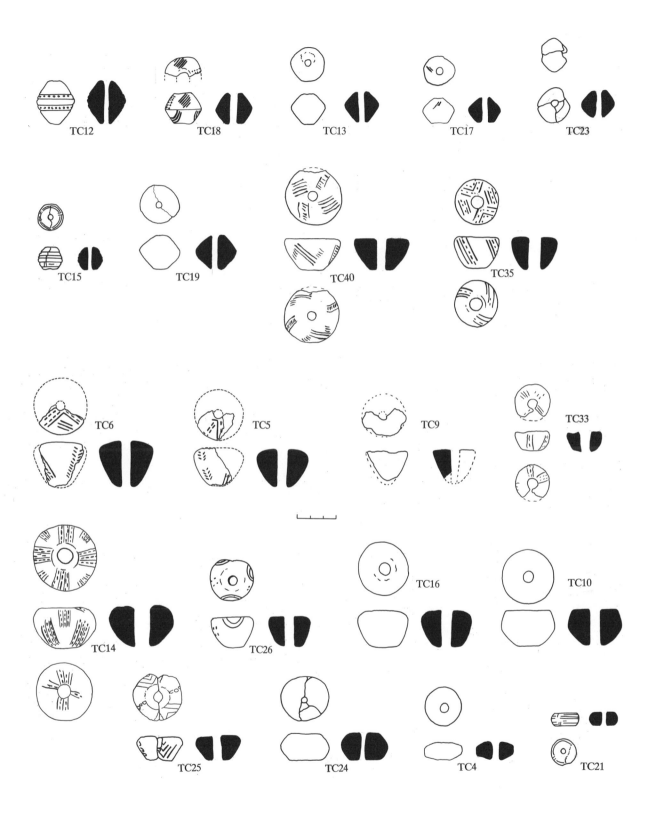

Fig. 9.1. Terracotta beads (TC18, 13, 17, 23, 15, 4, 21) and spindle whorls from Sotira *Kaminoudhia*.

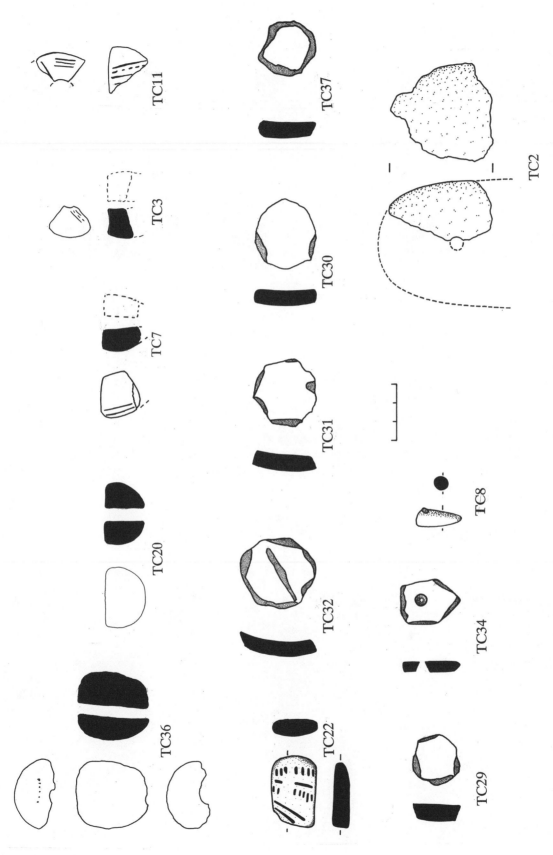

Fig. 9.2. Terracotta spindle whorls (TC36, 20, 7, 3, 11), figurine fragment (?) (TC22), modified sherds (TC32, 31, 30, 37, 29), pendent (TC34), tripod foot (?) (TC8) and loom weight (TC2) from Sotira *Kaminoudhia*.

TERRACOTTA CATALOGUE

All measurements in centimeters.

TC1. Loom weight, pyramidal. Area A Unit 1 Phase II. Only a small fragment preserved. H. 6.9; av. D. 5.5. Pink (7.5YR 7/4) fabric, coarse with pebble inclusions. Undecorated.

TC2. Loom weight, pyramidal. Fig. 9.2; Swiny 1985a: fig. 4:5. Area A Unit 1 Phase II. Fragmentary. Est. D: 6.4; pres. wt: 58.2 gr; est. wt 150 gr. Reddish-yellow (7.5YR 8/6) fabric, coarse with many pebble inclusions. Undecorated.

TC3. Spindle whorl. Fig. 9.2. Area A Unit 1 Phase II. Type 2, conical or truncated conical with incised decoration. Fragmentary. Reddish-gray (5YR 6/6) lustrous slip. Incised decoration with lime fill: two groups of vertical dots enclosed by lines.

TC4. RP (?) bead. Fig. 9.1. Surface. Discoidal, undecorated. Intact. H: 1.3; D: 3; D of perforation: 0.6; wt: 8.5 gr. Very pale brown (10YR 8/3) fabric with fine grit temper. Slip not preserved.

TC5. RP spindle whorl. Fig. 9.1; Swiny 1985a: fig. 4:4; Swiny 1986a: fig. 3:22. I4C 3, Cemetery A unstratified. Type 2, conical with incised decoration. fragmentary. H: 3.2; est. D: 3.2; pres. wt: 11.2 gr, est. wt: ca. 30 gr. Very dark gray (5YR 3/1) with heavy grit temper. Incompletely fired. Reddish-brown (2.5YR 4/4) lustrous slip. Incised decoration with lime fill. "Feather" pattern on body, broken and solid chevrons over two vertical lines on base.

TC6. RP spindle whorl. Fig. 9.1; Swiny 1985a: fig. 4:7. Area A Unit 1 Phase II. Type 2, conical with incised decoration. Fragmentary. H: 3.4; est. D: 4; pres. wt: 17.4 gr; est. wt: 40 gr. Red (10YR 4/8) fabric with very dark gray (2.5YR 3) core. Medium grit and few fiber inclusions. Dark reddish-gray (10YR 4/1) slip. Incised decoration with lime fill. "Leaf" pattern and framed punctures on body, chevrons of solid and broken lines over three horizontal lines on base.

TC7. RP spindle whorl. Fig. 9.2. Area A Unit 1 Phase II. Type 2, conical or truncated conical with incised decoration. Fragmentary. Pinkish-gray (5YR 6/2) fabric with grit temper. Very dark gray (5YR 3/1) slip. Incised decoration with lime fill. Two vertical lines on body.

TC8. Terracotta point (tripod foot?). Fig. 9.2. Area C Unit 10. Fragmentary and worn. H: 2.5; max D: 0.8. Lightish brown-gray (10YR 6/2) fabric with heavy grit temper. No slip.

TC9. BrP spindle whorl. Fig. 9.1. Area A Unit 1 Phase II. Type 2, conical, undecorated. Fragmentary. H: 2.2; D: ca. 3.5; pres. wt: 9.2 gr; est. wt: 25 gr. =Reddish-gray (5YR 5/4) slip.

TC10. RP spindle whorl. Fig. 9.1; Swiny 1985a: fig. 4:6; Swiny 1986a: fig. 3:21. Area C Unit 17. Type 2, truncated conical, undecorated. 95% intact. H: 2.6; max. D: 3.7; pres. wt: 45.4 gr; est. wt: 50 gr. Grayish-brown (10YR 5/2) fabric with grit temper. Dark-gray (10YR 4/1) slip.

TC11. RP spindle whorl. Fig. 9.2. Area A Unit 1 Phase II. Type 2, conical or truncated conical with asymmetrical decoration. Fragmentary. H: 2.2; Max. D: 3.0; pres. D: 0.4. Red (10R 5/6) fabric with grit temper. Reddish-black (10R 2.5/1) core. Red (10R 5/6) slip. Incised decoration with lime fill. Line of punctures framed by two vertical lines on left and one vertical line on right, three horizontal lines framed by diagonal lines on base.

TC12. RP spindle whorl. Fig. 9.1. I5B (unstratified above T17). Type 1, biconical with asymmetrical decoration. Almost intact. H: 3.2; max. D: 2.9; end D: 1; hole D: 0.5. Reddish-brown (5YR 5/4) fabric with fine grit temper. Very dark gray (7.5YR N3) core. Red (2.5YR 5/8) slip. Incised decoration with lime fill. Two parallel horizontal groups of framed punctures.

TC13. RP bead. Fig. 9.1. Area C Unit 8. Biconical, undecorated. Fragmentary and repaired. H: 2.2; max. D: 2.6; end D: 1.1; hole D: 0.5 -0.55; wt: 10.2 gr. Light brownish-gray (10YR 6/2) fabric with fine grit temper. No slip remaining.

TC14. RP spindle whorl. Fig. 9.1. Area C Unit 2. Type 2, conical, incised. Intact. H: 3; max. D: 5; hole D: 1.2 - 1.1. Black fabric with fine grit temper. Incised parallel lines and perforations running perpendicular to the axis.

TC15. BrP bead. Fig. 9.1. Area C Unit 2. Biconical, incised. Almost intact. H: 1.6; max. D:2.1; end D:1; hole D: 0.5; wt: 5.9 gr. Light reddish-brown (5YR 6/3) to dark gray (10YR 4/1) mottled fabric with fine grit temper. Dark brown (7.5YR 3/4) slip. Incised decoration with lime fill. Two bands of three parallel horizontal lines broken by two vertical lines.

TC16. RP spindle whorl. Fig. 9.1. Area A Unit 7. Type 2, conical, undecorated. Intact. H: 2.5; bottom D: 3.9; top D: 1.9; hole D: 0.9 - 0.8; wt: 45.6 gr. Light brown (7.5YR 6/4) fabric with fine grit temper. Light reddish-brown (2.5YR 6/4) slip.

TC17. Bead of uncertain fabric. Fig. 9.1. Area B Unit 12. Biconical. Fragmentary, three-fourths preserved. H: 2.2; D:2.4; hole D: 0.5; pres. wt: 8.5 gr; est. wt: 12 gr. Light reddish-brown (5YR 6/3) fabric with fine grit temper. No slip preserved. Incised decoration with lime fill. Two diagonal lines.

TC18. RP bead. Fig. 9.1. Area A Unit 4 Phase I. Biconical. One-half preserved. H: 2.2; max. D: 3.2; hole D: 0.6 - 0.5; pres. wt: 15 gr. Light gray (5YR 7/1) fabric with fine grit temper, reddish-black (5R 2.5/1) very lustrous slip. Incised decoration with lime fill. Upper register has one group of two parallel vertical lines of punctures and one group of six diagonal lines. Two groups of three parallel curving lines on lower register.

TC19. BrP spindle whorl. Fig. 9.1. Area A Unit 6. Type 1, biconical. Three-fourths preserved. H: 2.3; max. D: 3.1; end D: 1.4; hole D: 5; pres. wt: 16.6 gr; est. wt: 22 gr. Very pale brown (10YR 7/4) fabric with heavy grit and gravel temper. Dark gray (7.5 YR N4) core.

TC20. RP spindle whorl. Fig. 9.2. Area C Unit 2. Type 4, hemispherical. Intact. H: 2.2; max. D: 3.5; base D: 3.2; hole D: 0.7; wt: 29.6 gr. Reddish-brown (2.5YR 5/4) fabric with heavy grit temper. Red (7.5R 5/8) to dark gray (7.5R N/4) mottled fugitive slip. Asymmetrical central perforation.

TC21. RP bead. Fig. 9.1. Area A Unit 5. Discoidal. Intact. H: 1; D: 2.1; hole D: 0.4; wt: 3.7 gr. Light gray (7.5YR N7) fabric with very few fine grits. No slip preserved. Incised decoration: two horizontal bands, one of three lines, one of two, interrupted by two vertical strokes. Lime fill fugitive.

TC22. RP figurine arm fragment? Fig. 9.2. H24A (unstratified in Area C above Unit 21). H: 3.6; W: 2.2 - 2.5; max. the 1. Light reddish-brown (2.5YR 6/4) fabric with heavy grit temper, fugitive light red (10R 6/6) slip. Incised decoration with lime fill. One group of two diagonal lines, two vertical groups of punctures separated by vertical lines.

TC23. RP bead. Fig. 9.1. Tomb 15. Three-fourths preserved. H: 1.8; max. D: 2.7; hole D: 0.4 - 0.5; pres. wt: 8.1 gr; est. wt: 11 gr. Pink (5YR 7/4) fabric with fine grit temper. Pinkish gray (5YR 6/2) core. Light red (10R 6/8) slip.

TC24. RP spindle whorl. Fig. 9.1. Area B Unit 13. Type 5, discoidal, undecorated. Broken and restored, 90% complete. H: 2; max. D: 3.5; end D: 2.3; hole D: 0.5; wt: 29 gr. Red (2.5YR 4/8) to dark reddish gray (5YR 4/2) mottled fabric with medium grit temper. Dark gray (5YR 4/1) core. No slip preserved.

TC25. BrP spindle whorl. Fig. 9.1. Area A Unit 7. Type 2, conical, incised. Broken and restored. H: 1.8; max. D: 3.6; top D: 2.1; hole D: 0.8; wt: 20.6 gr. Pinkish-gray (7.5YR 6/2) fabric with fine grit temper. Reddish-brown (5YR 5/4) slip.

Incised decoration of two opposing groups of four chevrons, two opposing diagonal lines of three punctures.

TC26. BrP spindle whorl. Fig. 9.1. Area A Unit 7. Type 2, truncated conical. Intact, one small chip. H: 2.4; max. D: 3.4; top D: 2; hole D: 0.8 - 0.7; wt: 26.6 gr. Light brown (7.5YR 6/4) fabric with fine grit temper. Slip totally eroded. Incised decoration of three groups of concentric semicircles, one group of four punctures.

TC27. RP spindle whorl. Swiny 1986a: fig. 3:20. Area A Unit 6. Type 1, biconical, incised. Intact. H: 3.6; D: 3.7; top hole D: 0.84; bottom hole D: 0.80. Gray fine grit temper. Some evidence for a brown slip covering the mottled black/gray surface. Both cones decorated with four rather crude bands of four to six parallel incisions.

TC28. BrP spindle whorl. Area C Unit 2. Type 2, conical, incised. Intact. H: 2.9, D: 4.4; top hole D: 0.75; bottom hole D: 0.86. Fine dark brown grit tempered fabric. Flat base and rounded, roughly conical sides. Incised decoration on base consisting of two V's with opposing angles made of framed incisions. Between the V's there are two diagonally placed motifs of three framed incisions. Sides decorated with an unusual arrangement of chevrons and parallel lines bordered by chevrons.

TC29. RP sherd roundel. Fig. 9.2, pl. 9.1. Area A Unit 40, Ft. 9. Th: 0.92; D: 2.6. Sherd from closed vessel shaped into a rough circle. Weak red (2.5YR 5/2) fabric with heavy grit temper. Dark reddish-gray (5YR 4/2) core. Red (2.5YR 5/6) slip.

TC30. RP sherd roundel. Fig. 9.2, pl. 9.1. C19D in Area B, unstratified. Intact. Th: 0.8; D:3.4 to 3.8. Sherd from open vessel shaped into a rough ovoid. Red (10R 5/8) fabric with grit and gravel temper. Dark reddish-gray (10R 4/1) core. Red (10R 5/8) to weak red (10R 4/2) slip.

TC31. RP sherd roundel. Fig. 9.2, pl. 9.1. Cemetery A, I6D, unstratified east of T12. Intact. Th: 0.9; D: 3.4 to 3.7 Sherd from open vessel shaped into a rough circle. Red (7.5R 5/6) fabric with heavy grit temper. Weak red (7.5R 5/2) core. Red (10R 5/5-4/8) slip.

TC32. RP Mottled sherd roundel. Fig. 9.2, pl. 9.1. EW Trial Trench, unstratified. Intact. Th: 0.9; D: 4.1 to 4.2. Sherd from open vessel with pronounced curve, shaped into roughly circular form. Red (2.5YR 5/8) fabric with heavy grit temper, red (10R 4/8) slip.

TC33. RP spindle whorl. Fig. 9.1. Area C Unit 22. Type 2, truncated conical. Incised. Fragmentary. H: 1.4; D: 2.7; top hole D: 0.78; bottom hole D: 0.83. Fine gray brown grit tempered fabric. Probably slipped. Base decorated with two opposing sets of four lines radiating from center and two (only one preserved) sets of double framed incisions. Sides decorated with alternating bands of double framed incisions and four parallel lines. Unusually small for a spindle whorl.

TC34. RP sherd pendant. Fig. 9.1, pl. 9.1. Area A Unit 40. Intact. Th: 0.6; W: 2.5; L: 3.2. RP sherd from open vessel chipped into rough pentagram. Hole drilled from one side slightly off-center. Visible wear around perforation. Reddish-yellow (5YR 6/6) fabric with medium grit temper. Red (2.5YR 5/6) slip.

TC35. BrP spindle whorl. Fig. 9.1. Area C Unit 21. Type 4, hemispherical. Slightly damaged. Incised. H: 2.5, D: 3.6; top hole D: 0.86; bottom hole D: 1.00. Base decorated with two opposing sets of framed incisions separated on each side by a motif consisting of an outer single incised line followed by a row of incisions, then two parallel incised lines. The sides are decorated with three similar motifs consisting of a single incised line followed by a row of incisions and two more incised lines.

TC36. RP spindle whorl. Fig. 9.2. Area C Unit 8. Type 3, ovoid. Incised. Fragmentary, about one-third preserved. H: 3.9; D: 3.6. Roughly ovoid with one end flattened. Fine brown grit-tempered fabric. Matt brown slip. Undecorated except for a line of six small punctures on the flat base.

TC37. RP sherd roundel. Fig. 9.2, pl. 9.1. Area A Unit 42. Intact. Th: 0.9; D: 3.1 to 3.2. Roughly circular.

TC38. BrP spindle whorl. Area A Unit 42. Type 2, conical. Incised. Fragmentary, less than one-third preserved. H: 2.5; D: 1.6. Fragment of a rounded conical whorl. Brown fine grit tempered fabric with a brown lustrous slip. Incised decoration consisting of alternating (?) bands of chevrons and double framed incisions and another incomplete motif of incisions and punctures in between.

TC39. RP spindle whorl. Area A Unit 1 Phase I. Type 2, conical or rhomboidal. About one-fourth preserved. D: (est.) 3.5. Fine sandy fabric with a thin slip and carefully incised lime-filled decoration on sides and base. The base has two bands of framed incisions and the side has two incisions framed by parallel lines.

TC40. RP spindle whorl. Fig. 9.1. Area A Unit 20. Type 2, conical. Incised. One small chip at base. H: 2.2; D: 4.1; top hole D:0.75; bottom hole D: 0.77. pres. wt: 39 gr; est. wt 40 gr. Reddish brown fine sandy fabric (5YR 4/4) either unslipped or with a slip of the same color. Dark gray core (5YR 3/1). Incised lime-filled decoration consisting of two bands of opposing framed diagonal incisions separating two motifs consisting of three diagonal parallel lines with a band of three to four incisions on opposing sides at either end, thus forming a zigzag motif. Base has two bands of framed incisions separating two sets of five diagonal lines.

TC41. BrP spindle whorl. Settlement surface. Type 2, truncated conical. Incised. One-half preserved. H: 1.75; D: 3.51; est. wt 20 gr. Pink (5YR 7/4) fabric with fine grit temper. Dark reddish-brown (5YR 2.5/2) slip. Incised decoration with lime fill. One group of two diagonal punctured lines on body. One group of three diagonal solid lines on base.

TC42. RP sherd roundel from an open shape. Area C C19D, unstratified above Unit 12. One-half preserved. 3.4 x 3.2; Th: 0.7.

TC43. RP sherd roundel. Area C Unit 10. Possibly an open shape, worn. 3.6 x 3.4; Th: 0.7. Roughly circular.

TC44. RP Mottled sherd roundel from an open shape. Area A Unit 42. 5.4 x 4.8; Th: 1.3.

TC45. Sherd roundel. Pl. 9.1. Area A Unit 6. From an open shape, worn. Chalcolithic fabric? 2.4 x 2.3; Th: 1.1. Roughly circular.

TC46. RP Mottled sherd roundel. Pl. 9.1. Area A Unit 3 Phase II. From a closed shape. 2.7 x 2.5; Th: 1.2.

TC47. RP Mottled sherd roundel. Pl. 9.1. Area A Unit 6, found with P120. Fits into the neck of jug P120. 4.0 x 3.8; Th: 1.0. Roughly circular.

TC48. Sherd roundel. Pl. 9.1. Area A Unit 16. Unidentifiable fabric with large inclusions, black core and brown surfaces. 3.5 x 3.3; Th: 0.9.

TC49. RP sherd roundel. Pl. 9.1. Area A Unit 1 Phase II. From a small closed vessel, oval in shape; corner chipped. 2.8 x 2.1; Th: 0.7.

TC50. RP sherd roundel. Pl. 9.1. Area A Unit 3 Phase II. From an open shape. 4.0 x 3.6; Th: 0.5.

TC51. RP Philia sherd roundel. pl. P.1. Area A Unit 4 Phase I. From a closed vessel. 3.5 x 3.1; Th: 1.

TC52. RP sherd roundel. Pl. 9.1. Area C Unit 2. From a closed shape. Worn. 3.0 x 3.0; Th: 1.1.

TC53. RPSC sherd roundel. Pl. 9.1. Area A Unit 20. Worn. 2.6 x 2.2; Th: 0.8.

TC54. RP sherd roundel. Pl. 9.1. Area C Unit 2. From an open shape. 2.9 x 2.7; Th: 0.6.

10

THE HUMAN SKELETAL REMAINS

by Carola Schulte Campbell

INTRODUCTION

The excavation of the Early Cypriot burial ground and settlement at Sotira *Kaminoudhia* yielded a small but interesting collection of human skeletal material. The importance of this collection is not in its size or the excellence of its preservation, but the glimpse it provides into the demography and the health of the population at *Kaminoudhia*. The occurrence of non-metric traits and cultural practices provide an insight into the population's movements and interrelationships of this time. The sample is small and may not be truly representative of the ancient population. However, where appropriate, comparisons are made with other collections, such as those from Neolithic Sotira and Khirokitia.

METHODS AND MATERIALS

The technical study of this skeletal material took place well after excavation, therefore the writer had to rely on the excavation notebooks and photographs taken in the field. This investigation has used a variety of morphometric techniques to make a holistic assessment of this small but significant collection. Individually the skeletal material has been analyzed for:

a. Age at Death
b. Gender
c. Biological Affinities
d. Disorders caused by Trauma
e. Diseases
f. Cultural Modification

The values used for age at death based on cranial sutures are those proposed by Todd and Lyon (1924) and McKern and Stewart (1957). The sub-adult osseous material was assessed on bone development and tooth eruption, using the standards given in Steele and Bramblett (1988) and William Bass (1971).

The standard measurements of the skull and long bones are those that are described in Bass (1971), Brothwell (1963), Krogman (1973) and Steele and Bramlett (1988). Reference material for the identification of pathological conditions came from a number of sources, but the primary ones are Brothwell (1963), Steel and Bramlett (1988) and Angel (various). The collection, as representative of the ancient population, is assessed for demographic characteristics and cultural practices (e.g., burial customs, artificial cranial deformation).

THE HUMAN SKELETAL REMAINS

In general the bones were not well preserved, and the excavation process inevitably caused further damage. In some incidences, the bone fabric was damaged by the buildup of calcareous deposits, and in other cases the osseous material was demineralized and had a soft bark-like texture. Nevertheless, it was possible to clean and reconstruct a number of skulls and long bones.

CEMETERY A

TOMB 4

Overview of burial

The small fragments of bone were scattered throughout the fill of the chamber.

Description and measurements

Cranial and Dental

DESCRIPTION	MEASUREMENTS	COMMENTS
Parietal fragments	7 mm thick	Somewhat inflated bones. One small area near complicata may not be fully closed.
Left Mandible		Left side of mandible with mental foramen. The tooth sockets of P2, M1 & M2 have completely resorbed, indicating that tooth loss occurred sometime before death.
Occipital	13 mm thick	Central portion with nuchal lines visible, very thick 13 mm with endocranial pitting.

A number of individual crowns of teeth were recovered, which are not well preserved. The teeth are small to medium in size and show only moderate wear.

TOOTH TYPE	CUSP PATTERN	WEAR	COMMENTS
Mandibular Molar 3	+5	Very Light	
Mandibular Molar 3	+5	Very Light	
Maxillary Molar 2	4+	Moderate	
Maxillary Molar 2	4+	Moderate	
Maxillary Molar? 1	4-	Moderate	Small
Maxillary Molar? 1	4-	Moderate	Small
Mandibular Premolar 1		Light	Right?
Mandibular Canine		Light	
Mandibular Canine		Light	
Maxillary Incosor 1 or 2		Light	

Post-cranial

DESCRIPTION	MEASUREMENTS	COMMENTS
Fibula	None possible	Adult?

Hand -
Left lunate
Navicular
Triquetral
Capitate
Pisiform
Phalange
  1st row
  2nd row
  3rd row
		
		One
		Four
		One

Femur		Group of shattered femora fragments from an adult

Analysis

At least one individual is represented and, by the state of the dentition, would appear to be a relatively young adult. The cranial fragments from Tomb 4 associated with the dentition indicate that the individual suffered from a particularly intriguing pathology. The skull fragments show an unusual thickness and inflation of the diploe. In the case of the occipital fragment, there is endocranial pitting. This is fairly typical of porotic hyperostosis, indicating a homeopathic disorder, most likely an anemia. As this individual did reach adulthood, it is not possible to attribute this to full blown thalassemia.

Overall the dental health was good in the 10 individual teeth. However, in the left mandible fragment the alveolar bone has resorbed as the result of tooth loss. This may have been due to trauma rather than decay or ill health.

TOMB 5

No skeletal remains.

TOMB 6

Overview of burial

The dentition, cranial, and long bone fragments may come from a single individual. The bone fabric of all specimens is covered in calcareous deposit.

Description and measurements

Cranial and Dental

The only cranial evidence is the portion that centers around bregma encompassing the superior anterior portion of the parietals, and the superior portion of the occipital (pl.10.1a). It was not possible to remove the encrusted limestone: therefore suture closure could not be determined. There are no signs of artificial cranial deformation.

The dentition is nearly completely represented with 24 teeth. Nine mandibular teeth are still in their sockets and fifteen maxillary teeth were found loose. Three incisor crowns were so badly preserved that it is impossible to distinguish whether they were mandibular or maxillary. The mandible is represented from the ascending ramus on the left side to the first molar on the right. It is parabolic in shape and is also encrusted in a calcareous deposit (pl. 10.1b).

Mandible with Teeth in Sockets

TOOTH TYPE	CUSP PATTERN	WEAR	COMMENTS
Left Molar 3	+5	None	Small
Molar 2	+4	Very Light	Small
Molar 1	+4	Significant	Small
Premolar 2		Light	Small
Premolar 1		Moderate	Small
Canine			Missing
Incisor 2			Missing
Incisor 1			Missing
Right Incisor 1			Missing
Incisor 2			Missing
Canine		Significant	Large
Premolar 1		Light	Carie on Distal Area
Premolar 2		Light	
Molar 1	+4	Moderate	
Molar 2			Missing
Molar 3			Missing

Maxillary Teeth Found Loose

TOOTH TYPE	CUSP PATTERN	WEAR	COMMENTS
Left Molar 2	3+	Light	
Molar 1	3+ or 4-	Moderate	
Premolar 2		Light	
Premolar 1		Moderate	
Canine		Significant	
Incisor 2?		Significant	Uneven wear pattern
Incisor 1		Significant	Uneven wear pattern
Right Incisor 1?		Significant	Uneven wear pattern
Incisor 2?		Significant	Uneven wear pattern
Canine		Significant	
Premolar 1		Light	
Premolar 2		Light	
Molar 1	3+	Moderate	
Molar 2	3+ or 4-	Light	
Molar 3	3	Very Light	Small

Cranial Measurements

DESCRIPTION	MEASUREMENTS	COMMENT
Mandible	Min breadth of Ascending Ramus = 29.5 mm	Left side

Post-cranial

The three major long bones are represented: humeri, femora, and tibiae. The bone fabric is poorly preserved, exhibiting calcareous deposits in some areas and decalcification in others. Both humeri are represented with almost complete shafts, and show strong muscle markings along the deltoid tuberosity and radial groove. The mid portions of the femora are adult in size. The tibiae shafts are poorly preserved but have a pronounced anterior crest and are triangular in shape.

Postcranial Measurements

DESCRIPTION	MEASUREMENTS	COMMENT
Left Tibiae	Diameters at Nutrient Foramen Mediolateral = 23.10 mm Anterior-Posterior = 35.75 mm	Platycnemic index = 64.62, which is Mesocnemic indicating that the mediolateral flatness is not pronounced.

Analysis

The evidence indicates this is a youngish adult (25–30 age range) with good musculature. There are no signs of arthritis or deterioration of the bones.

The dental wear supports the analysis, with dental attrition ranging from slight to significant. The variation was due to malocclusion causing the teeth to wear at an uneven rate. The wear pattern is significant as it evidences orthognasion, or an edge-to-edge bite. Angel (1961) also found this type of malocclusion at Sotira. Overall dental health is quite good, with only one small carie found on the lower right first premolar.

TOMB 7

No skeletal remains.

TOMB 8

No skeletal remains.

TOMB 9

No skeletal remains.

TOMB 10

No skeletal remains studied. The excavation notes report some poorly preserved human long bone fragments and ribs, which were so securely bonded into the limestone matrix that they were impossible to retrieve without being broken into small fragments.

TOMB 11

Overview of Burial

A single burial that is thought not to have been looted, but which showed signs of later disturbance when the terraces were built. The burial had been laid out in a flexed position on its right side.

Description and Measurements

Cranial

Overall, the bone fabric was found to be in good condition and it was possible to reconstruct much of the cranium. Several key areas of the left parietal and the occipital were missing. Nevertheless, for this collection it is one of the better-preserved skulls, and it was possible to take a number of measurements.

The skull is represented by the entire vault, with the following exceptions:

- The frontal bone is missing the lateral end of right orbit at ectoconchion, and the left orbit, hardly better preserved, extends only to the frontotemporal line.
- The right parietal is complete with the exception of the inferior portion along the coronal suture. The right temporal bone is missing the superior anterior border, and is represented along asterica.
- The left parietal is missing the inferior borders, and the entire left temporal.
- The occipital is missing the left side, and the right side is constructed from two fragments.

The skull is small and mesocrane (pl. 10.2a, 2b). The occiput has a moderate curve and the temporals are moderate and high. The parietals region is short and the supramastoid crest is not pronounced. The parietal bone is quite thick. The mastoid process is small and occipital area rounded. The forehead has a full frontal curve with bregma set well back. The frontal bone and parietal eminencies are high and rounded. The supraorbital ridges are not pronounced and glabellar is raised.

The right orbit shows cribra orbitalia (pl. 10.1c). Wormian Bones are present, one in vertis along the sagittal sure and others along lambdoid.

Cranial Measurements

DESCRIPTION	MEASUREMENTS	COMMENTS
Max. Cranial Length	176.5 mm	1. Cranial Index = 78.47 indicating mesocrany or an average headed individual
Max Cranial Breadth	138.5 mm	
Max Frontal Breadth	104? mm	1. Break over right frontotemporal
Orbital Breadth (left)	37.5 mm	
Frontal Arc	133 mm	
Parietal Arc	108 mm	
Parietal Thickness	8.5 mm	
Frontal Chord	111.5 mm	
Parietal Chord	97.5 mm	
Biasterionic Breadth	92 mm	
Maximum Horizontal Perimeter	512 mm	
Minimum Breadth of Ascending Ramus (left)	33.25 mm	
Bigonial Breadth	90.5 mm	1. Reconstructed
Foramen Mentalia Breadth	44.25 mm	
Height of Ascending Ramus (left)	55.00 mm	

Height of Mandibular Symphysis	31.50 mm	
Maximum Projective Mandibular length	101.00 mm	
Coronoid Height	59.50 mm	

Dental

The mouth area and dentition are well represented, with nearly a complete mandible, large portion of the maxilla and 20 teeth. Two discrete maxillary fragments were found and reconstructed:

1. The left half extends from I1 to M3 but is missing the most central edge. Dental disease is rife. The canine socket appears to have been enlarged due to infection. Certainly the tooth next to it, a premolar (?), has been lost during life. The M1 has a carie on the distal cusps and the M2 and M3 were missing before death. The M1 socket shows considerable resorbtion of alveolar bone.

2. The right side of maxilla, the socket for I1 is broken and the fragment extends from I2 to P2. The P1 socket shows abscess.

The mandible is nearly completely represented with the exception of the right M3 and ramus. The mandible is small and parabolic in shape. The teeth are small and chin is rounded (pl. 10.1d).

Maxilla Portions

TOOTH TYPE	CUSP PATTERN	WEAR	COMMENTS
Left maxillary			
Molar 3			Lost ante-mortem
Molar 2			Lost ante-mortem
Molar 1	??	Significant	Distal cusps very badly worn, and/or decayed
Premolar 2		Significant	Found out of socket
Premolar 1			Lost ante-mortem
Canine			Socket enlarged due to dental disease
Incisor 2		Significant	Found out of socket
Incisor 1		Moderate	Found out of socket
Right incisor 1		Moderate	Found out of socket
Right maxillary			
Incisor 2			Missing
Canine		Moderate	Found out of socket
Premolar 1			ABSCESS
Premolar 2			Lost ante-mortem
Molar 1			Missing
Molar 2			Missing
Molar 3			Missing

Mandible

TOOTH TYPE	CUSP PATTERN	WEAR	COMMENTS
Left Molar 3	+4	Light	
Molar 2	+4	Moderate	
Molar 1			Lost ante-mortem, alveolar bone resorbed
Premolar 2		Significant	
Premolar 1		Significant	
Canine		Moderate	Slightly crowded and rotated so faces outward
Incisor 2		Moderate	
Incisor 1		Moderate	
Right incisor 1		Moderate	
Incisor 2		Moderate	
Canine		Moderate	
Premolar 1		Significant	
Premolar 2		Significant	
Molar 1			Lost ante-mortem
Molar 2	+4	Light	Wear more on distal buccal cusps. Has carie on the distal lingual cusp, medium in size
Molar 3	+4	Light	Found out of socket

Post-cranial

DESCRIPTION	MEASUREMENTS	COMMENTS
Right humerus	Least Circumference of shaft = 67.00 mm	Overall characteristics: 1. Strong insertions of deltoid muscle and groove or radial nerve. 2. Crest below lesser tubercle is marked. 3. Bone very oval in cross section. 4. 195 mm of shaft present.
Left humerus	Least circumference of shaft; Left 66.50 mm	1. 270 mm of shaft present
Right radius		1. Missing head and distal articulation. 2. Interosseous crest is medium and radial tuberosity not very marked. 3. Not measurable. 4. 195 mm of shaft present.
Left radius		1. Shaft is flat and interosseous crest is very sharp 2. 150 mm of shaft is present.
Right ulna		1. Interosseous crest is medium in size 162 mm of shaft present.
Left ulna		1. Missing proximal and distal ends. 2. The interosseous crest is moderately marked.

Right clavicle		1. Missing sternal articulation and distal end. The conoid tubercle is marked.
Pelvis		1. Right innominate pelvic fragment from region around sciatic notch. The a portion of the sciatic notch is represented and appears broad and shallow. (Female).
Right femur	Subtrochanteric Diameter Mediolateral 28.00 mm Anterior-Posterior 28.50 mm	1. Missing neck and head and also distal area around Lesser Trochanter. 2. Adult size, long and only moderately marked Linea Aspera. 3. Shafts show none or little bowing, 290 mm of shaft present. 4. Platymeric Index = 79.8 which indicates that it is Platymeric or Flat.
Left femur		1. Matches the above. 2. 310 mm of shaft is present.
Right tibia	Nutrient Foramen Diameter Anterior-posterior = 31.5 Mediolateral = 23.25	1. Missing proximal and distal, measures 250 mm. 2. Anterior crest only moderately pronounced and posterior part of shaft narrow. 3. The Platycnemic Index = 74.6 Eurycnemic or indicates that Mediolateral dimensions or more rounded than flat.
Left tibia		1. Missing both proximal and distal ends, measures 255 mm. 2. Description matches the above.
Right tibia		1. No distal and proximal ends. It has been reconstructed from 2 fragments. 2. Interosseous Crest pronounced.
Left fibula		1. Interosseous Crest pronounced.
3 & 4th metacarpals		1. Only fragments present.

Analysis

A female in her late twenties at death (27 years approx.). She displays a minor degree of cribra orbitalia and the parietals have an inflated diploe.

Overall, her dental health is poor with tooth loss during life, evidence of an abscess and caries. The teeth appear to have edge-to-edge wear pattern, which is not uncommon in this population. There was tooth loss during life, and it is very likely the individual suffered from periodontal disease.

The long bones do not display any unusual characteristics. The femurs are flat and are not bowed.

TOMB 12

Overview of Burial

This chamber tomb is the largest in the cluster of tombs that occupies the northwest corner of Cemetery A. Although it yielded few remains, it may be significant that it contained the only child burial.

Description and Analysis

Very few remains from a child approximately 3 years of age, including: 1) Immature epiphysis femur of young child (pl. 10.1e). Several boxes of small long bone fragments were recovered.

It is unfortunate that there is not more of this child to study. Its age at death falls into the range common to children suffering from untreated thalassemia.

TOMB 13

No skeletal remains.

TOMB 14

Overview of Burial

A single burial was found in a flexed position on its right side with the skull to the south pointing east. This skeleton showed no signs of disturbance and was well represented. The bone fabric of both the cranial and post-cranial remains is poorly preserved.

Description and Measurements

Cranial

The cranium is relatively well represented, missing only its face, frontal bone and right temporal bone. The inferior right portion of the parietal and right side of the occipital are somewhat distorted. The occipital has been reconstructed.

The left side of skull, parietal, and occipital are reflective of the crania's true shape. The left temporal has been broken and is missing the mastoid process. The zygomatic arch is broken and has been distorted. In the occipital the sagittal suture is well defined. The skull is small to medium in size and appears very smooth. The occipital area is high and rounded, as are the parietals (pls. 10.2c, 10.3a). The teeth are large.

Cranial Measurements

DESCRIPTION	MEASUREMENTS	COMMENTS
Max Cranial Length	138.5 mm?	Skull Reconstructed
Parietal Thickness	6 mm	
Occipital Chord	114 mm	Skull Reconstructed
Occipital Arc	92.5 mm	Skull Reconstructed

Dental

The mandible is intact though it has suffered significant post-humus damage and warping. The teeth and much of the alveolar bone are missing from P1 left through I1 right. The ramii are broken off. It was not possible to take any measurements. The chin is quite strong and the teeth appear large with very little wear.

Mandible with Teeth in Sockets

TOOTH TYPE	CUSP PATTERN	WEAR	COMMENTS
Left Molar 3	Y5	Very Light	Large
Molar 2	+4	Light	Large
Molar 1	Y5	Light	Large
Premolar 2		Very Light	
Premolar 1		Light	Found out of the socket
Canine		Light	Found out of the socket
Incisor 2		Light to Moderate	Found out of the socket
Incisor 1			Missing
Right Incisor 1			Missing
Incisor 2		Light	
Canine		Light	
Premolar 1		Light	
Premolar 2		Very Light	
Molar 1		Light	Large
Molar 2	+4	Very Light	
Molar 3	?	?	Cusp missing

Maxillary Teeth Found Loose

TOOTH TYPE	CUSP PATTERN	WEAR	COMMENTS
Molar	4+	Very Light	Large
Molar	3+	Very Light	Large

Post-cranial

DESCRIPTION	MEASUREMENTS	COMMENTS
Right Femur	Subtrochanteric Diameter Anterior–posterior = 29.5 Mediolateral 30.5	Reconstructed from 3 pieces and has no distal end. At the proximal end it is broken off in the region of lesser trochanter. Some measurements still possible. The Femur shows definite bowing and the linea aspera is moderately marked. There is no sign of arthritis or other signs of ageing. Platymeric Index is 96.72 or Eurymeric indicating that the bone was not flat.
Right Tibia	None possible	Badly preserved midshaft portion.
Left Humerus	None possible	Badly preserved midshaft portion.
Fibula side?		Badly preserved midshaft portion.
Right Humerus		Badly preserved shaft.
Pelvis Fragments		Badly preserved and no information available.

Analysis

An adult male (?) in his mid to late twenties at death. The skull is medium in size and is very smooth. It has a high and rounded occipital. The parietals are broad and somewhat inflated. There is no sign of any artificial cranial deformation. The chin is large and square. The dentition has only moderate wear. The associated femur has marked bowing.

TOMB 15

Overview of Burial

Three burials are reported for Tomb 15. This is the only example of tomb reuse in this collection. During the Late Bronze Age tombs were often reused for several burial episodes; however this practice is less common in earlier periods.

The excavation revealed that the original occupant was pushed to one side in order to make way for two subsequent burials. What is believed to be the first burial is in the best condition. The other skeletons were more disturbed, and this has made analysis more difficult.

Description and Measurements

Cranium 1 (fig. 3.6, Tomb 15, No. 12)

This is in better condition than Cranium 2 described below, but is still quite fragmentary. It was not possible to clean and restore this cranium because the calcareous deposit surrounding the bone is stronger than the bone fabric. There was not the time or the equipment to attempt the extensive restoration required, which would in any case be of limited success.

The specimen primarily comprised the top cap of the vault (pl. 10.3b), with the right side better preserved. The following bones are represented:

- Most of the frontal which was broken off at nasion, the left side of which is more fragmentary
- The entire right parietal and superior lateral part of the temporal bone
- Right half of the occipital
- Superior half of left parietal
- Missing is the face, left temporal, left portion of the occipital, sphenoid mastoids etc.:

Cranial Measurements

DESCRIPTION	MEASUREMENTS	COMMENTS
Max Cranial Length	165.00 mm	
Parietal Arc	115.00 mm	
Parietal Thickness	4.5 mm	
Parietal Chord	134.50 mm	

Cranium 2 (fig. 3.6, Tomb 15, No.14)

This skull is only very partially represented by the left parietal. The specimen is embedded in limestone and both endo and ecto cranially the fabric is damaged. Two areas of suture are visible on opposite corners of the piece. The suture is not fully closed along what appears lambdoid suture near asterica. Parietal is from a medium size skull.

Dentition from Crania 1 and 2

This dentition is not clearly differentiated, due to the disturbance of the skulls and other remains in this part of the tomb. As expected, two individuals are represented: one young person and the other, an older individual, showing considerable tooth wear. The excavation notes indicate that the younger is associated with Skull 1 and the other associated with Skull 2. However, this is impossible to substantiate.

Right Mandible Portion Attributed to Skull 1

TOOTH TYPE	CUSP PATTERN	WEAR	COMMENTS
Canine		Very Light	
Premolar 1		Very Light	
Premolar 2		Light	
Molar 1	+4	Light	
Molar 2	+4	Very Light	
Molar 3			Unerupted loose

Teeth from Sieving Attributed to Skull 1

TOOTH TYPE	CUSP PATTERN	WEAR	COMMENTS
Maxillary			
Left Molar 3	3	Very Light	
Molar 2	4+	Light	
Molar 1	4+	Light	
Premolar 1/2		Light	
Canine		Light	
Right Incisor 1		Light	
Incisor 2		Light	
Canine		Light	
Premolar 1		Light	
Premolar 2		Light	
Molar 1			Missing??
Molar 2	4+	Light	
Molar 3	3	Very Light	
Misc.			
Mandibular premolar		Light	
Mandibular premolar		Light	
Molar Cusp	??	Significant	
Molar Cusp	4+	Moderate	
Molar Cusp	4+	Light	

Mandible Portion Attributed to Skull 2 Extends from Left to I2 on Right (pl. 10.1f)

TOOTH TYPE	CUSP PATTERN	WEAR	COMMENT
Left Molar 3			Missing
Molar 2		Significant	Missing proximal cusps, carie?
Molar 1		Very Significant	
Premolar 2		Very Significant	
Premolar 1		Moderate	
Canine		Very Significant	
Incisor 2		?	
Incisor 1		Significant	
Right Incisor 1		Significant	
Incisor 2		Significant	

Teeth from Sieving Attributed to Skull 2

TOOTH TYPE	CUSP PATTERN	WEAR	COMMENTS
Maxillary			Found Loose
Left Incisor 2		Light/Moderate	
Incisor 1		Light/Moderate	
Right Incisor 1		Light/Moderate	
Incisor 2		Moderate	
Canine		Light/Moderate	
Premolar 1		Light/Moderate	
Premolar 2		Light/Moderate	
Misc.			
Canine			Worn without root
Molar			Split

Cranium 3 (fig. 3.6, Tomb 15, No.8)

This skull is one of the best represented in the collection: it was excavated whole and removed intact. Unfortunately it was encased in limestone, which had hardened since excavation (pl. 10.3c). Overall the bone fabric was differentially preserved, and it was not possible to further conserve given the equipment and time. A number of measurements were possible (see below).

The vault of skull is mostly complete; however the right parietal is crushed inward. Parts of occipital were missing (right half) and central superior area of left parietal missing. The face is represented though somewhat distorted.

Cranial Measurements

DESCRIPTION	MEASUREMENTS	COMMENT
Maximum Cranial Length	199 mm?	
Maximum Cranial Breadth		Not possible due to warping
Minimum Frontal Breadth	103.50 mm	
Nasal Height	47.5 mm	

Orbital Height	31.00 mm (left)	
Orbital Breadth	40.50 mm (right)	Orbital Breadth = 76.54 Chamaeconchy, wide orbits
Palatal Breadth	59.5 mm (exterior) 37.5 mm (interior)	
Breadth of Ascending Ramus	32.00 mm	
Bigonial Breadth	105.00 mm	
Foramen Mentalia Breadth	50.50 mm	
Mandibular symphysis	25.25 mm	
Maximum projective Mandibular Length	96.50 mm	

Dental (fig. 3.6, Tomb 15, No. 9)

The maxilla is embedded in calcareous deposits. The teeth show more wear on the right side, and the right second and third molars are separated by a gap, which may be congenital diastema. Damage makes it impossible to determine if there was any peridontal disease.

Maxilla

TOOTH TYPE	*CUSP PATTERN*	*WEAR*	*COMMENTS*
Left Molar 3	4-	Moderate	
Molar 2	3?	Moderate	
Molar 1	4-	Moderate	
Premolar 2			Missing
Premolar 1			Missing
Canine			Missing
Incisor 2			Missing
Incisor 1			Missing
Right Incisor 1			Missing
Incisor 2			Missing
Canine			Missing
Premolar 1			Missing
Premolar 2		Moderate	
Molar 1	4-	Significant	
Molar 2	3	Moderate	
Molar 3	4-	Light	
Misc. Teeth			
Maxillary 12		Moderate	
Maxillary 11		Moderate	
Premolar 1		Light	

The mandible is very well represented, only missing the right ramus (pl. 10.4a). The bone fabric is poor and the left ramus is reconstructed by 3 pieces. The left mandible M3 is congenitally missing. The mandibular teeth are large and the chin is square.

Mandible Teeth in Sockets

TOOTH TYPE	CUSP PATTERN	WEAR	COMMENTS
Left Molar 3			Congenitally missing
Molar 2	+4	Moderate	
Molar 1	Y??	Moderate	
Premolar 2			Damaged
Premolar 1		Significant	
Canine			Missing
Incisor 2			Missing
Incisor 1			Missing
Right Incisor 1			Missing
Incisor 2			Missing
Canine			Missing
Premolar 1		Significant	
Premolar 2		Significant	
Molar 1	Y-5?	Very Significant	
Molar 2	+4	Moderate	
Molar 3	+4	Moderate	

Postcranial

Associated with Cranium 1 and 2

DESCRIPTION	MEASUREMENTS	COMMENTS
Femur shaft	None possible	1. Reconstructed from 2 pieces. 2. Adult in size with average bowing.
Tibia shaft fragment	Diameters at Nutrient Foramen Anterior-Poster = 30. 4 mm Mediolateral = 19.5 mm	1. Poorly preserved. 2. Adult size. 3. Platycnemic Index is 67.33 indicating it is Mesocnemic.
Metacarpal fragment		No analysis possible.

Postcranial Bones Associated with Skull 3

DESCRIPTION	MEASUREMENTS	COMMENTS
Tibia (left)		Reconstructed from 2 pieces, missing distal and proximal ends. Adult in size. Flattened shaft with prominent anterior crest. Specimen matches below.
Tibia (right)		1. Reconstructed from 2 pieces, also missing both ends. 2. Matches above.
Humerus (left)	Least circumference of shaft 74.5 mm?	1. Reconstructed from 3 pieces Almost complete, broken off just below the neck and across top of olecranon process. 2. Deltoid tuberosity marked. 3. Adult in size. Not possible to confirm epiphyseal closure.

Humerus (right)		1. Reconstructed from 3 fragments, old breaks had mineralized so reconstruction not reliable. 2. Twin to the above, with marked deltoid tuberosity.
Femur (left)	Subtrochanteric Diameters Anterior–Posterior = 26.5 mm Mediolateral = 34 mm	1. Bone in good condition, minor reconstruction at proximal end of shaft. Still incomplete. 2. Bone is long and gracile. The linea aspera is sharp. 3. Shows pronounced bowing 4. Platymeric index = 77.4 or Platymeric indicating a broad or flat bone
Femur (right)	Subtrochanteric Diameters Anterior–Posterior = 27.5 mm Mediolateral = 35.5m	1. Shaft portion comes from proximal end but is without neck or head 2. Twin to above, also shows pronounced bowing 3. Platymeric Index = 77.46 or Platymeric as above.

Miscellaneous Bone

DESCRIPTION	MEASUREMENTS	COMMENTS
Mid shaft of adult clavicle		Right side, appears that sternal articulation had taken place (i.e., fused)
Femur		Shaft fragments
Fibula		Shaft fragments
Radius & Ulna		Shaft fragments
Innominate		Unidentifiable

Analysis

Individual 1

The individual is a young female (?) between 15–18 years of age. There is no evidence of any pathologies. The vault is infantile and short headed. It is broad though no measurements are possible. The occipital is high and gently protrudes. The forehead is high and the parietal rounded. The temporals are also high. There is no artificial cranial deformation. Overall size is small and smooth, with high forehead and infantile appearance resembling the individual in Tomb 11. It was not possible to attribute the few long bones to either Skull 1 or 2; in any case they were unremarkable.

Individual 2

Individual 2 is an adult in middle years (35 plus). The dentition is represented by 17 teeth: eight were still intact in the right mandible. These show considerable wear and one molar has a carie. The only other cranial evidence consists of a portion of the left parietal fragment. This is from a medium sized skull.

Individual 3

Individual 3 is a male in his mid-thirties at death (33–37 years of age). The skull is linear and appears dolicephalic. The forehead is high and steep with low, large orbits and pronounced brow ridges. The occipital is not particularly rugged or pronounced and the occipital bone is quite thick. The top view of the vault is ovoid and smooth. The zygomatic arches are strong and the face is long. The mouth is prone to flatness orthgnathism.

Nineteen teeth were found associated with this individual, 15 in their sockets. The wear was pronounced but otherwise the dental health was good. The palate is parabolic and the mandible has a strong square chin and large teeth.

The coronal suture is completely closed but not obliterated. The occipital suture is more than half closed. There is no evidence of artificial cranial deformation.

As with Tomb 6, the three major long bones are represented for this individual: humeri, femora, and tibiae. The femora are platymeric and have pronounced bowing (pls. 10.4e and 10.4f). The tibiae have a prominent anterior crest. The humeri are robust with a marked deltoid tuberosity.

TOMB 16

Overview of Burial

The tomb showed much disturbance, not the least of which was the destruction of its eastern portion by a footpath. The human skeletal remains were few and fragmented; it was not possible to ascertain burial position.

Description and Analysis

The tomb contained the few remains of an adult (?). The post-cranial material consisted of indistinct shaft fragments. A single upper premolar, P2 was recovered; it is an adult tooth showing light wear.

TOMB 17

Overview of Burial

The tomb showed evidence of ancient disturbance, both of the skeletal remains and the associated grave goods.

Description and Measurements

Cranial and Dental

No cranial evidence was found except a right mandible fragment (pl. 10.4b) and three individual teeth. The ramus is small, the teeth worn and the alveolar bone has receded. The following measurements were possible:

Cranial Measurements

MEASUREMENTS	*COMMENTS*
Maximum breadth of Ascending Ramus = 35.5 mm	Reflective of the small jaw
Coronoid height = 63.75 mm	

Right Mandible Portion with Teeth in Sockets

TOOTH TYPE	CUSP PATTERN	WEAR	COMMENTS
Molar 3	Y4	Moderate	Carie on distal lingual cusp
Molar 2	+4	Very Significant	
Molar 1	+4?	Very Significant	
Premolar 2		Significant	
Premolar 1		Moderate	
Canine		Light/Moderate	
Individual Teeth			
Maxillary Molar	4+	Significant	Lingual cusp uneven wear
Maxillary Molar	4+	Moderate	Uneven wear not as pronounced
Maxillary Premolar		Light	

Post-cranial

Several long bones were represented but none are complete. These without exception are missing their distal and proximal ends, but are adult in size. The following measurements and descriptions were possible.

Post-cranial Description and Measurements

DESCRIPTION	MEASUREMENTS	COMMENTS
Femur (right)	Portion of shaft is 235 mm	1. Linea aspera is moderately marked 2. Shaft not bowed
Femur (left)	None possible	1. Smaller fragment but the partner to above
Tibia	None possible	1. Assorted fragments no distinctive features

Analysis

An adult was middle-aged at time of death. The dentition is represented by nine teeth and a portion of the right mandible, which indicate that the individual suffered from malocclusion and some dental disease. The long bones were from the leg region and showed no distinctive features.

TOMB 18

No skeletal remains.

TOMB 19

No skeletal remains.

TOMB 20

No skeletal remains.

TOMB 21

No skeletal remains.

CEMETERY B

TOMB 1

No skeletal remains.

TOMB 2

Overview of Burial

The tomb was open and had been looted at some time in the relatively distant past.

Description and Measurements

Cranial and dental
        None, except for three individual teeth, described below:

TOOTH TYPE	CUSP PATTERN	WEAR	COMMENTS
Canine		Significant	
Premolar 2		Significant	
Premolar 1		Significant	

Post-cranial
        The following were the only post-cranial remains recovered:

DESCRIPTION	MEASUREMENTS	COMMENTS
Humerus (right)	None possible	1. Distal end with 100 mm of shaft 2. Several fragments of the shaft 3. Adult with marked margin to lateral epicondyles
Tibia (right)	None possible	1. Distal end with 160 mm shaft 2. Several shaft fragments with moderate anterior crest 3. Adult
Metatarsal	None possible	
Ulna (right)	None possible	1. Proximal end 2. Arthritic lipping on Olecranon Process

Analysis

        At least one adult individual is represented from these remains. Given the significant dental wear, the individual was at least in the middle plus years at time of death.

TOMB 3

No skeletal remains.

SKELETAL REMAINS FROM THE SETTLEMENT

UNIT 22 (figs. 2.15, 2.18; pl. 10.5b)

Overview of Skeleton

The presence of an intact human skeleton at the inner end of Unit 22, a long narrow room in Area C, was unexpected (see Chapter 2, Unit 22, fig. 2.15). To date no burials have been found associated with habitations at *Kaminoudhia*, as custom appears to have dictated that the dead should be interred extramurally in cemeteries at some distance from settlements. In his detailed description in Chapter 2 of Unit 22, where the skeleton was discovered, Swiny argues that this is not, in fact, a burial and that the presence of the skeleton should be explained in another way. The individual was very well represented.

Description and Measurements

Cranial and Dental

The skull was recovered in a block; the left side of the face was crushed into the right. The facial bones are very thin and have shattered. The sutures are wide open which resulted in the vault being very fragmented and fragile. The skull and face are small. The face appeared low with large orbits, and the forehead is rounded. The mouth appears prognathius. The inside palate is missing, and the atlas and axis vertebrae were found in the maxillary cavity.

Cranial Measurements

DESCRIPTION	MEASUREMENTS	COMMENTS
Orbital Breadth –left	32.50 mm	
Parietal Thickness	6 mm	
Minimum Breadth of Ascending Ramus	27.75 mm	Right Side
Foramen Mentalia Breadth	39.25 mm	
Symphysial Height	24.50 mm	
Max Projective Mandibular Length	87.50 mm	
Coronoid Height	46.00 mm	Right Side

Two Maxilla Portions - Right Extends M3 to I1 and Left Extends M2 to P2

TOOTH TYPE	CUSP PATTERN	WEAR	SIZE	COMMENTS
Left Molar 3				Missing
Molar 2	3+	Very Light		
Molar 1	Y4	Very Light		
Premolar 2		Very Light		
Premolar 1		Very Light		Found loose
Canine		Light		Found loose
Incisor 2		Light/Very Light		Found loose
Incisor 1		Very Light		Found loose
Right Incisor 1		Light		Bone represented to M3
Incisor 2				Lost post-mortem
Canine				Lost post-mortem
Premolar 1				Lost in life?
Premolar 2		Light		
Molar 1	Y4	Light		
Molar 2	3+	Very Light		
Molar 3	3 or 3+	Very Light		Erupting

Nearly Complete Mandible (pl. 10.4c)

TOOTH TYPE	CUSP PATTERN	WEAR	SIZE	COMMENTS
Left Molar 3				Missing
Molar 2	+4	Very Light		
Molar 1	Y4/Y5	Very Light		
Premolar 2		Very Light		
Premolar 1		Very Light		
Canine		Very Light		
Incisor 2		Very Light		
Incisor 1		Light		
Right Incisor 1		Light		
Incisor 2		Very Light		
Canine		Very Light		
Premolar 1		Light		
Premolar 2		Light		
Molar 1	Y4/Y5	Light		
Molar 2	+4	Very Light		
Molar 3				Erupting, hypoplasia line

Post-cranial

DESCRIPTION	MEASUREMENTS	COMMENTS
Humerus (right)	Least circumference of shaft = 45 mm	1. Reconstructed from 2 pieces (191 mm) 2. Complete shaft broken off at neck and the olecranon fossa with part of medial epicondyle remaining 3. Found with ulna and radius 4. Deltoid tuberosity is not pronounced
Humerus (left)		1. Matches the right 2. The shaft bone is 5 mm in diameter!
Ulna (right)	Least circumference of shaft is 28 mm Physiological length 188 mm	1. Reconstructed from 4 fragments 2. Olecranon process and the coronoid process are very small. 3. Only missing the distal articulation
Radius (right)		1. Reconstructed from 3 pieces, missing the head and distal articulation 2. The Radial tuberosity is not marked
Radius (left)		1. Matches the right 2. Reconstructed from 2 fragments (156 mm) 3. The head is not
Femur (right)	Established maximum length is 292 mm Subtrochanteric Diameters Anterior -Posterior = 20.75 mm Mediolateral = 23.00 mm	1. Found with the innominate (see below) 2. Reconstructed from 3 fragments, missing head - may be immature 3. Shaft is small with a marked linea aspera
Femur (left)		1. Reconstructed from 3 fragments. 2. It is a central shaft fragment (181 mm) missing both ends. 3. Matches the right. 4. Greater trochanter from immature femur
Tibia (left)		1. Matches above
Fibula (right)		1. Midshaft portion (135 mm) 2. Displaying flatness
Tibia (right)		1. Almost complete (217 mm) 2. Distal end may be missing due to immaturity 3. Small in size and musculature
Fibula (left)		1. 3 Fragments
Innominate (right)		1. From the sciatic notch area 2. Notch is broad and shallow (female)
Patella (right)	Height = 31.5 mm Width = 33.0 mm	
Hand Bones		1. 4 Metacarpals 2. 1-2nd Row Phalange 3. 2 -1st Row Phalange 4. 1- 3rd Row Phalange
Vertebral		1. Atlas and Axis 'cemented' in mandible 2. Sundry process fragments

Analysis

The skeleton is that of a young female between 16–18 years of age at death, with indications of poor health. The skull is small and paedomorphic. The vault sutures are open, reflecting the youth of the individual. Although not very thick in comparative terms, the parietals appear to have inflated diploe in relation to the other cranial bones. There is no metopism and no apparent artificial cranial deformation.

The dentition is nearly completely represented. The third molars are just beginning to erupt, a key indicator of age. Lunt (1983) noted in her study of this dentition that the crown of the right mandibular M3 appears to have a hypoplasia line. This is usually caused by a short-term disease or deficiency in Vitamin D at the time of tooth formation (Brothwell 1963:152).

All the long bones are at least partially represented, with the exception of the left ulna (pl. 10.5a shows selection of long bones). Where appropriate, reconstructions were made and measurements taken. These bones are small in size and still not fully mature. Of particular note is the left humerus shaft that has a very thick diameter (pl.10.4d). This condition may be the result of retarded remodeling during growth, and represents the non-resorbed shaft of an earlier age. The cranium and long bones exhibit features resulting from osteoporosis (see discussion in summary).

UNIT 6 (fig. 2.6)

The moderately well preserved femur and pelvis found on the habitation surface of Unit 6 were discovered after the present study was completed and will be included in any future research on the human skeletal remains from *Kaminoudhia*. The bones are plotted on fig. 2.6.

UNIT 16 (figs. 2.8, 2.16)

Overview

The three long bones lay scattered in a triangular arrangement (1.00 m x 30 cm) on the bedrock habitation surface of the room (see Chapter 2, Unit 16, and fig. 2.8 on which the bones are plotted). These bones were found near two unique picrolite tubular objects, perhaps serving as personal ornaments.

Description and Measurements

The humeri and femora are the only bones represented.

DESCRIPTION	MEASUREMENTS	COMMENTS
Humerus (right)	None	1. Shaft is broken off distally just above the eipcondyles and extends proximally to top of radial tuberosity. 2. Reconstructed from 2 shaft fragments (191 mm). 3. The deltoid tuberosity is pronounced. Overall the bone appears large and with strongly marked musculature.
Humerus (left)	Least circumference of shaft = 48.5 mm	1. Distal epiphysis is broken above the olecanon fossa and proximally just beyond the deltoid tuberosity (180 mm) 2. Matches the above
Femur		6 shaft fragments unidentifiable

Analysis

The bones are from an adult sized individual.

SUMMARY OF FINDINGS

Numbers of Individuals, Sex, and Age

The minimum number of individuals represented in this collection is thirteen. Three females and two males were identified. All the females died at a relatively young age—two adolescents and one in her late twenties. The males had an average older age at death—one in his mid-twenties, the other in his mid-thirties. The seven unsexed individuals showed a similar distribution—one young adult, one in its late twenties, three middle-aged plus, and two indeterminate. This collection contained only one child (approximately three years at death). Although it is not possible to ascertain a reliable average age at death, this distribution is not unusual for ancient populations.

Population Characteristics

The crania are very similar in form to those found at the Ceramic Neolithic site of Sotira *Teppes,* a few hundred meters to the southwest (Angel 1961). They are characterized by having high rounded vaults and are more mesocrane than brachycrane. Two crania display orthognathous mouth regions, which is marked by an edge to edge wear pattern of teeth. Wormian bones were present on one skull. Unusually there is no evidence of metopism, which is relatively common in Cypriot populations.

Several individuals in this collection have pronounced bowing of the femur. This is not of a pathological form (e.g., rickets) but is rather a natural variation, which may reveal a population trend (Steele and Bramlett 1988:219–20).

Artificial Cranial Deformation

Artificial cranial deformation was prevalent in many ancient Cypriot populations. While its absence in this collection may be explained by the smallness of the sample, it should be noted that the eight skulls from Sotira *Teppes* were also undeformed (Angel 1961:229). Therefore, this evidence may suggest that the Sotirans did not practice artificial cranial deformation on their young children.

Paleopathologies

Porotic Hyperostosis

Three of the thirteen adults found in this collection exhibit some evidence of porotic hyperostosis. There is osteoporotic pitting, cribra orbitalia, and extreme thickening of the diploe in the crania. One of the individuals, an adolescent, also has extreme thickening of the humerus shaft. This may result from non-resorbtion of shaft during growth periods at an earlier age.

Statistically this pathology affects a very high proportion (23%) of the adults in the collection, though this small sample may be biased. Higher instances of porotic hyperostosis (22%–40%) have been found in other Bronze Age skeletal collections from Greece and Cyprus, however these are predominantly children (Angel 1964). Perhaps of more significance is that Angel's study of Ceramic Neolithic crania from Sotira (1961) specifically states there was no evidence of this condition.

The cause of porotic hyperostosis has been debated over the last century. It is generally believed that this is the result of anemia, an acquired iron deficiency disease. It is often referred to as a nutritional stress factor. Where there is extreme porotic hyperostosis in children, it has been possible to identify specific genetic pathologies—such as thalassemia in Mediterranean populations.

Stuart-Macadam (1992:40) offers an alternative hypothesis to the traditional interpretation that this pathology is the negative result of disease. She postulates that its development is a positive defense in fighting disease. The hypothesis is based around two critical premises:

1. Except in cases of outright malnutrition, diet plays a minor role in the development of iron deficiency anemia.

2. Mild iron deficiency or hypoferremia is not necessarily a pathological condition but is one of the body's defenses against disease.

The hypothesis is that when faced with chronic and/or heavy pathogen loads, individuals become hypoferremic as part of their defense against these pathogens. Stuart-Macadam (1992:41) cites a number of studies that show that if the body withholds iron there is a decreased risk of infection. In other words, by withholding iron the system is strengthened as a positive and adaptive response to invading microorganisms.

Stuart-Macadam (1992:42) argues that a common factor between populations which show an unusually high incidence in porotic hyperostosis is a heavy pathogen load from parasites (e.g., malaria or hookworm). The increase of this pathology during the Neolithic is not seen as a function of iron-poor diets but rather of increased sedentism and population density leading to an increased pathogen load.

One of Angel's hypotheses is that the occurrence of porotic hyperostosis in adults may be attributed to the thalassemia heterozygote. Furthermore this is seen as a response to endemic malaria and increased disease as the result of irrigation practices (Angel 1964 and 1967).

If one assumes that both Stuart-Macadam and Angel are correct, this would indicate that the presence of the thalassemia gene in the heterozygote individual may induce a natural hypoferremia. This condition would benefit the health of individuals living in Sotira by enabling them to resist malaria and other parasites. Much more needs to be known about the population and the environment to substantiate such an hypothesis. But it does pose an interesting question—what changes occurred between the Ceramic Neolithic and Early Bronze Age to cause the occurrence of this pathology in the population of Sotira?

Dental Health

Overall the dental health in the *Kaminoudhia* collection is reasonably good. It is interesting to note that the three individuals who exhibit signs of porotic hyperostosis also have the poorest dental health.

11

THE ANIMAL REMAINS

by Paul Croft

INTRODUCTION

Although the sample of faunal remains from Sotira *Kaminoudhia* is small, it is of considerable interest since it represents the last third of the third millennium B.C.E., for which very little evidence concerning the nature of animal economies in Cyprus is known (Manning and Swiny 1994).

A total of more than five hundred pieces of mammalian bone were identified from *Kaminoudhia* (Table 11.1), of which the overwhelming majority are caprines, cattle, fallow deer (Dama Mesopotamia) and pig. A few bones of fox were present. A single cat bone, although from a stratified lot, appears to be intrusive (as does a single small rodent bone). Additionally, two different species of birds are represented by a few bones. The entire assemblage consists of 15 kg of animal bone, of which 42.6% by weight proved identifiable.

Table 11.1. Numbers of identified larger mammalian bone fragments.

MAMMAL	TOTAL SAMPLE	PERCENT	RELIABLE CONTEXT	PERCENT
Caprine	190	36.2	164	38.0
Cattle	168	32.0	128	29.6
Deer	96*	18.3	78*	18.1
Pig	64	12.2	56	13.0
Fox	6	1.1	5	1.2
Cat	1	0.2	1	0.2
Total	525	100.0	432	100.1

* Figures include 6 antler bases, but exclude several other small antler fragments.

It will be apparent from Table 11.1 that a fraction of the assemblage derives from insecure, mainly superficial, contexts (18% of identified fragments, representing 21% by weight). Since there is little stratigraphic or artifactual evidence for contamination with later material at *Kaminoudhia*, the bones from these insecure contexts are probably contemporary with the stratified faunal remains. However, to preclude the possibility of confusion, this material has been disregarded in the following discussion. A breakdown by weight of faunal remains from stratified contexts is given in Table 11.2.

An attempt was made to identify all skeletal elements except ribs and vertebrae, other than the atlas, axis, and sacrum. Teeth that retained less than half a complete tooth crown were also excluded from consideration.

Faunal material from *Kaminoudhia* was generally not well preserved, and this is reflected both in the relatively low identifiable proportion and in the high incidence of (mainly single) teeth in the assemblage. The material was very fragmentary, much of it was abraded, and an encrustation that commonly affects faunal remains from prehistoric sites on the calcareous soils of lowland Cyprus covered some of it. The poor condition of the assemblage has naturally served to minimize the amount of useful metrical data that it could provide. Since a pronounced degree of differential preservation of the bones of different animals, and of bones of mature and immature animals, occurred at *Kaminoudhia*, interpretations based upon the material must necessarily be viewed as tentative.

Identified postcranial fragments (Table 11.3) may provide a better guide than raw counts to the relative taxonomic abundance of the main animals at *Kaminoudhia*. Of these, caprine remains (39%) are the most abundant, followed by those of cattle (27%), deer (19%) and pig.

Table 11.2. Weights (gr) of animal bone from reliable contexts.

MAMMAL	*IDENTIFIED*	*PERCENTAGE*
Caprine	941	19.1%
Cattle	2536	51.6%
Deer	1060*	21.6%
Pig	363	7.4%
Fox	7	0.1%
Cat	7	0.1%

Total identified: 4914 (41.2% of sample)

SIZE	*UNIDENTIFIED*	*PERCENTAGE*
Cattle size	1976	28.2%
Deer size or smaller	5040	71.8%
Total Unidentified	7016	(58.8% of sample)
TOTAL SAMPLE	11930	

* Figures include all antler pieces

THE ANIMALS

CAPRINES

Fifteen items could be specifically attributed to sheep and ten to goat (Table 11.3). Both caprine genera were present at *Kaminoudhia*, and sheep may have been more abundant than goats. However, with such a small sample, it would be unwise to claim that these figures reflect the actual proportions in which the two genera were utilized in the economy of the site.

Epiphysial fusion data are not abundant. Of the earlier fusing bones represented, only six out of forty-three specimens (14%) are unfused (proximal radius, distal humerus and distal tibia, distal scapula and proximal phalanges 1 and 2) which fuse before one and a half to two years of age (Silver 1969: Table A). However, in view of the generally poor state of bone preservation at *Kaminoudhia*, it is likely that this ratio conveys a misleadingly low impression of mortality among young caprines. Since they are fragile, immature bones are liable to have been particularly vulnerable to attrition.

Permanent fourth premolars would have replaced deciduous lower third premolars at about two years of age (Deniz and Payne 1982: Table 2; Silver 1969: Tables E and F). Since teeth tend to be more durable than other skeletal elements, the equal representation of these among the caprine material from *Kaminoudhia* (three of each) supports the idea that mortality among young caprines has been underestimated based on the fusion data.

Table 11.3. Numbers of identified bone fragments of the main animals represented in stratified contexts at Sotira *Kaminoudhia*. NB. Figures include fragments specifically identifiable as either sheep or goat, and these are indicated in parentheses. An S or a G represents a single sheep or goat, while for multiple identifications these letters are prefixed by a number. For example, the entry for proximal radii of sheep/goat which reads 5 (G2S) means that of five identified caprine right proximal radii, one was specifically identifiable as goat and two as sheep.

	CATTLE				DEER				CAPRINE		
	L	**R**	**ND**	**TOTAL**	**L**	**R**	**ND**	**TOTAL**	**L**	**R**	**TOTAL**
Scapula		1	1	2		1		1	3	3	6(G2S)
p. Humerus			1	1							
d. Humerus	4	1		5	3	5		8	5	5	(1092G2S)
p. Ulna					2			2	1		1
d. Ulna	1			1							
p. Radius		1		1	1	2		3	3	3	6(G3S)
d. Radius					1	2		3		1	1
p. Femur									3		3
d. Femur									1	3	4
Patella						1		1			
p. Tibia						1		1			
d. Tibia					1	3		4	6	1	
Astralagalus	1	2		3		3		3	4	2	7
Calcaneum	5			5	1			1	1		6(2G3S)
p.m/Carpal	1			1					1	2	1(G)
p.m/Tarsal	1			1					2	2	3
d.m/Tarsal							3	3			4
Atlas								1			2
Axis				1				3			2
Pelvic fragments.				3							11(S)
Sacrum								2			
Carpals				4							
Tarsals											2(S)
Os mallelare											
Longbone shafts				19				8			17
Phalanx 1				13				9			16(G3S)
Phalanx 2				12				2			6
Phalanx 3				2				2			1
Total				—				—			—
Postcranial fragments				74				57			109
Cranial fragments				54				21			55(2G)
TOTAL FRAGMENTS				128				78			164

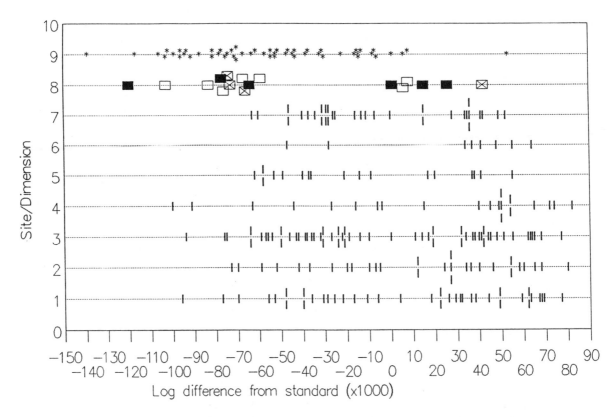

Fig. 11.1. Symbols represent measured (or, in a minority of cases, estimated) values for certain dimensions of selected mature (fused) skeletal elements of caprines from Sotira *Kaminoudhia*, Kissonerga *Mosphilia* and Marki *Alonia*.

Vertical dashes (on lines 1–7) represent specimens from Kissonerga *Mosphilia* as follows: 1) Radius proximal breadth; 2) Metacarpal & metatarsal proximal breadth; 3) Humerus breadth of distal trochlea; 4) Calcaneum anterior length of dorsal tubercle; 5) Scapula greatest length of distal articular process; 6) Naviculocuboid greatest breadth; 7) Tibia distal breadth.

Rectangles (on line 8) represent a small, pooled sample of these same elements/dimensions for *Kaminoudhia*. Solid = sheep, crossed = goat, open = undifferentiated caprine. Asterisks (on line 9) represent a pooled sample from Marki *Alonia*.

Measurements were all taken according to the specifications of von den Driesch (1976), except for that on the calcaneum, which is defined by Hué (1907:39 and pl. 14) as the length of the dorsal (anterior) edge from the most cranial point of the dorsal tubercle to the axial point on the lip of the articular surface for the astragalus.

Values are represented as logarithmic differences (x 1000) from a standard for each dimension. The standards adopted are the median values (in mm) for the large Kissonerga sample which are: 1) 36.4 2) 28.2 (metacarpal) 21.9 (metatarsal) 3) 34.9 4) 44.2 5) 36.0 6) 27.3 7) 30.9.

According to Silver (1969: Table A), the caprine distal radius, proximal ulna, calcaneum, and both ends of the femur fuse at between 2.5 and 3 years of age. Only one out of five specimens of these elements was fused at *Kaminoudhia*, and two out of four distal femora, reported by Silver to fuse at 3-3.5 years, were fused. This pattern suggests that only a minority of caprines at *Kaminoudhia* lived long enough to attain skeletal maturity.

Wear data for nine lower third molars, which erupt at about two years of age, concur with this fusion information from later-fusing elements. Six specimens were in less than full wear, represented by Payne's (1973:290) tenth stage, three were in full wear and none display a more advanced state of wear.

Figure 11.1 is a ratio diagram (Simpson et al. 1960:357) which plots the differences between the logarithms of various measured dimensions of mature caprine bones from *Kaminoudhia* and two other Cypriot prehistoric sites and presents a set of standard values for these dimensions. Ratio diagrams are a useful aid to the interpretation of small samples, since they permit size comparison to be made between dissimilar anatomical elements, which are not directly comparable through the intermediary of the standard values (Meadow 1981:160). The standard values used in fig. 11.1 represent median values for the large sample of Cypriot Chalcolithic caprine bones from the west coast settlement of Kissonerga *Mosphilia* (Croft 1998).

Lines 1 through 7 in fig. 11.1 represent measurements of various skeletal elements of caprines (mainly goats) from Kissonerga. In each case, a bimodal distribution of values roughly around the median is clearly indicated, reflecting sexual size dimorphism. Since specimens that could be specifically attributed to both sheep and goat occur on either side of the median, a size difference between the two caprine genera may be ruled out as an explanation for the existence of two size groups.

Line 8 in fig. 11.1 represents the limited range of metrical data for a pooled sample of the same elements from *Kaminoudhia*. Solid squares denote specimens attributed to sheep, crossed squares indicate goats, and open squares designate undifferentiated caprines. Bimodality is also clearly indicated. As with Kissonerga, both the larger and smaller size groups include specimens that are attributable to both caprine genera, so sexual size dimorphism provides the most likely explanation. It would appear that male caprines at *Kaminoudhia* were smaller on average than those at Kissonerga, while females were generally much smaller. This morphological difference may reflect the introduction of different breeds of goat, and probably sheep, at the beginning of the Bronze Age.

A pooled sample from Marki *Alonia*, dating to the early second millennium B.C.E. and thus broadly contemporary with *Kaminoudhia*, is represented by asterisks on line 9 of fig. 11.1. The overall size range of the Marki caprines, which include similar numbers of sheep and goats, corresponds better with that of *Kaminoudhia* than Kissonerga, perhaps suggesting that the same breeds of caprine were present at the two later sites (Croft 1996). In contrast to both Kissonerga and *Kaminoudhia*, sexual size dimorphism is not apparent in the Marki sample.

A conceivable explanation would be that castration was practiced at Marki, but not at *Kaminoudhia* or Kissonerga, although this is not the place for a discussion of this possibility. The small *Kaminoudhia* faunal sample did not provide evidence for the horn conformation of the goats, but if they were of the same breed as those at Marki then they would have had twisted horns rather than the untwisted "scimitar" type known from earlier periods in Cyprus.

The presence of equal numbers of males and females among the caprines of Chalcolithic Kissonerga, probably reflecting exploitation mainly for meat, is illustrated in fig. 11.1. The preponderance of females apparent in the small *Kaminoudhia* sample suggests that milk production may have been an objective here, although not necessarily the overriding (or even the primary) objective of caprine exploitation (cf. Payne 1973: fig. 2).

CATTLE

The larger size of isolated teeth of cattle than those of caprines makes them more visible during excavation, and therefore more likely to be recovered. This factor may be responsible for the lower proportion of the total number of identified fragments of cattle, which consists of postcranial fragments (Table 11.3). Furthermore, the rendering of a cattle carcass into packages of size suitable for domestic consumption might normally be expected to involve a greater degree of bone fragmentation than the preparation of a much smaller caprine carcass. Greater fragmentation of cattle remains is evidenced at *Kaminoudhia* by the fact that the average weight of an identified fragment (19.8 gr) is only about 3.5 times greater than that of the average caprine fragment (5.7 gr), while the disparity in the weights of whole bones of these two taxa is much greater than this. These two factors may have operated to reduce the amount of epiphysial fusion data available for cattle to a much lower level than for caprines, from samples of identified fragments of comparable size.

As with caprines, few of the earlier fusing bones of cattle were found in an unfused state. Four distal humeri, a proximal radius, and sixteen first and second phalanges were fused and only three second phalanges were unfused. This suggests that only 12.5% of cattle died before one and a half years of age (Silver 1969: Table A). Among the very few later fusing elements represented, a fused distal ulna and proximal humerus and an incompletely fused calcaneum hint that most cattle may have survived into adulthood.

Although such a small body of material cannot be interpreted with any degree of confidence, the impression gained is one of low mortality among immature cattle. Dental data, while insufficient to permit refinement of this picture, do not contradict it: out of 43 single teeth and tooth-bearing jaw fragments, only four included deciduous teeth.

As mentioned in Chapter 2, the finds from Unit 10 included the apparently complete frontal portion of a small cattle skull, which retained both horn cores. No other cattle remains were present in Unit 10. The other mammalian remains from this unit consisted of an undistinguished handful of caprine, deer and pig bone fragments. It thus seems likely that this substantial skull fragment had been deliberately placed here. The only other notable feature of the small faunal sample from Unit 10 is the presence of half a dozen bird bones, attributed to kestrel (*Falco tinnunculus*) (see below).

FALLOW DEER (*Dama mesopotamica*)

Out of 26 specimens of earlier fusing articular ends (proximal radius, first and second phalanges and distal scapula, humerus, tibia, and metapodial) only four were unfused, which suggests low mortality among young deer of less than perhaps two years of age. Among seven specimens of elements which fuse later than this, three were unfused or incompletely fused, suggesting that a greater proportion of deer died during sub adulthood, but that many survived into adulthood. Dental data were too sparse to be informative.

Ten pieces of antler, amounting to half the total weight of deer remains identified from *Kaminoudhia*, included four shed, one shedding, and one unshed antler bases. Antler was widely used for the manufacture of such items as hafts, beads, and hammers in Stone Age Cyprus (Croft 1983; 1985; 1998), and it is likely that it would have been brought onto the site as an industrial raw material. At least one shed antler, a rather straight unbranched specimen from the first head of a fallow buck, has been modified by the removal of the burr from around the base of the antler for use as a hammer for flint working (Unit 1 Lot 6). A second, abraded, shed antler base lacks all but the last vestiges of its burr, and may also represent the striking end of a hammer (Unit 21 Lot 5). Similar antler hammers are known from Chalcolithic Lemba *Lakkous* (Croft 1985:201) and Kissonerga *Mosphilia* (Croft 1998) in the Ktima Lowlands of western Cyprus. This general type has a widespread spatial and chronological distribution, and is known from as far away as the Solutrean of France (Bordes 1974).

PIG

Little may be said about pig based on the small amount of material recovered. Among the very limited amount of pig dental remains, deciduous teeth figured prominently, suggesting adherence at *Kaminoudhia* to the normal practice of killing a majority of pigs at a young age.

SMALL MAMMALS AND BIRDS

At *Kaminoudhia*, as on many prehistoric sites in Cyprus, fox was a minor component of the fauna. Five fragments were identified from as many separate contexts.

Since a small felid (*Felis* cf *lybica*) is known as early as the Aceramic Neolithic in Cyprus (Croft 1998, 1996; Davis 1987:307) there is no a priori reason why it should not be present at *Kaminoudhia*. However, the single cat bone recovered (from Unit 16 Lot 12), a complete humerus, is suspiciously well-preserved by comparison with other faunal material from the site. Therefore, it appears to be intrusive. An encrusted and broken rodent mandible is of Mus/Acomys size, but is not identifiable.

Among the bird bones a distal carpometacarpus is attributed to mallard (*Anas platyrynchos*) and six fragments of tibia, carpometacarpus, and tarsometatarsus to kestrel (*Falco tinnunculus*). The kestrel remains were all from Unit 10 Lot 7 and probably derive from a single individual.

Spatial Distribution of the Faunal remains

Most of the architectural units at *Kaminoudhia* yielded some stratified animal bone: thirty-four different units yielded between one and twenty-six identifiable pieces, one (Unit 2) yielded forty-five, and one (Unit 21) yielded 137. Thus, the small faunal sample is spread thinly across the site and a detailed, unit-by-unit, spatial analysis would not be meaningful.

A more general comparison of faunal sub samples by area (Table 11.4) suggests that the remains of the different animals were not randomly distributed across the site, and that distinct differences exist in the taxonomic composition of the area samples. A contrast is apparent in the composition of the Area A sample of 145 identified fragments and that from Area C, consisting of 253 items. In Area A, caprine remains outnumber those of cattle by 3.6:1 whereas in Area C cattle remains somewhat outnumber those of caprine. The relative abundance of pig remains appears greater in Area A than in Area C, while that of deer is the same in both Areas. The faunal sample from Area B (twenty identified fragments) is far too small to be reliable, but seems more similar in composition to that for Area C than Area A.

Since radiocarbon dates from the two areas reveal no evidence for a general chronological disparity, it seems most likely that distributional variability among the animal remains is functional in origin (Manning and Swiny 1994: Table 2). The physical condition of bone material from Areas A and C is similar, so differential preservation would seem to be an unlikely cause. Whether refuse disposal practices, dietary variability among different segments of society, or some other factor is responsible remains a matter for conjecture.

Table 11.4. Taxonomic composition of faunal sub samples from Areas A, B and C at Sotira *Kaminoudhia*.

AREA		BOS	CAPRINE	DEER	PIG	TOTAL
A	n=	20	72	26	27	145
	%	13.8	49.2	17.9	18.6	
B	n=	9	7	3	1	20
C	n=	98	82	46	27	253
	%	38.7	32.4	18.2	10.7	

ANIMAL REMAINS FROM TOMB 11

The only animal remains recovered from the *Kaminoudhia* tombs consisted of fragments of the skull and mandibles of a goat kid, which were presumably associated as a funerary offering with a human burial on the floor of the tomb. A mandibular fragment with an erupting second molar suggests an age of about one year (Silver 1969: Table F).

DISCUSSION AND CONCLUSIONS

If the main economic animals of *Kaminoudhia* are viewed purely as providers of meat, a rough estimate of their relative significance may be made based on the number of postcranial fragments identified for each taxon (Table 11.3). Interspecific differences in tooth number, in patterns of fragmentation of cranial bones, and in identifiability of individual cranial fragments suggest that cranial material should be excluded from consideration.

For the purposes of estimating relative meat yield, the main animals represented at *Kaminoudhia* are assumed to have provided meat in these proportions: cattle, 8: pig, 3: deer, 3.4: caprines, 1 (for an explanation of these figures see Croft 1998). Application of these meat-yield factors to counts of identified postcranial fragments from *Kaminoudhia* suggests the following relative contributions to meat supply: cattle 58%, deer 19%, pig 12%, and caprines 11%.

It must be stressed that the above estimates of contribution to meat supply are not claimed to be accurate. The imponderables of assemblage formation, the operation of a diversity of taphonomic factors, and possible biases in sampling and recovery always render the economic interpretation of animal bone collections from archaeological sites a hazardous process. However the faunal remains emphasize that despite the predominance of caprine remains over those of cattle at *Kaminoudhia*, it is highly probable that cattle were by far the major providers of meat. Caprines may have provided comparable quantities to pig and less meat than deer, both of which animals were represented by considerably fewer bones.

The adoption of a meat-orientated view has thus far simplified the discussion of animal exploitation at *Kaminoudhia*. As discussed above, it is likely that the caprines would have been exploited for their milk. This is probably also true of cattle, which might have been kept to provide traction as well. Wool production may also have been an objective of sheep management at *Kaminoudhia*. Consideration of these secondary animal products adds significantly to the uncertainties which have already been described as inherent in economic interpretation, and prompts us to view a "carnivorous" reconstruction of the animal economy with a high degree of skepticism.

Although antler may be classed as a secondary product, and a suggestion has been made that fallow deer were milked during the Bronze Age in Cyprus (Morris 1985:268), they are not normally considered as secondary producers. Pigs are unambiguous in yielding only primary products. It seems likely, therefore, that a purely meat-based assessment of the relative importance of the various animals in the subsistence economy tends to overvalue the deer and pig, possibly to a considerable extent, by comparison with cattle and caprines, which potentially yield secondary products, particularly milk.

Cattle are not known from Chalcolithic Cyprus, which—along with the widespread use of metal and novel ceramic fashions—seem to constitute part of the innovations which are associated with the inception of the local Bronze Age. Other animals which probably arrived in Cyprus at the same period include an equid and a screw-horned breed of goat (Croft 1996). It is therefore possible that the lack of evidence for equid at *Kaminoudhia* simply reflects the inadequately small size of the sample rather than a real absence.

As stated at the outset, the sample of faunal remains excavated at *Kaminoudhia* is of considerable interest despite its small size and poor state of preservation, since it provides the best available evidence for the exploitation of animals during the last few centuries of the third millennium B.C.E. Apart from the *Kaminoudhia* sample there exists only a relatively small assemblage from Kissonerga (Period 5) in which cattle and caprines are not as prominent and deer and pigs are considerably more abundant than at *Kaminoudhia* (Croft 1998). However, since it is possible that the Kissonerga assemblage could be heavily contaminated with Chalcolithic material, differences from the *Kaminoudhia* assemblage may be due more to this factor than to variations in contemporary animal economies.

The early second millennium faunal sample so far recovered by the ongoing excavations at Marki *Alonia* in the central lowlands of Cyprus (Frankel and Webb 1992, 1993) is much larger than that from *Kaminoudhia*, comprising more than 3,000 identified fragments. This is the only other near-contemporary assemblage, and it suggests an animal economy of a type broadly similar to that of *Kaminoudhia* (Croft 1996). A similar rough estimate of relative meat yield to that made above for *Kaminoudhia* indicates that at Marki cattle provided 57% of meat, deer 26%, caprines 13%, and pig 4%. At Marki equid, fox, dog, cat, and bird remains were also present in small numbers.

In conclusion, faunal remains from *Kaminoudhia* were not sufficiently abundant to permit interpretation at a very detailed level. Nevertheless, the overall impression gained from the material is that of a diverse animal economy dominated by cattle, in which caprines (mostly sheep) and pigs were also important. The hunting of deer supplemented production from the domestic sector of the animal economy, and were important as suppliers of both meat and antler.

WORKED BONE CATALOGUE

All measurements in centimeters.

B1. Needle. (Fig. 6.16) Area C Unit 2. Intact, broken in 3 pieces. L: 6.0, W: 0.5, Th: 0.24, D. of eye: 0.15. Highly polished. Flattened slightly irregular piece of bone with a broad rounded head, narrowing down to a point. The perforation at the flattened end was drilled from both sides.

B2. Bead. Area A Unit 4. One end damaged. Dark grey. L: 1.7, W: 0.9, Th: 0.6, D. of perforation: 0.4 x 0.2. Very smooth surface. Oval in transverse section, cylindrical, narrowing towards one end with central perforation.

B4. Antler hammer. (Fig. 6.16) Area C Unit 21. Fragment. L: 3.6, W: 3.3, Th: 2.8. Roughly mushroom shaped burr. Well-worn and faceted from use as a hammer.

B5. Needle. (Fig. 6.16) Area B Unit 12. Fragment. L: 4.5, W: 0.6, Th: 0.4. D. of eye: 0.4. Elongated, flattened in transverse section towards the eye, round towards the broken point.

B6. Point. (Fig. 6.16) Area C Unit 21. Fragment. L: 7.3, W: 1.8, Th: 1.3. Elongated point, semicircular in transverse section towards broken end. The other end has a rounded point.

B7. Antler hammer. (Fig. 6.16) Area A Unit 1 Phase II. Intact in several pieces. (See detailed description in Chapter 11).

B8. Point. (Fig. 6.16) Area C Unit 21. Fragment. L: 3.5, W: 0.8, Th: 0.25. Semicircular in transverse section. Very sharp point. Cut/shaping marks clearly visible on both edges.

B9. Point. Area C Unit 9. Intact? Chipped on one side and at very tip. L: 5.6, W: 1.3, Th: 0.3. Semicircular in transverse section.

B10. Point. Area C Unit 20. Fragment. Only medial portion preserved.

B11. Point. Area C Unit 9. Fragment. Only medial portion preserved.

12

THE BOTANICAL REMAINS

by Julie Hansen

INTRODUCTION

To understand the economy and subsistence of the settlement of Sotira *Kaminoudhia*, sediment samples from all areas excavated were processed through a water sieve to recover plant remains and other organic and inorganic material. Although the plant remains were not abundant, they provide an indication of the crops grown and wild plants exploited by the people at this site.

THE RECOVERY SYSTEM

Sediment samples of approximately 10 liters each were collected from contexts and features (such as pits and bins) that appeared to contain ash and carbon. The water sieve consisted of a fifty-gallon oil drum filled with water into which was set a nylon mesh (ca. 1.5 mm) that was attached around the top of the drum with clothespins. As water from a hose pipe flowed into the oil drum, sediment was poured into the net mesh and agitated lightly by hand. The drum had an overflow spout that allowed excess water and floating material to flow into a fine mesh (ca. 0.5 mm) sieve set into the top of an aluminum tub. The non-floating heavy fraction (residue) was collected in the nylon net. When the sample had been fully processed, the net was removed, dried, and later sorted. Material in the fine sieve was dumped onto a newspaper, set indoors to dry, and was sorted using a binocular microscope at 10X to 50X.

THE PLANT REMAINS

Table 12.1 provides the list of plant remains and other finds from the water sieve. Only a few samples produced identifiable remains. The paucity of plant remains from Sotira *Kaminoudhia* may be due to the shallow nature of the site: most deposits were less than 1 m from the surface. In a Mediterranean climate with very hot, dry summers, the ground and everything in it become dry. With the onset of rain in the autumn, the first percolation of moisture into the ground causes the very dry carbon to break apart into small fragments. Over time these fragments disperse and become too small to recover or identify. Nonetheless, we recovered enough remains to provide some indication of the plants exploited at this site.

Emmer wheat (*Triticum turgidum* ssp. *dicoccum*), grape (*Vitis vinifera*), almond (*Prunus dulcis*), and olive (*Olea europaea*) are the primary species represented. The wheat was undoubtedly a crop and is the most common type of crop in the Mediterranean during this period. However, it is uncertain whether the other plants were collected from the wild or also were cultivated. The single grape seed, although large, is insufficient evidence for domestication or viticulture at this site. In the Levant grapes were cultivated by at least 3,000 B.C.E. (Stager 1985). The olive also may have been cultivated, but there are too few remains to suggest large-scale storage or processing.[1] Distinguishing wild from domesticated olive is not possible based on pit size, and it is usually the presence of large numbers of pits and/or oil processing facilities, such as those found in the Late Bronze Age sites of Maroni *Vournes* (Cadogan 1984) and Kalavasos *Ayios Dhimitrios* (South 1992), that provide evidence of cultivation of this tree crop. The almonds probably were collected from the wild, although with so few remains, establishing evidence for their cultivation (such as increased nut size) is not possible.

Other plant remains include wild ryegrass (*Lolium* sp.), a common weed in cereal crops. Wild pistachios (*Pistacia* sp.) are also present and might have been collected for use as a flavoring in various foods. Terebinth *(Pasticia terebinthus)* is available in the Cypriot markets today for use in *loukanika* sausage. Wild pear *(Pyrus amygdaliformis)* was recovered from one sample. Numerous small fragments of wood were recovered, but most were too small to section and identify.

COMPARATIVE MATERIAL

Plant remains are not abundant in any site on Cyprus. In the Early Cypriot period this is even more the case because there has been little attempt to recover plant remains from the few sites excavated of this period. The Chalcolithic sites of Lemba *Lakkous* (College 1985) and Kissonerga *Mosphilia* (Murray 1991) have also produced short lists of plant remains including several species also found at Sotira *Kaminoudhia*. As noted above, emmer wheat is the most common cereal found on sites from the Aceramic Neolithic through the Bronze Age. Olives have also been identified from the Aceramic Neolithic sites of Khirokitia (Hansen 1989) and Cape Andreas *Kastros* (van Zeist 1981), as well as from the later Neolithic Ayios Epiktitos *Vrysi* (Kyllo 1982). Almonds were also identified from the latter site. Grape does not occur at sites on Cyprus until the Late Neolithic and is identified at *Vrysi*. Plants that have not been identified from *Kaminoudhia* but which have been recovered from contemporary or earlier sites include lentils (*Lens culinaris*), bitter vetch (*Vicia ervilia*), einkorn wheat (*Triticum monococcum*), and barley (*Hordeum vulgare*).

CONCLUSION

Although there are relatively few plant remains from Sotira *Kaminoudhia*, there are sufficient data to suggest that this was an agricultural site at which emmer wheat was cultivated. Olives, grapes, almonds, and pears were also exploited, but it is not known whether any of these were cultivated. Wild pistachios may have been collected for use as a flavoring in various foods.

---

[1] Two impressions that appear to be from olive leaves occur on a RP Mottled bowl (P48) from Tomb 18 (pl. 4.6b).

Table 12.1. Sotira *Kaminoudhia* Plant Remains (Sc.= Scientific sample)

Area A: Unit, Operation	DEPOSIT	SPECIES	NO.	COMMENT
Unit 5	Pit 1	Wood-Angiosperm	6	Too small to identify
Unit 1	Feature 3, Sc. 2	No finds		
Unit 3	Sc. 3, ashy	Wood-ring porous nutshell indet.		1 too small to identify, 5 Pottery, flint, bead from residue
Unit 4	Ashy	Cf. Bromus sp. Prunus dulcis Vitis vinifera Lilium sp. Nutshell frag. Indet. Wood-Angiosperm	1 2 1 1 1 5	Nutshell fragments Fragments too small to identify Bone, flint, pottery, from residue
Unit 15	4	No finds		Object 2 – seed cast in mudbrick Compositae sp.
Unit 4		Wood	2	Small fragments, indet.
Unit 4, Phase I	Ashy	Lolium sp. Triticum turgidum Ssp. Dicoccum Wood	5 1 4	 Fragments Indet.
Unit 6	Feature 2	Wood	3	Fragments indet. Flint from residue
Unit 4	Sc., 1 bin	No finds		
Unit 15	Sc. 3, pit 3	No finds		

Area B: Unit, Operation	DEPOSIT	SPECIES	NO.	COMMENT
Unit 12	Soil from mortar	No plants		Bone, pottery, flint, from residue

Area C: Unit, Operation	DEPOSIT	SPECIES	NO.	COMMENT
H23D2. Unstrat.	Feature 1 Lower level	Wood	2	Fragments indet. Bone, flint, pottery, from residue
H23D2. Unstrat.	Feature 1. Lower level	No finds		
Unit 22	Sc. 4, interior Spouted bowl	Wood-angiosperm	10	
Unit 22	Sc. 3, Feature 2 Lower level ash above bedrock	cf. *Prunus dulcis*	2	Nutshell fragments
Unit 22	Sc. 4, Feature 3	*Prunus* sp.	3	Wood fragments
Unit 22	Sc. 2, ash	No finds		
Unit 22	Ash	Wood		Too small to identify Bone, pottery, bead, flint, from residue
Unit 22	Pot near human remains	No finds		

Unit 23	Ash, middle of room	cf. Olea Wood-gymnosperm Wood	2 1 45	Wood Pottery, bone, from residue
Unit 16	Feature 2, bins	No plants		Flint from residue
Unit 21	W side of WL	cf. *Olea* sp. *Pistacia* sp. Wood indet.	2 3	Pit Fragments Pottery, flint, from residue
Unit 2	Feature 7 Interior	No finds		
Unit 2	Ash	No plants		Pottery from residue
Unit 8	Above floor	*Pistacia* sp. *Compositae* sp. Wood	1 1 6	 Indet; pottery, flint, from residue
Unit 8	Ashy NE section	*Prunus dulcis* cf. Leguminosae Wood Angiosperm-wood	3 1 30	Nutshell fragments Indet. Flint, pottery, stone beads 1 1/2 and possible bead blanks from residue
Unit 8	Above floor	Olea sp..	1	Wood, pottery, from residue
Unit 8	Ashy W of WL Just above floor	cf. Olea	2	Wood
Unit 2	Sc. 3, ash	No finds		
Unit 2	Sc. 1, ash	No plants		
Unit 2	Sc. 5, ash Top of walls	cf. Olea Wood-angiosperm	1 2	Wood
Unit 2	Sc. 6, ash	No finds		
Unit 2	Sc. 2, ash	No finds		
Unit 17	Sc, 7, ash	No plants		Flint from residue
Unit 17	Ash	No finds		
Unit 17		No finds		
Unit 2		No finds		
Unit 17	Ash	No finds		
Unit 9		cf. Leguminosae	1	Seed fragment, indet.
Unit 9		Wood	20	Fragments too small to identify
Unit 17	Ash Above floor	Wood	5	Fragments too small to section
Unit 2	Ash E side above Floor	Pinus sp.	9	Wood
Unit 2	Sc. 6, ash	No plants		Pottery, flint, from residue
Unit 2	Sc. 7	No plants		Pottery, flint from residue
Unit 2	Ash	No plants		Flint from residue
Unit 2	Sc. 8, ash	No finds		
Unit 2	Sc. 9, ash	No finds		
Unit 2	Sc. 10	Wood-angiosperm	1	Too small to identify
Unit 10		cf, Graminae	1	Fragment

Tombs	DEPOSIT	SPECIES	NO.	COMMENT
Tomb 11		Wood-angiosperm	2	Too small to identify
Tomb 11	Object 10	No finds		
Tomb 14		No plants		Bone from residue
Tomb 15		No plants		Bone, beads – 3 from residue

13

THE MOLLUSKS

by David S. Reese

INTRODUCTION

The Early Cypriot site of Sotira *Kaminoudhia*, today five kilometers from the sea on the south coast, produced 39 marine shell fragments, five crab claws, and several fossil shells (Table 13.1). The marine shells are more likely to be ornaments than food items.

THE REMAINS

MARINE SHELLS

There are nine *Cerastoderma edule glaucum*, with three fresh but most collected already dead. Of particular interest are three shells that might have been used as ornaments. Area A Units 1 and 3 produced shells with holes punched from inside, and from Area C Unit 2 came a shell holed on its body and also holed by a carnivorous gastropod.

Six *Charonia* fragments, all probably *Charonia sequenzae*, came from Area A (Units 1, 3, 4, and 7), Area B Unit 12, and from an unstratified lot in F20A. There are five *Dentalium*, with two unstratified from the cemetery area. Others come from Area A Units 5 and 7 and Area C Unit 9.

There are five *Phalium* remains. From Area A Unit 1 comes a burnt lip fragment. A body cut open with a curving body part present was located in Area B Unit 14. Three shells were found in Area C. Unit 21 produced a lip fragment broken from its shell, Units 22 and 23 yielded complete mollusks. The one found in Unit 23 was fresh, with a recent slit hole behind the lip, while that from Unit 22 was slightly worn. There are two *Glycymeris*, both collected dead and ground down and holed at the umbo, from Area A Units 5 and 34. There are three *Murex trunculus* from Area A Unit 33, Area C Unit 21 (fresh), and the surface (water-worn, hole opposite mouth). There are two *Murex brandaris* from Area A Unit 1 (fresh) and Area C Unit 21 (water-worn fragment, open body). There are two *Thais* from Area B (unstratified, rather fresh) and Area C Unit 21 (water-worn, open body).

There are single examples of *Cerithium* from Area A Unit 3 (water-worn apical fragment); *Monodonta* fragment from Area B Unit 12; water-worn *Arca* from Area B Unit 12; *Barbatia* (holed just below umbo) from Area B Unit 13; *Luria* fragment from Area C Area 10; and *Patella* from Area C (unstratified).

CRAB CLAWS

Crab claws came from Area A Unit 3 and Area A unstratified (2), Area C Unit 17, and from the East–West Trial Trench between Areas A and B.

FOSSIL SHELLS

Fossil oyster remains came from Area A Units 1, 6 (holed on upper part of valve), Unit 16 (2 fragments), Unit 39, and from Area C Unit 2. There are also 12 oyster fragments from five contexts on the surface outside the tombs of Cemetery A.

Two fossil sea urchin fragments were excavated from Area A Unit 4 and Area B Unit 14, and a fossil *Glycymeris* internal mold came from Area B (unstratified).

COMPARANDA

Several Cypriot Chalcolithic sites yielded shells. Erimi *Pamboula* had 51 shell fragments, including seven *Cerastoderma*, six *M. brandaris*, three *Cerithium*, two *Patella*, one *Glycymeris*, and one *Monodonta* (Wilkins 1953).

Early to Late Chalcolithic Lemba *Lakkous* Area I produced more than 53 individual shells, including 12 *Glycymeris* (some collected as dead), four *Charonia*, four *Patella*, more than three *Dentalium* (some also registered as finds), three *Phalium*, two *Cerithium*, two *Monodonta*, one *Murex trunculus*, one *Thais*, and 19 crab claws (Ridout-Sharpe 1985:104, 105).

Lakkous Area II yielded more than 99 individual shells including: 25 *Glycymeris* (many collected dead, two holed at umbo), one *Acanthocardia* (cockle larger than *Cerastoderma*), fifteen *Patella*, eight *Charonia*, six *Phalium*, more than four *Dentalium* (others registered as finds), three *M. trunculus*, two *Thais*, two *Monodonta*, one *Cerithium*, and 17 crab claws (Ridout-Sharpe 1985:213, 215).

Early Chalcolithic Kissonerga *Mylouthkia* yielded 41 shell individuals including one *Acanthocardia*, 28 *Patella* (fifteen found together), four *Monodonta*, three *Charonia*, one *Phalium*, and one *M. brandaris* (Ridout-Sharpe 1985:299).

From Middle to Late Chalcolithic Kissonerga *Mosphilia* Unit 1015 came 124 marine shell individuals including 100 *Monodonta*, 16 *Patella*, and two *Charonia* (Ridout-Sharpe 1991:84). This pit and Unit 1375 also produced crab remains (Croft 1991:74). *Mosphilia* Unit 1225 produced 14 marine shell individuals, including five *Monodonta*, one *Acanthocardia*, one *M. brandaris*, one *Barbatia*, and one *Patella* (Ridout-Sharpe 1991:84).

Dentalia are frequently found at Cypriot Neolithic and Chalcolithic sites. They are present at Early Chalcolithic Kalavasos *Ayious* (South 1985:73, fig. 4, nos. 24–25).

There are four restored necklaces of *Dentalium* from the Middle Chalcolithic Cemetery 1 at Souskiou *Vathyrkakas*, about six km from the south coast (Christou 1989:88–89, fig. 12.6; Goring 1988:53, fig. 33; Karageorghis 1973: fig. 69, 1982a: fig. 20; Nicolaou 1990: pl. XXIIIb). Dentalia are also known from *Mosphilia*, particularly Grave 563 (Peltenburg 1987b:221; 1992:27–31) and from Late Chalcolithic *Lakkous*, including a necklace of 37 shells from Grave 47 (Peltenburg 1979:29, 1984:56f., fig. 1, pl. XVII; 1990: fig. 2; Peltenburg et al. 1983:15, pl. III:4; Karageorghis 1983: fig. 38).

Chalcolithic Prastio *Ayios Savvas tis Karonos* Monastery, today 17 km from the sea in the west, produced 110 marine shell remains from about 98 individuals and two *Potamon* crab claws (Reese n.d.). There are 49 fresh *Cerastoderma* fragments from at least 37 individuals. There are 25 *Dentalium* present. Twenty-four small *Dentalium* and a picrolite cruciform figurine (from a necklace?) were found in an ossuary (Rupp and D'Annibale 1995:39, pl. IV:2).

There are two water-worn *Glycymeris* and one *Barbatia* fragment.

The six *Monodonta* and five *Patella* were probably food items. There are also four *M. trunculus* (three definitely collected dead), two *Cerithium* fragments (one water-worn fragment could have been strung), and two *Charonia* fragments.

Unmodified cockles were found at Kalopsidha *Tsaoudhi Chiftlik* in the Early Cypriot IC Tomb 34 (ca. 2075 B.C.E.). Another was found under the floor of a house where a tomb was also found (Biggs 1966), as well as from a female's tomb in Trench 3 (Gejvall 1966:128–29). A potsherd from here also had a *Dentalium* imprint (Biggs 1966).

Marine specimens

Table 13.1. Shells, crabs and fossils from Sotira *Kaminoudhia*. All measurements in millimeters. D = diameter; ext. = external; H = height; L = length; max. = maximum; W = width

PROV.	SPECIES	COMMENTS
AREA A		
Unit 1	*Charonia*	Fragment, worn, 29 x 33
Unit 1	*Murex brandaris*	Large, fresh, broken distal spine L 62
Unit 1	*Cerastoderma*	Left valve, worn, collected dead, W 22, H 21, hole punched from inside, exterior size of hole: 4.75 x 5
Unit 1	*Phalium*	Lip fragment, burnt, L 21.5, W 7.5-7.8
Unit 3	*Cerastoderma*	Worn, collected dead, left valve, hole punched from inside, W 18.75, H 17.75, hole 3.25 x 3.75
Unit 3	*Cerithium vulgatum*	Water-worn apical fragment, L 27, W 15
Unit 3	*Charonia*	Fragment of columella and siphonal notch, has ridges, 18.5 x 17
Unit 4	*Charonia*	Fragment of upper part of siphonal notch, worn, thick ridges, L 30, W 17.5
Unit 5	*Glycymeris*	Water-worn, pitted, W 21, H 18, broken distal end, ground-down and holed at umbo (now worn), hole 2.5 x 1.75
Unit 5	*Cerastoderma*	Partly worn exterior, fresh inside, left valve, H 24, W 25
Unit 5	*Dentalium vulgare/D. rubescens*	L 11.25, max. D 2.5
Unit 7	*Charonia sequenzae*	Fragment, L 19.5, W 14
Unit 7	*Dentalium*	Very thin lines, L 18, ext. D 3.75
Unit 33	*Cerastoderma*	Worn, right valve, W 28.5, H 28.5
Unit 33	*Murex trunculus*	L 32, W 22.25
Unit 34	*Glycymeris*	Worn, broken distal end, W 22, H 18, ground-down and holed at umbo, ground-down area 5.25 x 5.5, hole 2.5 x 1.5
Unstrat. I17A 7	*Cerastoderma*	Somewhat worn, small, right valve, W 12, H 11.5

AREA B		
Unit 12	*Monodonta*	Small fragment
Unit 12	*Charonia sequenzae*	Body fragment, broken lip and body whorl, L 80.5, W 76
Unit 12	*Arca noae*	Water-worn, left valve, not complete, W 35+, H 17+ bit
Unit 13	*Barbatia barbata*	Right valve, W 33, H 16, poor hole 3 x 2 below umbo, not definitely man made.
Unit 13		"Shell impression in clay" - curving, small, not identifiable
Unit 14	*Phalium*	Body cut open, only curving body part present, L 37.5, W 35
Unstrat. C19D 5	*Thais haemastoma*	Rather fresh, L 44, W 30
Unstrat. C20A 12	*Cerastoderma*	Fresh, small, right valve, H 16, W 16
Unstrat. C20B 1	*Cerastoderma*	Fresh, left valve, H 22, W 22
AREA C		
Unit 2	*Cerastoderma*	Badly worn and pitted, left valve, W 29.5, H 28.5, hole in body 6.25 x 4.25, also holed by carnivorous gastropod 3 x 3
Unit 9	*Dentalium dentalis*	L 20.5, W 6.5, fresh
Unit 10	*Luria*	Fresh, fragment, has brown spots, _ of one lip, L 21
Unit 21	*Phalium*	Lip fragment, broken off shell, not water-worn, L 35, W 6.5
Unit 21	*Murex trunculus*	Fresh, L 61.5, W 42
Unit 21	*Murex brandaris*	Fragment, open body, not quite complete apex, water-worn, L 53, W 24+
Unit 21	*Thais*	Water-worn, open body, L 31, W 21
Unit 22	*Phalium*	Complete, slightly worn, smooth, L 41, W 29
Unit 23	*Phalium*	Complete, fresh, bumpy bottom area, L 51, W 38, slit hole behind lip L 19, W 8 (probably recent hole)
Unstrat. I24B 1	*Patella*	Fresh, low type, 23 x 17
Unstrat. F20A 1	*Charonia sequenzae*	Upper body fragment, worn, L 34, W 26
Unstrat. Area A.	*Murex trunculus*	Water-worn, L 54, W 38, hole opposite mouth L 10, W 6, lip broken
Stratified E-W TT	*Cerastoderma*	Fresh, left valve, broken distal end, W 30, H 21.5 (broken) (See Chapter 2 Units 27-29).
Cemetery Sh 1	2 *Dentalium ulgare/ D. rubescens*	L 21, W 3.5; L 34.5, W 4

CRAB CLAWS		
Unit 3		
Unstrat. G17A 1		Broken, thin type
Unstrat. H17C 1		Claw fragment
Stratified E-W TT		Distal end fragment, thin type. See Chapter I Units 27-29
Unit 17		
FOSSIL SHELLS		
Unit 1	Oyster	Small fragment, 27 x 14
Unit 4	Sea urchin	Fragment, 22 x 12, thin, T 3.75
Unit 6	Oyster	Small, circular, 18.5 x 19.5, holed on upper part of valve 3.5 x 3.5
Unit 16	Oyster	2 fragments, 1 or 2 valves, 29 x 21; 18 x 18
Unit 39	Oyster	Small fragment, 25 x 13
Unit 14	Sea urchin	Large dorsal fragment, 22 x 13.5
Unstrat. C20B 3	*Glycymeris*	Internal mold, both valves, H 40, W 35
Unit 2	Oyster	Fragment - black, but not burnt, 25 x 19
CEMETARY A, SURFACE		
I5B	Oyster	5 fragments - rather large individuals: 70 x 63+, 71 x 37+, 71 x 45+, 74 x 56+, 88 x 60+
I6D	Oyster	2 fragments - small pieces
I6D	Oyster	Fragment - lower side fragment, flat
I6D	*Oyster*	3 fragments - 1 larger, 2 smaller, could be from one or two valves
I6D-C	*Oyster*	Fragment - 51 x 44.5

14

GEOLOGIC AND GEOMORPHIC SETTING AND RESOURCES

by George (Rip) Rapp

PHYSIOGRAPHY AND CLIMATE

Cyprus is the third largest island in the Mediterranean, covering 9,250 square kilometers. Lying along the 35th parallel of latitude, it rises from 2,000 meters beneath the sea, but it is separated from the Anatolian mainland only by a relatively shallow saddle, approximately 800 meters deep. During historic times of low sea level, it was never connected to the Anatolia Peninsula.

The landscape of Cyprus exhibits a general east/west trend. The topography reflects the underlying geology, which is largely made up of sedimentary rocks. The main landscape features of the island can be grouped into four subdivisions.

The main topographic feature, the Troodos Ophiolite Complex, occupies about one-third of the southwestern portion of the island (fig. 14.1). Consisting of mafic (low silica) igneous rocks including basalt, gabbro, and dolerite, it represents a section of oceanic lithosphere and underlying upper mantle that was formed about 80 million years ago. Uplift of the rock mass began about 40 million years ago and continues today. Much of this massif now lies more than 1,200 meters above sea level, with Mount Olympus at 1,900 meters. Massive cupiferous sulfide deposits are associated with the pillow lavas of the complex. Other mineralization includes chromite and asbestos. Copper has been mined from the Troodos Complex over many millennia, possibly since 2000 B.C.E.

The Pentadaktylos Range, which parallels the northern coast, has an average height of 600 meters and consists principally of slightly metamorphosed Jurassic limestone. The broad Mesaoria Plain (the historical "bread basket" of the island) lies between the two mountain systems and consists of Late Cretaceous to Pleistocene marine deposits that range from limestone and calcareous marls to sandstones. Alluvial deposits cover most of the surface of the plain, which now lies about 200 meters above sea level and extends essentially the full length of Cyprus from Morphou Bay on the west to Famagusta Bay on the east. In the northern part of the Mesaoria Plain the rocks are highly folded, giving rise to a hummocky topography. In the southern part, the rocks are little deformed. Perennial springs and good soils have made this a choice area for settlement from earliest times.

A narrow coastal plain, varying from 0.5 to 5 km wide, surrounds much of the island. Elevated marine terraces border the coastal plain; at least six levels of old marine terraces can be distinguished.

Today's island of Cyprus is of relatively recent geologic origin. During most of the Tertiary Period it existed as two separate islands in the Tethys Sea (a precursor to the Mediterranean). These two "islands" are now the Pentadaktylos Range on the north and the Troodos Massif on the south side of Cyprus. Marine sediments deposited between the two highlands formed the chalk plateaus of southern Cyprus.

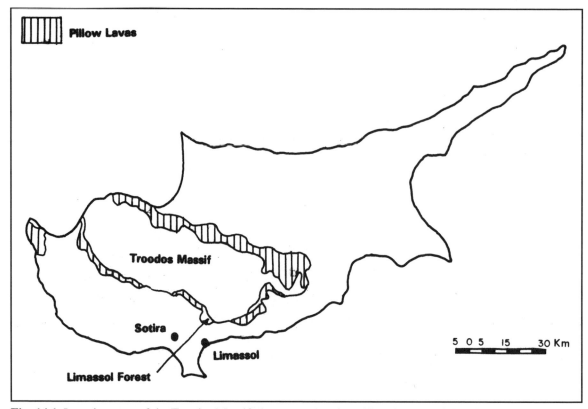

Fig. 14.1. Location map of the Troodos Massif, the copper-bearing pillow lavas, and the Limassol Forest.

The site of Sotira *Kaminoudhia* lies in the chalk plateau region. The surficial geology of the immediate area consists of chalky colluvium and alluvium, with thin soil that supports modest agriculture. A spring located just south of the site provides water.

The earliest methodical description of the geology of Cyprus, including a 1:250,000 sketch map, was done by A. Gaudry in the 1850s and early 1860s. E. Maurice translated this work in 1878 (Gaudry 1878). The Geological Survey Department of Cyprus was established in 1950, at which time systematic geologic mapping began. The first comprehensive bibliography and a revised 1:250,000 color geologic map were published by Bear (1961, 1962, 1963a).

The eastern and southern flanks of the Troodos Massif and the Limassol Forest (fig. 14.1) are typified by scarp and dip topography, with escarpments of gently dipping sedimentary rocks facing inwards toward the mountains. Additional landscape diversity stems from the deeply incised river gorges radiating from these mountains. These river valleys provided communication between the coast and the more remote areas. The majority of the rocks exposed in this scenic region are chalks, limestones, calcareous sandstones, and shales, with some salt deposits (including gypsum). The coastal margins of southern Cyprus in many places consist of low-lying flat plains with only a few meters of relief. These plains represent Pleistocene and Holocene marine terraces. Old sea cliffs often mark the inland edge of the younger terraces. The beaches and river mouths of southwest Cyprus would have provided adequate locations for landing ships during prehistoric times.

Some of the youngest deposits in southern Cyprus are salts that were precipitated in shallow water lakes, such as south of Larnaca. These salt deposits formed landward of coastal barriers during the last few millennia. The salts, derived from seawater migrating through the sand and gravel barriers, were precipitated in the hot and dry summer season. The major salt mineral is rock salt (halite), but gypsum and Epson salts also occur. The nearest salt lake to Sotira *Kaminoudhia* is about thirteen kilometers away on the Akrotiri Peninsula.

The predominant rock formation exposed in the Sotira *Kaminoudhia* area is the Pakhna Formation, consisting of reddish, marly chalks and limestones with shale and coquina lenses and some minor lenses of evaporite. Generally, the chalks and limestones are well-bedded and massive. The reddish color is due to weathering of ferrous material in the rock. The local limestones exhibit a great diversity in composition and resistance to weathering and erosion. The compact, dense, weather-resistant facies form many of the topographic highs. This rock material makes good building stone. In southern Cyprus, including the site of Sotira *Kaminoudhia,* the Pakhna contains a calcarenite (clastic) facies that includes detritus from Troodos igneous rocks. This facies functions as an aquifer, but it is unlikely that the inhabitants of the site utilized the subsurface water.

Despite the great variation in parent material—from limestones to mafic igneous rocks—the dominant soil of Cyprus is typical Mediterranean terra rossa. However, in southwest Cyprus, many (if not most) of the local soils are immature gray and brown-brown soils with limited pedogenic development. Some of these are lithosols, a large group of azonal soils characterized by lack of developed soil morphology and an abundance of poorly weathered rock fragments. In the Sotira village area, these lithosols are often found in shallow depressions in the bedrock. Mature brown and red soils, including pockets of the typical Mediterranean terra rossa, also occur in the region. These shallow pockets seem to be related to both the soft limestone called *havara* (Pantazis 1973) and the overlying, much harder calcareous crusts called *kafkalla*. Kafkalla (or *kafkallia*) is Greek-Cypriot for barren limestone crust lands. Havara is a secondary limestone deposited by the evaporation of calcium carbonate-rich water during the summer months. In the immediate area of Sotira *Kaminoudhia*, the soils are very thin and relatively immature. They are somewhat thicker under local pine forests.

Forests currently cover about twenty percent of the island, mostly confined to mountainous regions. Current vegetation patterns do not mirror the Early Bronze Age landscape because of deforestation from Roman times through the medieval period.

Perhaps sixty percent of the land is arable, but many of the soils are poor. The weathering and erosion of the terra rossa soils, which formed inland on the limestones, has produced the agriculturally fertile soils. The soils around Sotira *Kaminoudhia* are very shallow. Modern plowing has exposed bedrock in many places.

Of the many rivers in Cyprus, few are perennial except in their upper reaches, flowing usually from November through May. The largest rivers on the island have their sources in the Troodos Massif and drain radially from this topographic high. Most of the runoff is from the southern slopes, which receive more precipitation than the northern slopes. Melting of winter snow on the Troodos provides water for the major rivers until early summer. The upper reaches of these rivers are geologically young and filled with alluvium. Consequently, the surface water resources of Cyprus are not well-suited for perennial irrigation. Christodoulou (1959:39) observed that, "Where there is level, cultivable land there is not enough water and where there is abundant water there is not enough land."

Cyprus has no fresh-water lakes, only salt lakes at Larnaca and Limassol. Important groundwater aquifers underlie the western and southeastern Mesaoria Plain. Aquifers in the west are associated with the reef limestone, gypsum, and calcareous rocks surrounding the Troodos Massif. These aquifers give rise to springs, most of which derive water from joints and fissures in the rocks. Most of the springs are small. The largest springs south of the Troodos Massif yield more than one million cubic meters per year.

Cyprus has a semi-arid Mediterranean climate with hot, dry summers and cool, wet winters. Rainfall, confined to the months of November through March, averages 480 mm per year, varying from 350 mm in the Mesaoria Plain to 1,000 mm high in the Troodos, closely following the topographic contours. The climate is under pronounced continental influence, with most of the annual rainfall originating in winter low-pressure systems from the northwest. In the summer, temperatures on the coasts vary between 30° and 37° C. Temperatures are lower in the mountainous areas and during the winter months.

Since at least the beginning of the Middle Holocene (circa 7000 B.P.), environmental changes in the eastern Mediterranean have been of degree rather than kind. The climatic shifts have been moderate. The most dramatic physical changes have been in river valleys, estuaries (particularly infilling), and coastlines. Settlements and farming in these geomorphically unstable areas were constrained and impacted. The small valley in which Sotira *Kaminoudhia* was located was not subject to severe geomorphic changes. With poor quality soil, semi-arid climate, a paucity of surface water, and extreme evapo-transpiration, farming in the Sotira *Kaminoudhia* region of southwestern Cyprus would have been a tenuous endeavor.

ROCK AND MINERAL RESOURCES

The regional geologic resources likely to have been exploited by the inhabitants of Sotira *Kaminoudhia* were limestone for building blocks, umber, ochre, river gravel, and copper. An adequate supply of limestone for construction was available locally and needs no further comment here. A layer of sediments known as umbers often covers the pillow lavas of the Troodos. These brown earths are darker than ochre or sienna and consist largely of manganese oxides and hydrated ferric oxide. They are highly valued as a permanent pigment and are used either in their greenish-brown natural state (raw umber) or in their dark-brown or reddish-brown calcined state (burnt umber). For red and yellow pigments, the inhabitants had an abundance of ochres from the gossans capping the sulfide deposits to the northeast. River gravels from the Kouris bed provided tough, cohesive boulders of convenient size for making chipped and ground stone tools. The same river was the source of picrolite which appears to have played an important role in the economy of the settlement.

As Cyprus entered and moved through the Bronze Age, one aspect of the geology gained in importance. This was the nature and abundance of copper deposits, combined with the total lack of tin deposits. (The possible foreign sources of tin will not be addressed in this study.)

First, the nature of Cypriot copper deposits must be reviewed. For most of the ancient world, early copper metalsmiths utilized easily smelted copper minerals from the oxidized ores of sulfide deposits. Such ores were rare on Cyprus. Nevertheless, Early and Middle Cypriot metalsmiths were active. Balthazar (1990) records more than 300 analyses of copper and bronze from Early and Middle Cypriot times. There is evidence of copper mining and smelting in the Troodos as early as 2000 B.C.E. (Merrillees 1984; Olsson 1987).

Early Cypriot metal prospectors would have learned rapidly that subsurface copper minerals were represented at the surface by the bright yellows and reds of the gossans that form as sulfide deposits are oxidized by ground water. Virtually all of these gossans were investigated in ancient times (Constantinou 1982, 1992). There likely would have been minor amounts of malachite, azurite, and native copper associated with the gossans. Early Cypriot metalsmiths would have utilized these minerals until the deposits were exhausted.

In the Early Bronze Age of the eastern Mediterranean the dominant copper based alloy was an arsenical copper. In the opinion of this author, this arsenic initially was fortuitously derived from the high-arsenic copper sulfide deposits that were exploited (see Rapp 1988:25; 1999). Later metalsmiths might well have merely selected the arsenical copper ores that produced the best bronze. Tennantite ($Cu_{12}As_4Si_3$) occurs in the secondary enrichment zone above the primary copper-iron sulfide ores. For another view on Cypriot copper-arsenic production, see Zwicker (1986).

In any event, copper sulfide deposits with significant arsenic content are well known. Such deposits include the one at Limassol Forest, relatively near Sotira *Kaminoudhia* (Panayiotou 1980). At least nine arsenide minerals have been identified from this deposit. Although ancient mining at Limassol Forest has been suggested only for Classical and Roman times, the specific copper sources and mines for southwestern Cyprus during Early and Middle Cypriot times have not been identified.

The major copper-containing minerals throughout Cyprus are various copper-iron sulfides and cupiferous iron sulfides (pyrite and pyrrhotite). This author questions whether Early and Middle Cypriot metalsmiths could recover copper from copper-iron sulfides by normal roasting and smelting techniques. The flowering of bronze metallurgy on Cyprus during Late Cypriot seems to reflect the ability to smelt abundant copper-iron sulfide ores. The high sulfur content of Cypriot Bronze Age slags, an average of 1.48% for Enkomi and Kition slags (Rapp 1998), also indicates sulfide smelting by at least the Late Bronze Age.

The earlier copper production must have involved chiefly ore minerals derived from the secondary enrichment zone: the sulfides chalcopyrite, covellite, bornite, and chalcocite, and the copper oxides cuprite and tenorite. The latter are easily distinguished by their black color and are far easier to smelt. Bear (1963b) reports several occurrences of malachite and azurite in Cyprus. There is no doubt that rare, small deposits of these oxidized and easily smelted copper minerals occurred on Cyprus and must have been utilized during the initial stages of Cypriot copper metallurgy. However, this author has visited dozens of gossans and oxidized copper deposits without finding any trace of these minerals. On the other hand, Knapp and Cherry (1994:95–96) report finding both minerals in their surveys.

The copper-bearing deposits are located in the pillow lavas that have been eroded to form a discontinuous rim around the Troodos Mountains (fig. 14.1). The author spent parts of three seasons during the 1970s investigating the copper deposits of the Troodos. It is likely that, during the Bronze Age, ore was mined and possibly transported to smelting sites. There are no known slag heaps in the vicinity of Sotira *Kaminoudhia*, so evidence is lacking for local smelting during the period of habitation. There are slag heaps in the western part of the Limassol Forest (nearest Sotira *Kaminoudhia*) that are quite far from any recent copper mining.

Slag heaps from the Early and Middle Cypriot have not yet been found anywhere on Cyprus. Based on radiocarbon, the earliest slag heaps date only to the seventh century B.C.E. (Zwicker 1986). Steinberg and Koucky (1974; see also Koucky and Steinberg 1982) have suggested that hydrometallurgic methods may have been used to pretreat the sulfide ore before smelting. The product of this leaching process would be an impure copper-iron sulfate. It would be easier to recover copper by smelting this sulfate than smelting a copper-iron sulfide. Zwicker et al. (1977) report significant deposits of copper sulfate in the Troulli mine. Zwicker (1986) also showed experimentally that this copper sulfate could be easily smelted, with no production of slag.

THE SEISMIC REGIME

Cyprus is located in a tectonically unstable zone between two continental crustal masses. For the last 200 million years, the African plate to the south and southwest of Cyprus has been moving relative to the Eurasian plate to the north of Cyprus. The island is a remnant of oceanic crust, marooned between these two continental plates. The tectonic activity is expressed partly by frequent earthquakes. The southwestern coast near Paphos has been one of the most-affected areas over the last two millennia, with major earthquakes in 15 B.C.E., that led to the destruction of Old Paphos, and in C.E. 71, 332, 365, 1189, 1222, and most recently in 1953.

In her catalogue of ancient earthquakes in the Mediterranean area up to the tenth century C.E., Guidoboni (1994) lists 15 B.C.E. (perhaps 17 B.C.E.) as the earliest recorded earthquake. However, the frequency of earthquakes in southwestern Cyprus in the last two millennia, along with the active tectonic setting, indicates that third and second millennia B.C.E. inhabitants would have known the rumble of earth tremors.

Mudbrick is the construction material least resistant to seismic damage, although undressed stone construction with mud mortar or with no mortar is not much better. The buildings at Sotira *Kaminoudhia* would not have withstood an earthquake of intensity VIII (see Rapp 1986) without severe damage.

Two severe recorded earthquakes in the Sotira region will serve as examples. Soren (1985) has detailed the evidence of a major earthquake at the nearby Roman site of Curium (Kourion); with a likely date of 21 July 365 C.E., Soren estimated the intensity of the quake to be between IX and XII on the Modified Mercalli scale. A second quake, dated to 11 May 1222, completely destroyed Limassol and Paphos, with great loss of life (Ambraseys et al. 1994:40).

Although assessing archaeological evidence for seismic activity must be approached with caution (Rapp 1986), there is evidence of a possible earthquake during the habitation of Sotira *Kaminoudhia*. Wall tumble where the fallen blocks retained their original spatial arrangement is shown in pl. 14.1. Such a pattern would be expected if a wall fell, *en masse*, during an earthquake.

15

THE REGIONAL ARCHAEOLOGICAL
SURVEY

by Steve O. Held[1]

INTRODUCTION

The Sotira *Kaminoudhia* Survey (SKS) formed part of the second season of excavations. The primary investigations, directed by the writer, lasted from July 17 through August 27, 1983. They consisted of a systematic, intensive archaeological survey and a reconnaissance soil survey. A survey of the modern vegetation and land use in an arbitrarily defined circular area with a radius of 1 km, surrounding the modern village of Sotira and the prehistoric settlements of *Teppes* and *Kaminoudhia*, was also completed. The 1983 season also included a limited ethnographic study of the village. The aim of this study was primarily to supplement the archaeological information produced by both excavation and survey with data on local land use, animal husbandry, and vernacular building. An additional aim was to make a modest contribution to the record of traditional life in a depopulated Cypriot village. These secondary investigations were continued in the summer of 1984, when the author and Claudia Chang conducted a weeklong survey of the pastoral system of Sotira in order to expand the ethnoarchaeological database of the Sotira Project. The decision to include a multidisciplinary catchment analysis in the research design of the excavation reflects a systematic approach common in early prehistoric fieldwork in Cyprus (Legge 1982; Gomez et al. 1987; and Le Brun et al. 1987). Despite the limited scope of the investigations, this research has made it possible not only to put the settlement at *Kaminoudhia* into an ecological perspective but also to reassess and augment Dikaios' (1961) findings at the site of *Teppes*.[2]

SURVEY DESIGN

The fieldwork was scheduled as follows: one and one-half week reconnaissance survey by the writer to familiarize himself with the size, topography, vegetation/land use, hydrography, and archaeological remains of the survey area. This stage included a few spot checks on hills further afield, including the Sotira Culture site at Kandou *Kouphovounos*, 3 km to the east (CS 2074, Dikaios 1961:1;

---

[1] Ed. note. This chapter is an edited version of Held 1988. No references to surveys undertaken since 1988 have been included.

[2] Credit goes to the members of the archaeological survey field crew: A. Aristidou, C. Cummings, B. and I. Dispain, G. Ewing, A. Greenway, T. LaTourrete, S. Millspaugh, D. O'Connor, G. Panayiotou, C. Peaple, C. Roseen, J. Thompson, and A. Zournatzi, who endured the rigors of funicular surveying for various lengths of time. Bill Fox assisted in part of the systematic surface collection.

Megaw 1952:113; Stanley-Price 1979:135 no. Lm.14), where diagnostic Late Neolithic ceramics as well as a small quantity of chipped stone and ground stone material were noted on the surface.

The second stage consisted of a 3 1/2-week systematic survey, involving complete coverage on foot of 40 contiguous 50 m wide east/west transects by a crew of 3–5 whose members were spaced between 10 and 16.6 m apart. This required a total of 245 person-hours spread over thirteen days spent in the field, amounting to an average of approximately twenty-five person-hours/km² at a rate of 6.5 hours of field walking; this roughly represents the daily endurance limit in rugged terrain during the hot Cypriot summer months.

Assuming a positive correlation between survey intensity and the rate of site discovery (Plog et al. 1978:389–93), the systematic survey was therefore of a sufficiently high level of intensity to produce reliable data on the presence and absence of sites in the sample universe (Cherry 1983:387). The third and final stage of the Sotira *Kaminoudhia* survey consisted of one week of pin flagging, mapping and controlled surface collection of sites large enough to warrant further investigation.

As a systematic, intensive survey, the *observational* part of the design emphasized the blanket coverage of a relatively small (ca. 10 km²) area surrounding two major early prehistoric settlements. In the case of the *acquisitional* part, however, a flexible, non-probabilistic sampling strategy was used, consistent with the region's tiny scatters and isolated find spots. Many samples were therefore taken on a judgmental basis involving the collection in 50 m² quadrants of undiagnostic as well as diagnostic artifacts in order to skew the results as little as possible under the circumstances.

RESULTS

The initial impression of a rather ephemeral human presence beyond the vicinity of *Teppes* and *Kaminoudhia* was confirmed by the dearth of substantial scatters of any period that became apparent as the systematic, intensive survey progressed. Only four settlement sites were located: namely a Byzantine farmstead situated off the Sotira-Zanaja road by the "Sotira Pine" northeast of the modern village (S. 25: Sotira *Sternes* NE 2), which may have been the predecessor of a historically documented major feudal estate named "San Chitino" in the vicinity of Sotira (Goodwin 1984:477,1517); two sites of indeterminate age with rectilinear walls apparent in the topsoil but without associated artifacts, ca. 800 m east of Sotira (S. 85: Sotira *Limnia* South 2; S. 86: Sotira *Limnia* South 3); and a large MC settlement situated on a promontory on the far side of Symboulos Canyon, ca. 1.2 km west of Sotira, which is also the richest site the survey has produced (S. 84: Sotira *Troulli tou Nikola*). The remainder are eighty-three find spots (with fewer than five artifacts or with sherds from a single vessel), comprising early prehistoric ground stone tools, small quantities of worked and unworked chert, occasional oddities like tiny igneous pebbles, jasper nuggets, fossilized oyster shells, and *dhoukani* flake-blades as well as ceramics. The overwhelming majority of the pottery consists of undiagnostic red monochrome coarse ware sherds of various fabrics which may date from anywhere between the Hellenistic and Medieval periods and always vastly outnumber the Roman fine ware with which they are spatially associated in the scatters. Pottery of other prehistoric and later periods—notably MC, LC, and Cypro-Archaic decorated and plain wares—is entirely lacking from the survey collection (with the exception of the above-mentioned MC settlement), and a single Bichrome rim sherd (SKS 38-XXXII-317, FS. 79: Sotira *Vlisies/Vounon* SE) found by itself ca. 1 km southwest of Sotira near the perimeter of the survey area only accentuates the complete absence of ceramics of these periods.

Overlying these discrete sites and find spots is a diffuse scatter of the same historical red monochrome ceramics that covers the entire survey area and manifests itself in single or handfuls of sherds. This scatter, which is so thin that the term barely applies and is also found in other regions of the island, is seen simply as the result of pot breakage through centuries of human transit and not as representing, or relating to, specific loci of human activity. By contrast, most of the *sites* located by the survey consisted of clearly discernible artifact concentrations covering between 400 and 2,500 m².

CATALOGUE OF SELECTED SITES (fig. 15.1)

1. S. OX/Sotira *Kaminoudhia* (built-up settlement and cemeteries): Excluded from survey.
2. S. OOX/Sotira *Teppes* entire site, incl. slopes and Areas I–IV (Dikaios 1961): Excluded from survey.
3. S. 84/Sotira *Troulli tou Nikola*/Survey Extension /VD04861. 38414: Late (?) MC settlement. Promontory site at confluence of Symboulos River and tributary. 800 m due W of and inter visible with *Teppes*. Dense scatter on E and W slopes, incl. RP IV and DPBC, rubbers and saddle querns, grinders, rubbing stones, pounders, etc., chalcedony pecking stones, little chipped stone, numerous stone thresholds. Tombs located at base of promontory's SE slope above W bank of Symboulos River. Systematic surface collection.
4. S. 18/Sotira *Arkolies* Center 2.14,15,17-NW-XI-XX VD04867.38419: Prehistoric, with Roman/Early Christian component. Large cultivated field ca. 500 m NW of *Teppes*. Largest homogeneous scatter in survey area, with quantities of ground stone, chipped stone, some RL sherds, red monochrome coarse ware, one Ridge Ware sherd. Systematic surface collection.
5. S. 18A/Sotira *Arkolies* Center 2 (Hill 322)/15-NW-XVI/VD04866.38420; Early Prehistoric (?). Hillock in the middle of S. 18, with dense cluster of chipped stone. No ceramics. This site is a discrete locus within S. 18.
6. S. 22/Sotira *Arkolies* West/15.16-NW-IX-X/VD04864.38419: Early Prehistoric (?). Edge of cliff overlooking Symboulos Canyon, ca. 700 m WNW of *Teppes*. Dense chipped stone scatter and nine small igneous pebbles.
7. S. 36/Sotira *Arkolies* South/19.20-NW/22-SW-XVIII-XIX/VD04868.38417, VD04868.38416, VD04876.38417: Early Prehistoric. Cultivated field ca. 300 m NW of *Teppes*. Second largest scatter in survey area. Quantities of ground stone, chipped stone, small number of late red monochrome sherds and one RP (?) handle fragment.
8. S. 10/Sotira *Derji*/*Arkolies* North/08.09-NW- XIV/VD04866.38422: Early Prehistoric, with later (Roman?) component. Cultivated field on S side of Derji tributary, ca. 850 m NW of *Teppes*. Small ground stone scatter, two chert flakes, small ceramic scatter of late red monochrome sherds, incl. one Terra Sigillata.
9. S. 4/Sotira *Arkappies* West/04.05-NW-XXI/VD04870.38425, VD04869.38424: Late Roman/Medieval. Recent (19th century?). Uncultivated scrubland on weathered limestone, ca. 1 km N of *Teppes*. Large scatter of late red monochrome sherds, including glazed ware.
10. S. 45/Sotira *Kokkinoyi* 1/23. 24-SW-XIII-XIV/VD04866.38415: Early Prehistoric. Uncultivated field ca 250 m WNW of *Teppes*. Ground stone scatter incl. rubber and quern fragments, chipped stone scatter including one *dhoukani* flake-blade.
11. S. 58/Sotira *Plathkiastrata* /29-SW-XIV-VD04866.38412: Early Prehistoric, with later (Medieval?) component. Cultivated field overlooking Vathyronas drainage, ca 400 m SW of *Teppes*. Large ground stone scatter, incl. one quern fragment. Small quantity of chipped stone. One red monochrome wheel-made sherd.
12. FS. 63/Sotira *Plathkiastrata* South 1/31-SW-XIII-VD04866.38411, S70/Sotira *Plathkiastrata* South 2/32-SW-XV/VD 04867. 38411: Early Prehistoric. Cultivated field overlooking *Kliouphas* Canyon, ca. 500 m SSW of *Teppes*. Small ground stone scatter, incl. one quern fragment.
13. FS. 55/Sotira *Elies tou Ayiou Yeoryiou* 1/28-SW-XXI/VD04870.38413, S. 57/Sotira *Elies tou Ayiou Yeoryiou* 2/30-SW-XVIII-XX-VD04869.38412: Early Prehistoric. Cultivated field above Kliouphas Spring, ca. 250 m SSE of *Teppes*. Ground stone scatter, incl. one quern fragment.
14. S.56/Sotira *Kanjelli* 1/29-SE-XXXVIII/VD04878.38412, FS.62/Sotira *Kanjelli* 2/31-SE-XXXVIII/VD04878.38411: Early Prehistoric. Uncultivated field near abandoned sheepfold (illustrated in H.W. Swiny 1982:32, fig. 18), ca. 1.1 km ESE of *Teppes*. Ground stone scatter, incl. one intact and one fragmentary quern. A large igneous fragment with signs of use was found in one of the walls of the sheepfold (FS. 62).
15. S. 85/Sotira *Limnia* South 2/Survey Extension/VD04882.38415, S. 86/Sotira *Limnia* South 3/Survey Extension/VD04883.38414: Late Prehistoric/Historical? Pine forest, ca. 1.3 km E of *Teppes*. Two rectilinear

rubble walls with facing courses of orthostats in topsoil. No associated artifacts or diagnostic features

16. S. 25/Sotira *Sternes* Northeast 2/16-NE-XXXVIII-VD04879.38418: Byzantine settlement (farmstead?). Pine forest on ridge top, ca. 1 km ENE of *Teppes*. Plastered, rectangular well, large quantity of building debris, incl. rubble and roof tiles. Large quantity of late coarse ware sherds, incl. pithos rim fragments. One ground stone quern fragment.

17. S. 87/Sotira *Arkappies* East/07-NE-XXXI/VD04875.38423: Drystone wall buried in historical terrace fill. Upper Kliouphas drainage, ca 1.2 km NNE of *Teppes*. Test pit sunk by project geomorphologist J. A. Gifford. Probably old terrace retaining wall or dam. No associated artifacts

18. S. 2/Sotira *Arkappies* North/02-NE- XXXII/VD04876.38426: (Late) Roman (?), with prehistoric component. Cultivated field, ca. 1.3 km NNE of *Teppes*. Large scatter of red monochrome sherds. Two chipped stone tools: one scraper and one knife on backed blade (fragment).

DISCUSSION

Inferences from the distribution of the sites and find spots will not be attempted, because even an intensive survey such as this one cannot achieve a measurable approximation of its target population without an assessment of the factors affecting the visibility and survival of sites, such as vegetation and long-term disturbances by geomorphologic processes and rural land use activities. Since the density and composition of the encountered scatters, as well as the nature of the constituent archaeological materials, generally made for low site obtrusiveness, visibility had a pronounced effect on the probability of discovering what we were looking for (Schiffer et al. 1978:6–8).

The vegetation cover and terrain encountered within the 1 km radius did not seriously impede field walking and the recognition of surface material in any but a few locations such as the Symboulos Canyon (which is unlikely to contain sites anyway) and areas of dense tragacanthic maqis plants like spiny burnet and gorse in which the visibility of sites was reduced drastically on both level and sloping surfaces. These blanks in the ground scan may amount to perhaps five percent of the survey area; in the remainder site visibility may be rated fair to excellent, and thus it can be confidently stated that no sites, as defined above, were missed.

Destruction, dislocation, and concealment of sites through natural and anthropogenic agents such as erosion on ridgetops, plateau edges and drainage slopes; colluviation on drainage bottoms; as well as terracing and dry farming, which was practiced more extensively in the past, have certainly altered the original distribution of sites and find spots in the survey area. Therefore, an assessment of the extent to which secular changes in the overburden have reshaped the land surface should form the crux of a geomorphological contribution to the survey analysis. Particularly problematic in this respect is the drainage morphology in a number of small tributaries and "arroyos"—especially in the well-defined, bifurcated upper drainage of the Kliouphas Creek north–northeast of *Kaminoudhia*, where intensive terracing has obscured the depositional sequence of sediments. The chronology of this area remains poorly understood. From an archaeological viewpoint, undated terraces are simply artificial, arbitrarily inserted land surfaces that scramble the natural stratification of associated artifacts to the point where faithfully recording them on a distribution map becomes a somewhat futile exercise. Aside from scatters, local inhabitants may also displace single artifacts. An example is the use of heavy ground stone tools as ballast by villagers during the carob harvest when loading the panniers of their donkeys with jerry cans full of water. At the site of the harvest, the ballast is tossed and becomes once again part of the archaeological record, albeit in a new place. Without recognition of this distribution practice, the spatial analysis of ground stone distribution in a survey area runs the risk of conveying a spurious accuracy and is liable to lead to erroneous conclusions.

Few sites or find spots were located on terraces, which in the case of settlements might be explained as the result of a preference for open slopes and ridge tops over the narrow drainages, but which, as the "deep tomb" (Tomb 20) at *Kaminoudhia* suggests, probably reflects the burial of other types of sites under recent terrace fill. The small number of Early Prehistoric ground stone find spots and late ceramic scatters found on terraces in the drainages north and northeast of Sotira most likely surfaced from the backfill and eroded down the drainage slopes—they are therefore not in situ. Pending clarification of these points, however, the rough-grain distribution shows a much greater density of both Early Prehistoric lithic and historical ceramic scatters in the western half of the survey area, whereas the eastern half, east of the Sotira–Zanaja road, is almost devoid of material. In fact, all but one lithic site are located southwest, west, and northwest of Sotira *Teppes*, along the eastern edge of the Symboulos Canyon and its eastern side drainages. This area continues to be valued for farming, hunting, and for its sources of water, and these sites no doubt represent the agricultural focus of *Teppes* if not *Kaminoudhia* and *Troulli tou Nikola* as well. In one of these side drainages, that of the Vathyronas Creek, whose head is at the base of the southwest slope of *Teppes* (fig. 15.1), the survey located the spring (now dry) more likely to have been used by the inhabitants of the Early Prehistoric settlement than the village springs mentioned by Dikaios (1961:1) (S. 48: Sotira *Paleokhorka* NE). The historical ceramic scatters, on the other hand, are more frequent on the higher, undulating terrain north of the modern village. Their correlation with uncultivated areas of weathered limestone and a thin terra rossa soil cover under invading pine (*P. Brutia halepensis*) could be interpreted as a sign that settlement shifted away from the springline (fig. 15.1) onto the high ground north of Sotira, but may alternatively stem from the greater chance of survival for ceramic scatters in localities outside plow zones, of which there are few in the intensively cultivated southern half of the survey area.

The density of isolated lithic find spots evidences a similar falloff from west to east. Consisting predominantly of igneous rubbing stones, pounders, rubber-pounders, axes and adzes, and rubbers, along with an occasional spall or quern fragment, as well as a few small and morphologically unimpressive chipped stone implements, they seem to indicate casual procurement activities in a prehistoric catchment most likely covered with pine, oak, juniper, lentisc, and possibly wild olive (Held 1989).

The survey conducted during the 1984 season was designed to furnish data for a study of the Sotira herding system structured on the model described by Chang (1984) and, on a more theoretical level, to test the case for the ethnoarchaeological potential of pastoral research which has since been eloquently argued by Chang and Koster (1986). Ethnographic interviews were conducted and data collected on the village's thirteen sheep, goat, and sheep/goat flocks and the *mandres* (folds) at which they are kept. It is hoped that the information thus obtained will enable us to recognize and explain the spatial patterning of the folds, flock trails, grazing habits, and pasture locations, allow the definition and analysis of dimensional variables of folds, and ultimately permit us to address problems of prehistoric animal husbandry at *Teppes* and *Kaminoudhia* in a more cogent manner than would be possible through faunal analysis alone. A welcome outgrowth from these investigations will be the generation of an architectural "mandra database" which may prove useful to research into vernacular drystone building techniques and the way in which such simple structures turn into ruins after abandonment.[3]

CONCLUSION

What can be learned from the survey? Having produced so few settlements or other "attractive" site types, its results are going to tell us more about locational parameters which define the small diachronic focus at Sotira than fill blanks on the distribution map. Due to its limited extent, the Sotira *Kaminoudhia* Survey can only rank as a catchment survey rather than a regional site survey. Coupled

[3] Ed. note. This research was never undertaken.

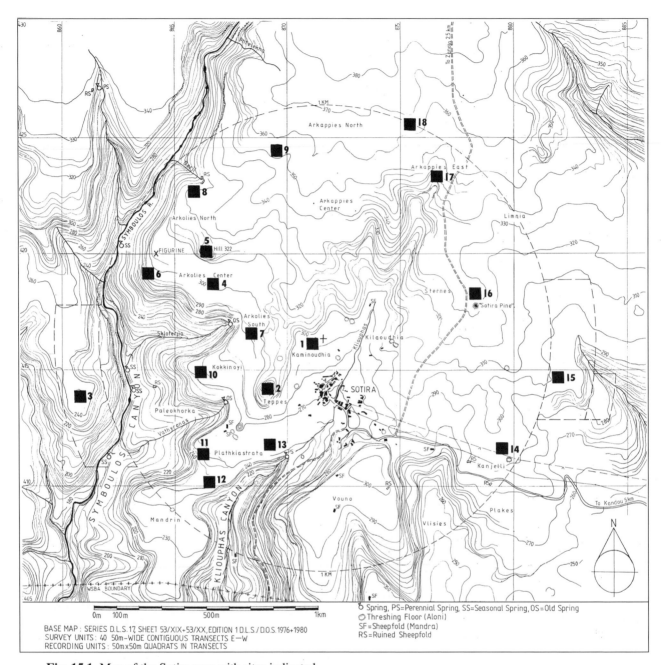

Fig. 15.1. Map of the Sotira area with sites indicated.

with the soil, vegetation, land use survey, ethnographic study of the village, as well as contributions on the geology and geomorphology, these investigations will put the settlements at *Teppes*, *Troulli tou Nikola*, and *Kaminoudhia* into an ecological perspective. The Sotira region does not appear to be a prime area for settlement like, for instance, the Vasilikos Valley or the Lemba area. Once this is recognized, the meager returns of the survey as far as substantial sites are concerned are easily explained. As a centralized survey it was too limited in its areal coverage to pick up the nearest settlements, and consequently found instead the archaeological background noise which covers the landscape in between (Gallant 1986:415–16). The nearest known early prehistoric settlement, Kandou *Kouphovounos*, is 3 km away to the east. This may indicate the magnitude of spacing that a regional survey would have to exceed in order to produce settlement sites. Kandou *Kouphovounos* is also in a more strategic position as far as raw material sources when the assumed location of prehistoric exchange networks are concerned. Sotira and its ancient settlements lie at the southern end of a large slab of *Pakhna* limestone, which slopes down gently from the southern edge of the Kryos Valley north of Pano Kividhes at an angle of approximately 5 degrees. Extensive open pine forests cover it, the result of natural reforestation in recent times through the invasive behavior of the local species. Appearances to the contrary, biotic diversity is considerable (see Chapter 16), and the carrying capacity of the land would certainly have been sufficient to provide a permanent subsistence base for small sedentary communities of several hundred inhabitants, provided they were not contemporaneous. The Symboulos River forms the major drainage of this region, and since it also originates there it contains no igneous boulders or cobbles from the Troodos Ophiolite Complex. Thus all rock utilized in the igneous ground stone technology of the Sotira area (i.e., gabbro, microgabbro, diabase, and pyroxene andesite) had to be collected either in the Kouris River immediately east of Kandou, or from a raised beach deposit where the Symboulos River enters "Happy Valley," southwest of Sotira. Similarly, the Lefkara chert of the chipped stone industry and the picrolite used at *Teppes* and *Kaminoudhia* occur nowhere closer than the Kouris Valley. The inconvenience involved in heavy raw material acquisition over a minimum distance of four kilometers would explain the relative frequency of limestone querns in the survey area and the apparent caching of igneous rocks at *Teppes* (Dikaios 1961:188, 190).

In terms of communication and exchange networks, the settlements at Erimi *Pamboula* and Episkopi *Phaneromeni* occupy a nodal position at the intersection of the east–west coastal corridor with a putative north-south link along the Kouris Valley and across the Amiandos Pass (cf. Swiny 1981:81–82). From this point of view, the region between Kividhes and Sotira is a backwater, lacking obvious incentives for settlement and patently unsuitable for the emergence of central places in the socio-economic sense. This probably accounts both for the lack of major sites in general and the absence of a well-known Early Prehistoric phenomenon in Cyprus: i.e., a dense cluster of sites belonging to *successive* periods which represents a pattern of shifting settlement locations inside a particular ecological niche. The reason why the higher topography of Sotira and Kandou attracted at least some settlement during the Early Prehistoric period may lie not so much in economic considerations as in the chronology of coastal alluviation at the western end of the Limassol plain, which could have resulted in the presence of an estuarine environment in the lower Kouris Valley during the fifth millennium B.C.E. and a delta which was still emerging as late as the fourth millennium B.C.E. The absence of the present fertile floodplain near Erimi and Episkopi would have confined habitation, as well as routes of communication, to higher elevations such as the foothills, an argument which finds strong support in the pattern of early prehistoric settlement locations throughout the Limassol District. However, while the causal relationship between site selection and environment will no doubt continue to be a hotly debated issue, the SKS, for all its modest micro-regional scale, has shown that whenever settlers arrived, they invariably opted for the small area around Sotira with its numerous springs, and for no other place.

Since testing hypotheses about site spacing and clustering is clearly beyond the scope of a centralized catchment survey, the next logical step would be to expand the Sotira *Kaminoudhia* survey into a regional survey covering the area between the Kouris River to the east, the Kryos River beyond Kividhes to the north, a line stretching from the lower Symboulos River to Ayious Amvrosios in the west, and the Western Sovereign Base Area boundary to the south, roughly 75 km². Using a stratified, systematic, unaligned sample with a fractation of 11 percent or 22 percent depending on the area, such an extensive survey could be conducted in a single field season with a small, experienced team and limited funding, covering a region in southern Cyprus which continues to be archaeological *terra incognita* aside from the important excavated settlements of *Teppes* and *Kaminoudhia*. Looking further ahead, an extensive survey should eventually be enlarged westwards to link up with the eastern limits of the Canadian Palaiopaphos Survey Project (Rupp 1987, Rupp et al. 1984), resulting in complete areal coverage of the archaeologically important southern seaboard between the Limassol Plain and the Ktima Lowlands.

16

AN ENVIRONMENTAL SURVEY NEAR PARAMALI VILLAGE, LIMASSOL

by Wouter van Warmelo

INTRODUCTION

This study is the result of observations recorded over a period of two years and eight months from October 1980 to May 1983. Frequent visits to the study area allowed the author to develop a detailed picture of a small but representative locality in the lower Troodos foothills of southern Cyprus.[1]

Reference sources for the identification of Cypriot flora and fauna at the time of writing (1983) were scarce and it has been necessary to rely on the generous help of individuals both in Cyprus and abroad who are acknowledged in the appropriate appendices.[2] With this assistance, a systematic and accurate survey was feasible. Any errors are mine alone. Details of species recorded are, in each case, as observed unless otherwise indicated. The results of the survey depend entirely on information gathered from the target area and obviously do not reflect the picture for Cyprus as a whole.

DURATION OF SURVEY

The findings are confined to a two year period from May 1981 through April 1983, partly to complete two full years from spring to spring, but also to exclude the steep learning curve of the first few months when many errors were made.

STUDY AREA (figs. 1.2, 16.1; pls. 16.1a, 16.1b)

The focus of the survey was a circular area approximately 1 km in radius with near its center a prominent hill 146 m high known as Klouva or Kloupha[3] about 1 km east of the now uninhabited Turkish Cypriot village of Paramali (also known as "Old Paramali Village"). Periodic visits were also made to the Sotira locality for control checks. The center of the survey lies 5.25 km on a bearing of 245

---

[1] As an officer serving in the Royal Air Force I have no specific scientific background in environmental studies, but my career has involved the meticulous observation and systematic recording of a wide range of data which facilitated the implementation of this study.

[2] The staff at the British Museum (Natural History) provided much appreciated assistance on several aspects of this research.

[3] The 146 m high hill has two British Sovereign Base Area bench marks, BP57 and BP58, clearly marked on the 1:5,000 topographical map: Series D.L.S 17 (D.O.S 155), Sheet 53/XXV, Edition 1 D.L.S./D.O.S. 1977.

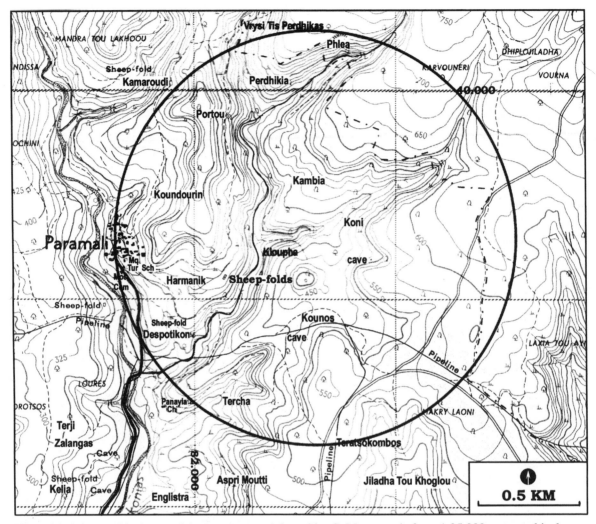

Fig. 16.1. Topographical map of the survey area. Adapted by C. Mavromatis from 1:25,000 topographical map: Series D.O.S. 355 (K8110), sheet 53, published by Directorate of Overseas Surveys, 1961 (Crown Copyright Reserved).

degrees true from Sotira *Kaminoudhia*. The edges of the two areas are 3.25 km apart. The highest point within the survey is an isolated hill 200 m above sea level, which forms part of the plateau framing the eastern perimeter of the study area. The lowest point, where the Perdhika River[4] joins the Pharkonias River, is 50 m, and the mean is about 120 m above sea level.

In the vicinity of Sotira Village the highest point is the Neolithic site of *Teppes*, 330 m above sea level and the lowest point is 170 m above sea level in the Symvoulos riverbed. The mean altitude of the Sotira area is around 290 m above sea level. The surveyed locality lies some 3 km inland, whereas Sotira is 5 km from the sea. The climatic and geographic differences between the two areas, however, are so small that observations from the one may be considered as broadly valid for the other.

---

[4] Although the watercourses shown on the map are described as "rivers," this term is purely one of convention. In reality these watercourses are mere seasonal streams which only flow during a wet winter or after major rainstorms. In some places, such as the bridge across the Pharkonias, they do remain perennial, but the sluggish summer flow soon disappears again beneath the rocky stream bed.

CLIMATE (Appendix 16.1)

Hot dry summers and cool rainy winters are typical in Cyprus. The micro-climate in the area fits this pattern, and any differences are matters of detail. For example, flowering periods are perhaps a week or two later than at Episkopi which is nearer the sea. Overall climatic conditions obviously vary from year to year. The winter immediately prior to the period of this survey was unusually wet. During the period of survey, however, total rainfall was some 70 mm per year below the average. Furthermore, temperatures averaged over the first twelve months produced a figure of about 0.5° C below the average and in the second year about 0.9° C below average. The figures relate to the conditions recorded at Royal Air Force, Akrotiri, 9 km to the southwest, and the nearest location where measurements were taken consistently.

TOPOGRAPHY (fig. 16.1)

The Middle Miocene alternating chalks are typical of the Pakhna Formation. Outcrops of harder rocks are evident as vertical cliffs in relatively deep gorges, where the slopes of the walls gradually reduce towards the river beds, although they never completely level off. The river beds of the Perdhikas and its unnamed tributary to the east are young scars through the detritus of the slopes. They remained dry throughout the period with the exception of a flow in the Perdhikas River on two brief occasions in February 1983. It should be noted that at the extreme southwestern edge of the survey zone, in the vicinity of the bridge across the Pharkonias or Paramali River, water flowed throughout the period over shallow, rocky steps. It was here that the brookweed and lesser bulrush flourished.

Above the gorges, the area is characterized by rolling hills covered with coarse, loose soil of fragmented chalky rocks, except where there are further rock outcrops. Several valleys and gorges terminate abruptly at their heads, in the northeastern sector of the survey with an amphitheater of harder rock, in which the shallow caves have occasionally been modified for sheepfolds (pls. 16.1a, 16.1b).

VEGETATION (Appendix 16.2)

The area seemed to have been uncultivated for many years prior to April 1983[5] when a small section of the plateau was plowed once and then left alone (pl. 16.2a). There is evidence at several locations of pre-modern terracing associated with numerous carob trees (*Ceratonia Siliqua,* pl. 16.2a) and a few olives (*Olea europea,* pl. 16.2b), which were still harvested every year. Lentisc *(Pistacia meniscus),* spiny burnet *(Sarcopoterium spinosum),* thyme *(Thymus capitatus),* prickly broom *(Calicotome villosa),* gorse (*Genista sphacelata,* pl. 16.3a), and various species of rockrose (*Cistus spp.,* pl. 16.4a) dominate the scene, providing several shades of green throughout the year and brighter colors during the flowering season. A point of interest demonstrated by the survey was that at any time of the year flowers brighten what could have been a monotonous picture.

After the initial autumn rainstorms, the purple and blues of tiny flowers like the autumn squill *(Scilla autumnalis)* and grape hyacinth *(Muscari parviflorum)* announce the appearance in shady areas of the autumn crocus *(Colchicum autumnale)* with its lilac petals. A little later in the winter huge

---

[5] The land in the survey area belongs to Paramali Village, inhabited by Turkish Cypriots, so it would have remained uncultivated at least since 1974 when the villagers left the area. Some of the less productive areas could well have been abandoned well before that date.

expanses of anemones *(Anemone coronaria)* in all their colors—mauve ones first—cover the growing grasses, and masses of yellow buttercups *(Ranunculus sp.)* appear everywhere. Little pockets of soil in limestone solution holes turn into miniature gardens with friar cowls *(Arisarum vulgare)* and narcissi *(Narcissus spp.)*. In spring the anemones are replaced gradually by the turban buttercups *(Ranunculus asiaticus)*, which look the same but belong to a different species. These are predominantly creamy-white in this area, whereas elsewhere in Cyprus they tend to be a brilliant yellow. At this time of the year field poppies *(Papaver rhoeas)* appear, as do the various species of yellow sun roses *(Helianthemum spp.)*, occasional blue irises *(Iris sisyrinchium)*, and the pinks and whites of the rockroses (*Cistus spp.*, pl. 16.4a). Here and there, almost hidden among the vegetation, are the wispy, very pale love-in-a-mist flowers *(Nigella damascena)*, while even more difficult to locate is the yellow and red dayglo *(Cytinus hypocistus)*, a parasite which grows on one species of rockrose *(Cistus parviflorus)*.

Spring is the best time for orchids: sixteen species and sub-species were recorded by the survey between September and May. Except where nibbled by goats, several species flower in extensive patches. For centuries, herds of goats have determined the growth of vegetation in this area. Although they tend to keep the overall height of much of the vegetation fairly low, fortunately at present they do not roam in such numbers that vegetation is actually destroyed. Some self-seeded olive trees, however, do not get a chance to grow beyond juvenile stage, when their leaves are dark green, smaller, and more rounded.

As the landscape begins to dry out, the first of many thistles appear: the purple Syrian thistle *(Notobasis syriaca)*, the white mottled holy or milk thistle (*Silybum marianum*, pl. 16.3b) and the yellow pale star thistle *(Centaurea pallescens)*. Oleander bushes *(Nerium oleander)*, particularly in the river beds, start sprouting pink flowers, and the isolated flowers of the unobtrusive violet larkspur (*Delphinium peregrinum*) can easily be missed. They look like tadpoles on stalks. In August, when the soil appears to be hard-baked and dry, the pokers of the sea squill *(Urginea maritima)* still manage to break the ground surface to develop into tall spikes of white flowers swaying in the breeze.

At the end of Appendix 16.2 are listed those ferns, mosses and lichens that were possible to identify.

REPTILES AND AMPHIBIANS (Appendix 16.3)

Lizards were frequently noted during the warmer months, mostly *Lacerta laevis* and *Ophisops elegans*, but they enjoyed brief outings on warm winter days. The agamas (*Agama Stellio,* pl. 16.4d), however, remained in their winter quarters, the hollow trunks of carob trees being very popular. In summer these dragon-like creatures with knobby skins enjoyed sunbathing on sloping slabs of rock, only their nodding heads indicating that they were alert to a human presence. By contrast, when disturbed the blunt-nosed vipers *(Vipera lebetina)* tended to "freeze" with head elevated just clear of the ground. Their escape maneuver was a slow turn around, accelerating smoothly until they were moving at great speed but with considerable friction noise (unlike the silent grass snake, *Malpolon monspessulanus)*. At a small pool in November 1982 three such vipers, two about 100 cm and one about 150 cm in length, were observed. The latter, beautifully colored, escaped slowly among some foliage and so did one of the others. However, the third remained in a "freeze" posture at the pool. Three minutes later it too had left. They were seen again two days later, when their behavior was similar. They were not recorded again until the next spring after coming out of hibernation. The Montpellier snake (*Malpolon monspessulanus)*, normally black and up to 200 cm long, was usually seen in flight across my path, while cat snakes *(Telescopus fallax)* were rarely recorded. On one occasion a cat snake was seen hanging from the nest of a magpie or hooded crow, where judging by the anguished calls it had just made a kill.

The only frogs visually recorded were tree frogs *(Hyla savignyi)*. More often they were heard "piping" their songs in winter along with the occasional and questionable marsh frogs *(Rana ridibunda)*.

MAMMALS (Appendix 16.4)

Without doubt goats currently have the greatest impact on the countryside. Fortunately their ravages were confined to two or three herds, one coming daily from Sotira Village. A flock of sheep from Paramali Village sometimes swept through the countryside.

Rats *(Rattus rattus)* were periodically sighted but hares *(Lepus europaeus)* only once or twice. Foxes *(Vulpes Vulpes)*, usually grayer and smaller than their European kin, lived in the gorges but did not inhabit one den for long. Sightings were rare as they remained under cover during the daylight; occasionally one was found asleep on a patch of grass in the sun or on a rocky ledge. Only once was a pair observed, when the female easily escaped the puzzled dog-fox after a farcical game of "hide and seek." Although hedgehogs are common throughout Cyprus, where they comprise a substantial percentage of road kills at night, none was recorded in the survey area, no doubt again because of their nocturnal habits.[6]

INSECTS (Appendix 16.5)

As expected, there were many invertebrates, most of which could not be identified by the writer (e.g., pl. 16.4c). Only the butterflies have been listed in Appendix 16.6 in alphabetical order. The latter provided a fine spectacle of color over the countryside like the golden yellows of the clouded yellow *(Colias crocea)*, the orange, white and black of the migratory painted lady *(Cynthia cardui)*, the strong black and red admiral *(Vanessa atalanta)*, and the whites (pl. 16.4b) and blues. Day flying moths were common, although grass moths "disappeared" when they landed on the dry stalks or leaves of grass. Dragonflies were usually a long way from water, but in later summer they frequently fell victim to small birds of prey like Eleonora's falcon *(Falco eleonorae)*. Most intriguing was the commonly noted female digger wasp *(Ammophila sp)*, which fills her nest hole in the ground with sand and small pebbles and then picks up another pebble to seal it properly. It uses this pebble in a steam hammer movement making a noise like that of a dental high speed drill! One unidentified curiosity noted was a 30 cm long, 1–2 mm thick, black swimming worm in the stream water, resembling a flexible bicycle spoke (horsehair worm ?). This specimen was seen twice in the same spot, but the river then dried up.[7]

BIRDS (Appendix 16.6)

Although hunting is allowed in this area, in the early 1980s few hunters visited Paramali and wildlife did not appear to have suffered directly. However, it is difficult to judge what effect the excessive shooting on the Akrotiri Peninsula has had on the bird populations inland, near Paramali and Sotira Villages. The traditional nesting sites continued to be used, and most, but not all, the casualties noted appeared to have resulted from natural causes, predation or accident. Two pairs of little owls *(Athene noctua)* occupied the same holes in their respective cliffs almost continuously, while one pair

---

[6] Ed. note. Several hedgehogs fell into the excavation trenches at Sotira *Kaminoudhia* in 1983.

[7] Ed. note. In the late spring of 1977 SS saw a large cluster of similar thread worms in an old oil drum half full of water in the Evdhimou Valley.

of kestrels *(Falco tinnunculus)* moved its site a few yards from year to year. The latter successfully produced four young in 1981 and five in 1982, assuming that it was the same pair.[8] The griffon vultures *(Gyps fulvus)* frequently drifted over from their residence on Episkopi cliffs.

Spring saw the arrival of black and yellow golden orioles *(Oriolus oriolus)* on their way north, as well as the much smaller but similarly colored black-headed buntings *(Emberize melanocephala)*, which used to sing their repetitive but tinkling refrain from the top-most branches of trees and shrubs. However from the depths of bushes occasionally came brief extracts of the nightingale *(Luscinia megarhynchos)* on passage to the mountains. Then came the cackles of the great spotted cuckoo *(Clamator glandarius)*.

The pied wheatears *(Oenanthe pleschanka)*, with their thin, buzzing song, were the most common summer residents. They would breed and stay until the autumn, when the more spectacular migrations take place. Cranes, both *Grus grus* and *Anthopoides virgo*, follow standard routes which are the reverse of their spring routes, and they come over in noisy, squawking flocks of anything from just forty to as many as two thousand.

This experience is only matched perhaps by the sight of a score or so of honey buzzards *(Pernis apivorus)* slowly and silently gliding southward. Some buzzards, usually *Buteo Buteo*, spend the night in the area resting up for the long water crossing. Then it is time for robins *(Erithacus rubecula)* to be heard calling in the gorges. The stonechats *(Saxicola torquata)* drive out the pied wheatears, and the cycle starts again.

The number of species identified during the study period must be only a proportion, albeit a large one, of the overall picture. It nevertheless typifies the great variety of wildlife which exists in this generally dry region of southern Cyprus.

SUMMARY

The variety of species recorded as the result of protracted, systematic observation was surprising. What initially seemed quite a desolate scene actually proved to be full of life–and it was not visited by the author at night when many other species are active. To some extent the impact of humans is currently much less than it could have been, except for the introduction of the goat, the carob and the olive.[9]

---

[8] It was interesting to be able to observe the progress of these five from the time that there were only three eggs, through their first tentative flights, until they were hunting strongly.

[9] Ed. note. The survey area is partially within the boundaries of the Western Sovereign Base Area, belonging to the United Kingdom. Development, and sometimes even access, is either prohibited or restricted, so the impact of the building boom occurring in Cyprus since 1974, which has drastically affected the environment of many regions, is minimal here. The situation could change soon.

APPENDIX 16.1

WEATHER, MAY 1981–APRIL 1983

Place: RAF Akrotiri, Cyprus

Information: Average Maximum Temperature for the Month.
Average Minimum Temperature for the Month.
Total Rainfall for the Month in Millimeters.
In brackets are the deviations from the 21-year period 1956–1977, except
that Feb–Apr 1983 period covers 1956–80.

MONTH	AV. MAX. (Dev)	AV. MIN. (Dev)	RAINFALL (Dev)
May 81	23.3 (-2.1)	14.4 (-1.8)	0.4 (-5.6)
Jun 81	29.5 (+0.9)	20.1 (+0.3)	0.4 (-0.6)
Jul 81	30.4 (-0.1)	22.1 (+0.3)	0 (0)
Aug 81	31.1 (0)	22.7 (+0.7)	0 (-1.0)
Sep 81	29.7 (0)	20.0 (+0.1)	0 (-3.0)
Oct 81	26.0 (-0.6)	17.5 (-0.8)	0.2 (-21.8)
Nov 81	20.7 (-2.0)	11.7 (-1.4)	84.7 (+32.7)
Dec 81	19.2 (+0.9)	11.3 (+0.7)	42.7 (-57.3)
Jan 82	17.4 (+1.0)	8.9	39.3 (-59.7)
Feb 82	15.0 (-1.8)	7.6 (-1.2)	106.5 (+48.5)
Mar 82	17.2 (-1.5)	8.1 (-2.3)	46.7 (+10.7)
Apr 82	21.4 (-0.2)	13.8 (+0.7)	7.2 (-10.8)
May 82	24.7 (-0.5)	15.7 (-0.5)	2.9 (-3.1)
Jun 82	28.1 (0.5)	19.1 (-0.7)	1.5 (+0.5)
Jul 82	29.4 (-1.1)	21.2 (-0.6)	0 (0)
Aug 82	30.8 (-0.3)	21.6 (-0.4)	0 (-1.0)
Sep 82	29.9 (+0.2)	20.1 (+0.2)	0 (-3.0)
Oct 82	26.8 (+0.2)	17.0 (+0.3)	6.3 (-13.7)
Nov 82	20.6 (-2.1)	11.0 (-2.1)	11.1 (-29.8)
Dec 82	17.3 (-1.0)	8.7 (-1.9)	46.6 (-53.6)
Jan 83	14.5 (-1.0)	6.3 (-2.6)	51.0 (-48.0)
Feb 83	14.8 (-2.0)	6.7 (-2.2)	142.8 (+80.6)
Mar 83	17.0 (-1.6)	8.6 (-1.8)	34.1 (-2.3)
Apr 83	20.8 (-0.7)	12.4 (-0.7)	15.4 (-1.0)

Reference: Monthly statistics issued by the Meteorological Office, Royal Air Force, Akrotiri.

APPENDIX 16.2

CHECKLIST OF PLANTS

The author has had to rely on available reference works and on visiting authorities in the fields covered by this research.[10] When the survey was undertaken no up-to-date published study existed for the identification of Cypriot flora and some species remained unidentifiable.[11]

Flowering Periods

These are based on those noted in the survey area. When in doubt the dates in brackets are those provided by published references.

Key to References

(1)   Matthews, A. Pers. Comm.
(2)   Briggs, M. Pers. Comm.
(3)   Demetropoulous, A. Pers. Comm.
(4)   Meikle 1977.
(5)   Matthews 1968.
(6)   Chapman 1967.
(7)   Philippou 1974.
(8)   Polunin and Huxley 1981.
(9)   Williams et al. 1978.
(10)   Fitter et al. 1974.

1.   *Ajuga chamaepitys* (Ground-Pine). Mar–May (Uncommon) (8)
2.   *Alkanna tinctoria* (Dyer's Alakanet). Aug–Apr (Uncommon) (8)
3.   *Allium neapolitanum* (Neapolitan Garlic). Jan–Apr (Common) (5,8)
4.   *Allium subhirsutum* (Hairy Garlic). Mar–May (Common) (5,8)
5.   *Anacamptis pyramidalis* (Pyramidal Orchid). Apr–May (Common) (3,9)
6.   *Anagallis arvensis ssp. foemina* (Blue Pimpernel). Jan–Jun (Common) (5)
7.   *Anchusa hybrida* Jan–Apr (Uncommon) (5)

---

[10] Ed. note. At the time of van Warmelo's study J. Meikle's *Flora of Cyprus*, Vol II, Kew 1985, had yet to be published. The lack of access to this basic reference work does not invalidate the results of his survey of an area of Cyprus which has already considerably changed since 1983.

[11] Thanks are due to the the following people who were consulted during the compilation of this report: Anne Matthews, who lived in Cyprus and was the author of *Lillies of the Field*; M. Briggs a visiting botanist, who gave me one day of her time; and Andreas Demetropoulous, Director of the Cyprus Department of Fisheries, who apart from general advice was most generous in sharing his knowledge of Cyprus orchids.

8.   *Anemone coronaria* (Anemone). Nov–Apr (Abundant) (4, 5)
     var.*coronaria* (scarlet)
     var. *rosea* (rose-pink)
     var. *cynea* (blue)
     var. *alba* (white)
9.   *Anthemis chia* (Chamomile). Feb–May (Abundant) (7, 8)
10. *Anthyllis tetraphylla* Mar–Apr (Uncommon) (8)
11. *Arisarum vulgare* (Friar's Cowl). Nov–Mar (Common) (5, 8)
12. *Arnebia hispidissima* Dec–Apr (1)
13. *Arum dioscorides* (Cuckoo-pint). Mar–Apr (8)
14. *Ballota integrifolia*. May–Jun (Common) (Endemic) (6)
15. *Bellevalia nivalis*. Feb (Fairly Common) (1)
16. *Bellevalia trifoliata*. Feb–Mar (Fairly Common) (7)
17. *Bosea cypria*. (Jun–Jul) (Uncommon) (Endemic) (6)
18. *Calendula arvensis* (Field Marigold). Dec–Apr (Common) (5)
19. *Calycotome villosa* (Prickly Broom). Dec–Apr (Common) (4, 5, 6)
20. *Capparis spinosa* var. *canescens* (Caper). May–Jul (Fairly common) (4, 5, 6)
21. *Carlina corymbosa ssp. involucrat*a (Carline Thistle). Aug–Sep (Fairly common) (5)
22. *Carlina pygmaea* (Dwarf Carline Thistle). Aug–Dec (Common) (Endemic) (5)
23. *Ceratonia siliqu*a (Carob). Jul–Nov (Common-harvested) (4, 6)
24. *Centaurea pallescens* (Pale Star Thistle). Apr–Jun (Fairly Common) (5)
25. *Centaurium tennuiflorum* (Centaury). Apr–May (Fairly Common) (7)
26. *Chrysanthemum coronarium* (Crown Daisy). Nov–Apr (Common) (5)
27. *Chrysanthemum segetum* (Corn Marigold). Mar–Jun (Fairly Common) (5, 8)
28. *Cichorium sp* (Dwarf Chicory). Apr–May (Uncommon) (identified by (7) as *C. pumilum* but I have my doubts)
29. *Cistus creticus* var. *creticus*. Nov–May (Common) (4, 6)
30. *Cistus parviflorus*. Nov–May (Common) (4, 6)
31. *Cistus salviifolius* (Sage-leaved Rockrose). Feb–May (Common) (4, 5, 6)
32. *Clematis cirrhosa* (Virgin's Bower). Dec–Jan (Uncommon) (4,6)
33. *Colchicum autumnale* (Autumn Crocus). Sep–Oct (Fairly Common) (8)
34. *Colchicum hiemale*. Nov–Dec (Fairly Common) (2)
35. *Convolvulus althaeoides* (Mallow-leaved Bindweed). Dec–May (Common) (5)
36. *Convolvulus oleafolius* (Olive-leaved Bindweed). Dec–May (Common) (1)
37. *Crupina crupinastrum*. Apr–May (Common) (8)
38. *Cupressus sempervirens* (Italian Cypress). Mar–Apr (Fairly Common) (4, 6)
39. *Cyclamen persicum* (Cyclamen). Nov–Apr (Uncommon) (5)
40. *Cynoglossum creticum* (Hound's Tongue). Mar–May (Fairly Common) (8)
41. *Cytinus hypocistus*. Apr–May (Uncommon-one location) (2,8) B2
42. *Delphinium peregrinum* var.*eriocarpum* (Violet Larkspur). Jul (Uncommon-two locations) (4)
43. *Echinops viscosus* (Viscous Gobe Thistle). Jun–Nov (Fairly Common) (5)
44. *Echium lycopsis* (Purple Viper's Bugloss). Mar–Jun (Uncommon) (8)
45. *Ephedra fragilis* ssp. *campylopoda* (Shrubby Horsetail). Jun–Jul (Two specimens) (4, 6)
46. *Erodium cicutarium* (Storksbill). Feb–Jun (Common) (4)
47. *Erodium gruinum* (Long-beaked Storksbill). Feb–Apr (Fairly common) (4)
48. *Erodium malacoides* (Soft Storksbill). Jan–Apr (Uncommon) (4)
49. *Eryngium creticum*. Jun (Fairly Common) (4)

50. *Euphorbia helioscopa* (Sun Spurge). Jan–Apr (Common) (5)
51. *Fagonia cretica*. Dec–Mar (Fairly Common) (4, 8)
52. *Ficus carica* (Fig). (Mar) (One specimen) (6)
53. *Fumaria densiflora*. Jan–Mar (Uncommon) (4)
54. *Fumaria macrocarpa*. Feb–Mar (One small area) (4)
55. *Gagea peduncularis* (Yellow Star of Bethlehem). Jan–Feb (Fairly Common) (5, 8)
56. *Genista sphacelata* var. *sphacelata* (Gorse). Mar–May (Common) (4, 6: who classifies it var. *Bovilliana*)
57. *Geranium molle* (Dove's-foot Cranesbill). Feb–Apr (Fairly common) (4)
58. *Geranium rotundifolium* (Round-leaved Cranesbill). Feb–Apr (Uncommon) (4)
59. *Geranium tuberosum* (Tuberous Cranesbill). Feb–Mar (Uncommon) (4)
60. *Gladiolus tryphyllis*. Mar–Apr (Fairly Common) (5)
61. *Helianthemum* spp. (Sun Rose - several spp. seen, but I have not separated this genus. According to (4), the following spp. could possibly occur in the district:
    a. *H. aegyptiacum*. Mar–Jun
    b. *H. obtusifolium*. Feb–May (Endemic)
    c. *H. salicifolium*. Feb–May
    d. *H. syriacum*. Apr–Jun
62. *Helichrysum siculum* (Everlasting or Sungold). Dec–Apr (Common) (5)
63. *Heliotropium europaeum*. Jun–Dec (Fairly Common) (8)
64. *Hyacinthella nervosa* spp. *millingeni*. Dec–Jan (Fairly Common) (1)
65. *Inula viscosa* (Inula). Sep–Jan (Common) (7)
66. *Iris sisyrinchium* (Iris). Feb–Apr (Uncommon) (5)
67. Juniperus phoenicia (Phoenician Juniper). Feb–Apr (Fairly Common) (4, 6)
68. *Lamium amplexicaule* (Red Dead-nettle). Feb–Apr (Fairly Common) (7)
69. *Lathyrus blepharicarpus* var. *cyprius*. Feb–Mar (Uncommon) (Endemic?) (4)
70. *Legousia speculum-veneris* (Venus's Looking Glass). Mar–Apr (One location) (5)
71. *Lithosphermum hispidulum*. Dec–Apr (Common) (1)
72. *Lloydia graeca*. Mar–Apr (Common) (7, 3)
73. *Mandragora officinarum* (Mandrake). Dec–Feb (Fairly Common) (5, 8)
74. *Medicago* spp. According to (4), seven spp. could possibly occur in the district, but I have not yet been able to separate those I have seen.
75. *Melilotus sulcatus* (Melilot). Feb–Jun (Uncommon) (4)
76. *Mercurialis annua* (Annual Mercury). Feb–Mar (Common) (2)
77. *Micromeria graeca*. Dec–May (Common) (8)
78. *Muscari atlanticum* (Grape Hyacinth). Feb–Apr (Uncommon) (8)
79. *Muscari comosum* (Tassel Hyacinth). Mar–May (Fairly Common) (5, 8)
80. *Muscari parviflorum* (Grape Hyacinth). Sep–Nov (Common) (5)
81. *Myrtus communis* (Myrtle). Sep–Oct (Uncommon) (4, 5, 6)
82. *Narcissus papyraceus* (Paper Narcissus). Mar (One specimen) (5, 8)
83. *Narcissus serotinus* (Late-flowering Naricissus). Sep–Dec (Uncommon) (5)
84. *Narcissus tazetta* (Polyanthus Narcissus). Dec–Jan (Fairly Common) (5, 8)
85. *Nerium oleander* (Oleander). May–Jul (Common) (6, 8)
86. *Nigella damascena* (Love-in-a-Mist). Mar–May (Uncommon) (4)
87. *Nigella fumariifolia* (Fennel Flower). May (One specimen) (4, 7)
88. *Notobasis syriaca* (Syrian Thistle). Mar–May (Common) (5)
89. *Odontites cypria*. Oct–Jan (Fairly Common, Endemic) (1)

90. *Olea europea* (Olive). May–Jun (Common-harvested) (6)
91. *Onobrychis venosa*. Mar–May (Common) (Endemic) (4, 5)
92. *Onosma fruticosum* (Golden Drop). Jan–Apr (Common) (1, 6)
93. *Ophrys apifera* (Bee Orchid). Mar–Apr (Uncommon) (9)
94. *Ophrys argolica as. elegans* (Eyed Bee Orchid). Feb–Mar (Common) (3, 9)
95. *Ophrys carmelii* (Mt. Carmel Ophrys). Jan–Mar (Common) (3, 9)
96. *Ophrys fuciflora* ssp. *bornmuelleri* (Short-petalled Orchid). Feb–Mar (Fairly Common) (3, 9)
97. *Ophrys fusca* (Sombre Bee Orchid). Mar (Fairly Common) (9)
98. *Ophrys fusca* ssp. *omegaifera*. Feb–Mar (Uncommon) (9)
99. *Ophrys lutea* (Yellow Bee Orchid). Mar (Common) (9)
100. *Ophrys scolopax* (Woodcock Orchid). Feb–Mar (Fairly Common) (9)
101. *Ophrys sphegodes ssp. sintenisii* (Early Spring Orchid). Feb–Mar (Very Common) (9)
102. *Orchis coriphora ssp. fragrans* (Bug Orchid). Apr–May (Common) (9)
103. *Orchis italica* (Naked Man Orchid). Mar–Apr (Fairly Common) (3, 9)
104. *Orchis morio* ssp *picta* var. *libani* (Green-winged Orchid). Feb–Mar (Common) (9)
105. *Orchis sancta* (Holy Orchid). Apr–May (Common) (9)
106. *Ornithogalum tenuifolium* (Slender-leaved Star of Bethlehem). Feb–Apr (Common) (5)
107. *Orobanche* spp. (Broomrapes). Mar–Apr (Several spp.) (8)
108. *Oxalis pes-caprae* (Cape Sorrel). Nov–Apr (Common) (4, 5)
109. *Pallenis spinosa* (Prickly Ox-eye). Mar–Jun (Common) (5)
110. *Papaver rhoes* var. *oblongatum* (Field Poppy). Mar–Jun (Fairly Uncommon) (4)
111. *Papaver hybridum* (Bristly Poppy). Mar–Jun (Uncommon) (4)
112. *Parentucellia latifolia* (Southern Red Bartsia). Mar–May (Common) (1, 2, 8)
113. *Phagnalon graecum* (Grecian Fleabane). Jan–Apr (Common) (5, 6)
114. *Pinus brutia* (Aleppo or Calabrian Pine, pl. 16.3c). Aug–Sep (Fairly Common) (4, 6)
115. *Pistacia lentiscus* (Lentisc). Feb–May (Very Common) (4, 6)
116. *Pistacia terebinthus* (Terebinth). Mar–Apr (Fairly Common) (4, 6)
117. *Plantago lagopus*. Mar–May (Common) (8)
     Note: There may be other *plantago* ssp. I have not differentiated.
118. *Prasium majus* (Spanish Hedge-Nettle). Dec–May (Common) (8)
119. *Quercus coccifera* (Holly or Kermes Oak ?) (Two specimens) (6)
120. *Ranunculus asiaticus* (Turban Buttercup). Mar–May (Abundant) (4)
     2 variants:
     a: var. *albus* predominates
     b: var. *sanguineus* rare
     However, var. *albus* occasionally tinged with red.
121. *Ranunculus bullatus* ssp. *cyntheraeus*. Nov–Jan (Common) (4)
122. *Ranunculus fiscaria* ssp. *ficariiformis* (Lesser Celandine). Feb–Mar (Fairly Uncommon) (4)
123. *Ranunculus millefoliatus* ssp. *leptaleus*. Feb–Apr (Fairly Uncommon) (4)
124. *Ranunculus muricatus*. Feb–Mar (Fairly Common) (4)
125. *Raphanus sativus* (Wild Radish) Feb–Mar (Uncommon) (4)
126. *Reseda lutea* (Wild Mignonette). Feb–Apr (Fairly Uncommon) (4)
127. *Rhamnus oleoides* ssp. *graecus* (Buckthorn). Apr–May (Fairly Common) (4, 6)
128. *Romulea tempskyana* (Romulea). Dec–Feb (Common) (2)
129. *Salvia horminum* (Red-topped Sage). Mar–Apr (Rare) (8)
130. *Salvia verbernaca* (Wild Clary). Feb–May (Uncommon) (8)
     Note: There were other sage-like plants I could not identify and (4) does not cover this family.

131. *Samolus valerandi* (Brookweed). Jun–Aug? (One location) (10)
132. *Sarcopoterium spinosum* (Spiny Burnet). Feb–Mar (Very Common) (4, 5, 6)
133. *Satureia thymbra* (Summer Savory). Mar–May (Fairly Common) (1, 8)
134. *Scilla autumnalis* (Autumn Squill). Sep–Dec (Common) (5, 8)
135. *Scolymus hispanicus* (Spanish Oyster Plant). May (Fairly Common) (8)
136. *Sedum porphyreum*. Mar–Apr (Fairly Common) (Endemic) (4)
137. *Sedum* sediforme (Stonecrop). Jun–Jul (Fairly Common) (4)
138. *Senecio sp.* (Groundsel). Early Spring (Fairly Common) (10) (Identification doubtful)
139. *Serapias vomeracea* (Long-lipped Serapias). Mar–May (3, 9)
140. *Sherardia arvensis* (Field Madder). Feb–Apr (Fairly Common) (4)
    Color normally lavender-blue, but white also seen.
141. *Silybum marianum* (Holy or Milk Thistle). Apr–Jun (Common) (8)
142. *Sinapis alba* (White Mustard). Feb–Apr (Common) (4)
    (species identification may be incorrect, however, family correct)
143. *Smilax aspera* (Green or Cat-briar). Sep–Nov (Fairly Common) (6)
144. *Smyrnium olusatrum* (Alexanders). Feb–Apr (One location) (4)
145. *Solanum nigrum* (Black Nightshade). Nov–May (Rare) (8)
146. *Sonchus* spp. Sowthistle). Mar–May (Common) (10)
    (I cannot identify Cyprus spp. as I have no source material.
147. *Spiranthes spirales* (Autumn Lady's Tresses). Oct–Jan (Rare) (9)
148. *Stellaria media* ssp. cupriana (Common Stitchwort). Jan–Mar (Fairly Uncommon) (4)
149. *Tetragonolobus purpureus* (Asparagus Pea). Feb–May (Common) (4)
150. *Thrincia tuberosa* (Tuberous Hawkbit). Sep–Jan (Common) (7)
151. *Thymus capitatus* (Thyme). Jun–Sep (Very Common) (6)
    Note: In one location plants continued flowering until Jan.
152. *Tordylium aegyptiacum*. Feb–Mar (Common)(4)
153. *Tragopon porrifolius* (Salsify). Mar–Apr (Fairly Common) (5, 7)
154. *Trifolium campestre* ssp. *campestre* (Hop Trefoil). Feb–May (Common) (4)
155. *Trifolium clypeatum*. Feb–May (Common) (4)
156. *Trifolium stellatum* var. *stellatum* (Star Clover). Feb–May (Common) (4)
    Note: There are several other *Trifolium* spp. I have noticed but have not identified. (4) lists a total of 13 spp. which could occur in the district.
157. *Typha angustifolia* (Lesser Bullrush). Jun–Jul (One location) (10)
158. *Urginea maritima* (Sea Squill). Aug–Oct (Abundant) (5)
159. *Urtica pilulifera* (Roman Nettle). Mar–May (Fairly Common) (8)
160. *Valantia hispida*. Mar–Apr (Common) (4)
161. *Verbascum sinuatum* (Mullein). Jun–Aug (Uncommon) (8)
162. *Veronica cymbalaria* (Speedwell). Feb–Apr (Uncommon) (8)
163. *Vicia* spp. (Vetch)
    Note: (4) lists 10 spp. and sspp. which could possibly occur in this district, but I have not separated these.

FERNS

Adiantum capillus-veneris (Maidenhair Fern)
Asplenium adiantum-nigrum (Black Spleenwort)
Ceterach officinarum (Rusty Black Fern)

MOSSES

Several spp. of mosses are evident, of which I was able to have only one identified:

Selaginella denticulata

Reference: Briggs, M. Pers. Comm.

LICHENS

Several spp. of lichens are evident, of which I have isolated the following possible *genera*:

Caloplaca
Verrucaria

Reference: Alvin and Kershaw 1963.

APPENDIX 16.3

CHECKLIST OF REPTILES AND AMPHIBIANS

The species identified are listed below:

LIZARDS

Agama stellio (Agama)
Lacerta laevis (Wall Lizard)
Acanthodactylus schreiberi (Schreiber's Spiny-footed Lizard)
Ophisops elegans (Snake-eyed Lizard)
Ablepharus kitaibelii (Snake-eyed Skink)
Chamaeleo chamaeleon (Chameleon)
Cyrtodactylus kotchyi (Kotchy's Gecko) (Seen once in May 83)

SNAKES

Typhlops vermicularis (Worm or Greek Blind Snake)
Telescopus fallax (Cat Snake)
Malpolon monspessulanus (Montpellier Snake)
Vipera lebetina (Blunt-nosed Viper)

FROGS

Rana ridibunda (Marsh Frog)
Hyla savignyi (Savigny's Tree Frog)

Reference: Arnold, E.N. Pers. Comm.

APPENDIX 16.4

CHECKLIST OF MAMMALS

There ought to be hedgehogs, mice, fruit bats, insectivorous bats and other mammals in the area, but I have seen only the following species:

Rattus rattus (Ship Rat)
Lepus europaeus (Brown Hare)
Vulpes vulpes (Red Fox)

Reference: Spitzenberger 1978 and 1979.

APPENDIX 16.5

CHECKLIST OF INSECTS

Some insects were identified with reasonable confidence.

BUTTERFLIES

1. *Pieris brassicae* (Large White)
2. *Pontia daplidice* (Bath White)
3. *Anthocharis cardamines phoenissa* (Orange Tip)
4. *Colias crocea* (Clouded Yellow)
5. *Gonepteryx cleopatra taurica* (Cleopatra)
6. *Vanessa atalanta* (Red Admiral)
7. *Cynthia cardui* (Painted Lady)
8. *Chazara briseis larnacana* (The Hermit) (Endemic)
9. *Maniola* sp. (Meadow Brown sp.) (Endemic)
10. *Pararge aegeria* (Speckled Wood)
11. *Lasiommata megera lyssa* (Wall Brown)
12. *Lasiommata maera orientalis* (Large Wall Brown)
13. *Glaucopsyche Paphos* (Paphos Blue) (Endemic)

References:
 (1) Parker, R. Pers. Comm.
 (2) Whalley 1981.

OTHER

Black Dragonfly
Red Dragonfly
Neutral-colored Dragonfly
Digger Wasp (*Ammophila* sp?)
Cicada
Migratory Locust
Grass moths
Hummingbird Hawk Moth (*Macroglossum* sp?)
Processionary Pine Moth (*Thaumetopoea wilkinsonii*)
Pond Skaters
Honey Bees
Bumble Bees

APPENDIX 16.6

CHECKLIST OF BIRDS

The "Voous" systemic order of spp has been followed here.

1. *Pernis apivorus* (Honey Buzzard). Autumn (Frequent)
2. *Milvus migrans* (Black Kite). Autumn (Occasional)
3. *Neophron neophron percnopterus* (Egyptian Vulture). May (Once)
4. *Gyps fulvus* (Griffon Vulture). All year (Breeding nearby)
5. *Circus cyaneus* (Hen Harrier). Winter (Rare)
6. *Circus macrourus* (Pallid Harrier). March (Once)
7. *Circus pyargus* (Montagu's Harrier). September (Twice – possibles)
8. *Accipiter nisus* (Sparrowhawk). Winter and Spring (Occasional)
9. *Buteo buteo* (Buzzard). Autumn (Occasional)
10. *Hieraaetus fasciatus* (Bonelli's Eagle). October (Once)
11. *Falco tinnunculus* (Kestrel). All year (One pair breeding)
12. *Falco subbuteo* (Hobby). Autumn (Twice)
13. *Falco eleonorae* (Eleonora's Falcon). Summer (Frequent-breeding nearby)
14. *Falco peregrinus* (Peregrine). Spring (Twice - breeding nearby)
15. *Alectoris chukar* (Chukar). All year (Resident)
16. *Grus grus* (Common Crane). Autumn and Spring
17. *Anthropoides virgo* (Demoiselle Crane). Migrant (Identification difficult - in huge flocks)
18. *Venellus venellus* (Lapwing). Winter (Occasional)
19. *Gallinago galinago* (Snipe). Winter (Twice)
20. *Tringa glareola* (Wood Sandpiper). Winter (Once)
21. *Columba livia* (Rock Dove). All year (Breeding atempted but breeding successful nearby)
22. *Columba oenas* (Stock Dove). August (Once)
23. *Columba palumbus* (Woodpigeon). All Year (Occasional-sometimes in flock of up to 14)
24. *Streptopelia turtur* (Turtle Dove). Summer (Breeding)
25. *Clamator glandarius* (Great Spotted Cuckoo). Early Summer (Frequent)
26. *Cuculus canorus* (Cuckoo). Spring (Frequent)
27. *Tyto alba* (Barn Owl). Spring (Once)
28. *Otus scops* (Scops Owl). Spring/Summer (often heard)
29. *Athene noctua* (Little Owl). All year (two pairs Breeding)
30. *Asio otus* (Long-eared Owl). November (Once)
31. *Asio flammeus* (Short-eared Owl). April (Once)
32. *Caprimulgus europaeus* (Nightjar). Late Summer (Occasional)
33. *Apus apus* (Swift). Summer (Frequent)
34. *Apus Melba* (Alpine Swift). Summer (Frequent)
35. *Merops apiaster*[12] (Bee-eater). Spring and Autumn (Frequent)

---

[12] According to the late Stellios Mavros (1981), who used to keep bees in traditional terracotta tubular beehives in the courtyard of his Sotira Village house, before DDT decimated the population bee-eaters were a common nesting species in the Symvoulos Gorge, west of the village. Since the 1950s, none has nested in the neighborhood. Bee-eaters still nest in gorges near Kakopetria and perhaps in other remote areas of Cyprus as well.

36. *Coracias garrulus* (Roller). Early Summer (Occasional)
37. *Upupa epops* (Hoopoe). Spring and Autumn (Occasional)
38. *Galerida cristata* (Crested Lark). All year (Resident)
39. *Lullula arborea* (Wood Lark). Winter (Frequent)
40. *Hirundo rustica* (Swallow). Summer (Frequent)
41. *Hirundo daurica* (Red-rumped Swallow). Summer (Frequent)
42. *Delichon urbica* (House Martin). Summer (Occasional)
43. *Anthus trivialis* (Tree Pipits). Autumn and Spring (Twice)
44. *Anthus pratensis* (Meadow Pipit). Winter (Frequent)
45. *Motacilla flava* (Yellow Wagtail). October (Once)
46. *Motacilla cinerea* (Gray Wagtail). Winter (Rare)
47. *Motacilla alba* (White Wagtail). Winter (Frequent)
48. *Prunella modularis* (Dunnock). December (Once)
49. *Erithacus rubecula* (Robin). Winter (Frequent)
50. *Luscina megarhynchos* (Nightingale). Spring (Occasional)
51. *Phoenicurus ochruros* (Black Redstart). Winter (Frequent)
52. *Phoenicurus phoenicuros* (Redstart). Autumn/Spring (Occasional)
53. *Saxicola rubetra* (Whinchat). Autumn (Occasional)
54. *Saxicola torquata* (Stonechat). Winter (Frequent)
55. *Oenanthe isabellina* (Isabelline Wheatear). Winter (Occasional)
56. *Oenanthe oenanthe* (Wheatear). Autumn/Spring (Frequent)
57. *Oenanthe pleschanka* (Pied Wheatear). Summer (Breeding)
58. *Oenanthe hispanica* (Black-eared Wheatear). Autumn/Spring (Occasional)
59. *Oenanthe finschii* (Finsch's Wheatear). November (Once)
60. *Monticola solitarius* (Blue Rock Thrush). Winter (Occasional)
61. *Turdus merula* (Blackbird). Winter (Frequent)
62. *Turdus philomelos* (Song Thrush). Winter (Frequent)
63. *Turdus viscivorus* (Mistle Thrush). November (Once)
64. *Hippolais pallida* (Olivaceous Warbler). Late Summer (Occasional)
65. *Sylvia conspicillata* (Spectacled Warbler). Winter (Occasional)
66. *Sylvia melanocephala* (Sardinian Warbler). Winter (Occasional)
67. *Sylvia melanothorax* (Cyprus Warbler). All year (Breeding)
68. *Sylvia rueppelli* (Ruppell's Warbler). Spring (Rare)
69. *Sylvia hortensis* (Orphean Warbler). April (Twice)
70. *Sylvia curruca* (Lesser Whitethroat). Autumn/Spring (Occasional)
71. *Sylvia communis* (Whitethroat). Late Winter (Rare)
72. *Sylvia borin* (Garden Warbler). Autumn/Spring (occasinoal)
73. *Sylvia atricapilla* (Blackcap). Winter/Late Spring (Frequent)
74. *Phylloscopus sibilatrix* (Wood Warbler). Autumn (Occasional)
75. *Phylloscopus collybita* (Chiffchaff). Winter (Frequent)
76. *Phylloscopus trochilus* (Willow Warbler). Autumn/Spring (Occasional)
77. *Musicapa striata* (Spotted flycatcher). Autumn/Spring (Frequent)
78. *Ficedula albicollis* (Collared Flycatcher). April (Frequent)
79. *Ficedula hypoleuca* (Pied Flycatcher). April (Occasional)
80. *Parus major* (Great Tit). All Year (Breeding)
81. *Oriolus oriolus* (Golden Oriole). April (Occasional)
82. *Lanius collurio* (Red-backed Shrike). Autumn (Occasional)

83. *Lanius minor* (Lesser Gray Shrike). Autumn (Occasional)
84. *Lanius senator* (Woodchat Shrike). Spring (Occasional)
85. *Lanius nubicus* (Masked Shrike). Summer (Frequent)
86. *Pica pica* (Magpie). All year (Breeding)
87. *Corvus monedula* (Jackdaw). All Year (Breeding)
88. *Corvus corone* (Hooded Crow). All Year (Breeding)
89. *Corvus corax* (Raven). All Year (Occasional)
90. *Sturnus vulgaris* (Starling). Winter (Frequent)
91. *Passer domesticus* (House Sparrow). All Year (Breeding)
92. *Passer hispaniolensis* (Spanish Sparrow). All Year (Occasional)
93. *Fringilla coelebs* (Chaffinch). Winter (Frequent)
94. *Serinus serinus* (Serin). Winter (Frequent)
95. *Carduelis chloris* (Greenfinch). All Year (Breeding)
96. *Carduelis carduelis* (Goldfinch). All Year (Breeding)
97. *Carduelis cannabina* (Linnet). Winter (Frequent)
98. *Emberiza hortulana* (Ortolan Bunting). Autumn/Spring (Rare)
99. *Emberiza caesia* (Cretzschamar's Bunting). Summer (Breeding)
100. *Emberiza melanocephala* (Black-headed Bunting). Early Summer (Occasional)
101. *Miliaria calandra* (Corn Bunting). September (Once)

17

CHRONOLOGY

by Ellen Herscher and Stuart Swiny

INTRODUCTION

Sotira *Kaminoudhia* is the first scientifically excavated site in Cyprus to provide evidence for nearly the entire Early Bronze Age period on the island. This chapter discusses the relative and absolute chronology as derived from the study of the ceramics and the radiocarbon determinations. The resulting chronological framework thus provides a fundamental extension and refinement to the standard chronology of the period as formulated by James Stewart (1962).

RELATIVE CHRONOLOGY

The cemetery and settlement at Sotira *Kaminoudhia* together span almost the entire Early Cypriot Bronze Age. Within this period, they can be divided into three broad stages (which do not correspond exactly to the traditional Early Cypriot I, II, and III as defined by Stewart [1962]).[1]

Philia Phase

Four tombs can be assigned to the Philia Phase, the earliest of them being Tomb 1, excavated by P. Dikaios in 1947 (Dikaios 1948; H.W. Swiny 1982:20–21). This tomb displays clear connections to the Chalcolithic period as well as marking the appearance of the distinctive Philia types of cooking pot and bottle.[2]

Among the tombs excavated by CAARI, the Philia Phase is best represented by Tomb 6, with its distinctive features of the typical "mosque lamp," the truncated juglet, beak spout fragments, and spiral earrings. Tomb 15 displays similar diagnostic traits. The few remains recovered from Tomb 10 also indicate a Philia Phase date.

At the type site of Philia *Vasiliko* the characteristic feature is numerous jugs with long beak or cutaway spouts; in addition to the Red Polished ware, Black Slip and Combed Ware (BSC) and White Painted (Philia) ware were present.[3] In contrast, at *Kaminoudhia* the distinctive jugs are scarce, tentatively identified in only small fragmentary form, and the BSC and WP (P) wares are not attested.

---

[1] They do appear to correlate quite closely with the three phases identified (at least provisionally) at Marki *Alonia* (Philia, EC I and/or II, EC III–MC I), although occupation at *Kaminoudhia* apparently ceases earlier, before the end of EC III: cf. Webb and Frankel 1999:37.

[2] For the Chalcolithic-Philia transition, cf. Webb and Frankel 1999:38–42.

[3] Dikaios 1962:160–76; Dikaios 1953:324. For the standard Philia Phase assemblage, see Webb and Frankel 1999: figs 3, 5; for Philia wares other than RP, see Webb and Frankel 1999:24–28.

Nevertheless, the affinities to other known Philia Phase sites are secure, in the form of several ceramic types (e.g., the incised ear-lug pots, the oddly truncated juglets ["neck juglets"], deep spouted bowls), metal, spindle whorls, and earrings.[4] While the differences between the *Kaminoudhia* tombs and other Philia Phase sites may be attributable to regional causes,[5] it seems more likely that in this case the differences are due to chronological factors, with *Kaminoudhia* representing a late stage of the period. The addition of a horizontal handle on Spouted Bowl A, the more developed shape of Juglet D,[6] and the variety of decorated ear-lug pots lends support to this interpretation.

In addition to the deposits that appeared to be associated with tombs, a number of Philia Phase vessels were found below the topsoil of the cemetery but without any surviving evidence for a burial context.[7] These may have once belonged to shallow pit graves that have been disturbed, or they were perhaps simply deposited on the surface (see Chapter 3).

Early Cypriot I/II

The second phase at *Kaminoudhia*, corresponding roughly to the traditional EC I–II, is best represented by Tomb 7. The most diagnostic attributes of the phase include short-necked amphorae with vertical (sometimes slightly angular) handles, round-spouted jugs, flat-based deep hemispherical bowls, and elaborately incised RPSC conical bowls and flasks. Such incised vessels, known at the time only from chance finds, were classified by Stewart as "Red Polished I South Coast" ware, which he dated to EC I or possibly II and noted its connections to Philia style decoration.[8] The *Kaminoudhia* excavations have shown Stewart's astute perceptions to be true. These vessels also show some similarities to RP I and II incised conical bowls and flasks from *Vounous*, although with a strong regional character. Seemingly close in date to this phase is a tomb at Psematismenos *Trelloukkas*, with comparable jugs, conical bowl, Type A large bowl, Type A small bowls, and potmark.[9] The flasks are also similar to EC I flasks from Arpera.

Tombs 14 and 17 can probably be assigned to the same date, although they lacked RPSC ware. The two amphorae (Types A and B) and large jug (P118) in Tomb 14 have general similarities to RP I vessels from *Vounous* and are closely paralleled at *Trelloukkas*, as are the two bowls from Tomb 17. Tomb 9 is dated to the same period on the basis of its single RPSC vessel. Tomb 18 has also been tentatively dated to the EC I/II phase, although its somewhat unusual contents included nothing that is precisely diagnostic.

Tomb 4 had been much disturbed and produced finds dating to both EC I/II and the subsequent EC III period (see below). From the earlier phase belong two RPSC flasks, a sherd of a RPSC ear-lug

---

[4] Philia ceramic types at *Kaminoudhia* include: Spouted Bowl A; Juglet D; Cooking Pot B; Ear-lug pots A, B, C, and an unclassified example (P11); Bottle D; Storage Vessel A; probably Jug E; possibly Jug F; Unclassified Small Bowls P54, Dikaios 1/4 and 1/6; and several Unclassified Flasks (see Chapter 4 for discussion of types).

[5] As suggested by Webb and Frankel 1999:42, n. 287.

[6] Comparable truncated juglets from other sites usually have the spout and lower end of the handle extending directly from the base.

[7] Ear-lug pots P7 and P41, flasks P9, P35 and 101, small bowl P54: see catalogue in Chapter 3.

[8] Stewart 1962:270; 1992:84, 90; see discussion of RPSC ware in Chapter 4. For the uninterrupted evolution of standard EC ceramics from Philia types, cf. Webb and Frankel 1999:42.

[9] Todd 1985; cf. Coleman et al. 1996:336–37. While the *Trelloukkas* tomb published by Todd (1985) contained no RPSC ware, a second tomb recently published from the site (Georghiou 2000) contained two RPSC flasks and other vessels with close parallels in *Kaminoudhia* T.7.

pot, and a jug with potmarked handle. Dating to EC III were two Type A Brown Polished bottles. While the appearance of RPSC ware and Brown Polished bottles together must raise the question of whether the two wares could be (at least partly) contemporary, there is no evidence from other undisturbed deposits that they were used at the same time. Thus if the Tomb 4 finds do in fact originate from a single tomb, the most likely interpretation is that two successive burials were made in it.

One RPSC flask, P34, was found in the topsoil immediately west of Tomb 6 (see Chapter 3).

Early Cypriot III

The latest tomb excavated at *Kaminoudhia* is Tomb 12, which appears to be nearly contemporary with the settlement, dating to early in the EC III period. Tomb 12 contained a DPBC tankard (the only DPBC vessel recovered from the cemetery), a Brown Polished bottle, and a Type A large jug with a distinctive type of incised decoration on the handle; the settlement produced similar diagnostic pottery.

Tomb 11 contained none of these clearly diagnostic ceramic types, although one jug (P58) was classified as Type A despite its undeveloped decorative scheme. It may be that this was simply a "poorer" tomb (the ceramics may have been poorly fired as well). The best dating evidence comes from the spouted bowl (P63), which places the tomb in EC III.

A fragmentary Brown Polished bottle constituted the only ceramic find from Tomb 8, suggesting that this deposit is contemporary with Tomb 12. The single Type A bowl from Tomb 13 provides less conclusive evidence, but the fact that the base of this bowl is nearly round may suggest a late date for the deposit, i.e., EC III. The two finds from Tomb 19 indicate an EC III date as well, although the Brown Polished bottle (P105) in this deposit is not the usual type.

SETTLEMENT

As mentioned above, the diagnostic features of Brown Polished bottles, Type A jugs, and DPBC ware provide evidence for the synchronism of Tomb 12 and the *Kaminoudhia* settlement, although a slightly later date for the settlement may be suggested by several factors. Sherds of Brown Polished bottles were found in Area A, Units 16 and 30, and on bedrock in Area C, Unit 23; their style of decoration most resembles that of P27 and P29 from Tomb 4. The settlement examples of Type A jugs are poorly preserved, but are well represented in Areas A and C.[10] Drab Polished Blue Core ware from the settlement occurred in Areas A and C, and includes two tankards, a large jug and other large jug fragments, and several fragmentary juglets.[11] Most importantly, the settlement produced a fragmentary bottle (P74) imported from the North Coast; its context suggests that it dates to the end of the use of the settlement, which was sometime before the end of the Early Cypriot period.

In addition to the key features noted, links between the latest *Kaminoudhia* tombs and the settlement are suggested by a few other ceramic types. Examples of bowl Type C come from both Area C and Tomb 11. The large spouted bowls Types B and C were found in the settlement and Tombs 12 and 11 respectively.

However, in general there is very little correspondence between cemetery and settlement ceramic types, raising the possibility that the settlement (at least in its latest occupation) was somewhat later than the latest tombs which were excavated in the cemetery. The decoration on some (but not all) of the

---

[10] Examples include P70, P120, P136; additional uncatalogued fragments were found stratified in Area A and unstratified in Areas B and C.

[11] P85, P72, P88, P137 (fig. 4.7); P109 (fig. 4.6).

Type A jugs from the settlement is more careless, and the examples there were much more poorly preserved. Drab Polished Blue Core ware, a more technologically advanced fabric, is more common and more decorated in the settlement. The settlement tankards may be slightly later versions of the type. Fewer Brown Polished bottles came from the settlement, although this could equally be attributed to functional or preservation factors, rather than chronological. In general, the Red Polished ware from the cemetery had less decoration than that from the settlement, while accidental impressions (of straw or other organic materials) were more common in the cemetery.

Small bowls, the most common type of vessel in both cemetery and settlement, have very few similarities between the two areas. Only Type A is definitely attested in both, and this is a very broad class. Furthermore, its settlement distribution is only in Area A; even there, it is not particularly frequent. The settlement in general produced a much wider variety of small bowls, all of which apparently had lugs; some cemetery bowls were lugless even in the latest phase (e.g., P97, fig. 4.1).

Also significant is the fact that all vessels from the cemetery have flat bases, except for the Philia Phase bottles and the probable "imports" Brown Polished bottles and DPBC ware, while some Red Polished pots from the settlement have round bases (including small bowls and juglets, e.g. P73, P123; Bowl Types D–E, G; Dipper Type A), or "dimple" bases (Bowl Types F–G). Notably more decoration appears on vessels from the settlement as well (cf. especially Unclassified RP juglets). While the fragmentary amphora P82 (fig. 4.13) from Area A can be tentatively compared to Type A amphorae, such as P100 (fig. 4.14) from Tomb 12, its unique elaborate decorative scheme must be regarded as a new feature.

A few other links to the standard RP sequence may help provide dating for the *Kaminoudhia* settlement, although drawing comparisons with north coast material is always a bit risky due to the strong evidence for south coast conservatism and north coast idiosyncrasy. Dipper Type A has EC III–MC I parallels; no dippers were found in the cemetery. Large storage vessels like the unclassified P141, from Area C, are generally not attested before EC IIIB/MC I (although this could be due to lack of EC excavated settlements). Spouted Bowl Type B, from both Tomb 12 and the settlement, has parallels at EC III *Vounous* (although with the usual north coast base). The unclassified large spouted bowl, P135 from Area C, may be related to large deep bowls, probably with ritualistic functions, that appear at the end of EC or beginning of MC (cf. Herscher 1997). The impressed relief band decoration on DPBC jug P109 (and occurring on two rim sherds of RP Mottled Type B large bowls) seems to be an EC III feature adopted from the north.

The tankards represent a precursor of a Middle Cypriot type: Types A and B, which are the most tankard-like, occur at *Kaminoudhia* in DPBC fabric. Comparable types appear on the north coast in Red Polished ware in EC III and increase in MC I.[12]

Comparisons with sites in central Cyprus help to provide a *terminus ante quem* for the *Kaminoudhia* settlement. At Marki *Alonia* most small bowls are hemispherical with round bases; horizontal handles rising from the rim become dominant in MC I (Frankel and Webb 1996b:117). Alambra follows a similar pattern (Coleman et al. 1996: fig. 63), as do the tombs at Kalavasos (cf. Todd 1986: fig. 26; Karageorghis 1940–1948: fig. 7 "first burial") and Larnaca *Ayios Prodromos* (Herscher 1988: fig. 1:2–6), but no bowls of this type were found at *Kaminoudhia*.[13] At both Marki and Alambra large spouted bowls from the settlements frequently have trough spouts; *Kaminoudhia* bowls only have tubular spouts. At Marki, deeper bowls with small flat bases and vertical lugs, like those from *Kaminoudhia* (Type A), were associated with levels dating before the EC III reconstruction. Like

---

[12] Type VIIK, Stewart 1992:157-62, esp. pl. XXIV:1, 6, 9; fig. 23:1.

[13] The tentative beginnings of such handles may be represented on P17 and P84 (fig. 4.1).

Kaminoudhia, Drab Polished Blue Core ware appears at Marki "at least" by EC III (Frankel and Webb 1996b:157). No Brown Polished ware was found in either the Marki or Alambra settlements, but only in the earliest Alambra tomb (T. 105).

It should also be noted that many of the "latest" features of the settlement—such as relief decoration (e.g., P137), twisted handles (P138),[14] and a nipple base (P88)[15]—are found in Area C, suggesting that this area may have seen the latest occupation at the site (although no great time difference is implied). A RP Mottled sherd of a large bowl rim from Area C had a horizontal impressed relief band below the rim; indeed, large bowls in general are more common in Area C than in the other areas. Also from Area C came the unclassified jugs P106 (with relief snake decoration and round base, the only large vessel from *Kaminoudhia* with a round base)[16] and P117, and juglet P55 (Type E), all with narrow neck and very globular body. These pots have close parallels in Kalavasos *Panayia Church* Tomb 36, dated to MC II.[17] Kalavasos Village Tomb 5 (Karageorghis 1940–1948:121–26) also provides parallels for several Area C vessels: juglet P60 (Type C), DPBC juglet P137, the unclassified storage vessel P141, the unclassified large spouted bowl P135, and an almost exact counterpart to juglet P55. The chronology of Tomb 5 is rather problematic,[18] but a date of EC IIIB/MC I seems most likely. The unclassified storage vessel P141 found additional parallels dating to EC III–MC I, including one from the Alambra settlement (early MC). The unclassified jug P106 is also closely paralleled in the Alambra settlement. The composite (?) bowl P87 is paralleled at Marki in EC III–MC I.

The strongest dating evidence for the settlement, of course, is the fragmentary imported RP III north coast style black-topped bottle, P74 (fig. 4.11). While a date of EC IIIB/MC I has previously been suggested for this and similar bottles (cf. Herscher 1991:46–47, with references), further analysis of the decorative style of this particular bottle—as well as the comparable and better preserved bottles from Kalavasos *Panayia Church* Tomb 46 (below)—indicates that it must fall within the EC III period.[19] Bottle P74 is clearly earlier than the RP III pottery from the well-known tomb Lapithos 6A, dated to EC IIIB/MC I, which contained the Middle Minoan I imported jar (Grace 1940).

While the last usage of the settlement can thus be dated fairly securely, its duration is more problematic. Alterations to the architecture suggest that the site was occupied for some length of time, but the deposits showed little depth and almost no stratification (except for limited areas in Units 1 and 3). From the ceramic point of view, as discussed above, most of the settlement finds that are datable fall within the conventional EC III period.[20] On the other hand, the corpus of settlement ceramics

---

[14] For twisted handles of IIIB/MC I date, cf. Stewart 1988:30; Grace 1940: pl. VIII:80; Stewart 1962: fig. LXV:5, 6; Coleman et al. 1996: fig. 54:F1. This last example, from the Alambra settlement (dated early in MC), also closely parallels the unclassified jug P106, which is also from Area C.

[15] Cf. Stewart 1988:82, fig. 19:2, in White Painted IA, probably MC I; Stewart 1962: fig. CLIII:6, 7 (in Black Polished ware), CLVI:6.

[16] See n. 14 above.

[17] Todd 1986:183. Tomb 36 also contained DPBC and White Painted wares, and a considerable amount of metal. The stratification in this tomb was very disturbed, so possibly there was a burial in it earlier than MC II.

[18] The so-called "upper burial" was not properly excavated, and the fact that this group is composed almost entirely of large vessels suggests that they were simply visible above the other offerings from the two (actual) burials when the tomb was discovered: cf. Karageorghis 1940–1948:121–23, fig. 7; Todd 1986:199.

[19] Cf. Stewart 1962: fig. LXXI:4, from Lapithos 314B[2] (EC IIIA–B). For additional discussion of the dating of this type in general, see Stewart 1992:68–69.

[20] But when dealing with undecorated red monochrome sherds, it is virtually impossible to distinguish RP III from early RP or RP Philia: cf. Webb and Frankel 1999:13–14.

exhibits considerable internal variation, which might be considered a sign of longevity. For example, three uncatalogued spouts of bowls were found in Unit 30 of Area A: their shapes are similar, but they were made in three very different fabrics. Also noteworthy are the wide variety of lug types on the small bowls. Does a lack of standardization imply a long chronological span or is it—as seems more likely at least in this case—an indication of small-scale domestic manufacture (cf. Frankel and Webb 1996b: 110–11)?

Nevertheless, a few diagnostic pieces earlier than EC III have been identified from the settlement. These include three stratified fragments of cutaway spouts from Type F jugs, two from Area A and one from Area C (see Chapter 4). Fragments of Type F jugs were also found in the cemetery (Tomb 6 and probably Dikaios Tomb 1), where they date to the Philia Phase, but the settlement examples have parallels with *Vounous* EC I types.[21] Also from Area A came four stratified incised sherds; one of them (from Unit 1) is definitely from a Philia style small closed vessel with the characteristic zigzag and herringbone decoration. The other three (from the floor level of Unit 6, and from Units 20 and 35) are probably RPSC ware, of EC I/II date. A spout from Area A Unit 41 could possibly have come from a Philia type spouted bowl (Type A), but was too fragmentary to support a certain conclusion. A lug from Unit 4 Phase I could have come from a Stroke-Burnished bowl of Philia type, but again was too small for certainty.

Among the catalogued vessels, the incomplete large bowl P146, from Area C, appears to have early parallels from the *Trelloukkas* tomb. The Type C juglet also has tenuous EC I/II links, occurring in Tomb 7 as well as in the settlement, although the two examples are not closely similar to one another and not necessarily contemporary. The storage vessel P140 (Type B) perhaps has connections with Vasilia Tomb 103, but it also has a parallel from Kalavasos Tomb 5, which cannot be earlier than EC III (further evidence for the problematic nature of the Vasilia chronology: cf. Swiny 1985a:23–24). While it might be argued that these few examples of earlier material demonstrate an extended period of use for the settlement, the evidence is extremely weak. Considering the proximity of tombs from the earlier periods, many of which lay near the surface and had been disturbed in the past, it is not surprising that a few stray sherds should have made their way into the settlement deposits.

The main period of the *Kaminoudhia* settlement and the last phase of its cemetery use are contemporary with Tomb 46 at Kalavasos *Panayia Church*, the earliest tomb excavated here by the Vasilikos Valley Project, and have close similarities to its ceramic assemblage. Kalavasos Tomb 46 contained a Type C small bowl like that from *Kaminoudhia* Tomb 11 and the settlement, a large Type B spouted bowl as found in *Kaminoudhia* Tomb 12 and the settlement, a dipper similar to P62 but with flat base, and a good parallel for the amphora P83 (Type D) from the *Kaminoudhia* settlement. This tomb also produced six Brown Polished bottles (plus two spindle whorls of the same fabric) and a total of seven north coast RP III black-topped vessels (both bottles and juglets are represented, and some are too fragmentary to make the distinction: Todd 1986: fig. 36).

Kalavasos Tomb 46 was dated to MC I by the excavator (Todd 1986:184), but in fact a date of EC III is more likely: the tomb does not appear to pass into MC I. The lack of White Painted ware could be attributed to regional factors, although WP II ware does occur in other Kalavasos tombs. More telling within the south coast context is the absence of small bowls with horizontal handles rising from the rim and the presence of a lugless small bowl (Todd 1986: fig. 35:2). Except for the Brown Polished and north coast bottles, all the vessels in the tomb have flat bases: yet there are almost no flat bases in any other Kalavasos tombs.

---

[21] For the development from Philia types, cf. Dikaios 1953:325.

The north coast bottles/juglets from Kalavasos Tomb 46 are all closely similar in style to P74 from *Kaminoudhia*, and because they are better preserved (retaining body decoration as well as neck), closer stylistic dating is possible: the best north coast parallels for the decoration are all EC III. Only one of the vessels (K-PC 419) has the body decorated in the net pattern (concentric circles joined by groups of parallel lines) which is characteristic of the north coast in EC III–MC I, and this example is decorated in the neat early (EC III) version of the motif.[22] It is also significant that Kalavasos Tomb 46 does *not* include any of the standard incised RP III ware that is found in other (later) tombs from the *Panayia Church* cemetery.[23] This later incised RP III from Kalavasos has closer affinities to the style of the RP III from Larnaca *Kition* than to that from the north coast (cf. Karageorghis 1974: pls. CVI, CIXCXI, CXV). Thus Kalavasos Tomb 46 provides strong evidence for dating *Kaminoudhia* P74 to early in the EC III period, a time when such bottles seem to have been widely exported from the north coast to other parts of the island.[24]

Probably of the same date are two tombs found earlier in Kalavasos village, just south of the *Panayia Church*.[25] Tomb 9 contained a north coast juglet in RP III style like that of P74 (also lacking net pattern decoration: cf., e.g., Stewart 1962: fig. XCIII:10), a Brown Polished bottle, and a Type D small bowl, and has been dated to mid-EC III (Todd 1986:201). A bottle in the same style was found in Tomb 10 along with numerous Brown Polished vessels. Kalavasos Tomb 10 also contained a cooking pot identical to the Type C examples from *Kaminoudhia*. This tomb has been dated to the end of EC III (Todd 1986:201–2), although no chronological difference from Tomb 9 is apparent from the evidence available.[26]

Also from Kalavasos and close in date to Tomb 46 is the first use of Tomb 48 (Todd 1986:150, fig. 36:7). It contained a Brown Polished bowl and RP vessels with flat bases; a few round-based pots were assigned to this burial as well, suggesting that the deposit may be slightly later than Tomb 46, but still within EC III. Also dating to EC III is Kalavasos Tomb 4, which produced a Brown Polished juglet and a DPBC amphora with simple punctured decoration recalling that on tankard P72 (Karageorghis 1940–1948:121, fig. 21.CI). Kalavasos Tomb 1 may be contemporary, with a DPBC flask and (possibly) two Brown Polished spindle whorls.[27]

Geographically closer to *Kaminoudhia* and also dating to EC III is Episkopi *Phaneromeni* Tomb 23E, which contained four Brown Polished bottles and two DPBC vessels with simple decoration (Swiny 1976:47–51, figs. 6–9); the DPBC jug P66 has punctured decoration much like that on the *Kaminoudhia* tankard P72. The tomb has previously been dated to early MC I, but this is unlikely, especially since most of the RP vessels from the tomb have flat bases. From an adjoining chamber, *Phaneromeni* 23D, of comparable date, came a north coast bottle much like P74 and a Brown Polished bottle (Herscher 1991: 46, fig. 5.1; Carpenter 1981:60–61, fig. 3–5). Also contemporary is *Phaneromeni* Tomb 12, which contained Brown Polished bottles, a north coast bottle like P74, and early DPBC ware.[28]

---

[22] Cf., e.g., Stewart 1962: figs. XCV:1, CI:2–4, 9. The motif degenerates into a much looser arrangement in EC IIIB–MC I: cf., e.g., Stewart 1962: fig. XC:7, 10, 19.

[23] E.g., Tombs 36, 40 and 47; cf. Todd 1986: fig. 31.

[24] Cf. Herscher 1991:46–48; for other examples, see Chapter 4.

[25] Karageorghis 1940–1948:130–32, figs. 12, 14, 18:G1, 24:A11.

[26] Many of the vessels are not illustrated, and features such as the presence of round bases for RP ware are not known.

[27] Karageorghis 1940–1948:119, fig. 24; the spindle whorls are not illustrated.

[28]Weinberg 1956:121, fig. 9: dated to EC IIIA.

To the north of Sotira lies Alassa, where the first burial in Tomb 1 appears to be contemporary with the *Kaminoudhia* settlement.[29] This deposit included a spouted bowl similar to P49 (Type D) and two north coast bottles.

In the center of the island, Nicosia *Ayia Paraskevi* Tomb 11 is dated to EC III (Hennessy et al. 1988:18–19, fig. 27). Most of the RP vessels from this tomb had round bases, so it may be slightly later than *Kaminoudhia*, although this may also be a regional difference. It contained two north coast bottles and a bowl with early net pattern decoration.

At Alambra, just south of Nicosia, Tomb 105 appears to be contemporary with *Kaminoudhia* (Coleman et al. 1996:318–22). The earliest tomb excavated by the Cornell University excavations, it contained a Brown Polished style juglet and some RP ware with flat bases, along with round bases and one dimple base. This tomb does not contain any standard RP III incised ware, as occurs frequently elsewhere at Alambra (e.g., T. 102), and the small bowls from T. 105 are deeper and more conical than the bowls from the settlement. The Alambra *Mouttes* settlement, dated by Coleman to early MC (Coleman et al. 1996:260, 334), is later than *Kaminoudhia*, but not by very much: no flat bases occurred, but it produced parallels to *Kaminoudhia* vessels P106 (jug), P138 (juglet), and P141 (storage vessel), all from Area C. A few sherds of DPBC ware were found at Alambra, with decoration that appears slightly more developed than that from *Kaminoudhia*.

In the same region, what has been excavated and published of the Marki *Alonia* settlement is mostly later than *Kaminoudhia*, but the earlier levels at Marki (the chronology of which is still being refined) show some similarities. Drab Polished Blue Core ware appears there in EC III; the pre-EC III (dated EC I and/or II) levels have deeper small bowls with small flat bases; pointed vertical lugs are associated with earlier deposits.[30] A Type C small bowl has been recovered. No Brown Polished ware has so far been identified. The lowest (Philia Phase) deposits at Marki have recently received systematic exploration, and connections to the Philia Phase tombs at *Kaminoudhia* are attested (cf. Webb and Frankel 1999:11, 31–34).

While no stratified occupation deposits of the Philia Phase were found at *Kaminoudhia*, the evidence from the cemetery supports the stratigraphic data from Marki indicating that it represents a distinct early phase separated from the EC III–MC I levels by occupation related to EC I/II as known on the north coast (Webb and Frankel 1999:37–38). This demonstrates conclusively that Stewart's view—that the "Philia Culture" was a regional variation contemporary with EC I–II on the north coast—is incorrect (Stewart 1962:269–70, 296–97). At *Kaminoudhia*, tombs of both the Philia Phase and those with links to the traditional north coast EC I/II (although with local variations) coexist side-by-side, with no intermingling of ceramic types.

The last phase at Sotira *Kaminoudhia* is a time when the strict regional isolation of the earlier Bronze Age appears to be breaking down. In addition to the appearance of imported north coast ceramics in the south, the western Drab Polished Blue Core ware begins to appear at southern and eastern sites. Round bases begin to appear on south coast ceramics, becoming firmly established by MC I.

ABSOLUTE CHRONOLOGY

The evidence for the absolute dating of the settlement was presented in comprehensive detail by Manning and Swiny (1994). No new evidence has appeared since then to require a revision of the chronology proposed in that article, which appears to have been accepted by the scholarly community.

---

[29] Flourentzos 1991:7–15. Alassa T. 1 continued in use into MC II or III.

[30] Webb and Frankel 1999:37–38; Frankel and Webb 1996b:117, 120, 156–57, fig. 7:3.

At the time of their initial publication (Hedges et al. 1993) and that by Manning and Swiny the following year, these were the first radiocarbon dates available for the Cypriot Early Bronze Age. Since then seventeen EC and three Philia Phase dates have been provided by Marki *Alonia* (Frankel and Webb 1996b:27, Table 4.5; 1997:87) which have further defined and refined the absolute chronology for the period under discussion and lend further weight to the chronological framework previously suggested by Manning and Swiny.

For the sake of convenience some of the information published in Manning and Swiny 1994 will be summarized here at the same time as it is linked to the relative chronology built around Herscher's study of the ceramic assemblage. Although some other classes of artifacts do provide corroboration of the relative chronology provided by the pottery, neither the metal nor the terracottas can provide such temporally well-defined striations.

As so rightly mentioned by Frankel and Webb (1996b:27), there is much more than meets the eye when it comes to the interpretation of radiocarbon dates, and questions of integrity (i.e., the physical qualities of the sample, be it a single piece of charcoal or an aggregate of small fragments), nature of sample (potentially long-lived wood or short life seeds and reeds etc.), as well as its stratigraphy and association with other cultural remains must all be taken into account.

Problems with radiocarbon dating were first encountered with *Kaminoudhia* material when a set of five human and animal bone samples submitted for dating in 1990 provided confusing and unreliable results (Manning and Swiny 1994: Table 1).[31] They had been obtained from Area A Units 3 and 33, Area C Unit 22, and Tomb 11 in Cemetery A. Varying degrees of carbonate contaminants seem to have been absorbed by the bones, which provided an unacceptable range of dates starting in 1917–1545 B.C.E. (ETH-6659) and ending in 988–783 B.C.E. (ETH-6660) which, apart from their inconsistency, were almost all far too recent to be considered seriously.

The second attempt, only using charcoal, was undertaken by Manning and Swiny in 1991. Thirteen charcoal samples—of which ten were selected—from wood and one from reed (?) were submitted to R. A. Housley at the Oxford University Radiocarbon Accelerator Unit for AMS dating. Two came from Phase I in Area A, and thus belong to the earliest buildings so far excavated at the site; the remaining eight came from Phase II deposits in Areas A (n = 3) and C (n = 5). Details not published in 1994 concerning the provenance of the samples follow below. The numbers (1–12) of the samples remain the same. Note that samples 6 and 11 were not dated.

Phase I

1. OxA-3038. Area A, Unit 1, Lot 51. Located 1 cm above bedrock on the floor in northeast corner of the unit. No hearth nearby and no visible source of contamination. Associated with the earliest occupation of the site. Date: 3890±90 BP. Manning cal 2583–2066 B.C.E.

2. OXA-3309. Area A, Unit 7, Lot 51. From a pit beneath Wall O, associated with the earliest occupation of the site. Date: 3780±90 B.C.E. Manning cal 2466–1932 B.C.E.

In terms of absolute chronology, the median date of the two determinations for Phase I is around 2300 B.C.E.—the precise date being 2296 B.C.E. Neither of these samples was located near a hearth but they probably did originate from firewood. There is no evidence to indicate how structures

---

[31] These AMS determinations were run by W. Wölfli at the Eidgenössische Technische Hochschule Zürich. They were submitted by S. O. Held.

of Phase I were destroyed, whether by neglect, intention or by fire or earthquake. The origin of the charcoal is most likely to have been from firewood burnt at some stage in the life of Phase I. Traditional societies tend to burn easily cut, gathered and transported twigs and branches, which, by definition, tend to be younger than wood from the trunks of large, mature trees. Even presuming that the wood originated from building material it is important to note that 26 out of the 37 beams and lintels roughly dated by tree ring counts from traditional buildings in nearby Paramali Village (see Chapter 2, Appendix 2.1) were 33 years old or less. Most, in fact, were in their teens and twenties, so young trees were obviously preferred, for the reasons mentioned in Appendix 2.1.

It is likely that the structures of Phase I had a life span of at least a generation and it is equally probable that the charcoal came from wood that was under 30 years of age, therefore an absolute date of around 2270 B.C.E. seems the most plausible for this phase. Barring the unlikely possibility that the samples belong to the very earliest occupation of the site, then a date of 2300 B.C.E. or a little earlier for the beginning of building activity in Area A seems reasonable.

This date raises the issue of the diagnostic Philia Phase and EC I–II burials in the cemetery. Although the Philia ceramics are of a late type, they do belong—along with the EC I–II ceramics from Tombs 7 and 14—to cultural phases that precede the occupation in any of the areas so far excavated. As noted by Herscher, virtually no Philia and EC I–II pottery was recorded from the settlement excavations. Where then did these people who buried their dead in Cemetery A live? We have systematically surveyed the area around *Kaminoudhia* on two occasions, once in 1978 by the Kent State University team directed by Swiny (this survey resulted in the discovery of the settlement) and again in 1983 by Steve Held and his team. No evidence of another settlement has been detected, and Swiny does not believe that one exists anywhere other than in the direct vicinity of the excavations. There is a good depth of deposit with well-preserved architectural remains between Areas A and B, and it is quite possible that habitations contemporary with the Philia tombs exist here. Phase I was only preserved—and poorly at that—in a few parts of Area A where the deposits are notoriously shallow, so it cannot be excluded that those who built the first structures of this phase buried their dead in Tombs 7 and 14. More stratified settlement data are required to resolve this issue.

Phase II

3. OxA-3310. Area A, Unit 7, Lot 50. About 50 cm to the east of the hearth against WAH. Date: 3780±90 BP. Manning cal 2466–1932 B.C.E.

4. OxA-3311. Area A, Unit 7, Lot 50. In southwest corner of the unit, about 30 cm north of WAK. Date: 3890±100 BP. Manning cal 2606–2049 B.C.E.

5. OxA-3312. Area A, Unit 4, Lot 6. 60 cm north of WD. No hearth recorded in this area. Date: 3690±100 BP. Manning cal 2376–1783 B.C.E.

7. OxA-3544. Area C, Unit 2, Lot 7a. From ash rich debris in southwest corner of the courtyard. Date: 3840±75 BP. Manning 2480–2046 B.C.E.

8. OxA-3545. Area C, Unit 2, Lot 18. From ash rich debris in northeast corner of courtyard, about 1 m from a hearth. Date: 3860±75. Manning cal 2518–2062 B.C.E.

9. OxA-3546. Area C, Unit 8, Lot 8. From north corner of the room, 20 cm north of Feature 23. No hearth recorded nearby. Date: 3760±75 BP. Manning cal 2414–1943 B.C.E.

10. OxA-3547. Area C, Unit 10 (not "Room 8" as incorrectly reported in Manning and Swiny 1994: Table 2), Lot 7. On bedrock about 2.3 m east of WA. Date: 3860±80. Manning cal 2536–2055 B.C.E.

12. OxA-3548. Area C, Unit 17, Lot 8. Almost in the center of the room. No hearth recorded nearby. Date: 3800±75. Manning cal 2460–1990 B.C.E.

The medial date for Phase II based on the eight determinations listed above is about 40 years later than Phase I, namely 2262 B.C.E., which translates to 2236 B.C.E. if 30 years are subtracted for the possible age of the wood.

The most accurately datable ceramic find from the settlement is P74, the imported RP III black-topped bottle attributed by Herscher (see above) to early in the EC III period. It is fortunate that P74 was found in a wall niche or cupboard in Unit 1, suggesting that it was a prized possession in use at the time of the settlement's abandonment. This synchronism suggests that the EC III period must have begun some time before 2236 B.C.E.

Herscher's meticulous study of the settlement ceramics notes that the wares and shapes recorded in Area C seem slightly more evolved—i.e., later—than those from Area A in particular, which creates a bit of a problem. There is clear evidence for coursed tumble in Areas A and B, but not in Area C, which on the other hand yielded an intact skeleton at the back of a room (Unit 22). Since this was not a burial it seems reasonable to suggest that it was an earthquake victim, like the poorly preserved remains of individuals in Units 6 and 16 in Area A. That the five radiocarbon determinations from Area C are statistically identical to those from Area A Phase II is not surprising in view of the standard errors involved, so the dates cannot be used to argue one way or another. If the skeleton in Unit 22 is that of an earthquake victim then it seems logical to argue that it was the same event that destroyed the habitations in Areas A and B. How then how does one explain the more evolved ceramic styles present? Is it a chronological or functional difference, i.e., were the rooms in Area C devoted to different activities? As noted in Chapter 2, there is some evidence for non-domestic activities in Units 8 and 10 and one wonders whether the surrounding units, especially Unit 8 with its unusual shape, may have been involved in what was happening nearby. More excavation needs to be undertaken in Area C to better understand both its chronological and functional relationship to the other parts of the settlement.

REFERENCES CITED

Addington, L. R.
  1986   *Lithic Illustration: Drawing Flaked Stone Artifacts for Publication.* University of Chicago Press, Chicago.

Adovasio, J. M., G. Fry, J.D. Gunn, and R. F. Maslowski.
  1975   "Prehistoric and Historic Settlement Patterns in Western Cyprus." *World Archaeology* 6:339–65.

Alvin, K. L., and K. A. Kershaw.
  1963   *The Observers Book of Lichens.* F. Warne, London.

Ambraseys, N. N., C. P. Melville, and R. D. Adams.
  1994   *The Seismicity of Egypt, Arabia, and the Red Sea: A Historical Review.* Cambridge University Press, Cambridge.

Angel, J. L.
  1972   "Ecology and Population in the Eastern Mediterranean." *World Archaeology* 4:88–105.

  1967   "Porotic Hyperostosis or Osteoporosis Symmetric." Chapter 29. In *Diseases in Antiquity*, edited by D. Brothwell and A. T. Sandisons, pp. 378–89. Charles C. Thomas, Springfield.

  1964   "Osteoporosis: Thalassemia?" *American Journal of Physical Anthropology* 22:369–74.

  1961   "Neolithic Crania from Sotira." Appendix 1. In Dikaios 1961, pp. 223–29.

  1953   "The Human Remains from Khirokitia." Appendix 2. In Dikaios 1953, pp. 416–30.

Åström, P.
  1972   *The Swedish Cyprus Expedition* IV:1B. *The Middle Cypriote Bronze Age.* The Swedish Cyprus Expedition, Lund.

  1969   "The Economy of Cyprus and its Development in the Second Millennium." In *Cyprus at the Dawn of Her History: The Collections of the Cyprus Museum, from the Neolithic to the Bronze Age*, pp. 81–88. Archaeologia Viva 2(3), Paris.

Åström, P., J. C. Biers et. al.
  1979   *Corpus of Cypriote Antiquities 2: The Cypriote Collection of the Museum of Art and Archaeology University of Missouri-Columbia.* Studies In Mediterranean Archaeology 20:2, Göteborg.

Aupert, P.
  1997   Amathus During the First Iron Age. *Bulletin of the American Schools of Oriental Research.* 308:5–25.

Aurenche, O.
  1981   *La maison orientale:l'architecture du Proche Orient ancien des origines au milieu du quatrième millénaire,* Bibliothèque archéologique et historique / Institut français d'archéologie du Proche Orient, Volume 109. P. Geuthner, Paris.

Bahadir Alkim, U., H. Alkim, and Ö Bilgi.
1988   *Ikiztepe I. The First and Second Seasons of Excavations (1974–1975)*. Türk Tarih Kurumu, Ankara.

Balthazar, J. W.
1990   *Copper and Bronze Working in Early through Middle Bronze Age Cyprus*. Studies in Mediterranean Archaeology and Literature, Pocket-book 84. Paul Åströms Förlag, Göteborg.

Bannerman, D. A., and W. M. Bannerman.
1971   *Handbook of the Birds of Cyprus and Migrants of the Middle East*. Oliver and Boyd, Edinburgh.

Barber, E.
1991   *Prehistoric Textiles: The Development of Cloth in the Neolithic and Bronze Ages with Special Reference to the Aegean*. Princeton University Press, Princeton.

Barlow, J. A., and S. J. Vaughan.
1999   "Breaking Into Cypriot Pottery: Recent Insights Into Red Polished Ware." In *Meletemata: Studies in Aegean Archaeology Presented to Malcolm H. Wiener as He Enters His 65th Year*, edited by P. P. Betancourt, V. Karageorghis, R. Laffineur and W.D. Niemeier, Volume 1, pp. 15–20. (Aegeum 20) Université de Liège, Belgium.

Barlow, J. A., D. L. Bolger, and B. Kling (eds).
1991   *Cypriot Ceramics: Reading the Prehistoric Record*. University Museum Monograph, University Museum, University of Pennsylvania, Philadelphia.

Bass, W.
1971   *Human Osteology*. The Missouri Archaeological Society, Columbia.

Baudou, E., and R. Engelmark.
1983   "The Tremithos Valley Project. A Preliminary Report for 1981." *Report of the Department of Antiquities, Cyprus, 1983*. Department of Antiquities, Nicosia, pp. 1–8.

Bear, L. M.
1963a   *A Geological Map of Cyprus (1:250,000)*. Republic of Cyprus Government Printing Office, Nicosia.

1963b   *The Mineral Resources and Mining Industry of Cyprus*. Bulletin 1. Republic of Cyprus, Ministry of Commerce and Industry, Geological Survey Department, Nicosia.

1962   *Additions to the Bibliography of Cyprus Geology*. Annual Report of the Geological Survey (1961) Cyprus, p. 39, Nicosia.

1961   *A Bibliography of Cyprus Geology*. Annual Report of the Geological Survey (1960) Cyprus, pp. 35–45, Nicosia.

Belgiorno, M. R.
1997   "A Coppersmith Tomb of Early-Middle Bronze Age in Pyrgos (Limassol)." *Report of the Department of Antiquities, Cyprus, 1997*. Department of Antiquities, Nicosia, pp. 119–46.

Ben Tor, A.
1992   *The Archaeology of Ancient Israel*. Yale University Press, New Haven.

Bernabò-Brea, L.
1976   *Poliochni. Città preistorica nell' isola di Lemnos*. Volume 2. L'Erma di Bretschneider, Roma.

1964   *Poliochni. Città preistorica nell' isola di Lemnos.* Volume 1. L'Erma di Bretschneider, Roma.

Betts, A.
n.d.   "The Chipped Stone." In *Vasilikos Valley Project* 8. *Excavations at Kalavasos-Ayious*, edited by I. A.
         Todd and P. Croft. Studies in Mediterranean Archaeology 71(8). Paul Åströms Förlag, Göteborg:
         Unpublished ms. in author's possession.

Betts, A.
1987   "The Chipped Stone." In "Excavations at Kissonerga *Mosphilia* 1986," edited by E. J. Peltenburg
         and Project Members. *Report of the Department of Antiquities, Cyprus, 1987.* Department of Antiq-
         uities, Nicosia, pp. 10–14.

1985   "The Chipped Stone." In Peltenburg 1985, pp. 94–95, 196–97, 276–78.

1979a   "The Chipped Stone from Lemba-*Lakkous* and Kissonerga-*Mylouthkia* (1976–77)." *Report of the
         Department of Antiquities, Cyprus, 1979.* Department of Antiquities, Nicosia, pp. 100–111.

1979b   "Lemba *Lakkous*—Two Caches of Chipped Stone." In Peltenburg 1979, pp. 42–43.

Biggs, H. E. J.
1966   "Report on Molluscs found at Kalopsidha, Cyprus." Appendix 8. In *Excavations at Kalopsidha and
         Ayios Iakovos in Cyprus*, edited by P. Åström, pp. 135–36. Studies in Mediterranean Archaeology 2.
         Paul Åströms Förlag, Lund.

Bittel, K.
1940   "Der Depotfunde von Soli-Pompeiopolis." *Zeitschrift für Assyriologie* 46:183–205.

Bolger, D. L.
1991   Early Red Polished Ware and the Origin of the "Philia Culture." In Barlow et al. 1991, pp. 29–35.

1988   *Erimi Pamboula: A Chalcolithic Settlement in Cyprus.* British Archaeological Reports International
         Series 443. British Archaeological Reports, Oxford.

1985   *Erimi-Pamboula: A Study of the Site in Light of Recent Evidence.* Ph.D. dissertation. University of
         Cincinnati, Cincinnati.

1983   "Khrysiliou-*Ammos*, Nicosia-*Ayia Paraskevi* and the Philia Culture of Cyprus." *Report of the De-
         partment of Antiquities, Cyprus, 1983.* Department of Antiquities, Nicosia, pp. 60–72.

Bonn, A. G.
1977   *The Domestic Architecture of Early Bronze Age Palestine.* Ph. D. dissertation, Bryn Mawr College,
         University Microfilms International, Ann Arbor, Michigan.

Bordaz, L. A.
1978   *The Metal Artifacts from the Bronze Age Excavations at Karataş-Semayük, Turkey and their Signifi-
         cance in Anatolia, the Near East and the Aegean.* Ph. D. dissertation, Bryn Mawr College, Univer-
         sity Microfilms International, Ann Arbor, Michigan.

Bordaz, J.
1970   *Tools of the Old and New Stone Age.* Natural History Press, New York.

Bordes, F.
    1974   "Un percuteur en bois de renne du Solutréen Superior de Laugerie Haute Ouest." In *Premier colloque international sur l'industrie de l'os dans la préhistoire*, edited by H. Camps Fabrer, pp. 97–100. Editions de l'Université de Provence, Provence.

    1968   *The Old Stone Age*. McGraw-Hill, New York.

    1961   *Typologie du Paléolithique Ancien et Moyen*. Mémoire 1. Institut de Préhistoire de l'Université de Bordeaux, Bordeaux.

Bordes, F., and D. Crabtree.
    1969   "The Corbiac Blade Technique And Other Experiments." *Tebiwa* 12(2):1–21.

Brandt, S. A.
    1994   *Woman the Toolmaker: Contemporary Use of Flaked Stone Tools in Ethiopia*. Institute of Human Origins Lecture Series, Spring 1994. Public Lecture, February 22nd. University of California, Berkeley.

Branigan, K.
    1974   *Aegean Metalwork of the Early and Middle Bronze Age*. Clarendon Press, Oxford.

Briois, F., B. Gratuze, and J. Guilaine.
    1997   Obsidiennes du site néolithique précéramique de Shillourokambos (Chypre), *Paléorient* 23:95–112.

Brothwell, D. R.
    1963   *Digging Up Bones*. 1st Edition. The Trustees of the British Museum, London.

Brown, A. C., and H. Catling.
    1980   "Additions to the Cypriot Collection in the Ashmolean Museum, Oxford, 1963–77." *Opuscula Atheniensia* 13(7):91–137.

    1975   *Ancient Cyprus*. University of Oxford, Ashmolean Museum, Oxford.

Buchholz, H.-G.
    1982   "Bronzezeitliche Brettspiele aus Zypern." *Acta Praehistorica et Archaeologica* 13/14:67–73.

    1981   "'Schalensteine' in Griechenland, Anatolien und Zypern." In *Studien zur Bronzezeit, Festschrift für Wilhelm Albert v. Brunn*, pp. 63–81. Von Zabern, Mainz am Rhein.

Buitron-Oliver, D.
    1996   *The Sanctuary of Apollo Hylates at Kourion: Excavations in the Archaic Precinct*. Studies In Mediterranean Archaeology 109. Paul Åströms Förlag, Jonsered.

Cadogan, G.
    1984   "Maroni and the Late Bronze Age of Cyprus." In *Cyprus at the Close of the Late Bronze Age*, edited by V. Karageorghis and J. Muhly, pp. 1–10. A. G. Leventis Foundation, Nicosia.

Calnan, K.
    1984   *The Architecture and Finds of the Tombs at Sotira Kaminoudhia*. M.A. Thesis, Drew University, Madison, New Jersey.

Carpenter, J. R.
1981   "Excavations at Phaneromeni, 1975–1978." In *Studies in Cypriot Archaeology*, edited by J. C. Biers and D. Soren, pp. 59–78. Monograph 13. Institute of Archaeology, University of California, Los Angeles.

Catling, H. W.
1971   "Cyprus in the Early Bronze Age." In *The Cambridge Ancient History*, 3rd edition. Volume 1, part 2, pp. 808–23. Cambridge University Press, Cambridge.

1969   "The Cypriote Copper Industry." In *Cyprus at the Dawn of Her History: The Collections of the Cyprus Museum, from the Neolithic to the Bronze Age*, pp. 81–88. Archaeologia Viva 2(3), Paris.

1964   *Cypriot Bronzework in the Mycenaean World.* Clarendon Press, Oxford.

1963   "Patterns of Settlement in Bronze Age Cyprus." *Opuscula Atheniensia* 4:129–69. C. W. K. Gleerup, Lund.

Cauvin, M. C.
1984   "L'Outillage Lithique de Khirokitia (Chypre) et le Levant." In *Fouilles Récentes à Khirokitia (Chypre) 1977–1981*, edited by A. Le Brun, pp. 85–87. Mémoire 41. Editions Recherche sur les civilisations, Paris.

Chang, C.
1984   *The Ethnoarchaeology of Herding Sites in Greece.* In University of Pennsylvania. Museum Applied Science Center for Archaeology. MASCA Journal. 3(2), Zooarchaeology Supplement, pp. 44–48.

Chang, C., and H. A. Koster.
1986   *Beyond Bones: Toward an Archaeology of Pastoralism.* Academic Press, New York.

Chapman, E.
1967   *Cyprus Trees and Shrubs.* Government Printing Office, Nicosia.

Charles, J. A.
1967   Early Arsenical Bronzes – A Metallurgical View." *American Journal of Archaeology* 71:21–26.

Cherry, J. F.
1983   "Frogs Round the Pond: Perspectives on Current Archaeological Survey Projects in the Mediterranean Region." In *Archaeological Survey in the Mediterranean Area*, edited by D. R. Keller and D. W. Rupp, pp. 375–416. British Archaeological Reports, Oxford.

1983   "Survey on Keos 1983." *Old World Archaeology Newsletter* 7(3):21.

Christodoulou, D.
1959   *The Evolution of the Rural Land Use Pattern in Cyprus.* Monograph 2. World Land Use Survey, London.

Christou, D.
1998a   *Annual Report of the Department of Antiquities for the Year 1992.* Department of Antiquities, Nicosia.

1998b   *Annual Report of the Department of Antiquities for the Year 1993.* Department of Antiquities, Nicosia.

1993   "Chronique des Fouilles et Découvertes Archéologiques à Chypre en 1992." *Bulletin de Correspondance Hellenique* 117:719–55.

1989   "The Chalcolithic Cemetery 1 at Souskiou-Vathyrkakas." In *Early Society in Cyprus*, edited by E. Peltenburg, pp. 82–94. Edinburgh University Press, Edinburgh.

Clark, J. E.
1986   "Another Look at Small Debitage and Microdebitage." *Lithic Technology* 15(1):21–33.

Cleuziou, S., and T. Berthoud.
1982   "Early Tin in the Near East, A Reassessment in the Light of New Evidence from Western Afghanistan." *Expedition* 25 (1):14–20.

Cluzan, S.
1984   "L'Outillage en Pierre." In Le Brun 1984a, Volume 1, pp. 97–110 and Volume 2, pp. 120–21.

Coleman, J. E.
1985   Investigations at Alambra, 1974–1984. In Karageorghis 1985b, pp. 125–41.

Coleman, J. E., J. A. Barlow, M. K. Mogelonsky, and K. W. Schaar.
1996   *Alambra: A Middle Bronze Age Settlement in Cyprus. Investigations by Cornell University in 1974– 1985*. Studies in Mediterranean Archaeology 118. Paul Åströms Förlag, Göteborg.

Coleman, J. E., J. A. Barlow, and K. W. Schaar.
1981   "Cornell Excavations at Alambra, 1980." *Report of the Department of Antiquities, Cyprus, 1981*. Department of Antiquities, Nicosia, pp. 81–98.

Coles, J.
1973   *Archaeology by Experiment*. Charles Scribner and Sons, New York.

College, S.
1985   "The Plant Remains." In Peltenburg 1985, pp. 101–2, 209–11, 297–98.

Collins, M.
1975   "Lithic Technology as a Means of Processual Inference." In *Lithic Technology, Making and Using Stone Tools*, edited by E. Swanson, pp. 15–34. Mouton, Le Hague.

Constantinou, G.
1992   "Ancient Copper Mining in Cyprus." In *Copper, Cyprus and the Sea*, edited by A. Marangou and K. Psillides, pp. 43-74. Government of Cyprus, Nicosia.

1982   "Geological Features and Ancient Exploitations of the Cupriferous Sulphide Orebodies of Cyprus." In Muhly et al. 1982, pp. 13–24.

Coqueugniot, E.
1984   "Premiers Éléments Concernant l'Utilisation des Outils en Silex de Khirokitia (Chypre). Campagne de 1981." In Le Brun 1984a, pp. 89–93.

Courtois, J.-C.
1962   "Sondages 1959." In "Contribution à l'Etude des Civilisations du Bronze Ancien à Ras Shamra – Ugarit." In Schaeffer 1962, pp. 415–75.

Courtois, L.

1981   "Examen Microscopique et Analyse à la Microsonde des Céramiques "Base Ring" du Chypriote Recent." *Palaeorient* 7:145–51.

1971   *Description Physico-Chimique de la Céramique Ancienne: la Céramique de Chypre au Bronze Récent.* Thèse, C.N.R.S., Paris.

Courtois, L., and B. Velde.

1984   Microscopic and Microprobe Analysis of Six Pottery Samples from *Phaneromeni*, Episkopi (Cyprus)." Preliminary Report (unpublished).

Crabtree, D. E.

1982   *An Introduction to Flintworking.* 2nd Edition. Idaho Museum of Natural History, Pocatello.

1972a   *An Introduction to the Technology of Stone Tools I.* Occasional Papers of the Museum 28, Idaho State University, Pocatello.

1972b   *A Glossary of Flint Working Terms II.* Occasional Papers of the Museum 28, Idaho State University, Pocatello.

1967   "Notes on Experiments in Flintknapping: 3. The Flintknapper's Raw Materials." *Tebiwa* 10(1):8–24.

Crabtree, D. E., and R. B. Butler.

1964   "Notes on Experiment in Flintknapping: 1. Heat Treatment of Silica Minerals." *Tebiwa* 7(1):1–6.

Craddock, P. T.

1995   *Early Metal Mining and Production.* Edinburgh University Press, Edinburgh.

1986   "Report on the composition of bronzes excavated from a Middle Cypriot site at Episkopi *Phaneromeni* and Some Comparative Cypriot Bronze Age Metalwork." In Swiny 1986, pp. 153–58.

Craddock, P. T., and N. D. Meeks.

1987   "Iron in Ancient Copper." *Archaeometry* 29(2):187–204.

Crewe, L.

1998   *Spindle Whorls. A Study of Form, Function and Decoration in Prehistoric Bronze Age Cyprus.* Pocket Book 149. Paul Åströms Förlag, Jonsered.

Croft, P. W.

1998   "The Bone and Antler Industry" and "Animal Remains." In Peltenburg 1998, pp. 199–200, 207–14.

1996   "Animal Remains from Marki-Alonia." In Frankel and Webb 1996b, pp. 217–22.

1991   "Man and Beast in Chalcolithic Cyprus." *Bulletin of the American Schools of Oriental Research* 282/283:63–79.

1991a   "The Animal Remains." In Peltenburg 1991a, pp. 73–74.

1985a   "The Bone and Antler Industry." In Peltenburg 1985, pp. 1, 96–97, 200–202, 294.

1985b   "The Mammalian Fauna." In Peltenburg 1985, pp. 98–100, 202–8, 295–96.

1983   "The Antler Industry of Kissonerga-Mylouthkia." In Peltenburg and Project Members 1983, pp. 18–23.

n.d.   "Mammalian Faunal Remains from Aceramic Kalavasos-Tenta." In *Vasilikos Valley Project* 7: *Excavations at Kalavasos-Tenta II*, edited by I. A. Todd. Studies in Mediterranean Archaeology 71(7). Paul Åströms Förlag, Jonsered.

Cuomo di Caprio, N., and S. J. Vaughan.
1983   "Differentiating Grog (chamotte) from Natural argillaceous Inclusions in Ceramic Thin Sections: An Experimental Study." *Archaeomaterials* 7(1):21–40.

D'Annibale, C.
1993   "Lithic Analysis." In Rupp et al. 1993, pp. 399–404.

1992   "Lithic Analysis." In Rupp et al. 1992, pp. 307–12.

Davis, S. J. M.
1987   "La faune." In "Le Neolithique Preceramique de Chypre," by A. Le Brun, S. Cluzan, S. J. M. Davis, J. Hansen, and J. Renault-Miskovsky, pp. 305-309. *L'anthropologie* 91, pp. 283-316.

Debney, T.
1997   "Flaked Stone: Changing Patterns of Manufacture and Raw Material Use." Appendix 1. In Frankel and Webb 1997, pp. 105–9.

1996   *Form and Function: Assemblage Variability and Use-Wear Analysis of a Flaked Stone Assemblage from Marki-Alonia, Cyprus.* B.A. Honors Thesis, School of Archaeology, La Trobe University, Melbourne.

de Contenson, H.
1969   "Les Couches du Niveau III au Sud de l'Acropole de Ras Shamra." In Schaeffer 1969, pp. 45–89.

de Jesus, P. S.
1980   *The Development of Prehistoric Mining and Metallurgy in Anatolia.* British Archaeological Reports International Series 74. British Archeological Reports, Oxford.

de Jesus, P. S., G. R. Rapp, and L. Vagnetti.
1982   "Cypriote Bronzes in the Art and History Museum at Geneva." *Studi Micenei ed Egeo-Anatolici* 23:7–29.

de Vaux, R.
1961   "Les fouilles de Tell el-Far`Ah." *Revue Biblique* 68: 557–92.

Deniz, E., and S. Payne.
1982   "Eruption and Wear in the Mandibular Dentition as a Guide to Ageing Turkish Angora Goats." In *Ageing and Sexing Animal Bones from Archaeological Sites,* edited by R. Wilson, C. Grigson, and S. Payne, pp. 155-205. British Archaeological Reports 109, Oxford.

Desch, C.H.
1950   "Spectrographic Analyses of Metal Objects." In E. and J.R. Stewart 1950, pp. 370–71.

des Gagniers, J., and V. Karageorghis.
1976   *Vases et Figurines de l'Âge du Bronze à Chypre: Céramique Rouge et Noire Polie.* Les Presses de l'université Laval, Québec.

Dibble, H. L.
1987   "The Interpretation of Middle Paleolithic Scraper Morphology." *American Antiquity* 52:109–17.

Dikaios, P.
1971   *Enkomi Excavations, 1948–1958.* Vol. II. Philipp von Zabern, Mainz am Rhein.

1969   *Enkomi Excavations, 1948–1958.* Vol. I. Philipp von Zabern, Mainz am Rhein.

1962   *The Swedish Cyprus Expedition* IV:IA. *The Stone Age*, pp. 1–204. The Swedish Cyprus Expedition, Lund.

1961   *Sotira.* University Museum Monograph, The University Museum, University of Pennsylvania, Philadelphia.

1960   "A Conspectus of Architecture in Ancient Cyprus." *Kypriakai Spoudai*, Volume D, pp. 3–30.

1953   *Khirokitia. Final Report on the Excavations of a Neolithic Settlement in Cyprus on Behalf of the Department of Antiquities, 1936–1946.* Oxford University Press, London.

1948   "Trial Excavations at Sotira, Site Teppes, on Behalf of the University Museum Cyprus Expedition." *Bulletin of the University Museum, University of Pennsylvania* 13(3):16–23.

1946   "Early Copper Age Discoveries in Cyprus: 3rd Millennieum B. C. Copper- Mining." *The Illustrated London News* 2, March, pp. 244–45.

1940   "The Excavations at Vounous-Bellapais in Cyprus, 1931–1932." *Archaeologia* 88:1–174.

1939   "Excavations at Erimi 1933–1935: Final Report." *Report of the Department of Antiquities, Cyprus, 1936.* Department of Antiquities, Nicosia, pp. 1–81.

Donovan, H.
1993   *Cyprus: An Island in Isolation? A Preliminary Analysis of the Chipped Stone Assemblage from Marki Alonia.* B.A. Honors Thesis. Department of Archaeology and Anthropology, Australian National *University*, Canberra.

Dunand, M.
1952   "Byblos au temps du Bronze Ancien et de la conqête Amorite." *Revue Biblique*59:82–90.

Duryea, D.
1965   *The Necropolis of Phaneromeni and Other Early Bronze Age Sites in Cyprus.* M. A. Thesis, University of Missouri, Columbia.

Earl, B., and H. Özbal.
1996   "Early Bronze Age Tin Processing at Kestel-Göltepe." In *Archaeometry 94. Proceedings of the 29th International Symposium on Archaeometry (Ankara 1994)*, edited by S. Demirci, A. M. Özer, and G. D. Summers, pp. 435–46. TÜBITAK, Ankara.

Eaton, E. R., and H. McKerrell.
1976   "Near Eastern Alloying and Some Textual Evidence for the Early Use of Arsenical Copper." *World Archaeology* 8(2):169–91.

Ehrich, R. W. (ed.)
  1992   *Chronologies in Old World Archaeology*. 3rd edition. University of Chicago Press, Chicago.

Elliott, C.
  1991   "Rock Sources of Ground Stone Tools of the Chalcolithic Period in Cyprus." *Bulletin of the American Schools of Oriental Research* 282/283:95–106.

  1985   "A General Assessment of the Ground Stone Industry." In Peltenburg 1985, pp. 70–93, 161–95, 271–75.

Elliott, C., C. Xenophontos, and J. G. Malpas.
  1986   "Petrographic and Mineral Analyses Used in Tracing the Provenance of Late Bronze Age and Roman Basalt Artefacts from Cyprus." *Report of the Department of Antiquities, Cyprus, 1986*. Department of Antiquities, Nicosia, pp. 80–96.

Elster, E.
  1989   "The Chipped Stone." In *Achilleion: A Neolithic Settlement in Thessaly, Greece, 6400–5600 BC*, edited by M. A. Gimbutas, S. M. M. Winn, and D. M. Shimabuku, pp. 273–306. University of California Press, Los Angeles.

Emre, K., B. Hrouda., M. Mellink, and N. Özgüç.
  1989   *Anatolia and the Ancient Near East. Studies in Honor of Tahsin Özgüç*. Türk Tarih Kurimu, Ankara.

Fasani, L.
  1988   "La sepoltura e il forno di fusione de La Vela di Valbusa (Trento)." *Preistoria Alpina* 24:165–81.

Fasnacht, W.
  1996   "Interview with Kosta Symeou Concerning the Use of Cherts in Threshing Sledges." In Coleman et al. 1996. Appendix 4, p. 431.

Finlayson, W.
  1987   "Preliminary Report on Use Wear Traces on Chert Tools." In "Excavations at Kissonerga-*Mosphilia* 1986," by E. J. Peltenburg and Project Members. *Report of the Department of Antiquities, Cyprus, 1987*, Department of Antiquities, Nicosia, pp. 14–15.

Fitter, R. A., and M. Blamey.
  1974   *The Wild Flowers of Britain and Northern Europe*. Harper Collins, London.

Flourentzos, P.
  1995   "A Unique Scene on a Cypriote Red Polished Jug." *Journal of Prehistoric Religion* 9:15–18.

  1991   *Excavations in the Kouris Valley I. The Tombs*. Department of Antiquities, Nicosia.

  1988   "Tomb Discoveries from the Necropolis of *Ayia Paraskevi*." *Report of the Department of Antiquities, Cyprus, 1988*. Department of Antiquities, Nicosia, pp. 121–25.

  1982   "Selected Antiquities of Red Polished Ware from Cypriote Private Collections." *Opuscula Atheniensia* 14:21–26.

  1975   "Notes on the Red Polished III Plank Shaped Idols from Cyprus." *Report of the Department of Antiquities, Cyprus, 1975*. Department of Antiquities, Nicosia, pp. 29–35.

Forde, C. D.
1963   *Habitat, Economy and Society: A Geographical Introduction to Ethnology.* E. P. Dutton, New York.

Fox, W.
1988   "Kholetria *Ortos*: A Khirokitia Culture Settlement in Paphos District." *Report of the Department of Antiquities, Cyprus, 1988.* Department of Antiquities, Nicosia, pp. 29–42.

1984   "Dhoukani Flake Blade Production in Cyprus." *Lithic Technology* 13(2):62–67.

Fox, W., and D. Pearlman.
1987   "Threshing Sledge Production in the Paphos District of Cyprus." In Rupp 1987a, pp. 228–34.

Frankel, D.
1988   "Pottery Production in Prehistoric Bronze Age Cyprus: Assessing the Problem." *Journal of Mediterranean Archaeology* 1(2):27–55.

Frankel, D., and J. M. Webb.
2000   "Excavations at Marki-*Alonia*, 1999–2000." *Report of the Department of Antiquities, Cyprus, 2000.* Department of Antiquities, Nicosia, pp. 65–94.

1999   "Excavations at Marki-*Alonia*, 1998–9." *Report of the Department of Antiquities, Cyprus, 1999.* Department of Antiquities, Nicosia, pp. 87–110.

1997   "Excavations at Marki-*Alonia*, 1996–7." *Report of the Department of Antiquities, Cyprus, 1997.* Department of Antiquities, Nicosia, pp. 85–109.

1996a   "Excavations at Marki-Alonia, 1995–6." *Report of the Department of Antiquities, Cyprus, 1996.* Department of Antiquities, Nicosia, pp. 51–68.

1996b   *Marki-Alonia. An Early and Middle Bronze Age Town in Cyprus. Excavations 1990–1994.* Studies in Mediterranean Archaeology 123(1). Paul Åströms Förlag, Jonsered.

1993   "Excavations at Marki-Alonia, 1992–1993." *Report of the Department of Antiquities, Cyprus, 1993.* Department of Antiquities, Nicosia, pp. 43–68.

1992   "Excavations at Marki-Alonia, 1991–1992." *Report of the Department of Antiquities, Cyprus, 1992.* Department of Antiquities, Nicosia, pp. 29–49.

Freestone, I. C.
1995   "Ceramic Petrography." In "Science in Archaeology: A Review," by P. E. McGovern, pp. 79–142, *American Journal of Archaeology* 99:111–15.

Fugmann, E.
1958   *Hama. Fouilles et Recherches 1931–1938. III. L'Architecture des Périodes Pré-hellenistiques.* Nationalmuseet, København.

Gale, N. H.
1991   "Metals and Metallurgy in the Chalcolithic Period." *Bulletin of the American Schools of Oriental Research* 282/283:37–61.

Gale, N. H., Z. A. Stos-Gale, and W. Fasnacht.
1996   "Copper and Copper Working at Alambra." In Coleman et al. 1996. Appendix 2, pp. 359–400.

Gallant, T. W.
  1986   "Background Noise and Site Definition: A Contribution to Survey Methodology." *Journal of Field Archaeology* 13:403–18.

Garstang, J.
  1953   *Prehistoric Mersin. Yümük Tepe in Southern Turkey: the Neilson Expedition in Cilicia.* Clarendon Press, Oxford.

Gaudry, A.
  1878   *Geology of Cyprus.* Trans. E. Maurice. H. M. Stationery Office, London.

Gero, J. M.
  1989   "Assessing Social Information in Material Objects: How Well Do Lithics Hold Up?" In *Time, Energy and Stone Tools*, edited by R. Torrence, pp. 92–105. Cambridge University Press, Cambridge.

Gejvall, N.-G.
  1966   "Osteological Investigation of Human and Animal Bone fragments from Kalopsidha." Appendix IV. In *Excavations at Kalopsidha and Ayios Iakovos in Cyprus*, edited by P. Åström, pp. 128–32. Studies In Mediterranean Archaeology 2. Paul Åströms Förlag, Lund.

Georghiou, Giorgos.
  2000   "An Early Bronze Age Tomb at Psematismenos-*Trelloukkas*." *Report of the Department of Antiquities, Cyprus, 2000.* Department of Antiquities, Nicosia, pp. 47–63.

Giardino, C.
  2000   "Prehistoric copper activity at Pyrgos." *Report of the Department of Antiquities, Cyprus, 2000.* Department of Antiquities, Nicosia, pp. 19–32.

  1998   *I metalli nel mondo antico. Introduzione all'archeometallurgia.* Laterza, Roma-Bari.

Giardino, C., G. E. Gigante, G. Guida, and R. Mazzeo.
  1996   "EDXRF and Metallography for In Situ Simultaneous Analysis of Archaeological Metal Artefacts." In *Art '96. Fifth International Conference on Non Destructive Testing, Microanalytical Methods and Environmental Evaluation for Study and Conservation of Works of Art (Budapest 1996)*, pp. 327–37. Budapest.

Gibson, A., and A. Woods.
  1990   *Prehistoric Pottery for the Archaeologist.* Leicester University Press, London.

Given, M., and D. Coleman.
  1998   "Threshing in its Technical, Social and Landscape Context." Paper presented at *Early Agricultural Remnants and Technical Heritage. Sophia Antipolis, 23rd – 27th November, 1998.*

Gjerstad, E.
  1926   *Studies on Prehistoric Cyprus.* Uppsala Universitets Årsskrift, Uppsala.

Gjerstad, E., J. Lindros, E. Sjöqvist, and A. Westholm.
  1935   *The Swedish Cyprus Expedition. Finds and Results of the Excavations in 1927–1931.* Volume II. Swedish Cyprus Expedition, Lund.

Goldman, H.
  1956   *Excavations at Gözlü Kule, Tarsus, Volume II. From the Neolithic through the Bronze Age.* Princeton University Press, Princeton.

Gomez, B., M. D. Glascock, M. J. Blackman, and I. A. Todd.
  1995   "Neutron Activation Analysis of Obsidian from Kalavasos-Tenta." *Journal of Field Archaeology*
          22:503–8.

Gomez, B., J. Hansen, and J. M. Wagstaff.
  1987   "The Vasilikos Valley." In Todd 1987, pp. 3–10.

Gonnet, H.
  1993   "Systemes de cupules, de vasques et de rigoles rupestres dans la region de Beyköy en Phrygie." In
          Aspects of Art and Iconography: Anatolia and its Neighbors: Studies in Honor of Nimet Özgüç,
          edited by M. J. Mellink, E. Porada, and T. Özgüç, pp. 215–24. Türk Tarih Kurumru, Ankara.

Goodwin, J. C.
  1984   *An Historical Toponymy of Cyprus I–II.* Fourth Rev. Edition, 2 Volumes. Jack Goodwin, London.

Gopher, A.
  1994   *Arrowheads of the Neolithic Levant: a Seriation Analysis.* Dissertation Series, American Schools of
          Oriental Research 10. Eisenbrauns, Winona Lake, Indiana.

Goring, E.
  1988   *A Mischievous Pastime: Digging in Cyprus in the Nineteenth Century.* National Museums of Scotland,
          Edinburgh.

Gould, R. A.
  1980   *Living Archaeology.* Cambridge University Press, Cambridge.

  1978   "Beyond Analogy in Ethnoarchaeology." In *Explorations in Ethnoarchaeology,* edited by R. A. Gould,
          pp. 249–93. University of New Mexico, Albuquerque.

  1969   *Yiwara: Foragers of the Australian Desert.* American Museum of Natural History. Charles Scribner's
          Sons, New York.

  1968   "Chipping Stones in the Outback." *Natural History* 77(2):42–49.

Gould, R. A., D. A. Koster, and A. H. L. Sontz.
  1971   "The Lithic Assemblage of the Western Desert Aborigines of Australia." *American Antiquity* 36:149–
          69.

Grace, V.R.
  1940   "A Cypriote Tomb and Minoan Evidence for its Date." *American Journal of Archaeology* 44:10–52.

Gramly, R. M.
  1992   *Guide to the Palaeo-Indian Artifacts of North America.* Second revised edition. Monographs in
          Archaeology. Persimmon Press, Buffalo.

Guidoboni, E.
  1994   *Catalogue of Ancient Earthquakes in the Mediterranean Area Up to the 10th Century.* Istituto Nazionale
          di Geofisica, Roma.

Guilaine, J., F. Briois, J. Coularou, J.-D. Vigne, and I. Carrère.
  1997/8 "Les Débuts du Néolithique à Chypre." *L'Archéologie* 33:35–40.

Guilaine, J., F. Briois, J. Coularou, and I. Carrère.
    1995a "L'Établissement Néolithique de Shillourokambos (Parekklisha, Chypre). Premiers Résultats." *Report of the Department of Antiquities, Cyprus, 1995*. Department of Antiquities, Nicosia, pp. 11–32.

    1995b "Le Site Néolithique de Shillourokambos (Chypre)." *Bulletin de Correspondance Hellenique* 119:737–41.

Guilaine, J., J. Coularou, F. Briois, I. Carrère, and S. Philbert.
    1993   "Rapport Sur Les Travaux de L'Ecole Française à Amanthonte de Chypre en 1992." *Bulletin de Correspondance Hellenique* 117:716–18.

Hansen, J.
    1989   "Khirokitia Plant Remains, Preliminary Report." In Le Brun 1989, pp. 235–50.

Hartmann, A.
    1970   *Prähistorische Goldfunde aus Europa, Studien zu den Anfängen der Metallurgie* 3, Gebr. Mann, Berlin.

Hayden, B.
    1987   "From Chopper to Celt: the Evolution of Resharpening Techniques." *Lithic Technology* 16(2–3):33–43.

Heider, K. G.
    1997   *Grand Valley Dani: Peaceful Warriors*. Third Edition. Holt, Rinehart and Winston, Fort Worth.

Heimann, R., and U. M. Franklin.
    1981   "Archaeo-thermometry: The Assessment of Firing Temperatures of Ancient Ceramics." *Journal of the International Institute of Conservation—Canadian Group* 4:23–45.

Held, S. O.
    1992   *Pleistocene Fauna and Holocene Humans: a Gazetteer of Paleontological and Early Archaeological Sites on Cyprus*. Studies in Mediterranean Archaeology 95. Paul Åströms Förlag, Jonsered.

    1990   "Back to What Future: New Directions in Cypriot Early Prehistoric Research in the 1990s." *Report of the Department of Antiquities, Cyprus, 1990*. Department of Antiquities, Nicosia, pp. 1–44.

    1989   *Contributions to the Early Prehistoric Archaeology of Cyprus: Environmental and Chronological Background Studies*. British Archaeological Reports, International Series. British Archaeological Reports, Oxford.

    1988   "Sotira-*Kaminoudhia* Survey: Preliminary Report of the 1983 and 1984 Seasons." *Report of the Department of Antiquities, Cyprus, 1988*. Department of Antiquities, Nicosia, pp. 53–62.

Hellweg, P.
    1984   *Flintknapping: the Art of Making Stone Tools*. Canyon Publishing Company, Canoga Park, California.

Hennessy, J. B.
    1973   "Cypriot Artists of the Early and Middle Bronze Age." In *The Cypriot Bronze Age: Some Recent Australian Contributions to the Prehistory of Cyprus*, edited by J. Birmingham, pp. 10–22. Australian Studies in Archaeology, Sydney.

Hennessy, J. B., K. O. Eriksson, and I. C. Kehrberg.
1988   *Ayia Paraskevi and Vasilia*. Studies In Mediterranean Archaeology 82. Paul Åströms Förlag Göteborg.

Herglotz, H. K., and L. S. Birks.
1978   *X-Ray Spectrometry*. M. Dekker, New York.

Herscher, E.
1998   "Archaeology in Cyprus." *American Journal of Archaeology* 102:309–54.

1997   "Representational Relief on Early and Middle Cypriot Pottery." In *Four Thousand Years of Images on Cypriote Pottery. Proceedings of the Third International Conference of Cypriote Studies, Nicosia, 3–4 May, 1996*, edited by V. Karageorghis, R. Laffineur, and F. Vandenabeele, pp. 25–36. Leventis, University of Cyprus, Vrije Universiteit Brussel, Université de Liège. Brussels-Liège-Nicosia.

1991   "Beyond Regionalism: Toward an Islandwide Middle Cypriot Sequence." In Barlow et al. 1991, pp. 45–50.

1988   "Kition in the Middle Bronze Age: The Tombs at Larnaca-*Ayios Prodromos*." *Report of the Department of Antiquities, Cyprus, 1988*. Department of Antiquities, Nicosia, pp. 141–66.

1981   "Southern Cyprus, the Disappearing Early Bronze Age and the Evidence from Phaneromeni." In *Studies in Cypriot Archaeology*, edited by J. C. Biers and D. Soren, pp. 79–85. Monograph 13, Institute of Archaeology, University of California, Los Angeles.

1979   "Cretan and Cypriote Ceramic Techniques in the Late Third Millennium B.C." In *Acts of the International Archaeological Symposium, The Relations Between Cyprus and Crete, ca. 2000–500 B.C.*, edited by V. Karageorghis, pp. 1–7, Nicosia.

1976   "South Coast Ceramic Styles at the End of Middle Cypriote." *Report of the Department of Antiquities, Cyprus, 1976*. Department of Antiquities, Nicosia, pp. 11–19.

1972   "A Potter's Error: Aspects of Middle Cypriote III." *Report of the Department of Antiquities, Cyprus, 1972*. Department of Antiquities, Nicosia, pp. 22–33.

Herscher, E., and S. C. Fox.
1993   "A Middle Bronze Age Tomb from Western Cyprus." *Report of the Department of Antiquities, Cyprus, 1993*. Department of Antiquities, Nicosia, pp. 69–80.

Herscher, E., and S. Swiny.
1992   "Picking Up the Pieces: Two Plundered Bronze Age Cemeteries." In *Studies in Honour of Vassos Karageorghis*, edited by G. C. Ioannides, pp. 69–86. Society of Cypriot Studies, Nicosia.

Herzog, Z., G. R. Rapp, Jr., and O.Negbi, (eds).
1989   *Excavations at Tel Michal, Israel*. The University of Minnesota Press, Minneapolis.

Heywood, H., S. Swiny, D. Whittingham, and P. Croft.
1981   "Erimi Revisited." *Report of the Department of Antiquities, Cyprus, 1981*. Department of Antiquities, Nicosia, pp. 24–42.

Hodges, H.
1964   *Artifacts: An Introduction to Early Materials and Technology*. John Baker, London.

Holloway, R. R., and S. S. Lukesh.
   1995   *Ustica. I: The Results of the Excavations of the Regione Siciliana, Soprintendenza ai Beni Culturali
           ed Ambientali Provincia di Palermo in Collaboration with Brown University in 1990 and 1991.*
           Center for Old World Archaeology and Art, Brown University, Providence.

Hordynsky, L.
   1996   "Determining Utilitarian Patterns: the Flaked Stone Evidence in Cyprus." Unpublished paper presented
           at the American Schools of Oriental Research Annual Meetings, Napa, California.

Hordynsky, L., and I. A. Todd.
   1987   "The Surface Survey of the Site." In Todd 1987, pp. 17–20.

Hordynsky, L., and A. Kingsnorth.
   1979   "Lithic Reduction Sequences in the Vasilikos Valley: Methods and Preliminary Results." In "Vasilikos
           Valley Project: Third Preliminary Report, 1978," by I. A. Todd and Project Members, pp. 287–90,
           Journal of Field Archaeology 6:265–300.

Hordynsky, L., and M. Ritt.
   1977   "The Chipped Stone Industry at Kalavasos-Pamboules." In "Vasilikos Valley Project: Second
           Preliminary Report," by I. A. Todd and Project Members, pp. 190–96. *Journal of Field Archaeology*
           5:161–96.

Hosler, D.
   1994   *The Sounds and Colors of Power: The Sacred Metallurgical Technology of Ancient West Mexico.*
           MIT Press, Cambridge, Mass.

Hué, E.
   1907   *Musée osteologique - étude de la faune quaternaire.* Scheicher Frères, Paris.

Humphreys, I. K.
   1987   *A Functional Analysis of the Structures at Sotira Kaminoudhia in Cyprus.* M. A. Thesis, Drew
           University, Madison, New Jersey.

Iakovides, S. E.
   1990   "Mycenaean Roofs: Form and Construction." *L' Habitat Égéen Préhistorique.* Bulletin de
           Correspondance Hellenique Supplément 19:147–60.

Ionas, I.
   1988   *La maison rurale de Chypre (XVIIIe-XXe siècle): Aspects et techniques de construction.* Centre de
           Recherche Scientifique de Chypre, Nicosia.

Joukowsky, M. S.
   1986   *Prehistoric Aphrodisias: An Account of the Excavations and Artifact Studies.* Archaeologia
           Transatlantica 3. Center for Old World Archaeology and Art, Brown University, Providence.

Kaiser, T., U. M. Franklin, and V. Vitali.
   1986   "Pyrotechnology and Pottery in the Late Neolithic of the Balkans." In *Proceedings of the 24th
           International Archaeometry Symposium,* edited by J. Olin and M. J. Blackman. Smithsonian Press,
           Washington, D.C.

Karageorghis, V.
   1991   *The Coroplastic Art of Ancient Cyprus I. Chalcolithic - Late Cypriote I.* A. G. Leventis, Nicosia.

1989   "Chronique des Fouilles et Découvertes Archéologiques à Chypre en 1988." *Bulletin de Correspondance Hellenique* 113:789–853.

1988   "Chronique des Fouilles et Découvertes Archéologiques à Chypre en 1987." *Bulletin de Correspondance Hellenique* 112:794–855.

1987   "Fouilles de Sotira-*Kaminoudhia*." In "Chronique des Fouilles et Découvertes Archéologiques à Chypre en 1986." *Bulletin de Correspondance Hellenique* 111:680.

1985a   *Ancient Cypriote Art in the Pierides Foundation Museum.* Pierides Foundation, Larnaca.

1985b   *Archaeology in Cyprus, 1960–1985.* A. G. Leventis Foundation, Nicosia.

1984   "Fouilles de Sotira-*Kaminoudhia*," pp. 936–39, figs. 132–34. In "Chronique des Fouilles et Découvertes Archéologiques à Chypre en 1983." *Bulletin de Correspondance Hellenique* 108:893–971.

1983   "Chronique des Fouilles et Découvertes Archéologiques à Chypre en 1982." *Bulletin de Correspondance Hellenique* 107:905–53.

1982a   *Cyprus, From the Stone Age to the Romans.* Thames and Hudson Inc., New York.

1982b   "Fouilles de Sotira-*Kaminoudhia*," pp. 715–18, figs. 81–83. In "Chronique des Fouilles et Découvertes Archéologiques à Chypre en 1981." *Bulletin de Correspondance Hellenique* 106:685–751.

1978   "Chronique des Fouilles et Découvertes Archélogiques à Chypre en 1977." *Bulletin de Correspondance Hellenique* 102:879–938.

1976   "Chronique des Fouilles et Découvertes Archéologiques à Chypre en 1975." *Bulletin de Correspondance Hellenique* 100:839–906.

1975   "Chronique des Fouilles et Découvertes Archéologiques à Chypre en 1974." *Bulletin de Correspondance Hellenique* 99:801–51.

1974   *Excavations at Kition I. The Tombs.* Department of Antiquities, Nicosia.

1973   "Chronique des Fouilles et Découvertes Archéologiques à Chypre en 1972." *Bulletin de Correspondance Hellenique* 97:601–89.

1968   "Chronique des Fouilles et Découvertes Archéologiques à Chypre en 1967." *Bulletin de Correspondance Hellenique* 92:261–358.

1966   "Chronique des Fouilles et Découvertes Archéologiques à Chypre en 1965." *Bulletin de Correspondance Hellenique* 90:275–370.

1940–1948   "Finds from Early Cypriot Cemeteries." *Report of the Department of Antiquities, Cyprus, 1940–1948.* Department of Antiquities, Nicosia, pp. 115–52.

Karageorghis, V., and M. Demas.
    1988   *Excavations at Maa-Palaeokastro 1979–1986.* Department of Antiquities, Nicosia.

Kardulias, P. N., and R. W. Yerkes.
    1998   "Microwear and Metric Analysis of Threshing Sledge Flints from Greece and Cyprus." *Journal of Archaeological Science* 23:657–66.

Keeley, L. H.
    1980   *Experimental Determination of Stone Tool Uses.* University of Chicago Press, Chicago.

    1974   "Technique and Methodology in Microwear Studies: A Critical Review." *World Archaeology* 5:323–36.

Keeley, L. H., and M. H. Newcomer.
    1977   "Microwear Analysis of Experimental Flint Tools: A Test Case." *Journal of Archaeological Science* 4:29–62.

Keswani, P.
    1997   "Hierarchies, Heterarchies, and Urbanization Processes: The View from Bronze Age Cyprus." *Journal of Mediterranean Archaeology* 9(2):211–50.

    1994   "The Social Context of Animal Husbandry in Early Agricultural Societies: Ethnographic Insights and an Archeological Example from Cyprus." *Journal of Anthropological Archaeology* 13:255–77.

Kingery, W. D., P. B. Vandiver, and M. Prickett.
    1988   "The Beginnings of Pyrotechnology. Part II. Production and Use of Lime and Gypsum Plaster in the Pre-Pottery Neolithic Near East." *Journal of Field Archaeology* 15:219–44.

Kingsnorth, A.
    n. d.   *Kholetria-Ortos, 1992–1994 Excavations: Ground Stone.* In preparation.

    1996a   "Sydney Cyprus Survey Project 1995: The Flaked Stone." Appendix 1, pp. 295–366. In Knapp and Given 1996.

    1996b   "The Chipped Stone." In Coleman et al. 1996, pp. 178–96.

    1982   "Excavations at Kalavasos-Ayious." In "Vasilikos Valley Project: Fourth Preliminary Report, 1979–1980," by I. A. Todd and project members, pp. 50–57. *Journal of Field Archaeology* 9:35–77.

Kloutsiniotis, R., and N. Faraclas.
    1984   *Tzia (Keos). Greek Traditional Architecture.* Melissa Publishing House, Athens.

Knapp, A. B.
    1994   "Problems and Prospects in Cypriote Prehistory." *Journal of World Prehistory* 8:377–452.

Knapp, A. B., and M. Given.
    1996   "The Sydney Cyprus Survey Project (SCSP) - Third Season (1995)." *Report of the Department of Antiquities, Cyprus.* Department of Antiquities, Nicosia, pp. 295–336.

Knapp, A. B., and J. F. Cherry.
    1994   *Provenience Studies and Bronze Age Cyprus: Production, Exchange and Politico-Economic Change.* Monographs in World Archaeology 2. Prehistory Press, Madison.

Knapp, A. B., S. O. Held, I. Johnson, and P. S. Keswani.
    1994   "The Sydney-Cyprus Survey Project (SCSP). Second Preliminary Season (1993)." *Report of the Department of Antiquities, Cyprus, 1992.* Department of Antiquities, Nicosia, pp. 329–43.

Knapp, A. B., S. O. Held, I. Johnson, and E. Zangger.
1992   "The Sydney-Cyprus Survey Project –First Preliminary Season (1992)." *Report of the Department of Antiquities, Cyprus, 1992.* Department of Antiquities, Nicosia, pp. 319–36.

Kosay, H. Z.
1966   *Alaca Höyük.* Türk Tarih Kurumu, Ankara.

Koucky, F. L., and A. Steinberg.
1982   "Ancient Mining and Mineral Dressing on Cyprus." In *Early Pyrotechnology: The Evolution of the First Fire-Using Industries,* edited by T. A. Wertime and S. F. Wertime, pp. 149–80. Smithsonian Institution Press, Washington, D.C.

Krogman, W. M.
1973   *The Human Skeleton in Forensic Medicine.* Charles C. Thomas, Springfield, Ill.

Kyllo, M.
1982   "The Botanical Remains." In Peltenburg 1982, pp. 90–93, 415–36.

Lamb, W.
1936   *Excavations at Thermi in Lesbos.* University Press, Cambridge.

Le Brun, A.

1995   "Khirokitia, un Village Néolithique." In *Chypre au cœur des civilisations méditerranéennes,* pp. 14–23. Les Dossiers d' Archéologie 205, Archéologia, Dijon.

1989   *Fouilles Récentes à Khirokitia (Chypre) 1983–1986.* Éditions Recherches sur les Civilisations. Mémoire 81. Editions A.D.P.F., Paris.

1984a   *Fouilles Récentes à Khirokitia (Chypre) 1977–1981.* Etudes Néolithiques. Mémoire 41. Éditions Recherche sur les Civilizations. Editions A.D.P.F., Paris.

1984b   "La Distribution Spatiale du Materiel. Essai d'Analyse." In Le Brun 1984a., pp. 191–97.

1981   *Un Site Néolithique Précéramique en Chypre: Cap Andreas-Kastros.* Études Néolithiques. Mémoire 5. Éditions Recherche sur les Civilisations. Editions A.D.P.F., Paris.

Le Brun, A., S. Cluzan, S. J. M. Davis, J. Hansen, and J. Renault-Miskovsky.
1987   "Le néolithique précéramique de Chypre." *L'Anthropologie* 91:283–316.

Legge, A. J.
1982   "Ayios Epiktitos: The Recent Farming Economy." In Peltenburg 1982, pp. 14–20.

Lehavy, Y.
1989   "Excavations at Dhali-Agridhi: 1972, 1974, 1976A. Part 2. Dhali-Agridhi: the Neolithic by the River." In *The American Expedition to Idalion, Cyprus 1973–1980,* edited by L. E. Stager and A. M. Walker, pp. 203–43. Oriental Institute Communications 24. University of Chicago, Chicago.

Lloyd, S. E., and J. Mellaart.
1962   *Beycesultan I. The Chalcolithic and Early Bronze Age Levels.* The British Institute of Archaeology at Ankara, London.

Lubsen-Admiraal, S. M.
    1999   "The T. N. Zintilis Collection of Early Cypriot South Coast Ware." *Report of the Department of Antiquities, Cyprus, 1999*. Department of Antiquities, Nicosia, pp. 35–70.

    1988   "A Red Polished Sextet from Amsterdam." *Report of the Department of Antiquities, Cyprus, 1988*. Department of Antiquities, Nicosia, pp. 127–31.

Luedtke, B.
    1992   *An Archaeologist's Guide to Chert and Flint*. Archaeological Research Tools 7. Institute of Archaeology. University of California, Los Angeles.

MacLaurin, M. L. G.
    1980   *Cypriot Red Polished Pottery and Its Regional Variations*. Ph.D. dissertation, University of London, London.

Maddin R., T. Stech Wheeler, and J. D. Muhly.
    1977   "Tin in the Ancient Near East: Old Questions and New Finds." *Expedition* 19(2):35–47.

Maniatis, Y., and M. S. Tite.
    1981   "Technological Examination of Neolithic-Bronze Age Pottery from Central and Southeast Europe and from the Near East." *Journal of Archaeological Science* 8:59–76.

Manning, S. W.
    1993   "Prestige, Distinction, and Competition: The Anatomy of Socioeconomic Complexity in Fourth to Second Millenium B.C.E." *Bulletin of the American Schools of Oriental Research* 292:35–58.

Manning, S., and D. Conway.
    1992   "Maroni Valley Archaeological Survey Project: Preliminary Report on the 1990–1991 Field Seasons." *Report of the Department of Antiquities, Cyprus, 1992*. Department of Antiquities, Nicosia, pp. 271–83.

Manning, S. W., and S. Swiny.
    1994   "Sotira *Kaminoudhia* and the Chronology of the Early Bronze Age in Cyprus." *Oxford Journal of Archaeology* 13:149–72.

Mantzourani, E.
    1994   "Έκθεση αποτελεσμάτων της ανασκαφής στη θέση Καντού-Κουφόβουνος." *Report of the Department of Antiquities, Cyprus, 1994*. Department of Antiquities, Nicosia, pp. 31–38.

Marder, O., E. Braun, and I. Milevski.
    1995   "The Flint Assemblage of Lower Horvat `Illin: Some Technical and Economic Considerations." `Atiqot 27:63–93.

Matsuzawa, T.
    1996   "Chimpanzee Intelligence in Nature and in Captivity: Isomorphism of Symbol Use and Tool Use." In *Great Ape Societies*, edited by W. C. McGrew, L. F. Marchant, and T. Nishida, pp. 196–209. Cambridge University Press, Cambridge.

Matthews, A.
    1968   *Lilies of the Field - A Book of Cyprus Wild Flowers*. Couvas and Sons, Limassol.

McAnany, P.
   1988   "The Effects of Lithic Procurement Strategies on Tool Curation and Recycling." *Lithic Technology*
           17(1):3–11.

McCartney, C.
   1993   "An Attribute Analysis of Cypriot Dhoukani 'Teeth': Implications for the Study of Cypriot Chipped
           Stone Assemblages." *Report of the Department of Antiquities, Cyprus, 1993.* Department of
           Antiquities, Nicosia, pp. 348–64.

McDonald, W. A., and G. R. Rapp, Jr. (eds).
   1972   *The Minnesota Messenia Expedition: Reconstructing a Bronze Age Regional Environment.* The
           University of Minnesota Press, Minneapolis.

McKern, T. W., and T. D. Stewart.
   1957   *Skeletal Changes in Young American Males: Analyzed from the Standpoint of Age Identification.*
           Technical Report EP-45. Environmental Protection Research Division, Quartermaster Research and
           Development Center, U.S. Army, Natick, Mass.

McKerrell, H., and R. F. Tylecote.
   1972   "The Working of Copper-Arsenic Alloys in the Early Bronze Age and the Effect on the Determination
           of Provenance." *Proceedings of the Prehistoric Society* 38:209–18.

Meadow, R. H.
   1981   "Early animal domestication in South Asia: A First Report of the Faunal Remains from Mehrgarh,
           Pakistan." In *South Asian Archaeology 1979: Papers from the Fifth International Conference of the
           Association of South Asian Archaeologists in Western Europe held in the Museum für Kunst der
           Staalichen Museen Preussischer Kulturbesitz,* edited by Herbert Härtel, pp. 143–79. D. Reimer Verlag,
           Berlin.

Megaw, A. H. S.
   1952   "Archeology in Cyprus." *Journal of Hellenic Studies* 72:113–17.

Meikle, R. D.
   1977   *Flora of Cyprus.* Volume 1. The Bentham-Moxon Trust, Royal Botanic Gardens, Kew.

Mellink, M. J.
   1991   "Anatolian Contacts with Chalcolithic Cyprus." *Bulletin of the American Schools of Oriental Research*
           282/283:167–75.

   1989   "Anatolia and Foreign Relations of Tarsus in the Early Bronze Age." In Emre et al. 1989, pp. 319–
           31.

   1973   "Excavations at Karataş-Semayük and Elmali, Lycia, 1972." *American Journal of Archaeology*
           77:293–303.

   1969   "Excavations at Karataş-Semayük in Lycia." *American Journal of Archaeology* 73: 319–31.

   1968   "Excavations at Karataş-Semayük in Lycia, 1967." *American Journal of Archaeology* 72:243–59.

Merrillees, R. S.
   1991   "The Principles of Cypriot Bronze Age Pottery Classification." In Barlow et al. 1991, pp. 237–40.

1986   "A 16ᵗʰ Century B. C. Tomb Group from Central Cyprus with Links both East and West." In *Acts of the International Archaeological Symposium Cyprus Between the Orient and the Occident, Nicosia, 8–14 September 1985,* edited by Vassos Karageorghis, pp. 114–48. Department of Antiquities, Nicosia.

1984   "Ambelikou-*Aletri*: A Preliminary Report." *Report of the Department of Antiquities, Cyprus, 1984.* Department of Antiquities, Nicosia, pp. 1–13.

1978   *Introduction to the Bronze Age Archaeology of Cyprus.* Studies In Mediterranean Archaeology-Pocket Book 9. Paul Åströms Förlag Göteborg.

1974   "Settlement, Sanctuary and Cemetery in Bronze Age Cyprus." In *The Cypriot Bronze Age: Some Recent Australian Contributions to the Prehistory of Cyprus,* edited by J. Birmingham, pp. 44–57. Australian Studies in Archaeology, Sydney.

Metcalfe, D., and K. M. Heath.
1990   "Microrefuse and site structure: The Hearths and Floors of the Heartbreak Hotel." *American Antiquity* 55(4):781–96.

Mogelonski , M. K.
1996   "Ground Stone." In Coleman et al. 1996, pp. 142–77.

Mohen, J.-P.
1990   *Métallurgie Préhistorique. Introduction à la paléométallurgie.* Masson, Paris.

Morris, D.
1985   *The Art of Ancient Cyprus.* Phaidon Press, Oxford.

Morris, H.
1977   *Chipped Stone Implements From Phaneromeni, Cyprus. (a) Preliminary (b) Catalogue and Analysis.* M.A. Thesis. University of Minnesota, Minneapolis.

Mortensen, P.
1970   "A Preliminary Study of the Chipped Stone Industry from Beidha, An Early Neolithic Village in Southern Jordan." *Acta Archaeologica* 41:1–54.

Muhly, J. D.
1985   "Sources of Tin and the Beginnings of Bronze Age Metallurgy." *American Journal of Archaeology* 89:275–91.

1978   "New Evidence for Sources of Trade in Bronze Age Tin." In *The Search for Ancient Tin,* edited by A. D. Franklin, J. S. Olin, and T. A. Wertime, pp. 43–48. Smithsonian Institution, Washington, D.C.

1976   "Supplement to Copper and Tin. The Distribution of Mineral Resources and the Nature of the Metal Trade in the Bronze Age." *Transactions of the Connecticut Academy of Arts and Sciences* 46:77–136.

1973   "Copper and Tin. The Distribution of Mineral Resources and the Nature of Metal Trade in the Bronze Age." *Transactions of the Connecticut Academy of Arts and Sciences* 43:161–535.

Muhly, J. D., R. Maddin, and V. Karageorghis.
1982   *Early Metallurgy in Cyprus, 4000–500 BC. Acta of the International Archaeological Symposium (Larnaca, Cyprus 1981).* The Pierides Foundation, Nicosia.

Murray, M. A.
 1991   "The Plant Remains." In Peltenburg 1991, p. 72.

Muscarella, O. W.
 1988   *Bronze and Iron: Ancient Near Eastern Bronzes in the Metropolitan Museum of Art.* The Metropolitan
         Museum of Art, New York.

Myers, J. W., E. E. Myers, and G. Cadogan.
 1992   *The Aerial Atlas of Ancient Crete.* University of California Press, Los Angeles.

Myres, J. L.
 1897   "Excavations in Cyprus in 1894." *Journal of Hellenic Studies* 17:134–73.

Myres, J. L., and M. Ohnefalsch-Richter.
 1899   *Catalogue of the Cyprus Museum.* Clarendon Press, Oxford.

Native Way
 n.d.   *Catalogue.* P.O. Box 159, Washington, MS. 39190.

Naumann, R.
 1971   *Architektur Kleinasiens von ihren Anfängen bis zum Ende der Hethitischen Zeit.* Wasmuth, Tübingen.

Netzer, E.
 1992   "Building Materials in the Prehistoric Periods Until the End of the Prehistoric Period." In *The
         Architecture of Ancient Israel from Prehistoric to the Persian Periods. In Memory of Immanuel
         (Munya) Dunayevski*, edited by A. Kepinski and R. Reich, pp. 17–27. Israel Exploration Society,
         Jerusalem.

Neuville, R.
 1934   "La Préhistoire de Palestine." *Revue Biblique* 43:237–59.

Newcomer, M. H.
 1976   "Spontaneous Retouch. Second International Symposium on Flint." *Staringia* 3:62–64.

Nicolaou, I.
 1990   "The Jewellery of Cyprus from Neolithic to Roman Times." *Archaeologia Cypria* 11:117–20.

Nicolaou, I., and K. Nicolaou.
 1988   "Dhenia-*Kafkalla* and *Mali* Tombs." *Report of the Department of Antiquities, Cyprus, 1988.*
         Department of Antiquities, Nicosia, pp. 71–120.

Nishiaki, Y.
 1990   "Corner-Thinned Blades: A New Obsidian Tool Type from a Pottery Neolithic Mound in the Khabur
         Basin, Syria." *Bulletin of the American Schools of Oriental Research* 280/281:5–14.

Northover, J. P.
 1989   "Properties and Use of Arsenic-Copper Alloys." *Der Anschnitt* 7:111–18.

Ohnefalsch-Richter, M.
 1893   *Kypros, the Bible and Homer.* Asher, London.

Olin, J., and M. J. Blackman (eds).
    1986   *Proceedings of the 24th International Archaeometry Symposium.* Smithsonian Press, Washington,
             D.C.

Olsson, I.
    1987   "Carbon 14 Dating and the Interpretation of the Validity of some Dates from the Bronze Age in the
             Aegean." In *High, Middle or Low, Acts of an International Colloquium on Absolute Chronology
             Held at the University of Gothenburg, 20th-22nd August, 1987,* edited by Paul Aström, pp. 4–38.
             Studies in Mediterranean Archaeology Pocket Book 56–57. Paul Åströms Förlag, Göteborg.

Orphanides, A. G.
    1983   *Bronze Age Anthropomorphic Figurines in the Cesnola Collection at the Metropolitan Museum of
             Art.* Studies in Mediterranean Archaeology Pocket Book 20. Paul Åströms Förlag, Göteborg.

Overbeck, J. C., and S. Swiny.
    1972   *Two Cypriot Bronze Age Sites at Kafkallia (Dhali).* Studies in Mediterranean Archaeology 33. Paul
             Åströms Förlag, Göteborg.

Özgüç, T., and R. Temizer.
    1993   "The Eskiyapar Treasure." In *Aspects of Art and Iconography: Anatolia and its Neighbors. Studies in
             Honor of Nimet Özgüç,* edited by M. J. Mellink, E. Porada, and T. Özgüç, pp. 613–28. Türk Tarih
             Kurumu, Ankara.

Panayiotou, A.
    1980   "Cu-Ni-Co-Fe Sulphide Mineralization, Limassol Forest, Cyprus." In *Ophiolites: Proceedings
             International Ophiolite Symposium, Cyprus 1979,* pp. 102–16. Cyprus Geological Survey Department,
             Nicosia.

Pantazis, T. M.
    1973   "A Study of the Secondary Limestones (Havara and Kafkalla) of Cyprus." *Geographical Chronicles*
             4:12–39.

Papageorghiou, A.
    1991   "Chronique des Fouilles et Découvertes Archéologiques à Chypre en 1990." *Bulletin de
             Correspondance Hellenique* 115:789–833.

Payne, S.
    1973   "Kill-off Patterns in Sheep and Goats: The Mandibles from Assvan Kale." *Anatolian Studies* 23:281–
             303.

Pearlman, D. A.
    1984   *Threshing Sledges in the Eastern Mediterranean: Ethnoarchaeology with Chert Knappers and
             Dhoukanes in Cyprus.* M.A. Thesis. Center for Ancient Studies. University of Minnesota, Minneapolis.

Peltenburg, E. J.
    1998   *Lemba Archaeological Project* II.1A. *Excavations at Kissonerga-Mosphilia, 1979–1992.* Studies In
             Mediterranean Archaeology 70:2. Paul Åströms Förlag, Jonsered.

    1996   "From Isolation to State Formation in Cyprus, c. 3500 – 1500 B.C." In *Development of the Cypriot
             Economy from the Prehistoric Period to the Present Day,* edited by V. Karageorghis and D. Michaelides,
             pp. 1–44. Lithographica, Nicosia.

1992   "Birth Pendants in Life and Death: Evidence from Kissonerga Grave 563." In *Studies in Honour of Vassos Karageorghis*, edited by G. K. Ioannides, pp. 27–37. Leventis Foundation, Nicosia.

1991   "Kissonerga-Mosphilia: A Major Chalcolithic Site in Cyprus." *Bulletin of the American Schools of Oriental Research* 282/283:17–35.

1991a   *Lemba Archaeological Project* II.2. *A Ceremonial Area at Kissonerga*. Studies in Mediterranean Archaeology 70(3). Paul Åströms Förlag, Göteborg.

1990   "Chalcolithic Cyprus." In *Cyprus Before the Bronze Age*, edited by C. Newman Helms, pp. 5–24. The J. Paul Getty Museum, Malibu.

1989   (ed.). *Early Society in Cyprus*. Edinburgh University, Edinburgh.

1988   "Lemba Archaeological Project, Cyprus, 1986." *Levant* 20:231–35.

1987a   "A Late Prehistoric Pottery Sequence for Western Cyprus." In Rupp 1987a, pp. 53–69.

1987b   "Lemba Archaeological Project, Cyprus, 1985." *Levant* 19:221–24.

1985   *Lemba Archaeological Project* I. *Excavations at Lemba-Lakkous, 1976–1983*. Studies in Mediterranean Archaeology 70(1). Paul Åströms Forlag, Göteborg.

1984   "Lemba Archaeological Project, Cyprus, 1982: Preliminary Report." *Levant* 16:55–65.

1982   (ed.) *Vrysi, A Subterranean Settlement in Cyprus. Excavations at Prehistoric Ayios Epiktitos Vrysi, 1969–1973*. Aris and Phillips, Warminster.

1979   "Lemba Archaeological Project, Cyprus, 1976–1977: Preliminary Report." *Levant* 11:9–45.

Peltenburg, E. J., and Project Members.
1986   "Excavations at Kissonerga-*Mosphilia* 1985." *Report of the Department of Antiquities, Cyprus, 1986*. Department of Antiquities, Nicosia, pp. 28–39.

1983   "The Prehistory of West Cyprus: Ktima Lowlands Investigations 1979–82." *Report of the Department of Antiquities, Cyprus, 1983*. Department of Antiquities, Nicosia, pp. 9–55.

Penhallurick, R. D.
1986   *Tin in Antiquity: Its Mining and Trade Throughout the Ancient World with Particular Reference to Cornwall*. Institute of Metals, London.

Perlès, C.
1992   "In Search of Lithic Strategies: A Cognitive Approach to Prehistoric Chipped Stone Assemblages." In *Representations in Archaeology*, edited by J. C. Gardin and C. S. Peebles, pp. 223–47. Indiana University Press, Bloomington.

1987   *Les Industries Lithiques Taillées de la Grotte de Franchthi, (Grèce)*. Tome I. *Présentation Générale et Industries Paléolithiques*. Indiana University Press, Bloomington.

Pernicka, E.
1990   "Gewinnung und Verbreitung der Metalle in prähistorischer Zeit." *Jahrbuch des Römisch-Germanischen Zentralmuseums Mainz* 37(1):21–129.

Perrot, J.
n.d.   "Procédés de débitage clactonien et levalloisien dans le Néolithique et le Chalcolithique de Chypre."
           Unpublished manuscript cited in Le Brun 1981.

Philippou, M.
1974   *From Cyprus With Love - Flowers of Cyprus.* Zavallis Press, Nicosia.

Pieridou, A.
1967   "Pieces of Cloth from the Early and Middle Cypriote Periods." *Report of the Department of Antiquities,
           Cyprus, 1967.* Department of Antiquities, Nicosia, pp. 25–29.

Pigott, V. C.
1990   "Bronze I, In Pre-Islamic Iran." In *Encyclopaedia Iranica* IV, edited by E. Yarshater, pp. 457–71.
           Routledge & Kegan Paul, London.

Pilides, D.
1996   "Storage Jars as Evidence of the Economy of Cyprus in the Late Bronze Age." In *The Development
           of the Cypriot Economy from the Prehistoric Period to the Present Day*, edited by V. Karageorghis
           and D. Michaelides, pp. 107–24. University of Cyprus, Nicosia.

Pingarrion, L.
1981   "Determinación de Temperaturas de Cocción de Cerámica Arquelógia por Métodos Dilamétricos."
           Antropologia y Tecnica 1:31–56.

Pingel, V.
1995   "Technical Aspects of Prehistoric Gold Objects on the Basis of Material Analyses." In *Prehistoric
           Gold in Europe. Mines, Metallurgy and Manufacture*, edited by G. Morteani, and J. P. Northover, pp.
           385–98. Kluwer Academic, Dordrecht.

Pinker, S.
1995   *The Language Instinct.* Harper Perennial, New York.

Pitzer, J. M.
1977   *Basic Sources for the Study of Burins.* Archaeological Research Facility. University of California,
           Berkeley.

du Plat Taylor, J.
1957   *Myrtou-Pigadhes: A Late Bronze Age Sanctuary in Cyprus.* Oxford University Press, Oxford.

1952   "A Late Bronze Age Settlement at Apliki, Cyprus." *Antiquaries Journal* 32:133–67.

Plenderleith, H. J.
1950   "Object of Gold, Tomb 164 B, no. 40." In Stewart, E., and J. R. 1950, p. 370.

Plog, S., F. Plog, and W. Wait.
1978   "Decision Making in Modern Surveys." In *Advances in Archaeological Method and Theory* 1, edited
           by M. B. Schiffer, pp. 383–421. Academic Press, New York.

Polunin, O., and A. Huxley.
1981   *Flowers of the Mediterranean.* Chatto and Windus, London.

Pope, S. T.
  1918   "A Study of Bows and Arrows." *University of California Publications in American Archaeology and Ethnology* 13(9):329–414.

Pullen, J. D.
  1990   "The Early Bronze Age Village on Tsoungiza Hill, Ancient Nemea." In *L' Habitat Égéen Préhistorique. Bulletin de Correspondance Hellenique Supplément* 19:331–46.

Ragette, F.
  1974   *Architecture in Lebanon: The Lebanese House During the 18th and 19th Centuries.* American University of Beirut, Beirut.

Rapp, G. R., Jr.
  1999   "Copper, Tin, and Arsenic Sources in the Aegean Bronze Age." In *Meletemata: Studies in Aegean Archaeology Presented to Malcolm H. Wiener as He Enters His 65th Year*, edited by P. P. Betancourt, V. Karageorghis, R. Laffineur and W.D. Niemeier, Volume 1, pp. 699–704. (Aegeum 20) Université de Liège, Belgium.

  1998   "Composition and Softening/Fluid Temperatures of some Ancient Cypriot Slags." In *Metallurgica Antiqua in Honour of Hans-Gert Bachmann and Robert Maddin. Der Anschnitt*, Beiheft 8:177–82.

  1988   "On the Origins of Copper and Bronze Alloying." In *The Beginning of Metals and Alloys*, edited by Robert Maddin, pp. 21–27. MIT Press, Cambridge.

  1986   "Assessing Archaeological Evidence for Seismic Catastrophe." *Geoarchaeology* 1(4):365–79.

  1982   "Native Copper and the Beginning of Smelting: Chemical Studies." In Muhly et al. 1982, pp. 33–38.

Rapp, G. R. Jr., and S. E. Aschenbrenner (eds).
  1978   *Excavations at Nichoria in Southwest Greece.* University of Minnesota Press, Minneapolis.

Reade, J. (ed).
  1981   *Chalcolithic Cyprus and Western Asia.* British Museum Occasional Paper 26. British Museum, London.

Reese, D.S.
  n.d.   "The Shells from Prastio-*Agios Savvas tis Karonis Monastery*." To appear in final excavation report.

Renfrew, C., and J. M. Wagstaff (eds).
  1982   *An Island Polity: the Archaeology of Exploitation at Melos.* Cambridge University Press, Cambridge.

Ridout-Sharpe, J. S.
  1985   "The Mollusca." In Peltenburg 1985, pp. 103–6, 212–16, 298–305.

  1991   "The Mollusca." In Peltenburg 1991, pp. 75–84.

Roberts, J.
  1963   "Determination of the Firing temperature of Ancient Ceramics by Measurement of Thermal Expansion." *Archaeometry* 6:21–25.

Robertson, L. F.
  1986   *Corpus of Cypriote Antiquities 11. The Brock University Collection of Cypriote Antiquities.* Studies in Mediterranean Archaeology 20:11. Paul Åströms Förlag, Göteborg.

Ronen, A.
    n.d.   *Threshing Flint Knapping in Cyprus*. Haifa: University of Haifa. (Video)

Rosen, S. A.
    1997   *Lithics After the Stone Age: A Handbook of Stone Tools from the Levant*. Alta Mira Press, Walnut
              Creek, California.

Rupp, D. W. (ed).
    1987a   *Western Cyprus: Connections. An Archaeological Symposium Held at Brock University, St. Catharines,
              Ontario, Canada*. Studies in Mediterranean Archaeology 77. Paul Åströms Förlag, Göteborg.

    1987b   "The Canadian Palaipaphos Survey Project: An Overview of the 1986 Season." *Echos du Monde
              Classique/Classical Views* 30 n.s. 6(2):217–24.

Rupp, D. W., and C. D'Annibale.
    1995   "Preliminary Report of the 1994 Field season of the Western Cyprus Project at Prastio-*Agios Savvas
              tis Karonis Monastery* (Pafos District)." *Report of the Department of Antiquities, Cyprus, 1995*.
              Department of Antiquities, Nicosia, pp. 33–48.

Rupp, D. W., J. T. Clarke, C. D'Annibale, J. Critchley, and P. W. Croft.
    1994   "Preliminary Report of the 1993 Field season of the Western Cyprus Project at Prastio-*Agios Savvas
              tis Karonis Monastery* (Paphos District, Cyprus)." *Report of the Department of Antiquities, Cyprus,
              1994*. Department of Antiquities, Nicosia, pp. 315–28.

Rupp, D. W., J. T. Clarke, C. D'Annibale, R. H. King, and P. W. Croft.
    1993   "The Western Cyprus Project: 1992 Field Season." *Report of the Department of Antiquities, Cyprus,
              1993*. Department of Antiquities, Nicosia, pp. 381–412.

Rupp, D. W., J. T. Clarke, C. D'Annibale, and S. T. Stewart.
    1992   "The Canadian Palaiopaphos Survey Project: 1991 Field Season." *Report of the Department of
              Antiquities, Cyprus, 1992*. Department of Antiquities, Nicosia, pp. 285–318.

Rupp, D. W., L. W. Sorensen, J. Lund, R. H. King, and W. A. Fox.
    1987   "The Canadian Palaiopaphos Survey Project: Third Preliminary Report, 1983–1985." *Acta
              Archaeologica* 57:27–45.

    1984   "Canadian Palaiopaphos (Cyprus) Survey Project: Second Preliminary Report, 1980–1982." *Journal
              of Field Archaeology* 11(2):133–54.

Rye, O. S.
    1981   *Pottery Technology: Principles and Reconstruction*. Manuals on Archaeology 4. Taraxacum,
              Washington, D.C.

Saghieh, M.
    1983   *Byblos in the Third Millennium B.C.: A Reconstruction of the Stratigraphy and a Study of the Cultural
              Connections*. Aris and Philips, Warminster.

Schaar, K. W.
    1990   "Aegean House Form: A Reflection of Cultural Behaviour." In *L' Habitat Égéen Préhistorique. Bulletin
              de Correspondance Hellenique Supplément* 19:174–82.

    1985   "House Forms at Tarsus, Alambra and Lemba." *Report of the Department of Antiquities of Cyprus,
              1985*. Department of Antiquities, Nicosia, pp. 37–44.

Schaeffer, C. F. A.
   1969   *Ugaritica VI*. Librairie Orientaliste Paul Geuthner, Paris.

   1962   *Ugaritica IV*. Librairie Orientaliste Paul Geuthner, Paris.

   1936   *Missions en Chypre 1932–1935*. Librairie Orientaliste Paul Geuthner, Paris.

Schiffer, M. B., A. P. Sullivan, and T. C. Klinger.
   1978   The Design of Archaeological Surveys." *World Archaeology* 10:1–28.

Seton-Williams, V.
   1936   The Implements of Flint and Chert." In Dikaios 1939, pp. 51–53.

Sharp, L.
   1952   Steel Axes for Stone Age Australians." *Human Organization* 11:17–22.

Sheets, P.
   1990   Review of *Time, Energy, and Stone Tools*, edited by R. Torrence. *Journal of Field Archaeology*, 17(4):501–2.

Shepard, A. O.
   1965   *Ceramics for the Archaeologist*. Carnegie Institution, Washington, D.C.

Silver, I. A.
   1969   "The Ageing of Domestic Animals." In *Science In Archaeology*, 2nd edition, edited by D. R. Brothwell and E. S. Higgs, pp. 283-302. Thames and Hudson, London.

Simmons, A. H.
   1996   Whose Myth? Archaeological Data, Interpretations, and Implications for the Human Association with Extinct Pleistocene Fauna at Akrotiri Aetokremnos, Cyprus." *Journal of Mediterranean Archaeology* 9(1):97–105.

   1992   "Preliminary Report on the Akrotiri Peninsula Survey, 1991." *Report of the Department of Antiquities, Cyprus, 1992*. Department of Antiquities, Nicosia, pp. 9–11.

   1991a   "Humans, Island Colonization and Pleistocene Extinctions in The Mediterranean: The View from Akrotiri-Aetokremnos, Cyprus." *Antiquity* 65:857–69.

   1991b   "Preliminary Report on the Interdisciplinary Excavations of Akrotiri-Aetokremnos (Site E): 1987, 1988, 1990." *Report of the Department of Antiquities, Cyprus, 1991*. Department of Antiquities, Nicosia, pp. 7–14.

   1989   "Preliminary Report on the 1988 Test Excavations at Akrotiri-Aetokremnos, Cyprus." *Report of the Department of Antiquities, Cyprus, 1989*. Department of Antiquities, Nicosia, pp. 1–5.

   1988   "Test Excavations at Akrotiri-Aetokremnos (Site E): an Early Prehistoric Occupation in Cyprus." *Report of the Department of Antiquities, Cyprus, 1988*. Department of Antiquities, Nicosia, pp. 15–23.

Simmons, A., and Kingsnorth, A.
   1997   "The Discussion Continues; Human Impact on the Environment in Prehistoric Cyprus." Unpublished paper presented at the 1997 Annual American Schools of Oriental Research Academic Meeting, Napa, California.

Simmons, A. H., and M. R. Rose.
1999   "A Comparative Study of the Aetokremnos Chipped Stone." Chapter 17. In *Faunal Extinction in an Island Society: Pygmy Hippopotamus Hunters of Cyprus*, edited by A. H. Simmons. Kluwer Academic/ Plenum, New York.

Simpson, G. G., A. Roe, and R. C. Lewontin.
1960   *Quantitative Zoology*. Harcourt, Brace and World, Inc., New York.

Singer, C., E. J. Holmyard, and A.R. Hall (eds).
1954   *A History of Technology*. 5 volumes. Oxford University Press, New York.

Skinner, E. J., J. L. Fagan, and P. W. Ainsworth.
1989   "Lithic Landscape: Technological Constraints of Size, Shape, and Amount of Cortex." Unpublished paper presented at the 47th Plains Anthropological Conference, Sioux Falls, South Dakota.

Smith, M. A.
1996   "The Chipped Stone Assemblage." In Frankel and Webb 1996b, pp. 102–9.

de Sonneville-Bordes, D., and J. Perrot.
1954–56 "Lexique de la typologie du paleolithique superieur." *Bulletin de la Societe Prehistorique Francaise* 1–9:51-59.

Soren, D.
1985   "An Earthquake on Cyprus. New Discoveries from Kourion." *Archaeology* 38(2):52–59.

Soren, D., and E. Lane.
1981   "New Ideas About the Destruction of Paphos." *Report of the Department of Antiquities, Cyprus, 1981*. Department of Antiquities, Nicosia, pp. 178–83.

South, A.
1992   "Kalavasos-Ayios Dhimitrios 1991." *Report of the Department of Antiquities, Cyprus, 1992*. Department of Antiquities, Nicosia, pp. 133–45.

1985   "Figurines and other Objects from Kalavasos-Ayious." *Levant* 17: 65–79.

Speth, J. D.
1985   "Experimental Investigation of Hard-Hammer Percussion Flaking." In *Experiments in Flintworking* 2, edited by D. E. Crabtree and J. D. Speth, pp. 51–80. Idaho State University Museum Special Publication 10. Idaho State University, Pocatello.

Spier, R. F. G.
1970   *From the Hand of Man: Primitive and Preindustrial Technologies*. Houghton Mifflin, Boston.

Spitzenberger, F.
1979   "Die Säugeitierfauna Zyperns, Tiel II, Chiroptera, Lagomorpha, Carnivora und Artiodactyla." *Annalen des Naturhistorischen Museums Wien* 82:439–65.

1978   "Die Säugeitierfauna Zyperns, Tiel I, Insectivora und Rodentia." *Annalen des Naturhistorischen Museums Wien* 81:401–41.

Stager, L.
1985   "The Firstfruits of Civilization." In *Palestine in the Bronze and Iron Ages: Papers in Honour of Olga Tufnell*, edited by J. N. Tubb, pp. 172–88. Institute of Archaeology, London.

Stanley-Price, N. P.
1979   *Early Prehistoric Settlement in Cyprus, 6500–3000 B.C.* British Archaeological Reports International Series 65. British Archaeological Reports, Oxford.

Steele, D. G., and C. A. Bramblett.
1988   *The Anatomy and Biology of the Human Skeleton.* Texas A&M University Press, College Station.

Steinberg, A., and F. L. Koucky.
1974   "Preliminary Metallurgical Research on the Ancient Cypriot Copper Industry." In *The American Expedition to Idalion, Cyprus*, edited by L. E. Stager, A. Walker, and G. E. Wright. BASOR Supplementary Volume 18:148–78. American Schools of Oriental Research, Cambridge.

Stekelis, M.
1961   "The Flint Implements." In Dikaios 1961, pp. 230–34.

1953   "The Flint Implement Technologies." In Dikaios 1953, pp. 409–13.

Stewart, E., and J. R. Stewart.
1950   *Vounous 1937–38: Field Report on the Excavations Sponsored by the British School at Athens.* Skrifter Utgivna av Svenska Instituet I Rom 14, Lund.

Stewart, J. R.
1992   *Corpus of Cypriot Artefacts of the Early Bronze Age.* Part. II. Studies In Mediterranean Archaeology 3(2). Paul Åströms Förlag, Jonsered.

1988   *Corpus of Cypriot Artefacts of the Early Bronze Age.* Part. I. Studies In Mediterranean Archaeology 3(1). Paul Åströms Förlag, Göteborg.

1965   "Notes on Cyprus." *Opuscula Atheniensia* 6:157–64.

1962   *The Swedish Cyprus Expedition* IV:IA. *The Early Bronze Age in Cyprus*, pp. 205–401. The Swedish Cyprus Expedition, Lund.

1957   "The Melbourne Cyprus Expedition, 1955." *University of Melbourne Gazette* 13(1):1–3.

1939   "Decorated Tomb Façades, Cyprus." *Antiquity* 13:461–63.

Stewart, S. T.
1992   "Chert Utilization." In Rupp et al. 1992, pp. 312–14.

1987   "A Model of Prehistoric Chert Acquisition in the Paphos District, Cyprus." In Rupp 1987a, pp. 43–51.

1985   "Socio-cultural and Functional Aspects of Lithic Raw Material Selections in the Paphos District, Cyprus." In *Status, Structure and Stratification: Current Archaeological Reconstructions: Proceedings of the Sixteenth Annual University of Calgary Archaeological Association Conference*, edited by M. Thompson, M. T. Garcia, and F. J. Kense, pp. 105–11. University of Calgary, Archaeological Association, Calgary.

Stockton, E.
1968   "Pre-Neolithic Remains at Kyrenia, Cyprus." *Report of the Department of Antiquities, Cyprus, 1968.* Department of Antiquities, Nicosia, pp. 16–19.

Stos-Fertner, Z., and N. H. Gale.
  1979   "Chemical and Lead Isotope Analysis of Ancient Egyptian Gold, Silver and Lead." In *Proceedings of the 18th International Symposium on Archaeometry and Archaeological Prospection (Bonn 1978) Archeo-Physica 10*. Bonn: 299–314.

Stuart-Macadam, P.
  1992   "Porotic Hyperostosis: A New Perspective." *American Journal of Physical Anthropology* 87:39–47.

Stokoe, J. (rev. by F. Rose).
  1965   *The Observer's Book of Ferns*. Frederick Warne, London.

Stronach, D. B.
  1957   "The Development and Diffusion of Metal Types in Early Bronze Age Anatolia." *Anatolian Studies* 7:55–88.

Swanson, E. (ed).
  1975   *Lithic Technology, Making and Using Stone Tools*. Mouton, Le Hague.

Swiny, H. W. (ed.).
  1982   *An Archaeological Guide to the Ancient Kourion Area and the Akrotiri Peninsula*. Department of Antiquities, Nicosia.

Swiny, S.
  1997   "The Early Bronze Age." In *A History of Cyprus*. Volume 1, edited by T. Papadopoulos, pp. 171–212. Archbishop Makarios III Foundation, Office of Cypriot History, Nicosia.

  1995   "Le Bronze Ancien et le Bronze Moyen." In *Chypre au coeur des civilisations méditerranéennes*, pp. 30–35. Les Dossiers d'Archéologie 205, Archéologia, Dijon.

  1991   "Reading the Prehistoric Record: A View from the South in the Late Third Millennium B.C." In Barlow et al. 1991, pp. 37–44.

  1989   "Prehistoric Cyprus: A Current Perspective." *Biblical Archaeologist* 52:178–89.

  1989   "From Roundhouse to Duplex: A Re-Assessment of Prehistoric Bronze Age Society." In Peltenburg 1989, pp. 14–31.

  1988   "The Pleistocene Fauna of Cyprus and Recent Discoveries of the Akrotiri Peninsula." *Report of the Department of Antiquities, Cyprus, 1988*. Department of Antiquities, Nicosia, pp. 1–14.

  1986a   "The Philia Culture and its Foreign Relations." In *Acts of the International Archaeological Symposium Cyprus Between the Orient and the Occident Nicosia, 8–14 September 1985*, edited by V. Karageorghis, pp. 29–44. Department of Antiquities, Nicosia.

  1986   *The Kent State University Expedition to Episkopi* Phaneromeni. Part 2. Studies in Mediterranean Archaeology 44(2). Paul Åströms Förlag, Nicosia.

  1985a   "The Cyprus American Archaeological Research Institute Excavations at Sotira *Kaminoudhia* and the Origins of the Philia Culture." In *Acts of the Second International Congress of Cypriot Studies, Nicosia, 20–25 April 1982,* Volume A, edited by T. Papadopoulos and S. A. Hadjistyllis, pp. 13–26. Society of Cypriot Studies, Nicosia.

1985   "Sotira-Kaminoudhia and the Chalcolithic/Early Bronze Age Transition in Cyprus." In Karageorghis 1985b, pp. 115–24.

1982   "A Spiral Game (Mehen) from Lemba Area II?" Appendix 4. In E. Peltenburg, "Lemba Archaeological Project, Cyprus 1980: Preliminary Report." *Levant* 14:53–54.

1982a   "Correlations Between the Composition and Function of Bronze Age Metal Types in Cyprus." In Muhly et al. 1982, pp. 69–79.

1982b   "Sotira Kaminoudhia" in H.W. Swiny 1982, pp. 20–22.

1981   "Bronze Age Settlement Patterns in Southwest Cyprus." *Levant* 13:51–87.

1980   "Bronze Age Gaming Stones from Cyprus." *Report of the Department of Antiquities, Cyprus, 1980.* Department of Antiquities, Nicosia, pp. 54–78.

1979   *Southern Cyprus, c. 2000–1500 B.C.* Ph.D. dissertation, Institute of Archaeology, University of London, London.

1976   "Stone 'Offering Tables' from Episkopi *Phaneromeni.*" *Report of the Department of Antiquities, Cyprus, 1976.* Department of Antiquities, Nicosia, pp. 43–56.

1972   "The Fortified Settlement." In Overbeck and Swiny 1972, pp. 24–31.

Swiny, S., and C. Mavromatis.
2000   "Land Behind Kourion: Results of the 1997 Sotira Archaeological Project Survey." *Report of the Department of Antiquities, Cyprus, 2000.* Department of Antiquities, Nicosia, pp. 433–52.

Szabo, A., and T. J. Barfield.
1991   *Afghanistan, An Atlas of Indigenous Domestic Architecture.* University of Texas, Austin.

Taramides, G.
1999   *Applied Thermodynamics in the Prehistoric Pottery of Cyprus.* G. Taramides, Nicosia.

Tatton-Brown, V., V. Karageorghis, E. J. Peltenburg, and S. Swiny.
1979   *Cyprus BC: 7000 Years of History.* British Museum, London.

Thalhammer, O., E. F. Stumpfel, and A. Panayiotou.
1986   "Postmagmatic, Hydrothermal Origin of Sulfide and Arsenide Mineralizations at Limassol Forest, Cyprus." *Mineralium Deposita* 21:95–105.

Thimme, J. (ed).
1977   *Art and Culture of the Cyclades. Handbook of an Ancient Civilization.* C. F. Müller, Karlsruhe.

Thomas, G.
1988   "The Maa Chalcolithic Excavations." In *Excavations at Maa-Palaeokastro 1979-1986*, edited by V. Karageorghis and M. Demas, pp. 267–89. Department of Antiquities, Nicosia.

Thuesen, I.
1988   *Hama. Fouilles et Recherches 1931–1938. Volume 1. The Pre-and Protohistoric Periods.* København, Nationalmuseet.

Tite, M. S.
  1969   "Determination of the Firing Temperature of Ancient Ceramics by Measurement of Thermal
          Expansion: A Reassessment." *Archaeometry* 11:131–43.

Tite, M. S., Y. Maniatis, N. Meeks, M. Bimson, M. Hughes, and S. Leppard.
  1982   "Technological Studies of Ancient Ceramics from the Near East, Aegean and Southeast Europe." In
          Early Pyrotechnology, edited by T. Wertime and S. Wertime, pp. 61–71. Smithsonian Institution
          Press, Washington, D.C.

Tixier, J.
  1974   "Glossary for the Description of Stone Tools, with Special Reference to the Epipalaeolithic of the
          Maghreb." Trans. M. H. Newcomer. *Newsletter of Lithic Technology, Special Publication 1.*
          Washington State University, Pullman.

  1963   *Typologie de l'Epipaleolithique du Maghreb*. Memoires du Centre de Recherches Anthropologiques
          et Ethnographiques 2. Arts et Metiers Graphiques, Paris.

Tixier, J., M.-L. Inizan, and H. Roche.
  1980   *Préhistoire de la Pierre Tailleé*. I. *Terminologie et Technologie*. Cercle de Recherches et d'Études
          Préhistorique, Valbonne.

Todd, I. A.
  1987   *Vasilikos Valley Project 6 . Excavations at Kalavasos-Tenta I*. Studies in Mediterranean Archaeology
          71(6). Paul Åströms Förlag, Göteborg.

  1986   (ed.) *Vasilikos Valley Project 1: The Bronze Age Cemetery in Kalavasos Village*. Studies In
          Mediterranean Archaeology 71(1). Paul Åströms Förlag, Göteborg.

  1985   "A Middle Bronze Age Tomb at Psematismenos-*Trelloukkas*." *Report of the Department of Antiquities,
          Cyprus, 1985*. Department of Antiquities, Nicosia, pp. 55–77.

  1982   "Vasilikos Valley Project: Fourth Preliminary Report, 1979–1980." *Journal of Field Archaeology*
          9:35–79.

Todd, T. W., and D. W. Lyon, Jr.
  1924   "Endocranial Suture Closure Part 1: Adult Males of White Stock." *American Journal of Physical
          Anthropology* 7(3)325–84.

Torrence, R.
  1982   "The Obsidian Quarries and Their Use." In *An Island Polity: The Archaeology of Exploitation at
          Melos*, edited by. C. Renfrew and J. M. Wagstaff, pp. 193–221. Cambridge University Press,
          Cambridge.

Toumazou, M. K., R. W. Yerkes, and P. N. Kardulias.
  1998   "Athienou Archaeological Project: Investigations in the Malloura Valley, Cyprus, 1990-1995." *Journal
          of Field Archaeology* 25:163–82.

  1992   "Excavation and Survey in the Malloura Valley, Central Cyprus: The 1991 Season." *Old World
          Archaeology Newsletter* 15(3):18–23.

Tylecote, R. F.
  1986   "Metallographic Examination of Copper-Base Alloy Specimens from Episkopi *Phaneromeni*, Cyprus,
          of the Middle-Late Cypriot Period (2000–1650 BC)." Appendix II. In Swiny 1986, pp. 159–63.

1981   "Chalcolithic Metallurgy in the Eastern Mediterranean." In Reade 1981, pp. 41–51.

1982   "The Late Bronze Age: Copper and Bronze Metallurgy at Enkomi." In Muhly et al. 1982, pp. 81–100.

1976   *A History of Metallurgy.* Metals Society, London.

Vagnetti, L.
1980   *Figurines and Minor Objects from a Chalcolithic Cemetery at Souskiou-Vathyrkakas (Cyprus).* Dell'Ateneo & Bizzarri, Roma.

1979   "Two steatite figurines of Anatolian type in Chalcolithic Cyprus." *Report of the Department of Antiquities, Cyprus, 1979.* Department of Antiquities, Nicosia, pp. 112–14.

van Zeist, W.
1981   "Plant Remains from Cape Andreas Kastros, Cyprus." Appendix VI. In Le Brun 1981, pp. 59–99.

van Zeist, W., and S. Bottema.
1982   "Vegetational History of the Eastern Mediterranean and the Near East during the last 20,000 Years." In *Palaeoclimates, Palaeoenvironments and Human Communities in the Eastern Mediterranean Region in Later Prehistory*, edited by J. L. Bintliff and W. van Zeist, pp. 277–323. Volume 133. British Archaeological Reports International Series, Oxford.

Vaughan, P.
1985   "The Burin-Blow Technique: Creator or Eliminator?" *Journal of Field Archaeology* 12:488–596.

Vaughan, S. J.
1995   "Ceramic Petrology and Petrography in the Aegean." In "Science in Archaeology: A Review," pp. 115–17. Edited by P. E. McGovern, *American Journal of Archaeology* 99:79–142.

1991   "Late Cypriot Base Ring Ware: Studies in Raw Materials and Technology." In *Recent Developments in Ceramic Petrology*, edited by A. P. Middleton and I. C. Freestone, pp. 337–68. British Museum Occasional Paper 81. The British Museum, London.

Vavouranakis, G., and G. Manginis.
1995   "Μεσοκυπριακοί ταροι στι Θέση Αυδήμου–καμάρες." ("Middle Cypriot Tombs from the Cemetery of Eudhimou-Kamares.") Report *of the Department of Antiquities, Cyprus, 1995.* Department of Antiquities, Nicosia, pp. 67–94.

Vermeule, E., and Wolsky, F. Z.
1990   *Toumba tou Skourou: A Bronze Age Potters' Quarter on Morphou Bay in Cyprus.* Harvard University Press for the Harvard University-Museum of Fine Arts, Boston Cyprus Expedition, Cambridge, Massachusetts.

Vita-Finzi, C.
1973   "Paleolithic Finds from Cyprus?" *Proceedings of the Prehistoric Society* 39:453–54.

von den Driesch, A.
1976   "A Guide to the Measurement of Animal Bones from Archaeological Sites." *Peabody Museum Bulletin* 1, Peabody Museum of Archaeology and Ethnology, Cambridge, Mass.

Waechter, J.
    1953   "A Comparison between the Flint Implements of Khirokitia and Erimi." In Dikaios 1953, pp. 414–15.

Waldorf, D. C.
    1984   *The Art of Flintknapping*. Third edition. Mound Builder Arts and Trading Co., Branson.

Warner, J.
    1979   "The Megaron and Apsidal House in Early Bronze Age Western Anatolia: New Evidence from Karataş." *American Journal of Archaeology* 83:133–47.

Warren, P.
    1992   "Myrtos-Phournou Koryphi." In *The Aerial Atlas of Ancient Crete*, edited by J. W. Myers, E. E. Myers, and G. Cadogan, pp. 198–201. University of California Press, Los Angeles.

    1972   *Myrtos: An Early Bronze Age Settlement in Crete*. Supplementary Volume 7. British School of Archaeology at Athens, London.

Watkins, T. F.
    1979   "Kataliontas-Kourvellos: The Analysis of the Surface Collected Data." In *Studies Presented in Memory of Porphyrios Dikaios*, edited by V. Karageorghis, pp. 12–20. Lions Club of Nicosia (Cosmopolitan), Nicosia.

    1973   "Some Problems of the Neolithic and Chalcolithic Period in Cyprus." *Report of the Department of Antiquities, Cyprus, 1973*. Department of Antiquities, Nicosia, pp. 34–61.

Webb, J. M.
    1997   *Corpus of Cypriote Antiquities 18: Cypriote Antiquities in Australian Collections* I. Studies In Mediterranean Archaeology 20(18). Paul Åströms Förlag, Jonsered.

Webb, J. M., and D. Frankel.
    1999   "Characterizing the Philia Facies: Material Culture, Chronology, and the Origin of the Bronze Age in Cyprus." *American Journal of Archaeology* 103:3–43.

Weinberg, S.
    1956   "Exploring the Early Bronze Age in Cyprus." *Archaeology* 9(2):112–21.

Weisman, R.
    1994   "Petrographic Analysis of Pottery From Alambra." In "Uncharted Vessels: Studies of Red Polished and White Painted Wares from Alambra, Cyprus," edited by J. Barlow. *Hydra* 11, Athens, pp. 25–60.

Wertime, T. A.
    1978   "The Search for Ancient Tin: the Geographic and Historic Boundaries." In *The Search for Ancient Tin*, edited by A. D. Franklin, J. S. Olin, and T. A. Wertime, pp. 1–6. Smithsonian Institution, Washington.

Whalley, P. E. S., and R. Lewington.
    1981   *The Mitchell Beazley Pocket Guide to Butterflies*. Mitchell Beazley, London.

Whittaker, J. C.
    1996   "Athkiajas: A Cypriot Flintknapper." *Lithic Technology* 21(2):108–20.

1994   *Flintknapping: Making and Understanding Stone Tools*. University of Texas Press, Austin.

Whittingham, D.
1981   "Erimi Pamboula Revisited." *Report of the Department of Antiquities, Cyprus, 1981*. Department of
          Antiquities, Nicosia, pp. 24–42.

Wilkins, G. L.
1953   "Shells from Khirokitia and Erimi." Appendix IV. In Dikaios 1953, pp. 438–40.

Williams, D. F.
1983   "Petrology of Ceramics." In *The Petrology of Archaeological Artefacts*, edited by D. R. C. Kempe
          and A. P. Harvey, pp. 301–29. Oxford University Press, Oxford.

Williams, J. G., A. E. Williams, and N. Arlott.
1978   *Orchids of Britain and Europe with North Africa and the Middle East*. William Collins, London.

Woolley, L.
1955   *Alalakh. An Account of the Excavations at Tell Atchana in Hatay, 1937–1949*. London, Society of
          Antiquaries.

Wright, G. R. H.
1992   *Ancient Building in Cyprus*. E. J. Brill, Leiden.

1985   *Ancient Building in South Syria and Palestine*. 2 volumes. E. J. Brill, Leiden.

Yener, K. A., E. Geçkinly, and H. Özbal.
1996   "A Brief Survey of Anatolian Metallurgy prior to 500 BC." In *Archaeometry 94. Proceedings of the
          29th International Symposium on Archaeometry (Ankara 1994)*, edited by S. Demirci, A. M. Özer,
          and G. D. Summers, pp. 375–91. TÜBITAK, Ankara.

Zois, A. A.
1992   "Vasiliki." In Myers et al. 1992, pp. 276–81.

Zwicker, U.
1986   "Ancient Metallurgical Methods for Copper Production in Cyprus: Parts 1 and 2, Oxide, Sulphate
          and Silicate Ore." *Bulletin of the Cyprus Association of Geologists and Mining Engineers* 3:79–111.

1982   "Bronze Age Metallurgy at Ambelikou-Aletri and Arsenical Copper in a Crucible from Episkopi-
          Phaneromeni." In Muhly et al. 1982, pp. 63–68.

Zwicker, U., E. Grembler, and H. Rollig.
1977   "Investigations on Copper-slags from Cyprus (second report)." *Report of the Department of Antiquities,
          Cyprus, 1977*. Department of Antiquities, Nicosia, pp. 309–31.

LIST OF AUTHORS

Paul Croft   Lemba Village, Paphos District, Cyprus

Claudio Giardino   Instituto Universitario Suor Orsola Benincasa, Naples, Italy

Giovanni E. Gigante   Università degli Studi La Sapienza, Rome, Italy

Steve O. Held   4 Zelgliweg, 8309 Breite CH, Switzerland

Ellen Herscher   3309 Cleveland Avenue NW, Washington, DC

Julie Hansen   Department of Archaeology, Boston University, Boston, MA

Alice Kingsnorth   Department of Anthropology, American River College, Sacramento, CA

George (Rip) Rapp   Archaeometry Laboratory, University of Minnesota, Duluth, MN

David Reese   Peabody Museum of Natural History, New Haven, CT

Stefano Ridolfi   Università degli Studi La Sapienza, Rome, Italy

Carola Schulte Cambell   Preston Hill Farm, Iwerne Minster, Blandford, Dorset, UK

Stuart Swiny   Institute of Cypriot Studies, Department of Classics, University at
                            Albany, Albany, NY

Sarah Vaughan   Institute for Theoretical Physics, University of California at Santa Barbara,
                            CA

Clark A. Walz   Department of Classics, Cornell University, Ithaca, NY

Wouter van Warmelo   50 Garfield Road, Claremont, Cape Town, South Africa

INDEX

PLATES

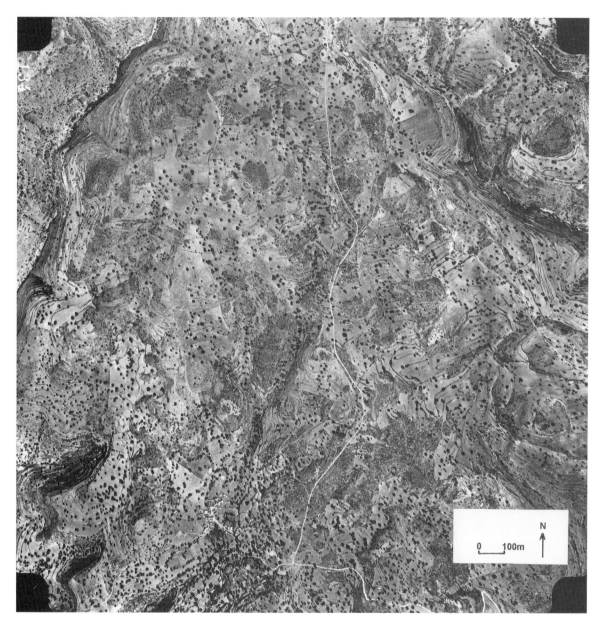

Pl. 1.1. Aerial photograph of the Sotira area taken on the 6th of October 1962. North is to the top of the photograph. The village is visible on the lower left. The small but prominent circular plateau to the west of the village is the Ceramic Neolithic site of *Teppes*. The *Kaminoudhia* settlement is 200 m north of the village center. The dirt road to Kandou Village is visible on the lower right, with that to Zanaja running through the center of the photograph. To the northwest, the Symvoulos Gorge is emphasized by the morning shadow. Courtesy Department of Lands and Surveys, Government of the Republic of Cyprus (State Copyright Reserved).

Pl. 1.2. Aerial view of the *Kaminoudhia* settlement. Cemetery A is located in the upper right hand corner. Autumn 1983.

Pl. 1.3. Aerial view of Areas A (to the east), B (to the west) and C (to the south). The top of the photograph is north. Autumn 1986.

Pl. 1.4. Area A from the east. The trench on the lower left measures 4 x 4 m. Autumn 1986.

Pl. 1.5. Area C from the southwest. The long north-south trench on the left is 4 m wide. Autumn 1986.

Pl. 2.1a. Tumble from Wall I looking west.

Pl. 2.1b. Unit 1, pits of Phase I in Floor 2 from the north.

Pl. 2.1c. Units 1 and 3 from the west. Note Phase I pits in the northwest corner of Unit 3.

Pl. 2.2a. Units 1 and 3 from the south.

Pl. 2.2b. Corridor into Units 1 and 3 on left, with in situ quern. From the northeast with Sotira *Teppes* in the background.

Pl. 2.2c. Unit 4 in foreground, Units 19 and 20 behind. The wall running diagonally across Unit 4 is of undetermined post Bronze Age date. From the south.

Pl. 2.3a. Lime plaster bin (Ft 15) in Unit 4 with a RP Mottled cooking pot (P122) smashed in situ.

Pl. 2.3d. Unit 5 from the south.

Pl. 2.3b. Unit 19 with west half of Unit 20 from the south.

Pl. 2.3c. Unit 20 from the south. Note hearth (Ft 16) against back wall.

Pl. 2.4a. Unit 5 mudbricks in section.

Pl. 2.4b. Unit 6 hearth (Ft 10) from the west.

Pl. 2.4c. Unit 6 from the south. Note monolithic threshold and trough (Ft 11) on the right.

Pl. 2.4d. Unit 6 from the north. Note in situ quern and lime-stone slab against back wall and the monolithic threshold on the left and trough (Ft 11) behind.

Pl. 2.5a. Unit 5 upper right, Unit 6 lower right, Unit 18 center left, Units 40 and 7 (with scale) upper left. Unit 32 in foreground.

Pl. 2.5b. General view of Area A from west. Unit 30 in foreground, Unit 5 in center with seated figures, Units 1 and 3 behind. Unit 7 on right.

PLATES

569

Pl. 2.6a Tumble in Units 12 and 13 (at top of photograph) from the north, with WH in course of excavation.

Pl. 2.6b. Street paving in Sotira Village with dry stone wall behind (1983).

Pl. 2.6c. View of wall tumble in Unit 13, looking west.

Pl. 2.6d. Section of wall tumble in Unit 12, looking north.

Pl. 2.7a Unit 2. Red Polished Mottled bowl (P86) in situ. Note ash above floor. From the northwest.

Pl. 2.7b. Unit 10 from the south with WA and Features 30 and 31 on left. Note P121 in situ on the lower right.

Pl. 2.7c. Floor and roof of an abandoned house in Old Paramali Village (1987). Note axe or adze marks on beam below scale.

Pl. 2.8a. Burnt house in Old Paramali Village (1987). Note blackening of the upper walls. On left, against the back wall, the stub of a charred beam protrudes 1.5 m into the room.

Pl. 2.8b. Abandoned house in Old Paramali Village (1987). The methods of roofing and wall construction are clearly distinguishable. The interior walls were originally covered with lime plaster and numerous layers of whitewash, now stained with mud dissolved from the roof by winter rains.

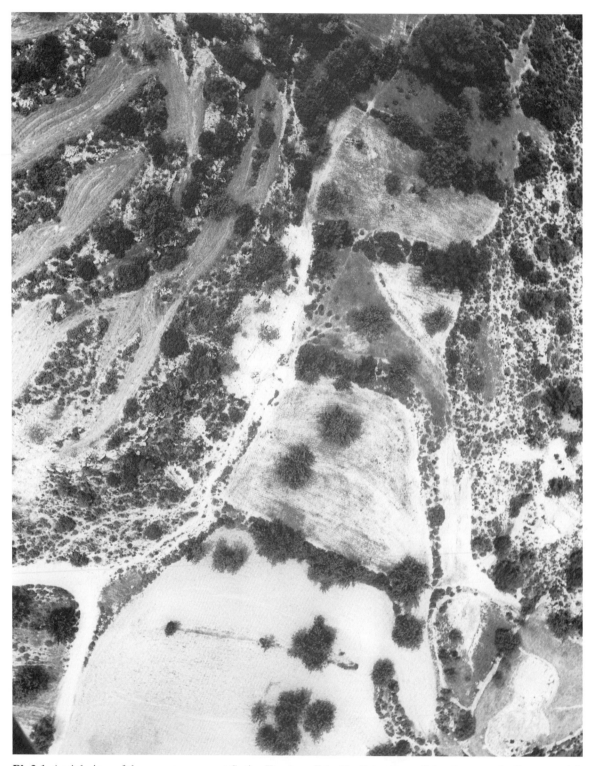

Pl. 3.1. Aerial view of the cemetery area at Sotira *Kaminoudhia*. North is at top of the photograph. Cemetery A is visible in the center as an elongated white patch on the west side of the path. The three open chambers of Cemetery B are visible as a row of dots just below the center on the right side of the photograph. Operations R4A and R4C are visible below. The flat terraces planted with carob trees between the two cemeteries stand out clearly.

Pl. 3.2a. General view of Cemetery A from the northwest before excavation of Tomb 17. The figure on the right facing the camera stands immediately above the chamber of Tomb 17. The recumbent figure on the left is excavating the dromos of Tomb 14, the seated figure in the center left with her back to the camera is excavating Tomb 15, and the dark figure facing left in the mid-distance stands above Tomb 7. One bent and one straight figure work in the dromos of Tomb 6, which lies behind the straight pine tree in the distance. Dikaios' Tomb 1 was located about 4 m behind and to the left of the camera.

Pl. 3.2b. Tomb 6 from the south in the course of excavation after removal of the skeletal remains. Note that the upper half of P53 in the center of the picture is missing because it protruded flush with the eroded bedrock surface. The arrow points to the intertwined gold (electrum) earrings M6, M7.

Pl. 3.2c. Tomb 6. Detail of human bone cluster against and below the base of P53. The nail in center left indicates findspot of bronze earrings, M13 and M21.

Pl. 3.3a. Tomb 6. Intertwined gold earrings M6 and M7 in situ.

Pl. 3.3b. Tomb 10. P65 and P66 in situ.

Pl. 3.3c. Tomb 7 finds in situ.

Pl. 3.4a. Tomb 11 in the course of excavation. The tomb chamber is visible through the rectangular opening at the bottom of the trial trench.

Pl. 3.4b. Tomb 14. Dromos and plaka in situ. This tomb was undisturbed.

Pl. 3.4c. Tomb 11. Ceramic vessels in situ: P92 (right), P63 (left), with P47 visible beneath its left side. The skull is visible above the center of the scale.

Pl. 3.5a. Tomb 15. General view of skeleton and dagger, M18, after removal of pottery.

Pl. 3.5b. Tomb 18. Ceramic vessels in situ: top left to right, P61, P47, P78; below, P59. (Ruler = 30 cm).

Pl. 3.5c. Tomb 20 with the removed plaka on left. The small size of the chamber is emphasized by the seven-year-old child crouching inside.

Pl. 3.6a. Tomb 6 pottery: P53, P52, P94, P14, P22, P11.

Pl. 3.6b. Tomb 7 pottery: P12, P23, P21, P80, P76, P31.

Pl. 3.6c. Tomb 12 pottery: P99, P100, P95, P96, P84, P97, P98.

Pl. 3.7a. Tomb 14 pottery: P90, P118, P68, P93.

Pl. 3.7b. Tomb 17 pottery: P104, P89.

Pl. 3.7c. Tomb 18 pottery: P61, P78, P48, P59.

Pl. 4.1a. Jug P69: wear on base.

Pl. 4.1b. Amphora P83: slip on interior of vessel.

Pl. 4.2a. Amphora P83: groove around rim interior.

Pl. 4.2b. Amphora P83: upper end of handle inserted through neck and smoothed on interior.

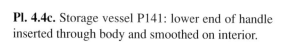

Pl. 4.3a. Large bowl P110, interior showing ancient mending holes.

Pl. 4.3b. Small bowls P5 and P6 fused together.

Pl. 4.4a. Jug P147: construction of neck.

Pl. 4.4b. Jug P147: upper end of handle inserted through neck and smoothed on interior.

Pl. 4.4c. Storage vessel P141: lower end of handle inserted through body and smoothed on interior.

Pl. 4.5a. Ear-lug pot P102: interior base construction.

Pl. 4.5b. Unstratified griddle fragment with mat impression.

Pl. 4.5c. Fragment of Type F jug from Area A Unit 20.

Pl. 4.5d. Fragment of Type F jug from Area C Unit 23.

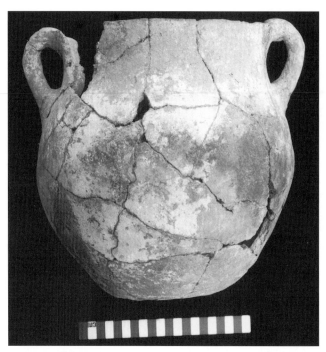

Pl. 4.6a. Type B Cooking Pot (Dikaios l/1).

Pl. 4.6b. Olive leaf impression on small bowl P48.

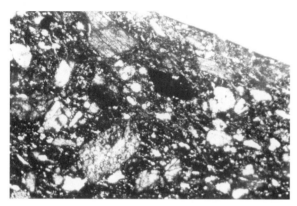

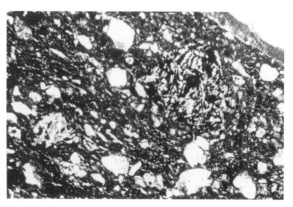

Pl. 5.1. SC26 Fabric 1. Red Polished Ware. Field of view 3mm. Plain polarized light (PPL). Abundant fine amphiboles and biotites, quartz, silt, thin red slip on a well-smoothed surface.

Pl. 5.2. SC56 Fabric 1. Red Polished IV. Field of view 3mm. PPL. Fine biotites exhibiting some parallel alignment, amphiboles and plagiogranite rock fragment, calcareous concretion layer on vessel surface.

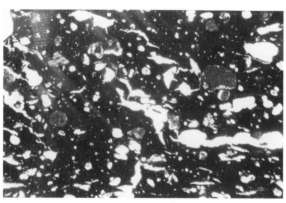

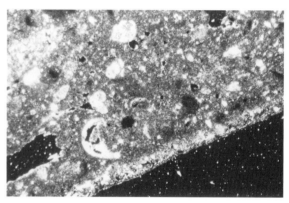

Pl. 5.3. SC19 Fabric 2. Red on White Ware. Field of view 3 mm. PPL. Abundant, fire elongated voids parallel to surface of vessel reminiscent of vegetal temper voids.

Pl. 5.4. SC7 Fabric 4. Red Polished Ware. Field of view 3 mm. PPL. Illustrates fine-grained groundmass, abundant discrete microfossils, thin red slip layer.

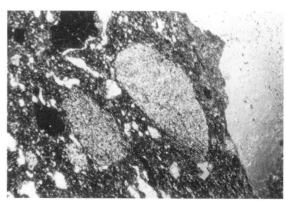

Pl. 5.5. SC25 Fabric 6. Drab Polished Blue Core Ware. Field of view 3 mm. PPL. Fragments of shale.

Pl. 5.6. SC1 Fabric 6. Drab Polished Blue Core Ware. Field of view 3 mm. PPL. Subround siltstone clasts, angular dark fragments of shale.

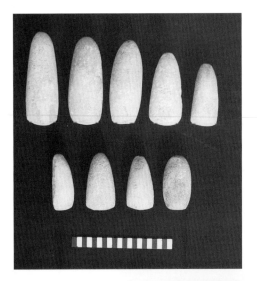

Pl. 6.1a (top left). Axes Type 1 & 2. Row 1: S238, 132, 549, 128, 159. Row 2: S9, 389, 521, 327.

Pl. 6.1b (top right). Axes Type 2, Adze (S450). Row 1: S326, 272, 524, 369. Row 2: S81, 186, 416, 450, 254.

Pl. 6.1c (center). Rubber pounders. Row 1: S130, 432, 8, 56, 164, 155, 365, 344. Row 2: S127, 311, 274, 342, 377, 211, 2, 1, 210. Row 3: S312, 313, 124, 180, 358, 515, 434, 18, 13.

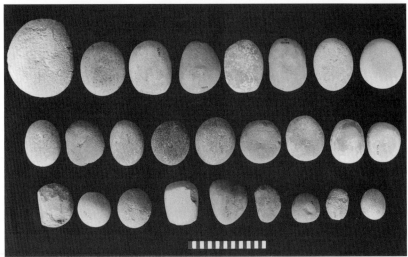

Pl. 6.1d (bottom). Pounders. Row 1: S402, 197, 104, 521, 383, 302, 113, 11, 350. Row 2: S49, 213, 172, 55, 265, 10, 304, 362, 156, 284. Row 3: S321, 276, 210, 537, 262, 170, 25, 345, 364, 537, 215.

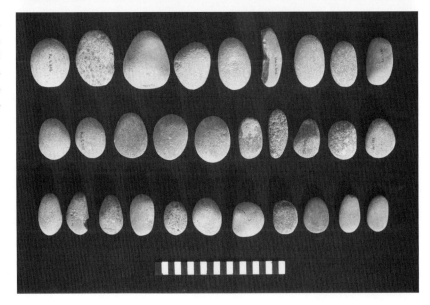

Pl. 6.2a. Pestle: S199.

Pl. 6.2b. Pecking stones. Row 1: S409, 279, 229. Row 2: S390, 241, 403. Row 3: S271, 407, 391.

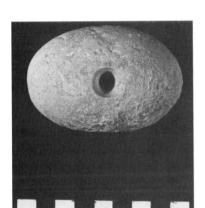

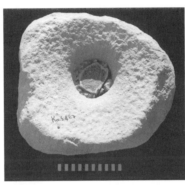

Pl. 6.2c. Mace head: 275.

Pl. 6.2d. Dish: S446.

Pl. 6.2e. Mortar: S239.

Pl. 6.2f. Mortar: S280.

Pl. 6.2g. Mortar: S427.

Pl. 6.2h. Mortar: S548 *in situ* from the north. Note trunnion on lower left.

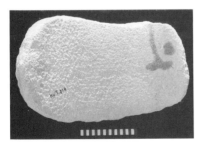

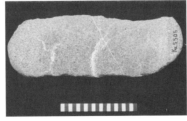

Pl. 6.2i. Quern: S426.

Pl. 6.2j. Rubber: S505.

Pl. 6.2k. Rubber: S236.

Pl. 6.3a. Senet: S467.

Pl. 6.3b. Senet: S425.

Pl. 6.3c. Senet: S330.

Pl. 6.3d. Senet: S234.

Pl. 6.3e. Senet: S424.

Pl. 6.3f. Mehen: S530.

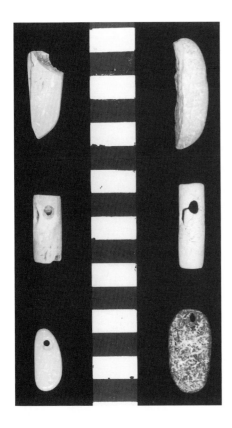

Pl. 6.3g. Worked picrolite: top left S463, top right S459. Personal ornaments, beads: middle left S461, middle right S460. Pendants: bottom left S469, bottom right S542.

Pl. 6.3h. Personal ornaments, bead: bottom S338, spacer, middle S473. Top. Bone bead, B2.

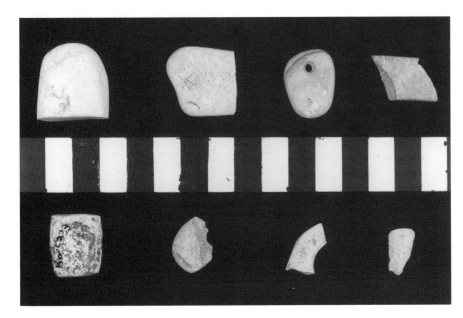

Pl. 6.3i. Worked picrolite except personal oranment, pendant S340. From left to right: top S332, S336, S340, S224; bottom S333, S335, S334, S337.

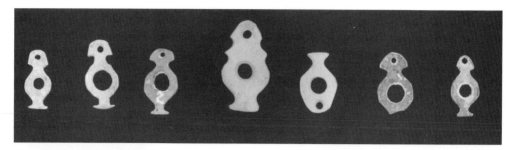

Pl. 6.4a. Anthropomorphic figurines used as pendants (left to right) S471/5, S471/6, S471/2, S471/7, S471/4, S471/3, S471/1. Height of largest figurine 1.9 cm.

Pl. 6.4b. S208, necklace reconstructed with beads and spacers surrounding Skull #3 in Tomb 6.

Pl. 6.4c. Antler hammer *in situ* with lithics in Unit 1.

Pl. 6.4d. Cattle skull in Unit 10.

Pl. 8.1a. M18, dagger from *Kaminoudhia*.

Pl. 8.1b. M12, billet from *Kaminoudhia*.

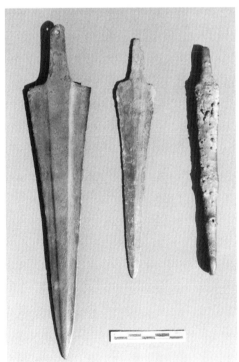

Pl. 8.1c. Daggers T5a/11 from Philia *Vasiliko* and M18 from *Kaminoudhia;* Billet M12 from *Kaminoudhia*.

Pl. 8.1d. Electrum earrings M6 and M7 from *Kaminoudhia*.

Pl. 8.1e. Electrum earring M6 being worn.

Pl. 9.1. Sherd roundels and pendant. Row 1: TC32, TC50, TC47, TC30, TC31; Row 2: TC48, TC37, TC51, TC52, TC46, TC54; Row 3: TC29, TC49, TC34, TC53, TC45.

Chapter 10

Pl. 10.1a. Tomb 6. Profile view of cranial fragment, centered around bregma.

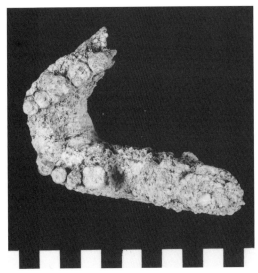

Pl. 10.1b. Tomb 6. Mandible incrusted in havara. Note the parabolic shape.

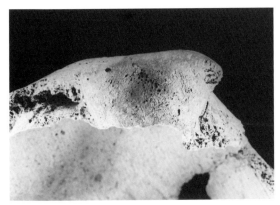

Pl. 10.1c. Tomb 11. Inside view of the right orbit displaying cribra orbitalia.

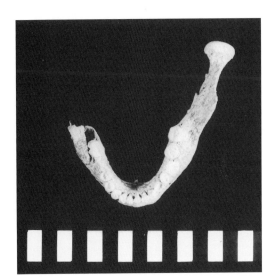

Pl. 10.1d. Tomb 11. Top view of mandible. Note the tooth wear.

Pl. 10.1e. Tomb 12. Immature epyphysis of a child's femur.

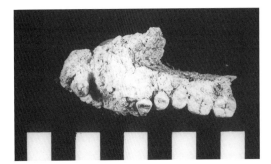

Pl. 10.1f. Tomb 15. Mandible attributed to Cranium 2.

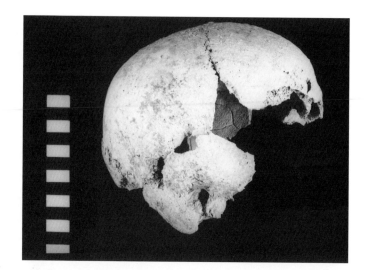

Pl. 10.2a. Tomb 11. Right profile view of skull. Note the full frontal curve and high parietal eminence.

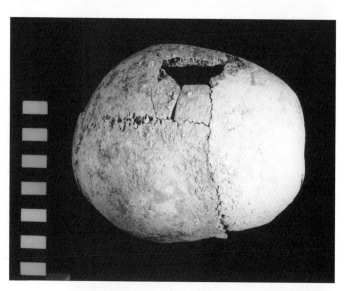

Pl. 10.2b. Tomb 11. Top view of skull.

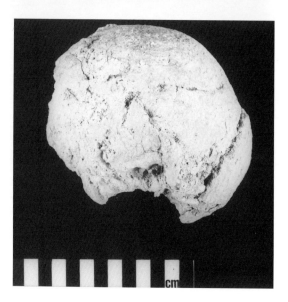

Pl. 10.2c. Tomb 14. Profile view of left side of skull. Note rounded occipital.

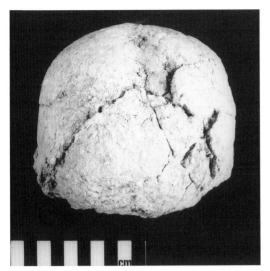

Pl. 10.3a. Tomb 14. Back of skull. Note the high occipital.

Pl. 10.3b. Tomb 15. Cranium 1 represented by top cap of vault.

Pl. 10.3c. Tomb 15. Cranium 3.

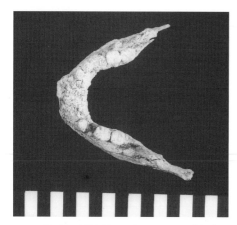

Pl. 10.4a. Tomb 15. Cranium 3 top view of mandible, complete except for right ramus.

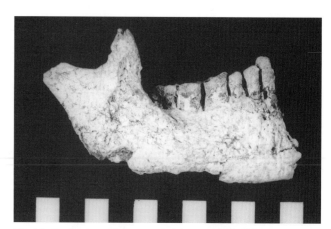

Pl. 10.4b. Tomb 17. Side view of right mandible.

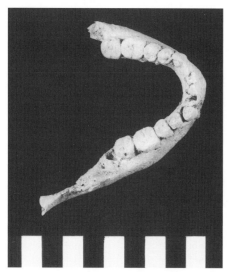

Pl. 10.4c. Unit 22. Top view of mandible. Note erupting third molar.

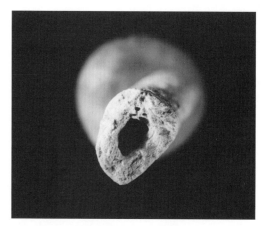

Pl. 10.4d. Unit 22. Cross section of left humerus shaft. Note the non-resorbed inner shaft indicative of retarded remodelling during growth.

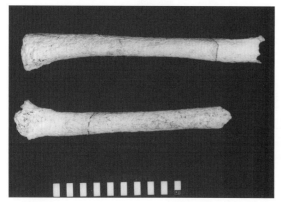

Pl. 10.4e. Tomb 15. Top view of femora from Individual 3.

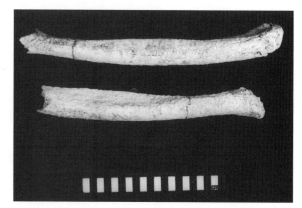

Pl. 10.4f. Tomb 15. Side view of femora from Individual 3. Note the pronounced bowing.

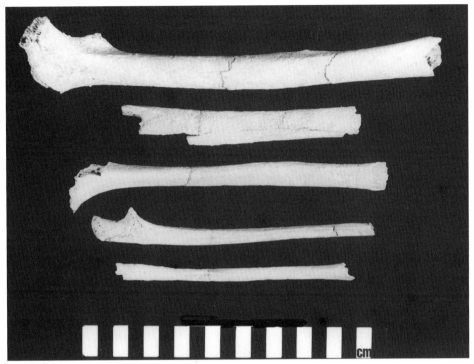

Pl. 10.5a. Unit 22. Long bones from young adult female.

Pl. 10.5b. Unit 22. In situ skeleton of young adult female with large bowl P110. North is at the top of the photograph.

Chapter 14

Pl. 14.1. Tumble from a wall in Area B. The retention of the spatial arrangement of the building blocks indicates that the wall fell as a unit, likely in an earthquake.

Pl. 16.1a. Survey area; view of gorge northeast of Kloupha.

Pl. 16.1b. Survey area; general view of gorge north-northeast of Tercha, looking north (now destroyed by road building).

Pl. 16.2a. Carob plantation with plowed ground.

Pl. 16.2b. Olive grove.

Pl. 16.3a. *Genista sphacelata* in flower.

Pl. 16.3b. *Silybum marianum* in flower.

Pl. 16.3c. *Pinus brutia*.

Pl. 16.4a. *Cistus creticus.*

Pl. 16.4b. *Pontia daplidice* – female.

Pl. 16.4c. Unidentified fly.

Pl. 16.4d. *Agama stellio.*